Publications of the Milman Parry Collection
of Oral Literature No. 6

WEATHERED WORDS

WEATHERED WORDS
FORMULAIC LANGUAGE AND VERBAL ART

edited by
Frog
and
William Lamb

Published by
THE MILMAN PARRY COLLECTION OF ORAL LITERATURE
Harvard University

Distributed by
HARVARD UNIVERSITY PRESS
Cambridge, Massachusetts & London, England
2022

Weathered Words: Formulaic Language and Verbal Art

Published by The Milman Parry Collection of Oral Literature, Harvard University
Distributed by Harvard University Press, Cambridge, Massachusetts & London, England
Copyright © 2022 The Milman Parry Collection of Oral Literature

EDITORIAL TEAM OF THE MILMAN PARRY COLLECTION

Managing Editors: Stephen Mitchell and Gregory Nagy
Executive Editors: Casey Dué and David Elmer

PRODUCTION TEAM OF THE CENTER FOR HELLENIC STUDIES

Production Manager for Publications: Jill Curry Robbins
Web Producer: Noel Spencer
Cover Design: Joni Godlove
Production: Kristin Murphy Romano

ON THE COVER

Pablo Picasso, *Violin and Grapes*. Céret and Sorgues, spring-summer 1912. The Museum of
Modern Art, New York, NY, inv. no. 32.1960. Mrs. David M. Levy Bequest. © 2022 Estate of
Pablo Picasso / Artists Rights Society (ARS), New York.
Digital Image © The Museum of Modern Art, Licensed by SCALA / Art Resource, NY.

ISBN: 978-0-674-27839-4
Library of Congress Control Number: 2022934846

Table of Contents

Acknowledgements

The concept of this volume and several of its chapters grew out of an international seminar-workshop held on 17–19 May 2017 in Helsinki, Finland: "Formula: Units of Speech—'Words' of Verbal Art," organized by Folklore Studies, University of Helsinki, and the Finnish Literature Society (SKS). Several chapters of this book (2, 5, 6, 11, 12, 14, 15, 16, and 17) are developed from papers published for circulation prior to the event (in *Formula: Units of Speech—'Words' of Verbal Art: Working Papers of the Seminar-Workshop*, Helsinki, 2017). We thank the Federation of Finnish Learned Societies and the Academy of Finland research project "Mythology, Verbal Art and Authority in Social Impact" (2016–2021) for their generous support towards this event.

Producing an edited book such as the present one relies on the cooperation, hard work and goodwill of numerous individuals. We thank Prof. David Elmer and the editorial board of the Milman Parry Collection of Oral Literature series at Harvard University Press for their belief in the project and their valuable assistance. We are grateful for the comments of two anonymous reviewers, which have strengthened many of the contributions and the manuscript as a whole. We also thank Jesse Barber for preparing the index, as well as Jill Curry Robbins and the team at the Center for Hellenic Studies for shepherding the book through the production process.

Finally, we thank the authors of this volume, who were all so willing to discuss and develop their chapters as the book advanced toward publication. Their enthusiasm, dedication, and insightful conversation have made this work a pleasure.

1

A Picasso of Perspectives
on Formulaic Language

FROG, UNIVERSITY OF HELSINKI
WILLIAM LAMB, UNIVERSITY OF EDINBURGH

FORMULAIC PHRASEOLOGY presents the epitome of words worn and weath-ered by trial and the tests of time. Scholarship on weathered words is, by nature, exceptionally diverse and interdisciplinary. Verbal art is in focus here, and this volume appears in the Publications of the Milman Parry Collection of Oral Literature. Given the centrality of Oral-Formulaic Theory (OFT, also called "Oral Theory"[1]) in discussions of verbal art—a paradigm initiated by Parry himself—it is addressed directly in some chapters and indirectly in most others. Yet, this is not a book about OFT per se. Weathered words are but a part of it and OFT is, itself, but a part of scholarship on weathered words. Rather, the present volume displays a diversity of approaches to, and perspectives on, a phenom-enon of language, rather than trying to obscure that phenomenon behind one theoretical arc. Each contribution has its own scope and degree of abstraction, and brings particular aspects of formulaic language into focus. Of course, no volume on such a diverse topic as formulaic language can be all-encompassing, but the eighteen chapters presented here highlight aspects of the phenom-enon that may be eclipsed elsewhere. It is worth noting that the contributions diverge not only in style, but sometimes even in the way they choose to define

---

[1] Whereas the term "oral-formulaic" spread principally through the title of an article by Francis Peabody Magoun, Jr. (1953), Albert Bates Lord did not use the term "oral-formulaic theory" and referred to OFT instead as "oral theory" (e.g. 1960:5; 1995:167), which established it as a synonym for OFT from 1960 onwards. A few scholars now use "Oral-Formulaic Theory" for Lord's and other early forms of OFT and use "Oral Theory" for its developments from mainly the 1990s and thereafter (a terminological distinction erroneously attributed to John Miles Foley in Acker 1998:xiv–xv). Owing to continuities in the gradual evolution of OFT research as it was refined, revised, and its scope of concerns expanded without a clear break, we distinguish Lord's formal-ization below as "Classic OFT."

"formula" and related phenomena. As such, these chapters offer eighteen over-lapping frames that complement one another both in their convergences and their contrasts. While they view formulaicity from multifarious angles, they unite in a Picasso of perspectives on which the reader can reflect and draw insight.

1. Background

A deep-rooted and enduring division exists between approaches to formulaic language in oral poetry and in other forms of human discourse. This gap emerged subtly and has been maintained on both sides, owing in large part to ideologies about poetry that now seem dated. Almost accidentally, the divide formed through the notion that poetry and language use more generally are somehow separate, so research was done on one or the other in isolation. Nevertheless, the divide was gradually recognized as illusory and approaches on both sides have begun to converge in recent decades: there has been a growing interest in interdisciplinary perspectives on weathered words. The present volume is a consequence of this interest beginning to precipitate into open discussion.

1.1 Classic Oral-Formulaic Theory and reification of the divide

The divide that became such an obstacle to cohesive discussion was not always there. The study of recurrent phraseology in any particular language was initially integrated. It may be tempting to assign the divide to modern disciplinary diversification, which centrally developed in the late nineteenth and early twentieth century, but it is not so straightforward. The divide did not begin as a segregation of poetic from non-poetic discourse. It was initially a pragmatic division of focus. Formulaic language in non-poetic discourse was primarily studied in the researchers' own languages—modern Germanic and Romance languages in the West. In these languages, poetry is generally seen as a literary art, in which unique expression is valorized. From that perspective, poetry is not deemed useful for studying conventional phraseology. Although studies of weathered words in oral poetry were unambiguously concerned with conventional phraseology, the traditions surveyed were in other languages and the studies were predominantly descriptive; recurrent phraseology was not theorized in these works to any great extent. However, that changed with Oral-Formulaic Theory.

Scholarship on formulaic language diversified as a result of the remarkable success story of OFT in Western scholarship. OFT was built on Milman Parry's studies of formulaic language in Homeric epics (e.g. 1928), which engaged an ongoing debate about whether these epics were oral or written (see also Foley 1988). The central idea was that long epics are not memorized texts: they are composed in performance, using a conventional phraseology that is pre-fitted to particular metrical positions. At the time, one of the more enduring questions of Western literature was whether Homer's poems were originally oral or literate. Parry's theory was that, if the phraseology of an epic was predominantly formulaic, it had been composed orally.

Parry went through the Homeric canon, identifying instances of phraseology that recurred in the same metrical positions of a line, and described what he found as formulae. This led him to define a formula as "a group of words which is regularly employed under the same metrical conditions to express a given essential idea" (Parry 1930:80, emphasis removed; adapted from Parry 1928:16). Parry's model had only modest impact at first, but it was further developed by Albert Bates Lord, whose dissertation (1949) produced a stir of interest in Harvard circles. Subsequently, Lord formalized OFT in his *Singer of Tales* (1960), introduced as "Parry's oral theory" (1960:5, also 12), and this produced a boom of discussion internationally. Lord's *magnum opus* propagates Parry's definition of formula, which is explicitly linked to meter (1960:4), and more generally frames formulaic language as a phenomenon distinctive of metered verse improvised within a tradition—what Lord described as *composition in performance*.

Lord's formalization can be distinguished as *Classic OFT*. Its international spread across the next two decades was remarkable. Karl Reichl (this volume) points out that Parry saw his definition as specifically for Homeric poetry; it was not meant to be universal and was rapidly considered too narrow even for Homeric poetry (Hainsworth 1968). Parry's statistical method for assessing the orality of a text based on formulaic density was also widely debated and shown to be problematic (Russo 1976). Nevertheless, the central idea of a relationship between formulaic language and improvisation was generally upheld. OFT was widely embraced and, already during its initial boom, it was energetically adapted to an ever-increasing variety of traditions, from stanzaically structured ballads (Holzapfel 1969) to prose narration (Bruford 1966). OFT gradually assimilated and superseded alternative approaches to how formulaic language works in practice. This does not mean that OFT became the only approach to verbal art—far from it. OFT was received enthusiastically because it provided a model for versification as language production, rather than simply for identifying and analyzing formal units (even if that is what much early OFT research did). Postmodernism was working its way through academia, bringing situations and contexts into focus for considering variation and interpretation that precipitated into, for example, the so-called performance-oriented turn (cf. Bauman 1975 [1984]; Ben Amos and Golstein 1975). OFT aligned with such interests:

unlike other approaches, it accounted for how performers can perform verbal art *in situ*, advancing far beyond Parry's original questions about the Homeric poems.

Prior to *The Singer of Tales*, formulae in prose verbal art had received scattered attention (e.g. Nutt 1890:448–450, 497; Thompson 1951:457–459). Yet, they were viewed collectively under the aegis of "style," not in terms of formal or functional features that would bring them into research focus and invite comparative analysis. Scattered applications of Classic OFT and its concepts to prose did not gain footing. Consequently, such formulae might be acknowledged, but discussions tended to remain both fragmented and also isolated from poetry, focusing on particular formulae or types thereof. Without gaining coherence, let alone momentum, discussions about formulaic language in prose verbal art remained relatively undeveloped (e.g. Lüthi 1990:57–67; Sävborg 2018).

Within a vast international discussion, OFT was flexed and developed in numerous ways. "Formula" became a trending term, which calved away from Parry's definition and was applied to almost any recurrent feature in lines ("syntactic formula," "structural formula," "metrical formula," etc.). Lord's *Singer of Tales* stood like a Maypole at the center of dynamic debate, and OFT rapidly evolved as a result. OFT sought to account for formulaic language, but also the content units that Parry called *themes*, and the whole text-types that Lord called *songs*. Its amorphousness allowed it to absorb approaches to similar units like a sponge. OFT's terminology became interdisciplinary, and earlier expressions like *locus communis, commonplace, cliché*, and *phrase* were replaced by *formula*. With such shifts in terminology, once separate discussions came into dialogue with OFT. Eventually, OFT became so encompassing that different approaches were considered to be integrated with it, rather than in competition. Although *The Singer of Tales* stood as a monolith in the midst of this heterogeneity, Classic OFT accounted for only one type of oral poetry: line-by-line improvisation in a periodic meter (e.g. Finnegan 1977:ch. 3). It became the *de facto* framework for analyzing formulaic language in verbal art, yet its conditions were obstacles for traditions that did not fit the profile. Ultimately, OFT's implicit ideology—that a formula is a phenomenon specific to oral, metered poetry—reified the divide in research on formulaic language at large.

OFT has evolved considerably since Lord's *Singer of Tales*. Around 1990, the movement to approach and understand forms of verbal art on their own terms reached a critical mass. Rejecting prescriptive Western models of poetics, Dell Hymes' *ethnography of speaking* (e.g. 1981) and Denis Tedlock's *ethnopoetics* (e.g. 1983) deconstructed the long-presumed contrast between "poetry" and "prose." They reconceptualized versification by explicating the organizational principles underlying certain forms of Native American verbal art. Their work was not aimed at formula research per se, but its implications pulled the rug out from under Parry's criterion of "under the same metrical conditions" (1928:16; 1930:80; Lord 1960:4). Interest shifted from formulae as poetic compositional building-blocks to their variation and meaningfulness in tradition-dependent patterns of use. Consequently, "formula" became more flexibly conceived "as an integer of traditional meaning" in much OFT research (Foley and Ramey 2012: 80).

OFT scholars began to move beyond propositional meanings. John Miles Foley was particularly influential here, through his development of a semiotic approach to the production and reception of expressions in oral tradition. His theory of *immanent art* (1991) built on the study of formal units developed in OFT to account for their propositional, but also their connotative semantics, which can be highly distinct within verbal art. Foley's work, and that of similar scholars, fed back into the sea of OFT research. Terminological distinctions from OFT developed in some networks and dissolved in others. "Oral-Formulaic Theory," or its variation "Oral Theory," stuck most widely to refer to frameworks for how formulae and themes "work" in a tradition. Immanent art, on the other hand, has become more commonly discussed as the *traditional referentiality* of such units (cf. Foley 1991:6–8).[2] Foley (1995) later systematically synthesized immanent art with OFT, Richard Bauman's theory of performance (e.g. 1984), Dell Hymes's ethnography of speaking (1981), and Denis Tedlock's ethnopoetics (1983). All of these approaches remain distinguishable, but through their centers rather than their boundaries; they have enriched one another at their sites of intersection and overlap.

The turn to tradition-dependent meanings revived interest in OFT and stimulated adaptations to traditions that did not fit the profile of Classic OFT. Polarized oppositions of "memorized" and "improvised," as well as "oral" and "written," were breaking down. Scholars adapted OFT as a tool for exploring regularities in different forms of verbal art without presuming or testing the sort of "composition in performance" emblematic of Classic OFT's models (Harvilahti 1992; cf. also Lord 1995), as well as in written text transmission, in traditions where "oral improvisation has changed its locus" (Parks 1986:650; see also Doane 1994). Foley's theoretical work contributed to this process. At the same time, the turn towards semantics was a turn away from defining abstract

---

[2]   Traditional referentiality is sometimes conceived through "intertextuality," although it is better seen as a response to the latter. Intertextuality developed in literature studies as a way of viewing meaning in texts through their networks of relationships to one another, customarily approached as independent of an interpreter. Traditional referentiality localized meaning in units of expression as signs (e.g. Foley 1991:7), as what could otherwise be described as the indexicality of those signs, which Foley developed in an experience-based framework rather than treating it as having an objective existence (esp. Foley 1995:47–59).

concepts like formula. Foley, for example, did concentrated work on formulaic language (e.g. 1990), but later found meanings came into better focus through performers' emic concept of a "word" as a unit of utterance, rather than as an orthographic unit (e.g. 2002:11–21). "Word" cut past technicalities of how to define a formula or theme. This avoided rather than developed a theory of what constitutes formulaic language versus something else, but the performance-centered concept of "word" provided a new instrument for talking about weathered words and the "loads" of meaning that they may carry, theorized through traditional referentiality. On the other hand, Parry's formula definition remains prominent in OFT (e.g. Foley 2002:110–112) and Lord's *Singer of Tales* is still the most common point of entry for scholars interested in formulaicity in verbal art.

1.2. Evolution across the gap

While OFT underwent its boom and evolution from the 1960s onward, research on recurrent phraseology also developed in leaps and bounds on the far side of the divide. In linguistics, partly due to the emphasis on structuralism in the mid-twentieth century—and generative syntax in particular (e.g. Chomsky 1957)—conventional expressions were seen as relatively insignificant for understanding language. However, situated language began to come into focus from the late 1960s, with the rise in functionalist and corpus-based studies (Bybee 2006), while new fields began taking shape at the intersections of linguistics and anthropology and of linguistics and sociology. These developments reached a watershed in the 1970s and set the stage for the next half-century of research (Pawley 2007).

Earlier research had commonly focused only on idioms that deviate in some way from the meaning, syntax, or lexicon of "normal" speech. The crucial development in the second half of the twentieth century was reconceptualizing formulaic language as also including phraseology analyzable through the lexicon and grammar. This development combined with new methodologies and changing interests to give new life to approaches focused on the linguistic lexicon within an objectified model of language. In parallel with this, the rise of interest in socially situated language and its links to social behavior and interaction came into focus at a multidisciplinary nexus that can be broadly described as discourse studies. These two trajectories of development can be viewed as at the extremes, with a continuum of research between them, but they are significant for understanding the different ways that formulaic language became conceived and understood. Research focused on language as an objective entity brought formulaic language into focus as a *formulaic sequence*, i.e. as constituted of multiple words or perhaps morphemes that collectively form a regular linguistic unit; the conception of such a sequence then gradually developed to include constructions more abstract than lexemes alone. At the other end of the continuum, research focused on situated discourse began looking beyond linguistic signs to include paralinguistic features like intonation and gesture, functions in interpersonal interaction, and so forth (Pawley 2009), which led such features to be considered in combination with lexemes as formulae. Formulaic language was sometimes conceived in incompatible ways, and these proliferated in parallel to the various uses of "formula" in OFT on the far side of the divide.

Later, as OFT research moved away from concerns about the role of formulae in composition at the rate of performance, researchers in other fields were realizing the variety and density of prefabricated linguistic units and constructions in everyday talk. Considerable work has occurred from a variety of angles on formal typologies and meanings or functions in discourse: questions of how humans produce and interpret language are now in focus.

Alison Wray's work has proven particularly influential in recent decades. Through Wray's principle of *needs-only analysis*, she articulated how formulaic phraseology alleviates the cognitive load involved in producing and interpreting language (2008:17–20). According to this principle, people will not normally analyze units of language in the flow of spoken or written discourse beyond what is necessary to interpret the message. In other words, they do not expend additional cognitive effort without a motivation of "need" (Wray 2008:130–132). This principle operates irrespective of how people learn a formulaic sequence; it is inconsequential whether they learn it holistically (without cognizance of its constituents) or by analyzing the sequence and only gradually internalizing it as a unit. This approach leads to her oft-repeated definition of a formulaic sequence, which has had wide-ranging utility:

> [It is] a sequence, continuous or discontinuous, of words or other elements, which is, or appears to be, prefabricated: that is, stored and retrieved whole from memory at the time of use, rather than being subject to generation or analysis by the language grammar.
>
> Wray 2002:9

More concisely, Wray describes the formula and formulaic sequence in terms of a *morpheme-equivalent unit* or *MEU* (2008:11–12), a concept that has proven particularly influential in recent years. Wray's innovative approach synthesizes long-developing discussions across the field of linguistics and related disciplines. She also presents it in an accessible way, which has facilitated its spread in numerous directions, becoming both an instrument and emblem of changes in formulaic language scholarship.

1.3. Convergence and communication

Already decades ago, attempts were being made to bridge different branches of research on weathered words (e.g. Kiparsky 1976; Kuiper and Haggo 1984). Some innovations in OFT research drew directly on research from across the divide (e.g. Acker 1983; 1998) and OFT also fed into research in other fields, for example, cognitive psychology (Rubin 1995). Such efforts never bloomed into open discussion, but the landscape has changed in recent decades. Independent developments on each side have led to a convergence of definitions and interests. However different their backgrounds and terminology, Foley's and Wray's approaches are fully aligned: a formula is a "word" of the register describable "as an integer of traditional meaning," corresponding to a "morpheme-equivalent unit" (cf. also Kuiper 2009). The convergence gives rise to both compatibility and relevance. The relevance, however, is most easily recognized from the side of verbal art research, because entry points into current, accessible, and broad discussions on formulaic language in other fields are easier to find. Weathered words have moved from the spotlight in research on verbal art, so concentrated discussions are fewer, narrower, and often embedded in a broader discussion, and books with "formula" or "formulaic" in the title have only been appearing on the other side of the divide. It is thus unsurprising that, for those attempting to engage with OFT from another perspective, Lord's and Parry's work remains as the main frame of reference (e.g. Wray 2008:ch. 4; Rubin 1995).

Although the gap persists, scholars' attitudes have changed in recent decades, especially among those working with verbal art. Repeated stumbling over Parry's definition generated a need for something better suited to a broader range of verbal art, for which Foley's broad concept of "word" provided a patch, but has not provided a solution for a more nuanced analytical tool. Refocusing on situational meaning in OFT research has also driven interdisciplinarity. Engagement across the divide has been facilitated by the convergence of interests and alignment in approaches to weathered words.

The present volume has emerged on this background and brings into focus the variety of current research on weathered words in verbal art. Some of the chapters focus on formulae that align fully with Parry's definition, while others focus on recurrent elements that fall well outside of it. This volume introduces current research on a phenomenon of multidisciplinary interest, with the hope that it will stimulate future discussion and innovation. The trend in current research on verbal art has been the exploration of situation-specific meanings, but such a focus requires accounting for both the formal and semiotic aspects of language. It is at this broad intersection that the present volume is positioned.

2. Organization

The contributions to this book could be grouped a dozen different ways. With each arrangement, connections between chapters are juxtaposed by unavoidable contrasts. We offer what we believe is the best arrangement, in five sections of three to four chapters each. OFT is still the dominant framework in Western scholarship for investigating how verbal art "works" in performance; therefore, it is appropriate to open this collection with the section, *Oral-Formulaic Theory and Beyond*. Each subsequent section brings a particular topic into focus that is of central concern for the collection. After considering some general perspectives on formulaic language in verbal art, and OFT as a widespread framework, the collection highlights additional theories and methodologies in formula research. Sections are organized around the role of the verse form in structuring formulae, the limits of formulaic language, and its roles in constructing different forms of discourse.

2.1. Oral-Formulaic Theory and beyond

In "Formulas in Oral Epics: The Dynamics of Meter, Memory, and Meaning," Karl Reichl opens Part I of the volume with perspectives on formulaic language going back to Parry's seminal work and explores its dimensions through more recent understandings. He then grapples with several issues that run through the book: the relationship of formulae to meter; the role of memory in performance; the significance of formulaic language in practice; and the possibility for long stretches of text to be more or less fixed even in an otherwise highly variable form of verbal art. Reichl provides valuable insights into these topics by considering poetry and song in the Kirghiz epic tradition.

Since the nineteenth century, scholarship on Old English alliterative poetry has discussed formulaic language and it has been an important nexus for advancing formula research. OFT's foundations are situated upon studies of Homeric and South Slavic epic poetry. Both poetic traditions are organized by similar metrical systems, based on counting syllables or syllables and their quantities. In contrast, Old English verse uses a stress-based system, where the number of syllables can vary. Furthermore, the meter requires alliteration, which drives variation in word choice. Parry's definition of formula was not transferrable to this poetry without adaptation, which produced rich discussions about how to define and distinguish concepts like formula, and how different concepts of OFT relate to it. In "Of *Scopas* and Scribes: Reshaping Oral-Formulaic Theory in Old English Literary Studies," Steven C. E. Hopkins elucidates the history of this rich vein of research, which exemplifies how OFT was adapted to one poetic tradition after the next. Hopkins introduces the reader to a vital arena of OFT research, one that also provided an abundance of valuable perspectives on oral-written interaction—some of the most significant insights produced to date.

Although OFT research built especially upon South Slavic epic as a living oral tradition, this has not been the only approach to that poetry. The turn from detailing the formal operation of language units to how their meanings and associations are constructed is also not exclusive to OFT. In "*Vlach Paupers: Formula and Layers of Meaning*," Sonja Petrović pursues these issues across several genres of South Slavic traditions. She offers a fresh and innovative perspective that complements Classic OFT research. Conducting a case study of one particular formula, she traces both its connections to historical social environments and its uses in different genres.

Anatoly Liberman brings the discussions of this section to a close by looking at formulaicity as a broad and fundamental phenomenon. In "Humans as Formulaic Beings," Liberman offers a wide, comparative context for the emergence of OFT, and he reminds us that formulae can be explored in diverse forms, rather than exclusively as a linguistic phenomenon. His learned discussion provides nuanced perspectives on how and why people engage with formulaic language, and significant observations about how patterns in idiom may change over the course of history.

2.2. Methodological approaches

Methodology is another key focus of formula research. Relevant scholarship has encompassed the theories that underpin analyses and interpretations, but also the strategies and procedures that form methods proper. Both concerns are advanced in Part II, "Methodological Approaches." Discussion is launched by Frog, who takes up *multiform theory*, which was initially formulated by Anneli and Lauri Honko (1995; 1998) as part of an alternative to OFT. The Honkos felt that their theory of linguistic multiforms could better account for certain phenomena of variation and flexibility in verbal art. In "Multiform Theory," Frog introduces this theory and its history, proposing that it reflects a basic linguistic phenomenon—one not limited to poetry. He distinguishes the multiform from the formula in its complexity and polysemic capability, arguing that it is a complementary type of unit, and also compatible with OFT.

In a similar strand, Raymond F. Person, Jr. considers the theory of *category triggering* presented by Gail Jefferson (1996). Category triggering concerns how the production of language in discourse activates networks of association in vocabulary. Jefferson's theory accounts for patterns and variation in conversational language, like when using a wrong word that is linked by sound or sense to the one intended. In "Formulas and Scribal Memory: A Case Study of Text-Critical Variants as Examples of Category-Triggering," Person combines this theory with OFT and its expansions through Foley's work, offering valuable insights into variations made by scribes in copying ancient biblical texts and Greek epics. This chapter illustrates the importance of balancing approaches to flexibility in language use with the sources for particular traditions, as well as relevant questions that the sources are equipped to answer.

The rise of meanings in formula research on verbal art has given little attention to how formulaic language may be used to structure relations between the performer and what is referred to, reflecting his or her stance toward it—i.e. stance-taking. Koenraad Kuiper and David Leaper investigate stance-taking in sports commentators' formulaic epithets, referring to players and the feats of local and foreign teams. In "*We Don't Support; We Observe*: Epithets and Modifiers in a Vernacular Formulaic Genre," they offer a sophisticated quantitative analysis of formulaic language in sports commentary, situating their discussion in relation to OFT research on epic. This chapter introduces the valuable concept of *formulaic genre*. Whereas Classic OFT's methodology built on statistical surveys of formulae and used formulaic density as a litmus test for orality, formulaic genre is a descriptive term for a verbal genre characterized by a high density of formulaic language, irrespective of whether it is oral or written (see also Kuiper 2009). Kuiper and Leaper illustrate how quantitative methods can be used to determine whether structures of social relations are built into formula usage.

Statistical methods are also at the forefront in William Lamb's "From Motif to Multiword Expression: The Development of Formulaic Language in Gaelic Traditional Narrative." An issue widely debated in Classic OFT research was the relationship between formulaic language and so-called themes, units of narrative content. Lamb takes up a corresponding question in prose narration. Using a corpus of traditional tales featuring motif annotation by Stith Thompson (MacKay 1940), Lamb explores how formulaic language links to international tale motifs and how these relations vary by genre. In this way, he attempts to provide an empirical basis for two proposed factors underlying the development of formulae: recurrence and semantic distinctiveness.

2.3. Language and form

Part III focuses upon relationships between formulaic language and the organizing principles of poetic discourse. The organizing principles of many traditions of oral poetry diverge from Homeric and South Slavic epics far more than Old English verse. James J. Fox starts off the section with "Form and Formulae in Rotenese Oral Poetry," in which he introduces formula constructions in a tradition of canonical parallelism that lacks periodic meter. In canonical parallelism, lexical pairs regularly recur in parallel lines. Fox elucidates how this type of lexical pair functions as a unified formula and reveals how sets of such formulaic pairings can develop complex patterning across a series of lines. Fox connects with the preceding section on methodology by presenting his system for mapping pairs through stretches of poetry. He then situates the operation of these formulaic pairings in relation to Roman Jacobson's approaches to poetics.

Naming formulae were central to Parry's (1928) early theorizations, in which he explored their fixity and variation, semantics, and patterns in their metrical structures. In "Formula and Structure: Ways of Expressing Names in the Northern Runosong Tradition," Jukka Saarinen takes up this classic topic in his study of how naming formulae are structured in so-called Kalevala-meter poetry. This poetry's short epic form led poems to be remembered and performed as "texts" rather than as improvised compositions in performance. It has a regular syllabic rhythm with often only two to four words per line, which stabilizes its phraseology. Saarinen shows that naming in this poetry follows formal patterns and outlines a typology of syntactic-metrical types, each of which he describes as a *formula system*, adapting a concept initially outlined by Parry (1928; 1930; cf. Lord 1960:35, 47–48; see also *syntactic formula* in Russo 1963). Saarinen considers how the dominance of particular metrical-structural formulae led to new formulations on the same pattern—i.e. they are generated within the framework of an established syntactic type.

To understand the relationship between formulae and poetic structure, it is valuable to examine what happens to them when they move between poetic systems. Yelena Sesselja Helgadóttir examines this phenomenon in "Formulae across the North Atlantic (from Continental Scandinavia to Iceland)." She traces the movement of formulaic language across genres and closely related languages, which may sometimes allow etymological translation and other times require alternative phrasing. Her study offers valuable insights into how language interacts with the organizing principles of a poetic form. She describes how the loss of a poetic feature like alliteration or rhyme in the movement of a formula to a new poetic system may be "compensated" by another poetic feature, revealing that such compensation may occur even when it is not necessarily required by the new metrical environment.

2.4. Explorations at the boundaries

Part IV, "Explorations at the Boundaries," carries discussions of weathered words to the peripheries of formulaic language. Ian Brodie leads the section by investigating formulaic language in stand-up comedy. He focuses, in particular, on how language crystallizes in stand-up performance routines and how situationally motivated variation for such language works in the genre. In "*I Am a Fan of Hilarity*: Possible Directions for Oral-Formulaic Theory and the Study of Stand-Up Comedy," Brodie illuminates the process of choosing between competing phrases as strategic choices for humorous effect. Bringing choice and variation into focus leads formulae to be framed as units in the lexicon that are used like non-formula units. This highlights the fuzzy boundary between whether particular units are or are not formulae.

Classic OFT was built on an idea that poets use phraseology pre-fitted to metrical positions in order to produce metrically well-formed lines at the rate of performance. Hans Nollet reveals that such recycling of weathered words can also occur in quite different traditions. In "Formulas in Neo-Latin Poetry as a Means to Language Enrichment and Self-Representation: Language Tips and Sociolinguistics in Justus Lipsius' Poems," Nollet illustrates that a corresponding motivation of ensuring the metricality of lines is found among Neo-Latin literary poets. Such practices were directed both towards displaying erudition and avoiding metrical mistakes. Neo-Latin poets composed in Classical Latin meters, which included rules related to syllabic quantities that were no longer distinguished in spoken Latin, which made the reuse of tried and tested turns of phrase from earlier poets the surest means to prevent an acoustically—but not analytically—unperceivable metrical error. These weathered words operate as formulae, but are not the formulae of an *oral* poetic idiom. This chapter situates some of the most basic perspectives on recurrent phraseology in oral poetry in relation to a formally identical phenomenon in literate compositions, where Nollet situates it in contradistinction to contemporary ideas of plagiarism.

Although most approaches to formulaic language stress the expression as forming a unit of meaning, Sergei Klimenko brings into focus *rhythmic fillers*. These have functional roles in regulating the flow of language in performance, but, because they do not communicate propositional meaning, they were sometimes omitted from early transcriptions of oral poetry. In "Rhythmic Fillers in Ifugao *hudhuds*," Klimenko applies a sophisticated linguistic approach to the operation of language in sung performance and reveals the importance of these fillers for realizing verse form. A filler of this type does not correspond to an "integer of meaning," or to a "morpheme-equivalent unit," yet Milman Parry (1928) argued that the epithet "swift-footed" could equally be used as a formulaic metrical filler, accompanying the name "Achilles" to complete required line positions without contextual meaning. Like the preceding chapters in this section, Klimenko's study explores weathered words at the boundaries of what is commonly addressed as formulaic language in verbal art.

2.5. Constructing worlds of discourse

The final section of the volume, Part V, considers what formulae do and how they operate, both formally and at the level of texture. In "Formulaic Expression in Olonets Karelian Laments: Textual and Musical Structures in the Composition of Non-Metrical Oral Poetry," Viliina Silvonen explores how linguistic and musical units are combined during the composition in performance of a regional form of Karelian laments. These laments are a form of sung, non-metrical poetry. Formulae may be structured through alliteration, but their length is flexible: such flexibility operates in tandem with the different durations of melodic units. Silvonen's investigation leads to the valuable observation that formulaic density and verbal regularity vary considerably between expressions that are personal to the performer and those that are ritually required in every lament of a particular type.

Formulaic language in genres of prose storytelling has been widely acknowledged but rarely received concentrated attention as a broad phenomenon. The density and use of weathered words in such genres vary, but they are particularly prominent in the Russian tradition. Tatiana Bogrdanova explores how translators have engaged with the highly formulaic quality of these folktales by comparing multiple translations of a particular collection. In "Folklore Formulas in Arthur Ransome's *Old Peter's Russian Tales* (1916)," Bogrdanova reveals how different renderings of formulaic language can manipulate a reader's experience of the text, and she considers how translators encode cultural differences in narration.

Although weathered words in folktales may be less researched, some—such as *Once upon a time*—have vast resonance for the genre. This section, and the book, ends with Jonathan Roper's investigation of key formulae in English fairy-tales. In "Opening and Closing Formulas in Tales Told in England," Roper reveals the functional differences of common formulae in structuring narration, as well as their potential to evolve on the oral–written continuum. He shows that a single complex formula may travel between very different cultural environments, and maintain features belonging to one, but not the other. In addition to variation through elaboration and simplification, Roper makes the important observation that, even when formulae originate in prose, they may exhibit poetic structuring at a phrasal level, a point of note that underscores the false division between "poetry" and "prose."

3. Warp and Weft

The five sections of *Weathered Words* move through general overviews, theoretical discussions, and case studies, to explore the limits of what might be considered formulae and the broader discourses constructed through them. Some of the threads of the individual chapters may be self-evident, yet others may escape view in the course of reading, especially when a particular chapter is read in isolation. In order to help readers to anticipate and map the diverse connections, the more prominent of these threads are briefly mentioned here.

3.1. The metrical criterion of Parry's definition of formula

The scholars of Old English poetry discussed by Hopkins were amongst the first to wrestle with the metricality condition of Parry's formula definition. This condition has been an obstacle for those working with oral poetry regularly organized on principles other than periodic meter, such as parallelism in the study by Fox, or poetry in which particular organizing principles are not uniformly applied, such as the traditions covered by Silvonen and Yelena Sesselja Helgadóttir. Parry's definition has remained a stumbling block to adaptations of OFT to prose, because scholars may feel that the failure to meet Parry's criterion of metrical conditions needs to be justified (cf. Lamb 2015; Sävborg 2018). More specifically, discussions of prose formulae are often disconnected from questions of how language is produced in performance, as seen in Roper's study, where language production is simply not relevant. Reichl highlights the disconnection between Parry's intentions, when formulating his definition, and its dissemination through *The Singer of Tales*. What often remains unrecognized is that Parry's criterion of "under the same metrical conditions" (1928:16; 1930:80) derives directly from his original methodology for identifying formulae by looking for the recurrence of words in the same metrical positions—i.e. his definition is a description of the things his method would find (Frog 2014:41; cf. Wray 2008:94–97). Without that criterion, however, Parry's definition as "a group of words which is regularly employed ... to express a given essential idea" (1928:16; 1930:80) corresponds to Wray's morpheme-equivalent unit (2008:12). While the issue of Parry's metrical criterion is often in the background of research, it is worth foregrounding here; it is widely encountered, and duly considered in some of the chapters of the current book.

3.2. Formula and poetics

We can identify the relation of poetics and formulae as another thread woven through certain chapters here. Part III, "Language and Form," examines the relationship between organizing principles of poetic form and the shape of formulae. Fox and Saarinen bring particular types of formulae into focus, and Yelena Sesselja Helgadóttir highlights what occurs as they move between poetic systems, yet the dynamics of weathered words in relation to poetic principles is a recurrent topic through the volume. Hopkins introduces the relationship between formulaic language, alliteration, and a rhetorical figure known as the "kenning" in Old English and Old Norse poetries. Frog sketches the relationships between poetic form and formula as a frame for considering types of variation, as well as more complex structures in which formulae participate. Klimenko explores the role of non-semantic fillers that complete what would otherwise be gaps in the flow of a performance. Nollet draws attention to literary uses of phraseology pre-fitted to meter. Silvonen and Roper each discuss formulae that are internally structured through alliteration or rhyme, independent of the surrounding unmetered discourse. The relationship between formulaic language and poetic form was of central interest already for Parry, but considerations of such phenomena have evolved considerably since that time. Now, they extend even to poetically organized formulae occurring in prose.

3.3. Fixity and variation

Alongside discussions of form are discussions of formula fixity and variation. Both fixity and variation concern weathered words of different sorts of scope, from a simple formulaic sequence to a stretch of language communicating one of OFT's themes. While most of the contributions examine how individual formulae vary—a fairly bread-and-butter topic—certain contributions highlight the phenomenon that Lord (1960:58–60) called a *run*. This is a term established by Alfred Nutt (1890:448–449) for stretches of recurrent text in metered or unmetered discourse that he, and later Lord, considered characteristic of oral traditions. More recently, multiform theory allows runs to be viewed in relation to a broader range of phenomena, as shown by Frog. Multiform theory focuses on complex verbal frameworks in the mind of a performer that work to produce stretches of discourse longer than a single line. These *linguistic multiforms* may also operate as *macro-formulae*, expressing a regular unit of narrative content, for instance. Shorter poetic forms with greater text stability were not initially well-suited to analysis through Classic OFT's focus on formulae within a verse line, yet their composition and variation becomes compatible with OFT when attention is on these larger units (see also Lord 1995:ch. 6).

Reichl highlights that Classic OFT's idea of "composition in performance" is linked not just to the long epic form, but more directly to the epic traditions on which it was developed. He reveals that the Kirghiz long epic form is characterized by long sequences of text that are reproduced with a high degree of fixity at a verbal level. Ian Brodie applies Anna-Leena Siikala's (1984 [1990]) concept of *crystallization* to understand how units of narration are linked together in the mind of a narrator. This concept avoids viewing fixed and free as a binary opposition, allowing a spectrum on which fixed memorization and free generative reformulation are extremes. Silvonen also uses this concept, well established in Finnish scholarship, to discuss the relative fixity of both individual formulae and complex formal units on a hierarchy of different scopes. The more complex units have remained outside of the interests of Classic OFT research, but both these and the phenomenon of crystallization have special relevance to unmetered forms of discourse.

3.4. Formulaic density

Salient to explorations on the relative fixity of runs and other long stretches of verbal art is formulaic density. The chapters in this volume do not adopt the spurious notion that formulaic density can be used to index a performance's "orality," but rather that it varies meaningfully across performances and genres of oral tradition. For example, Kuiper and Leaper observe that formulaic density is higher in so-called "calling" commentary of sports commentators—the play-by-play presentation of ongoing action—than in "color" commentary. In the latter, the pace is more relaxed and the topics more variable. Similarly, Silvonen observes that formulaic density is higher in ritual sections of Karelian laments than in non-ritual sections, where a performer may present a broader range of information. Lamb's statistical analysis produces complementary results in traditions of Gaelic storytelling. He finds a clear correlation between formulaic density and the recurrence of traditional motifs, and also shows that formulaic density varies, more generally, across different narrative genres. These discussions, in their turn, provide interesting frames of reference for considering comments on particular cases and examples in other chapters.

3.5. Oral and written discourse

In recent decades, scrutinizing the relationships between different forms of discourse (e.g. speech and writing) has become an independent research domain (see Biber and Conrad 2009). Several contributions to this volume engage with the topic in different ways. Issues of fixity and variation become particularly interesting in medieval and ancient *oral-derived texts* that have been produced at the intersection of oral tradition and writing technologies (Foley 1990:5). In addition to the initial process of writing out such texts, copyists may consciously or unconsciously vary these texts based on their own competence in the tradition, a phenomenon known as *scribal performance* (Ready 2019:203–215). As noted above, Hopkins surveys the rich discussions on this topic in research on Old English poetry, while Person explores its manifestation in biblical Hebrew and Homeric poetry. Classic OFT spread in an environment where orality was synonymous with the authenticity of tradition, yet the reality of many traditions is that there is interplay of composition, transmission, and re-composition between written text and oral practice. This is exemplified in the post-medieval poetry discussed by Yelena Sesselja Helgadóttir, as well as in the lively manuscript traditions of Iceland (Sävborg 2018) and Gaelic Scotland and Ireland (Bruford 1966; Lamb 2013), and in the English fairytales analyzed by Roper. So many tales were preserved in manuscripts and publications edited and recomposed for a literate audience that, inevitably, these literate stories reciprocally become the stuff of oral performers.

For Bogrdanova, this phenomenon is carried to yet another level; formulae rooted in the oral background of the Russian tale tradition are mediated, adapted, or omitted in the translation of these tales for popular English versions. Brodie, on the other hand, addresses stand-up comedy, where scripts may be formulated through a written medium to be performed orally, with the intention of appearing spontaneous. Alternatively, Nollet looks at parallels between formulaic language use, as described through OFT, and the reuse of phraseology in written poetry among Neo-Latin poets. When the topic of oral and written discourse is brought into focus across these chapters, their numerous and complementary perspectives provide a vibrant dialogue for the reader.

4. Cubism

In the wake of increasing institutional emphasis on bibliometrics and associated de-emphasis of monographs, books comprised of articles or chapters by diverse authors have been on the rise in the humanities. Even when they are systematically designed, and chapters strictly assigned, readers may perceive such books as lacking coherence. To an extent, this is due to the normal diversity found across individual authors' knowledge, interests, experience, and emphases. Yet, diversity can be unified and unifying. This is important to acknowledge because reader expectations are key to how a book is read and received. For instance, if realism is assumed as a frame of reference, a Picasso may look childish or aberrant; Carl Jung (1932 [1966]) observes that, if received from a patient, some of Picasso's works would be considered symptomatic of schizophrenia. As will be obvious from this introduction, rather than pruning divergences, we have nurtured diversity. In each chapter, the object of weathered words is taken up in different materials, bringing a particular aspect of a phenomenon, theory, or method into focus. Each chapter makes a valuable contribution to the topic of formulaic language. Together, these diverse and juxtaposed representations form a portrait of *Weathered Words.*

References

Acker, P. 1983. *Levels of Formulaic Composition in Old English and Old Icelandic Verse.* Unpublished PhD dissertation, Brown University.

——. 1998. *Revising Oral Theory: Formulaic Composition in Old English and Old Icelandic Verse.* New York.

Bauman, R. 1975 [1984]. *Verbal Art as Performance.* Prospect Heights, Brooklyn.

Ben Amos, D., and Goldstein, K., eds. 1975. *Folklore: Performance and Communication.* Approaches to Semiotics 40. The Hague.

Biber, D., and Conrad, S. 2009. *Register, Genre and Style.* Cambridge.

Bruford, A. 1966. "Gaelic Folk-tales and Mediæval Romances: A Study of the Early Modern Irish Romantic Tales and Their Oral Derivatives." *Béaloideas* 34:i-285.

Bybee, J. "From Usage to Grammar: The Mind's Response to Repetition." *Language* 82(4):711–733.

Chomsky, N. 1957. *Syntactic Structures.* The Hague.

Doane, A. N. 1994. "The Ethnography of Scribal Writing and Anglo-Saxon Poetry: Scribe as Performer." *Oral Tradition* 9(2):420–439.

Finnegan, R. 1977. *Oral Poetry: Its Nature, Significance and Social Context.* Cambridge.

Foley, J. M. 1990. *Traditional Oral Epic: The* Odyssey, Beowulf, *and the Serbo-Croatian Return Song.* Los Angeles.

——. 1991. *Immanent Art: From Structure to Meaning in Traditional Oral Epic.* Bloomington.

——. 1995. *The Singer of Tales in Performance.* Bloomington.

——. 2002. *How to Read an Oral Poem.* Urbana.

Foley, J. M., and Ramey, P. 2012. "Oral Theory and Medieval Studies." In *Medieval Oral Literature,* ed. K. Reichl, 71–102. Berlin.

Frog, ed. 2017. *Formula: Units of Speech—'Words' of Verbal Art: Working Papers of the Seminar-Workshop, 17th-19th May 2017, Helsinki, Finland.* Folkloristiikan Toimite 21. Helsinki.

Hainsworth, J. B. 1968. *The Flexibility of the Homeric Formula.* Oxford.

Harvilahti, L. 1992. *Kertovan runon keinot: Inkeriläisen runoepiikan tuottamisesta.* Helsinki.

Holzapfel, O. 1969. *Studien zur Formelhaftigkeit der mittelalterlichen dänischen Volksballade*. PhD dissertation, Johann Wolfgang Goethe-Universität zu Frankfurt am Main.

Honko, L., and Honko, A. 1995. "Multiforms in Epic Composition." *XIth Congress of the International Society for Folk-Narrative Research (ISFNR), January 6–12, 1995, Mysore, India: Papers I–IV*, II, 207–240. Mysore.

———. 1998. "Multiforms in Epic Composition." In *The Epic: Oral and Written*, ed. L. Honko, J. Handoo, and J. M. Foley, 31–79. Mysore.

Hymes, D. 1981. *"In Vain I Tried to Tell You": Essays in Native American Ethnopoetics*. Philadelphia.

Jefferson, G. 1996. "On the Poetics of Everyday Talk." *Text and Performance Quarterly* 16(1):1–61.

Jung, C. G. 1932. "Picasso." In *The Spirit in Man, Art, and Literature*, ed. Sir H. Kead, M. Fordham, and G. Adler, 135–141. London.

Kiparsky, P. 1976. "Oral Poetry: Some Linguistic and Typological Considerations." In *Oral Literature and the Formula*, ed. B. A. Stolz and R. S. Shannon III, 73–106. Ann Arbor.

Kuiper, K. 2009. *Formulaic Genres*. Basingstoke.

Kuiper, K., and D. C. Haggo. 1984. "Livestock Auctions, Oral Poetry and Ordinary Language." *Language in Society* 13:205–234.

Lamb, W. 2013. "Recitation or Re-Creation? A Reconsideration: Verbal Consistency in the Gaelic Storytelling of Duncan MacDonald." In *'A Guid Hairst': Collecting and Archiving Scottish Tradition*, ed. K. Campbell, W. Lamb, N. Martin, and G. West, 171–184. Maastricht.

———. 2015. "Verbal Formulas in Gaelic Traditional Narrative: Some Aspects of Their Form and Function." In *Registers of Communication*, ed. A. Agha and Frog, 225–246. Helsinki.

Lord, A. B. 1949. *The Singer of Tales: A Study in the Processes of Composition of Yugoslav, Greek, and Germanic Oral Narrative Poetry*. Unpublished PhD dissertation, Harvard University.

———. 1960. *The Singer of Tales*. Cambridge, MA.

———. 1995. *The Singer Resumes the Tale*. Ed. M. L. Lord. London.

Lüthi, M. 1990. *Das Volksmärchen als Dichtung: Ästhetik und Anthropologie 2*. ed. Göttingen.

MacKay, J. G. 1940. *More West Highland Tales*. Edinburgh.

Magoun, F. P., Jr. 1953. "Oral-Formulaic Character of Anglo-Saxon Narrative Poetry." *Speculum* 28:446–467.

Nutt, A. ("chiefly"). 1890. "Notes." In *Folk and Hero Tales*, ed. and trans. D. MacInnes, 395–491. London.

Parks, W. 1986. "The Oral-Formulaic Theory in Middle English Studies." *Oral Tradition* 1(3):636–694.

Parry, M. 1928. *L'épithète traditionnelle dans Homère*. Paris. [Translation available in M. Parry, *The Making of Homeric Verse: The Collected Papers of Milman Parry*, ed. A. Parry 1971, 1–190. Oxford.]

———. 1930. "Studies in the Epic Technique of Oral Verse-Making I: Homer and Homeric Style." *Harvard Studies in Classical Philology* 41:73–147.

Pawley, A. 2007. "Developments in the Study of Formulaic Language Since 1970: A Personal View." In *Phraseology and Culture in English*, ed. P. Skandera, 3–45. Berlin.

———. 2009. "Grammarians' Languages versus Humanists' Languages and the Place of Speech Act Formulas in Models of Linguistic Competence." In *Formulaic Language* I–II, ed. R. Corrigan, E. A. Moravcsik, H. Ouali, and K. M. Wheatley, I:3–26. Amsterdam.

Ready, J. L. 2019. *Orality, Textuality, and the Homeric Epics: An Interdisciplinary Study of Oral Texts, Dictated Texts, and Wild Texts*. Oxford.

Rubin, D. C. 1995. *Memory in Oral Traditions: The Cognitive Psychology of Epic, Ballads and Counting-out Rhymes*. Oxford.

Russo, J. A. 1963. "A Closer Look at Homeric Formulas." *Transactions and Proceedings of the American Philological Association* 94:235–247.

———. 1976. "Is 'Oral' or 'Aural' Composition the Cause of Homer's Formulaic Style?" In *Oral Literature and the Formula*, ed. B. A. Stolz and R. S. Shannon III, 31–54. Ann Arbor.

Sävborg, D. 2018. "The Formula in Icelandic Saga Prose." *Saga-Book* 42:51–86.

Siikala, A.-L. 1984. *Interpreting Oral Narrative*. Trans S. Sinisalo 1990. FF Communications 245. Helsinki.

Tedlock, D. 1983. *The Spoken Word and the Work of Interpretation*. Philadelphia.

Thompson, S. 1951. *The Folktale*. New York.

Wray, A. 2002. *Formulaic Language and the Lexicon*. Cambridge.

———. 2008. *Formulaic Language: Pushing the Boundaries*. Oxford.

2

Formulas in Oral Epics

The Dynamics of Meter, Memory, and Meaning

KARL REICHL, UNIVERSITY OF BONN

William Charke: "You vnderstande not then what Formula is!"
Edmund Campion: "Teach me then!"

IN THE SUMMER OF 1581 the Jesuit Edmund Campion held a disputation
with a number of Protestant clerics, among them Alexander Nowell, Dean of
St. Paul's, and William Charke, preacher at Lincoln's Inn. The disputation took
place in the Tower of London, three months before Campion was executed. In
the report of this event, published in 1583, the first written record of the word
formula in English is found according to the Oxford English Dictionary (Nowell
and Day 1583; OED Online). Campion and his opponents talk here about the
Second Commandment, and what they mean by "formula" recalls the predomi-
nantly legal use of *formula* in Latin; the OED glosses this meaning as "A set
form of words in which something is defined, stated, or declared, or which is
prescribed by authority or custom to be used on some ceremonial occasion."
The first written record of "formula" as used in literary criticism and hence in
the present context is according to the OED found in A. S. Cook's preface to his
edition of the Old English biblical epic *Judith*. The word occurs only once in the
preface and is, as it were, casually introduced: "Rimes and various forms of asso-
nance are occasionally employed by Old English poets, [...], rarely in formulas or
compounds within the same hemistich" (1888:lii). Cook does not explain what
he means by a formula, but he does give a list of fully and partially repeated
phrases at the end of his book (1888:67) and a list of "verbal correspondences
between *Judith* and other poems" (1888:57–65), where together with single words
and compounds also collocations such as *cene under cumblum* ('brave under the
banners') or *goldwine gumena* ('gold-friend [= LORD] of men') are listed, colloca-
tions today generally recognized as formulas by Anglo-Saxonists.

The OED refrains from giving a definition of "formula" as used in literary criticism and simply states: "In various technical and semi-technical uses (see quots.).)." The reader who expects more from a dictionary probably feels like exclaiming with Campion: "Teach me then!" The lexicographers' restraint was, however, a wise move. While there is a certain similarity between the various meanings of "formula" in the writings about formulaic style and formulaic diction, different authors generally differ in their definition of the concept. In the discussion that follows, I will start with Milman Parry's view of the formula, a view that is also represented among the OED's quotations.

Before proceeding, however, a short comment on the meaning of "oral epics" in the title of this chapter is called for. By "oral" I refer first of all to what Milman Parry was looking for in the former Yugoslavia, i.e. poetry orally performed, orally transmitted, and orally composed. It has, however, to be admitted that in a "real-world situation" an epic is often located somewhere on a running scale from oral to literate in a continuum, with written and oral transmission, as well as written and oral composition, crossing paths repeatedly (Reichl 2015). The examples discussed below are closer to Parry's ideal of "oral" than, for instance, to the medieval situation where whatever has been preserved of originally oral poetry has been written down and has come under the influence of literacy.

As to "epic," much has been written about the epic as a genre, but as yet no universally accepted definition is available (Martin 2005). Most approaches to the epic in Western literature and literary theory take the Homeric epics as prototypes and Aristotle's remarks on the epic in his *Poetics* as canonical (Hainsworth 1991:1–10). While many characteristics of the epic that are derived from Homer—concerning form, conception, and function—are shared by epics in non-Western literary traditions, others are not. It is a moot question which of these shared and non-shared features are essential and which are not. A move to ethnic genre classifications helps to focus on individual traditions without the dominant "Aristotelian view" (Ben-Amos 1976), but when comparing different traditions, some kind of non-normative "meta-genre," which is both flexible and variable, is necessary. For the present study I propose to take Sir Maurice Bowra's (admittedly Aristotelian) characterization of the epic as a working hypothesis, even if we might not share Bowra's confidence in a "common consent" and might also have some reservations about his humanistic view:

> An epic poem is by common consent a narrative of some length and deals
> with events which have a certain grandeur and importance and come
> from a life of action, especially of violent action such as war. It gives a

special pleasure because its events and persons enhance our belief in the worth of human achievement and in the dignity and nobility of man.

Bowra 1945:1

In the following I will illustrate the concept of the formula and the various problems connected to the analysis of formulaic diction with examples from my own fieldwork. With the goal of reaching a better understanding of the oral background to medieval traditional epic poetry such as *Beowulf*, the *Chanson de Roland*, or the *Nibelungenlied*, my research has taken me to the oral epics of the Turkic-speaking peoples, especially of Central Asia (Reichl 1992; 2000). In this chapter I will focus on the Kirghiz epic of *Manas*. Formulas in oral epics will be discussed from three perspectives, their relationship to meter, their function as a memory-device for the singer-narrator, and their meaning. I will argue that while Parry's insistence on meter in his definition of the formula is an important point of departure for the analysis of formulaic diction, meter is not a defining mark of all oral epic traditions. It will also be shown that oral epics like those of the Kirghiz have other memory-devices than formulas; these will have to be considered on a par with formulas. My final point is that the appreciation and interpretation of formulas depend on an "oral poetics," in which the traditionality of the poetic idiom is acknowledged.

1. Formula and Meter: Milman Parry

Our modern understanding of the term "formula" with regard to epic poetry has been significantly shaped by Classical philology and the study of the Homeric epics. In earlier scholarship the formulaic style of the Homeric epics was perceived as the occurrence of "fixed epithets" or *epitheta ornantia* ('ornamental epithets'). A typical view is expressed in the following passage, taken from a handbook of Homeric studies published in 1905:

> One very marked feature of the poems is the use of epithets. They are frequently *stereotyped* or *stock epithets*, referring to some general attribute, as νῆες θοαί, πολυφλοίσβοιο θαλάσσης ['the swift ships', 'of the loud-roaring sea', K.R.], even though the ships are *stationary* and the sea *calm*. So proper nouns have special epithets more or less appropriated to themselves, till they become sometimes like part of the proper names. This is so common that it is unnecessary to give examples.
>
> Browne 1905:75

The author is, of course, right. As it is, all the passages with *polyphloisboio thalassês* ('of the loud-roaring sea') in the *Iliad* and the *Odyssey* can be interpreted as describing a stormy sea, but the collocation *nêes thoai* ('swift ships') does certainly also occur when the ships are clearly stationary, as when Hector sends a spy to find out whether the Greeks are still keeping watch over their "swift ships" (*Iliad* X 309 and 396; Murray 1924–1925:I, 458, 464).

It is the study of the epithet in Homer that led Milman Parry in his Paris dissertation to the discovery of the relationship between formula and meter (Parry 1928; English translation in Parry 1971:1–190). Parry looks especially at collocations of noun and epithet, as in Browne's examples, and by meticulous analysis arrives at a number of conclusions. Early on he maintains:

> There is only one way by which we can determine with some degree
> of precision which part of Homer's diction must be formulary: namely,
> a thorough understanding of the fact that this diction, in so far as it is
> made up of formulae, is entirely due to the influence of the metre.

> Parry 1971:9

Parry presents interesting insights into the meaning of epithets, to which I will return briefly in my last section. While he develops the ideas for his view of the formula in his dissertation, his much-quoted definition of the formula is actually found in another work, in his 1930 paper published in *Harvard Studies in Classical Philology*. I will give a somewhat fuller quotation than is usual:

> The formula in the Homeric poems may be defined as *a group of words
> which is regularly employed under the same metrical conditions to express a
> given essential idea.* The essential part of the idea is that which remains
> after one has counted out everything in the expression which is purely
> for the sake of style. [...] The word-group is employed regularly when
> the poet uses it without second thought as the natural means of getting
> his idea into verse. The definition thus implies the metrical usefulness
> of the formula.

> Parry 1971:272

Note that Parry talks about the formula "in the Homeric poems," a qualification that is often ignored, although it is obvious that different meters and metrical systems will require adaptations of Parry's definition. Parry himself did in fact look at other metrical systems, in particular the South Slavic ten-syllable line (*deseterac*). In the then still vibrant tradition of South Slavic heroic songs (*junačke pjesme*) he found a laboratory for the analysis of formulas and formulaic diction and their function in oral epic poetry. He studied the impact of his South Slavic findings for Homeric scholarship in a number of articles, but it was Albert B. Lord's *The Singer of Tales* of 1960 in which the classic formulation of what came to be known as the Oral-Formulaic Theory is presented. Lord, together with Francis P. Magoun, applied formulaic analysis to the Old English *Beowulf*, claiming that, as in the case of Homer, the formulaic analysis of poetry that has only survived in writing, but which we suspect to have belonged to an oral milieu, can help clarify its either oral or written origin. This triggered an avalanche of studies on formulas and formulaic diction in medieval epics, in particular in Anglo-Saxon studies, but also in Romance and Germanic philology. Much energy has been expended on the definition of the formula in different metrical systems, on distinctions between formulas and formulaic systems, and on statistical evaluations of formulaic frequency and density (Reichl 1989a). In this voluminous scholarly literature, the Oral-Formulaic Theory was further developed, revised, and elaborated. One of the most productive scholars in this field was John Miles Foley, who compiled a comprehensive bibliography of works studying formulas (Foley 1985) and has also written the historiography of the Oral-Formulaic Theory or, as he called it, the Oral Theory (Foley 1988; Foley and Ramey 2012).

Classical scholars and medievalists have become sensitized to the oral background of the Homeric epics and also of much of medieval epic poetry, but one has to admit that, despite the enormous impact of the Oral Theory, those Homerists and medievalists who were skeptical have remained so. Scholars realized early on that while formulas and formulaic systems are typical of oral epics such as the South Slavic *junačke pjesme*, the presence of formulas in medieval epics, however frequent and dense, does not necessarily imply an oral provenance (Benson 1966). There is no syllogism allowing an inference from "all oral epics are formulaic" to "all formulaic epics are oral." Furthermore, as will be shown below, not all oral epics are formulaic in the way that is typical of the South Slavic tradition.

2. Formulas without Meter?

Parry's insistence on meter in his definition of the formula works well in a great number of epic traditions, but poses problems in others. One problem concerns the very concept of meter. As the linguist Joseph H. Greenberg has observed, "the vast majority of African peoples south of the Sahara, including here the non-Moslem peoples of West Africa and all the Bantu peoples except the Islamicized Swahili, do not possess prosodic systems" (1990:556). Although this statement has been somewhat modified later by Africanists, the editions of various African epics confirm Greenberg's observations. Nevertheless there is a correspondence to meter in the way these epics are performed. Gordon Innes, in his edition and translation of three Mandinka versions of the West African epic *Sunjata*, distinguishes between three performance modes: the speech mode, the recitation mode, and the sung mode. The epic is performed to the accompaniment of a musical instrument in all three modes. The first mode is close to narration in prose, though with a higher level of pitch than in speaking; in the second mode the words are delivered in a recitative, chant-like style, in an even higher pitch, while in the third mode the words are sung. Innes remarks about the recitation mode:

> The material in the recitation mode consists of formulae and formulaic expressions, resembling in this respect the Yugoslav epic material discussed by Lord (1960) and the Anglo-Saxon and middle English poetry discussed by Magoun (1953), Waldron (1957) and others.

Innes 1974:15

Clearly, the absence of a regular meter does not imply the absence of formulas. The rhetorical and musical performance provides a patterning of the spoken or rather chanted and sung word, with the words arranged into lines of free verse rather than some regular meter. The formula is here tied to performance rhythm and the melodic line rather than metrical structures.

Another problem arises in traditions where the epic is generally performed in a mixture of verse and prose. The common view of the epic stipulates that it is a narrative in verse, though not necessarily in hexameters as Aristotle would have it. There are, however, exceptions to this. In a number of epic traditions long narratives, which by content and conception conform to the Aristotelian view of the epic, are composed in a mixture of verse and prose. This is true of a number of epics and oral epic traditions in India (Wadley 1989:76–79) and in Central Asia. "Prosimetrum," the regular mixture of verse and prose is a characteristic of traditional narrative in many traditions, medieval and modern (Harris and Reichl 1997). Some of the "prosimetric" oral narratives of the Turkic peoples belong to the genre of romance, but many are heroic or mythological epics. The epic of *Alpamysh*, for instance, diffused mostly among the Uzbeks, Kazakhs, and Karakalpaks, is such a one, with close parallels to the return of Odysseus. Some versions of the epic are in verse only and hence agree fully with the Aristotelian view of the epic; some, however, are in verse with interlaced prose passages (Zhirmunsky 1974b; Reichl 1992:160–170, 333–353). With the exception of the presence or absence of prose both realizations of *Alpamysh* are the same. If we call the narratives in verse epics, should we then not also call the prosimetric narratives epics?

When analyzing the prose passages of these prosimetric epics (and romances), we find a number of phrases that are formulaic in the sense that they are repeated—with variations as allowed in formulaic systems (Lord 1960:47–48)—and that they occur in predictable contexts, e.g. at beginnings, narrative junctures, as introductions to speeches etc. The folklorist İlhan Başgöz has provided a detailed analysis of various types of such formulas in the prose parts of Turkish romances (*hikâye*) (Başgöz 1982). In Uzbek prosimetric epics, the prose portions are sometimes composed in rhymed prose; here the formulaic expressions are midway between formulas in verse and formulas in prose (Reichl 1985:35–37). These examples show that a discussion of formulas in oral epics will also have to consider collocations and phrases that lie outside the bounds of meter. In the present context, these verbal patterns cannot be further exemplified, analyzed, and defined, but it is important to be aware of the fact that a restriction of the term "formula" to metrical lines does not do justice to the variety of formulaic diction found in oral epics.

3. Formula and Meter: Kirghiz

Although Parry's experience of primary oral epic poetry was limited to what he heard and collected in former Yugoslavia, he was aware of other oral traditions. In an article of 1932, Parry gave a lengthy quotation from Wilhelm Radloff's preface to a collection of Kirghiz oral epics (1971:334–335). Radloff collected his Kirghiz texts in 1862 and 1869 and published them in the original language and in German translation in 1885 (Radloff 1885). His German translations of Kirghiz and other Turkic oral epics were well known in scholarly circles; Hector and Nora Chadwick, for instance, used them for the third volume of their *Growth of Literature* (1932–1940: III, 1–226; reprinted in Chadwick and Zhirmunsky 1969). Radloff made a number of observations on the art of the Kirghiz epic singer and formulated some ideas that were later taken up and developed by the Oral Theory. Although many features of the Kirghiz epics and their performers are also true of other Central Asian and Siberian Turkic and Mongolian oral traditions, I will here focus on Kirghiz to pursue some of the theoretical questions posed by Parry's approach.[1]

---

[1] The majority of the Kirghiz (also spelled *Kyrgyz*) live in the post-Soviet Republic of Kyrgyzstan, bordering on Kazakhstan, Uzbekistan, Tajikistan, and China; there is a Kirghiz minority of about 190,000 in the Chinese province of Xinjiang. In my transliteration of Kirghiz, 'q' denotes a velar k-sound, *gh* a velar fricative (similar to Parisian *r*); [kh] is pronounced like [ch] in Scottish *loch*; all other consonants are pronounced as in English; the vowels are pronounced as in Italian, with the following exceptions: *ö* and *ü* are rounded as in French *bleu* and *mur* (they correspond to German *ö* and *ü* or Finnish *ö* and *y*); *ï* is a lax *i*, comparable to the *i* in English *bit*.

The Kirghiz have a rich heritage of oral epics, among which the epic of *Manas* takes pride of place. Manas is the central hero of the Kirghiz, and it is indicative of his role in Kirghiz culture and ethnic identity that the first great international festival after independence was devoted to Manas ("Manas 1000" in 1995). *Manas* is a cycle of epics, of which the first part is devoted to Manas, the second to his son Semetey, the third to his grandson Seytek. Kirghiz singers are famous for the length of the *Manas* cycle. Sayaqbay Qaralaev's (1894–1971) version of the cycle extends to about half a million verse-lines, Saghïmbay Orozbaqov's (1867–1930) *Manas*—only the first part of the cycle was written down—comprises over 180,000 lines, and Jüsüp Mamay's (1918–2014) cycle, in which the epic is extended to eight generations, is about 220,000 lines in length. Given the extent of the epic cycle, no summary of its plot can be given here. A few remarks concerning the first part of the cycle must suffice.[2] Here the hero's deeds and feats of prowess are retraced from birth to death. Manas unites the Kirghiz tribes and, together with allies from other tribes, fights against the oppressors and enemies of the Kirghiz, identified in the epic as Kalmucks (Mongols) and Qïtay (Chinese). Manas's most faithful companion is Almambet, a Kalmuck (or Chinese) who converted to Islam. Apart from numerous episodes with wars and single combat, the plot of the epic also comprises bride-winning expeditions, struggles with slanderers and traitors, and the giving of feasts, of which the most outstanding is the memorial feast for Kökötöy Khan. The latter is the subject of the first Kirghiz epic that was written down.

The meter of the Kirghiz oral epic (and this is also true of other Turkic traditions) is syllabic. The Turkic epic verse *par excellence* comprises seven or eight syllables. To illustrate this, I will look at thirteen lines from the introductory section of Jüsüp Mamay's version of the epic *Manas* (ll. 87–99).[3]

(1)

> Bul jomoqtun ichinde,
> Ayarï köp, alpï köp,
> Aytïsh bolghus saltï köp.
> Abaylap uq qalayïq,

---

[2] Both the "Memorial Feast for Kökötöy Khan" (written down in 1856 by the Kazakh traveler and ethnographer Chokan Valikhanov) and Radloff's *Manas* have been re-edited and translated into English by Arthur Hatto (1977; 1990). On the role of Manas in contemporary Kyrgyzstan, see van der Heide 2008; Reichl 2016. An excellent introduction to Manas was written by the linguist and comparatist Victor Zhirmunsky (1974c; in Russian).

[3] During my fieldwork in Central Asia, I met Jüsüp Mamay, a Kirghiz epic singer from Xinjiang, several times, the first time in 1985. At present I am in the process of translating the first part of his *Manas* cycle, running to about 55,000 lines. Although more volumes are completed, due to circumstances beyond my control only two volumes have been published to date (Reichl 2014–2015).

5   Apïrtïp aytqan qalpï köp.
       Altïnï köp, kümüsh köp,
       Attanïp joogho jürüsh köp.
       Japaa tartqan qorduq köp.
       Jangha batqan zorduq köp.
10   Shamaldan külük atï köp.
       Saydïrïp iymey saatï köp.
       Oq ötpögön tonu köp.
       Opol toodoy chongu köp.

       In this epic tale there are
       Many men of witchcraft, many men of strength,
       Many traditions, difficult to say in words.
       If you listen carefully, dear people,
5   You will also hear of many things exaggerated.
       There is much gold, there is much silver,
       There is much riding out to meet the foe,
       There is much shame and much oppression,
       There is much suffering of violence.
10   Many horses are there, faster than the wind,
       Many obstacles, not avoided, overcome,
       Many coats that not one arrow ever pierced,
       Giants as huge as is the Opol-Too.

Looking at the last line (*Opol toodoy chongu köp*), the syllabic arrangement (when taking into account word boundaries) is 2 + 2 + 2 + 1. In performance we have four beats. These are realized as a sequence of 2 + 2 + 2 +1 notes, of which the first in each group is accented. Depending on the melody, we have four bars of two or three pulses:

(2)

These notes can be arranged into different melodic lines; two melodies (or rather melodic formulas) predominate. They are sung (or chanted) by the Kirghiz *manaschy* (singer-narrator of *Manas*) without the accompaniment of a musical instrument (Reichl 2014:50–55). This rhythmic-melodic line can be analyzed as consisting of two halves, of which the first half comprises four (in some cases, five) syllables, while the second half consists of three syllables. It is customary to speak of a caesura dividing these two halves.

In our extract, the three syllables of the second hemistich form either a word of three syllables (*i-chin-de*, l. 1, and *qa-la-yïq*, l. 4) or a combination of a two-syllable word with a one-syllable word (*chong-u köp*, l. 13, and all the other lines). All of these lines are performed as indicated above, with two syllables in the penultimate bar and the third syllable in the last bar. As to the first hemistich, we have four patterns in our extract:

(3)

2 + 2 syllables	O-pol too-doy	(line 13, also lines 3, 8, 9)
1 + 3 syllables	Bul jo-moq-tun	(line 1, also line 12)
3 + 1 syllables	A-ya-rï köp	(line 2, also lines 2, 4, 6)
3 + 2 syllables	A-pïr-tïp ayt-qan	(line 5, also lines 7, 10, 11)

When the first half of the line consists of four syllables, these are performed as indicated above, i.e. in two bars with two syllables in each bar. If, however, we have a combination of a three-syllable word with a two-syllable word in the first hemistich, the two words are distributed over two bars, with three pulses in the first bar and two pulses in the second bar. In this case the notes in the first bar will be shortened; musically speaking they will be rhythmically performed as a triplet.

This is only a rough characterization of Kirghiz meter. It is important to stress that we are dealing with oral poetry and will therefore encounter a number of variations in actual performance. From my remarks about the meter of *Manas* it emerges that there is a congruence between syllabic and rhythmico-melodic patterns. The melody of the epic is basically syllabic (i.e., one note per syllable) and furthermore stichic, i.e. repeated (with variations) for every line (or every two lines). Although a number of modifications would have to be made in a proper study of Kirghiz meter and musical performance, it is noticeable that for the singer metrical correctness comprises both the number of syllables and their rhythmico-melodic patterning. In my opinion the mold into which the singer "pours" his syllables in performance is a composite of syllabic and rhythmico-melodic patterns. A similar idea is voiced by Lord when he writes about the apprentice singer that "he absorbs into his own experience a feeling for the tendency toward the distribution of accented and unaccented syllables and their very subtle variations caused by the play of tonic accent, vowel length, and melodic line" (1960:32).

As to the combination of lines into formally coherent passages ("strophes"), both rhyme (or assonance) and line-initial (or vertical) alliteration are used. They are not coextensive. In our example there is only one rhyme (broken up, however, into five groups), but there are four groups of initial alliterations. Also, non-rhyming and non-alliterating lines may occur, which means that neither principle is entirely regular. Due to the agglutinative structure of the Turkic languages, rhymes are often "morphological," i.e. consist at least in part of suffixes. In our example, the rhyme (sometimes assonance) consists of a two-syllable word (*altï* : *salpï* : *qalpï*, *kümüsh* : *jürüsh* etc.) plus the unchanging word *köp* ('much, many'). This is a frequent type of rhyme in Turkic oral poetry, called in Kirghiz *tataal uyqash* ('complex rhyme') or *redif* ('repetition', from Arabic). In performance the verse passages are segmented into sections of irregular length (similar to the *laisses* of the Old French *chansons des gestes*), which generally end with a musical flourish (a kind of ornamental fermata on the last syllable or syllables of a "strophe").

The question now arises how to define and identify a formula in the Kirghiz epic. The clear caesura suggests that both the first and second hemistich might be formulaic, in addition to the whole line, of course. An analysis of these thirteen lines leads to a rather surprising result. For the analysis I have used as my corpus the first part of the *Manas* cycle, i.e. *Manas* proper, in the version of Jüsüp Mamay, comprising ca. 54,500 lines (Sïdïq et al. 1995), in the version of Saghïmbay Orozbaqov, comprising ca. 51,000 lines (Musaev et al. 1978–1982),[4] and in the version of Sayaqbay Qaralaev, comprising ca. 74,500 lines (Zhaynakova and Akmataliev 2010).

In this huge corpus we find no parallels at all for four lines (1, 2, 8, 9). In a further two lines we find parallels to one of their half-lines, but these do not justify their classification as formulaic. In one case (line 4) it is only the first word (*abaylap*) that is found frequently in the texts, but it does not add up to a hemistich. In the other case (line 6 *kümüsh köp*) there is only one parallel. Also, when analyzing Kirghiz epic poetry, it turns out that either only the first half-line or the whole line have parallels. The second hemistich is "reserved" for the rhyme, and rhyme-patterns work on a different level in Kirghiz (as will be seen below). This leaves seven lines in our extract. Of these seven lines, two have just one parallel each for the first hemistich (line 5 *apïrtïp aytqan* and line 10 *shamaldan külük*). A further three lines have two parallels each for the first hemistich, i.e. line 3 (*aytïp bolghus*), line 7 (*attanïp joogho*), and line 11 (*saydïrïp iymey*). This leaves two lines where we can clearly see formulas, i.e. lines 12 and 13. For line 12 we have forty whole-line parallels, of which four are two-line

---

[4]   This is a shortened version of Saghïmbay Orozbaqov's text; the full version was published in 2010, but is not available in digital form (Musaev and Akmataliev 2010).

formulas, and for line 13 there are six further instances in the corpus. It turns out that the formulaic density in *Manas* is surprisingly low.

Of course, thirteen lines are not enough to establish the formulaic character and density of a work. If we choose a line with a noun epithet of the kind Parry analyzed in the Homeric epics, we will indeed find a much greater number of formulas. There are more than twenty different words for the hero in *Manas* (*er*, *baatïr*, etc.) and there are a number of metaphors used for the hero, such as *qabïlan* ('tiger'), *arstan* ('lion'), etc.; in addition, there are also adjectival and other attributes like *chong* ('big'), *alghïr* ('with a firm grip'), *Opol toodoy* ('[as big] as Mount Opol'), etc. These words and expressions can be combined with personal names and also with one another. A short passage with the epithet "tiger" for Manas will exemplify this. In Jüsüp Mamay's version we find as part of a duel between Manas and Shooruq the lines:

(4)

> Qabïlan tuughan baatïrday,
> Mïnday adis qayda bar,
> Artïnan udaa jönödü.

> Like a tiger-born hero,
> As skilful and supple as can be found on earth,
> [Manas] raced behind him.

Looking at the three versions mentioned earlier (Mamay, Sayaqbay, Saghïmbay), we find to our surprise that *qabïlan tuughan* ('tiger-born') occurs only once in Mamay's version and not at all in Saghïmbay's. The expression does, however, occur twenty-two times in the first hemistich in Sayaqbay's version. Here the second hemistich has both *er Manas* ('hero Manas') and *Manastï* (accusative of the name) twice, and in three cases it has a different referent (Sïrghaq, Almambet and Töshtük). Mamay does, however, have an epithet formula for Manas with *qabïlan*, i.e. *qabïlan Manas* ('tiger Manas'). This hemistich is also found in Saghïmbay's version (seventy-five times with reference to Manas, twice referring to a different hero). This shows us that singers have marked preferences for formulas.

Looking more closely at the formula *qabïlan Manas* in Jüsüp Mamay's *Manas*, we first note that this phrase occurs thirty-one times in the first hemistich; *qabïlan* is also used as an epithet of other heroes (Baqay, Kökchö, Chubaq, Sïrghaq, Qoshoy, and Kerkökül) and the expression *qabïlan tuughan* ('tiger-born') is also used once with one of the other heroes. As to the linkage of *qabïlan Manas* to the rest of the line, two syntactic patterns prevail. In one, the formula in the first hemistich is followed by *baatïr* ('hero') + case suffix in the second hemistich, building a noun phrase with different syntactic functions:

(5)

Pattern I

Qabïlan Manas	baatïrgha	dative
	baatïrnïn	genitive
	baatïrdï	accusative
	baatïrï	possessive

Depending on the case used, the noun phrase acts as subject, indirect object, direct object or attribute in the sentence. In the second syntactic pattern the formula is followed by a verb in the second hemistich; the verb is either in a finite or in a gerundival or participial form, e.g.:

(6)

Pattern II

Qabïlan Manas	kelatat	is coming
	olturdu	sat down
	toqtoboy	without stopping
	eljirep	being moved

Out of the thirty-one occurrences of the phrase *qabïlan Manas* in the first half-line in Jüsüp Mamay's *Manas*, twelve have Pattern I, which is obviously a formulaic system. In three further lines we have *törö* ('lord') + suffix (accusative or possessive) instead of *baatïr*. The formulaic system then looks like this:

(7)

Pattern Ia

Qabïlan Manas	baatïr	+ suffix
	törö	

Pattern II occurs sixteen times. As the verbs keep changing (with no regular semantic relationship between them) it would be stretching the terms "formula" and "formulaic system" to speak of a formulaic patterning here. Nevertheless, a syntactic constraint is present and the singer is not entirely free to continue the line.

It is interesting to note that closely related Turkic languages and oral traditions like those of the Kirghiz and Kazakhs agree in many points, but also show differences. While *qabïlan tuughan* ('tiger-born') does occur as a formula in Kirghiz (in Sayaqbay's version), *arstan tuughan* ('lion-born') does not. This expression does, however, occur frequently in Kazakh oral epics and functions there as part of a formulaic system (Reichl 1989b:370; on epithet formulas in Kirghiz, see Hatto 1989).

4. Memory

In his writings Milman Parry shifted the analysis of formulas and formulaic diction from the text to the singer. He came to the conclusion that formulas have a specific function: they lighten the memory-load of the singer-narrators and help them to perform smoothly, without hesitation and lapses of memory. Singers do not perform a memorized text, but "compose in performance," for which formulas (together with themes) are a useful instrument. Although Parry and Lord acknowledged the importance of listening to heroic songs and learning to imitate them for the training process, they asserted that a South Slavic *pjevač* did not learn specific epics but rather a technique; this consisted in mastering a large store of formulas and a sufficiently comprehensive set of themes, i.e. typical scenes and motifs. "It may truthfully be said that the singer imitates the techniques of composition of his master or masters rather than particular songs" (Lord 1960:24).

This statement, however, is not of universal application. In all the oral epic traditions of the Turkic-speaking peoples much stress is laid on the apprentice singer's good memory. We hear of master singers insisting on verbatim repetition of what they recited and of correcting the performance of their pupils (Zhirmunsky and Zarifov 1947:35-38). Where we have enough documents, it can be shown that at least in some Turkic traditions there is stability in the actual wording of an epic over several generations. In the case of the Karakalpak versions of the epic of *Edige*, for instance, we can see that singers have preserved specific lines and passages over the span of a century, clearly without the support of written versions (Reichl 2007:81-97). The singers' ability to store specific lines and expressions in their memory should not be underestimated.

Furthermore, Turkic singers learn specific epics rather than a technique. These are the epics that belong to the repertoire of their teachers and then become part of their own repertoire. With specific epics they also learn the epic idiom; they become, as it were, competent speakers of the epic language. This includes, as a matter of course, formulas and themes.

The task of "remembering," as Lord preferred to call the work of memory, is indeed eased by formulaic diction. The formulas are integrated into the metric system of the language in question, whether it is Greek, Serbian, Croatian, Bosnian, or Kirghiz, but the formulas are also integrated into the syntax of the respective language. They do not stick out like erratic blocks inserted into the flow of speech, similar to exclamations, asides, or quotations. When one looks more closely at the integration into their context, one can specify several syntactic patterns, which are not formulaic in the strict sense, but which are "predictable" in the sense that they accord fully with the given syntax (see also Kiparsky 1976). At the same time, the phrases and sentences are arranged under metrical constraints concerning the syllabic patterning and also under metrical constraints concerning rhyme/assonance and alliteration. An example will illustrate this.

The strongest constraint is due to rhyme. A trait of a number of Turkic oral traditions is that onomatopoeic rhyme-words, often in a particular form (gerund, ending in the suffix *p*), are used. In Kirghiz these rhyme-words form rhyme-strings and are important generators of consecutive verse lines. These verb forms have a high memory-value: they are memorable on account of their sound-patterns (see Rubin 1998). As rhymes they come of course at the end of a line. What precedes them in the line is generally not formulaic. There is, however, a link between the rhyme-word and the preceding phrase. This link is semantic and triggered by the meaning of the rhyme-word. As to the status of the antecedents of the rhyme-word, an example will help to clarify this. The example comes from Saghïmbay's version of *Manas* (Musaev et al. 1978–1982:II, 85–86):[5]

(8)

    Zambirek ünü *kürküröp,*
    Qoqus nayza tiygendin
    Qoynuna qanï *bürküröp,*
    Qalqandar sïndï *bïrqïrap,*
    Qan tögüldü *shïrqïrap.*
    Jebenin oghu *qïrqïrap,*
    Mïltïqtïn oghu *chïrqïrap,*
    Jer titirep *künggüröp,*
    Qulaq tundu *dünggüröp.*

    The voice of the musket was *thundering,*
    He who was unexpectedly wounded by a spear,
    His blood was *gushing* from his arm-pit,
    The shields were splitting and *splintering,*
    The blood was spilt in *rushing* flows.

[5] For a fuller treatment of rhyme-strings in Kirghiz, see Reichl 2020.

> The bows' arrows were flying and *whizzing*,
> The guns' bullets were flying and *buzzing*,
> The ground was trembling and *groaning*,
> The ears were deafened by the *booming* noise.

There are a number of rhyme-strings of this kind in Kirghiz epic poetry. Here I will only look at the combinations of the verb *kürkürö-* ('to thunder') with other verbs of a similar sound-structure. The rhyme-string of the quotation above consists of the following eight verb forms:

(9)

kürküröp	thundering
bürküröp	gushing
bïrqïrap	splintering
shïrqïrap	rushing
qïrqïrap	whizzing
chïrqïrap	buzzing
künggüröp	groaning
dünggüröp	booming

In order to give a full analysis of this rhyme-string, the rhyme-strings in which every single verb form in this list occurs should be tabulated; furthermore, all verb forms not in this list, but in the rhyme-strings tabulated, should also be analyzed as to the additional rhyme-strings in which they occur. Just taking *kürküröp*, the first verb form in the list, we find that the verb form appears in rhyme-strings of two, three, four, five, six, and eight elements in the three versions of the *Manas* epic mentioned above. In Saghïmbay Orozbaqov's text there are thirty-nine rhyme-strings with *kürküröp*, in Sayaqbay Qaralaev's version there are twenty-eight, and in Jüsüp Mamay's version there are twenty-one rhyme-strings. For the building of these rhyme-strings all in all nineteen verb forms occur.

These rhyme-strings do not represent a fixed sequence of verb forms; they are a variable and flexible string of rhyme words, which acts as a device generating rhyming lines. Interestingly, the lines as such are not formulaic. As many of these verbs imitate sound and express movement, their subjects do show some similarity in meaning. To give just one example: *kürküröp* ('thundering') can be construed with a weapon giving off a thundering noise, a wild animal growling, a person shouting, the wind roaring, and "the sky" thundering. Only occasionally are lines repeated and can lines be grouped into a formulaic system. A subgroup of the lines with a weapon as subject of *kürküröp* can be analyzed as follows:

(10)

    qualification + *mïltïq* ('gun') + (extension) + *kürküröp*

Under "qualification" the name and type of gun is given: *töö* ('large', literally 'camel'), *Aqkelte*, the name of Manas' gun, *almabash*, a hero's gun, a blunderbuss (literally 'apple-headed'). The "extension" is added in the lines with the mono-syllabic word *töö*, as additional syllables are needed to complete the line. Here is the evidence (all found in Saghïmbay's *Manas*):

(11)

Töö mïltïq ünü kürküröp	The voice of the big gun (was) thundering
Töö mïltïq atïp kürküröp	Shooting the big gun, thundering
Aqkelte mïltïq kürküröp (twice)	The gun Aqkelte (was) thundering
Almabash mïltïq kürküröp	The blunderbuss (was) thundering

It should be stressed that in over half of the occurrences of *kürküröp*, the first hemistichs cannot be placed in such semantically related groups. Where such a grouping is possible, we can see that the elements of these different sets form a web of semantically and partially formally related items which in some cases can be analyzed as formulaic systems, but in others lie outside formulaic analysis as practiced (in general) by the proponents of the Oral Theory.

What the Kirghiz case (which is supported by other Turkic traditions) shows is that the formula as defined by Parry is only part of the story. The Kirghiz singers' competence in the epic idiom consists clearly in being able to manipulate formulaic systems, i.e. the patterns underlying formulas like *Qabïlan tuughan er Manas* ('the tiger-born hero Manas') with their paradigmatic sets for the various positions (*Manastï* for *er Manas* etc.). The other part of the story is the use of a different generative device: the combination of rhymes, more specifically of *memorable rhymes*, i.e. *colorful* onomatopoeic or unusual verb forms, into variable rhyme-strings. These rhymes have, of course, a semantic content and their use within the phrase or sentence is constrained by both syntax and meaning. This implies that rhyme-strings are both stored as webs of phonetically similar words and as words occurring in syntactically and semantically possible contexts. Hence the possibility of arranging lines (as with *kürküröp*) into semantically defined groups.

This is not a complete picture of how the singer's memory works, or, to use Lauri Honko's term, of his "mental text" (Honko 1996). Themes are an important element, as Radloff stressed for the Kirghiz and Parry and Lord for the South Slavic oral traditions. There is no time to include themes in my discussion of the formula and formulaic diction. I will simply mention that the rhyme-strings exemplified are often linked to specific scenes or themes. One is the description of a whip, which in *Semetey* (the second part of the cycle) is a component of a larger scene, in which the hero lashes out at his wife. In this theme specific elements of language (verb forms describing the making and shape of the whip, generally in rhyme-position) interact with a number of concepts (the whip is made of ox or calf hide, the handle is covered in precious cloth, the lash is plaited, the whip is admired, etc.). Here sound and meaning, word-forms and elements of narrative build a web of associations, enabling the singer to "compose in performance." The formula in the narrow sense is here part of a wider patterning of the epic idiom (Reichl 1992:223–235).

5. Meaning

In his writings, Milman Parry looked at the Homeric formula basically from three points of view: from a text-oriented, formal point of view; from a singer-oriented, productive point of view; and from a reader/listener-oriented, semantic point of view. Much of his dissertation is devoted to defining and analyzing the formula. A large part is, however, also devoted to the question of the meaning of epithets (and hence formulas). How are we as readers to interpret the meaning of epithets in Homer's epics? How do the singer and his audience understand the meaning of epithets?

Parry like other classicists argues that in Homer fixed epithets have an "ornamental" rather than a particularized meaning. Taking up the quotation from Browne at the beginning of my chapter, we can say that it is characteristic of ships to be swift and of the sea to be stormy even if the ships are stationary and the sea is calm. Some epithets are fixed for one person or object—Achilles is always *podôkês* ('fleet-footed') and no one else is (except horses)—while other epithets are used for a group of persons or objects: Achilles is *dios* ('divine'), but so are a number of other heroes. Parry calls the former distinctive, the latter generic epithets. In his discussion of the epithet, he shows "first, that the fixed epithet in Homer is invariably used without relevance to the immediate action whatever it may be, and second, that the generic epithet does not define any characteristic that distinguishes one hero from another, but only the characteristic that makes him a hero" (Parry 1971:118). A proper understanding of this presupposes an audience steeped in traditional diction:

> The experience of a member of Homer's audience must have been fundamentally the same as that of a modern student, only much wider and deeper. From their earliest childhood, his audience must have

heard again and again long recitations of epic poetry, poetry composed always in the same style. The diction of this poetry, accessible to the modern reader only by way of long study, was familiar to them in its smallest details. The experience we have described of the beginner, who learns how to understand θοήν in νῆα θοήν, or δαΐφρονος ['swift' in 'swift ship', or 'of a martial mind', K.R.] with the name of a hero, must have come quickly to a member of Homer's audience, and long before he heard a line sung by Homer. And so with other noun-epithet combinations which a modern student learns to associate in thought after years of reading: Homer's audience would have made these associations easily.

Parry 1971:129

According to Parry a proper understanding of the fixed epithet is only possible on the basis of an "oral poetics." If we recognize the character of the fixed epithet, he writes, "we find ourselves at grips with a conception of style entirely new to us. We are compelled to create an aesthetics of traditional style" (1971:21).

Not all scholars, however, approach epics with Parry's attitude. In his *Literary History of Persia*, Edward G. Browne, professor of Arabic at the University of Cambridge in the early twentieth century, writes about the *Shāhnāma*, "The Book of Kings," one of the great epics of world literature:

> [...] I cannot help feeling that the *Sháhnáma* has certain definite and positive defects. Its inordinate length is, of course, necessitated by the scope of its subject, which is nothing less than the legendary history of Persia from the beginning of time until the Arab Conquest in the seventh century of our era; and the monotony of its metre it shares with most, if not all, other epics. But the similes employed are also, as it seems to me, unnecessarily monotonous: every hero appears as "a fierce, war-seeking lion," a "crocodile," "a raging elephant," and the like; and when he moves swiftly, he moves "like smoke," "like dust," or "like the wind."

Browne 1928:142

The similes Browne criticizes are, of course, formulas or constituents of formulas. Browne partly excuses his negative view of a formulaic style with what he calls "a constitutional disability to appreciate epic poetry in general" (1928:142). Many scholars who do not suffer from such a "constitutional disability," nevertheless share Browne's assessment of formulas as monotonous and artistically inferior. Such negative evaluations of a formulaic and repetitive style are often found when the creations of literary poets are set off against popular poetry and the works of oral tradition. When E. Talbot Donaldson interpreted the fourteenth-century English poet Chaucer's *Miller's Tale* he referred to the idiom of popular poetry as "that conventional diction—those clichés—by which the whole vernacular tradition was infected" (Donaldson 1970:14). "Infection" is a strong term, but an even more drastic voice is that of William Calin, who in a meeting of the *Société Rencevals* violently attacked all attempts at interpreting the Old French *chansons de geste* in the light of Milman Parry's findings in South Slavic oral epic poetry and expressed his belief that most of the members of the Society would rather read the Bible, Virgil, or Chrétien de Troyes than the South Slavic *Wedding of Smailagić Meho* (1981:227). Why waste one's time on oral epics?

These examples of a negative view of formulas and formulaic style show that misunderstandings easily arise if oral and popular poetry is measured against written literature and if the function and the poetics of the formula in oral narrative poetry are ignored. Formulaic diction has to be understood in the context in which it occurs, and it has to be interpreted within the framework of an oral poetics. This applies also to works which, while not oral themselves, are heavily indebted to oral poetry and composed in a traditional style. Ferdowsi's *Shāhnāma*, completed in about 1010 CE, is a case in point. Goethe issued a noteworthy warning in the commentary to his *West-östlicher Divan*, published in 1819, where he disadvises comparing the *Shāhnāma* to the Homeric epics. These epics stand in different traditions, respectively, with their own poetics; what is appreciated as particularly well-crafted in one tradition might meet with opprobrium in another.[6]

While the idea of an oral poetics dates back at least to the eighteenth century, the time of Herder and Goethe, this idea has received a new impetus in the second half of the twentieth century both in the context of the Oral Theory (e.g. Foley 1991) and of other theoretical orientations, such as ethnopoetics (e.g. Hymes 1981; Tedlock 1983) or "interpretative" literary criticism (e.g. Zumthor 1983). In these approaches, formulas and formulaic diction play an important role in defining the style of oral poetry. Audience expectations and associations connected to formulaic phrasing have also been explored (e.g. Renoir 1988 for Old Germanic). Comparative analyses have from early on concentrated on the epithet and the formula, showing both fundamental similarities and specific

---

[6]   In the notes to his *West-östlicher Divan*, published in 1819 (Goethe 1961:175–176). It is interesting to note that the Iranist Reuben Levy came to an appraisal of Firdowsi's style quite different from that of Browne quoted above; speaking of laments for fallen heroes and kings and of the descriptions of sunrises, Levy states that the poet "borrows a prevalent and highly-regarded art form, namely theme and variations, and proves himself a consummate master" (Levy 1967:xix).

differences in the use of epithets (e.g. Whallon 1965 for Homer and *Beowulf*; Detelić and Delić 2015 for Balkan and Turkic traditions).

I will end with a quotation from one of the early comparative studies of the fixed epithet, a little-known article published in the yearbook of an Austrian *Gymnasium* in Villach in 1886, written by one of the teachers of the school, Anton Filipský, and entitled "The Fixed Epithet in the Oral Epic" (*Das stehende Beiwort im Volksepos*). Filipský makes comparative remarks on the Homeric epics, Serbian heroic songs, Russian *bylinas*, the *Nibelungenlied*, and the *Kalevala*. It seems appropriate following the context of a conference held in Finland to close my chapter with a quotation from Filipský's article on epithets in the *Kalevala*:

> Also in the Finnish epic, which differs otherwise so significantly from the narrative poetry of the Indo-Europeans, we meet the same phenomenon [i.e. fixed, context-independent epithets, K.R.]. Väinämöinen, the main hero of the Finnish folk legend, has as *epitheta perpetua* 'old' and 'truthful'. The latter epithet adorns him also at times when he unabashedly tells lies (*wenn er recht wacker darauf loslügt*).

> Filipský 1886:xiii

Filipský gives two quotations from Runo XVI of the *Kalevala*, where "Väinämöinen, old and steadfast" (*vaka vanha Väinämöinen*), several times tells lies to Tuoni's daughter. Here, of course, Filipský was relying on the German translation of the *Kalevala*, in which *vaka* was translated as 'truthful' (*wahrhaft*). 'Steadfast' in Kirby's translation (1907) seems to be closer to the meaning of the adjective. But the point Filipský was making is probably still valid. The appreciation of epithet-formulas, and more generally of formulas and formulaic diction in oral epic poetry, presupposes an understanding of traditional style or, in Parry's words, the creation of "an aesthetics of traditional style."

References

Sources

Cook, A. S., ed. 1888. *Judith: An Old English Epic Fragment.* Boston, MA.

Goethe, J. W. 1961. *West-östlicher Divan: Noten und Abhandlungen zu besserem Versändnis des West-östlichen Divans.* Ed. P. Boerner et al. dtv Gesamtausgabe 5. Munich.

Hatto, A. T., ed. and trans. 1977. *The Memorial Feast for Kökötöy-Khan (Kökötöydün ašy): A Kirghiz Epic Poem.* London Oriental Series 33. Oxford.

———. 1990. *The Manas of Wilhelm Radloff.* Asiatische Forschungen 110. Wiesbaden.

Innes, G., ed. 1974. *Sunjata: Three Mandinka Versions.* London.

Kirby, W. F., trans. 1907. *Kalevala: The Land of Heroes.* London.

Levy, R., trans. 1967. *The Epic of the Kings: Shah-Nama, the National Epic of Persia by Ferdowsi.* Persian Heritage Series 2. London.

Murray, A. T., ed. 1924–1925. Homer. *The Iliad, with an English Translation,* 2 vols. London.

Musaev, S. et al., eds. 1978–1982. *Manas: Saghïmbay Orozbaq uulunun variantï boyuncha,* 4 vols. Frunze.

Musaev, S., and A. Akmataliev, eds. 2010. *Manas: Qïrghïz elinin eposu. Saghïmbay Orozbaq uulunun variantï boyuncha.* Bishkek.

Nowell, A., and W. Day. 1583. *A True Report of the Disputation or Rather Priuate Conference Had in the Tower of London, with Ed. Campion Iesuite, the Last of August, 1581.* London. https://quod.lib.umich.edu/e/eebo/A08426.0001.0 01?rgn=main;view=fulltext#DLPS170.

Radloff, W., ed. and trans. 1885. *Proben der Volkslitteratur der nördlichen türkischen Stämme, V: Der Dialect der Kara-Kirgisen.* St. Petersburg.

Reichl, K., trans. 1985. *Rawšan: Ein usbekisches mündliches Epos.* Asiatische Forschungen 93. Wiesbaden.

Reichl, K., ed. and trans. 2007. *Edige: A Karakalpak Oral Epic as Performed by Jumabay Bazarov.* FF Communications 141. Helsinki.

———. 2014–2015. *Manas: In the Version of Jüsüp Mamay,* 2 vols. Xinjiang "Manas" Research Centre Publications 4. Beijing.

Sïdïq, Sh. et al., eds. 1995. *Manas: Qïrghïz elinin tarikhiy eposu. Aytuuchu: Jüsüp Mamay,* 2 vols. Rev. ed. Urumqi.

Zhaynakova, A., and A. Akmataliev, eds. 2010. *Manas: Baatïrdïq epos: Sayaqbay Qaralaevdin variantï boyuncha.* Bishkek.

Literature

Başgöz, İ. 1982. "Formula in Prose Narrative Hikâye." In *Folklorica: Festschrift for Felix J. Oinas,* ed. E. V. Žygas and P. Voorhuis, 27–57. Bloomington.

Ben-Amos, D. 1976. "Analytical Categories and Ethnic Genres." In *Folklore Genres*, ed. D. Ben-Amos, 215–242. Austin.

Benson, L. D. 1966. "The Literary Character of Anglo-Saxon Formulaic Poetry." *PMLA* 81:334–341.

Bowra, C. M. 1945. *From Virgil to Milton*. London.

Browne, E. G. 1928. *A Literary History of Persia. II: From Firdawsí to Saʻdí*. Cambridge.

Browne, H., S.J. 1905. *Handbook of Homeric Study*. London.

Calin, W. 1981. "L'Épopée dite vivante: Réflexions sur le prétendu caractère oral des chansons de geste." *Olifant* 8(3):227–237.

Chadwick, H. M., and N. K. Chadwick. 1932–1940. *The Growth of Literature*, 3 vols. Cambridge.

Chadwick, N. K., and V. Zhirmunsky. 1969. *Oral Epics of Central Asia*. Cambridge.

Detelić, M., and L. Delić, eds. 2015. *Epic Formula: A Balkan Perspective*. Belgrade.

Donaldson, E. T. 1970. *Speaking of Chaucer*. New York.

Filipský, A. 1886. "Das stehende Beiwort im Volksepos." In *Siebzehnte Jahresschrift des k.k. Gymnasiums in Villach*, ed. A. Zeehe, iii–xxii. Villach.

Foley, J. M. 1985. *Oral-Formulaic Theory and Research: An Introduction and Annotated Bibliography*. New York.

———. 1988. *The Theory of Oral Composition: History and Methodology*. Bloomington.

———. 1991. *Immanent Art: From Structure to Meaning in Traditional Oral Epic*. Bloomington.

Foley, J. M., and P. Ramey. 2012. "Oral Theory and Medieval Literature." In *Medieval Oral Literature*, ed. K. Reichl, 71–102. Berlin.

Greenberg, J. H. 1990. "A Survey of African Prosodic Systems." In *On Language: Selected Writings of Joseph H. Greenberg*, ed. K. Denning and S. Kemmer, 553–578. Stanford.

Hainsworth, J. B. 1991. *The Idea of Epic*. Berkeley.

Hainsworth, J. B., and A. T. Hatto, eds. 1989. *Traditions of Heroic and Epic Poetry, II: Characteristics and Techniques*. London.

Harris, J., and K. Reichl, eds. 1997. *Prosimetrum: Crosscultural Perspectives on Narrative in Prose and Verse*. Cambridge.

Hatto, A. T. 1989. "Epithets in Kirghiz Epic Poetry 1856–1869." In Hainsworth and Hatto 1989:71–93.

Honko, L. 1996. "Epics along the Silk Roads: Mental Text, Performance, and Written Codification." *Oral Tradition* 11:1–17.

Hymes, D. 1981. *"In Vain I Tried to Tell You": Essays in Native American Ethnopoetics*. Philadelphia.

Kiparsky, P. 1976. "Some Linguistic and Typological Considerations." In *Oral Literature and the Formula*, ed. B. A. Stolz and T. S. Shannon, 73–106. Ann Arbor.

Lord, A. B. 1960. *The Singer of Tales.* 2nd ed. with CD. Ed. S. Mitchell and G. Nagy 2001. Cambridge, MA.

Magoun, F. P., Jr. 1953. "Oral-Formulaic Character of Anglo-Saxon Narrative Poetry." *Speculum* 28:446–467.

Martin, R. P. 2005. "Epic as Genre." In *A Companion to Ancient Epic*, ed. J. M. Foley, 9–19. Oxford.

Oxford English Dictionary. London. http://www.oed.com (March 13, 2018).

Parry, M. 1928. *L'épithète traditionelle dans Homère. Essai sur un problème de style homérique.* Paris.

———. 1971. *The Making of Homeric Verse. The Collected Papers of Milman Parry.* Ed. A. Parry. New York.

Reichl, K. 1989a. "Formulaic Diction in Old English Epic Poetry." In Hainsworth and Hatto 1989:42–70.

———. 1989b. "Formulaic Diction in Kazakh Epic Poetry." *Oral Tradition* 4:360–381.

———. 1992. *Turkic Oral Epic Poetry: Traditions, Forms, Poetic Structure.* Repr. 2018. New York.

———. 2000. *Singing the Past: Turkic and Medieval Heroic Poetry.* Ithaca.

———. 2014. "'Sing, O Muse!': Reflections on the Singing of Oral Epics." In *Song and Emergent Poetics*, ed. P. Huttu-Hiltunen, Frog, K. Lukin, and E. Stepanova, 45–63. Kuhmo.

———. 2015. "Memory and Textuality in the Orality-Literacy Continuum." In *Orality and Textuality in the Iranian World: Patterns of Interaction across the Centuries*, ed. J. Rubanovich, 19–42. Leiden.

———. 2016. "Oral Epics into the Twenty-First Century: The Case of the Kyrgyz Epic *Manas*." *Journal of American Folklore* 129(513):327–344.

———. 2020. "'The True Nature of the *Aoidos*': The Kirghiz Singer of Tales and the Epic of *Manas*." In *John Miles Foley's World of Oralities: Text, Tradition, and Contemporary Oral Theory*, ed. M. C. Amodio, 185–206. Leeds.

Renoir, A. 1988. *A Key to Old Poems: The Oral-Formulaic Approach to the Interpretation of West-Germanic Verse.* University Park, PA.

Rubin, D. C. 1998. *Memory in Oral Traditions: The Cognitive Psychology of Epic, Ballads, and Counting-out Rhymes.* New York.

Tedlock, D. 1983. *The Spoken Word and the Work of Interpretation.* Philadelphia.

van der Heide, N. 2008. *Spirited Performance: The Manas Epic and Society in Kyrgyzstan.* Amsterdam.

Wadley, S. S. 1989. "Choosing a Path: Performance Strategies in a North Indian Epic." In *Oral Epics in India*, ed. S. H. Blackburn, P. J. Claus, J. B. Flueckiger, and S. S. Wadley, 75–101. Berkeley.

Waldron, R. A. 1957. "Oral-Formulaic Technique and Middle English Alliterative Poetry." *Speculum* 32:792–804.

Whallon, W. 1965. "Formulas for Heroes in the 'Iliad' and in 'Beowulf'." *Modern Philology* 63(2):95–104.

Zhirmunsky, V. M. 1974a. *Tyurkskiy geroicheskiy èpos*. Leningrad.

———. 1974b. "Skazanie ob Alpamyshe i bogatyrskya skazka." In Zhirmunsky 1974a:117–348.

———.1974c. "Vvedenie v izuchenie èposa 'Manas'." In Zhirmunsky 1974a:23–116.

Zhirmunsky, V. M., and Kh. T Zarifov. 1947. *Uzbekskiy narodny geroicheskiy èpos*. Moscow.

Zumthor, P. 1983. *Introduction à la poésie orale*. Paris.

3

Of *Scopas* and Scribes

Reshaping Oral-Formulaic Theory in Old English Literary Studies

STEPHEN C. E. HOPKINS, UNIVERSITY OF CENTRAL FLORIDA

ALTHOUGH ORAL-FORMULAIC THEORY (OFT) was first introduced in Homeric scholarship, its development has been fundamentally shaped by application to the field of Old English literature. This chapter traces the development of OFT in Old English studies from its early appearance in the work of Francis Peabody Magoun, Jr. onwards, highlighting the major advances fostered by the poetry's structure and unique manuscript situation. Furthermore, given the romanticizing nationalism that shaped early Germanic literary scholarship, it becomes evident that these fixations have quietly shaped the concerns and work of OFT analysts over the years. Drawing upon OFT, scholars have excavated the complexity of oral epic across linguistic boundaries, as well as the cultural and mental shifts demanded by the introduction of literacy to previously oral cultures. Yet previous scholarship has often favored a handful of older texts, hampering inquiries into varieties of synchronic oral cultures or even of the possible persistence of oral culture diachronically, making Old English oral poetic practice appear more insular and static than it may have been.

1. Defining Old English Formulaicity

Old English poems tend to announce themselves, calling audiences to attention with formulaic openers. They might employ first-person plural pronouns to summon up a sense of communal memory about old tales and traditional narratives, lay or biblical. A pair of instructive examples can be found in the openings of *Beowulf* and *Exodus*. The first few lines of these two heroic poems are strikingly similar, hinging upon formulaic framings of the tale about to be told:

(1)

> Hwæt, we Gar-dena   in geardagum,
> þeodcyninga   þrym gefrunon,
> hu ða æþelingas   ellen fremedon

> Yes, we have heard of the greatness of the Spear-Danes' high kings in
> days long past, how those noble princes practiced bravery[1]

Compare this to the beginning of *Exodus*:

(2)

> Hwæt! We feor and neah   gefrigen habað
> ofer middangeard   Moyses domas,
> wræclico wordriht,   wera cneorissum [...]

> Listen! Far and near throughout middle-earth we have heard tell of the
> judgements of Moses, and of promises in exile made to generations of
> men [...]

The two rely upon similar formulas to prime audiences for the performance of
story: both open with the interjective *hwæt + we* ('we'), both remind their audiences
of great deeds in former days, and both feature names central to the unfolding
narrative.[2] The earliest admirers and scholars of the poetry were aware of these
speech-like formulas. Anticipating the concerns of Lord and Parry by a century, as
early as 1830, some Old English scholars were noting differences between poems
composed from within oral or from within literate frameworks (Olsen 1986:550).
It was only natural that, once Lord's and Parry's works arrived, they should be
seized upon by scholars of Old English. The formulas in Old English poetry were
not the focus of sustained inquiry until philologists later in that century began
asking about their origins: where did these texts and their formulas come from?
Of what source material were they woven?[3] And, at more than a century's remove,
we might do well to ask about how early scholarship, with its fixation on prob-
lematic romanticizations of race and nationalism, has shaped the development
of OFT in Old English studies, since the two have gone hand in hand for so long.[4]

[1] *Beowulf* is quoted from *Klaeber's Beowulf*; translations are from Fulk 2011. All other Old English
   poetry is from the *Anglo-Saxon Poetic Records*, and translations are my own.
[2] For work on Old English poetic formulaic openings as genre markers, see Battles 2014. For anal-
   ysis of poetic openings in terms of OFT, see Foley 1991:214–223.
[3] For a detailed review of Old English studies focused on formula, see Olsen 1986. For a linguistic
   discussion of what constitutes a "formula," see Wray 2009.
[4] For the ways in which "heritage politics" have been a fundamental aspect of Old English (and
   especially "Anglo-Saxon") studies, see Miyashiro 2019. For a study demonstrating the shifting
   meaning of the "Anglo-Saxon" era, often bound up in nationalist and racially inflected discourses,

2. The Question of Anonymous Style

Initially, Old English and Homeric scholars shared a common burden: that of authorship. Classicists began to realize that the works attributed to "Homer" were diffuse and probably represented a range of voices and compositions over time; Old English scholars arrived at a similar conclusion eventually, though only with great reluctance. Early on, despite the anonymity of the poetry, scholars were preoccupied with establishing authorship, perhaps hoping to divine an "Anglo-Saxon Homer" to glorify this "native" body of literature. Cædmon and Cynewulf were popular candidates, since they were among the few named *scopas*. The Beowulf Poet was another, especially since much early Old English poetry appeared to be pre-Christian (and, they hoped, pre-literate). Nineteenth-century scholars had debated the extent to which Old English poems reflected oral lays or sophisticated monastic works of literature, and debate over the precise nature of this oral background reached a new high in the 1870s. Early ammunition in this debate came from pioneering scholars like Eduard Sievers, who created corpora of formulaic phrases (see Liberman, in this volume, section 1). Along similar lines, Moritz Trautmann (1876) brought the importance of Old English "style" to the fore, attempting to assign texts to specific named authors on this basis alone. Though he raised an important issue, his endeavor was not highly successful because he only loosely defined "style." There is great difficulty in establishing authorship of anonymous poems, since matters of style belong as much to the tradition as to an individual composer of poetry within it. Another impediment was that only a handful of named Old English vernacular poets were (and still are) known at all.[5] In short order, most of the poetic corpus was being assigned to Cynewulf. Against this, Ellen Buttenwieser (1898) argued that since an oral-based formulaic style was behind these correspondences, authorship could not be satisfactorily proven on the basis of formulaic diction alone. Despite the enthusiasm of some, it was eventually decided, on grounds of common sense as well as philology, that Cynewulf could not have composed every "good" poem in the corpus.

Other early works, especially those related to folkloric studies, viewed Old English poems as texts that represent reworkings of now lost lays. On the basis of intertextual references that span centuries, as, say, when independent tales recount strikingly similar legends (such as the Sigmund episode in *Beowulf* and the Völsung legendarium in Old Norse), scholars recognized that these

---

see Rambaran-Olm 2017:114–115. For a study of the ways in which the flexible concept of "race" was fashioned within medieval studies, see Heng 2018.

[5] For the names of all known Old English writers, see Thornbury 2014:243–249.

references are echoes of yet-older bodies of legend.[6] Karl Lachmann's text-critical approach was imported and modified so that, on the basis of comparing cognate versions of the same legend, one might reconstruct the *Ur*-lays which were thought to have been behind these literary siblings.[7] This approach, known as *Liedertheorie*, was not without merit, as it prompted much fruitful source study and allowed scholars a better view of which legends circulated across time, space, and language. Still, its practitioners were sometimes overly reductive, valuing conjecturally reconstructed lays as much as the actual literature under consideration. In his "allegory of the tower," J. R. R. Tolkien memorably lamented that reductive *Quellenschaft* and *Liedertheorie* approaches took texts like *Beowulf,* that are valuable and artistic in their own right, and reduced them to debitage that was being mechanically sifted for fossilized hints of putative ancient lays. In this environment, the formulas were valued primarily as a window into poetic pre-history, to the detriment of the poems in which they survived (Tolkien 1936 [1991]:15–16).

3. Growing Side-by-Side: Oral-Formulaic Theory Grafted onto Old English Literature

As soon as his dissertation appeared in 1949, Lord's ideas were influential in many fields. They took especially deep root once planted in Old English studies; its scholars became some of the chief OFT innovators in the ensuing decades, and its concerns became crucial theoretical frontiers for OFT. One of the first to employ the approach was Francis Peabody Magoun, Jr. He had been considering poetic formulas as early as 1929, in his article on name elements in *Beowulf* and the *Poetic Edda*. In a landmark article (Magoun 1953), he went on to synthesize Lord's and Parry's approach to Homeric and oral epic in a manner specifically tailored to the structures and peculiarities of Old English poetry.

Building upon Parry's early principles, Magoun argued that the appearance (or lack) of repetitive formulas or formulaic phrases in an Old English poem could be used to determine whether it was an oral or literate composition, noting the malleability of formulas in Old English poetry as parts of a phraseological system constrained by meter (Magoun 1953:447, 450–453). He also pointed out the central paradox of studying oral-formulaic poetry in Old English, namely, that we can access it only in writing (1953:448–449). Initially, Magoun relied on Parry for definitions of technical terms like "formula" and "formulaic system,"

---

[6] For a thorough catalogue of attested heroic legends, see Wilson 1952. For a recent investigation of the Völsung legends attested in *Beowulf* and *Vǫlsunga saga*, see Abram 2017.

[7] For the influence of *Liedertheorie* on subsequent Old English studies, see Fulk and Cain 2013:esp. 291. For its application to structural analyses of *Beowulf*, see Shippey 1997.

and by means of these and corpus analysis, he declared that roughly seventy percent of the phrases in *Beowulf* appear elsewhere in the poetic corpus and are, therefore, formulaic. Furthermore, the overlap between Christian and possibly pre-Christian formulas was, to his eye, proof that most Old English poetry was the product of oral composition (1953:454, 458). Subsequent scholars have found his assessment overly reductive and reject the idea that density of oral features necessarily signals an oral composition. Nevertheless, Magoun's concerns and methodology were influential. He subsequently catalogued all instances in the corpus of formulaic type-scenes like the Beasts of Battle (Magoun 1955a), and sketched what he imagined to be the typical career of an early medieval English *scop* by analyzing Bede's account of Cædmon (Magoun 1955b). As in Magoun's work, much mid-century scholarship was bent on adapting OFT for use in Old English literary study; it was like hammering a square Cædmonian peg into a round Homeric hole, given the major differences between the cultural contexts. Still, the centrality of this new field was crucial for the development of OFT, since it required modification of the theory, and steered OFT studies in the direction they are now headed.

For example, it was possible to compare Homeric and South Slavic verse without modifying OFT much, because their respective moraic and syllabic meters, lacking regular alliteration or rhyme, are quite similar. Old English is quite a different beast: its poetry is alliterative-accentual, with the accentual rhythm allowing variability in the number of syllables or morae in a verse and alliteration on stressed elements linking the two halves of each poetic line.[8] The phonic metrical principle of alliteration requires words beginning with the same sound to link half-lines across a caesura and thus drives variation both within the formulaic idiom and between formulas. The variation of poetic diction is a hallmark of Old English formulas, which Parry's definition did not readily accommodate, so, if OFT was to be applied, its definitions had to be adapted: a crucial and difficult task (cf. Hainsworth 1968).

On the level of diction, Old English poetry features two specific ways of satisfying metrical and alliterative constraints. The first is by drawing upon a robust poetic diction. The second is a way of expanding that poetic diction by adapting noun phrases to accommodate the principle of variation: the kenning. However, while this structure is easy to identify, it is not always easy to define precisely. In the kenning, a self-contained poetic image is crafted in a noun phrase, for example, the *ganotes bæð* ('gannet's bath') (*Beowulf* 1861b). This is one possible

---

[8] For an introduction to Old English poetic form, see Terasawa 2011. For a schematic of verse types and sub-types, see Sievers 1893; but the field of Old English metrics is vibrant. For recent discussions, see Cable 1974; Russom 1987; Fulk 1992; Hartman 2011. For the argument that Old English poetic formulas continued in a living tradition after the Norman Conquest, see Weiskott 2016.

formula for the sea, though apposition and variation may, along with meter and alliteration, demand others, such as *hron-rad* ('whales' riding') (*Beowulf* 10). Likewise, the sun might be the *heofon-candel* ('heaven-candle') (*Exodus* 115b) or *heofenes gim* ('heaven's gem') (*The Phoenix* 183). In this way, metrical and alliterative demands are satisfied even when alliterative or syllabic demands might rule out some formulations of the head noun about which one is composing.

Scholars disagree widely on how to define kennings, however, and although this metaphorical construction can seem easy to pick out on the page, there is also disagreement about whether kennings are formulaic. One common definition sees the kenning as a formula that is *ein zweigliedriger Ersatz für ein Substantivum der gewöhnlichen Rede* ('a two-part substitution for a substantive of everyday speech') (Meissner 1921:2). This succinct definition has been criticized for its vagueness, especially since it does not speak to the metaphorical dimension of many kennings (Gardner 1972:464).[9] These definitional matters make a great difference: while Thomas Gardner (1969), drawing upon Heusler's strict definition, found only 122 true kennings in the entire corpus of Old English poetry, Alvin Lee (1998:58), with a looser definition, counted some seventy in *Beowulf* alone. Surely some kennings are more formulaic: *rodora wealdend* ('master of the heavens') (*Elene* 482) is one of several kennings for God constructed via the formulation [word for HEAVENS + word for LORD]. But in some poems, kennings can be quite original, such as the compound *mearhcofa* ('marrow-chamber') (*Paris Psalter, Psalm 101, 3, 3*). This is a kenning and compound, but can it be called a formula if there are no other comparable kennings attested for BONE or that use "marrow" as a constituent? Since not all compounds are formulaic, it is probably safer to conclude that not all kennings are, either.

It seems that skilled *scopas* could create new kennings to satisfy formal requirements while also providing a striking image, although scholars of Old English have often pointed to alliterative needs as the primary function of their use and variation. Later in the present volume, Frog addresses the ways in which formulas can be shaped by the form of a given discourse. In his analysis, a kenning may form the core of a linguistic multiform that can span clauses in the Old Norse *dróttkvætt* meter (Frog, in this volume, section 4), a more metrically demanding form than the Old English line. Applying this view to Old English kenning usage and variation helps explain how this poetic circumlocution may have been a method for satisfying not only alliterative needs, as has often been pointed out, but also metrical needs across the half line.[10] Viewed

---

[9] For non-metaphorical kennings, see van de Merwe Scholtz 1927 and Marquardt 1938. Heusler 1922:129 emphasizes the metaphorical. Against this, see Molinari 1983:34.

[10] For recent work on Old Norse poetics and kennings that confirms this point, see Quinn 2016. For a careful study and history of the *dróttkvætt* form, see Gade 1995.

from a cognitive perspective, then, kennings, along with collocate phrases, may have helped *scopas* deploy whole lines easily fitted to a poetic context in performance at minimal cognitive cost, providing a different kind of "thrift" than Homeric scholars have sought, keyed to satisfying the principles of apposition and variation. In previous studies, it has been assumed that a *scop*'s compositional skill can be measured by the originality of their kenning usage. That is, a good *scop* should employ kennings as frequently as needed, but should seldom use the same one twice; the *Exodus* poet might be viewed as exceptionally skillful in these terms, since that brief work features an astonishing number of otherwise unknown kennings.

4. Kennings and Dating: The Question of Scandinavian Influence

Poets such as those behind *Exodus* and *Beowulf* are famed for skillful kenning deployments. Yet their Old English kennings are also constructed very differently from skaldic kennings.[11] Given the strong influx of Scandinavian peoples in the ninth and tenth centuries, the question of Scandinavian influence upon the Old English kenning merits investigation. Some see the above poems as older and more pure specimens of Old English poetic practice—did the elaborate but repetitive skaldic kennings dilute a native tradition? This imagining of a more pure era of Old English oral poetry is tethered to an early dating for those texts, and sometimes feeds into a romanticizing view (or at least classicizing) of earlier poems as products of a more culturally pristine era. Scholars who reject early dates for these poems have asked whether the influence went the other way round. Roberta Frank (1987), expanding upon Dietrich Hofmann's ideas, has argued that *Exodus* is the product of skaldic influence. Since so many Scandinavians inhabited the Danelaw for so long, she suggests, we should expect to see their influence in the language as well as in the literature (Frank 1987:338). Even though she claims that *Exodus'* kennings are "extraordinarily responsive to a 'skaldic' reading" (1987:339) she does not explain what this means, leaving some unconvinced. Jonathan Watson (2002) has taken the question to another text, the *Finnsburgh Fragment*, to further explore the possibility of cross-linguistic influence. The question of Scandinavian influence remains vexed, however. In a recent essay, Leonard Neidorf and Rafael Pascual have systematically reassessed Frank's evidence for skaldic influence (especially in *Beowulf*) from a linguistic perspective, finding that *Beowulf* bears affinities to other Old Germanic poems "not because its author consciously imitated the

---

[11] For a typology of Old Norse poetic forms and kennings, see Clunies Ross 2005:esp. 236–246.

speech of foreign Germanic speakers, but because the early composition of this poem resulted in its conservation of a wider array of features that were probably characteristic of Proto-Germanic usage" (Neidorf and Pascual 2019:4). The focus on the poem as a "composition," a settled text rather than a performance that happened to be copied down, only underscores the strength of the authors' assumptions about *Beowulf*. At play in all of these investigations are competing ideologies that directly affect which texts and elements of texts are deemed worthy of study, both by chronology and by notions of indigeneity or foreign influence.[12] The issue is fraught, since conceding to one argument or another is implicitly conceding to a pedigree of poetics or poems as either inherited/indigenous or foreign, questions further complicated by the thorny issue of chronology.

One reason that scholars have fixated on the question of influence and its directionality is that the kenning only appears in Old English and Old Norse of all the Germanic languages.[13] Of course, investigating the origins of a poetic form can also feed into ideologies of cultural superiority, and so nationalistic pride sometimes creeps into such investigations. For example, one early theory (Heinzel 1875) was that Old English's simple kennings represent a degenerated practice of a more elaborate Common Germanic poetic inheritance, a view that implicitly sees continental Germanic peoples as culturally superior to the Germanic tribes who migrated and colonized England later, as though leaving the Black Forest region somehow weakened them. Less ideologically laden stances can be found from James Rankin (1909–1910:366–367), who proposed that the Old English kenning was simply a more archaic form, and that skaldic use represented the innovation, a view with which Heusler (1951 [1957]:136) agrees. Two other explanations have been proposed: either that Old English poets learned kennings from skalds (Hofmann 1955; although see also Irving 1959:7) or else that kennings are not traditional oral features at all, but a literary invention adapted from classical literature by Old English scribes and ultimately taught to the Scandinavians by them (Gardner 1969). Recently, however, R. D. Fulk (forthcoming) has furnished a highly detailed linguistic study of kenning construction in both languages, finding that Rankin's and Heusler's view is defensible. Rather than pointing to a period of archaic glory and purity (either for Old English or Old Norse), the evidence points to something much more interesting: to the kenning as a feature commonly inherited by Old English and

---

[12] For a different approach, which considers medieval globalisms and connections rather than provincialisms and isolation, see Kinoshita 2007.

[13] See Gardner 1969:111. He considers *The Heliand*'s *līkhamo* ('body') the only kenning attested in the language. However, as Fulk points out (forthcoming:26n10), this compound does not meet Gardner's definition of a kenning.

Old Norse eddic poetry; skaldic usage, by implication, is simply a later oral-formulaic development.

Variation in relation to alliteration is complemented by a practice referred to as apposition, when two or more syntactically parallel phrases are juxtaposed. That is, in the best Old English poetry, characters, and items are named and renamed multiple times in a row, allowing for subtle descriptions and characterizations. The process is illustrated as the Beowulf poet admires the poetic practice of Hrothgar's *scop*:

(3)

> [...] Hwilum cyninges þegn,
> guma gilp-hlæden, gidda gemyndig,
> se ðe eal fela eald-gesegena
> worn gemunde, word oþer fand
> soðe gebunden; secg eft ongan
> sið Beowulfes snyttrum styrian
> ond on sped wrecan spel gerade,
> wordum wrixlan [...]

Beowulf 867b–874a

> At times an attendant of the king,
> a man laden with glorious words, with a memory for stories,
> who remembered all the many multitudes of tales of old,
> came up with other words accurately assembled;
> the man in turn began sagely to recite Beowulf's exploit,
> to deliver successfully a skillful account,
> to make variations with words [...]

Thus, formulaic speech was foundational because knowing more formulas allowed one to "make variations with words" better, skillfully weaving apposition after apposition at the level of the hemistich, yielding a tension between alliterative formulaicity and the need for felicitous and even novel expression.[14] Trying to account for the Old English poetic principle of variation was the cause of one of the early major divisions between OFT as conceived for Homeric epic and its application to Old English. Scholars of Homer understood one advantage of poetic formulas as providing "thrift" for the poet (see e.g. Parry 1971:276–279).[15] From this perspective, variation, with all its repetitions, might be seen by

---

[14] For other features, see Olsen 1986; 1988.

[15] That is not to say that formulas are created for the purpose of thrift. Rather, formulas evolve on a principle of thrift for greater economy in composition. Over time, a once fresh and original

Homeric scholars as excessive or redundant. Still, the central poetic principle of apposition was studied early on by John O. Beaty (1934) and refined later still by Robinson (1985), whose works demonstrate the subtle ways in which skilled composers could produce poetic effects and complicated narrative commentary by means of appositive formulas.

Old English poetry features additional formulaic terms, including patronyms, as well as type-scenes and themes.[16] It should be noted that these features are not unique to Old English poetry: Reichl has pointed out that Medieval Russian literature—*The Song of Igor*, for example—contains the Beasts of Battle type-scene, and that formulaic attributive tags (i.e. *Beowulf maðelode* ['Beowulf spoke'], *sunu Ecgþeowes* ['son of Ecgþeow']) exist in many languages.[17] Still, Old English metrical and alliterative constraints leave their mark on these features, as has been documented by John Miles Foley (1990), whose comparative work focuses on the metrical, phrasal, and thematic as categories of oral-derived formulas across languages and literatures. However, as insightful as OFT can be for the study of Old English literature, it has not gone unquestioned. Larry D. Benson (1966) voiced some important caveats, bringing to scholars' attention a certain fallacy latent in some OFT approaches to Old English literature: just because a work is formulaic does not necessarily mean that it is also oral.[18] Calvin Kendall (1996) has also demonstrated that there were early English poets who were fully literate, like Cynewulf, who still employed formulas well. Joseph Dane (1994) has voiced even stronger skepticism about the methodology from a post-structuralist perspective. These misgivings should not be seen as debunking OFT, however. Instead, scholars have taken note of the objections, reformulating assumptions about how porous the boundary may have been between orality and literacy for Old English poets.

5. From Indexical Consideration to Aesthetic

Once OFT had been accepted in Old English studies, scholars began detecting local signs of oral indexicality in the poetic formulas along with their aesthetic purposes. One early and important contributor was Robert Creed, whose work drew attention to the relationship between formulas and complex units of content by studying "formulaic systems" such as the "*andswarode* system" or "*maðelode* system." He argued that some verbal formulas act as auditory

---

expression becomes calcified through conventional use, until it is a stock phrase that later composers can draw upon with little thought.

[16] For an overview see Olsen 1986:577–588.

[17] For comparative work between Turkic epic and medieval epic, see Reichl 2000.

[18] Holoka agrees: "formulae do not necessarily indicate orality" (1976:570).

punctuation markers for listeners, "essentially a verse-pair system designed to make a whole line of the song" (Creed 1957:527). In other words, set phrases and formulas might provide a functional and practical, while still metrical, way of suturing together speeches into longer narrative segments, which he expanded to a proposed lineation of poems in larger units he called "measures" (Creed 1982). However, Randolph Quirk was quick to articulate the limits of such "verse paragraphs," highlighting the differences between oral formulas and phrases chosen for metrical demands, and demonstrating that these do not always overlap (Quirk 1963:150). Another early contribution came from A. C. Spearing, whose work anticipated the aesthetic turn of OFT during the 1990's. He called attention to the affective impact that oral audiences might have felt from well-deployed oral formulas (Spearing 1964:20). Charles Wrenn (1967), in his *Study of Old English Literature*, argued that Old English poetics, though they remained formally stable, drifted from emphasizing the heroic to the hagiographical, but never entirely (*Elene* and *Judith* were at the core of his analysis). This was an important expansion because it considered the adaptation of oral formulas into written works, moving analysis towards texts later than *Beowulf.*

Amidst all the work being carried out on local formulaic features, there was some terminological confusion in the field, since terms were often borrowed from Lord very loosely (who was sometimes vague himself) and then used differently by different scholars, who only occasionally provided precise definitions.[19] Ann Watts (1969) called for a rigorous redefinition, so that approaches that drew analogies between Old English orality and other traditions—Homeric or Serbian, for example—might be more productive. Her work paved the way for later comparativists like Jeff Opland and Foley, and encouraged scholars to consider how "theme" and "formula" are separate aspects of a larger poetic system. Alain Renoir also undertook large-scale comparative work, urging his readers that "ignoring oral-formulaic features used functionally by a writer thoroughly and actively steeped in oral-formulaic rhetoric would also result in probable misinterpretation" (Renoir 1988:159). Despite Renoir's rigorous application of carefully defined OFT terminology to provide compelling readings of individual texts, on a broader conceptual level, his work does not distinguish between oral-formulaic composition and orally delivered texts. This crucial distinction would have to wait until the following decade for deeper consideration.

---

[19] See Olsen 1986:578–588, where she traces the refinement of these ideas. Major developments include Lord's own definition of theme ("a grouping of ideas") (1960:69), Creed's "sameness with difference" (1961:99), Fry's redefinition of the three as a hierarchy of motif, type-scene, and theme (1968:49), and Griffith's reassertion of Quirk's scheme, with especial emphasis on formulaic convention (1993:179).

Even while catalogues of formulas, type-scenes, and themes were being compiled, some scholars proceeded from this structuralist concern to more aesthetic ones. If a poem like *Beowulf* bore traces of oral formulas, then how much of it, as a literary experience, could be attributed to a single author in any meaningful sense? One answer to this question was Adrien Bonjour's study and assessment of the use of a single type-scene across the corpus of Old English poetry (Bonjour 1957). Taking up Magoun's catalogue of the Beasts of Battle instances, Bonjour analyzed the deployment of each formula linked to the type-scene to consider which poems' uses were most artful, and to see what connotations the formulaic set-piece might bear in context. In the end, he judged the *Beowulf* poet's use of them the best, while the Beasts of the supposedly lesser poets behind *The Battle of Brunnanburh* or *Genesis A* were merely set-pieces included out of a desire for conventional embellishment. In Bonjour's analysis, the Beasts of Battle theme spells doom, and "casts the shadow of death and slaughtered corpses in advance, and thereby implies [...] the inexorability of fate" (Bonjour 1957:565–566). Since then, scholars have fruitfully weighed the affective and artistic merits of the deployment of such themes (e.g. on the Beasts of Battle, see Frank 1987; Griffith 1993; Honegger 1998; Harris 2006; Hopkins 2018). Thanks to these conversations, Old English studies have furnished, arguably, the richest discussion on the relationship of formulaic language to larger units for the time, including foundational concepts like "ring composition" and "echo words," which Foley (1990) redubbed "responsions."[20] These discussions have had broad impacts on OFT, and their development can be linked again to the flexibility of idiom in Old English.

In short, the introduction of OFT to Old English studies brought both clarity and complexity to the question of "the poet" behind any Old English text to reach us by manuscript. Instead of identifying particular named *scopas*, scholars began to investigate the network of formulaic traditions drawn upon by the poets. Yet, in shifting away from seeking named figures to studying formulas, scholarship focused increasingly upon the oldest Old English texts, under the assumption that older would provide more evidence for orality, sometimes overlooking the possibility of oral evidence from later works. Chief among the innovations in the field from this period were the delineations between motif, type-scene, and theme. By the mid-1970s, literacy itself began to be theorized and scrutinized more carefully, sparked by important works like M. T. Clanchy's *From Oral Memory to Written Record* (1979).

---

[20]   For examples, see Leyerle 1967 and Niles 1979.

6. Written Oral Formula: Peculiarities of Old English Transitional Literacy

Both early adopters and opponents of oral-formulaic approaches saw Old English literature in polarized terms: a text was either oral or literate. Yet over time, as Katherine O'Brien O'Keeffe has suggested, scholars have augmented and synthesized each other's findings, and the field's "interest has shifted from construing orality and literacy as discrete and impermeable social states to envisioning them as complex social conditions coexisting with one another and affecting each other" (O'Brien O'Keeffe 2012:121). This conception became more nuanced after Eric Havelock's 1963 work, which argued that, in the Ancient Greek world, the introduction of writing radically changed conceptions of language in Athens. Walter Ong refined the idea further by exploring the implications of literacy as a laboriously acquired and epochal technology.[21] The continuum between primary orality (a culture which has no conception of literacy) and literacy (a culture in which most people are literate) is relative. It is thus useful to examine the spectrum and the gradations that exist along it; for the field of Old English literature, the more we understand the hues of residual orality, the more refined our understanding of early medieval England's transitional literary culture will be.

One common starting point for investigating the nature of oral poetry on the eve of Old English literacy is Bede's story about the first person to compose vernacular poetry on biblical subjects in traditional formulas.[22] In Book IV Chapter XXIV of his *Historia ecclesiastica*, Bede reports the famous story of Cædmon, an illiterate herdsman, who, by divine gift, miraculously masters poetic composition overnight. It seems that poetic formulation and adaptation of it to Christian thought constituted the miracle itself, for Bede mentions that Cædmon still needed to be taught a scriptural narrative and mull it over before he could compose.[23] The implications behind these tantalizing details have, in their turn, been the object of much critical rumination. For example, Magoun (1955b) argued that this account chronicled the typical career of an early English oral poet during the transitional period.[24] While this oversimplification has been questioned and nuanced over time, Cædmon is still

---

[21] For the classic articulation of levels of orality, see Ong 1982.

[22] For critical positions taken on the Cædmon narrative, see the opening paragraph of Orchard 2009.

[23] For the relative status of oral poetry in an increasingly literate culture, see Amodio 2004.

[24] For further considerations of Cædmon's career, see Fritz 1969, Wormald 1977, Clanchy 1979, Opland 1980, and O'Brien O'Keeffe 2012. For medieval formulaic mnemotechnology, see Carruthers 1990.

taken as an important figure of liminality, bridging oral and traditional Old English poetics to the monastic and memorative.

Shifting the question from *What were poets like during the transitional period?* to *What was writing like?*, Malcolm Godden has asked "Did King Alfred Write Anything?" (2007). The question aptly captures the transition in the way the field conceives what it meant to be a "writer" in the Late West Saxon context in the first place. King Alfred, who had commissioned an ambitious translation project, was, in the nineteenth century and most of the twentieth, considered the author of these texts in a sense not far from our own today.[25] Godden, drawing upon statistical analysis of verbal variation in this body of texts, suggests that Alfred may have commissioned some of them, but that others diverge more, and were, perhaps, merely attributed to him posthumously. The argument has been influential, but Janet Bately (2009) reexamined the statistical work and reminded readers that it is difficult to determine what factor(s) motivated the translator(s) of these texts, which represent different genres and textual traditions. As scholars continue to re-evaluate traditionally ascribed authorship in light of OFT and stylistics, one promising avenue of research might be suggested by Jane Stevenson's *Women Latin Poets* (2005:ch. 4), which features preliminary work on women composing in early medieval England in the circle of St. Boniface. Consideration of these eighth-century audiences for Latin poetry raises another question: what influence might oral stylistics have had on Anglo-Latin poetic composition? As we can see from discussions surrounding the Cædmonian and Alfredian narratives, the Old English textual situation, oral or literate, was complex because, like Cædmon's poetic gift, oral-written literature was liminal (see Harris and Reichl 2012).

7. Challenges Inherent to the Corpus

The haphazard survival of Old English manuscripts has increased the difficulty of assessing the oral-literate continuum.[26] The nature of the corpus and its preservation became crucial factors in the development of Old English formula research. Old English texts present methodological challenges and raise issues that were not salient in Homeric or South Slavic traditions. Once OFT research had built momentum, it had to face these challenges. Early manuscript evidence has been interpreted as indicating the primacy of Latin in writing. As a corollary,

---

[25] Godden 2007 reports that it is commonly believed that King Alfred personally translated the following: Gregory the Great's *Dialogi* and *Cura Pastoralis*, Boethius' *De consolatione Philosophiae*, Orosius' *Historia contra Paganos*, Augustine's *Soliloquiae*, and Bede's *Historia*. Treschow et al. 2009 also draws upon statistical analysis of lexical choices to dismantle Alfredian authorship.

[26] For the transmission process, see Fulk and Cain 2013:esp. ch. 2.

the vernacular's rise is often seen as the result of waning Latinity. This historical sketch is derived in two ways: first, from King Alfred's preface to the *Pastoral Care* and second, from the work of Michael Lapidge (1996:409–454), who demonstrates the poor Latinity even of English bishops in the ninth century. In light of this finding, it is commonly assumed that Old English oral culture existed alongside a scribal literary culture before admixture occurred. Then, so the story goes, in the destructive wake of the Vikings, many things began to be written in the vernacular under King Alfred's patronage. Having survived centuries of war, fires, and decay, Old English poetry is largely represented in single manuscripts, sparking debate over how accurate each textual witness is.

The corpus of Old English has also spurred innovations in OFT research because many Old English poems are shorter than texts from the epic traditions in which OFT was first developed. For this reason, James P. Holoka (1976) proposed that some of these brief compositions may have been circulated as more stable textual entities (see also Frog, this volume, section 3). This makes Old English literature a sort of test case for theories of emendation. Whether to emend a text is always a weighty decision, even under more normal circumstances where, say, one has several manuscripts or traditions from which to trace variants and manuscript families. When only a single copy of a text remains, scribal mediation of Old English texts becomes a much thornier issue. As Fulk has noted, due to these unusual circumstances, "the decision not to emend often involves more conjecture than to emend" (2007:149). Applying this idea, Neidorf (2014) provides examples from *Beowulf*, demonstrating that the early eleventh-century scribes of the present copy seem to have misunderstood the archaic and obscure lexical and metrical items in their exemplar, formulaic or not. His analysis suggests that they seem to have replaced unfamiliar words and formulas with more familiar ones (a process known as "trivialization" in textual editing), a finding that suggests a sort of shelf-life for oral formulas (see also Bozzone forthcoming); they are effective only as long as the associated traditions are remembered. Neidorf (2014), while he acknowledges that scribal performance is worthy of study, remains unconvinced that the Old English scribal variants we have provide plausible evidence that the scribes in question understood the technical aspects of Old English poetry well enough to compose on a substantial scale.

On the other hand, A. N. Doane (1991) has argued that, in cases where we have multiple copies of an Old English poem, and have a clearer picture of what sources and oral traditions lie behind the text, the variants do give evidence for sustained scribal performance—i.e. that scribes, drawing upon their own intuitive knowledge of the (originally) oral-formulaic tradition improvised while copying a text, replacing an exemplar's reading with formulaic insertions of their own. One major methodological division between these scholars is their focus: Neidorf focuses almost exclusively on texts considered early, assuming that the oldest texts are closer to a living oral tradition. This fetishization of early texts is, however, detrimental to rigorous study of the question: the only texts that survive in multiple copies are later ones, which is why Doane's work focuses on these less prized texts. Philological scrutiny across the period is needed in order to reassess these very old assumptions: if texts were composed by *someone* later in the period, as we know they were, then the oral traditions were alive *somewhere* (even if not in the scribes themselves). Until we carefully study later texts with the scrutiny lavished upon *Beowulf*, it will remain uncertain whether scribes were badly imitating *scopas* or misunderstanding their exemplars, and, more importantly, whether the oral tradition was evolving. This last possibility merits greater consideration since some sort of alliterative-accentual poetic practice survived as late as the fifteenth century, as attested by the works of the alliterative revival.[27]

8. Oral-Literate Culture

Now that a general typology of Old English formula has been established, we can return to a question that has loomed over discussions of OFT in Old English studies all along: if literacy was imported to the early English only after 597 CE, then how were pre-existing attitudes to oral formulas and oral culture reconciled with the new high-status Latinity and literacy that were fast taking hold? One way to answer this has been to turn to the pivotal story, mentioned above, of Cædmon, miraculously made a Christian *scop* overnight. Because we have few poems that we can confidently assign to the start of the period, but a great many Anglo-Latin ones, some have posited a great gulf in attitudes towards the vernacular; perhaps Old English was deemed unworthy of the new technology of writing, or perhaps it was felt to be ill-suited or inappropriate for the medium.[28] Recently, O'Brien O'Keeffe (2012) has shifted the conversation, suggesting that it is more fruitful to think about the two languages not in competition, but as linguistic/cultural forces that influenced each other.

Another source to which scholars can look is the material remains of the manuscripts themselves. O'Brien O'Keeffe (1990) has been foundational in bringing material culture and new philological methods into the conversation by investigating Old English manuscripts for what they can tell us about the scribes who produced them: their methods as well as their attitudes towards

---

[27] For the persistence of the alliterative tradition, see Weiskott 2016.

[28] This is not to suggest that we are utterly in the dark concerning the chronology of Old English poetry. The classic philological and metrical assessment is Fulk 1992; see also Fulk and Cain 2013.

the texts they were transmitting. She writes, "The presence of variant readings which are semantically, metrically, and syntactically appropriate suggests a strong overlay of oral habits of transmission in the copying of Old English formulaic verse" (1990:21). Over the course of her investigation, she posits a scribal culture amidst "transitional literacy." The idea is that scribes, who had, to some extent, access to oral tradition and formulas, felt free to improvise even while transcribing a text before them, because both oral and nascent literate cultures were in play in early medieval England, neither overriding the other yet. Because of this simultaneity, the exemplar of an Old English poem was not "the text" for a scribe as it might be for us; she argues that such a notion is anachronistic.[29] Rather, the manuscript and its text represent the recording of a single moment, of one possible breathed performance; revising it while copying (scribal performance) is merely continuing the living tradition in a new medium, one which, for subsequent historical reasons, strikes modern readers as more definitive and finalized than it would be to eyes conditioned by the prevailing contemporary oral culture.

From this perspective, a manuscript delivers us a moment of variance rather than a perfect text, yielding up traces of residual orality. For example, among the scribal variants of *The Battle of Brunanburh*, O'Brien O'Keeffe (1990:108–137) points out that many of those found in the D manuscript (British Library, MS Cotton Tiberius B. iv, ff. 3–86) suggest a lack of familiarity with traditional formulas—in line five, for instance, the annalist copies *heord weal clufan* ('they clove the care-wall' (?)) instead of the traditional formula *bordweal clufan* ('they clove the shield-wall'); and although one could imagine this to be a misreading of an exemplar's 'b' for the letter 'h', the blunder could have been corrected because of the formulaic demand for alliteration—but it was not. On the other hand, the variants in manuscript B are not defective in this obviously clumsy manner; the scribes of B employ different formulas, but their substitutions make sense. O'Brien O'Keeffe interprets the work of the B annalists as scribal improvisation with formulas, a cultural trend that scholarship on the copies of *The Soul and Body* fragments has also suggested.[30] Her influential work has sparked much discussion and debate.[31] The evidence is fragmentary—since so few Old English texts exist in multiple copies, it is difficult to determine how common these scribal practices really were, let alone how those added up, in the aggregate, into "scribal culture." Still, we get a glimpse of the complicated ways in which acts of remembrance mediated and informed vernacular texts

---

[29] Another important theorist on textual *mouvance* is Zumthor 1972.
[30] Moffat 1987 examines the Soul and Body poems. On these, see also Orton 2000.
[31] For additional New Philological approaches, see Niles 1993; also Doane 1991; 2002; Moffat 1992; Muir 2006. Contra her claims, see Lucas 1993 and Neidorf 2014.

that scribes understood as oral formulations, and how these differed qualitatively from their approach to written Latin.

9. Layers of Textual Transmission

A related complication is that the relative status of vernacular writing seems to have increased over the period. The reasons are unclear, but what was once an activity restricted to glossing became almost as common as Latin writing by the time of Alfred. There is evidence for some vernacular writing before Alfred's day, but how best to interpret this sudden rise is disputed since so many Old English prose texts come to us filtered through a Late West Saxon dialect (a "modernization" from the standpoint of the scribes of our surviving manuscripts). Even as early as 1903, Felix Liebermann, while sorting out the many transmissional layers of the early Kentish laws of Æthelbert (ca. 600), argued that legal texts, at least, were likely composed and written down in the vernacular rather than in Latin.[32] Beyond this, there is evidence for other vernacular genres written down early in the period. Fulk (2010), after sifting early anonymous prose texts to analyze their mixed dialectical features, concludes "the likeliest explanation, then, is that most texts displaying a considerable admixture of Anglian features are of Anglian origin" (2010:77). He also demonstrates why "a likelier period for the composition of much of it is thus before the destruction of the monasteries in the middle of the ninth century" (2010:78). Perhaps as a result of Viking depredations, most of our vernacular texts come to us in tenth-century (or later) manuscripts, generating the appearance that the vernacular was suddenly being written down at a much higher rate than before. Such an argument, based upon absence of evidence, must remain conjectural. Regardless of when exactly one assumes vernacular writing to have begun, it still raises the question: how did oral culture interact with scribal culture before, during, and in the wake of this cultural and linguistic revolution? Behind this is the question of what early English *scopas* were like across the period. Frank (1993) has proposed that such knowledge is lost to us and that the few literary representations of early English poets that we have are merely constructs, figments of an imagined past. However, J. D. Niles expresses skepticism that this agnostic position is all we can know about the early English oral poet. Instead, he suggests that each age in the wake of the early English conversion re-invented the literary figure of the oral poet until:

---

[32] For the evidence and the historical debates surrounding early vernacular composition, see Fulk 2010.

the models of oral performance that emerged during that long period of the Middle Ages became the source of layers upon layers of nostalgia that have been a potent aspect of the Western sensibility up to the present day [...] and there is no reason to think that the last bard will ever die. On the contrary, the mythos of the oral poet is likely to continue to thrive long after our present world has become the substance of future nostalgia.

Niles 2003:42

That is, the early medieval past is a layered palimpsest that consists of layers of nostalgic reinvention of figures, constantly remade as anchors for the ever-shifting present.[33] Literary nostalgia in Latin was anchored to named authors, emphasizing the *auctoritas* that comes with that construction; Old English oral texts, however, usually remained anonymous, even while Anglo-Latin literacy did not (Thornbury 2014). Anonymity makes the shadowy oral singer difficult for scholars to approach. Nevertheless, in the wake of O'Brien O'Keeffe (1990), scholars have continued to investigate what scribal attitudes may have been towards the words and formulas they inked on parchment.

10. Oral-Scribal Culture

Given the decentered nature of anonymous texts, what kind of accuracy did scribes strive for in copying? Or to what extent did they feel free to participate in the oral compositional process even while writing? To what extent can we trust their reports? The question of scribal attitudes and aptitudes has been a subject of debate for most of the last century. Kenneth Sisam's classical training and close work with textual editing left him with a low opinion of scribal trust-worthiness; early English scribal works "show a laxity in reproduction and an aimlessness in variation which are more in keeping with the oral transmission of verse [...] [scribes are] often ignorant, or inattentive to meaning" (Sisam 1946:34, 38). In such a view, the scribes make copying errors because the work is monotonous and the material beyond their comprehension. Lack of interest and knowledge combine to yield increasingly haphazard copies of works which must have always appealed to more erudite audiences than scribes. The task of the editor, therefore, is to purge the text of scribal meddling and restore it to its pristine and classical state. This view, characteristic of nineteenth- and early to mid-twentieth-century scholarship, is an outgrowth of Lachmannian

---

[33] For an illuminating development of this position, see Trilling 2009. She explores the memorative and commemorative implications of early English oral-scribal representations of the past.

and Housmanian textual criticism. Its practitioners have made immense strides in making the works of the ancient world more accessible and comprehensible than their (usually) late manuscripts could.

However, the methodology has some weaknesses when it comes to the transmission of vernacular literature, and the past fifty years or so has seen work which demonstrates that scribal attitudes towards the vernacular differed from Latin. O'Brien O'Keeffe (1990) is one example of work in this vein, and others have gone further. Doane's (1994:421–422) conception of scribal performance assumes a much higher degree of scribal competency, coupled with a much higher rate of scribal intervention.[34] He suggests that Classical and Latinate literary culture of medieval scribes was radically different from the common oral/traditional culture that encompassed Old English poetry. This difference, essentially that Latin texts were meant to be *read* (and were therefore thought of by scribes as more fixed) while vernacular compositions were meant to be *heard* (and were therefore thought of as more improvisational or ephemeral), manifests itself in the different manuscript apparatus that accompany texts in each language. Regarding scribal variants, Doane goes so far as to suggest that "this variation [...] is so massive yet textually so indifferent and so omnipresent in all poetic texts that it must be seen as the norm, not as a set of emendable exceptions" (2002:50). Because of the improvisational nature of oral-formulas, every variant that conforms to meter or other formulaic constraints is considered potentially scribal-performative. As Neidorf notes, O'Brien O'Keeffe's approach is more closely tethered to manuscript and formulaic evidence, and is less conjectural than that of others. However, he also suggests that "a serious impediment [...] is that few of the pertinent variants occur in the context of known formulae" (Neidorf 2017:111n4).

For all the points of disagreement between these perspectives on interpreting the manuscript evidence, the idea that scribes may not be entirely to blame for variants in manuscripts is also shared by Neidorf (2017). He proposes a "lexemic theory" of scribal culture, which takes account of the copying process not as a performative moment, but as a mechanical and redundant morpheme-by-morpheme task. While he maintains, as in his 2014 essay, that the *Beowulf* manuscript bears many traces of textual corruption, he later offers a more robust treatment of scribal behavior, writing:

---

[34] See also Kiernan 1981; Moffat 1992; Pasternack 1995. For the oral and formulaic inheritance as adapted and reworked in ecclesiastical circles during the Benedictine Reform, see Maring 2011; O'Camb 2016.

The scribes responsible for the poem's transmission have emerged from these chapters not as the "monastic blockheads" lambasted in classical textual criticism [...], but as earnest laborers who were charged with a task beyond their capabilities. They simply lacked the knowledge required for the transcription and simultaneous modernization of this centuries-old poem, the text of which was replete with archaic and dialectal spellings, rare words, artificial syntax, and unfamiliar proper names.

Neidorf 2017:103

That is, the lexemic theory suggests that when early English scribes copied a text, they did so to the best of their ability. However, as we know from the transmission of classical literature, some texts are recopied very infrequently. If, as linguistic and metrical analyses suggest, our copy of *Beowulf* is a copy of a much older poem, then it is not surprising that, as traditional and conservative as the oral-formulaic poetic tradition was, it should nevertheless contain words, phrases, and spellings unfamiliar to scribes because they are even older than their already venerable manuscripts. In his view, we can hardly blame tenth-century scribes for lacking deep knowledge of subtle linguistic and dialectal change. In moments of doubt, Neidorf suggests, the scribe, while modernizing orthography, simply guessed to the best of their ability, replacing an unfamiliar lexeme with a familiar and orthographically similar one. Rather than participating in an improvised composition of the text, "the scribes were engaged in a mechanical task whose success was continuously predicated on one critical operation: the identification of the lexeme present in a sequence of graphemes in the exemplar" (2017:103). If scribes recognized an old word or Anglian spelling, they then updated it to the Late West Saxon dialect of their scribal training. If they did not know it, they tried to update it—often wrongly but creatively. The theory offers an alternative account for textual variants by foregrounding the monotonous mechanical realities of the scribe's task.

11. Tangled in the Troubled Past

Looking back on the evolution of OFT in Old English studies, it is clear that scholars connected with Harvard University played an early and crucial role in devising the theory (Lord) and then applying it to Old English literary study (Magoun). Lord's endeavor was, in some respects, anti-classicizing, for it sought to deconstruct the idea that a single primordial poet named Homer was responsible for the *Iliad* and the *Odyssey*, two works that were, at the time, considered cornerstones of "Western Literature."[35] Yet Magoun's application of the theory to Old English seems to have been enveloped in a doubled action: on the one hand, it sought to raise the prestige of Old English literature by treating it as comparable to Classical literature, an endeavor undertaken in England during the previous century. On the other hand, as it did in Classics, OFT also greatly complicated our understanding of Old English poetic composition by emphasizing the performances and transmissional layers involved, undercutting simplistic narratives of authorship. Still, in both cases, the work effectively echoed nineteenth-century scholarly ideologies, rooted in a Romanticized nationalism. For by elevating Old English poetry to the level of cultural prestige alongside Greek epics, early OFT scholars inaugurated a quixotic quest for "authentic" Old English poetry. In their wake, much ink has been spilled in pursuit of classifying which works are closest to the living oral tradition; this quest has, in turn, led to a myopic focus on the texts that can be dated as earliest.

One consequence is that *Beowulf* has been elevated in OFT studies for a century, especially after Tolkien's influential essay gave it such critical prominence. As a result, when Magoun began importing OFT, many of the features he saw as most indicative of orality were trademarks of the *Beowulf* poet. This is not to say that *Beowulf* is not among the older Old English poems or that it is overrated; but if some portions of it are indeed ancient, we should also be open to the idea that its features may be "of their time." We know that as a living tradition, oral culture changes over time, and this fact puts demonstrably later works, such as *The Battle of Brunanburh* or even the Exeter Book's extravagant *Rhyming Poem*, at a critical disadvantage. They often go ignored, left to gather dust on the shelf since they are not classic Old English, and the assumption often runs that what few features of orality they happen to possess are merely evidence of the durability of the tradition in the hands of lesser *scopas*. But given the haphazard survival of Old English poetic texts, and the variation (intentional or not) attested to within those manuscripts, we would do well to pay more heed to non-classical texts, and to shed the notion of "non-classical" itself. For what might a non-classical (that is, later) Old English oral-formulaic habitus have looked like? Did the status of the *scop* change after the Danelaw was established? In what ways might the side-by-side cultivation of Anglo-Latin and Old English poetry have led to a hybrid stylistics? Such questions cannot be answered by fixating upon the earliest or supposedly "purest" texts.

This movement away from an obsession with purity is especially important since Old English began as a subfield of what was considered Germanic

---

[35] On the problematic artificiality of the myth of such a "Western canon," see Hall (2018:90–93). For problems with the boundaries of Old English and Middle English, see Cannon 2004.

Philology, a byproduct of the nineteenth-century obsession with finding ancient status and legitimacy in nationalism (Miyashiro 2019). Yet even before this, when Old English was thought of as belonging to England, it was used for political purposes, as ideology always is. Beginning with the sixteenth-century pioneers of Old English study, each era has rooted among its Old English roots in search of an origin story (Rambaran-Olm 2017).[36] By remaining so fixated upon notions of classical oral-formulaic poetry, scholars have also tacitly introduced this baggage to more recent debates on OFT within Oral Scribal culture.

12. Conclusion: Orality's Miliaux?

Given the complicated transmissional layers apparent in most Old English texts and the ambiguity of oral-scribal culture's contours, some scholars have sought to simplify matters by focusing on the earlier texts in the corpus, hoping that by gravitating towards an era of putative oral purity they might gain some measure of clarity. However, recent work on poetic audiences raises questions about even this assumption. Although many kinds of poetic practice and composition existed, it is clear that, oftentimes, a single person might cross these lines and participate in a range of poetic styles. We hear, for instance, of Aldhelm's ability to recite traditional heroic verse on bridges to draw crowds for his preaching. This practice suggests a widespread appreciation for traditional oral compositions, but it also suggests that a literate Latin poet was fully capable of changing language and form. It also raises another question: did Old English oral-formulaic practices have influence on Anglo-Latin poetics, or vice versa?[37]

Further work needs to be carried out on the many audiences that existed for these diverse compositional traditions. Emily Thornbury (2014) has brought this question to the fore for Old English and Anglo-Latin poetry. However, if *Egils saga* chapters 62–64 are to be believed, there was an eager English audience for skaldic poetry during this period as well. Should we assume that each stylistic tradition had its own distinct audience, that skalds entertained different audiences from monastic Old English poetry?[38] And who participated in medical and charm compositions? Andy Orchard (1994) has drawn attention to Aldhelm's alliterative stylistics, and Christopher Abram (2007) has further demonstrated that the division between insular Latin and vernacular compositions is, to a large extent, a false dichotomy. More could also be made of material culture—there are a number of artifacts that bear poetic fragments that afford us an

---

[36] For an interpretation of the Elizabethan motivations for studying Old English, see Brackmann 2012.

[37] See Orchard 1994.

[38] See Bredehoft 2009.

opportunity to study texts usually considered singular. Consider the Ruthwell Cross, inscribed as it is with a portion of the *Dream of the Rood*. What audiences were expected to appreciate its hybridity? The Franks Casket is another even more perplexing witness to multiple milieaux: its literate references are many (the nativity of Christ, the Romulus and Remus narrative, the Siege of Jerusalem), but so, too, are its references to oral compositions (the legend of Weyland, the archer "Egil" on its lid, and the undeciphered legend). Its Latin is quite rustic, but nothing else about the object comes across as anything less than sophisticated. If we are to better understand early Medieval England and the literature it produced, we need to turn our attention to the full complexity of its population: to migrants from Saxony, monks from Ireland and the continent, travelers and traders from all around the North Sea and the Mediterranean, and learned ecclesiastics from the Middle East and North Africa. Moving OFT studies towards other and later texts than *Beowulf* is a crucial step forward if the field is to confront its troubling past, rooted as it is in nationalism and racism.[39] This is not to discard the painstaking work of past generations of scholars; rather, it is to suggest that the kind of careful, sustained, and devoted attention lavished upon a handful of fetishized texts might be well spent on texts not traditionally seen as ideal specimens of Old English OFT, taking new texts and new textual situations into account.

Acknowledgements

I would like to express gratitude to R. D. Fulk, Kari Ellen Gade, Brian O'Camb, and Brandon Hawk for providing insightful feedback on various iterations of this chapter; any infelicities that remain are my own.

---

[39] Ellard (2019) draws crucial links between the troubling politics and scholarly practice of much of Old English's foundational scholarship. She excavates the ways nationalism and racism have quietly shaped (and skewed) our inquiries over the past two centuries. See also Rambaran-Olm 2019; Miyashiro 2019; Wilton 2020.

References

Sources

Fulk R. D., Bjork, R. E., and Niles, J. D. 2008. *Klaeber's Beowulf*, ed. 4. Toronto.

Krapp, G. P., and Van Kirk Dobbie, E., eds. 1931–1953. *The Anglo-Saxon Poetic Records*, 6 vols. New York.

Literature

Abram, C. 2007. "Aldhelm and the Two Cultures of Anglo-Saxon Poetry." *Literature Compass* 4:1354–1377.

———. 2017. "Bee-wolf and the Hand of Victory: Identifying the Heroes of *Beowulf* and *Vǫlsunga saga*." *The Journal of English and Germanic Philology* 116:387–414.

Amodio, M. 2004. *Writing the Oral Tradition: Oral Poetics and Literate Culture in Medieval England*. South Bend.

Bately, J. 2009. "Did King Alfred Actually Translate Anything? The Integrity of the Alfredian Canon Revisited." *Medium Ævum* 78:189–215.

Battles, P. 2014. "Toward a Theory of Old English Poetic Genres: Epic, Elegy, Wisdom Poetry, and the 'Traditional Opening'." *Studies in Philology* 111:1–33.

Beaty, J. O. 1934. "The Echo-Word in *Beowulf* with a Note on the *Finnsburg Fragment*." *Proceedings of the Modern Language Association* 49:365–373.

Benson, L. D. 1966. "The Literary Character of Anglo-Saxon Formulaic Poetry." *Proceedings of the Modern Language Association* 81:334–341.

Bonjour, A. 1957. "Beowulf and the Beasts of Battle." *Proceedings of the Modern Language Association* 72:563–573.

Bozzone, C. Forthcoming. "Homeric Constructions, Their Productivity, and the Development of Epic Greek." *Proceedings of the Conference Language Change in Epic Greek and Other Oral Traditions* (ed. L. Van Beek). Leiden.

Brackmann, R. 2012. *The Elizabethan Invention of Anglo-Saxon England*. Woodbridge, Suffolk.

Bredehoft, T. A. 2009. *Authors, Audiences, and Old English Verse*. Toronto.

Buttenwieser, E. C. 1898. *Studien über die Verfasserschaft des Andreas*. Heidelberg.

Cable, T. 1974. *The Meter and Melody of "Beowulf."* Urbana.

Cannon, C. 2004. *The Grounds of English Literature*. Oxford.

Carruthers, M. J. 1990. *The Book of Memory: A Study of Memory in Medieval Culture* ed. 2. Cambridge.

Clanchy, M. T. 1993. *From Memory to Written Record: England 1066–1307* ed. 2. Oxford.

Clunies Ross, M. 2005. *A History of Old Norse Poetry and Poetics*. Cambridge.

Creed, R. 1957. "The *andswarode*-System in Old English Poetry." *Speculum* 32:523–528.

———. 1982. "The Basis of the Meter of *Beowulf*." *Approaches to Beowulfian Scansion* (eds. A. Renoir and A. Hernández) 27–36. Berkeley.

Dane, J. A. 1994. "The Lure of Oral Theory in Medieval Criticism: From Edited 'Text' to Critical 'Work'." *Text* 7:145–160.

Doane, A. N. 1991. "Oral Texts, Intertexts, and Intratexts: Editing Old English." *Influence and Intertextuality in Literary History* (eds. J. Clayton and E. Rothstein) 75–113. Madison.

———. 1994. "The Ethnography of Scribal Writing and Anglo-Saxon Poetry: Scribe as Performer." *Oral Tradition* 9(2):420–439.

———. 2002. "Spacing, Placing, and Effacing: Scribal Textuality and Exeter Riddle 30a/b." *New Approaches to Editing Old English* (eds. S. Keefer and K. O'Brien O'Keeffe) 45–66. Woodbridge, Suffolk.

Ellard, D. B. 2019. *Anglo-Saxon(ist) Pasts, postSaxon Futures.* Santa Barbara.

Foley, J. M. 1990. *Traditional Oral Epic: The Odyssey, Beowulf, and the Serbo-Croatian Return Song.* Berkeley.

———. 1991. *Immanent Art: From Structure to Meaning in Traditional Oral Epic.* Bloomington.

Frank, R. 1987. "Did Anglo-Saxon Audiences Have a Skaldic Tooth?" *Scandinavian Studies* 59:338–355.

———. 1993. "The Search for the Anglo-Saxon Oral Poet." *Bulletin of the John Rylands Library* 75:11–36.

Fritz, D. W. 1969. "Cædmon: A Traditional Christian Poet." *Medieval Studies* 31:334–337.

Fry, D. K. 1968. "Old English Formulaic Themes and Type-Scenes." *Neophilologus* 52:48–54.

Fulk, R. D. 1992. *A History of Old English Meter.* Philadelphia.

———. 2007. "The Textual Criticism of Frederick Klaeber's *Beowulf*." *Constructing Nations, Reconstructing Myths: Essays in Honour of T. A. Shippey* (eds. A. Wawn, G. Johnson, and J. Walter) 131–153. Turnhout.

———. 2010. "Localizing and Dating Old English Anonymous Prose, and How the Inherent Problems Relate to Anglo-Saxon Legislation." *English Law Before Magna Carta: Felix Liebermann and Die Gesetze der Angelsachsen* (eds. S. Jurasinski, L. Oliver, and A. Rabin) 59–79. Leiden.

———. Forthcoming. "Kennings in Old English Verse and in the Poetic Edda." *European Journal of Scandinavian Studies.*

Fulk, R. D., and Cain, C. M, with Anderson, R. S. 2013. *A History of Old English Literature* ed. 2. Chichester.

Gade, K. E. 1995. *The Structure of Old Norse Dróttkvætt Poetry.* Ithaca.

Gardner, T. 1969. "The Old English Kenning: A Characteristic Feature of Germanic Poetical Diction?" *Modern Philology* 67:109–117.

———. 1972. "The Application of the Term 'Kenning'." *Neophilologus* 56:464–468.

Godden, M. 2007. "Did King Alfred Write Anything?" *Medium Ævum* 76:1–23.

Griffith, M. S. 1993. "Convention and Originality in the Old English 'Beasts of Battle' Typescene." *Anglo-Saxon England* 22:179–199.

Hainsworth, J. B. 1968. *The Flexibility of the Homeric Formula*. Oxford.

Hall, S. "The West and the Rest: Discourse and Power." *Race and Racialization: Essential Readings* (eds. T. Das Gupta, C. E. James, C. Anderson, et al.) 85–93. Toronto.

Harris, J. 2006. "Beasts of Battle, South and North." *Source of Wisdom: Old English and Early Medieval Latin Studies in Honour of Thomas D. Hill* (eds. C. Wright, F. Biggs, and T. N. Hall) 3–25. Toronto.

Harris, J., and Reichl, K. 2012. "Performance and Performers." *Medieval Oral Literature* (ed. K. Reichl) 141–202. Berlin.

Hartman, M. E. 2011. "The Hypermetric Line in Germanic Alliterative Verse." PhD dissertation. Indiana University.

Havelock, E. 1963. *Preface to Plato*. Oxford.

Heinzel, R. 1875. *Über den Stil der altgermanischen Poesie*. Quellen und Forschungen 10. Strassburg.

Heng, G. 2018. *The Invention of Race in the European Middle Ages*. Cambridge.

Heusler, A. 1922. Review of R. Meissner, *Die Kenningar der Skalden: Ein Beitrag zur skaldischen Poetik* (Bonn, 1921). *Anzeiger für deutsches Altertum und deutsche Litteratur* 41:129–132.

———. 1951. *Die altgermanische Dichtung* repr. 1957. Darmstadt.

Hofmann, D. 1955. *Nordische-englische Lehnbeziehungen der Wikingerzeit*. Bibliotheca Arnamagnaeana 14. Copenhagen.

Holoka, J. P. 1976. "The Oral Formula and Anglo-Saxon Elegy: Some Misgivings." *Neophilologus* 60:570–576.

Honegger, T. 1998. "Form and Function: The Beasts of Battle Revisited." *English Studies* 79:289–298.

Honko, L. 1998. *Textualising the Siri Epic*. FF Communications 264. Helsinki.

Hopkins, S. C. E. 2018. "Snared by the Beasts of Battle: Fear as Hermeneutic Guide in the Old English *Exodus*." *Philological Quarterly* 97:1–25.

Irving, E. B., Jr. 1959. "On the Dating of the Old English Poems *Genesis* and *Exodus*." *Anglia* 77:1–11.

Kendall, C. B. 1996. "Literacy and Orality in Anglo-Saxon Poetry: Horizontal Displacement in *Andreas*." *Journal of English and Germanic Philology* 85:1–18.

Kiernan, K. 1981. *Beowulf and the Beowulf Manuscript*. New Brunswick, NJ.

Kinoshita, S. 2007. "Deprovincializing the Middle Ages." *The Worlding Project: Doing Cultural Studies in the Era of Globalization.* (eds. R. Wilson and C. L. Connery) 61–75. Santa Cruz.

Lapidge, M. 1996. *Anglo-Latin Literature 600–899.* London.

Lee, A. 1998. *Gold-Hall and Earth-Dragon: 'Beowulf' as Metaphor.* Toronto.

Leyerle, J. 1967. "The Interlace Structure of *Beowulf.*" *University of Toronto Quarterly* 37:1–17.

Liebermann, F. 1903. *Die Gesetze der Angelsachsen,* vol. 2. Halle.

Lord, A. 1960. *The Singer of Tales.* Cambridge, MA.

Lucas, P. J. 1993. Review of K. O'Brien O'Keeffe, *Visible Song: Transitional Literacy in Old English Verse* (Cambridge 1990). *The Review of English Studies* 44(175):401–403.

Magoun, F. P., Jr. 1929. "Recurring First Elements in Different Nominal Compounds in *Beowulf* and the *Elder Edda.*" *Studies in English Philology, a Miscellany in Honor of Frederick Klaeber* (eds. K. Malone and M. Ruud) 73–78. Minneapolis.

———. 1953. "Oral-Formulaic Character of Anglo-Saxon Narrative Poetry." *Speculum* 28:446–467.

———. 1955a. "The Theme of the Beasts of Battle in Anglo-Saxon Poetry." *Neuphilologische Mitteilungen* 56:81–90.

———. 1955b. "Bede's Story of Cædman: The Case-History of an Anglo-Saxon Oral Singer." *Speculum* 30:49–63.

Maring, H. 2011. "Bright Voice of Praise: An Old English Poet-Patron Convention." *Studies in Philology* 108:299–319.

Marquardt, H. 1938. *Die altenglische Kenningar: Ein Beitrag zur Stilkunde altgermanischer Dichtung.* Halle.

Meissner, R. 1921. *Die Kenningar der Skalden: Ein Beitrag zur skaldischen Poetik.* Bonn.

van der Merwe Scholtz, H. 1927. *The Kenning in Anglo-Saxon and Old Norse Poetry.* Utrecht.

Miyashiro, A. 2019. "Our Deeper Past: Race, Settler Colonialism, and Medieval Heritage Politics." *Literature Compass* 16(9–10). https://doi.org/10.1111/lic3.12550.

Moffat, D. 1987. "A Case of Scribal Revision in the Old English 'Soul and Body'." *The Journal of English and Germanic Philology* 86:1–8.

———. 1992. "Anglo-Saxon Scribes and Old English Verse." *Speculum* 67:805–827.

Molinari, M. V. 1983. "Per un' analisi tipologica della kenning anglosassone." *Annali: Filologia germanica / Istituto universitario orientale, Sezione germanica* 26:29–52.

Muir, B. J. 2006. "Issues for Editors of Anglo-Saxon Poetry in Manuscript Form." *Inside Old English: Essays in Honour of Bruce Mitchell* (ed. J. Walmsley) 181–202. Oxford.

Neidorf, L. 2014. "Cain, Cam, Jutes, Giants and the Textual Criticism of 'Beowulf'." *Studies in Philology* 112:599–632.

———. 2017. *The Transmission of Beowulf: Language, Culture, and Scribal Behavior.* Ithaca.

Neidorf, L., and Pascual, R. J. 2019. "Old Norse Influence on the Language of *Beowulf*: A Reassessment." *Journal of Germanic Linguistics* 31:298–322.

Niles, J. D. 1979. "Ring Composition and the Structure of *Beowulf*." *PMLA* 94:924–935.

———. 1993. Review of K. O'Brien O'Keeffe, *Visible Song: Transitional Literacy in Old English Verse* (Cambridge 1990). *Speculum* 68(3):851–853.

———. 2003. "The Myth of the Anglo-Saxon Oral Poet." *Western Folklore* 62(1/2):7–61.

O'Brien O'Keeffe, K. 1990. *Visible Song: Transitional Literacy in Old English Verse.* Cambridge.

———. 2012. "Orality and Literacy: The Case of Anglo-Saxon England." *Medieval Oral Literature* (ed. K. Reichl) 121–140. Berlin.

O'Camb, B. 2016. "Isidorean Wolf Lore and the *felafæcne deor* of *Maxims I.C*: Some Rhetorical and Legal Contexts for Recognising Another Old English *wulf* in Sheep's Clothing." *English Studies* 97:687–708.

Olsen, A. H. 1986. "Oral-Formulaic Research in Old English Studies I." *Oral Tradition* 1(3):548–606.

———. 1988. "Oral-Formulaic Research in Old English Studies II." *Oral Tradition* 3(1–2):138–190.

Ong, W. J. 1982. *Orality and Literacy: The Technologizing of the Word.* London.

Opland, J. 1980. *Anglo-Saxon Oral Poetry: A Study of the Traditions.* New Haven.

Orchard, A. 1994. *The Poetic Art of Aldhelm.* Cambridge.

———. 2009. "The Word Made Flesh: Christianity and Oral Culture in Anglo-Saxon Verse." *Oral Tradition* 24:293–318.

Orton, P. 2000. *The Transmission of Old English Poetry.* Turnhout.

Parry, M. 1971. *The Making of Homeric Verse: The Collected Papers of Milman Parry.* Ed. by A. Parry. Oxford.

Pasternack, C. B. 1995. *The Textuality of Old English Poetry.* Cambridge.

Quinn, J. 2016. "Kennings and Other Forms of Figurative Language in Eddic Poetry." *A Handbook to Eddic Poetry: Myths and Legends of Early Scandinavia* (ed. C. Larrington, J. Quinn and B. Schorn) 288–309. Cambridge.

Quirk, R. 1963. "Poetic Language and Old English Meter." *Early English and Norse Studies Presented to Hugh Smith in Honour of His Sixtieth Birthday* (eds. A. Brown and P. Foote) 150–171. London.

Rambaran-Olm, M. 2017. "Medievalism and the 'Flayed-Dane' Myth: English Perspectives between the Seventeenth and Nineteenth Centuries." *Flaying in the Premodern World: Practice and Representation* (ed. L. Tracy) 91–115. Cambridge.

———. 2019. "Bede, Bath & Beyond: Difficulties with Race and Periodization in Anglo-Saxon England." Unpublished paper presented at Race Before Race Symposium, American University, Washington, DC, September 7, 2019.

Rankin, J. 1909–1910. "A Study of the Kennings in Anglo-Saxon Poetry." *The Journal of English and Germanic Philology* 8:357–422; 9:49–84.

Reichl, K. 2000. *Singing the Past: Turkic & Medieval Heroic Poetry*. Ithaca.

Renoir, A. 1988. *A Key to Old Poems: The Oral Formulaic Approach to the Interpretation of West Germanic Verse*. University Park, PA.

Robinson, F. C. 1985. *Beowulf and the Appositive Style*. Knoxville.

Russom, G. 1987. *Old English Meter and Linguistic Theory*. Cambridge.

Shippey, T. A. 1997. "Structure and Unity." *A "Beowulf" Handbook* (eds. R. Bjork and J. D. Niles) 149–174. Lincoln, NE.

Sievers, E. 1893. *Altgermanische Metrik*. Halle.

Sisam, K. 1946. "The Authority of Old English Poetical Manuscripts." *The Review of English Studies* 22:257–268.

Spearing, A. C. 1964. *Criticism and Medieval Poetry*. London.

Stevenson, J. 2005. *Women Latin Poets: Language, Gender, and Authority from Antiquity to the Eighteenth Century*. Oxford.

Terasawa, J. 2011. *Old English Metre: An Introduction*. Toronto.

Thornbury, E. 2014. *Becoming a Poet in Anglo-Saxon England*. Cambridge.

Tolkien, J. R. R. 1936. "*Beowulf*: The Monsters and the Critics." *Proceedings of the British Academy* 22 (1991):245–295.

Trautmann, M. 1876. *Über Verfasser und Enstehungszeit einiger alliteriender Gedichte des Altenglischen*. Leipzig.

Treschow, M., Gill, P., and Swartz, T. B. 2009. "King Alfred's Scholarly Writings and the Authorship of the First Fifty Prose Psalms." *The Heroic Age* 12. https://www.heroicage.org/issues/12/treschowgillswartz.php.

Trilling, R. R. 2009. *The Aesthetics of Nostalgia: Historical Representation in Old English Verse*. Toronto.

Watson, J. 2002. "The Finnsburh Skald: Kennings and Cruces in the Anglo-Saxon Fragment." *The Journal of English and Germanic Philology* 101:497–519.

Watts, A. 1969. *The Lyre and the Harp: A Comparative Reconstruction of Oral Tradition in Homer and Old English Epic Poetry*. New Haven.

Weiskott, E. 2016. *English Alliterative Verse: Poetic Tradition and Literary History.* Cambridge.

Wilson, R. M. 1952. *The Lost Literature of Medieval England.* London.

Wilton, D. 2020. "What Do We Mean by Anglo-Saxon? Pre-Conquest to the Present." *The Journal of English and Germanic Philology* 119:425-454.

Wormald, P. 1977. "The Uses of Literacy in Anglo-Saxon England and Its Neighbors." *Transactions of the Royal Historical Society* 27:95–114.

Wray, A. 2009. "Identifying Formulaic Language: Persistent Challenges and New Opportunities". *Formulaic Language: Distribution and Historical Change* (eds. R. Corrigan, E. A. Moravcsik, H. Ouali, and K. M. Wheatley) 27–51. Amsterdam.

Wrenn, C. L. 1967. *A Study of Old English Literature.* New York.

Zumthor, P. 1972. *Essai De Poetique Médiévale.* Paris.

4

Vlach Paupers

Formula and Layers of Meaning

SONJA PETROVIĆ, UNIVERSITY OF BELGRADE

IN THE NINETEENTH-CENTURY, philologists began to recognize patterns that we now regard as formulaic in South Slavic oral poetry and prose. These included introductory and closing formulae, as well as recurring descriptions, figures of speech, and tropes. Common formulae—such as wishes, heroic encounters, greeting kings, and intentions to move—were conveyed by established rhetorical and stylistic forms. Texts in the dominant meter of South Slavic epic, the asymmetrical decasyllable (4 + 6 syllabic positions, divided by a caesura), lent themselves to formulaic analysis. It was not only the meter of traditional oral song, but was also used in written and orally derived texts. Occasionally, it was also used in satirical public speech; decasyllable accounts of contemporary political events are encountered from the nineteenth century to the present day.

From the mid-twentieth century, Serbian folklorists began to adopt variety of approaches to studying formulae, including literary-historical and literary-theoretical perspectives, as well as approaches rooted in genre, performance, and poetic aesthetics (Milošević-Đorđević 2008; Detelić and Delić 2015). More recently, they have gravitated towards contemporary semiotics and anthropology. Serbian and Croatian folklorists accepted research on epic formulae by Milman Parry (1971), Albert Bates Lord (1960; 1995), and John Miles Foley (1995), albeit with certain constraints and criticisms (Bošković Stulli 1978; Detelić 2010). For example, they have provided their own insights regarding formulae from different genres of oral tradition, as well as comparative parallels between South Slavic and Homeric epics (Dukat 1988). Several decades ago, it was pointed out that formulae did not only facilitate song composition by helping to generate verses, but that they also condensed content (Bošković-Stulli 1978:32).

Milošević-Đorđević conceived the formula as a "creative, dynamic pattern that served oral artistic improvisation" (1984:85). She also observed that "the essential feature of oral literature [is] to create formulae in order to use them as a fundamental means of expression and artistic design" (1984:85). The vitality of formulaic language results from "the very nature of oral literature, from the relationship between tradition and creator, which is reciprocal and dialectical but dominated by tradition" (1984:85).

In the current chapter, we shall build upon this theoretical heritage and incorporate recent research (e.g. Reichl 1992; Honko 1998; Frog 2016; 2017) to elucidate the complex of meaning associated with the formula *Vlasi siromasi* ('Vlach paupers' or 'poor Vlachs'), as encountered in Serbian and South Slavic oral tradition. First, we shall consider its history and etymology, then its application in various folklore genres, and finally its semantic and lexical associations, in related formulae.

1. Historical Context of the Term *Vlasi* ('Vlachs')

The name *Vlasi* ('Vlachs', sg. *Vlah*), with its specific meanings for ethnic, professional, social, and religious groups, is not clearly distinguished in South Slavic oral tradition. Scholars provide different perspectives on the origin and diasporic movements of the "Vlachs." Confusingly, the name can mean both an ethnicity and a more specific occupational category, that of Balkan nomadic cattle-herders (Dvoichenko-Markov 1984; Winnifrith 1987). According to Czamańska:

> The term Vlachs or Wallachians has been used to refer to: 1. People speaking Eastern Romance languages or dialects; 2. People living according to a particular lifestyle, mostly dealing with mountain pastoralism (sometimes specific features of the pastoral economy are mentioned, for example cheese-making); 3. People who in their historical past had a defined social status (the Vlachian/Wallachian Right—*Ius Valachicum*); 4. People who in the Middle Ages established Romanian principalities.
>
> Czamańska 2015:7

In the "Vlachs" mentioned in Serbian Medieval sources, historians saw the remnants of "Romanised indigenes who, after the settling of the Slavs, remained as cattle herders in smaller or larger groups in various parts of the Balkan peninsula" (Dinić-Knežević 1999:86). From the second half of the tenth century, the Vlachs were recognized as a distinct social and political group throughout the Balkans: as cattle herders and soldiers, they lived in communes (*katun*), with a separate social order and local self-governance. In the thirteenth century, they were Slavicized. By the following century, they formed a unique social and economic category with particular obligations, especially to religious orders. They kept livestock (*ćelatori*), transported goods, accompanied abbot and monastery officials on their travels, conveyed their belongings, furnished the monastery with woolen coverlets and worsted material (*poklonici*), and tended monastery cattle (Dinić-Knežević 1999:87). 'Poor Vlachs' (*ubogi vlasi*)—"probably those who were indigent or incapacitated"—were mentioned in *Laws on the Vlachs*, in the charter which Serbian Emperor Dušan issued to the Monastery of St. Archangels near Prizren (1348–1354): their duty was to process wool that belonged to the Church (Isailović 2017:30; Mihaljčić 2006:128).

Traditionally, herder Vlachs were shepherds. They were renowned throughout the Balkans for their enormous flocks of sheep. They were also dairy farmers. Vlach cheese was held in high regard on the tables of Byzantium; it is praised by Anna Komnene in 1091, Theodore Prodromos in the mid-twelfth century (Antonijević 1982:28), and in Dubrovnik in the mid-fourteenth century (Jireček 1988/2:153). Various Serbian folk sayings attest to these reputations: *Bog sreću dijeli, a Vlahinja surutku* ('God dispenses happiness and a Vlach woman whey') (Karadžić 1987a:#284), *Turci vino piju, a vlasi surutku* ('The Turks drink wine and the Vlachs whey') (Daničić 1871:#5128).

The Vlachs had another traditional obligation: to guard the borders. This is mentioned in the *Despot's Kanun*, the law of Despot Stefan Lazarević (1377–1427). The provisions of the *Despot's Kanun*, incorporated into Ottoman laws for the "Smederevo Vlachs," remained in force up to 1516. At this point, some Vlach rights, such as the right to organize *zbor* ('council') and assemblies to elect a *kmet* ('a prominent peasant who mediates in inter-village disputes'), were excluded as unacceptable to the Ottoman legislators (Bojanić 1974:140; Kursar 2013:140).

Vlachs were considered itinerant and, due to this, distinct from the natives (Antonijević 1989:151–154). Fine writes that, in Serbia, Dušan's *Law Code* (1349):

> refers to 'Serbs' and 'Vlachs', and though at first sight this might seem to be an ethnic distinction, more detailed examination of the code shows that it was in fact occupational; Dušan was separating the Serb agriculturalists from the Vlach pastoralists, since their differing life-styles required very different tax policies.
>
> Fine 2009:129

Croatian sources from the second half of the fifteenth century show that Vlachs from the Ottoman territory and the Venetian Republic were brought in and settled in the area of Knin (the village of Promina, 1484). From there, they expanded to Cetina and Mt. Velebit, and then to Krk, around Učka and into Istria. They had military duties and a separate internal organization. Fine observed that "the Vlachs were a community with both ethnic characteristics (clearly recognized as a separate people) and also legal ones with special and separate rights" (2009:130).

In sources from the Ottoman period, the ethnic, professional, and social aspects of the Vlach name were closely intertwined. The term *Vlach* denoted people who:

> were not commoners and who did not have a master, but lived grouped in villages on "Vlach land", the land which they received for popu-lating and defending it. They carried out their military duties through their headmen and were therefore exempt from all taxation relating to agriculture and commoner [*rayah*] status.
>
> Bojanić 1974:174

In the Ottoman Empire, the Vlachs (*Eflaklar*) retained many of the rights granted to them by the Serbian Despot Stefan Lazarević. They had their own military and civic hierarchy, an independent internal organization, greater personal freedom, and an ability to move around. Indeed, Vlach villages "enjoyed terri-torial immunity and could not be assigned to timar landowners" (Bojanić 1974:175). In Ottoman legislation, certain expressions relating to the Vlachs have been preserved: for measures ('the Vlach sack'), taxes (*Vlach adet-i* ['old customs'], *Vlach resm-i* ['taxes'], *Vlach ducats* ['gold coins']), and handicrafts ("the Vlach blanket")—coverings and material for costumes and rain capes were particularly esteemed (Bojanić 1974:175).

> In the first decades of Ottoman rule, numerous bands of these Vlach shepherds flooded into our [Serbian] lands, not only into mountain regions but also parish areas, so it may be concluded that many farmers joined the ranks of these cattle herders.
>
> Zirojević 1974:170

It suited the Ottoman conquerors to settle these mobile and organized cattle herders in sensitive border areas and entrust them with their defense. While some of the Vlachs had military duties and carried out their military service in forts, others turned to agriculture. By the beginning of the sixteenth century, the Vlachs were internally stratified and Islamized to an extent. In 1536, the Vlach status in northern Serbia and the Zvornik sanjak was abolished; all Vlachs were converted into ordinary commoners, or *rayah*. Despite this, Vlach lords retained an important role as intermediaries between the common people and the Ottoman authorities (Zirojević 1974:176).

The official term *Vlasi* ('Vlachs'), meaning Christian hired soldiers—which included Vlachs, Serbs, and Croats—is encountered in the late seventeenth century in the Banska and Kostajnička Krajina. From the documents of the time, it is not always easy to figure out to whom the name actually refers. The terms "Vlach infidels," "Vlach schismatics," and *Vlach-Rasciani* ('Serbs')[1] were apparently used for "Vlachs who are ethnic Serbs, but were called Vlachs because of their social status" (Bojanić 1974:175). Opposed to this, the terms "Vlach Catholics" or "Hungarians" referred to Croats (Gavrilović 1986:62–63). The name *Morlaci* ('Morlachs') was "both imprecise and relative, for Dalmatians could use the term rather freely to distinguish themselves from other Dalmatians," and "Venetians invested the term with their own civilizing ideology of empire" (Wolf 2001:12). As different kinds of military forces (*voynuks, derbendci, dogancis*), they were also known as *Hajduci, Uskoci,* and *Martolosi* (Sugar 1996:39, 243).

In South Slavic folklore material, we see that the appellation "Vlach" also acquired specific regional nuances. In his *Serbian Dictionary* (1852), Serbian language reformer and collector of folklore Vuk Karadžić defines the meaning of this term in the different geographical and ethno-religious South Slavic environments:

> Vlah. 1) (po sjeveroist. kr.) der Walach, Valachus; ove Vlahe narod dalje k jugu i zapadu zove Karavlasi, a zemlju njihovu Karavlaška. 2) Srbi zakona Turskoga u Bosni i u Hercegovini, a tako i oni zakona Rimskoga, kako u Bosni i u Hercegovini, tako i u carstvu Austrijskome izvan Dalmacije zovu i to kao za porugu Vlasima braću svoju zakona Grčkoga: Ni u tikvi suda, ni u Vlahu druga. 3) u Dalmaciji građani i varošani i ostrvljani zovu Vlahom svakoga seljaka sa suhe zemlje, koje mu drago vjere, što se našijem jezikom onamo zove Vlah, ono se Talijanskijem i po ovome Njemačkijem zove Morlak (Morlacco). Riječ ova Vlah onamo nije nikaka poruga, jer i sami Vlasi za sebe reku, n. p. kad se kakav pravda da kakvoga gospodina nije dočekao i ugostio kao što treba: "oprostite gospodine, mi smo Vlasi; u vlaškijem kućama ovako se živi."

> Karadžić 1987b:118, s.v. "Vlah"

Vlach. 1) (northeastern parts) der Walach, Valachus; those Vlachs further towards the south and west, the people call *Karavlachs*, and

---

[1]   Rascia (*Raška*) was a center of the Serbian Kingdom in the 11–13th century. In that time, and also later, the name *Rasciani* was used for Serbs, esp. in Hungary and Habsburg Monarchy.

their country *Karavlachia*. 2) The Serbs of the Turkish law in Bosnia and Herzegovina, and also of the Roman law, as in Bosnia and Herzegovina and in the Austrian Empire outside of Dalmatia, derogatively call these Vlachs their brothers of the Greek law: [you will not find] a jug in a gourd [calabash] nor a friend in a Vlach. 3) In Dalmatia, citizens and inhabitants of smaller towns and islanders call every peasant from dry land [the mainland] a Vlach, whatever his religion, that which in our language is called Vlach, is in Italian and German called *Morlacco*. Over there the word Vlach is no insult, since the Vlachs themselves say, for example when making excuses for not welcoming a gentleman or offering him due hospitality: "Excuse me, sir, we are Vlachs; in Vlach homes this is how we live."

Contemporary etymological research of a broad sweep of South Slavic material confirms and expands Karadžić's observations. The Croatian etymologist, Skok, singles out the following meanings for "Vlach": 1) Latin [obscure]; 2) Romanian [nationality]; 3) Italian [nationality]; 4) Tzintzar [Aromanian]; 5) a man from a group of Vlach shepherd's huts, a nomadic shepherd; 6) among the Venetians, a Slav who moved to their area from Turkey; among the Croats, an Orthodox Serb who has moved to the military border from Ottoman territory; among Muslims in Kosovo, *Rišjanin*—an Orthodox Serb; among Muslims in Bosnia—an Orthodox person (1973:606).

Although the meaning of *Vlasi* has different regional, occupational, and social nuances, one consistent connotation is their mobility. This is reflected in historical sources and oral tradition, and has been encoded formulaically. The mobility of the Vlachs is connected to their occupation as cattle herders and as protectors of the borders. As keepers of the border, the Vlachs were settled in areas that were volatile during Ottoman rule; this added to their nomadic reputation. The attitudes of the natives towards the settled Vlachs varied, but a certain attitude of superiority can be sensed. From the standpoint of the natives, mobility was not a desirable attribute; it had connotations of unreliability. The differences between natives and settlers, farmers and cattle herders, and neighborly disputes and shifting human relations were encoded in various sayings relating to the Vlachs. According to Skok, because of the perception of the natives that, as newcomers and wanderers, Vlachs could not be trusted, the word "Vlach" had negative connotations, as seen in sayings such as: *Ni u loncu suda, ni u Vlahu druga* ('Neither a vessel in a pot, nor a friend in a Vlach'), *Ni u moru mire, ni u Vlahu vire* ('Neither the sea has boundaries, nor should the Vlach be trusted') (Skok 1973:608); *O Turčine, za nevolju kume, a ti Vlaše, silom pobratime* ('O Turk, a godfather of trouble, and you Vlach, by force a blood-brother') (Karadžić

1987a:#4157). The animosity of natives and neighbors towards the Vlachs may be seen in sayings that mock gluttony, like *Ofukao kao Vlah pitu* ('He devoured it like a Vlach does a pie') (Karadžić 1987a:#4159), or discord, like *Ne ujedini, Bože, Vlaha! Kažu da se tako Turci mole Bogu* ('God, do not unite the Vlachs!—They say that Turks pray to God with these words', i.e. if the Vlachs unite, they could defeat the Turks) (Karadžić 1987a:#3577).

Rivalry between neighbors is openly expressed in lampoons, with verses arising from mutual friction. Here is an example from Duži near Neum (Bosnia and Herzegovina), recorded in 1957–1958:

(1)

O ti, Vlaše repati	Hey you, Vlach with a tail,
sutra ti je krepati!	Tomorrow you will die!
Kuku ruci koja će te vući	Woe to the hand that will drag you
i lopati koja će te kopati.	And the spade that will dig you.
Latinine, revo,	[You] Latin ass,
ispalo ti cr'jevo;	Your guts have fallen out;
mačke ti ga vuku	Cats are dragging them
po kraljevu putu.	Along the King's road.

Simić 1959:199, #193

According to the eighty-year-old women who sang this song, the Herzegovians call the Dalmatians asses (*revo*), and they in turn call the Herzegovians devils ('with a tail'), "and when they fall out or get into a fight, they usually sing this song to each other." She explains the context: "They would sing this when tending cattle with the Christians (Orthodox Serbs), so we would mock them, and they us" (Simić 1959:199). The same text has also been recorded in Duboka near Slivno, Croatia.

2. The *Vlasi* ('Vlachs') Sequence and Expressing Identity in Formulae

Portrayals of the Vlachs in oral tradition are contradictory, inconsistent, and dependent on context and perspective. This is due to the socio-economic history of the Balkans, and the aforementioned tensions between natives and Vlachs newcomers. In the corpus of Serbian and South Slavic folklore, the term *Vlasi* usually denotes Christians of any ethnic or regional affiliation, but it may also imply Romanians. Christian Vlachs are usually placed in opposition to Muslims (Turks) and sometimes to the inhabitants of an area—whether Christian or Muslim—as newcomers opposed to the natives. When opposed to

Muslims, Vlachs are usually additionally denoted as *kauri* (Turkish *giaour*, *gawur* ['infidel, non-Muslim']): religiously, socially, and professionally, this is a derogative appellation.

Vlasi may encompass different ethnic and cultural groups, yet some singers use the term with more precision. For instance, a singer from Montenegro wishing to evoke the strength of the fighters of the First Serbian Uprising against the Ottomans (1804–1813), ascribes admiration for the Serbs to the Turkish Pasha Skopljanin, using the formula *Šumadija Vlasi* ('Vlachs of Šumadija'); Šumadija is a region in central Serbia:

(2)

Da ti znadeš, bego Mušovića,	If you knew, Bey Mušović,
Kakovi su Vlasi Šumadijnski,	What heroes the Šumadija Vlachs are
A da dođe Mutape Lazare,	And if Mutap Lazar came,
Da uljeze Kolašinu gradu,	And entered into Kolašin town
Primio bi Kolašina tvoga,	He would conquer your Kolašin
Izagna' bi Kolašinske Turke.	He would drive out the Kolašin Turks.

Karadžić 1986:227, #41

In epic songs, we encounter other similar formulae: Alaj-Bey Čengić vows to attack Montenegro to plunder *Vlasi Crnogorci* ('Montenegrin Vlachs') (Karadžić 1900b:73–74, #15) and Osman Ćustović pursues *Vlasi Kotarani*, *Vlasi Pločani*, *Vlasi Ledničani*, *Vlasi Crnovičani* in order to find a kidnapped girl (Hörmann 1990:II, 442, #65). Specifying the Vlachs' regions in these and similar examples serves to differentiate characters and situations while also highlighting local identity. This helps the listeners to identify and empathize with the protagonists.

When singers wish to accentuate the ethnic dimension of characters, for instance those of Romanian origin, they use formulaic names or surnames derived from the relevant ethnonym, like Radul Vlašić, Denalija Vlahović, or Vlah Alija. These are stereotypical folklore names and act as signals that listeners recognize.

Thanks to the way in which they compress and concentrate meaning, the formulae may add religious, social, ethical, occupational, or other dimensions in addition to Vlach ethnicity. An interesting combination of ethnic and religious components in Vlach characters is to be found in the *bugarštica*. This is an older stratum of South Slavic song with a long line, usually of 7 + 8 syllables, in which the singer toys with the perspectives of the narrator and characters to signify different aspects of Vlach identity. The heroine of the song is abducted by a "Turk" servant, and she uses her wits to free herself and return to her brother's court. The girl does not call her kidnapper a Turk, as the narrator does, but rather a *vlaška poturica* ('Vlach convert to Islam') (Bogišić 1878:103, #38). This formula is an implicitly negative judgment on the kidnapper and affects the song's message in several ways. First, the epithet is scornful and comes from the perspective of a Christian woman; converts in certain environments were considered to be moral turncoats and national traitors. Second, the girl's shrewdness and gender superiority are underlined: she has tricked the kidnapper servant—a person of lower social status—as he previously tricked her. Finally, the girl's independence within the family circle is emphasized, in comparison to her brother. These resonances and tropes are typical in this type of warrior maiden narrative.

3. The *Vlach Paupers* Formula and Kindred Concepts: Meanings in Context

The *Vlasi siromasi* ('Vlach paupers') formula blends the concept of "Vlachs" with that of "the poor" and creates a new, independent concept. Depending on genre, context, and the singer's predilections, the *Vlach paupers* formula may resonate as serious, humorous, ironic, or derisive. In Serbian and South Slavic folklore, poverty is a complex notion, within which social, economic, mythological-ritual, religious, anthropological, and other aspects meet and mingle. The image projected by "the poor," as with other marginal figures, is both positive and negative: they may be intermediaries between the people and the sacral, or outcasts from the community and religious ritual practice. They may even be viewed as delinquents. Meanings become ramified, since the category "poor" is extremely diverse. Each use of the formula has acquired specific attributes, especially in the attitude of the poor towards work and how they express themselves, such as their ethical opinions, their position in the family, and their community, gender, and age.

Influenced by Christian concepts and symbols adopted into the folk culture, certain dogmatic ideas and Biblical parables have brought about a transvaluation of ideas about the poor and how their characters are constructed in folklore. For instance, this is seen in the divesting of earthly goods to save one's soul, the high status awarded to choosing poverty in ascetic philosophy, condemning the rich and avaricious, and the lauding of charity and almsgiving as a form of exchange with the deity. The *Vlach paupers* formula interweaves these various associations of poverty with the complex semantics of "the Vlach population"—in its broadest sense—resulting in new associations and dimensions.

This formula is famously encountered in the curses, maledictions, and laments of the poor. As a verbal ritual, curses have powerful effects due to a widely held belief in the magical power of words. These effects multiply, since the poor are held to be intermediaries with the otherworld. The symbolism of laments is linked to ritual behavior, the cult of the dead, and communication with the dead. The dead are regarded as powerful helpers, but also demonic adversaries. With all this in view, even the greatest heroes fear the curses and laments of the poor and try not to challenge them.

The motif of the curses and laments of poor Vlachs is encountered in both the older and younger strata of epic songs, where it functions as an ethical corrective and contributes to the idealization of the epic hero. In a *bugarštica* from the first half of the eighteenth century, the story is sung of a Turk who kidnapped the wife of the famous Serbian hero, Ban Strahinjić (Banović Strahinja) and set fire to his court. Strahinjić asks his father-in-law to help him pursue the kidnapper and reclaim his wife, but the latter is afraid, offering to marry him to another woman and build a new court, for which he will raise the money in an immoral way—by taxing Vlachs from the "Vlach country." As an upright and compassionate hero, Strahinjić refuses his father-in-law's proposal:

(3)

> Ostavi me, moj šura, radi Boga velikoga:
> Što ti meni govoriš o mojemu b'jelu dvoru,
> Da ćeš stavit carine po lijepom vlaškom zemljom,
> I da mi ćeš iznova dvore moje ponoviti –
> N'jesu meni, Stjepane, tuđe suze od potrebe,
> Ni da mene proklinju tužni Vlasi siromasi.

Bogišić 1878:106, #40

> Let me be, my father-in-law, for the sake of God Almighty:
> What are you saying to me about my white court,
> That you will impose taxes on the beautiful Vlach country
> And that you will rebuild my court?
> I do not need, Stjepan, the tears of others,
> Nor to be cursed by the sad Vlach paupers.

In another example, a decasyllabic account from the first half of the nineteenth century, the Vlach paupers are shown as a disenfranchised workforce, mercilessly exploited by the Turks:

(4)

Što mi kažeš uzurlije Turke,	What say you of dawdling Turks,
Lasno im je činiti junaštvo,	It is easy for them to do heroic deeds,

| Ćeraju im kola i volovi, | Others plough with their carts and oxen |
| A rade im Vlasi siromasi. | The Vlach paupers work for them. |

Milutinović 1990:542–543, #133

These examples speak of the dependent position of Vlachs in relation to the Christian gentry or Turkish landlords, and they concur with historical data. The image of the poor who pay taxes and work as day laborers is a general one, in keeping with the poetic rules of the epic, but it is also a faithful picture of feudal relations during Ottoman rule in the Balkans.

The *Vlach paupers* formula is connected to a kindred formulaic sequence: *kabanice vlaške siromaške* ('rain capes of the Vlach paupers'). Long, caped cloaks— made of sheepskin, goatskin, or hand-woven wool—are characteristic of Balkan herder attire. Cultural and historical artifacts attest to this; the Vlachs were famous for the manufacture of textiles and garments (Dinić-Knežević 1999; Kursar 2013). In folk songs, Vlach rain capes are part of social, professional, and sometimes ethnic marking. The image describes and actualizes the characters, or suggests a nomadic way of life—one that is hardworking, but that provides relative independence from local Ottoman authorities. The capes can also serve as a disguise, when epic heroes wish to conceal their identity in order to trick an opponent or spy on the enemy. As formulae, both epithets are included in the decasyllable form and are linked by anadiplosis, thus concatenating single units of the phrase: *Na nji meći vlaške kabanice, / kabanice vlaške siromaške* ('Dress them in Vlach rain capes, / the rain capes of the Vlach paupers') (Karadžić 1900a:288, #25).

In some folk songs, poor Vlachs are equated to beggars in their appearance. Heroes disguise themselves in Vlach rain capes and assume the character of a beggar:

(5)

Svuče sebe delinsko ođelo,	He takes off the clothes of the hero,
A obuče prosjačko ođelo,	And puts on beggar's clothes,
Učini se Vlaše siromaše,	Turning into a poor Vlach,
Ode pitat' od vrata do vrata,	He goes a-begging,
Dokle dođe Jašaru na vrata:	Until he comes to Jašar's door:
....	....
– O, Jašare, dragi gospodare,	– O, Jašar, dear master,
Na vratima Vlaše siromaše,	At the door is a poor Vlach,
Pita štogođ za očinu dušu,	Begging a trifle for his father's soul,

91

Za očinu i za materinu!	For his father's and mother's!
A kada je Jaša razumio,	And when Jaša understood him,
Metnu ruku u džep od dolame,	He put his hand in the pocket of his dolman,
Pa izvadi dva dukata žuta:	And took out two yellow ducats:
– Na' ti, Jela, te daj siromahu!	– Take it, Jela, and give to the poor man!

Karadžić 1974:257, #82

Vlach rain capes indicate poverty only when the epithet "poor" is added to them. In proverbs and sayings, poverty is communicated formulaically by notions of nakedness: *Od gola Vlaha gola para* ('From a naked Vlach a naked coin', i.e. a poor Vlach cannot hide his penury) (Karadžić 1987a:#3944). Here nakedness is understood in its primary meaning, as a body unclothed out of want; torn and ragged clothes signify paupers and beggars.

The formulae summarize the poverty of the Vlachs as a professional, ethnical, religious, and social group. When "the Vlachs" is used in this disparaging way, it reflects social and cultural contexts, as well as inter-ethnic and inter-religious relations. Such pejorative formulae are derived from ethnic stereotypes. In one folk saying, the poverty of the Vlachs is compared with the poverty of the Šokci. The Šokci are a group of ethnic Croatian natives settled in Serbia, Bosnia, Croatia, and Hungary, who migrated from west Bosnia between the sixteenth and eighteenth centuries. The saying *Šokci ubokci, vlasi siromasi* ('Needy Šokci, poor Vlachs') is accompanied by an explanation from the collector of sayings, Vuk Karadžić: "Daklem nijedni nemaju ništa, nego oboji jednaki" ('So neither have anything, and both are equal') (Karadžić 1987a:#6208). Here the lexeme *Vlasi* is used in the pejorative meaning of Orthodox Serbs, as opposed to Catholic Croats, who are derogatively referred to as *Šokci*. By the sense and the synonyms *ubogi* ('needy') and *siromasi* ('poor'), however, this saying nullifies their differences, maintaining that they are identical in their poverty.

The *Vlach paupers* formula and the motif of Vlach poverty also occur in Serbian humorous folktales. For example, the *Vlach paupers* formula occurs in a narrative about a hungry Serb who earns his dinner at a Vlach wake by pretending to lament over the deceased. This is a version of ATU 1699, "Misunderstanding Because of Ignorance of a Foreign Language." In a variant from Vranje (south Serbia), newcomers are opposed to the natives and their customs, and the plot is built on a farcical reversal of roles: the Vlachs who intend to make fools of the people of Vranje are themselves made to look foolish:

(6)

Neki majstori vranjanci, iz sela Vlase, bili na radu u krajinskom okrugu, pa vraćajući se kućama, ostanu bez hleba. Kako su išli preko sela, a toga dana bile zadušnice, oni svrate na jedno groblje koje je bilo nekih naseljenika iz Rumunije.

Vranjanci, videći kako se tu obilato jede, zamole da dadu i njima da štogod jedu.

Jedan koji je pomalo znao srpski, da bi pravio komendiju s njima, reče im da moraju i oni kukati na groblju, pa će dobiti da jedu i piju.

Majstori čučnu na jedan grob i razdernjaju se:

— Kuku Vlasi, crni siromasi,

dobri beste, što svi ne pomreste.

Na to jedan stari Vlah, čovek bolećiva srca, dotrča, i stade ih dizati i ćutkati, da ne plaču. Dobiće svega.

I tada im dadoše te se siti najedoše i napiše, i veselo produžiše put.

Kića 1925:4

Some Vranje craftsmen from the village of Vlase were working in the Negotinska Krajina district. Returning to their home, they found they had no bread. As they were passing through a village on All Souls Day, they came upon a cemetery belonging to some settlers from Romania.

The Vranje men, seeing the abundance of food, asked for something to eat.

One man, who spoke a little Serbian and wanted to play a joke on them, told them they had to wail at the cemetery, then they would get food and drink.

The craftsmen squatted by a grave and began bellowing:

— Alas you Vlachs, black paupers,

you were [so] good, why didn't you all die?

On hearing this an old Vlach, a man with a soft heart, ran up to them and began to raise them up and hush them, [telling them] not to cry, that they would be given everything.

And then they gave [food] to them and they ate and drank to their heart's content, and went merrily on their way.

The story activates the ethnic stereotype of the Vlachs, who emerge as stupid since they do not understand Serbian (Sikimić 2002:190). At the center of the plot is the international motif of outwitting con men, while the subtext is the violation of customary norms—ridiculing the custom of lamenting the dead. In their mock lament, the Vlachs become "black paupers" and are sent to the other world, which satirizes the whole situation. It is similar to Bakhtin's grotesque overturning of worlds where the dead give food to the living. The epithet "black" in this formula is symbolic of death by analogy. Kindred idioms exist in the Serbian language, for example: "the black bird" as a herald of death; "to don black garb" as a sign of grieving for the deceased; and "to spin black wool for someone," meaning to lose someone close to you.

The story of the Vranje craftsmen has two older variants published in the nineteenth century. In these, the characters are set in a different historical context and their attitudes are decidedly those of rivals. They concern the relations between a Turkish landlord and his subjugated dependent, a Christian farmer. In a short story published in 1836 by Vuk Karadžić, to explain a saying, only the final point is emphasized:

(7)

Jao, moj Vlaho! ni ti rad tu ležati ni se ja više tebe derati, ali ne dadu Vlasi za badava piti i jesti. Pripovijeda se da je kazao Turčin kad mu na Hrišćanskom groblju nijesu dali da jede dok ne plače.

Karadžić 1987a:#1786

Alas, my Vlach! Neither do you like to lie here, nor [do] I like to grieve over you, but the Vlachs do not give one something to drink and eat for nothing. The tale is told that this is what a Turk said when, at a Christian cemetery, they would not give him something to eat until he cried.

In the story from Vranje, it was the Vlachs who were fooled, but in this variant, the Christians triumph over the Turk and force him to show respect for their deceased.

As mentioned previously, the associations triggered by "Vlach" formulae vary across culture and context. A very different case occurs in South Slavic folklore, where we encounter Vlach formulae that signify their wealth. To a degree, these are linked to social history, cultural experience, and stereotypical judgments of character. In some cases, natives observe the wealth of the Vlach newcomers or ascribe it to them. Their wealth is explained as Vlach resourcefulness, which is generally interpreted as a positive trait since it conveys wit and shrewdness. Connected formulae may also evoke a clandestine struggle against authorities. For instance, the saying *Bogata Vlaha i šteta pomaže* ('To a rich Vlach, even damage is helpful') (Knežević 1957:72) alludes to their ability to turn an unfavorable situation to their advantage. The saying *U bogata Vlaha i goveda su pametna* ('With a rich Vlach, even the cattle are clever') (Karadžić 1987a:#5731) has two different interpretations. According to Vuk Karadžić, the cattle are noted as clever to flatter the Vlach. The second explanation presupposes that the herding skills of the Vlachs are interpreted as wisdom, and so the human trait of intelligence is ascribed to the animals they own. According to the latter interpretation, the adroitness of the Vlachs refers to their resourcefulness in raising and keeping cattle without paying dues to the Turks, who seized cattle in lieu of tax (Avagjan 2017:61). The saying *U bogata Vlaha skupa pšenica* ('With a rich Vlach, expensive wheat') (Karadžić 1987a:#5732) speaks of the dearth of cereal crops among Vlach herders; since cattle herding was their main occupation, they sowed less wheat and were therefore reluctant to sell it.

In some epic songs and ballads, such *rich Vlach* formulae evoke a type of wealthy, autonomous herdsman. This was a well-respected member of rural community—usually the head of a patriarchal extended family *Zadruga*—and a keeper of traditional values. In a song written down in the early eighteenth century, rich Vlachs are depicted as integrated in a multilayered society and as respectful of traditional values, while poor Vlachs are depicted as marginal characters. The song revolves around a plan of highwaymen (*Hajduci*) to attack the wedding party of the daughter of Jovan, "a rich Vlach," and seize the bride's gifts. There is a formulaic, embellished description of the precious gifts of the Vlach girl, but the context of the events is realistic and historical.

(8)

Sjutra ćemo na stara drumova	Tomorrow we will take to the old roads
tu će proći bogati svatovi	This is where the rich wedding party will pass
i provesti bogatu devojku	Leading the rich girl
od Jovana, vlaha bogatoga.	Of Jovan, the wealthy Vlach.
Prid njom idu dve kamile blaga,	Before her go two loads of treasure,

za njom idu dve kamile dara,	Behind her go two loads of gifts,
nad njom viju dva alaj-barjaka,	Above her float two wedding banners,
obadva su od zelene svile,	Both made of green silk,
na njojzi parte od trista dukata.	On her cap three hundred ducats.

Gesemann 1925:16–17, #15

In this description, we notice the ethnographic artifacts—the girl's dowry and obligatory gifts for the bridegroom's family and guests—followed by the wedding banners. The ducats on the girl's cap are a token of her social status. They are also a talisman to protect the bride in her *rite de passage*, especially from demonic powers like the evil eye. Regarding the main topic, there is historical evidence that attacks by highwaymen on rich caravans were a common occurrence in the Balkan countries under Ottoman rule (i.e. from the fifteenth to the nineteenth century). In oral tradition, attacks on bridal parties were strongly condemned, since they blatantly violated customary laws and ethics. According to Serbian belief, jeopardizing a girl's marriage was a great sin. In this song, conflict is overcome thanks to the girl's wisdom and the power of spiritual kinship: the girl makes a blood brother of the highwayman so that he will not spoil her "first happiness" (i.e. her marriage). The brigand is mollified, returns her gifts, and even escorts her to the court.

The flexibility and open semantics of the *Vlach paupers* formula foster a degree of creative usage. Certain aspects of meaning can be suppressed, or become arbitrary or unmotivated. This is particularly the case when puns and rhymes or used: e.g. *vlasac; Vlasi sredomasi;* and the rhyme collocations *lasi-vlasi* and *lasi-malasi,* which are encountered in spells "of bugs in the head" (Radenković 1982:317–324). The meaning of the lexemes *sredomasi, lasi, malasi* is opaque. In the Homolje (east Serbia), the word "bugs" is used for two kinds of illnesses: "swollen cuticles filled with pus on the fingers and gumboils around the teeth." Bugs are a painful and unpleasant disease: "People believe that there is a bug there that bites the flesh so it hurts, and the pus that collects is its excrement" (Milosavljević 1913:223). In spells, the disease is named as *Vlasi sredomasi.* Magical chants count backwards to the expulsion of the disease into nothingness ("anti-space"), or else the parts of the body infected by the bugs are named, with a demand for them to be returned to the charmer:

(9)

Zahvatili ste se	You have infested yourselves
vlasi-sredomasi,	Vlachs-sredomasi,
da izedete (Stanće) srce.	To eat up the heart (of Stanće).

Daj ruku za ruku,	Give an arm for an arm,
daj nogu za nogu... (itd.)	Give a leg for a leg... (etc.)

Radenković 1982:317

In the *vlasac* spells, this is a homonym—the *vlasac* (*vlas* ['a hair']) disease is linked to the hair or strands of hair. According to one description, "this disease most often occurs in the nose, less in the eyes, on the neck, and other parts of the body" and is equated with syphilis. The charming involves the patient inhaling hot steam through the flower of summer savory (*Satureja hortensis*), while the charmer recites the magical text:

(10) Razvijajte se vlasi iz klupčeta crnog, belog, žutog, zelenog, crvenog, plavog, sedog, smeđeg, surog, sinjeg, riđeg, morastog, belovinastog, rujog, rujnog, pa idite u goru, u vodu i gde nigde nikoga nema: gde pevac ne peva, gde vatra ne gori, gde stoka ne riče, gde psi ne laju, gde mačka ne mauče, gde kokoška ne kakoće. Idite u goru, u vodu, gde nigde nikoga nema!

Petrović 1948:357–358

Unwind the strands from the ball of black, white, yellow, green, red, blue, grey, brown, ash, grey-blue, sea color, of the color of white wine, red, dark red, so go to the mountain, into the water, and where there is no one: where the rooster does not crow, where the fire does not burn, where the cattle do not low, where the dogs do not bark, where the cat does not mew, where the hen does not cluck. Go to the mountain, into the water, where there is no one!

After chanting the spell, the patient's hairs are found, having fallen under the pressure of the air into the receptacle through which the sick person inhales, and the disease is thus symbolically banished.

These charm formulae have been selected for their rhyming and metrical patterns, and they suit the magical texts precisely because of their mysterious meaning. In the *Vlasi sredomasi* formula, the second word also exists as *srdomasi*, which in folk medicine means inflammation of the brain. The form *sr(e)domasi* was probably derived from the noun *srdobolja* ('an infectious intestinal disease, dysentery'). Unlike the *lasi-vlasi* and *lasi-malasi* formulae, whose meaning is opaque, the formula *Vlasi sredomasi* is understood as being connected to disease; etymologically, it is related to heart disease.

4. Conclusions

In examining meaningful connections of lexemes in the formula *Vlach paupers*, we have attempted to point out the elasticity of the form, the significance of the context, and the condensation of different layers of meaning. Historical, cultural, and social circumstances have influenced the formula's different connotations. The lexeme *Vlasi* is encountered as an ethnonym, an appellative, or as a general term for the opposing Other ("us" ~ "them"), and the meaning changes depending on the area and context in which it is used. In the examples provided, the term "Vlachs" usually denotes Serbs, Orthodox Christians, or Christians from a Muslim perspective (especially in Bosnia and Herzegovina), but also the inhabitants of the Romanian province of Vlachia. The formula has a derogatory meaning when indicating affiliation to another religion or area, or membership of a newly settled population as opposed to the native one.

The lexical collocations in the formulae *tears and curses of Vlach paupers, poor Vlach rain capes, rich Vlachs, black Vlachs*, etc. are made by analogy with other established common phrases and folklore formulae. The collocations and lexical associations are constructed so as to underline social and ethnic meanings, and both synonymic and homonymic connections. Folklore genres include these formulae in established clusters of motifs, but each in its own domain recalls older historical circumstances and relationships (e.g. epic song). At the same time, they are sufficiently elastic to be adjusted to typical heroes and subjects, including humorous stories and anecdotes. Special cases of the formula, such as when it occurs in magical charms, expand the semantic range and create unexpected connections.

References

Sources

Bogišić, V., ed. 1878. *Narodne pjesme iz starijih, najviše primorskih zapisa*, I [Cyr.]. Belgrade.

Daničić, Gj., ed. 1871. *Poslovice*. Zagreb.

Gesemann, G., ed. 1925. *Erlangenski rukopis starih srpskohrvatskih narodnih pesama* [Cyr.]. Sremski Karlovci.

Hörmann, K., ed. 1888–1889. *Narodne pjesme Muslimana u Bosni i Hercegovini*, 2 vols. Ed. by Đ. Buturović 1990. Sarajevo.

Karadžić, V. S., ed. 1900a. *Srpske narodne pjesme*, VII [Cyr.]. Ed. by Lj. Stojanović. Belgrade.

——, ed. 1900b. *Srpske narodne pjesme*, VIII [Cyr.]. Ed. by Lj. Stojanović. Belgrade.

——, ed. 1974. *Srpske narodne pjesme iz neobjavljenih rukopisa Vuka St. Karadžića* [Cyr.], vol. 2. Ed. by Ž. Mladenović and V. Nedić. Belgrade.

——, ed. 1986 [1862]. *Srpske narodne pjesme*, IV [Cyr.]. Ed. by Lj. Zuković. Belgrade.

——, ed. 1987a [1849]. *Srpske narodne poslovice* [Cyr.]. Ed. by M. Pantić. Belgrade.

——, ed. 1987b [1852]. *Srpski rječnik (1852)*, 2 vols. [Cyr.]. Ed. by J. Kašić. Belgrade.

Kića 1925. *Kića: list za šalu, zabavu i skupljanje narodnih umotvorina* [Cyr.] (6 December 1925, 10(49): 4) Niš.

Knežević, M., ed. 1957. *Antologija narodnih umotvorina* [Cyr.]. Novi Sad, Belgrade.

Milosavljević, S., ed. 1913. *Srpski narodni običaji iz Sreza Omoljskog* [Cyr.]. Srpski etnografski zbornik 19, Običaji naroda srpskoga 3. Belgrade.

Milutinović, S. S., ed. 1990 [1833]. *Pjevanija crnogorska I hercegovačka* [Cyr.] Ed. by D. Aranitović. Nikšić.

Petrović, P. Ž., ed. 1948. *Život i običaji narodni u Gruži* [Cyr.]. Srpski etnografski zbornik 58. Drugo odeljenje. Život i običaji narodni 26. Belgrade.

Radenković, Lj., ed. 1982. *Narodne basme i bajanja* [Cyr.]. Niš (et al.).

Simić, Lj., ed. 1959. "Narodne pesme: Etnološko-folkoristička ispitivanja u Neumu i okolini." *Glasnik Zemaljskog Muzeja Bosne i Hercegovine: Etnologija* 14:169–207.

Literature

Antonijević, D. 1982. *Obredi i običaji balkanskih stočara* [Cyr.]. Belgrade.

——. 1989. "Cattlebreeders' Migrations in the Balkans through Centuries." *Migrations in Balkan History* (ed. I. Ninić) 147–156. Belgrade.

Avagjan, K. 2017. *Stereotip stranca u jezičkoj slici stvarnosti Rusa i Srba* [Cyr.]. PhD dissertation, University of Belgrade. http://nardus.mpn.gov.rs/handle/1 23456789/9030?show=full.

Bojanić, D. 1974. *Turski zakoni i zakonski propisi iz XV i XVI veka za Smederevsku, Kruševačku i Vidinsku oblast.* Belgrade.

Bošković-Stulli, M. 1978. "Usmena književnost." *Povijest hrvatske književnosti*, I, 7–353. Zagreb.

Czamańska, I. 2015. "The Vlachs—Several Research Problems." *Balcanica Posnaniensia: Acta et studia* 22(1):7–16.

Detelić, M. 2010. "Parry-Lord-Foley: And What We Can Do with Them." *Serbian Studies Research* 1(1):5–17.

Detelić, M., and Delić, L., eds. 2015. *Epic Formula: A Balkan Perspective.* Belgrade.

Dinić-Knežević, D. 1999. "Vlasi." *Leksikon srpskog srednjeg veka* [Cyr.] (eds. S. Ćirković and R. Mihaljčić) 86–87. Belgrade.

Dukat, Z. 1988. *Homersko pitanje.* Zagreb.

Dvoichenko-Markov, D. 1984. "The Vlachs: The Latin Speaking Population of Eastern Europe." *Byzantion* 54(2):508–526.

Fine, J. V. A. 2009. *When Ethnicity Did Not Matter in the Balkans: A Study of Identity in Pre-Nationalist Croatia, Dalmatia, and Slavonia in the Medieval and Early-Modern Periods.* Ann Arbor.

Foley, J. M. 1995. *The Singer of Tales in Performance.* Bloomington.

Frog. 2016. "Linguistic Multiforms: Advancing Oral-Formulaic Theory." *FF Network* 48:6–14.

———, ed. 2017. *Formula: Units of Speech – 'Words' of Verbal Art: Working Papers of the Seminar-Workshop 17th-19th May 2017, Helsinki, Finland.* Helsinki.

Gavrilović, S., ed. 1986. *Istorija srpskog naroda: Četvrta knjiga, prvi tom. Srbi u XVIII veku* [Cyr.]. Belgrade.

Honko, L. 1998. *Textualising the Siri Epic. FF Communications* 264. Helsinki.

Isailović, N. 2017. "Legislation Concerning the Vlachs of the Balkans before and after Ottoman Conquest: An Overview." *State and Society in the Balkans before and after Establishment of Ottoman Rule* (ed. S. Rudić and S. Aslantaş). Belgrade.

Jireček, K. 1988. *Istorija Srba*, 2 vols. [Cyr.]. Ispravljeno i dopunjeno izdanje (ed. J. Radonić). Belgrade.

Kursar, V. 2013. "Being an Ottoman Vlach: On Vlach Identity(ies), Role and Status in Western Parts of the Ottoman Balkans (15th–18th Centuries)." *OTAM* 34:115–161.

Lord, A. B. 1960. *The Singer of Tales.* Cambridge, MA.

———. 1995. *The Singer Resumes the Tale.* Ed. by M. L. Lord. Ithaca.

Mihaljčić, R. 2006. *Zakoni u starim srpskim ispravama: Pravni propisi, prevodi, uvodni tekstovi i objašnjenja* [Cyr.]. Belgrade.

Milošević-Đorđević, N. 1984. "Formula." "Formulativnost." *Narodna književnost* (eds. R. Pešić and N. Milošević-Đorđević) 84–85. Belgrade.

———. 2008. "Srpski folklor na razmeđi dva milenijuma: Osvrt na istoriju istraživanja." *Slovenski folklor i folkloristika na razmeđi dva milenijuma* [Cyr.] (ed. Lj. Radenković) 89–109. Belgrade.

Parry, M. 1971. *The Making of Homeric Verse: The Collected Papers of Milman Parry.* Ed. by A. Parry. Oxford.

Reichl, K. 1992. *Turkic Oral Epic Poetry: Tradition, Forms, Poetic Structure.* New York.

Sikimić, B. 2002. "Etnički stereotipi o Vlasima." *Junir: Yugoslav Society for the Scientific Study of Religion* 9:187–203.

Skok, P. 1973. "Vlah." *Etimologijski rječnik hrvatskoga ili srpskoga jezika*, vol. 3, 606–609. Zagreb.

Sugar, P. F. 1996. *Southeastern Europe under Ottoman Rule, 1354-1804.* Seattle.

Winnifrith, T. J. 1987. *The Vlachs: The History of a Balkan People.* London.

Wolf, L. 2003. *Venice and the Slavs: The Discovery of Dalmatia in the Age of Enlightenment.* Stanford.

Zirojević. O. 1974. *Tursko vojno uređenje u Srbiji (1459-1638)* [Cyr.]. Belgrade.

5

Humans as Formulaic Beings

Anatoly Liberman, University of Minnesota, Twin Cities

1. The Formulaic Language of Literature

SINCE THE STUDY OF EUROPEAN PHILOLOGY BEGAN with a detailed examination of Homer, it was noticed centuries ago (indeed, this fact could not be missed) that phrases like *ox-eyed Hera* and *wine-colored sea* kept turning up in the *Iliad* and the *Odyssey* with great, even monotonous, regularity. Quite early, German researchers coined the adjective *formelhaft* ('formulaic'). When the turn came for Old Germanic poetry to be analyzed according to the principles, tested on the material of Greek epics, exhaustive compendia of Old English, Old Saxon, and Old Icelandic formulas were put together. The contribution of Old High German was minimal, because almost no traditional alliterative poetry in that language has come down to us. Eduard Sievers's index of formulas appended to his edition of the Old Saxon *Heliand* ('The Savior') (1878) and Richard Meyer's corpus (1889) are still fully usable classics.

The key term in any study of formulas is repetition, or recurrence. Standard epithets attached to certain nouns do not exhaust the repertoire of formulas, for whole sentence-like blocks turn up in the poems again and again. It would be wrong to say that such blocks fit metrical conditions: they gained their popularity, perhaps sometimes were even coined, because the meter favored them. An in-depth analysis of such phrases is the achievement of the Parry-Lord, or Oral-Formulaic, Theory (OFT). Its practitioners showed why improvisation depends on such units in predictable places; they made it clear that, in oral tradition (at least in epics), composition is inseparable from improvisation. But OFT dealt not only with recurring verbal blocks. It also revealed, or at least described in detail, a great number of so-called themes, or type scenes.

Here is a characteristic example. When the hero is challenged, we never see him rushing into battle at once. If the episode is told in full, his wife or mother will try to dissuade him from attacking a dangerous enemy. He dismisses their fears and travels to the place of the encounter. An exchange of speeches between the contestants follows their coming face to face. The fight may be described in great detail (but again in formulaic terms: broken shields, flying spears, split helmets) or in a few evocative sentences, as though the minutiae could be taken for granted. If the hero perishes, we witness ceremonial obsequies and lamentations. Such type scenes are surprisingly numerous. The enormous literature on OFT was collected and annotated by John Miles Foley, who also provided an introduction to the theory and traced its evolution and influence on folkloristic research in the twentieth century (1988).

From a somewhat different angle and at approximately the same time, recurring elements in folklore (here in prose) were described by Vladimir Propp. His book, titled *Morfologiia skazki* ('Morphology of the Folktale'), appeared in 1928, but made no stir because it was written in Russian. Moreover, during the darkest years of Soviet history, the book incurred the accusation of formalism (a highly charged term of abuse), while its continuation on the origin of the wonder tale fell victim to another postwar purge, now directed at the "antipatriots" who were slow to realize that everything from the steam engine to the fairy tale had originated in Russia. But in 1958, Propp's early book was translated into English (at the initiative of Roman Jakobson) and became an academic bestseller.[1] In 1960, Harvard brought out Albert B. Lord's book *The Singer of Tales*. It also won immediate recognition, and the two strands of structural folklore met. Comparison of them is now commonplace. More than half a century has passed since 1958 and 1960, so that scholars have had ample time to think of the books' strong and weak points. There is of course a difference between them. Before 1958, Propp's name meant nothing in the West, except to those who dealt with Russian folklore (as a rule, such people were more interested in texts than in the achievements of the humanities), whereas *The Singer of Tales* was prepared for by numerous works of the late Milman Parry and the extremely active A. B. Lord, but without the book, the world-wide recognition of OFT would not have occurred.

Propp showed that the classical fairy tale follows a rigid structure. Although intuitively all have always known it, as Propp was the first to point out, for the plot runs along the easily recognizable lines—the hero (a despised third son, a so-called male Cinderella) leaves home, meets a magical helper, performs the tasks required of him by his prospective bride (most often a princess), and marries her—Propp showed that what often looks like a different motif is in fact a variation on the familiar one. Unlike the practitioners of OFT, Propp,

---

[1] See more on the ups and downs of Propp's career in the introduction to Propp 1984.

who, as noted, dealt with prose, addressed only content. In his tales, verbal formulas were few and played an insignificant role (cf. *once upon a time, and they lived happily ever after*, and their analogs in other languages). Both Parry-Lord's followers and Propp analyzed oral tradition, which inevitably depends on the use of recurring formulas. Neither the so-called singers of tales nor storytellers reproduce the text verbatim. They are rather like jazz musicians, who improvise according to the rules learned during the long years of apprenticeship.

The predictability of the situations neither spoils nor improves a poem and a tale, because everything depends on the inured tastes of the listeners and readers. It is only expected that the storyteller will remain within the limits imposed on the piece of art by tradition. A typical example of such dependence is the situation described in the first part of the Old English heroic poem *Beowulf*. After the conquest over the monster Grendel, the court poet found "other words" to celebrate the victory. But, as we know from the literature of that period, every "other" song was a variation composed within the same formulaic mold. The audience would hardly have accepted anything else. Some old masters displayed remarkable talent, even though they remained true to their school. Originality, as we understand it, developed with the growth of individual authorship. There is some attraction in predictability: it requires less mental strain from the listeners and confirms their perspicacity: they always get what they expect.

Type scenes also occur in prose. The so-called sagas of Icelanders (which artistically far exceed the other sagas) are full of them, partly because they inherited their worldview from Old Scandinavian epic poetry (eddic lays). We know that, if a worthy man is killed, his sons and brothers may remain passive and will be goaded into action by their womenfolk (mothers, sister, or widows). Other recurring incidents do not derive from heroic lays. For example, when a ball game on ice (a kind of hockey) or a horse fight (another favorite entertainment) is described, it is almost always followed by a violent quarrel that has dire consequences. Moreover, there would have been no point in describing a game or a horse fight unless it resulted in a quarrel. The saga does not focus on events that have no serious consequences. Every detail is important. Even when we are told how many guests attended a celebration and where they were seated, we are supposed to pay attention. This circumstance is made especially clear by love scenes. Old poetry taught us to watch heavily formulaic scenes of heroic wooing. Wooing in the sagas is quite different, for marriage is usually presented as a friendly bargain, though the woman is never forced to marry against her will. Such scenes are also formulaic from beginning to end, down to the response of the prospective bride's father (always the father: "I am for the bargain, but we have to ask my daughter").

Sometimes (and not too rarely), a man begins to pay court to a young woman without the consent or tacit approval of her kin. Her relatives do not explode immediately; rather they tell the man to stop his visits, which are hardly innocent (though premarital sex is not always taken for granted). The wooer persists in his folly, and the drama unfolds according to one or two predictable scenarios. The creation of a new family is too serious to be treated lightly. Daniel Sävborg has explored the treatment of love in the sagas and shown its formulaic nature in all its ramifications (see Sävborg 2018, with reference to his dissertation). It probably won't be an exaggeration to say that all medieval literature, both poetry and prose, is formulaic, even though each genre is formulaic in its own way.

In the nineteen-fifties, Propp, who, much to his surprise and even dismay, became a world celebrity, noted that his scheme, let alone the "morphology" he had laid bare, cannot be applied to other literary genres. Yet in a rather general way, formulaic structures are common. This statement needs no proof with regard to picaresque novels, but in a typical nineteenth-century novel like *David Copperfield*, and even the less predictable *Pendennis*, events develop more or less as they do in the fairy tale. In a classic detective story (Conan Doyle, Agatha Christie), the plot also unfolds "per plan": every character is suspected in turn, but the murderer, as we find out, is the one whom no one would have thought of casting for such a role. Every turn in the plot makes the great detective approach the solution but confuses the reader more and more. Textbooks, manuals, and instructions (directions) of all kinds are inevitably formulaic with regard to both content and language.

In a way, art, anonymous, as in the past, or individual, as in the modern epoch, always draws on formulas. Otherwise, there would not have existed the combination of the distinctive features of composition we call style. That is why we hear an unfamiliar piece of music and say it must be Mozart, Chopin, Brahms, or Tchaikovsky. In literature, the situation is the same. Who will fail to recognize Gogol or Thomas Mann from half a page of their works? Their greatness is inseparable from their limitations. Art historians are able to guess the painter of an unsigned picture with an astounding degree of precision. Lev Tolstoy (himself a good musician) was fond of Edvard Grieg. Yet once, after listening to his new piece, he praised it but added that it sounded too "Grieg-ish."

The power of individual formulas on the level of content is particularly instructive to observe. Roman Jakobson (1937) noticed that Pushkin had kept reproducing the same collision: a statue kills the protagonist. The best-known example is *The Bronze Horseman*, but there are many others. Pushkin was probably unaware of his obsession. By contrast, Lermontov realized that a demonic creature had been following him all his life. He even declared that he had got rid of his pursuer by means of verses (his main narrative poem is called *The Demon*), but he probably did not. However, Lermontov certainly composed his lyrics and prose in ignorance of the fact that all the characters he loved have blue eyes. Perhaps the prototypes did have blue eyes. What matters is that he included this detail because he could not resist the subconscious pressure.

The same holds for many other highly talented modern authors, who, as we may suspect, recreated near-identical turns of the plot unwittingly. Did Dickens realize that he twice used the model "a selfish father neglects a loving daughter": in *Dombey and Son* and in *Little Dorrit*? Or that the heroine's chosen man is also sent away twice, to reemerge, Peer Gynt-like, when no one expects him (in *Dombey and Son* and in *Bleak House*)? Was Dostoevsky aware of his predilection to so-called mass scenes with scandal? There is a "formulaic machine" inside every great master.

It need not bother a student of Lermontov how true to life his descriptions were, but a similar question requires greater attention when we deal with old literature. Nearly all of it features stock figures and stock situations, be it a generous king, an impotent or kind but weak old monarch cuckolded by his wife, an evil counselor, a doughty warrior (followed by a faithful retainer), a persecuted stepdaughter, a lascivious monk, cursed treasure, fratricide, prophetic dreams—the familiar makeup of any motif index.

Perhaps our life does run according to the ever-recurring patterns, but, when we compare medieval narratives (heroic poetry and romances), Icelandic sagas, the later picaresque novel, the vaudeville, and the Victorian novel, with the novels by Balzac, Flaubert, and especially Dostoevsky, Tolstoy, and those who came after them, we observe how gradually but inexorably modern authors strove to get rid of the familiar and the predictable. In the memory of the people still living, even the thriller has moved away from Conan Doyle's model (which does not mean that the production has become better). Literature and art develop by shaking off old formulas. That is why Sterne began his hero's biography with conception rather than birth. The insistent desire to avoid formulas and to parody them also becomes formulaic. We have all witnessed the aging and degradation of the avant-garde. Iconoclastic painters, poets, and musicians violated old canons, shocked the public, and attained glory, but very soon, being "abnormal" became the norm. Sergei Prokofiev prefaced his early piano concerto with the instruction *col pugno* ('with the fist'), a far cry from *appassionato*. The old formula was shattered, only to give way to a new one.

As time went on, the focus in literature shifted from the expected and typical to the unexpected and individual, so that, when creative arts were forced to return to the trodden path, the results were catastrophic, as we know from the experience of socialist realism, with its embarrassingly predictable clichés.

Apparently, formulaic literature, whatever its mold, should correspond to the mental attitude of a given society. The mold arises, dies, and arises again "in season." Once it becomes a thing of the past, it acquires antiquarian charm. That is why the *Iliad*, *The Lay of the Nibelungen*, *Don Quixote*, and *The Pickwick Papers* are, in a way, immortal.

In 1963, Eric Havelock published the book *Preface to Plato*. It was subjected to severe criticism (see Liberman 1994:43), but here we are not interested in how accurately Havelock's picture of Homeric Greece and the rise of literature was. Incidentally, now that more people have had a chance to get acquainted with this book, one keeps encountering references to it by literary historians who find Havelock's approach inspiring. It is Havelock's characterization of Plato's Athens that we should not miss:

> The whole memory of a people was poeticized, and this exercised a constant control over the ways in which they expressed themselves in casual speech. The consequences would go deeper than mere queerness or quaintness (from our standpoint) of verbal idiom. They reach into the problem of the character of the Greek consciousness itself, in a given historical period, the kind of thoughts a Greek could think, and the kind he would not think. The Homeric state of mind was, it will appear, something like a total state of mind.
>
> Havelock 1963:134

Havelock probably went too far when he said that the *whole* memory of a people was poeticized, but we should note the concepts he risked introducing: *a total state of mind* and *a formulaic state of mind*. It seems that a formulaic state of mind is the curse or blessing (depending on the point of view) of every society. We are slaves of religious, political, and scholarly formulas. Under Stalin and Hitler, the state of their subjects' minds was indeed "total," but in today's Western democracies, the situation is not radically different. The ever-recurring terms of abuse are applied to the candidates of the opposite party, the same vapid slogans are invoked again and again, and few people realize to what extent so-called free speech is formulaic speech, be its content praise or vituperation. This brings us to the question about the linguistic aspect of the formula.

2. The Formula as a Concept of Linguistics

A look at any moderately thick dictionary of English, French, German, etc. reveals an astounding number of phraseological units. Even those people whose speech is devoid of collocations like *hand over fist, by the skin of one's teeth, to buy a pig in a poke, in a brown study* ('in a state of deep meditation'); picturesque similes (*merry as a grig, happy as a clam at high tide*), binomials like *gall and wormwood, fine and dandy, safe and sound,* and verbal phrases like *to call a spade a spade* and *to pull one's leg* depend on such semi-free groups as *to make a mistake, to draw a (the) line, to set a limit, to shine bright, open access, old age,* and hundreds of others. Phraseology has long since become a branch of linguistics in its own right (*long since* and *in its own right* are of course also among the units phraseology studies, and so is *of course*). Some such units are "mildly idiomatic." Thus, mistakes (in English) can be only made, not done, whereas homework can be only done, not made. Other (almost free) collocations acquire a higher degree of idiomaticity. For example, *to make one's bed* does not presuppose constructing this piece of furniture (though it may!).

Phraseology as an object of study was initiated by Charles Bally (1905), whose name is familiar to many, because, together with Albert Sechehaye, he edited Saussure's posthumous *Course*. However, as a branch of linguistics, phraseology burst into bloom in the Soviet Union, where countless articles, books, and even specialized dictionaries were devoted to this subject (see Amosova 1961 and Kunin [or Koonin] 1970). East German linguists took the cue from their Soviet colleagues, and it is thanks to their efforts that phraseology acquired a measure of popularity in the West, for German, much more so than Russian, is accessible to linguists everywhere.

In the English-speaking world, phraseology has not been neglected either, but it never made it to the forefront of linguistics. However, it found an enthusiastic following among language teachers, predictably those who deal with English for foreigners. The literature in this area is huge. The collocation *formulaic language* occurs in it all the time, and a strict distinction has been made between idioms (*go the whole hog* and its likes) and so-called lexical bundles (*kind of, to begin with,* and so forth). Language teachers paid attention to several aspects of phraseology that seldom interested earlier theoreticians, namely, the frequency of idioms and "bundles" in oral speech and the differences of their use in speaking and writing. I became seriously interested in this literature in connection with my prospective explanatory and etymological dictionary of English idioms. Here, I will refer to four publications, because they are fully informative and because they appeared in the journals seldom consulted by theoretical linguists: Biber, Conrad, and Cortes 2004; Ädel [and] Erman 2012; Hyland 2012; and Ju-Hua Chen and Baker 2010.

The battles once fought in professional publications concerned the definition of a phraseological unit, the classification of such units, their structure, the variability of their elements, and the degree of their idiomaticity. Those battles need not delay us here, because all will agree that a unit in question should consist of at least two words, and, as a general rule, it is reproduced by speakers ready-made, rather than created anew, despite a possible variability of its constituents (cf. *get it into one's head ~ take it into one's head, cut to bits ~ cut to pieces,* and so forth—one variant is usually more frequent). Such units may be equal to whole sentences, some of which are proverbs: cf. *it is raining cats and dogs, never say die, one swallow does not make a summer,* and the like. Familiar quotations like *more in sorrow than in anger* belong here too. The formulaic blocks of a literary composition can be identified by their recurrence and their role in the making of the whole, while phraseological units reveal their nature by the degree of cohesion of their elements. A single occurrence of *dead season* or *merry as a grig* will suffice for its being recognized as such a unit, because most of us have no idea what *grig* means, and a season cannot be "dead," because it is not a living creature. Yet all of them are formulas in the broadest sense of this term.

Apart from similes like *red as a rose* and *speak like a book*, enigmatic phrases of the *Hooker Walker* type (an expression of ridicule or disbelief), phrases with currency in a limited area, and such descriptive phrases as *a cat in hell without claws* ('in the position of utter helplessness'), there still remain thousands of units familiar to most speakers of a given language. As far as I can judge, it has not been recognized that in the modern European languages, idioms appeared comparatively late. If one knows all the words in an Old English or Old French sentence, and can disentangle the syntax, one will understand everything in it. Old Icelandic and less so Middle High German do use metaphorical expressions (here I will ignore the complicated systems of metaphors prevalent in Old Icelandic skaldic poetry, so-called kennings, when, for example, the eye could be called the moon of the forehead), but, on the whole, the metaphor and idioms are the inheritance of the Renaissance, and so is the modern sense of humor, which permeates so many of them. (Greek and Latin are different; here I am speaking only about the "barbarian languages.") A student of a medieval European text should be ready to encounter recurring blocks and type scenes, but no one in it will be said to kick the bucket, show the white feather, or buy something for a song. At one time, I hoped to promote the study of Germanic historical phraseology in the United States and wrote an article on this subject (Liberman 1994:356–373), but only one dissertation bears fruit to my attempt (Janus 1994).

Thus, a total or near total state of mind we may associate with antiquity and the Middle Ages, and the efflorescence of the metaphor that resulted, among other things, in the rise of modern idioms, belong to different epochs. But this does not mean that we have not produced our own analog of a "total state of mind." Usually, the less talented a piece of writing and the more trivial an oral communication, the deeper its debt to highfalutin banalities and the higher its dependence on familiar verbal blocks. This phenomenon comes to the foreground in the periodical press and sloganeering, but not only there. Editors fight a losing battle against buzzwords, because the impulse to speak like everybody else cannot be dislodged. Journalists become deaf to repetition especially often. For instance, every time presidents and prime ministers meet, they are said "to huddle" (all my examples are from American newspapers). Meetings and projects are invariably "off to a robust start." Interest rates are no longer increased: they are "ratcheted up."

Even if we disregard the horror of the jargon in the humanities (gobbledegook makes every banality look and sound profound), we will notice that to survive in a society whose state of mind is "total," we have to abide by its rules. Every academic department (college, university) swears by equity and diversity. This is like buying a medieval indulgence. No grant application (I am again speaking about the humanities) will be funded unless the meaningless word *interdisciplinary* turns up in the first paragraph. Dedication to buzzwords results in the catastrophic impoverishment of young people's speech. One can spend the first twenty years of one's life using only four epithets: *great, fascinating* (variant: *fantastic*), *awesome*, and *weird*. There is no situation that won't be covered by *OK, cool, wow, no way,* and *big deal.* Even the slang of young Americans has lost its glow and become boringly predictable, because popular culture provides the same inspiration to everybody, while the once daring variations on the theme of the F word have long since lost their glamour. *The NWOAD* contains a list of locutions to be avoided (pp. 2011–2014). This is a heterogeneous list. For example, I see no danger in the phrases *down in the mouth* and *from time immemorial* (perhaps worn a bit threadbare, but not irritating); however, *above and beyond the call of duty, ripe old age,* and *join the club* irk me too. Everybody's threshold, it appears, is different, but one thing remains obvious: we are human because we are endowed with the power of speech, and we are social beings because our speech is formulaic.

However, an important line separates pre- from post-Renaissance mentality. In the remote past, the formulaic state of mind was probably the only one that could have existed. (Classical antiquity is a special case, and here I will not deal with it.) Thousands of years ago, the extreme instability of daily life resulted in the belief that one could not fight destiny. People believed that their fate was controlled by the spirits, gods, and other supernatural creatures. In both hunting and agricultural societies, nothing ever seemed to change. To use Mircea Eliade's (1954) term, the myth of the eternal return reigned supreme. Indeed, spring always followed winter, and the harvesting season followed summer. Even death meant going elsewhere (departing, as we say), rather than the end of life, and new animals were the old ones reborn. Formulaic language was a natural component of that attitude toward life.

It took millennia to shake off the myth of the eternal return. In the last two thousand years, even the triumph of Christianity with its accent on the immutability of the once established world order could not stop people from realizing that things did change. This liberating process or the process of enlightenment ran parallel to the gradual freeing of the individual from the "herd." To be sure, the herd instinct did not go anywhere, for humans are gregarious beings, but it no longer dominated the scene. The introduction of literacy accelerated and, in most places, inaugurated the development of individual authorship, and an awareness of an individual style was one of its side effects. Another natural side effect was the erosion of the formulaic way of expression in transmitting the knowledge of the past. The final victory over the formula is neither possible nor desirable, but at present, it is a matter of personal conviction how formulaic one's speech should be. To be sure, the tyranny of set phrases of the *make a mistake* versus *do one's homework* cannot be shaken off. Language imposes its limitations on our mentality. It may be profitable to view the history of the formula in conjunction with the entire history of civilization.

References

Ädel, A., and Erman, B. 2012. "Recurrent Word Combinations in Academic Writing by Native and Non-native Speakers of English: A Lexical Bundles Approach." *English for Specific Purposes* 31:81–92.

Amosova, N. N. 1963. *Osnovy angliiskoi frazeologii [Foundations of English Phraseology]*. Leningrad.

Bally, C. 1905. *Précis de stylistique. Esquisse d'une methode fondée sur l'étude du français moderne*. Genève.

Biber, D, Conrad, S., and Cortes, V. 2004. "*If You Look at* ... : Lexical Bundles in University Teaching and Textbooks." *Applied Linguistics* 23:150–169.

Chen, J.-H., and Baker, P. 2010. "Lexical Bundles in L1 and L2 Academic Writing." *Language Learning and Technology* 14:30–49.

Eliade, M. 1954. *The Myth of the Eternal Return*. Transl. W. R. Trask. Bollingen Series 46. Princeton University Press. First published in French in 1949.

Foley, J. M. 1988. *The Theory of Oral Composition*. Bloomington.

Havelock, E. A. 1963. *Preface to Plato: A History of the Greek Mind: Volume One*. Cambridge, MA.

Hyland, K. 2012. "Bundles in Academic Discourse." *Annual Review of Applied Linguistics* 32:150–169.

Jakobson, R. 1937. "Socha v symbolice Puškinově." *Slovo a slovesnost* 3:2–24. An expanded English version appeared in Volume 5 of Jakobson, R. 1979. *Collected Writings: On Verse, Its Masters and Explorers*, 237–280. Eds. S. Rudy and M. Taylor. The Hague.

Janus, L. 1994. *The Phraseology of* Egils saga. PhD dissertation, University of Minnesota.

Koonin [= Kunin], A. V. 1970. *Angliiskaia frazeologiia (teoreticheskii kurs)* [*English Phraseology (A Theoretical Course)*]. Moscow.

Liberman, A. 1994. *Word Heath: Wortheide: Orðheiði*. Episteme dell'Anticità e oltre 1. Rome.

Lord, A. B. 1960. *The Singer of Tales*. Harvard Studies in Comparative Literature 24. Cambridge, MA.

Meyer, R. M. 1889. *Die altgermanische Poesie nach ihren formelhaften Elementen beschrieben*. Berlin.

NWOAD = *The New Oxford American Dictionary: Second edition*. Ed. Erin McKean. New York.

Propp, V. 1928. *Morfologiia skazki* [*Morphology of the Folktale*]. Leningrad.

———. 1958. *Morphology of the Folktale*. Transl. L. Scott. Austin.

———. 1984. *Theory and History of Folklore*. Transl. A. G. Martin and R. P. Martin, et al. Ed. with an Introduction and Notes by A. Liberman. Minneapolis.

Sävborg, D. 2018. "The Formula in Icelandic Saga Prose." *Saga-Book* 42:51–86.

Sievers, E. 1878. "Formelverzeichnis." *Heliand* (ed. E. Sievers) 391–496. Halle.

6

Multiform Theory

FROG, UNIVERSITY OF HELSINKI

WHEN IS A FORMULA NOT A FORMULA? The question of where to draw the line between a formula and a word concerns a formula's threshold of minimum complexity, and it comes into focus because "word" and "formula" are considered to refer to distinct, complementary categories. However, there is no similarly common term for a category greater than a formula, and the question of a formula's threshold of maximum complexity generally goes unasked. C. M. Bowra, for example, considered that an epic formula could be "a set of lines up to a dozen or so in number" (1952:222)—which could make a formula of about eighty-nine words based on the first twelve lines of the *Odyssey*. Yet, can such a stretch of text carry a meaning in the same way as *fleet-footed Achilles*? And will the variation of such a large unit be comparable to a line-internal formula?

The present chapter introduces *multiform theory*, an approach to verbal systems that produce stretches of text in verse or prose that may considerably exceed a line or clause. Whereas the word offers a category in relation to which the minimum complexity of a formula is considered, the *linguistic multiform* presents a corresponding category for considering its maximum complexity. The present discussion is organized with an initial overview of some relevant terms and concepts and an overview of the background of multiform theory, followed by a survey of several types of multiforms in metered poetry, and finally a consideration of multiforms in prose and conversational dialogue.

1. A Definition of Formula

The distinction of linguistic multiforms from formulae is dependent on how "formula" is defined. Research on formulaic language has developed in different branches or strands. These can be viewed in terms of: (*a*) research centrally concerned with the lexicon of a language or Saussure's *langue* (i.e. language as an abstract system); (*b*) research centrally concerned with language as it operates in discourse or Saussures' *parole* (i.e. language as it varies in situated use); and (*c*) language as it works in oral poetry. The lexicon-centered and discourse-centered branches have developed in varying degrees of dialogue with one another and there is a continuum of research between them. Formula research on oral poetry has evolved more independently owing in large part to the long-standing tendency in Western cultures to treat "poetry" and "prose" as clear and distinct categories, reflected even in how each is arranged on a printed page. The tendency has been reinforced, on the one hand, by Western literary poetry's manipulation of any and all linguistic resources available for the production of unique works (cf. Hasan 1989). Oral poetry, however, develops and maintains a distinct register that relies on social recognizability for its communicative efficacy (Foley 1990; 1995; 1996; Frog 2015). On the other hand, Western research on oral poetry gradually became dominated by Oral-Formulaic Theory (OFT), reifying ideas that set "poetry" apart by initially propagating a "theory" that accounted for, and indeed defined, formulaic language through its relationship to metered verse (Frog and Lamb, this volume, section 1). The form of OFT that was disseminated through Albert Bates Lord's *Singer of Tales* (1960) belongs to an earlier era, here described as "Classic OFT," distinct from its more dynamic manifestations today. In a current register-based approach to oral and oral-derived verbal art the gap between language use in "poetry" and "prose" dissolves like a mirage.

The artificiality of a binary poetry/prose divide became clear as forms of verbal art were brought into focus on their own terms through Dell Hymes's ethnography of speaking (1962) and Dennis Tedlock's ethnopoetics (Rothernberg and Tedlock 1970), which highlighted how poetics operate on a spectrum. Nigel Fabb (2015:9–10) situates the breakthrough into poetry at the point where poetic principles such as meter, alliteration, rhyme, or parallelism are given priority over syntax and prosody in organizing a text into units (rather than only organizing units scattered within a text). From this perspective, the difference in language's operation in poetry is that poetic organizing principles become primary rather than complementary stylistic and rhetorical devices. In this case, syntax and prosody become subordinated and evolve along with use of the lexicon in relation to conventions of the formal organizing principles. Thus, some registers may have distinctive formulaic lexicons that might seem to work very differently from language in conversational speech, yet the phenomenon of formulaic language remains the same; its manifestations are simply shaped in relation to the particular hierarchy of organizing principles through which discourse is organized. The constraints that poetic organizing principles place on lexical choices can facilitate the crystallization of phraseology or drive variation (e.g. by requiring that a word begin with a particular sound for alliteration), as well as shape lexical semantics, particularly in a register that is used to express a limited range of things. As a result, formulae in poetic discourse may become more saliently observable, as may more complex verbal systems.

The diversity of forms that formulae may take has proven challenging to pin down with a simple definition (Schmitt and Carter 2004:2; cf. Harvilahti 1992a:29–67, 141–147). In recent decades, however, the different branches of research increasingly tend to agree on defining formulae in relation to three criteria: (*a*) a formula concerns linguistic signs, (*b*) operates with unitary meaning or function, yet (*c*) is distinguished from simple "words" by its complexity.[1] The unitary nature of a formula as a linguistic sign tends to be more or less straightforward, although it may be described in various ways, for instance as a "morpheme-equivalent unit" (Wray 2008:11–12) or as a linguistic "integer of meaning" (Foley and Ramey 2012:80). A formula's complexity, on the other hand, may focus exclusively on lexical items as a phrase or idiom; it may be a combination of a lexeme and syntactic structure that generates a formulaic sequence, or a combination of a lexeme and a poetic structure like meter or parallelism, or a combination of a lexeme with paralinguistic features or discourse structures. In all cases, a formula is viewed as a linguistic and cognitive reality that becomes established as a distinct unit with an exclusive entry in the mental lexicon of users, even if the same unit of meaning may be arrived at by analyzing the formula through the lexicon and grammar (Wray 2002:9–21). As a practical working definition, a formula is here considered *a linguistic sign or equivalent signifier that is more complex than a single word yet has unitary meaning or functional value so that it operates as a distinct unit of the lexicon.*

2. Collocation versus Formula

Defining a formula in terms of unitary meaning or function also distinguishes it from other phenomena in many forms of verbal art that are also sometimes called formulae. Prose is centrally organized through syntax and prosody in relation to meanings, so formulae emerge and evolve through the interaction of the lexicon with those organizing principles for expressing meanings or discourse functions. Where poetic principles receive precedence, these affect the formation of units of language, shaping formulae, but, in some poetries, also

---

[1]   During the OFT boom of the 1960s and 1970s, "formula" became a trendy term to label a variety of types of phenomena in oral poetry research, several of which left phraseology to focus on syntactic, structural, or semantic patterns recurring "under the same metrical conditions." Much of the terminology developed during this period has dropped out of use, although Joseph Russo's (1963) concept of "structural formula" continues to be taken up (see also Saarinen, this volume).

driving the development of units for meeting *purely formal* needs such as rhyme or alliteration, to which syntax and meaning or discourse function may be incidental (Frog 2015:82–89; Frog with Tarkka 2017:217–221).

Lexemes or phraseology linked by sound rather than sense have been explored especially in Old English verse (e.g. Reinhard 1976; Tyler 2006). Oversimplifying somewhat, this poetry's meter demands that the two halves of a line should be linked by the alliteration of prominent syllables, and pairs and sets of alternative words developed to meet that metrical need. However, meeting the metrical need was complementary to syntax and meaning rather than bound to it, and it was common to conclude an independent clause in the first half of a line and begin a new one in the second (i.e. with the effect that the meter "requires" the performer to continue with the next sentence). For example, the pair *word* ('word') and *wuldor* ('glory') could be spread across the grammatical subject and object, as in *and þæt word acwæð / wuldres aldor* (*Genesis* 639) ('and the *word* decreed, / *glory*'s elder [= Lord]', i.e. 'God decreed the word'), or it could equally be used across independent clauses in a line like *wuldres aldor. / Wordhleoðor astag* (*Andreas* 708) ('*glory*'s elder [= Lord]. / *Word*-speech arose'). The *word*-*wuldor* pair is based on a *metrical* function without a unitary meaning or discourse function qualifying a formula above and thus needs to be terminologically distinguished.

The (conventionalized) occurrence of things together or things that (conventionally) occur together are described as a *collocation*.[2] The *word*-*wuldor* pair is a collocation organized by alliteration while other linguistic collocations are shaped by different principles. A formulaic sequence is a type of collocation distinguished by its parts having unitary meaning. Here, *collocation* without other specification is used to refer to *collocations that are not also formulaic sequences*. In Old English research, discussions of alliterative collocations have focused on their potential for connotative semantics or to operate as cues in narration (Reinhard 1976; Tyler 2006; in Old Norse, see also Rugerrini 2016), a potential for meanings that is important to recognize, but does not necessarily meet the criteria of a formula above. The collocation's constituents' meanings or discourse functions are not collectively unitary and operate *relative to syntax* as independent linguistic signs (or within formulae as linguistic signs). Regular connotative meanings or associations of the collocation operate *independent of the syntax governing its constituents*. Thus, the collocation's semantics do not operate on the same level of syntagmatic relations as basic units of the lexicon, formulaic or otherwise. Moreover, formally driven collocations

---

[2] Collocation is sometimes also used for alternative words that occur in a single position in a phrase or other unit of discourse (Halliday and Hasan 1976).

do not necessarily develop connotative semantics at all, nor does developing such semantics mean that they were not also used simply to meet formal parameters by some people or in some cases (cf. Frog with Tarkka 2017:225). Alongside formally driven collocations like *word-wuldor*, collocations may also emerge in relation to other factors, such as semantic association (Tyler 2006). Distinguishing formula and collocation in relation to unitary meaning or function on the one hand and syntax on the other provides a foundation for formally distinguishing a formula's upper limit of complexity; it predicts that a formula is unlikely to exceed the scope of a clause.

3. The Background of Multiform Theory

Classic OFT offers a model for how oral epic singers can versify at the rate of performance, which it explains through: (*a*) Milman Parry's model of metrically pre-fitted phraseology forming an idiom that equips a performer to speak in verse on familiar subjects (1928; 1971); (*b*) *themes* as "groups of ideas regularly used in telling a tale" (Lord 1960:68), sometimes distinguished from *typical scenes* or *type-scenes* and *motifs* (see Foley 1990:esp. 240–245, 279–284, 329–335);[3] and (*c*) the *song*, which "the singer thinks of [...] in terms of a flexible plan of themes" (Foley 1990:99; see also Parry 1971:453). OFT's formulae and themes operate at two levels of syntagmatic relations, the combination of which distinguishes Lord's "composition in performance" from "improvisation" (Lord 1987:335–336). Classic OFT research remained focused on distinguishing and analyzing units of each type—the lexicon of a tradition's *langue* at the levels of language and narrative content. OFT's themes have often been qualified by having recurrent language in verbalization,[4] yet the relationship between formulae and themes generally remained unclear (Zumthor 1983 [1990]:92).

There is nothing new in recognizing that an oral tradition may have resources for expressing a stretch of text. In 1890, Alfred Nutt claimed that

---

[3] These terms have all been defined in various ways across time, with the distinction between *theme* and *motif* initially being quite vague and problematic (Propp 1928 [1968]:12–13), not least because they tended to be treated as practical rather than analytical terms (Thompson 1955–1958; Lamb, this volume). *Typical scene* or *type-scene* started off more or less as another term for the same thing (Arend 1933). Parry was developing a typology of themes (1971:446, 448, 450, 454) that was not developed further. Discussion was particularly sophisticated in Old English research, where some scholars sought to distinguish both terms from *motif* (Fry 1968; see also Hopkins, this volume; for a semiotic approach, see also Frog 2015:38–41), while, to complicate matters, *theme* is sometimes used in Indo-European studies for the semantic unit expressed by a formula (Watkins 1995:chs. 1, 15, 30, 36; *pace* Lord e.g. 1995:62).

[4] John Miles Foley (e.g. 1996, 1999) discusses themes in addition to formulae as "words" of verbal art, leveling the difference between the linguistic register and narrative or information that it is customarily used to mediate.

"stereotyped descriptive passages in verse or rhythmic prose, of a general character, so that they can be used indifferently with various incidents— are necessarily common in all bodies of myth or romance preserved orally" (1880:448–449). Nutt dubbed such a passage a *run* (1880:448–449), which became established especially in connection with Gaelic storytelling. Nutt's contemporary A. F. Gil'ferding (1894:24) similarly describes North Russian *bylina*-epics as having stable stretches of text while other stretches were quite variable. Finno-Karelian kalevalaic epic poetry is predominantly constituted of verbally stable units, making 'line sequences' (*säejaksot*) prominent in discussion (e.g. Krohn 1918). *Epithet* and *cliché* were used as complementary terms, whereas *formula* became common for a larger unit of language from relatively early on (e.g. Chadwick and Chadwick 1936:72).

Albert Lord picked up Nutt's term *run* (1960:58–60), a unit he describes as "a cluster of formulas" (1960:60) that "marks one of the characteristic signs of oral style" (1960:58; see also 1991:89). However, the term *run* did not gain the traction of OFT's other terminology,[5] probably because Lord only sought to show that runs were not memorized and did not contradict his theory of composition in performance, rather than exploring how they work and vary (e.g. Lord 1981:453; 1991:83). He later proposed a new term, *block of lines*, though without definition (Lord 1991:3 and ch. 5),[6] and made some observations linked to these units' memorability (1991:84, 89; 1995:62). In his posthumous monograph, he went on to argue that lyric poetry and ballads were not "memorized" by approaching them in terms of blocks of lines (Lord 1995:ch. 2, esp. 62; cf. also 1991:84), yet research was already moving away from concern about formal units and the operation of such verbal systems—however described—and such units did not receive interest in the evolution of OFT (although cf. e.g. Holzapfel 1980).

Terms like *run* or *block of lines* suggest a more or less continuous stretch of prefabricated text (e.g. McCarthy 1990:152). Particularly on the backdrop of Classic OFT's ideas of formulaic language, they give the impression of a chain of formulae with limited flexibility and variability. Classic OFT's emphasis in formulaic phraseology led non-formulaic verbal systems to generally remain in the shadows. John Miles Foley introduced *cluster* as an alternative to *run* that he applied equally to line series in South Slavic epic (1990:181) and also to the concentrated co-occurrence of lexical roots (rather than formulae) across a stretch of Old English verse (1990:211–212); he later used *paradigm* for a loose and variable verbal system with a coherent discourse function (Foley

---

[5] E.g. Lauri Harvilahti (1992b:91–96; 2004) offers the term *standard sequence* instead.

[6] *Run* is used in three other chapters of the same book (Lord 1991:22–23, 152, 161, 183) and once in chapter 5 (1991:90); there is also inconsistency in whether a block includes a couplet (cf. Lord 1991:77, 82, 88).

1991:214–221), addressed in section 7 below. In the mid 1990s, Lauri and Anneli Honko (1995; 1998) were working on the question of the remarkable variability in length that they observed in different performances of long epics. The Tulu epic performer they were working with, for example, once condensed a performance of a full epic to twenty minutes in order to fit the schedule of a radio broadcast (Honko 1998:30). Classic OFT's model of formulaic language was a poor fit for the extremely variable Tulu epic phraseology (Honko 1998:112–113), but the Honkos observed that stretches of text exhibited recurrent verbal frameworks of words and phrases that contracted or expanded in their different uses. They proposed *multiform* as a technical term to designate this type of verbal system established in the mind of an epic singer as a flexible and variable framework for producing a stretch of text.

The Honkos considered OFT handicapped by its point of departure from the minimal units of traditional language and narration—formula and theme—that were in such sharp focus that researchers had difficulty seeing beyond them. They felt that OFT left the "the enigma of epic composition" unsolved (Honko 1998:105; Honko and Honko 1998:73) because it paid too little attention to the production of longer stretches of verbal text (Honko 1998:103–105; Honko and Honko 1998:72–73). Lauri Honko advocated his own model of *mental text* to account for narration on a broader scope (e.g. Honko 1998:92–99). Classic OFT accounted for verbal composition in performance by *the existence of* a tradition's formulaic lexicon, whereas runs or blocks of lines appear as regular chunks of texts of greater scope. A multiform was, in contrast, a looser collocative system of vocabulary—both formulae and individual words—that could be elaborated or abridged to its core elements, yet was not bound to a consistent unit of meaning or narrative content like a theme. This initial model of a multiform is the foundation of multiform theory.

The word *multiform* had circulated in discussions of OFT owing to its use in *The Singer of Tales*. It was carried along with terms like *formula* and *theme*, but Lord uses *multiform* colloquially and inconsistently. He handles it as a practical adjective and noun to refer to anything with multiple forms, but he also uses it in the place of *variant* (a term prominent in text-oriented paradigms of comparative folklore), making *multiform* a term for any single manifestation of something like a theme that takes multiple forms (e.g. Lord 1960:100, 112–113, 133; see also Honko 1998:101–102; Honko and Honko 1998:40).[7] The Honkos turned this around and formalized *multiform* as a term for the linguistic framework that generates something with multiple forms. This use can also be extended beyond

---

[7]   John Miles Foley lists "multiforms" in the index of his 1988 review of OFT (1988:168); he formalizes the term "multiform" in *The Singer of Tales in Performance* (1995:2), yet the index headword is "multiformity" rather than "multiform" (1995:232; see also Honko 1998:101–102).

language to iconography, narrative motifs, themes, and so forth (as in Drout 2011:447).[8] I view multiforms as a general semiotic phenomenon, and therefore distinguish those addressed by the Honkos as *linguistic multiforms*.

The proposal that a skilled singer would develop such verbal systems for producing stretches of text is not surprising. A decade earlier, Anna-Leena Siikala (1984a:85–93; 1984b [1990]:80–86) observed that language *crystallizes* in the mind of a teller of legends as a variable framework for expressing a unit of narration. Siikala uses *crystallization* to refer to fixity and variability on a spectrum of degree rather than being either fixed or free, invariable or variable, memorized or improvised, as a binary opposition. Linguistic multiforms are the product of crystallization, which she observed as linked to semantically central units in repeated prose narratives (see also Kaivola-Bregenhøj 1988a:305–313; 1988b [1996]:192–199; Brodie, this volume). Siikala also explored this phenomenon in her work on the corpora of kalevalaic epics and incantations (1986; 1992 [2002]:111–112). Kalevalaic epic is a short epic form; epics are usually about 75–300 lines in length, depending on the plot and the region. Individual epics can be remarkably stable at a verbal level in transmission, in contrast to the long epics on which Classic OFT was developed (Harvilahti 1992a; Frog 2016b). Crystallization was saliently reflected in the poetry's transmission and accounted for how units of mythic knowledge and narrative or ritual elements were linguistically "ready-coded" (Siikala 1986:201) or "precoded" (1992 [2002]:111) for verbal performance (also Frog 2019:241–242). Siikala's extension of the concept to kalevalaic poetry advanced crystallization from something occurring within the mind of an individual to something bound up with a tradition's transmission, observable through the quantitative empirical data of a corpus.

The 1990s exhibit a scattered rise in interest in complex verbal units, including new terms for these units as *clusters* (Foley 1990) or *blocks* (Lord 1991; 1995). The Honkos' major innovation was to shift attention from units of content like themes to the verbal framework that may be used to express them. This shift in focus allowed the linguistic multiform to be tracked through a corpus across different contexts of use rather than starting from the unit of narration and looking at language that recurs with it. Foley's cluster of Old English word stems moves in the same direction and is easily identified with the

---

8   The Honkos' working definition of multiforms makes no reference to language: *"repeatable and artistic expressions of variable length which are constitutive for narration and function as generic markers"* (1995:211; 1998:35, original emphasis). This definition's parameter of functioning as generic markers would be problematic even for many linguistic multiforms because it excludes the same multiform operating freely across genres, whether within a broader poetic system (e.g. Tarkka 2013) or in the broad category of "prose."

Honkos' multiform. Foley, however, saw this as a tradition-specific phenomenon corresponding to Lord's formula-dense *runs*, and his interest was in potential associations with meaning rather than exploring the cluster as a flexible framework for producing a stretch of text (Foley 1990:206, 211–212). In contrast, the Honkos brought into focus the operation of multiforms at the level of verbal texture rather than meaning, and thus their potential to be polysemic (Honko and Honko 1998:36).

Multiform theory is not widely known and even less widely used. Lauri Honko promoted it (1995; 1996; 1998; 2003), but not in a way that made it generally relevant to, or applicable by, other scholars. First, multiform theory was presented and discussed only in relation to the quite narrow research question about the flexible length of long epics in performance: it accounted for one thing in a type of oral poetry with a very particular profile; it was not shown to have a broader utility. Second, multiforms were only demonstrated for the mind of one individual: they were not shown to circulate like formulae, which would make them relevant for the analysis of social aspects of a tradition. Third, multiform theory was presented as an *alternative* to OFT rather than as complementary it. In sum, multiforms only seemed relevant to variation in long epics as performed by a particular singer; they were also introduced as potentially incompatible with the dominant framework for studying variation in that type of poetry.

I started working with multiform theory more than a decade ago. I initially took up the concept when wrestling with a complex verbal system that clearly circulated between poets for producing a metrically well-formed line, yet could vary considerably in syntax and also in the referents of particular words, as discussed in the following section. The Honkos' multiform offered a means of bringing all of the complementary moving parts of the unit and their variation into focus as a verbal system that could be used to communicate *different meanings* and manipulated for *aesthetic effects*. The multiforms studied by the Honkos are like verbal latticeworks that can be stretched or collapsed in performance to prolong or condense epic narration, whereas the verbal system I faced was of invariable length but flexible in alternative word choices and word order; both, however, operate as complex formal linguistic resources for producing a stretch of text without forming a regular unit of meaning. I decontextualized the concept from the Honkos' specific questions and tradition-type: rather than latticework multiforms defining the concept, I view them as one among several types of multiforms in a practice-driven approach. This approach views multiforms as verbal systems that evolve and operate in relation to the organizing principles of a type of discourse and how that type of discourse is used, acknowledging that individual multiforms may vary considerably in their degree of crystallization. Working with the Honko's concept rapidly led me to use it as an approach to variation in the standard sequences or runs of kalevalaic epic poetry (Frog 2010b). Since that time, I have tested and refined multiform theory in relation to several types of oral poetry, including kalevalaic epic and incantations, Old Norse eddic and skaldic verse, Modern Icelandic *sagnakvæði*, and, to a lesser degree, Russian *bylina*-epics, Scandinavian ballads, Scandinavian verbal charms, and Rotenese ritual poetry.

Rather than conceiving a multiform simply as a set of words and formulae, I have extended the Honkos' model to consider syntax, equivalence sets of vocabulary (e.g. for meeting alternate alliterations or rhymes), and slots that are semantically, metrically, or functionally conditioned (Frog 2016a). Classic OFT was not well-suited to approaching shorter poetic forms (e.g. Holoka 1976:572), whereas multiform theory offers a framework for addressing mechanisms behind such poetries' more stable sequences of text (see also Lord 1995:ch. 2). When multiform theory is applied within the framework of OFT, short and long forms of poetry appear within a unified framework. The difference in length of the poetic form affects the degree to which multiforms crystallize. Depending on the tradition, such multiforms may become specific to a certain identity-bearing text, like a poem or song that is socially recognized as a particular thing made of language distinct from other poems or songs. It may even be specific to a particular part of a certain poem as opposed to others, as when a certain stanza is recognizable as a stanza of a particular episode of a particular ballad. In the context of the present chapter, an understanding of linguistic multiforms enables a distinction of a formula's upper threshold of complexity.

4. Formally Driven Multiforms

Some multiforms evolve primarily to meet formal rather than semantic needs. An exemplary case is found in Old Norse poetry in the *dróttkvætt* meter, although it is necessary to sketch out basic features of the poetic form and prominent features of the register to be understandable to an unfamiliar reader. *Dróttkvætt* is exceptionally demanding. It is composed in couplets of six-position lines that are normally formed with one syllable per position. Ideally, a pair of stressed syllables rhyme within each line and two stressed syllables in the first line of a couplet alliterate with the first syllable of the second—i.e. there are three to four sound requirements in each six-position line, on top of which are rules governing syllabic quantity. To accommodate these demands, the poetic register developed remarkably flexible (though still rule-governed) syntax that can scramble a clause across paired couplets—i.e. four lines—and embed one independent clause inside another so that words from different clauses may be in the same line.

What makes this poetry interesting from the perspective of multiform theory is that the constraints and flexibility of the poetic form interact with an elaborate system for generating equivalence expressions called kennings. Although it is not necessary to explore this system in detail here, it is important to at least give a sense of its dynamism. A kenning is a rhetorical figure formed of two nouns in a genitive construction or a compound that refers to a third nominal category, like saying *geira hríð* ('storm of spears') or *geir-hríð* ('spear-storm') for BATTLE. Although kennings could be generated for anything, their referents are generally predictable, centering around war, wealth, women, poetry, and patronage as poets' favored subjects. This predictability allows tremendous flexibility in word choice for the two elements along three trajectories: (*a*) equivalence within a semantic category, so *geirr* ('spear') could be any word for WEAPON or ARMOR, and *hríð* ('storm') any word for WEATHER or WIND; (*b*) functional equivalence across categories, so words for WEAPON can be replaced by any of over one hundred names of the god Odin, the name of any valkyrie, or any mythic hero (MYTHIC AGENT OF BATTLE) without affecting the kenning's meaning, and words for WEATHER can be replaced by any word for NOISE or GATHERING; and (*c*) a word within a kenning can itself be replaced by a kenning. In principle, this enables a poet to formulate a kenning for central referents of the kenning system that will fit any combination of syllabic requirements, alliteration, and/or rhyme (or their avoidance). On the other hand, this system allows different combinations of the same words to express different things, a potential compounded by *dróttkvætt*'s syntax, which allows a syntactic break within a line.

Dróttkvætt's flexibility and transmission as personal compositions attributed to individual poets with minimal variation led to the common view that the poetry is not "formulaic." Some years ago, while looking for something completely unrelated, I observed in *dróttkvætt* what would have been called a "formula(ic) system" in Classic OFT (Lord 1960:48; see also Parry 1928) but which can be abstracted as an *open-slot formula*, i.e. a formula with a *slot* (X) that can be completed by different *slot-fillers* (see also Acker 1983:45; 1998:40): *[1 2 3] í dyn X* ('... in the din of X [= BATTLE]'; numbers indicate additional metrical positions). I then noticed that two of the slot-fillers were linked to a collocative rhyme system *hjalmr–malmr–almr–(hilmir)* ('helmet–metal–elm–[prince]'), although in one case a poet had formed the kenning with the words at the beginning of the line while the word in the final position, expected for the slot-filler, belonged to a different independent clause: *málmskúrar dyn | hjálmar* ('metal-shower's din [= BATTLE] | helmets'). I gradually discovered that *dynr* ('din') alternated with *gnýr* ('roar') while the combination of either of these with the *hjalmr-malmr-almr-* (*hilmir*) collocative system exhibited recurrent vocabulary in the remaining positions. As diagrammed in (1), this system was used in a variant form where *dynr/gnýr* was transposed into the second of the line's six positions (-INFL and -GEN.PL indicate an inflectional syllable; variant word order and its occasional use of *himir* is in italic font below the double line; lexical choices only attested once are not shown; for data, see Frog 2009:239–240).

(1)

1	2	3	4	5	6
hjalm- malm- alm-	-skúr -þing ——— dyn- gný-	í ——— -skúr- -við-	dyn gný ——— -INFL	hjalm- malm-	-GEN.PL
				hilmi	

1	2	3	4	5	6
helm- metal- elm-	-shower -assembly ——— din- roar-	in ——— -shower- -wood-	din roar ——— -INFL	helmet- metal-	-GEN.PL
				prince	

This multiform is a case where lexical density and regularity likely made the unit recognizable as a formal resource, at least to skilled poets, although it was used in different contexts to express different semantic content and there is no reason to think it carried particular connotative semantics. However, the exceptional example that placed the syntactic break between positions 4 and 5 rather than earlier in the line contradicts expectations of usage in a composition where the poet is actively displaying his virtuosity. This case is most likely an example of the poet playing with expectations for aesthetic effect (Frog 2009:236).

Many multiforms in this poetry are much less complex, but they often seem to form around a kenning that has become *metrically entangled*,[9] which combines with a rhyme collocation or collocative system. Although a kenning is better viewed as a rhetorical figure than a formula, kennings used for a particular referent gravitate to conventions of use in particular metrical positions. Some of these are metrical-syntactic patterns common for kennings of different referents (cf. Russo 1963; Saarinen, this volume), but, even in these, conventional patterns of usage are reflected in preferred lexical choices. The *[1 2 3]* *(dyn/gný) X* formula (also used outside of (1)) is unambiguous in this respect: nineteen examples use *dynr*, twenty-two use *gnýr*, and fourteen use eight other words in that position (Frog 2014). In a case study of 340 kennings for BATTLE in their metrical positions in *dróttkvætt* lines (Frog 2016c), sixty examples formed a compound filling the first two positions of the second line in a couplet. Of these, nine had *hríð* as a base-word, as seen in (2), with an additional example from outside the earlier dataset. Six of the ten examples rhyme *hríð* with *síðan* ('then') at the end of the line (*dróttkvætt* rhyme concerns stressed syllables, not word endings), while *hríð* is not rhymed with *síðan* elsewhere in the 340 examples of the original case study. The rhyme appears as conventional specifically in connection with this semantic formula, so that *hríð* is not simply metrically entangled as a preferred lexical choice, but further entangled with a preferred rhyme collocation (noting that in viii and ix, rhyme is on the determinant rather than being regularly on *hríð*).

(2)

	X-*hríð*	[3 4]	[5 6]		
i.	malm-*hríð*	jǫfurr	síðan	X-storm ... then	Edáð *Banddr* 4^I.2[10]
ii.	odd-*hríð*	vakið	síðan	X-storm ... then	Hskv *Útdr* 10^{II}.2
iii.	odd-*hríð*,	ok, brátt	síðan	X-storm ... then	Kolli *Ingdr* 1^{II}.2
iv.	egg-*hríð*	né mun	síðan	X-storm ... then	Arn *Þorfdr* 16^{II}.2
v.	eld-*hríð*	es varð |	síðan	X-storm ... | then	Arn *Þorfdr* 20^{II}.6
vi.	vápn-*hríð*	konungr |	síðan	X-storm ... | then	Arn *Magndr* 8^{II}.2
vii.	vápn-*hríð* |	sonar	bíða	X-storm | ... await	EValg *Lv* 1^I.7–8
viii.	egg-*hríð*,	framir	seggir	X-storm ... say	ESk *Harsonkv* 2^{II}.4
ix.	geir-*hríð*	fregit	meiri	X-storm ... more	ÞjóðA *Magnfl* 6^{II}.8
x.	stál-*hríð*,	búendr	fríðir	X-storm ... good	Anon (*GBpA*) 3^{IV}.2

Examples (2.i–vi) reflect a complex unit X-*hríð [3 4] síðan* ('BATTLE ... then'). If *síðan* had a consistent syntactic relation to X-*hríð*, like 'then BATTLE' followed

---

[9] On *metrical entanglement*, see Frog 2021.
[10] All skaldic poetry quotations are referred to by sigla according to the Skaldic Project Database.

by a verb, this would operate as a formula expressing a regular unit of meaning, but the kenning and *síðan* are distributed across independent clauses in two of the six examples, comparable to the Old English *word-wuldor* collocation above. Conversely, the rhyme pair is linked to the particular semantic formula, so describing *X-hríð [3 4] síðan* simply as a collocation marginalizes the complexity of including a variable formula. I therefore distinguish this as a multiform.

5. Formula-System Multiforms

I use *formula-system multiform* to refer to a type of metrically driven multiform consisting of complementary sets of formulae that are associated in the mind of an individual to complete a metrical unit or its equivalent. This use of "system" is different from uses of the term in Classic OFT, where that word has been used in multiple ways, warranting prefatory comment to avoid confusion.

It is commonplace to use *formulaic system* to refer broadly to a formulaic genre's[11] idiom and principles of operation. Parry, however, used *system* to describe any network of formulae (in the sense of completed phrases) associated in the mind of a singer, looking especially at similar phrases in the same metrical positions and phrases expressing the same idea in different metrical positions (1928; 1930). Some of Parry's "systems" dissolve when metrical variation is accepted, but Lord propagated use of *system* to describe completed variants of an open-slot formula (1960:35–36, 47–49; cf. Saarinen, this volume). The extreme variability of Old English poetic phraseology led Donald K. Fry to shift emphasis from formulae as completed phrases to a generative model, defining a formula as "the direct product of a formulaic system" (1967:204, emphasis removed). Fry abstracted such a "system" to a template with fixed elements and variable slots (1967:199–203). Paul Acker adapted the concept of formulae having slots and slot-fillers from an independent strand of linguistic research (1983:94–96; 1998:63–66), an innovation that reconceived Classic OFT's systems as variable formulae. Parry's hierarchies of such formulae remain relevant, but can be viewed as hierarchies of metrically entangled slot-fillers, which may also crystallize into discreet formulae.

Where formulae used in the same metrical position can be assumed to be linked in the mind of a singer, potentially as alternatives, I would describe these as an *equivalence set*. This is contrasted with an *equivalence class* as the broader category of possible alternatives, irrespective of whether they are linked in anyone's mind. In metrical poetry, such alternatives form a metrical-semantic or metrical-syntactic equivalence set when the set of alternatives is linked in

---

[11] On the concept of *formulaic genre*, see Kuiper 2009; Kuiper and Leaper, this volume.

the mind through some type of equivalence or belongingness to a common category used in particular metrical positions. I reserve *system* for formulae that get used *together* in complementary interaction, rejecting Parry's usage for sets of formulae. The operation of a whole formulaic idiom can thus be considered as forming a system. A system as a set of formulae, associated in the mind of a performer, to complete complementary sets of metrical positions or equivalent units is a *formula-system multiform*, as in the example from kalevalaic epic in (3).

Kalevala-meter is a trochaic tetrameter, so lines normally consist of eight syllables, with rules governing stressed-syllable placement and systematic alliteration. Names of mythic heroes often have a four-syllable form like *Väinämöinen* or *Ilmarinen* and an optional two-syllable epithet (see also Saarinen, this volume). These naming formulae form equivalence sets in the minds of performers, as becomes apparent when performers accidentally transpose them (e.g. Frog 2016b:68–69, 76). These formulae are complementary to equivalence sets of words completing the first two positions followed by an open slot for a six-syllable noun phrase in the nominative case. Syntactically, the noun phrase may be the grammatical subject or a vocative naming of the addressee. The two sets combine to form an epic formula-system for generating well-formed lines in the flow of epic performance ("is" in parentheses reflects use of the verb as an expletive particle to complete a metrical position; see also Frog 2016b:75).

(3)

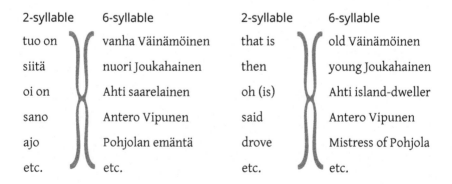

2-syllable	6-syllable	2-syllable	6-syllable
tuo on	vanha Väinämöinen	that is	old Väinämöinen
siitä	nuori Joukahainen	then	young Joukahainen
oi on	Ahti saarelainen	oh (is)	Ahti island-dweller
sano	Antero Vipunen	said	Antero Vipunen
ajo	Pohjolan emäntä	drove	Mistress of Pohjola
etc.	etc.	etc.	etc.

A single formula completed in a limited variety of ways does not itself qualify as a multiform. For example, the formula *annan {ainoan} X* ('I will give {my only} X') is used in a certain kalevalaic epic that takes the following forms in one local dialect:

(4)

i.	annan *kultia kyperän*	I will give *of gold a helmetful*
ii.	annan ainoan *orihin*	I will give my only *stallion*
iii.	annan ainoan *sisäreni*	I will give my only *sister*

Frog 2016b:73

When the lines are presented together out of context, *annan {ainoan} X* may look like a generative system, but the stability of the expression becomes apparent when it is presented within the multiform of which it is the variable core, and when it is recognized that the three forms are each used in three cycles of question-and-answer dialogue. In (5), X_1 indicates the slot-filler of the *annan {ainoan} X* formula; X_2 is a parallel full-line repetition of the grammatical object:

(5)

{Oi on vanha Väinämöini}	{Oh (is) old Väinämöinen}
Myössytäs pyhät sanasi	Make your holy words harmless
Perävytä lauhiesi	Turn back your sentences
Annan {ainoan} X_1	I will give {my only} X_1
{X_2}	{X_2}
{Oman pääni päästimeksi	{For liberating my own head
Itscheni lunastimeksi}	as a ransom for myself}

Frog 2016b:85

Annan {ainoan} X does not form a dynamic and generative system with an equivalence set of slot fillers and instead produces a set of crystallized alternative lines that are used within a particular, more complex multiform.

6. Formula-System Multiforms of Different Scope

The unit completed by a formula-system multiform may be greater than a single line. For example, the formula *[1 2] vanha Väinämöinen* in (3) forms a collocation with the semantically parallel complete line *tietäjä iän ikuinen* ('sorcerer of age eternal'). Use of the *vanha Väinämöinen* formula in the formula system can thus generate a couplet, although, in practice, the parallel line is not systematic and in many cases is not found more than once in a poem. Since the parallel line regularly follows the *vanha Väinämöinen* formula, forms a coherent unit of meaning with it, and is not used independently, it can be viewed as part of a single formula: *[1 2]* *vanha Väinämöinen / {tietäjä iän ikuinen}*. A formula that can expand or contract can be described as a *telescoping formula*. This formula can also be completed with the additional epithet *vaka* ('sturdy') or contracted by omitting *vanha* ('old') in order to be used in combination with a four-syllable open-slot formula: *{{vaka} vanha} Väinämöinen / {tietäjä iän ikuinen}*. The point here is that even the simple system presented in (3) may extend across more than one line where participating formulae are parts of collocations for producing verse parallelism.

Formula-system multiforms may be quite complex. The Old Norse eddic poem *Alvíssmál* is organized as a dialogic test of knowledge in which the god Thor asks how something is called "in all of the worlds" thirteen times, and the dwarf *Alvíss* ('All-Wise') offers thirteen corresponding replies. Each of Alvíss' answers is organized in a regular stanza in the *ljóðaháttr* meter. The stanza is formed of two half-stanzas, each of which is comprised of one long line, made up of two half-lines joined by alliteration as in Old English verse (marked Ia–b and IIIa–b in (6)), followed by a *Vollzeile* (literally 'full line') which is shorter, has a particular rhythm, and line-internal alliteration (marked II and IV). Each half-line and *Vollzeile* is constituted of a simple open-slot formula that refers to a race of beings or the realm of the dead and is completed with a word or kenning for how the respective thing is called by those beings / in that place. The stanza on how CORN is called is presented in (6):

(6)

   ^{Ia}*Bygg* heitir með mǫnnom ^{Ib}enn *barr* með goðom
         ^{II}kalla *vaxt* vanir
   ^{IIIa}*æti* iotnar ^{IIIb}álfar *lagastaf*
         ^{IV}kalla í helio *hnipinn*

                                        Alvíssmál 32, punctuation removed

   Barley it is called among men   but *barleycorn* among gods
         call [it] *growth*, the *vanir*
   oat [call it] giants   elves [call it] *staff of laws*(?)
         call [it] in Death's realm *drooping*

The thirteen stanzas of the dwarf's replies are each constituted of six open-slot formulae. The total of seventy-eight half-lines and *Vollzeilen* exhibit only fourteen formulae, shown in (7), with three minor variations that each occur on a formula's first use (formulae #3, #12, and #14; variations in parentheses).[12]

---

[12]   The formulae are otherwise remarkably regular in spite of the potential for flexibility in phraseology allowed by the metrical form (Frog 2011:48–50; forthcoming).

(7)

	#	Formula	Line type	Stanza													
				10	12	14	16	18	20	22	24	26	28	30	32	34
Line I	1	*X heitir með mǫnnum*	a-line	10	12	14	16	18	20	22	24	26	28	30	32	34
	2	*en X með goðum*	b-line		12	14	16	18	20	22	24		28	30	32	
	3	*en með ásum (álfum) X*	b-line	(10)								26				34
Line III	4	*X jǫtnar*	a-line	10	12	14	16	18	20	22	24	26	28	30	32	34
	5	*álfar X*	b-line	10	12		16	18	20	22	24		28	30	32	
	6	*en X dvergar*	b-line			14						26				
	7	*en í helju X*	b-line													34
Line II/IV	8	*kalla X vanir*	*Vollzeilen*	10	12			18		22	24	26	28		32	34
	9	*kalla X halir*	*Vollzeile*										28			
	10	*kalla X Y-regin*	*Vollzeilen*	10					20					30		
	11	*kalla X Y synir*	*Vollzeilen*				16									34
	12	*kalla dvergar X (dv. X)*	*Vollzeilen*		(12)		16			22	24			30		
	13	*kalla álfar X*	*Vollzeile*			14										
	14	*kalla í helju X (k. X helju í)*	*Vollzeilen*			(14)		18	20			26			32	

In each half of the stanza, the first formula (Ia, IIIa) does not vary. The slot-filler in that formula is required to carry alliteration, which drives the choice of the formula in the following half-line (Ib, IIIb). If that slot-filler requires vocalic alliteration (i.e. the stressed syllable must begin with a vowel; in Old Norse, all vowels alliterated with one another), it is carried by the poetic word for 'gods' (*æsir*) in Ib and 'elves' (*álfar*) in IIIb; if consonantal alliteration is required, another formula with different word order is used in which it is carried by the slot-filler, with a single variation in the final stanza (Acker 1983:94–96; 1998:63–66).[13] A *Vollzeile*'s structure requires alliteration of the first noun of the formula with its slot-filler. The three open-slot formulae used in IIIb all have equivalents in *Vollzeilen* with slightly different phrasing; these can be seen as metrically driven variations of a single formula (ten examples of #5 ~ one of #13, two examples of #6 ~ five of #12, one example of #7 ~ five of #14), in which case the multiform exhibits only

---

[13] The final exception might be interpreted as driven by alliteration, since the formula carries *h*-alliteration on *hel* ('death; Death; realm of the dead'), but it could also be rhetorically driven in anticipation of Alvíss' death in the following stanza.

eleven potential open-slot formulae with variations (Frog forthcoming). Within the context of other variation, selection of the formulae in *Vollzeilen* appears more likely driven by the slot-filler than vice versa.

Viewed in isolation, each long line of this unit might be seen as a simple, generative formula system for the long line of each half-stanza. However, the whole stanza is governed by a condition of non-repetition of the main noun in each formula. The same category of GODS, GIANTS, or MEN can be mentioned, but the same word cannot be used for it twice. Non-repetition means that formulae are not being selected at the level of the individual line, but at the level of a whole stanza. Variation in these thirteen stanzas only becomes understandable when the formula-system multiform in the background is recognized.

7. Macro-Formula Multiforms

Especially in narrative discourse, multiforms crystallize around units of what language is used to communicate or "do" (see also Siikala 1986:201; 1992 [2002]:111). Such multiforms can be similar to sets of formulae connected with a theme in Classic OFT (cf. Foley 1990:240–245, 279–284, 329–335), although how these relate depends on how theme is defined (Honko and Honko 1998:72–73). If theme is identified as a relatively short narrative unit, like a ballad stanza (cf. McCarthy 1990:152–153), multiform and theme may align. The more complex plot unit as conceived by Lord (1960:68–98) might be expressed and elaborated through a number of multiforms, much as he considered blocks of lines in lyric poetry as "intermediate between the formula and the theme" (1995:62). Formulae linked to a theme as a broader unit may not develop the regularity and density suggestive of a coherent verbal system per se, and may become linked to individual constituents of the theme rather than to one another in the mind of a performer. The co-occurrence of certain formulae with a theme may also simply result from their conventional use for expressing certain things that happen to be part of that theme (cf. Magoun 1955; Fry 1968). A formula may also become a metonymic cue of a narrative unit (e.g. Foley 1995:96) without being linked to a more complex verbal system (see also Roper, this volume). Only when a multiform becomes socially recognizable as a linguistic unit for expressing a regular meaning or function does it have the potential to operate as a complex linguistic sign comparable to a formula (cf. Foley 1990:206). Owing to its greater complexity, a multiform that functions in this way is here distinguished as a *macro-formula*.

Crystallization does not inherently lead a multiform to become a salient linguistic unit with a regular meaning or discourse function. This was seen in the *dróttkvætt* multiforms in (1) and (2) above. The Honkos foreground multi-forms' polysemy in Tulu epic (1995; 1998; also Honko 1998:100–116), yet the words of this epic register express regular, literal, propositional meanings. Thus, polysemy of the multiform would be in tandem with the fairly straightforward relationships between its constituent words or formulae and what is narrated, similar to collocations like the *word-wuldor* pair above. Both the Honkos (1998:41; also Honko 1998:102) and Lord (1981:459–460) doubted the social stability of linguistic multiforms or runs in highly variable long epic poetries, a view which would preclude use as a macro-formula. A multiform may also be regularly employed as an integer of traditional communication, as in what Foley (1991:214–223) calls the *Hwæt* paradigm in Old English. Foley describes this as "a collection of signals, not all bound by linear prosody, that cumulatively indicate the start of a tale" (1991:214). He summarizes this verbal system thus:

> the *Hwæt* paradigm [...] consists regularly of the interjection [i.e. *Hwæt!*], a verb of speaking or hearing, and identification of the speaker as 'we' or 'I'. It may also attract to itself other metonymic structures, such as the *þeod-/þrym* collocation, the 'in days of old/yore' phrase, and the whole line pattern involving *æðeling-* and *ellen*, but these latter items are most productively viewed as signals in their own right that may or may not appear with the *Hwæt* convention.
>
> Foley 1991:222–223

The three core elements of Foley's "paradigm" form a semantically and syntactically flexible unit that operates collectively as a discourse marker. As with Old English collocations, significance as a discourse marker operates at a different level than the propositional semantics of the phraseology. Variation in the first-person pronoun between singular and plural may be considered morphological, but variation in the verb produces different meanings in ways inconsistent with the definition of formula above. Formally, this multiform has a regularly structured onset, beginning with the interjection, which is followed immediately by the pronoun, whereas the verb may be used in the same half-line or follow some lines later and additional collocated elements may either precede or follow the verb. Constituents also appear on a hierarchy in which the three core elements are the most regular and others are optional.[14]

Where a poetic form is shorter and especially where it also imposes formal constraints on variation, sequences of text can become much more regular and recognizable as narrating a specific unit or type of unit. The multiform's

---

[14] The nature of the sources leaves it impossible to assess factors of regional or diachronic variation.

complexity affects its potential for variation in relation to the poetic form. For example, ballads with a rhymed stanzaic structure configure syntax within stanzas as formal units with breaks between them, and this correspondingly organizes the presentation of information. A rhymed quatrain structure can support the stability of a ballad stanza in social circulation, which is not to deny the poetic system's flexibility or performers' potential for creativity (see also McCarthy 1990). When the verbal unit becomes recognizable, it operates as a macro-formula for the unit of narration (sometimes addressed simply as a formula: see e.g. Holzapfel 1980: 21–27).

Finno-Karelian epic is stichic poetry—i.e. it is not composed in couplets or stanzas. Nevertheless, its macro-formula multiforms are remarkably crystallized and an epic may be performed almost entirely as a chain of such units (Frog 2016b; cf. Honko 2003:113–122). Someone competent in the poetry immediately recognizes certain lines as linked to a particular macro-formula or particular epic (Virtanen 1968:55; see also Tarkka 2013:90). They can make judgments about whether lines are "correct," or whether they align with one dialect of singing as opposed to another (Frog 2010b:99–100). The kalevalaic corpus is remarkably large, so a hundred or more examples of a particular epic may be collected across numerous regions and generations of singers. This allows nuanced perspectives on variation. The stichic poetic form opens these macro-formulae to potential variation in length, which does not seem so pronounced between performances in contrast to social variation on an individual, local, or regional basis. Several formal types of macro-formula multiforms are distinguishable according to how they vary.

The macro-formula in (5) above expresses a hero's offer of ransom in exchange for being released. This can be described as a *verbal core multiform*, a type common when dialogue is organized in cycles. The multiform will not appear without a particular core line or couplet while additional lines, such as a vocative phrase, parallel lines, and various, if conventionally established, elaborations can be omitted or sometimes added (see also Saarinen 1994:183). Some can be found expanded to perhaps ten lines or reduced to a single line or couplet without compromising narration. Singers generally did not capitalize on these multiforms' potential for variation. When a singer used the same multiform more than once within an epic, and even when singing the epic on different occasions, variation is not generally noticeable except for salient features linked to narration, like alternating slot-fillers or morphological variation between a request and a character's compliance (Frog 2016b:66–72). Nevertheless, verbal core multiforms exhibit flexibility in social circulation.

Kalevalaic macro-formulae that describe things in the third-person do not exhibit the same variability in length. In verbal-core multiforms, additional lines surrounding the core normally only include information that can be inferred from the surrounding narrative or context, whereas the information presented in third-person narration more commonly adds detail. This information is often presented in an ordered series, although the order of elements may also be variable or less crystallized. The first kalevalaic multiform that I explored in detail was a description of a fire seen on an island at the opening of a certain epic, found in over a hundred examples and often presented as two couplets in fixed order (Frog 2010a:372–376), as illustrated in (8):

(8)

Savu soarella palave	Smoke on the island burns
Tuli niemen tutkamessa	Fire on the peninsula's tip
Suur' ois paimenen paloksi	Great would be for the blaze of a shepherd
Pien' ehk' ois' sovan savuksi	Small perhaps would be for the smoke of war

SKVR I₁ 722.1–4, punctuation removed

As is common for a crystallized series multiform, the opening lines are quite regular. Variation increases as the lines progress (Frog 2016b:76; see also Siikala 1986:198–199). Kalevalaic verse parallelism does not allow syntactic elements to be elided in the first line of a series, which inhibits inversion of the first couplet because the verb for burning is elided in its second line. In the second couplet, the verb *olla* ('to be') allows flexibility because it has monosyllabic forms and its vocalic onset allows apocope of a preceding vowel. Thus, *suuri* ('great') can be contracted to *suur'* followed by *on* ('is') or *ois* ('would be') without impacting the meter, as here. When this singer performed the same epic fifteen years later, she reversed the order of the couplet and sang *suuri* ('great'), eliding the verb (*SKVR* I₁ 722a.7). Singers also occasionally invert *suuri* ('great') and *pieni* ('small') in this couplet, which is semantically nonsensical but creates alliteration between three words in each line. This variation only becomes understandable when the phraseology is viewed as a complex system rather than viewing the lines as independent formulae. Inverting the couplets or omitting only the first of them is inhibited by the second's reference to a fire that has already been introduced. This type of two-part structure is common in the tradition, with the first part usually more socially stable than the second. The propositional meanings of each couplet operate as complementary to the more complex unit's coherent expression of a mythic image as a linguistically mediated sign.

Other multiforms are not so regular: crystallization often occurs for the individual performer, but the multiforms look much more variable in the corpus because crystallization is not (as) integrated in social transmission. Among multiforms of this type, paired couplets may sometimes be interspersed with lines such as inquit formulae, creating variations in whether lines are or are not presented as direct speech, or whether they are presented as monologue as opposed to dialogue (cf. Frog 2010:365–371). Although kalevalaic crystallized series multiforms generally resist additional lines or multiforms being interposed into them, such variations can be found, as when the singer of example (8) later added the line *sanopa lieto Lemminkäini* ('Said loose Lemminkäinen') after the first couplet, so that the second became direct speech of the hero (*SKVR I$_1$* 722a.3–7). This variation is doubly exceptional, because it is not simply idiolectal; it varies between one singer's performances. Here, the multiform may operate as a macro-formula emblematic or iconic of a particular situation in an epic, yet that macro-formula works at a different level than what the particular lines and their organization express.

Parallelism is a potential indicator of complexity exceeding a formula, especially where parallelism appears variable. A significant mythic image in the same epic as (8) is a fiery eagle described as in a fiery birch on a fiery skerry in a fiery river. This is expressed in a series of grammatically parallel lines with lexical repetition that can be expanded, as in (9):

(9)

Tuloop' on tuliñi joki	Comes (is) a fiery river
Joess' on tuliñi koski	In the river (is) a fiery rapids
Kosess' on tuliñi luoto	In the rapids (is) a fiery skerry
Luuvoss' on tuliñi koivu	In the skerry (is) a fiery birch
Koivuss' on tuliset oksat	In the birch (is) fiery branches
Oksiss' on tuliñi kokko	In the branches (is) a fiery eagle

SKVR I$_2$ 754.128–133, punctuation removed

When this part of the image (the first of the two-part multiform) is expressed in only three lines, it could easily be viewed as a formula much as some couplets might be. However, it varies differently than most formulae: the first line opens with the verb in the formula (here) *tuloop' on tuliñi X* ('comes (is) a fiery X'), following which the slot-filler X fills slot Y in a "terrace" series of uses of the formula *Y-ss' on tuliñi X* ('in the Y (is) a fiery X') until X = "eagle" (or occasionally "talons"). The multiform telescopes or contracts according to the number of elements used in the series, though the order of elements remains fixed as a progression of narrowing focus or size. Whereas a formula may telescope through the presence or absence of potential elements, as in *{{vaka} vanha}*

Väinämöinen / {tietäjä iän ikuinen}, variation here is only understandable when the operation of slot-fillers in the system is acknowledged.

The conjuration of the tenth-century Old High German Second Merseburg Charm in (10a), operates similarly, although each slot-filler remains exclusive to one use of the recurrent formula *X zi X* ('X to X'):

(10a)

> ben zi bena bluot zi bluoda lid zi geliden
> bone to bone, blood to blood, limb to limb

Merseburger Domstiftsbibliothek Hs. 136

This conjuration can be observed across a millennium of oral-derived texts, with a more recent Danish variant offered in (10b):

(10b)

> Sener i Sener i Aare i Aare i Kjød i Kjød Blod i Blod etc.
> sinew to sinew to vein to vein to flesh to flesh, blood to blood, etc.

Hansen 1942 [1960–1961]:166

The conjuration is structurally, semantically, and even functionally regular. The slot-fillers are consistently elements that make up a human or animal limb, yet their number and order all vary (*pace* Watkins 1995:ch. 57). Whether a conjunction or preposition links the parallel units in series also varies, yet the slot-fillers are consistently governed by a principle of non-repetition, comparable to that in (6) above. A structure in which the same formula is used recurrently with non-repeating variations is widely found. It can be seen above in the *annan {ainoan} X* formula (4) in its repeating multiform (5), as well as in other contributions to this volume, such as the Norwegian rigmarole formula-pair *der sit X / s.VERB paa gull-Y* ('there sit X / [alliterating].VERB the gold-Y') discussed by Yelena Sesselja Helgadóttir that produces a series of non-repeating units of information (this volume, section 2). An internal recurrence or parallelism is not a prerequisite of a macro-formula multiform, but it is a potential indicator of greater complexity that affects how the unit operates and varies.

8. Multiforms in Aesthetically Unmarked Spoken Discourse?

To my knowledge, a concept corresponding to multiform has not been applied outside of discussions of verbal art, where it has mainly been considered in verse, although also in certain prose narrative traditions (Nutt 1890; Bruford, A.

1966 [1969]:ch. 16; see also Roper, in this volume). In this section, the primary interest is not in a particular analysis, but a more general question of the applicability of multiform theory outside of verbal art.

Koenraad Kuiper finds that formulaic density increases where speech behavior becomes regularly structured and recurrent or ritualized (2009:chs. 1–2, 4, 6, 9; see also Silvonen, this volume). He analyzes the formulaicity of cashiers' speech at supermarket check-outs in New Zealand and reveals several complex sequences that he calls formulae, such as the one for a cash-call in (11). Kuiper's diagrammatic representation (2009:106, fig. 6.3) is here adapted to a textual sequence with curly brackets around each optional element; each of the four elements of this recurrent formulation is identified with a superscript letter-code. The value of this example is in the issues that it raises when trying to distinguish a formula and a multiform:

(11)

^{A}{That's} ^{B}X ^{C}{for the lot} ^{D}{thanks / thank you}.

If we accept a formula as a complex unit of language established in the mental lexicon, elements A (*That (i)s*) and C (*for the lot*) are multi-word strings each distinguishable as an independent formula. In D, we might quibble over whether to consider *thanks* as a formula, but *thank you* is a formulaic sequence. The order of elements A–C is invariant owing to situational conventions syntax, and they cannot be interrupted by D, presumably for the same reason. That the language could offer a greater range of variations without a grammatical violation (e.g. *For the lot, that's X, thanks, *That's X, thank you, for the lot*) is a potential indicator of formulaicity or macro-formulaicity (Wray 2008:ch. 8). The only stable element is B, the slot-filler of the amount which the client must pay; all elements surrounding B are optional. The unit looks comparable to a verbal-core multiform like (5) above, where the function in dialogue can be completed by the core element alone; other elements elaborate and prolong the core but they are not essential, even if they are not normally omitted. On the other hand, we can turn comparison on its head: (5) differs from (11) in that the poetic meter leads its formulae to be perceived as discreet units of text (lines of verse) and semantic parallelism between lines is an indicator of higher complexity among these units. The elements of (11) form a regular, ordered four-part sequence expressing a regular unit of meaning. Formulae operate as unitary integers of discourse, so there is no reason that they could not also be integrated into a more extensive formulaic sequence. From this perspective, (11) looks like a telescoping formula comparable to *{{vaka} vanha} Väinämöinen / {tietäjä iän ikuinen}*, although with an alternating element in D rather than elements organized in a hierarchy like *vaka* not appearing without *vanha*. The question of how the unit is best understood becomes a question of how it is perceived by someone with native-like fluency.

The objectifying diagrammatic analysis of (11) makes all the elements appear atomic and the links between them equally weak, but syntax binds elements of the sequence A–C differently than their relationship to D. This is New Zealand English, and I might be assessing it with native-like fluency in the wrong English (cf. Kuiper 2009:ch.4). I have a number of years of experience in retail in the 1990s in Midwestern American English and, reflecting on my own linguistic competence (Searle 1969:12–15; Wray 2008:107–108), the corresponding formula would probably be:

(12a)

^{A}{That / It / Your total + (wi)ll be / (i)s / comes to} ^{B}X ^{C}{please$_{marked formality}$}.

Or, more abstractly:

(12b)

^{A}{pronoun / NP + *be*.INFL / comes to} ^{B}X ^{C}{please$_{marked formality}$}.

This expression can also be atomized as a number of alternative expressions constituting A, a verbal core B, and an extending element C. How the sequence of discourse is represented in analysis can affect how it is interpreted. It can equally be presented as an open-slot formula *That'll be X, please* with (*a*) minor variations in *That'll be*, (*b*) *please* as an optional formalizing extension, and (*c*) *That'll be* as easily omitted without corrupting the communication or leaving it ambiguous (an omission that might increase the probability of including *please*, or at least reduce its markedness). The perspective of native-like fluency is nevertheless not unambiguous here: my intuitive view is that this is a formulaic construction—but is it a formula or a macro-formula multiform?

At a theoretical level, an additional factor to consider is that the expression can reduce to the slot-filler without disrupting communication: if the slot-filler in B is expressed alone—if a cashier simply says "X"—can that be considered a variation on the "formula"? This question is complicated by the fact that the slot-filler is itself a construction in which the two consecutive numbers are pragmatically apprehended as an amount in dollars and cents of payment required, as opposed to the cashier's *Ten twenty-five* being understood as "Twenty-five minutes past ten o'clock."[15] A kenning like WEATHER OF WEAPONS in particular metrical positions was considered a semantic formula above, although the

---

[15] In American English, the construction requires two elements to be interpretable, so *Ten* alone would not be understandable as a monetary amount; it would have to be *Ten dollars* or *Ten cents*.

words completing it might vary. In contrast, the numbers completing B express situation-specific amounts: the construction provides the means of interpreting the numbers used to complete it rather than the numbers completing it forming a regular unit of meaning. As a native user, I can see *Ten twenty-five* as a situational variation of (12), but this returns to the question of whether (11) and (12) should be viewed as formulae that can be completed with the slot-filler only, or whether they should be viewed as a more complex and variable system of language. Viewed as a multiform, the collocative system of elements is a cognitive reality as a potential framework for expression (and interpretation). The framework has a verbal core of a monetary amount construction (whether or not this is considered as a formula proper), which is the only mandatory element for successful communication.

The expressions in (11) and (12) are quite variable, but each forms only a simple clause. Kuiper presents what he calls a change-counting formula (2009:107, fig. 6.6) that has been adapted as (13):

(13)

$$^A\{\text{That's / There's your / And}\} \quad ^B\text{X} \quad \{^C\text{change} \quad \Big| \begin{array}{l} ^D\{\text{thanks \{very much\}\}}. \\ | \ ^E\{\text{thank you \{very much \}\}\}}. \end{array}$$

This system is complicated by a hierarchical structure: whether D or E is used appears determined by the use or omission of C. I am not certain how the sequence operates in New Zealand English, but, within my own experience, this sequence of utterance or its equivalent would be conceived as two, distinct units of communication (separated by "|" above, not present in Kuiper's diagram): (*a*) a change-counting expression proper, referring to the immediate event of giving change, followed by (*b*) a thanking formula as a separate unit of discourse, referring to the whole interaction event of the financial transaction. In use, these would be separated by a brief pause as independent clauses. Since (11) and (13) are from the same study group, the potential for the alternative thanking formulae to be prolonged with *very much* in (11) is an indicator of a different relationship between the thanking formula and the preceding clause. This difference supports the interpretation that D/E in (13) is a separate unit of discourse from A–C. At the same time, the relation of C as a condition on use of D or E indicates that the two parts do not operate independently. Together, the complexity of this sequence is higher than in most units addressed as formulae: they form a stretch of text of multiple clauses and discourse functions that are not necessarily unitary in meaning. It thus seems relevant to distinguish the more complex type of unit from the expressions for change-counting and thanking that constitute it.

9. Concluding Remarks

Distinguishing multiforms from formulae is ultimately a question of utility rather than a theoretical necessity. I have proposed that the basic distinction between these analytical categories concerns complexity, which in turn has implications for differences in how the respective integers of language vary and how they relate to units of meaning. The organizing principles that distinguish oral poetry as verbal art make the relevance of multiforms more apparent and accessible, but, once multiforms are distinguished, questions of complexity and variation are brought into focus for this phenomenon in other contexts as well. Multiform theory offers a new frame of reference for considering formulaicity. It may also enable researchers to recognize and explore systems of multiple co-occurring formulae for producing or even coproducing stretches of discourse—systems that may have been generally overlooked because they remained beyond the scope of formula analysis proper.

References

Sources

Alvíssmál. Edda: Die Lieder des Codex Regius nebst vewandten Denkmälern I: Text ed. 4. (eds. G. Neckel and H. Kuhn 1962) 124–129. Heidelberg.

Andreas. The Vercelli Manuscript (ed. G. P. Krapp 1932) 3–51. London.

Genesis. The Janius Manuscript (ed. G. P. Krapp 1931) 1–87. London.

Hansen, H. P. 1942. *Kloge folk: Folkemedicin og overtro i Vestjylland*, 2 vols. ed. 2. 1960–1961. Copenhagen.

Skaldic Project Database. http://skaldic.abdn.ac.uk/db.php.

SKVR. Suomen Kansan Vanhat Runot, I$_1$, I$_2$, 1908a, 1908b. Helsinki.

Literature

Acker, P. 1983. *Levels of Formulaic Composition in Old English and Old Icelandic Verse.* Unpublished PhD dissertation, Brown University.

———. 1998. *Revising Oral Theory: Formulaic Composition in Old English and Old Icelandic Verse.* New York.

Agha, A. 2007. *Language and Social Relations.* Cambridge.

Agha, A., and Frog, eds. 2015. *Registers of Communication.* Helsinki.

Arend, W. 1933. *Die typischen Scenen bei Homer.* Berlin.

Bowra, C. M. 1952. *Heroic Poetry.* London.

Bruford, A. 1966. "Gaelic Folk-Tales and Mediæval Romances: A Study of the Early Modern Irish 'Romantic Tales' and Their Oral Derivatives." *Béaloideas* 34 (1969): i–v, 1–165, 167–285.

Chadwick, H. M., and Chadwick, N. K. 1936. *The Growth of Literature*, II. Cambridge.

Drout, M. D. 2011. "Variation within Limits: An Evolutionary Approach to the Structure and Dynamics of the Multiform." *Oral Tradition* 26(2):447–474.

Fabb, N. 2015. *What is Poetry? Language and Memory in the Poems of the World.* Cambridge.

Foley, J. M. 1988. *The Theory of Oral Composition: History and Methodology.* Bloomington.

———. 1990. *Traditional Oral Epic: The Odyssey, Beowulf, and the Serbo-Croation Return Song.* Los Angeles.

———. 1991. *Immanent Art: From Structure to Meaning in Traditional Oral Epic.* Bloomington.

———. 1995. *The Singer of Tales in Performance.* Bloomington.

———. 1996. "*Guslar* and *Aoidos*: Traditional Register in South Slavic and Homeric Epic." *Transactions of the American Philological Association* 126:11–41.

Foley, J. M., and Ramey, P. 2012. "Oral Theory and Medieval Studies." *Medieval Oral Literature* (ed. K. Reichl) 71–102. Berlin.

Frog. 2009. "Speech-Acts in Skaldic Verse: Genre, Formula and Improvisation." *Versatility in Versification: Multidisciplinary Approaches to Metrics* (eds. T. K. Dewey and Frog) 223–246. New York.

———. 2010a. *Baldr and Lemminkäinen: Approaching the Evolution of Mythological Narrative through the Activating Power of Expression.* PhD dissertation, University College London.

———. 2010b. "Multiformit kalevalamittaisessa epiikassa." *Kalevalamittaisen runon tulkintoja* (eds. S. Knuuttila, U. Piela, and L. Tarkka) 91–113. Helsinki.

———. 2011. "*Alvíssmál* and Orality I: Formula, Alliteration and Categories of Mythic Being." *Arkiv för Nordisk Filologi* 126:17–71.

———. 2014. "Mythological Names in *dróttkvætt* Formulae I: When is a Valkyrie Like a Spear?" *Studia Metrica et Poetica* 1(1):100–139.

———. 2015. "Registers of Oral Poetry." In Agha and Frog 2015:77–104.

———. 2016a. "Linguistic Multiforms: Advancing Oral-Formulaic Theory." *FF Network*, 48:6–11, 14.

———. 2016b. "Linguistic Multiforms in Kalevalaic Epic: Toward a Typology." *RMN Newsletter* 11:61–98.

———. 2016c. "Metrical Entanglement and *dróttkvætt* Composition—A Pilot Study on Battle-Kennings." *Approaches to Nordic and Germanic Poetry* (eds. Kristján Árnason et al.) 149–229. Reykjavík.

———. 2019. "Approaching Ideologies of Things Made of Language: A Case Study of a Finno-Karelian Incantation Technology." *Journal of the Serbian Folklore Society* 4(1):211–257.

———. 2021 (in press). "Metrical Entanglement: The Interface of Language and Meter." *Versification: Metrics in Practice* (eds. Frog, S. Grünthal, K. Kallio, and J. Niemi). Helsinki.

———. Forthcoming. "Text Ideology and Formulaic Language in Eddic Mythological Poems." *Saga-Book* 45.

Frog in collaboration with Tarkka, L. 2017. "Parallelism in Verbal Art and Performance: An Introduction." *Oral Tradition* 31(2):203–232.

Fry D. K. 1967. "Old English Formulas and Systems." *English Studies* 48:193–204.

———. 1968. "Old English Formulaic Themes and Type-Scenes." *Neophilologus* 52(1):48–54.

Gil'ferding, A. F. 1894. *Onezhskiya byliny, zapisannyya Aleksandrom Fedorovichem Gil'ferdingom letom 1871 goda*, I. St. Petersburg.

Halliday, M. K. A., and Hasan, R. 1976. *Cohesion in English.* London.

Harvilahti, L. 1992a. *Kertovan runon keinot: Inkeriläisen runoepiikan tuottamisesta.* Helsinki.

———. 1992b. "The Production of Finnish Epic Poetry—Fixed Wholes or Creative Compositions?" *Oral Tradition* 7:87–101.

———. 2004. "Vakiojaksot ja muuntelu kalevalaisessa epiikassa." *Kalevala ja laulettu runo* (eds. A.-L. Siikala, L. Harvilahti, and S. Timonen) 194–214. Helsinki.

Hasan, R. 1989. *Linguistics, Language, and Verbal Art.* Oxford.

Holoka, J. P. 1976. "The Oral Formula and Anglo-Saxon Elegy: Some Misgivings." *Neophilologus* 60:570–576.

Holzapfel, O. 1980. *Det balladeske: Fortællemåden i den ældre episke folkevise.* Odense.

Honko, L. 1995. "Multiformit ja pitkän eepoksen arvoitus." *Sananjalka* 37:117–145.

———. 1996. "Epics along the Silk Roads: Mental Text, Performance, and Written Codification." *Oral Tradition* 11(1):1–17.

———. 1998. *Textualising the Siri Epic.* Helsinki.

———. 2003. *The Maiden's Death Song and The Great Wedding: Anne Vabarna's Oral Twin Epic Written down by A. O. Väisänen.* Helsinki.

Honko, L., and Honko, A. 1995. "Multiforms in Epic Composition." *XIth Congress of the International Society for Folk-Narrative Research (ISFNR), January 6–12, 1995, Mysore, India: Papers,* 4 vols. (ed. anonymous) vol. II, 207–240. Mysore.

———. 1998. "Multiforms in Epic Composition." *The Epic: Oral and Written* (eds. L. Honko, J. Handoo, and J. M. Foley) 31–79. Mysore.

Hymes, D. 1962. "The Ethnography of Speaking." *Anthropology and Human Behavior* (eds. T. Gladwin and W. C. Sturtevant) 15–53. Washington DC.

Jakobson, R. 1960. "Closing Statement. Linguistics and Poetics." *Style in Language* (ed. T. A. Sebeok) 350–377. New York.

Kaivola-Bregenhøj, A. 1988a. *Kertomus ja kerronta.* Helsinki.

———. 1988b. *Narrative and Narrating: Variation in Juho Oksanen's Storytelling.* Trans. S. Sinisalo 1996. Helsinki.

Kuiper, K. 2009. *Formulaic Genres.* Basingstoke.

Krohn, K. 1918. *Kalevalankysymyksiä,* 2 vols. Helsinki.

Lamb, W. 2015. "Verbal Formulas in Gaelic Traditional Narrative: Some Aspects of Their Form and Function." In Agha and Frog 2015:225–246.

Lord, A. B. 1960. *The Singer of Tales.* Cambridge, MA.

———. 1981. "Memory, Fixity, and Genre in Oral Traditional Poetry." *Oral Traditional Literature: A Festschrift for Albert Bates Lord* (ed. J. M. Foley) 451–461. Columbus.

———. 1987. "The Nature of Oral Poetry." *Comparative Research on Oral Traditions: A Memorial for Milman Parry* (ed. J. M. Foley) 313–349. Columbus.

———. 1995. *The Singer Resumes the Tale.* Ithaca.

Colbert, D. 1989. *The Birth of the Ballad: The Scandinavian Medieval Genre.* Stockholm.

McCarthy, W. B. 1990. *The Ballad Matrix: Personality, Milieu, and the Oral Tradition.* Bloomington.

Nutt, A., in collaboration with MacInnes, D. 1890. "Notes." *Folk and Hero Tales* (ed. and trans. D. MacInnes) 395–491. London.

Magoun, F. P. Jr. 1955. "The Theme of the Beasts of Battle in Anglo-Saxon Poetry." *Neuphilologische Mitteilungen* 56(2):81–90.

Parry, M. 1928. *L'épithète traditionnelle dans Homère*. Paris.

———. 1971. *The Making of Homeric Verse: The Collected Papers of Milman Parry*. Ed. by A. Parry. Oxford.

Pawley, A. 2009. "Grammarians' Languages versus Humanists' Languages and the Place of Speech Act Formulas in Models of Linguistic Competence." *Formulaic Language, I: Distribution and Historical Change* (eds. R. Corrigan, E. A. Moravcsik, H. Ouali and K. Wheatley) 3–26. Amsterdam.

Propp, V. 1928. *Morphology of the Folktale*. Trans. L. Scott 1968. Bloomington.

Reinhard, M. 1976. *On the Semantic Relevance of the Alliterative Collocations in Beowulf*. Bern.

Rothenberg, J., and Tedlock, D., (eds.) 1970. *Ethnopoetics*. Special issue of *Alcheringa* 1(1).

Rugerrini, M. E. 2016. "Alliterative Lexical Collocations in Eddic Poetry." *A Handbook of Eddic Poetry: Myths and Legends of Early Scandinavia* (eds. C. Larrington, J. Quinn, and B. Schorn) 310–330. Cambridge.

Saarinen, J. 1994. "The Päivölä Song of Miihkali Perttunen." *Songs Beyond the Kalevala: Transformations of Oral Poetry* (eds. A.-L. Siikala and S. Vakimo) 180–196. Helsinki.

Schmitt, N., and Ronald C. 2004. "Formulaic Sequences in Action: An Introduction." *Formulaic Sequences* (ed. N. Schmitt) 1–22. Amsterdam.

Siikala, A.-L. 1984a. *Tarina ja tulkinta*. Helsinki.

———. 1984b. *Interpreting Oral Narrative*. Trans. S. Sinisalo 1990. Helsinki.

———. 1986. "Variation in the Incantation and Mythical Thinking: The Scope of Comparative Research." *Journal of Folklore Research* 23(2–3):187–204.

———. 1992. *Mythic Images and Shamanism: A Perspective on Kalevala Poetry*. Trans. S. Sinisalo and L. Stark-Arola 2002. Helsinki.

Tarkka, L. 2013. *Songs of the Border People: Genre, Reflexivity, and Performance in Karelian Oral Poetry*. Helsinki.

Thompson, S. 1955–1958. *Motif-Index of Folk-Literature* rev. ed. Copenhagen.

Tyler, E. M. 2006. *Old English Poetics: The Aesthetics of the Familiar in Anglo-Saxon England*. York.

Virtanen, L. 1968. *Kalevalainen laulutapa Karjalassa*. Helsinki.

Watkins, C. 1995. *How to Kill a Dragon: Aspects of Indo-European Poetics*. Oxford.

Wray, A. 2008. *Formulaic Language: Pushing the Boundaries*. Oxford.

Zumthor, P. 1983. *Oral Poetry: An Introduction*. Trans. K. Murphy-Judy 1990. Minneapolis.

7

Formulas and Scribal Memory

A Case Study of Text-Critical Variants
as Examples of Category-Triggering

RAYMOND F. PERSON, JR., OHIO NORTHERN UNIVERSITY

A S NOTED IN EARLIER DISCUSSIONS and throughout this volume, Milman Parry's initial definition of "formula" has required revision as the comparative study of oral traditions expanded into epic poetry beyond Homer and South Slavic epic, into prose traditions, and into literature that was obviously composed in writing but was nevertheless formulaic. Thus, any definition of "formula" must allow for variations, seriously taking into account the following questions: *How much does a formula exhibit verbal fixity versus flexibility? What is the difference between formulas in prose and poetic traditions? Can formulas produced orally be distinguished from formulas used in written compositions? Which formulas are generically connected to only one theme and which transcend thematic boundaries? Are formulas more common or dense in certain themes (for example, openings and closings) than in others?* Despite the various answers given by scholars to these questions, a consensus has emerged that every specific formulaic system has close semantic and syntactic connections to the tradition's language. That is, what Albert Lord called the "special grammar" (1960:35–36) and John Miles Foley called the "oral traditional register" (1995:15, 82–92) is an adaptation of the grammar of the everyday talk within the linguistic community of the performer and the audience.[1] "The formulas are the phrases and clauses and sentences of this specialized poetic grammar" (Lord 1960:36). Furthermore, formulas carry

---

[1] For my fuller discussion of "special grammar" and "register," see Person 2017a; Person 2017c. Although Lord's "special grammar" and Foley's "oral traditional register" are not synonyms, I understand Foley's term as refining and expanding Lord's, so that when I use "special grammar" below I am not limiting its meaning to Lord's definition, but refer to how Foley has broadened the understanding of Lord's original idea to include traditional phraseology and thematic structures. See further Person 2016. For a wider discussion of "register," see Agha and Frog 2015.

traditional meaning so that they "are not just compositional; they are also cognitive" (Foley 1991:60) and, much like *thank you* and *please*, they "come to our minds as a learned reflex" (Lord 1981:451).

If formulas are adaptations of practices in everyday conversation for the purpose of carrying traditional meanings, then a better understanding of how everyday conversation works may provide a helpful lens to understanding formulas better. For this purpose, Gail Jefferson's "On the Poetics of Ordinary Talk" (1996) provides excellent insights. She identified two phenomena for word-selection, what she called *sound-triggering* and *category-triggering*. In sound-triggering, there is a "a tendency for sounds-in-progress to locate particular next words" (Jefferson 1996:3). In category-triggering, words early in a conversation establish a category from which other words in the following discourse are selected.

As the comparative study of oral traditions has been applied to litera-ture, especially that with roots in oral traditions, the creative flexibility found within oral composition has been applied to the scribal process of copying literary texts, so that various scholars have argued for scribes as performers, including Anglo-Saxon scribes (O'Keeffe 1990; Doane 1994), ancient Israelite scribes (Person 1998), and scribes of Homeric epic (Ready 2019). That is, *scribal performance* can include the following observation concerning the transmission process: even the presence of a written manuscript in the transmission process did not negate the possibility that the scribe as performer will substitute one word or phrase for another or even substitute entire sections.[2] Any manuscript represents but a single instantiation of a particular literary text within a broader tradition. A scribe's familiarity with that broader tradition equipped him with a range of acceptable substitutions within the special register with potential to consciously or unconsciously produce what we might perceive as a variation, *even* when copying a manuscript (Person 2015). That is, scholars of literature too often think of the transmission process in a much too linear manner, in which the manuscript being copied is understood to be (or should be) the sole text that determines what the new copy should be; rather, the manuscript simply represents the larger collective memory of the community in relationship to

---

[2]   *Scribal performance* should not be understood as being limited to this one scribal function—that is, the copying of texts. Rather, *scribal performance* can refer to how scribes perform all of the various tasks that they undertake in ways that are somewhat analogous to oral-traditional performers, including copying from physical manuscripts to produce a new copy, reciting texts by memory, reading texts aloud in various scribal contexts (whether within the guild itself or in public), and instruction based on texts within the scribal guild or in public (including, when necessary, translation). For an excellent summary of the secondary literature on scribes as performers and the most thorough development of the idea of scribal performance in its many forms, see Ready 2019:192–215.

the literary text being copied that exists in multiple manuscripts (not simply the one before the scribe) and in the communal memory embodied in the scribe. Furthermore, even though it may have significant influence on the copy being made, the existing manuscript is not the sole influence. In this way scribal performance depends significantly on *scribal memory*, which refers to the knowledge of traditional texts held in the collective memory of scribes.[3] That is, the scribe's "copying" of a literary text in a way that is analogous to oral performance (scribal performance) may be based on a written manuscript, the oral text as remembered by the scribe, or in many cases some combination of the two (based on scribal memory), whether or not a manuscript is physically present.[4] As a result, scribal memory may influence how an individual scribe "copies" a manuscript, producing readings that from our anachronistic perspective may "differ" from other readings but from the scribe's perspective are nevertheless the "same," because they simply reflect the scribe's conscious or subconscious appropriation of alternative forms of the same literary text or other texts (oral and/or written) in the broader tradition that is characterized by multiformity, all of which use the tradition's special grammar.[5] Thus, to paraphrase the above quote from Lord, the words and phrases, including formulas, that the scribes may substitute in their production of the new manuscript may have come to their minds as a learned reflex.

Arguments for scribal performance and scribal memory have depended not only on the analogy of oral composition, but importantly upon text-critical "variants" of literary texts preserved in divergent manuscripts. That is, in the presence of the textual plurality and textual fluidity of some ancient and medieval texts, most text-critical "variants" appear to be so traditional that text critics have difficulty identifying which reading is "original" and in some cases have completely abandoned the endeavor of searching for the "original text." This is especially the case with those variants that Shemaryahu Talmon called "synonymous readings" and that David Carr called "memory variants." Talmon defined *synonymous readings* as follows:

    a.   The variant resulted from the substitution of a word or phrase by a lexeme which is used interchangeably with it in the text of the Hebrew Bible.

---

[3] For a summary of the secondary literature on scribal memory, see Person 2017b.

[4] For an excellent recent discussion of "oral text," see Ready 2019:16–27.

[5] For an excellent discussion of "difference" versus "sameness" in oral traditions and its application to literature (specifically Homer), see Ready 2018:74–77.

    b.   The variant does not adversely affect the structure of the verse, nor its meaning or rhythm, and therefore cannot have been caused by scribal error.

    c.   No sign of systematic or tendentious emendation characterizes such a variant, which must be taken at face value. Synonymous readings are not marked by a clearly definable ideological purpose, but rather are characterized by the absence of any difference between them in content or meaning.

    d.   As far as we can tell, synonymous readings do not stem from chronologically or geographically distinct literary sources.

Talmon 1961:336 [= 2010:172]

Explicitly building upon the work of Talmon and others, Carr defined *memory variants* as follows: "the sort of variants that happen when a tradent modifies elements of texts in the process of citing or otherwise reproducing it from memory" (2011:17).[6] With such text-critical variants as synonymous readings and memory variants, some of the standard explanations of these variants (such as "scribal error" or ideologically motivated revisions) simply do not apply, so that the question *Why would a scribe make such a change in the process of copying an existing text?* and the related question *Why would a culture accept different versions of literary texts?* become more pressing. However, when we consider Lord's insight that "[i]n oral tradition the idea of an original is illogical," then "we cannot correctly speak of a 'variant', since there is no 'original' to be varied" (1960:101). Rather, we need to consider the characteristic of multiformity in oral traditions (1960:99–102). Lord's insights seem to apply well to those ancient and medieval texts that exist in textual plurality, so that in a real sense we should consider ancient and medieval scribes as performers of texts in ways that are somewhat analogous to oral performers, thereby explaining what we often perceive as "variants" (Person 2015).

Lord noted that orally dictated texts of oral traditions and their subsequent editing differed from those that were carefully documented. "A certain amount of normalizing occurs during both the dictating and editing processes, so that the published song does not by any means exactly reproduce the formulaic style of the sung performance" (Lord 1953:127). Similarly, Jonathan Ready has argued convincingly that literary texts that come "from a process of dictation

---

6   Talmon's and Carr's examples differ somewhat. Talmon's examples are exclusively from the Hebrew Bible, often from different manuscripts of the same literary text. Carr's examples not only come from the Hebrew Bible, but also from other literature from the ancient Near East and the Mediterranean Basin. Both use examples from parallel biblical texts—for example,

should be understood as co-creations of the poet, scribe, and collector" (2019). That is, scribes must be considered as a potential part of the creative processes that have led to some ancient and medieval literature, whether the scribes were producing a dictation of an orally composed epic for the very first time or were copying an existing manuscript. This chapter builds upon these notions of scribal performance, but for the first time uses Jefferson's identification of category-triggering as a means to understand better the cognitive-linguistic processes operative in scribal memory, specifically as it relates to synonymous readings and memory variants. Examples come from ancient Hebrew, Aramaic, and Greek literature, specifically the Hebrew Bible, the Dead Sea Scrolls, Homer, and the New Testament. My Hebrew examples come from studies in which the terms "synonymous readings" and/or "memory variants" have been used to describe the variants. In some cases, the application of these terms to the Aramaic and Greek examples are my own; however, these examples are sometimes taken from secondary studies in which the authors are making arguments related to scribal performance and, as we will see, these examples nevertheless fit the definitions for these terms well. However, before discussing specific examples, I will first discuss further category-triggering, including how it may be adapted in the movement from conversation to oral traditions and literature with roots in oral tradition.

1. Word-Selection and Category-Triggering

As mentioned above, word-selection in everyday conversation can occur on the basis of sound-triggering and category-triggering. *Category-triggering* occurs when speakers choose among various options as they select their next word based on some category created by a preceding word or words. Jefferson described category as a loose term involving "objects that very strongly belong together, sometimes as contrasts, sometimes as co-members, very often as pairs. Up-down, right-left, young-old, husband-wife" (1996:9). Below are three

---

Chronicles is generally understood to be a later revision of the books of Samuel-Kings. Although in previous works I have focused on parallel biblical texts (see especially Person 2010), in this chapter I will generally limit my discussion to examples from different manuscripts of the same literary text, unless a parallel text provides additional insight into the textual variation. See also Talmon 1989b.

of Jefferson's many examples from three different conversations. Note that Jefferson placed brackets around the words she considered in the same category.

(1)

> Russia's the worst. We went twenty four hours once without [eating] a thing. I just got [fed] up waiting.
>
> Jefferson 1996:17

If we ask why the speaker chose "fed up" rather than something like "reached my limit," "eating" that precedes "fed up" provides a good explanation, since "fed up" is not only a verb that communicates the intended meaning here, but does so by a metaphorical use of "eating" until one has reached one's limit. Thus, "eating" suggested a category that included "fed up" that was then selected as the verb. Although the following example may require some ethnographic knowledge about livestock, an analogous explanation is available concerning word-selection.

(2)

> I wanted to go to an [agricultural] college but my mother [steered] me away from that.
>
> Jefferson 1996:17

If we ask why the speaker chose "steered me away from" rather than something like "discouraged me from," "agricultural" that precedes "steered" provides a good explanation, since "steer" is not only a verb that communicates the intended meaning here by metaphorically referring to driving, but is also a noun for male cattle. The last example from Jefferson also illustrates category-triggering in its use of "deeper" / "hole."[7]

(3)

> I hope to become more consistent as I get [deeper] into this w[hole] problem.
>
> Jefferson 1996:17

---

[7] Here we should note that transcription standards tend to favor the lexemes that make sense in the context of the spoken grammar, even when silent letters are involved. That is, "whole" and "hole" can be indistinguishable when spoken alone, but transcription standards obviously place such lexemes in their grammatical-pragmatic contexts, thereby choosing one spelling over the other and emphasizing a visual difference between these homophones.

Although such explanations may seem somewhat fantastical—thus, Jefferson's admission that poetics is the "wild side of Conversation Analysis" (1996:2)—her extensive collection of examples nevertheless supports her analysis well. Her examples include what she labeled as "category-flurries," sequences in which words from the same category occur throughout a conversation multiple times. One type of a category-flurry is "body-part flurries," in which words that are homophones to or have homophonous syllable(s) to body parts reoccur. She gave an example that took thirty-six lines to transcribe from a conversation by two women, both of whom contributed to the flurry containing the following: "[back] from Europe," "never come [back]," "that I [faced]," "any[body]," "thirty six square [feet]," "on my [neck]," "don't har[ass] me," "go right a[head]," and "here's my [body]" (1996:35). Thus, despite the presumed "wildness" of these observations, her identification of both sound-triggering and category-triggering is widely accepted within conversation analysis.

In *From Conversation to Oral Tradition* (2016), I argued that different formulaic systems use sound-triggering, category-triggering, or both as they adapt different linguistic characteristics of the everyday language for aesthetic purposes within the special grammar of the tradition. For example, the "heroic decasyllable" of the South Slavic Muslim epic tradition includes an adaptation of category-triggering as illustrated by the following formulaic system:

(4)

Jalah reče,	zasede djogata
Jalah reče,	posede dogina
Jalah reče,	posede hajvana
I to reče,	posede dorata
A to reče,	zasede hajvana

Lord 1960:48, his translation;
see also Foley 1990:160

"By Allah," he said,	she mounted the white horse
"By Allah," he said,	he mounted the white horse
"By Allah," he said,	he mounted the animal
And he said this,	he mounted the brown horse
And he said this,	he mounted the animal

Thus, the metrical requirements of the traditional decasyllable can be met in various ways by this formulaic system using a range of verb forms with the same number of syllables (*zasednu, zasedem, zasede, zasedi, zaseo*) in the same category with a range of nouns with the same number of syllables (*djogata, kočiju, dorata, paripa, hajvana, maljina, binjeka, mrkova, vranina, menzila, sturika, zekana, ezdralja)* also in the same category (Lord 1960:48). Moreover, this particular formulaic system consists of the combination of a verb and a noun, both of which can be understood as coming from the same category—that is, the verb means "he/she mounted" and the noun describes the type of "mount" that he/she is riding (Person 2016:75–79).

If category-triggering explains word-selection in conversation, what does word-selection look like in oral traditions? In order to answer this question, we should review briefly an observation that has been referred to in other chapters in this volume—specifically, Foley's (1981:92 n. 11; 1991:6–7) discussion of how "word" (in South Slavic *reč*; similarly, in biblical Hebrew דבר, see Person 1998:603–604; Person 2010:48–49) can be a vernacular term for a unit of utterance that corresponds to a traditional unit of meaning, including formulas. Thus, if a formulaic system can include category-triggering within specific synonymous formulas in terms of individual words/lexemes (as noted above), then the formulas themselves can be understood as somewhat synonymous "words"/phrases, so that it may not matter whether, for example, "he mounted the white horse" or "he mounted the brown horse," for within the special grammar both of these formulas may be in some sense synonymous, despite their lexical variance.

2. Synonymous Readings and Category-Triggering

As argued above, category-triggering is not only a phenomenon in everyday conversation, but can also occur in the special grammar of oral traditions, thereby preparing the way further for an argument that category-triggering may also occur when scribes as performers draw from their memory of the tradition, allowing them to substitute words, phrases, and formulas (all of which in some sense are traditional "words"/units of meaning) that occur in the same category, *even when* they are copying an existing manuscript to produce a new manuscript. In this section, I will provide examples of synonymous readings, including the following types: (1) different, single lexemes, (2) the same words in a different order, (3) different formulas, and (4) double readings, in which a manuscript preserves two synonymous readings found singly in other manuscripts. We will see that these various types of synonymous readings (all of which are memory variants) are evidence that category-triggering is a phenomenon in scribal memory in the process of scribal transmission of texts.

For those unfamiliar with the different textual traditions of the Hebrew Bible/Old Testament, I provide the following explanations. "Masoretic Text" (MT) refers to a group of medieval Hebrew manuscripts that is the received tradition—that is, the Hebrew text used in Jewish worship and the basis of Jewish and most Christian translations. "Septuagint" (LXX) refers to a group of manuscripts of the ancient Greek translation of the Hebrew Bible, first used in Jewish communities but then became mostly used by Christians. "Samaritan Pentateuch" (SamP) refers to a group of Hebrew manuscripts for the first five books of the Hebrew Bible (Genesis, Exodus, Leviticus, Numbers, Deuteronomy) used by Samaritans in their worship, both historically and today. The "Dead Sea Scrolls" refers to manuscripts (mostly Hebrew and Aramaic, a few in Greek) found in caves near Khirbet Qumran. The individual manuscripts are identified by the cave in which they were found, the literary text of the manuscript, and for those texts in which multiple copies are found in the same cave a letter denoting which manuscript. Therefore, "1QIsaᵃ" denotes the first/main Isaiah scroll found in cave 1 of Qumran; "1QIsaᵇ" the second Isaiah scroll found in cave 1; and so forth. The Dead Sea Scrolls and other texts found in the Judean Desert are the earliest extant manuscripts of the Hebrew Bible and the textual plurality found among these manuscripts shows that the other textual traditions have roots at least as early as the late Second Temple period (first century BCE and first century CE). All English translations are my own unless otherwise noted. All retroversions of the Greek into Hebrew or Aramaic (that is, the reconstruction of the Semitic text behind the Greek translation) are also my own, unless otherwise noted.[8] Examples are given in each section based on their illustrative value for my purpose, generally moving from simpler to more complex examples.

2.1. Synonymous readings: different, single lexemes

Although his definition of "synonymous readings" includes "words and phrases" (1961:336), Talmon's examples are primarily phrases in which only one lexeme differs. This is illustrated well in his discussion of synonymous readings based on a substitution of בני ('sons of') and בית ('house of') (1961:346–348). Here is a selection of his examples. The first three examples show synonymous readings within the tradition of the Masoretic Text itself (that is, between the "majority" text and other manuscripts):

---

[8] For the most widely accepted introduction to these different textual traditions and how biblical scholars approach them, see Tov 2012.

(5)

Judges 1:22

| MT | בית יוסף | the house of Joseph |
| mss | בני יוסף | the sons of Joseph |

Talmon 1961:346

(6)

Ezekiel 5:4, 12:24, 13:9, 14:5, 18:29

| MT | בית ישראל | the house of Israel |
| mss | בני ישראל | the sons of Israel |

Talmon 1961:346

(7)

Hosea 3:1

| MT | בני ישראל | the sons of Israel |
| mss | בית ישראל | the house of Israel |

Talmon 1961:347

The following example is a case in which the Masoretic Text has a different reading from the Samaritan Pentateuch:

(8)

Leviticus 17:13; 20:2

| MT | ואיש איש מבני ישראל | anyone from the sons of Israel |
| SamP | ואיש איש מבית ישראל | anyone from the house of Israel |

Talmon 1961:348

Based on these and other examples, Talmon concluded that בני ('sons of') and בית ('house of') "are used as synonyms when they serve in construct with a noun, or proper name, to denote a close connection or blood-relationship" (1961:346). In Jefferson's terminology, when combined with the same proper noun, the construct nouns בני ('sons of') and בית ('house of') access the same category of close kinship. Talmon reached similar conclusions in his discussions of many other pairs, including, for example, אדמה ('ground') and ארץ ('land')

(Talmon 1961:348–349) as well as ארץ ('land') and שדה ('field') (Talmon 1961:348–349), all of which access the same category in Jefferson's terminology.

The following two examples come from Jonathan Ready's *Orality, Textuality, and Homeric Epic* (2019), where he argues for scribal performance in the text-critical history of Homeric epic. Ready provides an excellent review of the secondary literature on the various arguments for scribal performance, including Carr's idea of "memory variants" (2019:205). Therefore, although he does not explicitly label the two examples I give below as "synonymous readings" or "memory variants," such labeling is certainly consistent with his argument. Examples (9–10) compare the "vulgate" text of Homer to Ptolemaic papyri. In example (9), note how Nausikaa's father is referred to in different ways.

(9)

> *Odyssey* vi 256

> "vulgate"   πατρὸς ἐμοῦ πρὸς δῶμα δαΐφρονος, ἔνθα σέ φημι
>   to the house of my prudent father, where I am confident

> P110   Ἀλκινόου πρὸς δῶμα δαΐφρονος, ἔγ[θα σέ φημι
>   to the house of prudent Alkinoos, where I am confident

> Ready 2019:256; West 1967:220

Both readings preserve the hexameter line, since they are metrically equivalent. The "vulgate" simply uses πατρὸς ἐμοῦ ('my father') when referring to Nausikaa's father, Ἀλκινόου ('Alkinoos'), obviously both of which belong to the same category. In example (10), note that there are synonymous readings for both what Hera is sitting on and for Olympus' response.

(10)

> *Iliad* VIII 199

> "vulgate"   σείσατο δ' εἰνὶ θρόνῳ, ἐλέλιξε δὲ μακρὸν Ὄλυμπον
>   she shuddered on her throne and made high Olympus
>   quake

> P7   [... ἐν] κλισμῷ, πελέ[μιξε δὲ μακρὸν Ὄλυμπον
>   ... on her couch and made high Olympus shake

> Ready 2019:259; West 1967:87

Both readings fit well within the special grammar of Homeric epic, including the hexameter line, simply using synonymous words or at least words from the same category. Both θρόνῳ ('throne') and κλισμῷ ('couch') refer to furniture upon which the gods sit or recline and ἐλέλιξε ('quake') and πελέμιξε ('shake') are synonyms, describing bodily movements of shuddering. Therefore, we can conclude that a comparison of these two hexameter lines reveals two synonymous readings, both of which are the substitution of a lexeme, one which draws from the category of furniture and the other from the category of shuddering.

2.2. Synonymous readings: same words, different order

Talmon noted the following:

> a word in the [Old Testament] can be replaced by its synonym [...] and the order of the synonymous expression in the parallel members of a verse can be inverted [...] without causing any distorting of the author's original intention or any disturbance of the syntax and rhythm of the verse.

Talmon 1961:336–337

Below I will provide four examples of the same words given in a different order as synonymous readings. The first example compares the Masoretic Text with a manuscript of Exodus from Qumran Cave 4 and involves a simple change in word order.

(11)

    Exodus 26:10

MT	ועשית המשים ללאת	You shall make fifty loops
4QpaleoExod^m	[ועשית ללא]ות המשים	[You shall make lo]ops fifty

Sanderson 1986:115

The difference here ("fifty loops" // "loops fifty") is grammatically permissible and insignificant in meaning.

    The second example comes from different manuscripts of the Greek New Testament.

(12)

Matthew 15:38

| B C L | γυναικῶν καὶ παιδίων | women and children |
| א D | παιδίων καὶ γυναικῶν | children and women |

Metzger 1971:40

These two readings are clearly synonymous, referring to the same group of non-adult males. The variation in the order of the two lexemes does not change the referent at all. Although γυναικῶν καὶ παιδίων ('women and children') was included in the published critical text, the editorial committee judged their argument for its inclusion as among the weakest, giving their decision the lowest ranking "D," which denotes that "there is a very high degree of doubt concerning the reading selected for the text" (Metzger 1971:xxviii). The reason for such doubt is that they are synonymous readings, referring to the same category of those who are not adult males.

The third example compares the "vulgate" text of the *Iliad* with a quote of the *Iliad* in the writings of Zenodotus, in which the verb stems are transposed between the main verb and the participle.

(13)

Iliad VIII 526

"vulgate"	εὔχομαι ἐλπόμενος Διί τ' ἄλλοισίν τε θεοῖσιν
	I pray, hoping to Zeus and the other gods ...
Zenodotus	ἔλπομαι εὐχόμενος Διί ἄλλοισίν τε θεοῖσιν
	I hope, praying to Zeus and the other gods ...

Bird 2010:57–58

These two synonymous readings refer to the same attitude of hopeful prayer/prayerful hope. Because these are "equivalent variants" in meaning and preserve the poetic meter, Graeme Bird concluded that "both variants have a right to be considered authentic" (2010:57).

The final example of synonymous readings in the form of the same words in different order compares a reading in the Masoretic Text with the Isaiah Scroll from Qumran Cave 1. This is a clear example of what Talmon described as "the order of the synonymous expression in the parallel members of a verse can be inverted" (1961:336).

(14)

Isaiah 49:6

MT להקים את שבטי יעקב ונצירי ישראל

to raise up the tribes of Jacob and the survivors of Israel

1QIsaᵃ להקים את שבטי ישראל ונצירי יעקב

to raise up the tribes of Israel and the survivors of Jacob

Talmon 1961:336–337

According to the tradition (for example, see Gen 32:28), "Jacob" and "Israel" are two names for the same individual; therefore, this exchange of proper names does not change the meaning of either noun phrase in this parallel construction. That is, "tribes of Jacob," "tribes of Israel," "survivors of Israel," and "survivors of Jacob" are synonymous readings, all referring the descendants of Jacob/Israel in the surviving tribes as one category.

2.3. Synonymous readings: different formulas

Although Talmon's definition of "synonymous readings" included "words and phrases" (1961:336), most of his examples really concern single lexemes. However, many studies that apply Talmon's insights to other texts include more examples of phrases, including formulas. The following examples come from studies that are drawing from Talmon's works or other works influenced by Talmon (Person 1998; Carr 2011). The first three examples come from the work of Ian Young in his comparison of the Masoretic Text of Daniel and the Septuagint (LXX) of Daniel. Note that I have provided my own retroversion of the LXX text into Aramaic for a more detailed comparison between the purported Aramaic *Vorlage* of the LXX and the Aramaic of the MT. Concerning example (15), the immediately preceding phrase in both texts describes King Belshazzar as drinking wine, so that the two synonymous readings here refer to his mood under the influence of the alcohol.

(15)

Daniel 5:2

MT בלשאצר אמר בטעם חמרא להיתיה

Belshazzar said, under the influence of the wine, to bring

LXX[OG]   κ‍α‍ὶ‍ ἀ‍ν‍υ‍ψ‍ώ‍θ‍η‍ ἡ‍ κ‍α‍ρ‍δ‍ί‍α‍ α‍ὐ‍τ‍ο‍ῦ‍, κ‍α‍ὶ‍ ε‍ἶ‍π‍ε‍ν‍ ἐνέγκαι

Aramaic   ⁹ ורם לבבה ואמר להיתיה

And his heart was exalted and he said to bring

Young 2016:273, his translation[10]

That is, "under the influence of the wine" "his heart was exalted" are two descriptions that access the category of possible alcohol-induced moods.

In the following example, we see different ways of referring to the category of idols or false gods.

(16)

Daniel 5:4

MT   לאלהי דהבא וכספא נחשא פרזלא אעא ואבנא

the gods of gold and silver, bronze, iron, wood, and stone

Daniel 5:23

MT   לאלהי כספא ודהבא נחשא פרזלא אעא ואבנא
          די לא חזין ולא שמעין ולא ידעין

the gods of silver and gold, bronze, iron, wood, and stone
who do not see and do not hear and do not know

Young 2016:274, 281, his translation

First, we should note that we have a transposition of "gold" and "silver" between these two phrases, thereby providing us with another example of a synonymous reading of the same words in different orders. Second, the description of the gods of metal, wood, and stone found in Dan 5:4 is repeated in Dan 5:23, but with the additional phrase of "who do not see/hear/know." That is, gods made of inanimate objects do not have perception and knowledge. Looking at the

---

⁹   For my retroversion of the Greek, see Dan 5:20; 11:12.

[10]   The translations of the Aramaic are Young's. For the Greek translations, Young used *New English Translation of the Septuagint* (NETS), which is available online at http://ccat.sas.upenn.edu/nets/edition/. In some cases, he adapted NETS to provide a better comparison with the Aramaic. See Young 2016:273n8.

parallel verses of Dan 5:4 and Dan 5:23 in the LXX, we find two other synonymous phrases for the category of false gods/idols.

(17)

> Daniel 5:4
>
> LXX[OG]   τὰ εἴδωλα τὰ χειροποίητα <u>αὐτῶν</u>
>
> Aramaic   אלהיהון עובדי בידיהין
>   idols made by their hands
>
> Daniel 5:23
>
> LXX[OG]   τὰ εἴδωλα τὰ χειροποίητα <u>τῶν ἀνθρώπων</u>
>
> Aramaic   אלהיהון עובדי ידי אנשא
>   the idols made by human hands

Young 2016:274, 281, his translation

These phrases are clearly synonymous, simply substituting the pronoun "their" for "human" (or vice versa). When we combine examples (16–17)—that is, we compare Dan 5:4 in the MT and LXX and Dan 5:23 in the MT and LXX—we see how the way I have presented these synonymous readings above is somewhat misleading, in that the comparison between the MT and LXX of the two passages has what appear to be (from our modern perspective) phrases that contain more variation, in that the lexical variation is greater. That is, "the gods of gold and silver, bronze, iron, wood, and stone" in MT Dan 5:4 and "the idols made of their hand" in LXX Dan 5:4 differ more significantly as do "the gods of silver and gold, bronze, iron, wood, and stone who do not see and do not hear and do not know" in MT Dan 5:23, and "the idols made by human hands" in LXX Dan 5:23. However, if the two phrases in the MT of Dan 5:4 and Dan 5:23 are synonymous and the two phrases in the LXX of Dan 5:4 and Dan 5:23 are synonymous, then we must consider all four phrases synonymous. In other words, the description of "the gods of gold and silver, bronze, iron, wood, and stone" is explicitly a reference to the observation that these gods/"idols made by their/human hands" cannot see, hear, or know anything. Therefore, these are four synonymous readings that access the category of false gods/idols.

Examples (18–19) come from different versions of the *Community Rule* of Qumran, one found in Cave 1 and one in Cave 4. In example (18), this section of these two manuscripts of the *Community Rule* begins with a different line introducing what follows.

(18)

Community Rule

1QS V 1   זה הסרך לאנשי היחד
This is the rule for the men of the community

4QSᵇ IX 1   מדרש למשכיל [על אנשי התורה
A midrash for the wise leader [over the men of the Torah

Carr 2011:86, his English translation; Metso 1997:27–28

Although the first lines of these two versions differ, they can nevertheless be understood as synonymous, because "the wise leader" is charged in both documents to oversee the application of "the rule" within the life of the community. In example (19), these two synonymous readings explain under whose authority interpretation of the community's rules fall, in the first this is quite explicit but in the second the single lexeme must have been understood within the community to refer to the list of individuals in the first.

(19)

Community Rule

1QS V 2–3   על פי בני צדוק הכוהנים שומרי הברית
ועל פי רוב אנשי היחד המחזקים הברית

under the authority of the Zadokites, the priests, who keep the covenant and under the authority of the majority of the men of the community who hold fast to the covenant

4QSᵇ IX 3   ועל פי הרבים
under the authority of the many

Carr 2011:86; Metso 1997:27–28

Although the reading from 1QS is certainly more specific, these two phrases could have been understood as synonymous within the community—that is, members of the community already knew who "the many" were in their communal structure, so the specification given in 1QS was not necessary to repeat in every reference to "the many" but could nevertheless be substituted easily in the process of copying due to scribal memory. In Jefferson's terminology, both phrases refer to the same category—that is, the leaders who have the authority in the community.

The last example of synonymous formulas comes from Homer, comparing the "vulgate" with one of the Ptolemaic papyri. Although fragment P31 does not include lines 500–501, P31 substitutes line 522 as found in the vulgate with lines 500–501 as found in the vulgate. That is, in this case, we have a substitution of two lines of hexameter for one as if they are synonymous.

(20)

    Odyssey ix 500–501, 522

"vulgate"   ὣς φάσαν, ἀλλ᾽ οὐ πεῖθον ἐμὸν μεγαλήτορα θυμόν,
             ἀλλά μιν ἄψορρον προσέφην κεκοτηότι θυμῷ·

             ὣς ἔφατ᾽, αὐτὰρ ἐγώ μιν ἀμειβόμενος προσέειπον·
             So they spoke, but could not persuade the great heart
               in me,
             but once again in the anger of my heart I cried to him:

             So he spoke, but I answered him again and said to him:

P31   [lines 500–501 are missing from ms]

             [ὣς ἔφατ᾽, ἀλ]λ᾽ οὐ πεῖθεν [ἐμὸ]ν μεγαλήτορα θυμόν,
             [ἀλλά μιν ἄψο]ρρον πρ[οσέφη]ν κεκοτηότι θυμῶι·
             [lines 500–501 are missing from ms]

             So he spoke, but could not persuade the great heart
               in me,
             but once again in the anger of my heart I cried to him:

                      Ready 2019:251; West 1967:230

Lines 500–501 and 522 in the vulgate are synonymous readings and can be easily substituted within the special grammar of Homeric epic. Note that both begin with ὣς φάσαν / ὣς ἔφατ᾽ ('So he spoke') and emphasize the repetitious nature of the following first-person speech (μιν ['again']).

2.4. Double readings

Talmon extended his identification of synonymous readings with his discussion of double readings (1960; see also 1961:343, 345). Talmon described *double readings* as a scribal technique of "preserving equally valid readings" and "the conflation of alternative readings" that are synonymous within the same manuscript

(1960:150 [2010:224]). In Jefferson's terminology, the scribes simply provided two synonymous readings from the broader tradition that are accessing the same category. Below I provide four examples of double readings, the first two concerning the conflation of a single lexeme and the other two showing how formulaic phrases can occur in double readings. Note that, although I generally arrange the variants in order from shortest to longest for the ease of my readers, I do not necessarily agree with the consensus that the longest reading is the latest.[11] In fact, my argument is that these synonymous readings should be understood as equally "original" or, better, equally "authentic." Interestingly, I have not (yet?) identified examples of double readings in Homer and the New Testament. The hexameter line of Homer would rule out the possibility of double readings within the verse, so that any double readings would have to be the inclusion of two hexameter lines that are synonymous (a possibility I have not [yet?] observed). Since my primary expertise is with the Hebrew literature, I will not attempt to make some conclusion based on this apparent difference, since I may have missed some evidence. However, despite the apparent differences, I think that the above evidence nevertheless supports the idea of scribal performance based on scribal memory for all of the literature discussed in this chapter, even if the degree of variation may differ.

The first example comes from a comparison of the parallel biblical passages of 2 Kings 18–20 and Isaiah 36–39, in which the double reading is found in the Isaiah Scroll of Qumran Cave 1.

(21)

Isa 37:9 // 2 Kgs 19:9

MT Isa 37:9   וישמע וישלח מלאכים
                     and he heard and he sent messengers

MT 2 Kgs 9:9   וישב וישלח מלאכים
                     and he returned and he sent messengers

1QIsa[a]   וישמע וישב וישלח מלאכים
                     and he heard and he returned and he sent messengers

Talmon 1989:86; Person 1998:605;
Tov 2012:225

The readings in the two texts from the Masoretic Text contain synonymous readings in which "he heard" and "he returned" are substituted. The Qumran

---

[11] For my position on such general rules as *lectio brevior potior*, see Person and Rezetko 2016.

reading simply conflates the two synonymous readings into a third synonymous reading.

The second example is similar to example (21) in that the two readings using synonymous verbs are conflated.

(22)

2 Samuel 12:16

LXX[B]   καὶ εἰσῆλθεν καὶ ηὐθλίσθη ἐπὶ τῆς γῆς
ויבוא ולן ארצה
and he came and spent the night on the ground

4QSam[a]   ויבוא וישכב בשק ארצה
and he came and lay down in sackcloth on the ground

MT   ובא ולן ושכב ארצה
and he was coming and spending the night and lying down on the ground

LXX[LMN]   καὶ εἰσῆλθεν καὶ ηὐθλίσθη καὶ ἐκάθεθδεν ἐν σάκκῳ ἐπὶ τῆς γῆς
ויבוא ולן ושכב בשק ארצה
and he came and spent the night and lay down in sackcloth on the ground

Young 2014:23, his translation

As in the previous example, here we have two versions with two verbs—"he came and spent the night" and "he came and lay down"—that are conflated in other versions ("he came and spent the night and lay down" with the variant verb tenses) with the variant plus of "in sackcloth" occurring in one of the shorter versions and in one of the longer versions.

The third example—the first one of a double reading containing obvious formulaic phrases—comes from a comparison of the parallel passages of 2 Kgs 24:18–25:30 and Jeremiah 52 in the Masoretic Text with the Septuagint reading of Jeremiah.

(23)

2 Kings 25:30 // Jeremiah 52:34

MT 2 Kgs 25:30   כל ימי חיו
all the days of his life

LXX Jer 52:34	ἕως ἡμέρας, ἧς ἀπέθανεν
	עד יום מותו
	until the day of his death
MT Jer 52:34	עד יום מותו כל ימי חיו
	until the day of his death, all the days of his life

Person 1998:605; Tov 2012:225–226

MT Kings and LXX Jeremiah contain two synonymous formulas referring to the length of the king's life that are conflated in MT Jeremiah.

The last example of double readings comes from Judith Sanderson's study of an Exodus Scroll from Qumran Cave 4. This example shows the flexibility that can occur within a formulaic system in that she showed how the text-critical evidence of Exod 32:11, Deut 9:26, and Deut 9:29 are especially illuminating concerning the formulaic phrases referring to the people of Israel as those whom God brought out of Egypt. Sanderson's analysis included evidence from the Masoretic Text, the Samaritan Pentateuch, an Exodus Scroll from Qumran Cave 4, and the Septuagint, including in one case an important variation within the Septuagint tradition itself.

(24)

Exodus 32:11 // Deuteronomy 9:26 // Deuteronomy 9:29
Exod 32:11

MT	אשר הוצאת מארץ מצרים בכח גדול וביד חזקה
	whom you brought out of the land of Egypt with great power and with a mighty hand
SamP	אשר הוצאת ממצרים בכח גדול ובזרוע נטויה
	whom you brought out of Egypt with great power and with a raised arm
4QpaleoExod[m]	אשר הוצ[את ו]בזרוע חזק]ה
	whom you brought [out with] a raised arm
LXX	οὓς ἐξήγαγες ἐκ γῆς Αἰγύπτου ἐν ἰσχύι μεγάλῃ καὶ ἐν τῷ βραχίονί σου τῷ ὑψηλῷ
	אשר הוצאת מארץ מצרים בכח גדול ובזרוע חטויה
	whom you brought out of the land of Egypt with great power and with a raised arm

Deut 9:26

MT   אשר הוצאת ממצרים ביד חזקה
whom you brought out of Egypt with a mighty hand

SamP   אשר הוצאת ממצרים בידך החזקה
whom you brought out of Egypt with your mighty hand

LXX   οὓς ἐξήγαγες ἐκ γῆς Αἰγύπτου ἐν τῇ ἰσχύι σου τῇ
μεγάλῃ καὶ ἐν τῇ χειρί σου τῇ κραταιᾷ καὶ
ἐν τῷ βραχίονί σου τῷ ὑψηλῷ

אשר הוצאת מארץ מצרים בכחך גדול ובידך החזקה
ובזרעך חנטויה
whom you brought out of the land of Egypt with
your great power, with your mighty hand,
and with your raised arm

Deut 9:29

MT   אשר הוצאת בכחך הגדל ובזרעך חנטויה
whom you brought out with your great power and
with your raised arm

SamP   אשר הוצאת ממצרים בכחך הגדול ובזרעך חנטויה
whom you brought out of Egypt with your great
power and with your raised arm

LXX   οὓς ἐξήγαγες ἐκ γῆς Αἰγύπτου ἐν τῇ ἰσχύι σου τῇ
μεγάλῃ καὶ ἐν τῷ βραχίονί σου τῷ ὑψηλῷ
אשר הוצאת מארץ מצרים בכחך הגדל ובזרעך חנטויה
whom you brought out of the land of Egypt with
your great power and with your raised arm

LXX[B]   οὓς ἐξήγαγες ἐκ γῆς Αἰγύπτου ἐν τῇ ἰσχύι σου τῇ
μεγάλῃ καὶ ἐν τῇ χειρί σου τῇ κραταιᾷ καὶ ἐν
τῷ βραχίονί σου τῷ ὑψηλῷ
אשר הוצאת מארץ מצרים
בכחך הגדל ובידך החזקה ובזרעך חנטויה
whom you brought out of the land of Egypt with
your great power, with your mighty hand, and
with your raised arm

Sanderson 1986:146

All of these phrases—from the shortest (Exod 32:12 in 4QpaleoExod[m]; "whom you brought out with a raised arm") to the longest (Deut 9:26 in LXX, Deut 9:29 in LXX[B]: "whom you brought out of the land of Egypt with your great power, with your mighty hand, and with your raised arm")—are synonymous and are made up of various possible options that can be represented in the following chart, so that every instantiation begins with the phrase in the first column, selects a phrase (or not) from the second column, and then selects one or more of the phrases in the last column, but nevertheless keeping those selected from the third column in the same order as given in the chart. Note that each column can be understood as a category in Jefferson's terminology.

(25)

	[lacking]	with [your] great power
whom you brought out	of Egypt	with [a/your] mighty hand
	of the land of Egypt	with [a/your] raised arm

All of the readings begin with "whom you brought out," a phrase that even by itself implicitly denotes "out of Egypt/the land of Egypt" (the category of the place of enslavement) and is then followed by a phrase referring to God's "power"/"hand"/"arm" (the category of "power" sometimes represented by body parts). Sanderson noted that all of these synonymous readings are "possible and defensible" (1986:147). Furthermore, since the variation occurs within the textual traditions of each of the three verses as well as among the three verses, we can conclude that this formulaic system worked within the scribal memory of the tradents of each of these texts, so that in one sense the substitution of one particular instantiation for another has not changed the text at all, because it maintains the same meaning contained within the formulaic system itself.

3. Conclusion

In previous work I have demonstrated how Jefferson's identification of category-triggering as a mechanism for word-selection in conversation (1996) is useful in helping us to understand how traditional phraseology, including formulas, works in the special grammars of oral traditions (Person 2016). In this chapter, I have demonstrated how Jefferson's insight can extend to our understanding better of how formulas work within the context of scribal performance of literary texts with roots in oral tradition – that is, even when a scribe is "copying" a manuscript that is physically present, the scribe may nevertheless draw from his memory of the way the literary text exists in the broader collective memory of the tradition, including oral texts and other manuscripts of the same text, in such a way that the "new" manuscript that the scribe is creating may draw from the multiformity allowed within special grammar of the tradition in relationship to this particular literary text. Therefore, scribal memory allows the scribe to produce a manuscript that from our modern perspective differs from the manuscript the scribe is "copying," because any manuscript is understood by the scribe as simply one instantiation of the literary text that exists in the multiformity within the tradition, including textual plurality. Nevertheless, the scribe would understand the "new" manuscript as reproducing the "same" text as the manuscript from which the scribe is copying, despite any variations at the lexical, phraseological, or thematic levels. Some of the "differences" that we perceive from our perspective are "synonymous readings" and "memory variants" that from the perspective of the ancient scribes do not really change the text. That is, the scribes are simply substituting one lexeme, phrase, or formula for another one that is understood as synonymous, because it is drawing from the same category. Category-triggering is simply working within scribal memory for word-selection and phrase/formula-selection (another type of "word") within the special grammar of the tradition.

Although I am not prepared to provide answers to all of the questions concerning formulas I asked in the introduction, an answer to the question concerning formulas in prose and poetic traditions has emerged. Category-triggering in scribal memory can work differently in prose and poetic traditions, at least in those poetic traditions with clearly defined poetic lines. That is, scribal performance and scribal memory are constrained by the special grammar of the tradition, including formal conventions like meter. For example, although prose traditions may allow significant variance in terms of the length of phrases that are synonymous readings (see example (24) above), poetic traditions with fixed poetic lines like Homeric hexameter may require synonymous readings to have the same number of syllables or at least to be able to adapt other words within the line to produce the same number of syllables. Of course, two poetic lines may be substituted for one poetic line that is synonymous (see example (20) above). At least, it appears that synonymous readings in Homer preserve the hexameter line. Therefore, the special grammar restricts how category-triggering works within scribal performance with some special grammars (especially in poetic traditions) being more restrictive than others.

Acknowledgements

I have often profited from past conversations with the following colleagues, including their comments concerning an earlier draft of this chapter: Ian Young, Jonathan Ready, Robert Rezetko, and Werner Kelber. This is my first time interacting with Frog and his editorial guidance—both in terms of additional secondary sources and restructuring my argument for a broader audience—has been valuable. The current version is stronger because of all of their suggestions, for which I sincerely thank them.

References

Agha, A., and Frog, eds. 2015. *Registers of Communication*. Helsinki.

Antovič, M., and Cánovas, C. P., eds. 2016. *Oral Poetics and Cognitive Science*. Berlin.

Bird, G. D. 2010. *Multitextuality in the Homeric Iliad: The Witness of the Ptolemaic Papyri*. Washington, DC.

Carr, D. M. 2011. *The Formation of the Hebrew Bible: A New Reconstruction*. Oxford.

Doane, A. N. 1994. "The Ethnography of Scribal Writing and Anglo-Saxon Poetry: Scribe as Performer." *Oral Tradition* 9:420–439.

Foley, J. M., ed. 1981. *Oral Tradition Literature: A Festschrift for Albert Bates Lord*. Columbus.

———. 1991. *Traditional Oral Epic: The* Odyssey, Beowulf, *and the Serbo-Croatian Return Song*. Los Angeles.

———. 1995. *The Singer of Tales in Performance*. Bloomington.

Jefferson, G. 1996. "On the Poetics of Ordinary Talk." *Text and Performance Quarterly* 16:11–61.

Lord, A. B. 1953. "Homer's Originality: Oral Dictated Texts." *Transactions of the American Philological Association* 84:124–134.

———. 1960. *The Singer of Tales*. Cambridge, MA.

———. 1981. "Memory, Fixity, and Genre in Oral Traditional Poetry." In Foley 1981:451–461.

McLay, R. T., trans. and ed. 2014. "Daniel." In Pietersma and Wright 2014:991–1022.

Metso, S. 1997. *The Textual Development of the Qumran Community Rule*. Leiden.

Metzger, B. M. 1971. *A Textual Commentary on the Greek New Testament*. London.

O'Keeffe, K. O. 1990. *Visible Song: Transitional Literacy in Old English Verse*. Cambridge.

Person, R. F., Jr. 1998. "The Ancient Israelite Scribe as Performer." *Journal of Biblical Literature* 117:601–609.

———. 2010. *The Deuteronomic History and the Book of Chronicles: Scribal Works in an Oral World*. Atlanta.

———. 2015. "Text Criticism as a Lens for Understanding the Transmission of Ancient Texts in Their Oral Environments." In Schmidt 2015:197–215.

———. 2016. *From Conversation to Oral Tradition: A Simplest Systematics for Oral Traditions*. New York.

———. 2017a. "Register." In Thatcher et al. 2017:331–332.

———. 2017b. "Scribal Memory." In Thatcher et al. 2017:352–355.

———. 2017c. "Special Grammar." In Thatcher et al. 2017:379–382.

Person, R. F., Jr. and Rezetko, R. 2016a. *Empirical Models Challenging Biblical Criticism*. Atlanta.

———. 2016b. "Introduction: The Important of Empirical Models to Assess the Efficacy of Source and Redaction Criticism." In Person and Rezetko 2016a:1–35.

Pietersma, A. and Wright, B. G., eds. 2014. *A New English Translation of the Septuagint and other Greek Translations Traditionally Included Under that Title (NETS)*. Oxford. http://ccat.sas.upenn.edu/nets/edition/.

Ready, J. 2018. *Homeric Simile in Comparative Perspectives: Oral Traditions from Saudi Arabia to Indonesia*. Oxford.

———. 2019. *Orality, Textuality, and Homeric Epic: A Study of Oral Texts, Dictated Texts, and Wild Texts*. Oxford.

Sanderson, J. E. 1986. *An Exodus Scroll from Qumran: 4QpaleoExod^m and the Samaritan Tradition*. Atlanta.

Schmidt, B. B., ed. 2015. *Contextualizing Israel's Sacred Writings: Ancient Literacy, Orality, and Literary Production*. Atlanta.

Talmon, S. 1960. "Double Readings in the Masoretic Text." *Textus* 1:144–184.

———. 1961. "Synonymous Readings in the Textual Traditions of the Old Testament." *Scripta Hierosolymitana* 8:335–383.

———. 1989a. "Aspects of the Textual Transmission of the Bible in Light of Qumran Manuscripts." In Talmon 1989c: 71–116.

———. 1989b. "Observations on Variant Readings in the Isaiah Scroll (1QIsa^a)." In Talmon 1989c:71–116.

———., ed. 1989c. *The World of Qumran from Within: Collected Studies*. Jerusalem.

———., ed. 2010. *Text and Canon of the Hebrew Bible: Collected Essays*. Winona Lake.

Thatcher, T., Keith, C., Person, R. F. Jr., and Stern, E., eds. 2017. *The Dictionary of the Bible and Ancient Media*. London.

Tov, E. 2012. *Textual Criticism of the Hebrew Bible*. Minneapolis.

West, S., ed. 1967. *The Ptolemaic Papyri of Homer*. Cologne.

Young, I. 2014. "The Dead Sea Scrolls and the Bible: The View from Qumran Samuel." *Australian Biblical Review* 62:14–30.

———. 2016. "The Original Problem: The Old Greek and the Masoretic Text of Daniel 5." In Person and Rezetko 2016:271–301.

8

We Don't Support; We Observe
Epithets and Modifiers
in a Vernacular Formulaic Genre

Koenraad Kuiper, University of Canterbury
David Leaper, the Royal College of Pathologists of Australasia

I N THIS CHAPTER WE EXAMINE the co-constructed tale of two small armies, latter day Myrmidons, doing battle in the form of a rugby union test match to see what role modifiers play in the live radio commentary of the battle. Our study is based on a corpus of two commentaries: one by New Zealand (NZ) commentators, the other by United Kingdom (UK) commentators. Our approach is quantitative being based on the corpus of transcribed recordings of these two teams of commentators. To begin we establish that radio broadcast rugby commentaries are an oral-formulaic genre (Kuiper 2009). We briefly outline relevant features of the game of rugby union football and show how it is, for the purposes of analysis, a slow sport using the metric provided by Koenraad Kuiper, Neda Bimesl, Gerard Kempen, and Masayoshi Ogino (2017). We then show the commentaries to be co-constructed narratives. This description will illustrate how a team of commentators distributes the task of "calling" the game by taking various roles including play-by-play commentary and color commentary. We then define traditional Homeric epithets, and modifiers in general, and examine the use of modifiers in our transcripts in detail to show how these function.

1. Radio Broadcast Rugby Union Commentaries as an Oral-Formulaic Genre

Our point of departure for this study is the assumption that those contingencies that give rise to oral heroic poetry being performed in the ways that it is also exist in diverse vernacular genres. This hypothesis was first explored in detail in Koenraad Kuiper's *Smooth Talkers: The Linguistic Performance of Auctioneers and Sportscasters* (1996) and "On the Linguistic Properties of Formulaic Speech" (2000), and in Alison Wray's *Formulaic Language and the Lexicon* (2002). This assumption is now common in linguistics (Sailer 2013). The crucial determinants are those outlined by Albert Lord in *The Singer of Tales* (1960). The speaker is subject to processing pressures during speech production which makes accessing lexical units longer than one word advantageous. Further these longer formulaic units must have predetermined conditions of use, for example, arming formulae in Homer or bid calling formulae in auction speech. Learning such formulae is contextually determined as a speaker learns the genres in which they play a part.

Turning now to radio broadcast commentary, it is self-evident that radio broadcast rugby union commentaries are a strictly oral genre. Radio rugby commentaries were first broadcast in the 1920s preceding spoken TV commentaries, which in turn preceded the much more recent on-line written blog commentaries.[1] The only transmission medium available for radio commentary genres is oral.

We define a formulaic genre as follows.

First, formulae are phraseological units, also termed phrasemes (and many other terms). A phraseological unit is a phrase (or clause) held in long-term memory as an item of vocabulary (Burger 2010). For our purposes we note at this point that some phraseological units cannot conventionally take a syntactic modifier, as in *make hay while the sun shines*; cf. *#make much hay while the bright sun shines*.[2] Modifiers can be an invariant constituent of a phraseological unit, as in the case of *a cock and bull story* and *cut a long story short*, or they can be optional (and perhaps also conventional), as in *come to a conclusion, come to the inescapable conclusion* and *make progress, make significant progress*.

Second, the speakers of a formulaic genre must utilize a significant number of formulae, lexically listed forms of words (phrases and clauses) which are associated with idiosyncratic conditions of use, i.e. they are specialized for the genre.[3] In the case of sports commentaries the formulae in use in a particular sport are

---

[1] The first radio rugby commentary in New Zealand by Allan Allardice was of a game between High School Old Boys and the Christchurch club broadcast on 29 May 1926.

[2] Phraseologists tend to make a distinction between conventional modification and artistic deformation, namely one-off word play modification such as *make economic hay while the sun shines* (Mel'čuk 1995).

[3] Just what constitutes a significant number is difficult to calibrate. Almost all human speech contains formulae. Oral-formulaic speech contains many but exactly what proportion for a genre to be oral-formulaic has yet to be determined. In sports commentary the proportion of formulae rises as a function of the pressure on the commentator for retrieval of lexical material from working memory. In horse-race calling, for example, almost everything a caller says is a formula (Kuiper et al. 2017).

related to or denote ritual episodes in the game (its moves), i.e. episodes which are repeated periodically in each game. So, for example, in cricket, a bowler bowls a ball towards a batsman (Pawley 1991). In baseball the pitcher throws a ball towards a batter. We can establish that radio rugby commentaries contain many episodes during the calling of which the commentator uses formulae. One of those moves, the lineout, has been documented in detail (Kuiper et al. 2013; Kuiper and Lewis 2013). Here is a further example, the shot at goal. Under two conditions, the awarding of a penalty or converting a try, an attempt may be made to kick the rugby ball over the goal posts, i.e. between the uprights and over the cross bar from a given position.[4] This process, termed *taking a shot at goal*, consists of the following sequence of events:

(1)

1. Kicker places the ball on the kicking tee facing the direction of the kick
2. stands up
3. paces backwards a set number of steps away from the direction of the kick
4. steps sideways a set number of steps
5. looks towards the goalposts
6. strides towards the ball
7. swings the kicking leg
8. strikes the ball.
9. The ball is elevated in the direction of the goal posts.
10. The ball either crosses between the goal posts and over the cross bar or not.

As with the lineout episode not all these sub-episodes receive commentary. A typical commentary taken from the New Zealand commentary transcript with formulae underlined follows:

---

4   Taking a shot at goal is different from a field goal, or drop goal, where a player attempts to kick the ball between the posts and over the cross bar during play.

(2)

Transcript 1

> *Here's Farrell, <u>dead in front</u>.*
> *22 metre mark.*
> *He's maybe half a metre inside that,*
> *is he?*
> *<u>Rocks his hips.</u>*
> *<u>Sways his body.</u>*
> *<u>Leers at the goalpost</u> away to the southern end.*
> *<u>Now he steps back</u>*
> *<u>Straightens the body</u>*
> *<u>Brings the right leg through</u>*
> *And, as he invariably does, smacks it <u>straight down the middle</u>.*

An example from the United Kingdom commentary depicts the action more concisely:

(3)

Transcript 2

> *And the Lions have their first <u>kick at goal</u>*
> *Owen Farrell <u>steps forward</u>*
> *Right footed*
> *It <u>sails between the uprights</u> into the Lion's fans,*
> *behind the posts away to our left-hand side*

Formulae related to the move of tackling a player from the other team include: *be driven to the ground, be driven into the turf, be wrestled to the ground, be sunk to the ground, be brought to the ground*. Formulae related to the forwards acting as a unit to move the ball forward include: *looking to drive, to drive it up*. The reverse move where forwards are being pushed in the opposite direction by their opponents: *be driven backwards*. When kicking the ball, the kicker *put it down the touchline/ middle of the pitch/right hand side of the pitch* (UK commentary). Taking a catch when the ball has been kicked high often begins with *coming forward is (name of player), coming after it is (name of player)*. When a ball which has been kicked lands on the ground, the New Zealand commentator often asks *Will it sit up (nicely)?* since the bounce of the ball is unpredictable.

This is just a small selection of formulae in regular use but sufficient to suggest that rugby commentary utilizes formulae and may thus be a formulaic genre. However, as we will show later, only one third of the commentary actually relates the ongoing action of the game, i.e. is commentary of currently on-going moves of the game. So only one third of the commentary is subject to the kinds of processing pressures which tend to lead to the selection by speakers of formulae.[5] The rest is commentary on the events which have happened. The traditional way this separation is made is to term the direct relation of currently ongoing action as play-by-play commentary while the rest is termed color commentary (Holmes 2001). In color commentary there are also formulae since the social constraints of color commentary are that the color commentary should deal with the events which have preceded the commentary and which will have contained the kinds of conventional moves that are associated with formulae. On occasion, however, there is time for originality, which is not possible in play-by-play mode, which is produced under time pressure.

(4)

Transcript 3 (NZ commentary)

> *There is a dude wearing a bane mask walks up the concourse with four beers in his hands. God I love Wellington.*

There may also be time to air obscure statistics:

(5)

Transcript 4 (UK commentary)

> *There is only one player in the 23 who hasn't scored an international point...*
> *There hasn't been a test match team who has managed to put 23 point scorers as a group.*

Third, a genre has a place in particular social niche (Hanks 1987). The genre of obituaries has a place in newspapers. Minutes of a previous meeting belong in the papers of a committee meeting. It is clear that radio sports commentary occupies such a niche. It has social conventions surrounding its broadcast and it fits with other types of sports reportage such as television commentary, press reports, and blog commentary within a broader sphere of sports culture.

We take it therefore that radio commentary of rugby union football is oral, formulaic, and a genre.

---

[5] We chose radio commentary because this puts greater pressure on speakers during play-by-play periods because silence is not an option.

2. Rugby Union as a Slow Sport

The intricacies of rugby union football are well outlined in the entry for rugby union in Wikipedia ("Rugby Union"). However, a few significant properties of the game need to be mentioned for what follows in this chapter. The game is played by two teams of fifteen players. Each team consists of two subsets of players: the forwards, who are often physically large, allocated to various positions and often collectively termed "the pack," and the backs who are the runners and who score most of the points by way of tries or successful kicks at goal.

In order to understand the way in which commentaries of sport are constructed it is important to note the perceptual nature of the speed at which the sport is seen as being played. In previous work it has been noted that some sports are slow while others are fast. This feature refers to the rate at which perceptually significant episodes occur. In horse racing, the rate is seen as high. In association football the pace is a little slower but breaks in play are infrequent. Even a throw-in in football takes a mere few seconds. In test cricket there are short periods when there is a lot of action while there are long periods when little of note happens (Kuiper et al. 2017). In rugby union football there are "moves" that are slow, such as rucks when the ball disappears beneath a stack of forwards, while passing moves among the backs where the ball passes quickly from one player to another are rapid. There are also long breaks between some moves, for example, when a scrum goes down or players gather for a lineout. So significant episodes occur in bursts, as also happens in cricket. This gives a good deal of time for color commentary as indicated below.

3. Radio Rugby Union Football Commentary as a Co-Constructed Narrative

Unlike the bards who composed oral heroic poetry and unlike horse-racing commentators, rugby union radio commentators build their discourse in teams, i.e. they co-construct their narratives. Why is this? The main reason is that the action that must be provided with commentary constitutes only a third of the commentary. This is shown in Table 1.

The ratio of play-by-play vs color is about 1:2. Comparing the NZ and UK commentary teams use of these two modes of commentary results in the chi-square statistic of 0.0656.[6] The *p*-value is 0.79779. This result is *not* significant

---

[6] Chi squared testing shows, for two or more variables, in this particular case the first variable being the New Zealand or UK commentary teams, and the second being their use of play-by-play versus color commentary, whether the differences between the two teams' use of play-by-play and color commentary differ significantly. The number of times each commentary

	play-by-play	color commentary	totals
NZ	1276	2311	3587
UK	1135	2029	3164
Totals	2411	4340	6751

Table 1. Play-by-play vs color in radio rugby commentary
(the units of analysis are explained in section 4.2)

at $p < 0.05$. The chi-squared result shows that there is no significant difference between the NZ and UK commentary teams as regards the ratio of play-by-play and color commentary.

In Tables 2 and 3 the commentators are reported as having one of three roles, the play-by-play commentator and two different kinds of color commentator, expert commentator(s) and sideline commentator, as seen in Table 2 for the NZ commentary and Table 3 for the UK commentary.

While an investigation of the co-construction in the two commentary traditions is beyond the scope of this chapter, it is clear from Tables 2 and 3 that there are significant differences in the way the two teams allocate the co-constructional commentary roles.

4. Method

4.1 The data set

The data on which this study is based consists of two transcribed radio commentaries of a test match in the series between the British and Irish Lions and the New Zealand All Blacks, played in New Zealand between June and July of 2017. While the games themselves have a running time of eighty minutes, breaks in

---

team uses both commentary modes is tested by the chi squared equation and gives a resulting number, the *p* value, which shows whether the differences are significant or not. The level of significance can also be assessed at different values (more or less demanding), the standard one being 0.05 (5%) which we have used in all cases. Another way to look at the way the chi squared statistic works is to suppose that we propose a hypothesis that the two commentary teams are going to utilize play-by-play and color commentary in very much the same way given that they are providing commentary on the same game. The chi squared test shows that our hypothesis is corroborated. There is no statistically significant difference between the two commentary teams in their use of play-by-play and color commentary.

	Play-by-play commentator Nigel Yalden	Expert commentator Ross Bond	Sideline commentator Daniel McHardy
Play-by-play	32.9%	0.5%	2.2%
Color	32.3%	13.1%	19%

Table 2. Co-construction of New Zealand rugby commentary.

	Play-by-Play Andrew MacKenna	Expert 1 Ben Kay	Expert 2 Shane Williams	Expert 3 James Haskill	Sideline Russell Hargreaves
Play-by-play	35.6%	0.1%	2.2%	0%	0%
Color	26.5%	14.1%	9.1%	12.0%	2.7%

Table 3. Co-construction of United Kingdom rugby commentary.

play when the clock is stopped mean that the commentaries are just over two hours. One commentary was by the commentary team accompanying the tour and employed by talkSPORT in the United Kingdom. The other was the RadioNZ Sport team from New Zealand.

Each commentary team had a play-by-play commentator, Andrew McKenna for talkSPORT and Nigel Yalden for RadioNZ Sport, as well as expert comments (color) commentators, Shane Williams, Ben Kay, and James Hassel for talkSPORT, and Ross Bond for RadioNZ Sport, and sideline commentators Russ Hargreaves for talkSPORT and Daniel McHardy for RadioNZ Sport. Andrew McKenna and Nigel Yalden are professional play-by-play commentators.

4.2 Segmentation

The transcripts were subdivided into clauses and, where there was no clause in an utterance, phrases for ease of later data coding and analysis. Each verb-based construction was given a separate cell as were small clauses where the verb was "understood" from context as were pro drop clauses.[7] Noun phrases such as the names of players, where they were not part of a clause, and interjections such

---

[7] A pro drop clause has a missing subject.

as *Gee*, *Yea*, and *Ooh* were given a separate cell. Little hangs on the exact nature of the units of analysis since this division was mainly for coding convenience. The numbers and percentages in the text and tables are in terms of these units of analysis. Each match yielded around 3,500 units of analysis.

The New Zealand commentary was transcribed by the first author and the British commentary by the second author. Coding was checked by both authors.

4.3 Coding

Each segment of the transcript was coded for the speaker who produced it. The content was coded for whether it was in play-by-play or color mode. Play-by-play was coded as such only if the segment dealt with what was actually happening at the time. So, for example, commentary of replays on television monitors where past actions were related was not coded as play-by-play. All "strong" modifiers (see below) were coded for whether they involved positive (praise) or negative (blame) evaluation. Praise was considered to be expressions of "admiration or approval of the achievements or characteristics of a person or thing" (*Cambridge Dictionary*, s.v. "praise") and blame for expressions in which "someone [...] did something wrong or is responsible for something bad happening" (*Cambridge Dictionary*, s.v. "blame"). The team which received praise or blame was noted, along with the actual modifier and whether the head of the modification was an entity or an action.

5. Modifiers and Epithets

Within the tradition of research begun by Milman Parry and Albert Bates Lord, epithets play a significant role (Parry 1928; Taylor 1990).[8] The heroes in formulaic epics such as the *Iliad* and *Beowulf* had the tales pertaining to their exploits told long after they were dead. The bards who sang of their exploits were thus able to embroider the tales as they wished and as their tradition allowed. The heroes were known to both the audience and the singer with the tales of their deeds also communally known. One of the features of the *Iliad* and *Odyssey* is the use of epithets, which were permanent attributes of heroes such as Achilles, *swift-footed Achilles*, of entities such as the *wine-dark sea*, etc. It is not our purpose to review the many studies of such epithets. However, we will make use of a distinction made by Paul Beekman Taylor who notes that, "[b]esides the customary division of epithets into identifications of family, social rank, and

---

[8] The use of fixed Homeric epithets echoes through into modern poetry in the last line of W. H. Auden's *Shield of Achilles* who calls Achilles not *the fleet footed Achilles* but *the strong, iron-hearted, man-slaying Achilles*.

personal accomplishment, epithets can be profitably classed as either "light" or "heavy"; that is, as either neutral and descriptive, or affective and critical" (Taylor 1990:195).

It is our purpose to explore the use of epithets, if there are any, and modifiers in general in a contemporary vernacular oral tradition and in a linguistic rather than a literary framework.

In many accounts of the syntax of human languages it is conventional to make a distinction between heads of a phrase and modifiers within the phrase. Within noun phrases the noun is the head, the essential part of speech without which there would be no noun phrase. Within such a phrase there can be optional modifiers. These conventionally have the function of narrowing the denotation of the phrase if the head noun is a common noun. So, for example, *a red ball* has a narrower denotation than *a ball*, i.e. *red ball* denotes a subset of the set denoted by *ball*. *The man in the moon* has a narrower denotation than *the man*. However, in the case of proper nouns, modifiers do not usually change the denotation of the head noun. *Red-headed Captain James Cook* denotes only James Cook (unless there are two or more Captain James Cooks). The modifier provides only an additional property. One class of modifiers are adjective phrases whose head word is an adjective (traditionally also termed "epithets"). A subclass of such epithets are fixed Homeric epithets, many but not all of which are adjectives. Parry (1928) also identifies generic epithets which are used more generally.[9] Some epithets are apositional noun phrase modifiers such as *son of Atreus*. If we look at fixed Homeric epithets for their criterial features, they have a non-narrowing denotational property perforce where they are employed as modifiers of proper nouns. *Bright-eyed Athena* has the same denotation as *Athena*. This property extends to the way in which Homeric epithets are used with common nouns. Wine-dark is an invariant property of sea not a modifier to distinguish one sea from another. The dawn is conventionally (and maybe perpetually) rosy-fingered. A further significant property of fixed Homeric epithets is that they are unique identifiers in that they apply to no other than their conventional head noun. Only Achilles is fleet-footed. Only the dawn is rosy-fingered. Let us suppose these properties of modifiers in general are able to be modelled as distinctive features.

(6)

Modifiers:

Head noun is a proper noun ±
Modifier alters denotation ±
Modifier is a unique identifier ±

---

[9] See Reichl (this volume) for further discussion.

A fixed Homeric epithet has the features: [±proper, -denotation narrowing, +unique identifier]. A general Homeric epithet has the features: [±proper, -denotation narrowing, -unique identifier].

Our contemporary bards, like Homer, make a living by the telling of tales, sometimes in addition to other professions. Sports commentators do not tell the tales of the heroes of the past. They relate the doings of the heroes of the present as they are performing their heroic deeds. This places different constraints on the commentators than those operating on traditional singers of tales, including not having to compose in metrical verse. Notwithstanding the differences in composition, the possibilities available to sports commentators may mean that some heroes might come to have associated conventional epithets or that there are conventional expressions (formulae) which have epithets inserted in them, as noted above.

Why have we chosen radio commentary to study modifiers? Since there is time in radio commentaries of rugby football to evaluate both the way the game is being played and the way in which individual players are performing, commentators make use of this time to express opinions on both the way the game is being played, the contribution of individual players, and even the refereeing; this is in contrast with horse-race callers who do not have time and do not express affective stances during the calling of a race. There is also an expectation on the part of the community of speakers and listeners that commentators will do this. It is part of the commentator's job. Since radio listeners cannot see the game being played, it is important to them to know how well the game is being played. Again, by contrast, there is no such expectation for horse-racing commentary, although race callers will evaluate the performance of horses and riders after the race has concluded when they have time to do so.

Our leading hypotheses relating to the function of modifiers in commentary are thus the following:

1. Given the transitory nature of the fame of sporting heroes and the fact that the tales of their individual actions are seldom repeated in a retelling of an event, few if any will have fixed (Homeric) epithets associated with them.

2. Given the enduring nature of the moves of the game, fixed conventional epithets might be expected for these.

There is a further aspect of the use of epithets which is of interest. While epithets can, as Taylor (1990) states, express physical, psychological, social, attitudinal, and many other aspects of a hero's nature, they can also express the narrator's attitude to the hero and his actions by way of positive or negative affect with "heavy" epithets. The narrator may admire or despise the hero. As well as denoting characteristics of the hero, "heavy" epithets can also denote the actions of heroes in the same way. We will investigate how our bards utilize these two options, those associated with the heroes and other entities and those associated with actions. Our hypothesis is that:

3.   Sports commentary, since it follows the action, will devote more affective modifiers to actions than to entities.

Given the time pressure the commentator is under, a further factor of note is the influence of the events being narrated. When immediate narration is taking place, i.e. the commentator is in play-by-play mode, it is less likely that modifiers will be used. This follows from J. Lachlan MacKenzie's generalization that there is a positive correlation between the grammatical complexity of the commentators' call and the degree of time pressure under which (s)he is operating at any specific juncture of the broadcast, to the effect that the greater the pressure on the commentator at any particular point in time, the simpler the syntax of the commentary becomes (Mackenzie 2005).

We investigate whether this generalization has an effect on the use of modifiers in commentary speech and hypothesize that:

4.   Color commentary will contain more modifiers than play-by-play commentary.

It is also not *a priori* clear whether tellers of tales will, on balance, be more likely to exhibit positive or negative effect towards heroes and their actions. We will investigate this hypothesis by looking at how the commentary teams praise and blame players and their actions. Given that the commentary is of sports heroes and their deeds our next hypothesis is that:

5.   Praise and blame will be allocated towards positive affect in rugby union sports commentary.

Finally, we will address the question of commentator bias, which has received attention in the literature. Bias can be of many types. Jacco van Sterkenburg, Annelies Knoppers, and Sonja de Leeuw (2012) investigate racial and ethnic bias in Dutch association football commentary. Pia Lundquist Wanneberg (2011) notes that the print media have sexualized views of women's sport. Susan Tyler Eastman and Andrew C. Billings (2001) investigate commentary bias for the factors of race and gender. Olan K. M. Scott, Brad Hill, and Dwight Zakus (2014) provide a detailed content analysis of commentary speech showing that particular properties of players and teams are drawn attention to, presumably at the expense of others. Andrew C. Billings and Fabio Tambosi (2004) explore "home team bias." "Home team bias" is a further focus of our analysis of modifiers. We will take it that the UK commentary team has the British and Irish Lions as their home team (even though they are not playing at home). We will investigate home team bias in the use of modifiers and hypothesize that:

6. Home team bias will be apparent in the use of modifiers.

6. Results: Modifiers in Radio Rugby Union Commentary

We have found no fixed Homeric epithets in the commentaries. There may be one that was in use previously in the case of the New Zealand All Black, Colin Meads, who was often referred to by his nickname "Pinetree" as "Pinetree Meads." This meets the criteria [+proper noun head, -denotation narrowing, +unique identifier]. But he was just called *Meads* in commentary speech. The closest modifier to a Homeric epithet in the commentary data is the adjective *big* which is used non-uniquely of a number of forwards, e.g. *big Ardie, big Brodie, big Owen Franks*. The only modifier used in this way is *big. Big* has the distinctive feature properties of [+proper noun head, -denotation narrowing, -unique identifier] similar to a general Homeric epithet.

There appear to be no Homeric epithets in use devoted to ritual events, i.e. set plays, notwithstanding such events making frequent appearance in any one game and in the historical evolution of the sport.

Turning now to "strong" modifiers, those expressing praise or blame, we find them distributed as in Tables 4 and 5. We have included in this count any expression which is "strong" including both single word modifiers and "phrasal" modifiers, namely phrases and clauses. Note that affective modifiers occur in about one in ten units of analysis.[10]

The chi-square statistic is 27.2904. The p-value is < 0.00001. This result is significant at $p < 0.05$, showing that the ratio of praise to blame in single word modifiers and phrasal modifiers in the NZ commentary is significantly different. There is a higher proportion of blame modifiers being expressed by phrasal modifiers than in the figures for single word modifiers. For the UK, the chi squared statistic 16.7774 and p-value of 0.00042 is significant at $p < 0.05$. The UK commentary team has a higher proportion of blame being expressed by phrasal modifiers, as does the NZ commentary team.

The significantly higher proportion of phrasal modifiers being used to express blame is probably not surprising, given the elite skill level of these teams.

---

[10] Note that we are not here counting formulae (phrasal lexical items) with a view to establishing whether or not our texts are formulaic. We are counting only modifiers.

Single word modifiers	210	34	244
Phrasal modifiers	43	31	74
Totals	253	65	318

Table 4. Affect by modifier type in NZ commentary.

Single word modifiers	158	31	189
Phrasal modifiers	75	44	119
Totals	233	75	308

Table 5. Affect by modifier type in the UK commentary.

Alongside this, the overall preference in "strong" modifiers towards praising good play may be the simple ease with which something can be said to be *good* or *great*. These were the two most common positive single word modifiers used by the NZ and UK teams, being used over sixty-eight and forty-eight times, respectively, in the commentaries. By contrast, there were no words in common between even the four most common single-word modifiers expressing blame in the NZ (*poor, dumb, clumsy, yawning*) and UK (*awful, cynical, terrible, confusion*) commentaries. Adding to this is the use of phrases to make the blame less direct, and perhaps more palatable for their listeners who may be fans. An example from the UK commentary is of a player's mistake being "in the unforced errors category," and another in the NZ commentary who "doesn't have his kicking boots on." The NZ team could also be playful in blame, when they describe slow moving forwards who "wander over like a herd of Friesians going in for milking on a Sunday morning."

Do commentators of radio rugby union commentary devote more affect to actions than to entities as proposed in hypothesis 3? Table 6 shows that this is the case.

The chi-square statistic is 1.3476. The p-value is 0.245698. The result is not significant at $p < 0.05$. There is no significant difference between the commentary teams in the ratio of entities to actions being the subject of the modifier. The overall ratio is around 1:3 in favor of actions.

NZ	70	248	318
UK	80	228	308
Totals	150	476	626

Table 6. Affective modifiers devoted to actions and entities.

	Play-by-Play Commentary		Totals	Color commentary		Totals
	praise	*blame*		*praise*	*blame*	
NZ	51	7	58	202	58	260
UK	60	11	71	173	64	237
Totals	111	18	129	375	122	497

Table 7. Distribution of "strong" modifiers by commentary mode.

What of the distribution of affect by commentary mode? Given that the ratio of play-by-play to color commentary is about 1:2, Table 7 shows that "strong" modifiers are over-represented in color commentary as predicted by MacKenzie's generalization.

For a comparison between the allocation of praise and blame in play-by-play as opposed to color commentary in the two commentaries combined, the chi-square statistic is 3.9976 and the p-value is 0.261719. This result is *not* significant at $p < 0.05$. This shows that the influence of commentary mode does not significantly differ with respect to the amount of affective modification which takes place in each.

Are the commentary teams more prone to being censorious than they are to be affectively positive? Table 8 shows that there is a strong bias toward positive affect in the ratio of about 5:1. This may well be because at this international level play is recognized as superior by the commentators in a series that involves many of the best rugby players in the game.

The comparison between the ratio of praise to blame for the two commentary traditions presented in Table 8 shows that there is no significant difference between the two.

	Praise	Blame	Totals
NZ	253	65	318
UK	233	75	308
Totals	486	140	626

Table 8. Affect in modifiers for two commentary traditions.

Commentry to...	Home Team		Other Team	
	praise	blame	praise	blame
UK Commentary Team	139	40	80	27
NZ Commentary Team	110	26	120	35
Totals	250	66	200	62

Table 9. Home team bias in modifier affect.

The chi-square statistic is 3.1779. The p-value is 0.240453. This result is *not* significant at $p < 0.05$ showing that there is no difference in the ratio of praise to blame between the two teams of commentators: both are more likely to praise than to blame.

What of home team bias? Results for this are shown in Table 9. Here, the comparison is between the praise and blame of the commentators' respective "home teams" with that they offer for the other team. The chi square tests were conducted for each commentary team, but no significant differences were found in either the UK commentary team ($\chi^2 = 0.3112, p = 0.5769$) or the NZ team ($\chi^2 = 0.5243, p = 0.4690$). It seems there is no statistical difference between praise and blame the commentaries use with either team.

This is not to say that there is no difference in the way in the use of praise and blame between the two teams, which does show a different bias. When the respective counts of praise and blame of their home team and the other team by one commentary team is compared to the other, the relationship is significant at $p < 0.05$ (χ^2 = 15.3373, p = 0. 00155). The use of praise and blame modifiers by the NZ and UK commentary teams differ significantly. The markedly contrasting ways the commentary teams used praise and blame with respect to their home team can be seen in Table 9. The UK team praised their team more and blamed their home team less, as might be expected for UK commentators calling a game involving the Lions. However, the NZ team surprisingly praised the other team more and blamed the other team less than their home team.

Various explanations can be put forward for this unexpected finding. It may be postulated that it is the unique circumstances arising from the intersection of those particular commentators' individual communication styles and the action they were observing that resulted in that particular co-constructed sample. Contributing to this may be the commentators' positioning related to the status of rugby as the national sport of New Zealand with the All Blacks rated internationally as the number one team, against the Lions as the strongest opposition they could hope to meet. Praising the Lions and blaming the All Blacks may be how the commentators build drama into the commentary for the edification of their home audience. However, this finding demands further research to prove that it is not an aberration, and a wider perspective to tease out the implications.

7. Discussion

The definitions which we have made for modifiers including Homeric epithets have enabled us to focus in detail on how such modifiers contribute to an understanding of the ways in which oral-formulaic narrators contribute affect to a narrative. Specifically, we have explored a number of ways of understanding "strong" modifiers in a vernacular oral-formulaic genre. These methods use as data a reasonably large text corpus from two oral traditions and the investigation is hypothesis-driven. Such methods can be applied to other oral-formulaic genres including those performed by traditional singers of tales. For instance, they could be applied to South Slavic epic to see if home team bias exists as between Christian and Muslim bards. One of Albert Lord's singers sang both Christian and Muslim traditional epics. Was the distribution of "strong" modifiers different in each? That our approach has been numerical has allowed us to test for the reliability of our conclusions. We intend to broaden our corpus to investigate in greater detail whether the two commentary traditions have different formulaic inventories since, notwithstanding the fact that the game of rugby union is played in both the United Kingdom and New Zealand, it is likely that the oral traditions for its commentary have been acquired in relative isolation of each other. By interrogating a larger data set in future work we want to follow up our proposal that the two commentary teams have different co-constructional styles for producing their narratives. Again, such findings have relevance to the study of oral traditions in general. The approach we have taken will also allow us to look at lexical choice in the two commentary teams, and to see whether there is lexical innovation.

8. Conclusion

In this study we have examined the transcripts of commentaries made by two different teams of radio commentators. We have shown that such texts instantiate an oral-formulaic genre. We have defined a range of modifiers including Homeric epithets in a distinctive feature style. This has allowed us to investigate a number of hypotheses relating to the occurrence of "strong" modifiers, namely modifiers that express affect, in this genre. The following hypotheses have received corroboration. Traditional Homeric fixed epithets are not in evidence either as modifiers of entities, such as people, or of actions such as kicking goals. While it is unlikely that there should be such Homeric epithets associated with individual players, given their transitory presence in the game, we would have predicted that set moves which often recur might have acquired Homeric fixed epithets over the time that radio commentaries of rugby football have been produced. However, that has not taken place and we have no idea why not. We have also shown that affective modification in general is found more in evidence in the color commentary than in the play-by-play commentary because the action during play-by-play proceeds at a rate where syntactic simplification, which includes the non-appearance of optional modifiers, action which is subject to MacKenzie's generalization, namely that the faster the action proceeds the more simplification there will be.

Turning now to "strong" modifiers, praise and blame for particular players or related events are not evenly distributed. Commentators are much more likely to praise teams, players and their actions than to blame them or their actions for poor play. Differences emerge in how "strong" modifiers express praise and blame, with phrases being significantly more likely to be used to express blame than praise by both commentary teams. This is likely due to the quality of play and the easy use of single words to express it. Blame, on the other hand, is more likely to involve mitigation and longer expressions that, for example, involve humor. As for home team bias, neither of the commentary teams showed significant bias with respect to the praise and blame for their home or the other team. However, the two commentary teams showed significantly different patterns of use: the UK team favoring their own side with more praise and less blame, whereas the NZ commentators praised the other team more and blamed them less than their home team, a finding that demands further research to confirm.

Since affect is commonly carried in a range of modifiers, we have suggested that the methodology we have employed in this study could be useful in exploring the ways in which affect is distributed in other narrative oral-formulaic genres.

References

Allardice, A. 1926. First radio rugby commentary in New Zealand. https://teara.govt .nz/en/speech/42794/allan-allardyce-on-making-the-first-live-rugby-commentary-in-1926.

Billings, A. C., and Tambosi, F. 2004. "Portraying the United States vs Portraying a Champion: US Network Bias in the 2002 World Cup." *International Journal for the Sociology of Sport* 39(2):157–165.

Burger, H. 2010. *Phraseologie: Eine Einführung am Beispiel des Deutschen*, 4 ed. Berlin.

Cambridge Dictionary. https://dictionary.cambridge.org/dictionary/english/.

Eastman, S. T., and Billings, A. C. 2001. "Biased Voices of Sports: Racial and Gender Stereotyping in College Basketball Announcing." *The Howard Journal of Communication* 12:183–201.

Hanks, W. F. 1987. "Discourse Genres in a Theory of Practice." *American Ethnologist* 14(4):668–692.

Holmes, J. 2001. *An Introduction to Sociolinguistics*. London.

Kuiper, K. 1996. *Smooth Talkers: The Linguistic Performance of Auctioneers and Sportscasters*. Mahwah, NJ.

———. 2000. "On the Linguistic Properties of Formulaic Speech." *Oral Tradition* 15(2):279–305.

———. 2009. *Formulaic Genres*. Basingstoke.

Kuiper, K., Bimesl, N., Kempen, G., and Ogino, M. 2017. "Initial vs. Non-Initial Placement of Agent Constructions in Spoken Clauses: A Corpus-Based Study of Language Production under Time Pressure." *Language Sciences* 64:16–33.

Kuiper, K., King, J., and Culshaw, D. 2013. "Whence Maori Rugby Commentary?" *He hiringa, he pūmanawa: Studies on the Māori Language* (eds. A. Onysko, M. Degani, and J. King) 149–179. Wellington.

Kuiper, K., and Lewis, R. 2013. "The Effect of the Broadcast Medium on the Language of Radio and Television Sports Commentary Genres: The Rugby Union Lineout." *Journal of Sports Media* 8(2):31–52.

Lord, A. B. 1960. *The Singer of Tales*. Cambridge, MA.

Mackenzie, J. L. 2005. "Incremental Functional Grammar and the Language of Football Commentary." *The Dynamics of Language Use: Functional and Contrastive Perspectives* (eds. C. S. Butler, M. de L. A. Gómez-González, and S. M. Dorval-Suárez) 113–128. Amsterdam.

Mel'čuk, I. 1995. "Phrasemes in Language and Phraseology in Linguistics." *Idioms: Structural and Psychological Perspectives* (eds. M. Everaert, E.-J. van der Linden, A. Schenk, and R. Schroeder) 167–232. Hillsdale, N.J.

Parry, M. 1928. *L'Épithète traditionelle dans Homère: Essai sur un problème de style homérique.* Paris.

Pawley, A. 1991. "How to Talk Cricket." *Currents in Pacific Linguistics: Papers in Austronesian Languages and Ethnolinguistics in Honour of George W. Grace* (ed. R. Blust) 339–368. Honolulu.

Sailer, M. 2013. "Idiom and Phraseology." http://www.oxfordbibliographies.com/view/document/obo-9780199772810/obo-9780199772810-0137.xml?rskey=a3XAUO&result=1&q=Sailer#firstMatch.

Scott, O. K. M., Hill, B., and Zakus, D. 2014. "Framing the 2007 National Basketball Association Finals: An Analysis of Commentator Discourse." *International Review for the Sociology of Sport* 49(6):728–744.

Taylor, P. B. 1990. "The Epithetical Style of *Beowulf.*" *Neuphilologische Mitteilungen* 91(2):195–206.

van Sterkenburg, J., Knoppers, A., and de Leeuw, S. 2012. "Constructing Racial/Ethnic Difference in and through Dutch Televised Soccer Commentary." *Journal of Sport and Social Issues* 36(4):422–442.

Wanneberg, P. L. 2011. "The Sexualization of Sport: A Gender Analysis of Swedish Elite Sport from 1967 to the Present Day." *European Journal of Women's Studies* 18(3):265–278.

Wray, A. 2002. *Formulaic Language and the Lexicon.* Cambridge.

9

From Motif to Multiword Expression

The Development of Formulaic Language in Gaelic Traditional Narrative

WILLIAM LAMB, UNIVERSITY OF EDINBURGH

A S THE PRESENT VOLUME DEMONSTRATES, research on formulaic language is vital, growing, and interdisciplinary. Little is known, however, about how such phraseology develops in the first place (see Pawley 2007). Some have suggested that formulas typically arise in recurrent situations (Coulmas 1981:2), such as greeting acquaintances or conducting supermarket transactions (Kuiper 2009:ch. 6). Presumably, these situations cue and constrain our communications and how we express them. Clearly, some themes of communication—or what are called here *discourse tropes*[1]—are more amenable to formulaic expression than others. For example, the tropes of everyday conversation tend to be associated with formulaic language (e.g. GREET FRIEND INFORMALLY:[2] *hi, how're you doing?*), but those associated with more novel, general, or informational purposes (e.g. INTRODUCE RESEARCH TOPIC TO VARIED AUDIENCE) may be less so.

We can imagine that when a new situation or communicative need arises and recurs in a community of speakers, the once idiosyncratic phrases associated with it may spread and crystallize. Through repetition, these phrases can become useful, group-vetted solutions for expressing particular discourse

---

[1] The term *discourse trope* is meant to refer to the semantic component of a unit of utterance, or roughly what is encoded by surface language. It is not bound by limits of scope or complexity. This allows it to include what is expressed by a single formula, or by potentially more complex units. Such conceptual breadth is necessary for the present pilot study, which attempts to relate the semantics and formulaicity of traditional narrative to other language domains.

[2] In the main text, discourse tropes are in small caps and formulas are in italics.

tropes, to the extent that we may refer to them as *conventionalized formulas*. Yet, while repetition may be necessary for formulaic language to develop and conventionalize in this way, it seems unlikely to be sufficient in all cases.

Another factor that may be instrumental in formulaicity is *semantic distinctiveness*, which describes the extent to which a discourse trope is set apart from others. This distinctiveness may be situation-specific, such as in a trope like INITIATE FORMAL PUBLIC ADDRESS. Relatively few individuals will ever deliver a formal public address. The distinctiveness of the occasion may explain why certain phrases index it so strongly, such as *Good evening, ladies and gentlemen*. This formula—or something similar—must have been uttered by a single individual at some point and subsequently conventionalized. It does not seem particularly repetitive, but it is semantically distinct. Similarly, Jonathan Roper (this volume) suggests that it is the "oddness" and "very unusualness" of *Once upon a time* that makes it so effective as a storytelling boundary marker. We can observe that the underlying trope, SIGNIFY BEGINNING OF WONDER TALE, is also distinctive in terms of its place in human communication. Citing J. B. Hainsworth (1968:25) and Eila Stepanova (2014:86), Frog (2021) states that the extent to which an individual formula varies in form correlates positively with its range of usage. The corollary of this is that the more restrictive the range of usage, the more likely it is that the language associated it will be crystallized. This observation is aligned to the claims made for semantic distinctiveness here.

Most of the above tropes are expressed by formulas marking discourse structure, but marking discourse structure is only one aspect of communication. Others tropes may concern discourse-internal messages. Scholars investigating traditional narrative refer to tale-internal tropes—the stuff out of which tales are made (Thompson 1955:7)—as *motifs* (see section 1). Live narrators respond to external circumstances like any participant, but the operant situation for traditional narrative is the story-world itself (Biber and Conrad 2009:132). Due to this, narrative motifs (e.g. GIANT STEALS CHILD THROUGH CHIMNEY) are somewhat different from the tropes we can identify for other registers. Although motifs and discourse tropes both refer to the semantics underlying units of utterance, motifs may be greater in scope and semantic complexity. Yet, motifs themselves vary in complexity (see section 3.1) and this variation allows us to examine two questions relating to formulaicity at large:

- Do semantically distinct motifs correlate more strongly with formulaic language than semantically less distinct ones?
- Or, is bare repetition of motifs the most salient factor for the development and conventionalization of formulaic language?

Allied to semantic distinctiveness is the notion of genre. Some genres, for instance, are clearly more formulaic than others (Kuiper 2009; Kuiper and Leaper, this volume). Citing V. Edwards and T. J. Sienkewicz (1990), Koenraad Kuiper defines a formulaic genre as: "a variety of a language (either spoken or written) which contains discourse structure rules which in turn index formulae for particular roles in the discourse and where a significant amount of the discourse is made up of formulae" (2009: 17). Yet, to what extent can we differentiate genres on the basis of their formulaic qualities (cf. Wray 2008:117)?

The current chapter is an attempt to explore these questions through a case study of Scottish Gaelic traditional narrative, a domain known for its rich formulaicity (Bruford 1966; Lamb 2015). Kevin O'Nolan (1971:236, 243) has previously noted a relationship between motifs and formulas[3] in Gaelic narrative and certain genre differences in formulaicity, but these have yet to be empirically evaluated. The corpus data deployed here (58,779 words) were constructed from a digitized, multi-genre book of orally garnered narratives from the nineteenth century, *More West Highland Tales* (*MWHT*) (MacKay 1940). This source is attractive for our purposes, because it has been independently annotated for motifs by none other than Stith Thompson[4] himself. The principal aim of this chapter is to conduct a preliminary investigation of the correlations between motifs, formula, and genre, contextualized to Gaelic storytelling. In this connection, I propose the concept of *formulaic motif* for a motif conventionally expressed in part or whole through formulaic phraseology in a particular genre or across genres. This is contrasted with *non-formulaic motif* for a motif typically not found to co-occur with formulaic phraseology.

Before proceeding, we should note that the formulas of prose narrative have been understudied to date (Sävborg 2018:51). With few exceptions, most of the research on formulaic language in narration has dealt with metered, epic poetry, such as that in *Beowulf* (Foley 1990), Yugoslavian hero narrative (Lord 2000), and the works of Homer (Parry 1930). This orientation harkens back to Parry's original definition of formula as "a group of words which is regularly employed under the same metrical conditions to express a given essential idea" (1930:80). Parry's protegee, Lord, stressed that formulas in metrical poetry were motivated by the exigencies of composition-in-performance. While this

---

[3] Corresponding observations have been made for verse narration in discussions of the theme in OFT research. From the present perspective, discussions are complicated by the tendency to focus on narrative units associated with co-occurrent phraseology without developing a model for the relationship of such units to formulaic phraseology generally (Foley 1990:ch.7; see also Frog, this volume).

[4] Thompson was a scholar associated with the Historic-Geographic Method and best known for his *Motif-Index of Folk-Literature* (1955–1958).

perspective may be suitable for some types of poetry, it is less so for others, and certainly does not help us to understand how and why prose narrative formulas develop, especially those of literary and sub-literary genres, such as Icelandic sagas (Sävborg 2018:56) and Goidelic hero tales (Bruford 1966). Presumably, they respond to different requirements and develop along different lines. I will touch on some of these divergences throughout this chapter.

Let us begin by evaluating the motif construct, followed by some preparatory considerations about genre and formulaicity in Gaelic narrative.

1. Formulaic Folklore: Motifs and Genres

To examine whether repetitive and semantically distinctive discourse tropes are more likely to be communicated formulaically, it is necessary to separate the tropes from surface expression. For example, the formulas *Back in a sec* and *Please excuse me* are both surface expressions of the trope SIGNIFY INTENTION TO DEPART TEMPORARILY, but they index different levels of formality. On the other hand, formal leave-taking can be encoded both by saying "Please excuse me" and "I hereby signal my intention to temporarily leave, but intend no offense," but the first phrase is formulaic and the second is not. One of the aims of this chapter is to uncover which motifs in Gaelic traditional narrative tend to be communicated formulaically and why. To do this, we must be able to map between motifs and formulas. For a loosely constrained domain (e.g. spontaneous conversation), mapping between formulas and discourse tropes would be difficult to achieve: not only are "discourse trope" and "motif" somewhat vague concepts, especially when not contextualized, but few sources provide the kind of information we seek. The motifs of traditional narrative, however, have been researched extensively, a modicum of agreement exists about them, and different sources are available for exploring their textual distribution.

Stith-Thompson's *Motif-Index of Folk-Literature* (1955–1958) is a six-volume listing of the tropes associated with international traditional narrative. As we are employing a corpus of tales annotated with this resource, we can measure whether motifs observed in the text are more likely to be expressed formulaically when frequent and more semantically distinctive. We can also note whether tales with frequently occurring motifs are generally more formulaic than others. Yet, before doing this, it is important to establish that the motif construct is fit for purpose.

Thompson specifies three types of motifs in his *Index*: 1) actors; 2) items in the background (e.g. a magical object); and 3) actions. Motifs are organized thematically across twenty-three categories, moving from more supernatural tropes to more realistic ones (Conrad 2008:644). An example of an action is

R137: *Mermaid rescues hero (boy) from shipwreck* ("Rewards and punishments" in Thompson 1955–1958). It is worth noting that the motifs included in Thompson's *Index* originate from a fairly wide range of oral literature, as discerned by its subtitle: *A Classification of Narrative Elements in Folk-Tales, Ballads, Myths, Fables, Mediæval Romances, Exempla, Fabliaux, Jest-Books, and Local Legends.*

One of the problems with the motif concept is that no structural criteria exist for distinguishing it, apart from the requirements that it is found in narrative and conveys a thematic element that is usually, but not always, smaller than the tale itself (Jason 2000:22). This fuzziness is evident in Thompson's own description:

> Certain items in narrative keep on being used by story-tellers; they are the stuff out of which tales are made. It makes no difference exactly what they are like; if they are actually useful in the construction of tales, they are considered to be motifs.

> Thompson 1955:7

Like the international tale-type (Uther 2004), the motif is useful for the purposes of taxonomy and comparative study, but is not rigorous in any theoretical sense. As Heda Jason observes, in the *Motif-Index*, full narrative episodes are found alongside single actions and characters (2000:22); the scope of the item is indiscriminate. Although Alan Dundes praised the *Motif-Index* as one of "the most valuable tools in the professional folklorist's arsenal" (1997:195), he criticized the three types as misconceived, because they overlap. For example, an "actor" always implies an accompanying "action" (Dundes 1997:197; cf. Bruford and MacDonald 2003:17). Vladimir Propp himself commented (1968:12–15) that the motif is insensitive to tale structure and too variable. He noted, for example, that a single tale-type may have multiple forms of an antagonist in its different variants: it may be a dragon in one, a falcon in another and a sorcerer in a further tale (Propp 1968:12–15). Yet, as valid as the above criticisms are from the perspective of tale taxonomy and plot structure, they do not weaken our proposal to use the motif to evidence discourse tropes in narrative, at least at this preliminary stage.

Consider, for example, Dundes's and Jason's criticism that motifs are polynomial constructs with indiscriminate scope. When we examine prose narrative formulas, we see that some are short and simple, while others are longer and more complex. At the short and simple end is the epithet, where an actor may be represented in monomial fashion. That is, an epithet—referring to a single actor (i.e. without an action)—can stand alone as a stretch of formulaic language. At the more complicated and lengthier end are the runs that typify Gaelic heroic narrative (see Example 2). For a preliminary study such as this, it is advantageous to use a functional inventory capable of representing what is found in the text—expanding or contracting as necessary—as the motif is able to do. In the tales used here, where a character such as *a' Chailleach Chearc* ('Henwife': a domestic witch) occurs but does not perform an action, it is useful to have recourse to the simple motif G200: *Witch*. On the other hand, if a "Henwife" or another witch carries out an action, we can label it with the accompanying action, e.g. H935: *Witch assigns tasks*. The compounded nature of the motif is not a problem here. In fact, it is beneficial.

Apropos of Propp's criticisms, it is not clear how formulas in traditional tales depend upon and, in turn, influence plot structure. Although it would be interesting to map between Propp's functions and formulaic content,[5] that is not the focus of the current study. Additionally, while motifs may be too variable for a discrete task such as tale classification, it seems useful to understand formulaic language in a less discrete fashion. For example, Wray has discussed conceptualizing it as a continuum (2012:239–240; cf. Lamb 2015:228–232). Until we fathom better what a formula is and is not, we should keep an open mind about its semantic architecture (cf. Wray 2008:99).

Let us now briefly consider the relationship between genre, formulaicity, and formula type. A large body of research (e.g. Biber 1988; Miller and Weinert 1998) has demonstrated how we alter our linguistic output according to non-linguistic factors: "Variability is inherent in human language: people use different linguistic forms on different occasions, and different speakers of a language will say the same thing in different ways" (Biber and Conrad 2009:5). Of course, synonyms—"saying the same thing[s] in different ways"—occur across both simple and phrasal lexemes, but absolute synonyms are rare in natural languages (Lyons 1995:61). One of the reasons for this is that our utterances and what they index change according to context. Interestingly, the greater their association with a context, the greater their indexical potential. Indeed, certain formulas are so tightly bound to a specific context that they uniquely index it. Biber and Conrad (2009:54) term these formulas *register markers*, giving an example of the "count formula" in baseball (e.g. "the count is '0' and '2'," i.e. zero balls and two strikes). Most formulas, however, are not so rigidly bound and can float between language domains to an extent.

In the case of Gaelic traditional narrative, there are genre-sensitive ways for expressing similar motifs. For example, while altercations between protagonists and antagonists occur in both hero tales and international folktales, narrators

---

[5] It may well be the case that the functions identified by Propp for *Märchen* correlate strongly with formulaic language.

tend to express them distinctly in the two genres (see section 3.3 for examples). One of our present objectives is to examine how the genres represented in *MWHT* differ in the types and proportions of formulas that they use.

Alan Bruford (1966:182) and Kevin O'Nolan (1968:18) discuss the overwhelming diversity of formulas found in Gaelic oral tradition, and the ability of expert Gaelic storytellers to artfully draw upon this special, enregistered lexicon.[6] Commonly, it is heard that Gaelic hero tales are more formulaic than other types of oral narrative, but this perspective is not universal amongst Gaelic scholars. One key difference between hero tales and other forms of oral narrative in Gaelic is that the hero tale genre was influenced by a high-register, literary prose tradition (Bruford and MacDonald 2011:15–16; cf. Bruford 1966:1–7 *et passim*); many oral versions of these tales, collected in the nineteenth and twentieth centuries, have precursors in Classical Gaelic[7] manuscripts (Bruford 1966). Due to this connection, I have suggested elsewhere that the oral hero tales might have been transmitted with a quasi-literate aesthetic, detectable in the tales' verbal conservativism (Lamb 2013:172). Bruford and Donald A. MacDonald (2011:17) state that hero tales were so valorized by Gaels that the formulas indexing them began to be used in other types of narrative, such as international folktales, to increase their prestige. Bruford indicates that these formulas were not specific to one genre, and could be "introduced by storytellers into any hero-tale or *märchen* where the appropriate action comes in" (Bruford 1966:36; cf. Zall 2010:214). This is similar to Kuiper's assertion that "speakers will borrow appropriate formulae from elsewhere in their speech repertoire to perform the necessary functions in a formulaic genre" (2009:199). On the other hand, O'Nolan seems to define the hero tale genre, at least in part, by its "extensive formulaic content" (1971:243). This suggests that formulas are more common in hero tales than in other types of oral narrative. So far, no scholar has attempted to empirically discern the differences between hero tales and other narrative genres in terms of their overall formulaicity and the types of formulas occurring in them. Again, doing this one of the objectives of the present chapter.

In section 2, the corpus data is described in more detail, along with the coding procedures and hypotheses that inform this study. The results and discussion are outlined in three subsections (3.1, 3.2, and 3.3), followed by the

---

[6] "If we realize that a storyteller in the heyday of such traditions had a really incredible range of such formulae, we realize that he was speaking a language within a language, but speaking it with exceptional fluency. His artistry would depend on his command of such formulae" (O'Nolan 1968:18).

[7] Classical Gaelic, also known as Early Modern Irish, was a conservative grapholect employed by the Scottish and Irish Gaelic intelligentsia from about the twelfth century (Ó Cuív 1973 [1983]:3) until about the seventeenth (Ireland) and eighteenth (Scotland) centuries.

conclusions in section 4. For reference, all of the data employed are presented in tabular form in the Appendix to this chapter.

2. Methodology

In this section, I describe the corpus in more detail, followed by the procedures for genre classification adopted here. After this, I outline how "formula" was defined for this study. Finally, I provide information on my coding procedures and data structures, and describe the four hypotheses that were tested. The statistical tests and results are described in section 3.

As mentioned above, texts from a PDF of *More West Highland Tales* (MacKay 1940) were used to investigate relationships between motifs, formulas and genres. Two things make *MWHT* attractive for our purposes. First, it represents vernacular nineteenth-century Gaelic narrative, taken down directly from tradition bearers. Second, as mentioned previously, it contains motif annotations by Stith Thompson himself. An alphabetical index at the back of the book provides all of the motifs found, according to the system that Thompson devised (see Thompson 1955–1958). I relied on Thompson's decisions as to what textual elements constituted motifs, but verified all of the annotations used in the dataset. Only recurrent motifs were of interest here; hapax motifs were not useful, as they provide no evidence of being conventionalized in the tradition.

The tales were assigned to one of three genres dependent on their subject matter and whether the tale was accompanied in the text by an Aarne-Thompson (AT) index number. The genres were: 1) hero tales; 2) international tales; and 3) miscellaneous tales. The model for *hero tales* was the five tales in *Sgialachdan Dhunnchaidh* (MacDhòmhnaill and Craig 1950), taken orally from a twentieth-century master storyteller from South Uist: Duncan MacDonald (see Lamb 2012). These tales all adhere to Ó hÓgain's definition of hero tales, as "adventures of some real or imagined warrior of old acting in a pre-medieval or medieval setting" (2006:284). Many of them also occur in imagined or geographical Ireland, and the heroes are often described as sons of Irish or Scandinavian kings. Additional trappings of these tales are references to medieval pursuits, such as playing *tàileasg* ('chess') or *iomain* ('shinty'), and the appearance of stereotyped figures such as *a' Chailleach Chearc* ('the hen-wife'). Where an ATU number was present, the tale was assigned to the *international tale* genre, apart from one instance of a tale being categorized as a hero tale.[8] Finally, the *miscellaneous tale*

---

[8] The exception was *Smeuran dubha 's an Fhaoillteach* ('Bramble Berries in February'). This tale matches the description of ATU 953 rather poorly: it is not a frame tale and it is missing several key motifs (see Uther 2004: I, 592–593). On the other hand, it does resemble a hero tale. For instance, the protagonist is described as the son of the king of Ireland, and specific references

Index #	Description	Pages	Refs	Tales	Formula	Example of Formula
E 55.1.1	Resuscitation by shouting at [...] the bones of the dead	19, 21, 41, 43, 239, 261, 273, 275	8	4	Y	*thòisich na cnàmhan air leantuinn ri chèile* (p 42) ('the bones began to join together')

Figure 1. Except from Datasheet 1.

category was used for narratives that were neither hero tales nor international tales. The tales assigned to it are mostly legends and historical anecdotes.

Formulas were defined as multiword expressions that appear to be prefabricated and conventionalized in the linguistic community (Lamb 2015:227, via Wray 2002:9; cf. Wray 2008:8n). When a formula occurred in more than one tale in *MWHT*, or when it was common to the greater oral tradition, I took this as evidence of conventionalization (cf. Zall 2010:217). For the purposes of this chapter, I did not distinguish between fixed expressions and lexico-grammatical templates,[9] nor between short formulas and longer formula-systems, also known as *runs* (see Bruford 1966:182–209; see also Frog, this volume). Thus, a run was considered to be a single formula. As a consequence of this approach, a small number of motifs occasionally mapped onto different sections of a larger formula-system. The classification of formulas is far from a trivial matter, as demonstrated by Sävborg (2018), and additional distinctions regarding length and plasticity would be useful for future research.

Two datasets, described below, were created to test several hypotheses. The following pieces of information were entered into Datasheet 1—a table of recurrent motifs—by examining the text and Thompson's motif index in *MWHT*:

---

to Ireland occur—e.g. *còig còigean na h-Èireann* ('the five provinces of Ireland')—in addition to medieval Irish life—e.g. *iomain* ('shinty'). The hen-wife character, so common in the hero tale genre (cf. Bruford and MacDonald 2011:452), also appears. Finally, some of the action and formalized dialogue are typical of the hero tale genre, such as *geas* ('be-spelling') sequences (cf. Craig 1944:60; see Ó hÓgáin 2006:265).

[9] Templates are expressions showing a mix of obligatory (closed) and flexible (open) elements, such as the English phrase, *NP put NP on*, where *put* and *on* are obligatory, but the NPs and syntax are flexible: "they *put* a show *on*"; "they *put on* a show."

- Index numbers ("Index #"), descriptions ("Description"), and page numbers ("Pages") of recurrent motifs
- How many times motifs occurred in the text ("Refs"), and in discrete tales ("Tales")
- Whether motif annotations coincided with recognizable formulas in the text ("Formula")
- Excerpts of the formulas themselves ("Example of Formula")

Figure 1 shows the first row of Datasheet 1. One of Thompson's motif annotations can be seen in Figure 2, along with a coincident formula, in highlighted text.

Datasheet 1 was used to test two hypotheses: 1a) that formulaic motifs occur more frequently than non-formulaic ones; and 1b) that formulaic motifs are more semantically distinct than non-formulaic motifs. If support is found for Hypothesis 1a, it would suggest that motifs which frequently occur in Gaelic oral tradition are more likely to be expressed formulaically. This would provide evidence that discourse tropes that recur tend to correlate with the development of formulaic language in a register. If support is found for Hypothesis 1b, this would suggest that repetition is not the only conditioning factor at play in the development of formulaic language and that semantic distinctiveness is also important.

Q 414·3	**Thill an Rìgh Og air ais a rithist far an robh a athair, is thuirt e ris, 'Tha brath air, is mur an innis thu e, beiridh mi ort is loisgidh mi thu, is leigidh mi an luaith leis a' ghaoith—mur an coisinn thu an fhalaire dhomh.'** [a]

Figure 2. Motif annotation and formula in *MWHT*.[10]

Datasheet 2 was compiled by manually reading the *MWHT* text in PDF form and highlighting formulas on the PDF as they occurred, regardless of motif annotations. The text and page information for these formulas was automatically extracted and formatted as a comma-separated (CSV) file. These data captured the full range of formulaic language in *MWHT*, permitting the evaluation of two further hypotheses: that motif-heavy texts also tend to be formulaically dense (Hypothesis 2); and that hero tales are more formulaic than the other types of Gaelic traditional narrative evaluated here, *viz.* international tales and

---

[10] English translation of the highlighted Gaelic text: 'I will burn you, and throw the ash to the wind'.

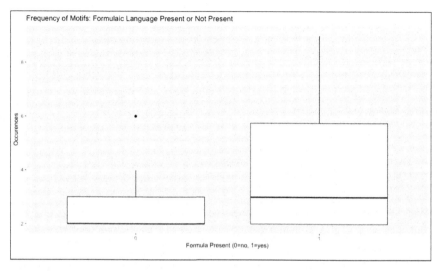

Figure 3. Motifs with and without formulaic coincidence.

miscellaneous tales (Hypothesis 3). Once the raw data had been reviewed, they were imported into R (R Core Team 2017) for further processing and analysis. The raw counts can be seen in the Appendix. To enable inter-genre comparisons, I normalized the data to counts per 1000 words.

In the following section, I describe the statistical tests employed and report the results. The findings should be regarded as preliminary due to the limitations discussed above and the relatively small numbers of texts included. However, support was found for each of the four hypotheses.

3. Results and Discussion

3.1. Differences between formulaic and non-formulaic motifs

To examine Hypothesis 1a, I compared the two groups from Datasheet 1 (i.e. formulaic motifs vs non-formulaic motifs) using a Wilcoxon rank sum test with continuity correction (i.e. the Mann-Whitney). There were 101 instances of recurrent motifs in total across *MWHT*. Thirty of these showed formulaic coincidence and seventy-one did not.

The results of the Wilcoxon test ($W = 651$, $p < 0.001$) indicate that formulaic motifs occur with greater regularity in the sample than non-formulaic ones, as the boxplot in Figure 3 shows. The solid lines in the boxplot represent the median values of occurrence, which were three for the formulaic motif group and two for the non-formulaic ones. As indicated by box heights, formulaic motifs also had a greater interquartile range,[11] suggesting that a greater proportion of the formulaic motifs were very repetitive. The vertical lines and dot above the boxes represent outliers,[12] which are also higher in the formulaic motif group. Although we cannot definitively probe cause and effect here, it does seem that the more frequently a motif is expressed, the more likely it is to be encoded formulaically.[13]

To examine whether formulaic motifs were more semantically specific than non-formulaic ones, I compared the descriptions of the top ten most frequent motifs from the formulaic (Table 1) and non-formulaic groups (Table 2), respectively. The wording of the motif labels was Thompson's, although I confirmed that they accurately described the elements present in the Gaelic formulas.

It is assumed here that the more syntactically complex a motif, the more semantically distinct it is as well. By counting each discrete syntagm (e.g. subject, verb, object), while omitting repeated grammatical categories (e.g. or window$^{\text{oblique noun}}$), conjunctions and prepositions,[14] we can derive a proxy for "semantic distinctiveness."[15] This procedure is illustrated in Figure 4.

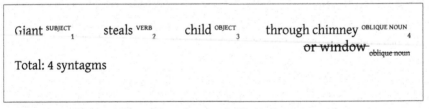

Giant $^{\text{SUBJECT}}_1$ steals $^{\text{VERB}}_2$ child $^{\text{OBJECT}}_3$ through chimney $^{\text{OBLIQUE NOUN}}_4$
~~or window~~ $_{\text{oblique noun}}$

Total: 4 syntagms

Figure 4. Illustration of semantic distinctiveness scoring

Semantic distinctiveness scores are listed under "Syntagms"[16] in Tables 1 and 2. Individual syntagms are marked using subscript numbers in the "Motifs" column of both tables. Based upon this analysis, it seems that the most frequent formulaic motifs ($\bar{x}$ = 3.4 syntagms) are more semantically specific than the most

---

[11] The interquartile range indicates the central 50% of the data, from 25% below the mean (or median, in this case) to 25% above.

[12] Outliers are particularly high or low scores; they lie outside the typical range of the data.

[13] Frog points out that a feedback loop may exist, where a linguistically pre-coded formula is easier to express, interpret and remember as a structured unit. Thereby, it is more appealing to use owing to both communicative and cognitive economy.

[14] Conjunctions and prepositions are semantically thin.

[15] This is similar to Veselovskij's decomposition of themes (see Propp 1968:12).

[16] A syntagm is any syntactic element in an utterance, for example a noun.

Rank	Index	Motifs (annotated with syntagms)	Freq	Tales	Syntagms
1	F360	Malevolent$_1$ or destructive fairy$_2$	9	2	2
2	G261.1	Giant1 steals$_2$ child$_3$ through chimney$_4$ or window	9	2	4
3	E55.1.1	Resuscitation$_1$ by shouting$_2$ at [...] the bones$_3$ of the dead$_4$	8	4	4
4	C650	The one$_1$ compulsory thing$_2$	8	3	2
5	K2155.1	Blood$_1$ smeared$_2$ upon innocent$_3$ person$_4$ (or dog) brings$_5$ accusation$_6$ of murder$_7$	8	3	7
6	H935	Witch$_1$ assigns$_2$ tasks$_3$	6	3	3
7	N2.0.1	Wager$_1$ not agreed$_2$ upon but announced$_3$ after game$_4$	6	3	4
8	G275.3	Witch$_1$ burned$_2$	5	4	2
9	D5.1	Person$_1$ be-spelled$_2$ not to move$_3$	5	3	3
10	Q414.3	Burning$_1$ and scattering$_2$ ashes$_3$	4	3	3
		MEAN	6.8	3.0	3.4

Table 1. The most frequent formulaic motifs.

frequent non-formulaic ones ($\bar{x}$ = 2.3 syntagms). It is also worth noting that they are more repetitive than the non-formulaic motifs ($\bar{x}$ 6.8 vs $\bar{x}$ 4.8).

In principle, motifs expressing a dramatis personae, or motifs that are static nominal categories (i.e. images), equate to a single syntagm and could potentially be regularly expressed through a single formula. Three of the non-formulaic motifs in Table 2 consist of a bare *dramatis persona*: i.e. G200: *Witch*, S31: *Cruel stepmother*, and L10: *Victorious younger son*. It is difficult to imagine how these motifs, on their own, could be communicated in formulaic language

Rank	Index	Motifs (annotated with syntagms)	Freq	Tales	Syntagms
1	G200	Witch$_1$	6	4	1
2	S31	Cruel$_1$ stepmother$_2$	6	4	2
3	D683.2	Transformation$_1$ by witch$_2$	6	3	2
4	G510	Ogre$_1$ killed$_2$	6	3	2
5	L10	Victorious$_1$ youngest son$_2$	4	4	2
6	D131	Transformation$_1$: man$_2$ or woman to horse$_3$ or filly	4	3	3
7	D 113.1	Transformation$_1$: man$_2$ to wolf$_3$	4	1	3
8	H1337	Quest$_1$ for sword$_2$ of light$_3$	4	1	3
9	H1378.1	Quest$_1$ for wood$_2$ that is neither bent$_3$ nor straight	4	1	3
10	D 610	Repeated$_1$ transformations$_2$	4	1	2
		MEAN	4.8	2.5	2.3

Table 2. The most frequent non-formulaic motifs.

in prose, except for the ubiquitous "[wicked] witch."[17] On the other hand, almost all of the frequent formulaic motifs include a subject and a verb, and sometimes an object and other elements, as illustrated in Figure 4. If all motifs equating to static images are removed from the data, the differences between the two groups become even more pronounced. For formulaic motifs, we have 6.1 (Freq), 3.4 (Tales), and 3.8 (Syntagms), and for non-formulaic motifs, 4.6, 1.9, and 2.6, respectively.

---

[17] In some cases, common characters are associated with epithets, but only a few of these remain consistent in Gaelic oral narrative, such as *a' Chailleach Chearc* ('the hen-wife') and *an eachrais-ùrlair* ('domestic witch'). J. F. Campbell provides extensive commentary on the latter character, including its derivation and different forms (*MWHT*:492–499). The general absence of epithets in Gaelic prose narrative suggests that they may have functional differences in prose and metrical poetry. In the latter, formulaic epithets seem to be more common, and their *raison d'être* may stem partly from the need to fill metrical slots, which is irrelevant for prose.

These results suggest that repetitiveness and semantic distinctiveness act together in the development of formulaic expression: the more often that a motif occurs and the more semantically distinctive it is, the more likely it is to be encoded formulaically. It is worth noting, however, that the most frequent formulaic motif in this sample, F360: *Malevolent or destructive fairy*, is semantically bare. Its high frequency is due to the fact that a "wild fairy-woman" is mentioned in one of the most common Gaelic formulas, the *geas* ('be-spelling') formula (see Lamb 2015:238). Yet, a fairy-woman does not play a part in the tales themselves; the associated language of the run is only decorative and incidental. Thus, this does not challenge the proposal that formulas develop from repetitive and semantically distinctive communicative needs. However, it does show that formulas can be linked in an associative framework or *schema* in the minds of participants in an oral tradition (see Rubin 1995:21–24; Lamb 2015:234–235).

3.2. The relationship between overall motif and formula density

Hypothesis 2 attempts to generalize from Hypothesis 1a: I predicted that motif-heavy texts would also be formula-heavy. To examine this, I carried out a test of correlation between the number of recurrent motifs and formulas across the twenty-seven tales examined here (see *MWHT* Data). The data were monotonic, but not normally distributed, so I used a Spearman's rank correlation. The results (r_s = 0.59, p < 0.01) indicate a statistically significant, moderate correlation between the incidence of motifs and formulas across the individual texts. Figure 5 visualizes the result. The regression line represents the expected values given a particular frequency of formulas or motifs in a text. Although this result must be considered preliminary given the small number of texts and formulas investigated, it does appear that motif-heavy texts tend to be formula-heavy, and vice versa.

In Figure 5, it is notable that tales tend to be formulaic or not, and have numerous motifs, or not. It may be the case that over a certain density point, formulas beget other formulas and motifs beget other motifs. Perhaps what we are seeing here is "traditional resonance" in action: the build-up of associative networks or schemas (Foley 2002:134; cf. Lamb 2015:234–235). Yet, most international and miscellaneous tales have few formulas and motifs. Of the six texts that are both motif- and formula-heavy, four are hero tales, but only two are international tales. This suggests that hero tales are inherently more formulaic in Gaelic tradition than international tales, but it begs the question why some international tales are so formulaic and motif-heavy.

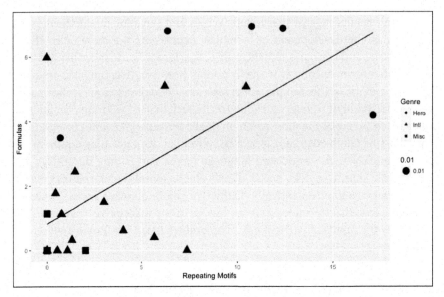

Figure 5. Correlation between formulas and recurring motifs
(frequencies per 1000 words).

3.3. Formulaicity: genre differences

This final results section examines Hypothesis 3; i.e. that hero tales show more formulaicity than international tales or miscellaneous ones. The rationale here was to examine whether related genres can be distinguished according to the proportions and types of their formulaic content. Although it is commonly heard that Gaelic hero tales are more formulaic than other oral narrative genres, one of the most esteemed Gaelic scholars, Alan Bruford, seemed to make no distinction between hero tales and international tales in this regard (1966:36, 182; cf. Ross 1959:10). On the other hand, hero tales often have literary analogues (Bruford 1966), which feature runs resembling the semi-calcified formulas of oral variants. Moreover, hero tales had a more constrained context than international tales in Gaelic tradition. For instance, some individuals in the past would doff their caps before renditions of heroic narrative (Maclean 1959:172; Collinson 1966:49), and most of the recorded hero tales have been narrated by men,[18] suggesting certain gender roles in the tradition. Given these factors, I

---

[18]   The rarity of female hero narrators is encapsulated in the Irish proverb, *tráthaire circe nó fiannaí mná* ('a woman telling hero tales or a crowing hen') (Sayers 1978:ix). Unfortunately, little work

predicted that hero tales would have a higher proportion of formulas[19] than the other two genres explored here.

The data for this part of the investigation came from Dataset 2 (see Appendix). They were not normally distributed, so I opted for a non-parametric measure, the pairwise Wilcoxon rank sum test with continuity correction. The hypothesis was that hero tales would show more formulas than international tales, and international tales more than miscellaneous tales. Accordingly, I used a one-sided test with FDR ("false detection rate") adjustment for multiple comparisons. The results indicated a statistically significant difference between hero tales and international tales ($p_{\text{one-tailed}}$ = 0.025), and also between hero tales and miscellaneous tales ($p_{\text{one-tailed}}$ = 0.025). The difference between international tales and miscellaneous tales was not statistically significant ($p_{\text{one-tailed}}$ = 0.063). Summary statistics for the three tale types are presented below in Table 3 and visualized in Figure 6 as a box and whisker plot.

Thus, formulas are significantly more frequent in hero tales ($\tilde{x}$ = 5.49/1000 words) than in international tales ($\tilde{x}$ = 0.51/1000 words) or miscellaneous tales ($\tilde{x}$ = 0/1000 words). Although formulas do appear in the international tales sampled here, they are far less common than in the hero tales. Considering the outliers in Figure 6, only one of the hero tales is devoid of formulaic language: *Sgeulachd Choise Chéin* ('The Healing of Kane's Foot'). However, the version of this tale included in *MWHT* is a fragment, which is inferior in style, length, and formulaic content to other renditions of the same tale (cf. Lachlan MacNeil's 1870 version in Craig [1950], which runs to eighty-three pages and is highly formulaic). The most formulaic of the international tales is *Mòr Nighean Smùid*, which has 5.99 formulas per 1000 words. This is a short cumulative tale (ATU 20c/2023), which is formulaic by definition.

There are clear differences in formula frequency between hero tales and the other types of tales in this sample. The question remains, how did the formulas themselves differ according to genre? To investigate this, I manually sorted the individual formulas found in the hero tales and international tales into five categories, utilizing a simple taxonomy developed for an earlier publication (Lamb 2015:236). This taxonomy is presented in Table 4 (NB: only top-level classes are used here).

---

has been done on gender roles in Gaelic narrative to date and this gap should be addressed. It is worth noting that heroic ballads were often sung by women (MacInnes 2006:206–207).

[19] Another way to calculate formulaicity would be to count the total number of formulaic words per 1000 words. This could be a useful method for a future study, although it is not immediately clear how to deal with open slots in templates. Additionally, it would defeat comparisons between formulas and motifs, which is crucial here.

Measure	Hero	Int'l	Misc
Min	0.00	0.00	0.00
Q1	3.67	0.00	0.00
Median	5.49	0.51	0.00
Mean	4.72	1.52	0.227
Q3	6.86	1.95	0.00
Max	6.94	5.99	1.14

Table 3. Genre variation in formulaicity—summary statistics
(formulas per 1000 words).

I. Boundary markers
    a. Openings
    b. Closings
II. Character expression and interaction
    a. Greetings and partings
    b. Emotive-expressive language
III. Power transactions
    a. Cursing
    b. Be-spelling
    c. Battle
IV. Descriptions and transitions
    a. Temporal transitions
    b. Geospatial transitions
    c. Descriptions (e.g. arming)
V. (Incidental and miscellaneous formulas)[20]
    a. Couplets and triplets
    b. Other incidental or miscellaneous formulas

Table 4: A Short Taxonomy of Gaelic Narrative Formulas
(from Lamb 2015:236).

---

[20] For the purposes of this study, Category 5 refers to miscellaneous or incidental formulas (e.g. *sgoil is ionnsachadh* ['school and learning']). In Lamb (2015), it indicated names and epithets, which were not explored here.

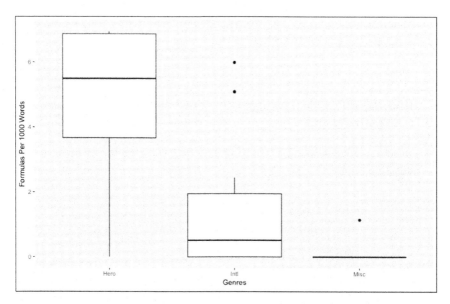

Figure 6. Genre variation in formulaicity—boxplot showing outliers.

The barplot in Figure 7 displays the proportions (i.e. out of 1.0) of formulas in each of the five categories, organized by genre. Two main observations can be made about differences in the two genres' formulaic content. The first is that, proportionately, formulas relating to "power transactions" occur three times more often in the hero tales than in the international tales. The second is that twice as many "incidental and miscellaneous" formulas occur in the international tales than in the hero tales. The first observation is no surprise, as battling, gaming, be-spelling, and cursing are mainstays of the hero genre. While the hero tales show elaborate and dramatic formulas, the international tales sampled here do not. For instance, compare the following two power transaction formulas, one very typical of Gaelic international tales and another of hero tales (translations by the present author):

(1)

  International Tale (Power Transaction Formula)

  Rinn a mhàthair an so, dà bhonnach. "A nis," ars ise, "gabh do roghainn, am fear mór le mallachd do mhàthar, no am fear beag le a beannachd."

"Thoir thusa dhomhsa do bheannachd, a mhàthair, agus beag no mór am bonnach, tha mi toilichte."

MWHT:50

Here, the mother made two bannocks. "Now," she said, "take your pick, the big one with your mother's curse, or the wee one with her blessing."

"Give me your blessing, oh mother, whether the bannock is small or big, I am happy."

(2)

Hero Tale (Power Transaction Formula)

Dhèanadh iad bogan air a' chreagan,[21]
Agus creagan air a' bhogan,
An uair a b'ìsle rachadh iad fodha,
Rachadh iad fodha gu an sùilean,
5   'S an uair a b'àirde rachadh iad fodha,
Rachadh iad fodha gu an glùinean.
Ach smuaintich Iain Og an so
Gu robh e fad o a chàirdean,
Agus goirid o a nàimhdean.
10   Thug e an togail shunndach, shanntach, aighearach ud da,
'S chuir e seachad air mullach a chinn e,
'S bhuail e chliathach ris an talamh,
'S bhrisd e dà aisinn fodha, 's té os a chionn.

MWHT:232

They made a bog of the rock,
And rock of the bog,
When they were least underground,
They went down to their knees,
5   When they were furthest underground,
They went down to their eyes.
But Young Ian thought now
That he was far from his friends,
And near to his enemies.
10   He gave a happy, lusty, joyous hoist to [his enemy],

---

[21] Another version of this run is discussed in Lamb 2015:239.

[Clear] over the top of his head,
And crushed his side on the ground,
And broke two ribs underneath him and one above.

The power transaction formula example from an international tale—the longest formula in *MHWT* for that genre—is laconic and colloquial compared to the one from a hero tale. The latter is longer and more elaborate, using devices such as strong images (e.g. terraforming), strung adjectives (*shunndach, shanntach, aighearach*), alliteration (*shunndach, shanntach*), and parallel phrases (e.g. *bogan air a' chreagan agus creagan air a' bhogan*). In these aspects, it resembles poetry more than prose (cf. Frog, this volume; Roper, this volume). The types of formulaic language seen here seem to be conditioned by genre-specific requirements and expectations.

Regarding the second observation above, the international tale formulas are more incidental and less thematic as a whole. Proportionately, a greater number of couplets and triplets occurs in them versus the hero tales, such as: *latha is bliadhna* ('a day and a year'); *sgoil is ionnsachadh* ('school and learning'); *gu math agus gu ro mhath* ('well and very well'); *beannachd no mollachd* ('blessing or curse'); *meal is caith* ('wear and enjoy'); and *mo chluas a chuala, mo shùil a chunnaic, mo bhonn a mhothaich* ('my ear that heard, my eye that saw, and my foot

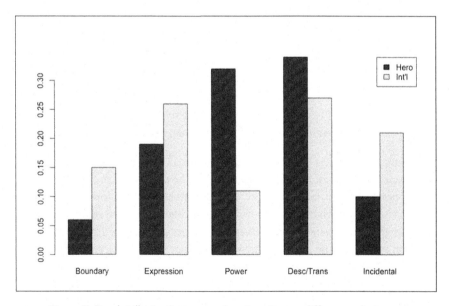

Figure 7. Barplot illustrating proportionate category differences between hero and international tale formulas.

that felt'). What they lack is the poetic, picturesque, and sometimes purple formulas that characterize heroic prose tales. On the basis of the current data, Bruford (1966:36, 182) was incorrect: there are significant differences between the frequency and types of formulas found in Gaelic hero tales and international tales.

4. Conclusions

Formulaic language is ubiquitous in human language, but it is difficult to observe formulas in the process of their development. While it has long been assumed that formulaicity arises from repetitive communicative needs and situations, no scholarship known to me has provided firm evidence for this. Furthermore, it is not clear whether repetition is the only predictor involved: factors such as semantic distinctiveness may be instrumental too. These were the departure points for this current chapter, which deployed folklore motifs to represent discourse tropes, and measured their coincidence with formulaic language across a corpus of traditional Gaelic tales. Genre differences in the texts were also assessed, to consider the extent to which formulaic language was responsive to context and purpose in this sample.

Four hypotheses were advanced, based upon a short survey of past research and informal observation, and statistical measures were conducted to assess them. They were as follows:

1a. Formulaic motifs recur more often than non-formulaic motifs.

1b. Formulaic motifs are more semantically distinct than non-formulaic motifs.

2. Motif-heavy texts are more formulaically dense than less motif-heavy texts.

3. Gaelic hero tales are more formulaic than other types of Gaelic tales.

The results support the notion that repetitive discourse tropes are a key stimulus for the development of formulaic language. In the Gaelic oral narrative context, the more frequent a motif, the more likely it is to be encoded formulaically. The results also suggest that formulaicity is conditioned by at least one factor other than repetition: semantic distinctiveness. The most frequent formulaic motifs tend, on average, to be more semantically distinct than the most frequent non-formulaic motifs.

Various scholars have weighed in on the proportion of formulas in different varieties of Gaelic oral narrative. Three varieties were examined here—hero tales, international tales, and miscellaneous tales—and hero tales were found to be more formulaic than the other two varieties. A post-hoc examination of the types of formulas found in hero tales versus international tales showed clear differences: hero tales had proportionately more formulas associated with "power transactions" and less "incidental" formulas than international tales. Furthermore, formulas in hero tales tended to be lengthier; very few long runs were found in the international tale sample. These results suggest that certain types of formulas in Gaelic traditional narrative strongly index the hero genre. Thus, they could be considered to be register markers. Based upon this *MWHT* sample, formulas do not appear to be easily transferred from hero tales to international tales, as Bruford suggested. Overall, it may be possible—at least in Gaelic traditional narrative—to distinguish between closely related genres according to the density and types of formulas present.

While this is not a diachronic study, per se, we can assume that formulaic language is more likely to develop and to be maintained in a language community when the underlying communicative needs occur regularly and are semantically distinct. Additionally, for these data, formulas are strongly indexical of the genres in which they developed; although international tales and hero tales in Scottish Gaelic resemble each other, their formulaic inventory is rather distinct.

This is a pilot study, and further investigation with a larger corpus is required before the queries considered here can be firmly answered. To properly address the diachronic development of formulas in Gaelic narrative, one must examine narrative texts throughout the history of the language. This would take many years and a diverse skillset, but it would elucidate many questions about intertextuality in Gaelic narrative. Future work could also usefully refine the constructs employed here; motif, formula, and discourse trope all require more rigorous models. A future study also could make further distinctions in the types of formulas classified (e.g. fixed phrase; template; multiform) and consider other contexts and thematic taxonomies beyond the motif. Much remains to be done on formulas in Gaelic oral tradition and formulaicity at large.

Acknowledgements

Many thanks to Frog and John Shaw for their helpful comments on a draft of this chapter. My thanks as well to Pavel Iosad for checking the statistics and assisting with the visualizations.

Appendix *MWHT* Data
Table 5: *MWHT* data.

Chapt	Title	Pg Beg	Pg End	Genre	Words	Formulas	Formulas/ 1k words	Motifs	Motifs/ 1k words
1	Mar a chuireadh an Tuairisgeul Mór gu Bàs	2	24	Hero	3632	25	6.88	45	12.39
2	An Tuairisgeul Mór	28	46	Hero	2631	11	4.18	45	17.10
3	Balgam Mòr	48	60	Intl	1768	9	5.09	11	6.22
4	Mòr Nighean Smùid	62	64	Intl	501	2	5.99	0	0.00
5	Sgeulachd Choise Chéin	68	72	Hero	550	0	0.00	0	0.00
6	Na Trì Chomairlean	74	82	Intl	1331	2	1.50	4	3.01
7	Mac an Tuathanaich	84	88	Misc	881	1	1.14	0	0.00
8	MacCuain	92	102	Hero	1430	5	3.50	1	0.70
9	Srìob Liath an Earraich	104	112	Intl	1172	0	0.00	0	0.00
10	Bilidh	118	128	Intl	1786	0	0.00	0	0.00
11	Iosbadaidh	130	146	Misc	2464	0	0.00	5	2.03
12	An Nighean Bhrèagha Leisg	148	166	Intl	2846	0	0.00	3	1.05
13	Alasdair, Mac an Impire	168	184	Intl	2614	0	0.00	0	0.00
14	Grùthan an Eòin is an Sporan Òir	188	202	Intl	2471	1	0.40	14	5.67
15	Gille a' Bhuidseir	210	224	Intl	1899	0	0.00	14	7.37
16	Iain Òg, Mac Rìgh na Frainge	228	274	Hero	6908	47	6.80	44	6.37
17	An dà Chraoibh Ghaoil	278	288	Intl	1879	0	0.00	1	0.53
18	An Nighean a Reiceadh	292	306	Intl	2249	4	1.78	1	0.44
19	An Leanabh gun Bhaisteadh	308	328	Intl	3081	1	0.32	4	1.30
20	An Duine Bochd, Beairteach	330	344	Intl	3227	2	0.62	13	4.03

Chapt	Title	Pg Beg	Pg End	Genre	Words	Formulas	Formulas/ 1k words	Motifs	Motifs/ 1k words
21	Na Trì Léintean Canaich	346	370	Intl	3154	16	5.07	33	10.46
22	An dà Sgiobair	372	388	Intl	2669	3	1.12	2	0.75
23	Mac a' Bhreabadair	394	406	Intl	2046	5	2.44	3	1.47
24	Smeuran Dubha 's an Fhaoillteach	410	432	Hero	2881	20	6.94	31	10.76
25	Dìol-Déirce Dhùn-Éideann	438	444	Misc	987	0	0.00	0	0.00
26	An Duine a Thug ris a' Mhèairle, agus a Chreach Mèarlach	446	452	Misc	947	0	0.00	0	0.00
27	Uisdean Mór MacGille Phàdruig, agus a' Ghobhar Mhaol Bhuidhe	454	458	Misc	775	0	0.00	0	0.00
28	Mac Gille Mhaoil, na	462	468	unused					
29	Donnchadh Eilein Iù, agus An Gille Glas	474	476	unused					
30	Gille Dubh Locha Dring	480	484	unused					

References

Sources

Craig, K. C. 1950. *Leigheas Cas O Céin. Sgialachd air a gabhail am Paislig an 1870 le Lachlainn Mac Nèill ... agus air a cur sìos air son Iain Òig Ìle le Eachann Mac 'Ill 'Eathainn. MSS. Iain Òig Ìle*, XVII. Stirling.

MacDhòmhnaill, D., and Craig, K. C. 1950. *Sgialachdan Dhunnchaidh*. Glasgow.

MacKay, J. G. 1940. *More West Highland Tales* (e-book). Edinburgh.

Software

R Core Team. 2017. *R: A Language and Environment for Statistical Computing* version 3.2.4. R Foundation for Statistical Computing. Vienna. http://www.R-project.org.

Literature

Biber, D. 1988. *Variation across Speech and Writing*. Cambridge.

Biber, D., and Conrad, S. 2009. *Register, Genre, and Style*. Cambridge.

Bruford, A. 1966. "Gaelic Folk-Tales and Mediæval Romances: A Study of the Early Modern Irish 'Romantic Tales' and Their Oral Derivatives." *Béaloideas* 34:i–285.

Bruford, A., and MacDonald, D. A. 2003. *Scottish Traditional Tales*. Edinburgh.

Campbell, J. F. 1872. *Leabhar na Feinne (Heroic Gaelic ballads): Collected in Scotland Chiefly from 1512 to 1871, Vol. I: Gaelic Texts*. London.

Collinson, F. M. 1966. *The Traditional and National Music of Scotland*. London.

Conrad, J. 2008. "Motif." In Haase 2008:643–645.

Coulmas, F., ed. 1981. *Conversational Routine: Explorations in Standardized Communicative Situations and Pre-Patterned Speech*. The Hague.

Dundes, A. 1997. "The Motif-Index and the Tale Type Index: A Critique." *Journal of Folklore Research* 34(3):195–202.

Edwards, V., and Sienkewicz, T. J. 1990. *Oral Cultures Past and Present: Rappin and Homer*. Oxford.

Foley, J. M. 1990. *Traditional Oral Epic: The* Odyssey, Beowulf, *and the Serbo-Croation Return Song* (e-book). Berkeley. http://ark.cdlib.org/ark:/13030/ft2m3nb18b/.

———. 2002. *How to Read an Oral Poem*. Urbana.

Frog. 2021 (in press). "Metrical Entanglement: The Interface of Language and Meter." *Versification: Metrics in Practice* (eds. Frog, S. Grünthal, K. Kallio, and J. Niemi). Helsinki.

Haase, D., ed. 2008. *The Greenwood Encyclopedia of Folktales and Fairy Tales.* London.

Hainsworth, J. B. 1968. *The Flexibility of the Homeric Formula.* Oxford.

Jason, H. 2000. *Motif, Type and Genre: A Manual for Compilation of Indices and A Bibliography of Indices and Indexing.* FF Communications 273. Helsinki.

Kuiper, K. 2009. *Formulaic Genres.* Basingstoke.

Lamb, W. 2012. "The Storyteller, the Scribe, and a Missing Man: Hidden Influences from Printed Sources in the Gaelic Tales of Duncan and Neil MacDonald." *Oral Tradition* 27(1):109–160.

———. 2013. "Recitation or Re-creation? A Reconsideration: Verbal Consistency in the Gaelic Storytelling of Duncan MacDonald." *"A Guid Hairst": Collecting and Archiving Scottish Tradition* (eds. K. Campbell, W. Lamb, N. Martin, and G. West) 171–184. Maastricht.

———. 2015. "Verbal Formulas in Gaelic Traditional Narrative: Some Aspects of Their Form and Function." *Registers of Communication* (eds. A. Agha and Frog) 225–246. Helsinki.

Lord, A. B. 2000. *The Singer of Tales* ed. 2. London.

Lyons, J. 1995. *Linguistic Semantics: An Introduction.* Cambridge.

MacInnes, J. 2006. "Twentieth-Century Recordings of Scottish Gaelic Heroic Ballads." *Dùthchas nan Gàidheal* (ed. M. S. Newton) 184–210. Edinburgh.

Maclean, C. I. 1959. "A Folk-Variant of the Táin Bó Cúailgne from Uist." *Arv: Tidskrift för nordisk folkminnesforskning* 15:160–181.

Miller, J., and Weinert. R. 1998. *Spontaneous Spoken Language.* Oxford.

Ó hÓgáin, D. 2006. *The Lore of Ireland: An Encyclopaedia of Myth, Legend and Romance.* Woodbridge.

O'Nolan, K. 1968. "Homer and the Irish Hero Tale." *Studia Hibernica* 8:7–20.

———. 1971. "The Use of Formula in Storytelling." *Béaloideas* 39/41:233–250.

Ó Cuív, B. 1973. *The Linguistic Training of the Mediaeval Irish Poet.* Edition 1983. Dublin.

Parry, M. 1930. "Studies in the Epic Technique of Oral Verse-Making, I: Homer and Homeric Style." *Harvard Studies in Classical Philology* 41:73–147.

Pawley, A. 2007. "Developments in the Study of Formulaic Language since 1970: A Personal View." *Phraseology and Culture in English* (ed. P. Skandera) 3–45. Berlin.

Propp, V. 1968. *Morphology of the Folktale.* Trans. L. Scott. Austin.

Rosenberg, B. 1987. "The Complexity of Oral Tradition." *Oral Tradition* 2(1):73–90.

Ross, J. 1959. "Formulaic Composition in Gaelic Oral Literature." *Modern Philology* 57(1):1–12.

Rubin, D. C. 1995. *Memory in Oral Traditions: The Cognitive Psychology of Epic, Ballads, and Counting-Out Rhymes.* Oxford.

Sävborg, D. 2018. "The Formula in Icelandic Saga Prose." *Saga-Book* 42:51–86.

Sayers, P. 1978. *An Old Woman's Reflections*. Oxford.

Stepanova, E. 2014. *Seesjärveläisten itkijöiden rekisterit: Tutkimus äänellä itkemisen käytänteistä, teemoista ja käsitteistä*. Kultaneiro 14. Joensuu.

Thompson, S. 1955. *Narrative Motif-Analysis as a Folklore Method*. FF Communications 161. Helsinki.

———. 1955–1958. *Motif-Index of Folk-Literature: A Classification of Narrative Elements in Folk-Tales, Ballads, Myths, Fables, Mediæval Romances, Exempla, Fabliaux, Jest-Books, and Local Legends* (e-book). Bloomington. https://archive.org/details/Thompson2016MotifIndex/page/n0.

Thompson, S. 1977. *The Folktale*. Berkeley.

Uther, H.-J. 2004. *The Types of International Folktales: Animal Tales, Tales of Magic, Religious Tales, and Realistic Tales, with an Introduction* repr. 2011. Helskinki.

Wray, A. 2008. *Formulaic Language: Pushing the Boundaries*. Oxford.

———. 2012. "What Do We (Think We) Know about Formulaic Language? An Evaluation of the Current State of Play." *Annual Review of Applied Linguistics* 32:231–254.

Wray, A., and Perkins, M. R. 2000. "The Functions of Formulaic Language: An Integrated Model." *Language and Communication* 20(1):1–28.

Zall, C. S. 2010. "Variation in Gaelic Storytelling." *Scottish Studies* 35:210–244.

10

Form and Formulae in Rotenese Oral Poetry

JAMES J. FOX, THE AUSTRALIAN NATIONAL UNIVERSITY

IN THIS CHAPTER, I wish to define and contrast two kinds of "formulae" in Rotenese oral poetry. For purposes of exposition and analysis, I intend to use a set of recognizable distinctions derived from the work of my initial mentor in this research, Roman Jakobson, who encouraged me to focus my attention on the comparative study of parallelism.[1] I then wish to concentrate on an examination of the patterning of compositions in one of these kinds of formulae and to show how such formulae are creatively varied among different Rotenese master poets. To begin, I wish to introduce my research.

1. A Primary Research Focus

For more than fifty years now, I have been studying the ritual language poetry of the Rotenese, a population in eastern Indonesia. The Rotenese possess a tradition of strict canonical parallelism requiring that virtually every word in every poetic utterance be paired according to well-established and well-recognized cultural rules. I estimate that to achieve fluency requires a knowledge of the pairing of several thousand words—perhaps a minimum of three thousand such terms. It is an inherited linguistic system that poets gradually come to master.

My concern over many years has been to understand which words may be paired and, by the same token, which words may not. There once existed a fear among poets of improper pairing of terms, especially in the most important of ritual language utterances; and even today, a poet—often a younger poet in an early attempt to perform—will be verbally "tisked" (a clicking of the tongue against the teeth) in public rejection, if he does not pair terms correctly.

[1] The publication of an entire issue of the journal *Oral Tradition*, volume 31, number 2 (2017), devoted to the parallelism in verbal art and performance with diverse contributions drawn from Finnic, Mayan, Tai, Austronesian, and Arandic languages and with an introduction by Frog and Lotte Tarkka may signal a possible revival in comparative interest in these poetic traditions.

In the course of my research, I have come to realize that the pairing of terms is both a compositional question and a historical question. To deal with these questions, I have developed a formal vocabulary to describe the various dimensions of pairing. I refer to each acceptable pair as a recognized *dyadic set* and each component of a set as a term. In simple notation, a dyadic set can be represented as: (a1//a2). For some years, I have been compiling a dictionary of these dyadic sets based on the dialect of the central domain of Termanu. This is still a work in progress as I continue to add sets. In defining terms, it is essential to have a specific dialect focus because "Rotenese" consists of a dialect chain that extends east-west across the length of the island. Neighboring dialects are generally intelligible but there is increasingly less intelligibility between more distant dialects. On the basis of reported mutual intelligibility, more distant dialects could be considered separate languages. One can distinguish as many as four to six related Rotenese languages. In addition, the political divisions on the island dating to the seventeenth century all claim to have their own separate language. Ritual performances are based on these seventeen small domains and therefore the recitations in ritual language are identified by domain. What is critically important is that the dialects are a "resource" for the creation of dyadic sets.

In this *Rotenese Dyadic Dictionary*, I list and define individual terms according to root form and specify the other terms with which they pair. In defining terms, I distinguish between terms used in ordinary speech (Termanu dialect) and those used only in the ritual poetic register, many of which originate from another dialect. Rotenese has many unrelated but homologous terms, such as for example, *alu(k)* for 'shoulder' and *alu(k)* for 'pestle' (final *-k* is a definite marker). In native exegesis, folk etymologies are often fashioned to link these homologous forms.

A word/term in ritual language has a definable range that consists of the number of other terms with which it is paired. This range varies. Some terms have a range of one and therefore occur only with another specific term while a small core of terms have a wide range of up to ten or more possible pairs. The terms at these two extremes have been of particular interest. Each term forms a single, specific dyadic set. Many, possibly a majority, of these single-range terms are identifiable as "dialect" terms derived from another dialect on Rote or possibly from another closely related regional language. Thus, for example, the term for 'day, daytime' (*fai(k)*) has a range of one because it only pairs with the term for 'sun, time' (*ledo(k)*). *Ledo(k)*, however, has a range of four. It can pair with separate terms such as 'moon' (*bulan*), 'heat' (*hana*) and 'dew' (*a'u*) in addition to (*fai(k)*). Out of just over 1,500 semantic terms in the current Dyadic Dictionary, 1,125 terms (70%) have only one linkage and thus form single dyadic

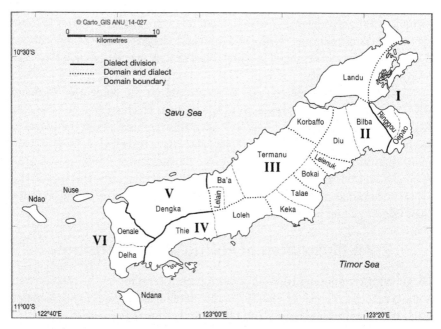

Figure 1. Dialect and Domain Map of the Island of Rote. Dialect divisions are indicated by Roman numerals: Dialects II and III, encompassing much of east central Rote, are closely related to one another and tend, despite differences, to be mutually intelligible. The eighteen historical domains (*nusak*) of the island are named and their borders indicated by dotted lines. A majority of these domains were given recognition by the Dutch East India Company in the seventeenth century and remain, to this day, socially distinct. Each domain claims to possess its own "language" or way of speaking (*dede'ak*).

sets; 347 elements (22%) have two, three, or four linkages, and are thus part of one or more networks, while thirty-five terms (0.02%) have multiple linkages (five linkages or more): these are core elements at the hub of a large and complex network.[2]

This defined pairing of words can be considered as one kind of formulaic creation. In the terminology of Roman Jakobson, these canonical complementary pairs, defined as metaphoric correspondences, constitute paradigmatic constructions that stand in contrast with the syntactic or metonymic relations of such terms in poetic utterances. It is the syntactic arrangement of terms—their

---

[2] For a longer and more considered consideration of this network analysis, see Fox 2014a:379–383.

formulaic combination—that I wish to focus on in this chapter.[3] I refer to these syntactic arrangements as "syntactic formulae." They can consist simply of two dyadic sets generally arranged in paired lines or they may be extended to three or even four dyadic sets.

Initially my field research was concentrated on the domain of Termanu with important subsidiary research in the domain of Thie (Ti'i). For the past ten years or more, however, I have extended this research across the island to record a broad spectrum of dialect recitations. I have recorded recitations from more than fifty poets.[4] In this chapter, my illustration of Rotenese syntactic formulae will be focused and selective. I will first illustrate the use of the syntactic formulae in the dialect of Termanu and then, where relevant, consider their usage in a number of other dialects.

2. An Illustration of Formulaic Composition

I begin with a simple eight-line composition from Termanu by the master poet, Meno Tua, "Old Meno," or simply "Meno" (Stefanus Adulanu), with whom I worked closely in 1965–1966. As an illustration of formulaic construction, this composition is one of several short ritual recitations that I have published previously (Fox 1974:76–77 / 2014a:140–141) and commented on briefly.[5] This ritual poem, in a botanic idiom, describes the succession of generations and can be used as a prayer for the prosperity of a male child.

(1)

Lole faik ia dalen	On this good day
Ma lada ledok ia tein na	And at this fine time [sun]
Lae: tefu ma-nggona lilok	They say: The sugar cane has sheaths of gold
Ma huni ma-lapa losik.	And the banana has blossoms of copper.
Tefu olu heni nggonan	The sugar cane sheds its sheath
Ma huni kono heni lapan,	And the banana drops its blossom,
Te hu bei ela tefu okan	Leaving but the sugar cane's root
Ma huni hun bai.	And just the banana's trunk.
De dei tefu na-nggona seluk	But the sugar cane sheaths again

---

[3] For another, earlier analysis that compares the formulaic features of Rotenese recitations among five Rotenese poets, see Fox 2010.

[4] Photos of many of the poets cited in this chapter can be found in *Master Poets, Ritual Masters* (Fox 2016).

[5] Michael Silverstein has selected a different one of these short recitations (Fox 1974:74 / 2014a:138) and has done his own analysis of its succession of formulae (Silverstein 2004:168).

Fo na-nggona lilo seluk	The sheaths are gold again
Ma dei huni na-lapa seluk	And the banana blossoms again
Fo na-lapa losi seluk.	The blossoms are copper again.

This poem is composed of just eight dyadic sets: (a1//a2), (b1//b2), etc:

(2)

lole//lada	good//fine	(a1//a2)
fai(k)//ledo(k)	day//sun	(b1//b2)
dale(n)//tei(n)	inside//belly	(c1//c2)
tefu//huni	sugarcane//banana	(d1//d2)
-nggona//-lapa	sheath//blossom	(e1//e2)
lilo//losi	gold//copper	(f1//f2)
olu//kono	shed//drop	(g1//g2)
oka//hu	root//trunk	(h1//h2)

This composition also includes various connectives, emphatics, time markers, and verbal elements, all of which are invariant: *ia* ('this'), *ma* ('and'), *tehu* ('but'), *de* ('then')[6], *fo* ('that'), *heni* ('away, off'), *bei* ('still'), *bai* ('also'), *seluk* ('again'), *lae* ('they say').

Using simple dyadic notation to mark separate paired terms, the composition can be represented formulaically as follows:

(3)

Lole faik ia dalen		
a1 b1 c1	a1, b1, c1
Ma lada ledok ia tein na		
a2 b2 c2	a2, b2, c2
Lae: tefu ma-nggona lilok		
d1 e1 f1	d1, e1, f1
Ma huni ma-lapa losik.		
d2 e2 f2	d2, e2, f2
Tefu olu heni nggonan		
d1 g1 e1	d1, g1, e1
Ma huni kono heni lapan		
d2 g2 e2	d2, g2, e2

---

[6] The particle *de* has the sense of 'then' in English. It marks the next in a sequence of actions. In short poetic sequences taken out of context, I have translated *de* as 'then' to mark its presence in a line. In longer sequences, I have left *de* untranslated because English tacitly recognizes a sequence of actions that need not be marked as they are in Rotenese.

Tehu bei ela tefu okan
d1   h1   d1, h1
Ma huni hun bai.
   d2 h2   d2, h2
De dei tefu na-nggona seluk
     d1   e1   d1, e1
Fo na-nggona lilo seluk
     e1   f1   e1, f1
Ma dei huni na-lapa seluk
    d2   e2   d2, e2
Fo na-lapa losi seluk.
   e2 f2   e2, f2

3. Syntactic Formulae and Their Use in Composition

Syntactic formulae are used to enhance composition: they are not rigid templates but rather modular verbal constructions. They can be extended, restricted, modified, or varied to meet the requirements of composition. The better and more able the poet, the more he uses such formulae for aesthetic advantage.

Paired poetic lines can have from one to three and sometimes even four dyadic sets. As in the poem on banana and sugarcane, these syntactic formulae can be represented in simple notation as:

(4)

    a1, b1, c1, [d1]
    a2, b2, c2, [d2]

As an illustration of the variety of the possibilities available for composition, I have chosen to focus on one of the most common sets of formulae found across numerous compositions: formulae built around the dyadic set: *fai(k)//ledo(k)*. These syntactic formulae may consist of *fai(k)//ledo(k)* on its own with one or another invariant modifier or, more commonly, with either one or two dyadic sets that qualify the *fai(k)//ledo(k)* dyadic set. The following examples are from the master poet, Meno.

Faik is 'day'; *ledok* is 'sun' but, to make sense in English, I often translate *ledok* as 'time'. The first two lines of the poem on sugarcane//banana illustrates one such possibility.

(5)

> Lole faik ia dalen
> 　a1　b1　　c1　　　　　　　a1, b1, c1
> Lada ledok ia tein na
> 　a2　b2　　　c2　　　　　　a2, b2, c2

An even simpler use of this basic framework can be seen in the lines that rely only on *fai(k)//ledo(k)*. In these lines, *lo* (for *leo*) ('as'), *ia* ('this'), and *boe* ('also') are invariant forms and *ma* ('and') connects the two lines.

(6)

> Lo faik ia boe　　　　　　　As on this day too
> Ma lo ledok ia boe　　　　　And as at this time too

A variation on this formula framework uses the dyadic set *leo//deta*, both of which have the meaning 'as, like', together with *fai(k)//ledo(k)*:

(7)

> De leo faik ia boe　　　　　But as on this day too
> Ma deta ledok ia boe　　　 And like at this time too

Yet another common usage are the paired lines where *nai* ('at, on, during') and *ia* ('this') are invariant forms and the dyadic set *dale//tei* – *dale* ('inside') and *tei* ('stomach, guts, insides') are added:

(8)

> Nai faik ia dalen　　　　　 During this day
> Ma nai ledo ia tein　　　　 And during this time

Another common usage with two dyadic sets is demonstrated by the lines where the *fai//ledo* dyadic set occurs in the plural (*-kala*) and another dyadic set *basa//no'u* – *basa* ('all') and *no'u* ('enough, sufficient') is added.

(9)

> De basa fai-kala　　　　　　But on all the days
> Ma no'u ledo-kala　　　　　 And enough of the time

More interesting but equally common is the usage involving three dyadic sets in two paired lines where the numerals *esa//dua* ('one, two') and the adjectival forms *nunin//teben* ('definite, certain, true') are used to modify *fai//ledo*.

(10)

Faik esa ma-nunin	On one definite day
Ma ledok dua ma-teben	And at a second certain time

Although Meno used the previous formula (5) with its pairing of *esa//dua*, he tends, more often, to use a formula that relies on a single invariant modifier, *esa* ('one').

(11)

De faik esa ma-nunin	On one definite day
Ma ledo esa ma-teben	And at one certain time

In 1965–1966, the other master poet of Termanu was Stefanus Amalo who was of the same age as Meno and his equal in composition. Most of his formulaic usages were indistinguishable from those of Meno. Some examples of his use of the *fai//ledo* formulae follow. One simple use of the *fai//ledo* pair is the following:

(12)

De fai-a neu fai	But from day to day
Ma ledo-a neu ledo	And time (sun) to time (sun)

Another simple usage combines the pair *losa//nduku* ('to, up to, until') with *fai//ledo*:

(13)

Losa faik-ka	To this day
Ma nduku ledok-ka	And until this time

Like Meno, Stefanus Amalo frequently used the three-dyadic formulae as in the short poem on banana and sugarcane:

(14)

Lole faik ia dalen	During this good day
Ma lada ledok ia tein	And at this fine time

Peu Malesi was another poet whom I recorded in 1965–1966 and again in 1972–1973 when he had come to be considered the leading poet in Termanu, following on the deaths of both Meno and Stefanus Amalo. His use of the *fai//ledo* formula framework was barely distinguishable from that of either Meno or Stefanus Amalo. One can compare the following lines with Meno's lines (8) or Stefanus Amalo's lines (14).

(15)

De leo faik ia dalen	But as on this day
Ma leo ledok ia tein	And as at this time

One can compare the following lines from Peu Malesi with those of Meno (10).

(16)

Faik esa ma-nunin	On one definite day
Ma ledok dua ma-teben	And at two certain times

However, Peu Malesi often used two variations on this formula framework. In the first of these, he replaced the *nunin//teben* dyadic set with the equally acceptable *-nunin/-nda* dyadic set where the verbal form *-nda* has the meaning 'to meet, to agree, to target, to be specific':

(17)

Ledok dua ma-nunin	The second definite time
Ma faik telu ma-ndan na	And the third specific day

In the second of these usages, he simply used the dyadic set *-teben//-nda*:

(18)

Ledok dua ma-nda	The second specific time
Ma faik telu ma-teben	And the third particular day

In technical terms, the terms *-nunin, -teben, -nda* are interlinked and any two can be used to form a dyadic set. The numerals, one, two, three (*esa, dua, telu*) are similarly interlinked.[7]

In his compositions, Peu Malesi tended to use the dyadic set *dua//telu* ('two//three') more than the set, *esa//dua* ('one//two'), as for example in the following lines:

(19)

Ledo telu, mu mete	On the third dawn [sun], go and see
Fai dua, mu mete	On the second day, go and see

---

7 The use of numerals is strictly ordered in ritual language: it is possible to pair one//two, two//three, and three//four as well as seven//eight (though this pair tends to be associated with inauspicious matters) and eight//nine (which invariably signify auspiciousness and completeness.). The term for five is *lima* which also refers to the hand. Some poets (Seu Bai, for example, in Termanu) use the dyadic set *lima//ne* ('five//six') to signify one hand and the other hand, while other poets reject this possibility.

Another poet, a contemporary of Peu Malesi, Seu Bai (Eli Pellondou) tended to use the formula with *tetu//tema* ('right, proper, full, complete') (the sun at its zenith is *tetu*; the moon at its fullest is *tema*):

(20)

| Faik esa ma-tetuk | On one right day |
| Ledok esa ma-temak | At one proper time |

Most of the *fai//ledo* formulae used in Termanu are also used by poets in other domains across dialect areas. This formula is recognizable, despite minor sound changes (*dale* (Termanu) > *lalan* (Dengka)) as used by the master poet from the domain of Dengka, Simon Lesik (see example (14)):

(21)

| Lole faik esa lalan | On this good day |
| Ma lada ledok esa tein | And on this fine time |

The master poet Ande Ruy from the domain of Ringgou also regularly uses this formula:

(22)

| Tehu lole fai ia dalen | But on this good day |
| Ma lada ledo ia tein | And on this fine time |

Like Meno, the master poet of Thie (Ti'i), N. D. Pah often used the term *esa* ('one') rather than the dyadic set, *esa//dua* ('one//two') in his compositions:

(23)

| Faik esa no dalen | On one day |
| De ledok esa no tein | Or at one time |

Yet he would also use the numerical set *telu//ha* ('three//four') in other contexts:

(24)

| Tada ledok telu | Then in three suns |
| Do sodak fai ha | Or in four days |

I have also recorded another poet from Thie, G. Foeh who used a variant of the Termanu formula in examples (17), (18), and (19) based on the dyadic set (*-nda//tetu*):

(25)

Fo faik dua mandan	That on the second specific day
Ma ledok telu matetun	And on the third right time

All of these formulae are relatively simple. They punctuate recitations at various points and are easily mastered by fledgling poets. More extended formulae are of greater significance and require more compositional skills.

4. Extended Syntactic Formulae:
The Genealogical Introduction

More interesting than these relatively simple formulae are the syntactic formulae that extend over a succession of lines. They can occur on their own but often skilled poets interweave extended formulae with one another. One of the most prominent of these formulae is what I call the "genealogical introduction" which introduces the principal characters in a chant. These introductions usually begin with a marriage and go on to describe the birth of a child or children. Such genealogical introductions are essential to both origin narratives and funeral chants. They are often interwoven with other extended formulae to elaborate, for example, on the food cravings of a pregnant mother that foretell the character of the child and frequently include formulae for the development of the child after the birth.

An eight-line example of a genealogical introduction is one by Meno which begins the funeral chant entitled *Boni Balo ma Tola Delu*. This particular introduction is simple but contains the main features of most introductions: the "carrying" of a woman who is given a dual name to marry with a man who is also given a dual name and then the birth of a child (or children) whose dual names follow that of their father whereby the first name of the father (or a part thereof) becomes the second name of the child. In basic notation, "father's name" (a1, a2)//(b1, b2) becomes the child's name (c1,a1)//(d1, b1).

In these lines, the woman is named Ndao Meo//Bala Iu, her husband's name is Boni Balo//Tola Delu, and their child is Loma Boni//Natu Tola. The child is a girl and referred to by the formula *ke-fetok//tai-inak*.[8] The three key verbal dyadic sets are *soku//ifa* ('to lift, cradle, carry'), *sao//tu* ('to marry, wed') and *bongi/lae* ('to give birth to, to bring forth'). The arrangement of dyadic sets in these eight lines can best be understood by providing notation of their expression:

---

[8] The *ke//tai* set in this expression is, I believe, a reference to the specific cloth straps that a woman wears wrapped around her body at the time of marriage.

(26)

Ala soku-la Ndao Meo	They lift Ndao Meo
a1 b1 c1	
Ma ifa-la Bala Iu.	And they carry Bala Iu.
a2 b2 c2	
De sao-na Boni Balo	She marries Boni Balo
d1 e1 f1	
Ma tu-na Tola Delu	And weds Tola Delu
d2 e2 f2	

5 Boe te bongi Loma Boni — She gives birth to Loma Boni
   g1   h1   e1

Ma lae Natu Tola. — And brings forth Natu Tola.
   g2   h2   e2

De ke-fetok — She is a girl child
   i1 j1

Ma tai-inak. — And a female child.
   i2 j2

One can compare Meno's eight-line genealogical introduction with Stefanus Amalo's sixteen-line introduction in the funeral chant *Ndi Lonama ma Laki Elokama*. These lines retain most of the formulae used in Meno's introduction. Stefanus Amalo does, however, substitute the verb *lali* ('to transfer, shift') with *soku* in the dyadic set, thus *soku//lali* rather than *soku//ifa*. He also introduces another formula for marriage, *lelete//fifino*, which is the partially reduplicated form of *lete//fino* ('to bridge//join'). However, he retains the use of the dyadic sets, *tu//sao* and *bongi//lae*. In this poem, the woman named Lisu Lasu-Lonak//Dela Musu-Asuk marries the man Ndi Lonama//Laki Elokama and then has two children: a boy named Solu Ndi//Luli Laki and a girl, Henu Ndi//Lilo Laki. The formula for a girl is *ke-fetok//tai-inak* and for a boy the formula is *popi-koak//lanu-manuk* ('cock's tail feathers//rooster's plume').

(27)

Soku Lisu Lasu-Lonak	They lift Lisu Lasu-Lonak
Ma lali Dela Musu-Asuk.	And they transfer Dela Musu-Asuk.
De lelete neu sao	She bridges the path to marry
Ma fifino neu tu.	And she joins the way to wed.
5 De ana tu Ndi Lonama	She weds Ndi Lonama
Ma sao Laki Elokama.	And she marries Laki Elokama.
Boe ma ana bongi-	She gives birth to Solu Ndi na Solu Ndi

Ma ana lae-na Luli Laki	And she brings forth Luli Laki
Fo popi-koak Solu-Ndi	A cock's tail feathers, Solu Ndi
10 Ma lano-manuk Luli Laki.	And a rooster's plume, Luli Laki.
Boe te ana bei boe bongi	But she still continues to give birth
Ma bei boe lae.	And still continues to bring forth.
Lae-nala Henu Ndi,	She brings forth Henu Ndi,
De ke-fetok;	She is a girl child;
15 Ma lae-nala Lilo Laki,	And she brings forth Lilo Laki,
De tai-inak.	She is a woman child.

Most of the formulae of the genealogical introduction are recognizable across the different dialects of the island. Thus, for example, in an origin chant from Thie, the master poet, N. D. Pah (known as Guru Pah), provided this extended introduction to recount the royal marriage of the woman, Pua Kende//No Rini, to the Sun and Moon, Ledo Horo//Bula Kai, and the birth of their son, Adu Ledo//Ndu Bulan, who in his recitation goes on to encounter the Lords of the Ocean and Sea.

Guru Pah elaborates on this royal wedding by identifying Pua Kende//No Rini as the child of Kende Balasama//Rini Balasama and by inserting a set of formulaic lines that describe how this woman is regally dressed for her wedding. Instead of the dyadic set *soku//lali*, which Stefanus Amalo relies on, Guru Pah uses the dyadic set *lali//keko* ('to transfer, move, shift'). However, like Meno and Stefanus Amalo, he also uses the dyadic sets *sao//tu* and, as expressed in Thie dialect, *bonggi/rae*.

(28)

Lali rala Kende Balasama anan	They transfer Kende Balasama's child
Inak kia Pua Kende	The woman Pua Kende
Neu sao Bula Kai	To marry with Bula Kai
Keko rala Rini Bala-Sama anan	They move Rini Balasama's child
5 Fetok kia No Rini	The girl No Rini
Neu sao Ledo Horo.	To marry with Ledo Horo.
Ara pasa pendi neu tain	They wrap a long cloth around her waist
Ma ara henge deras neu tein.	And they tie a red cloth on her stomach.
Ara olu lelen	They place an armband
10 Ma te ara pada suen	And they ornament her breasts
Kela nai eis daan	A bracelet on her ankle
Ma ndeli nai lima kuku.	And a ring on the finger.
Bonggi heni Ndu Bulan	She gives birth to Ndu Bulan
Ma rae heni Adu Ledo.	And brings forth Adu Ledo.

One can contrast the various elaborate genealogical introductions from Termanu and Thie with this succinct introduction by the master poet from Oenale, Hendrik Foeh, known for his concise poetic style. At the core of these formulaic lines are the island-wide dyadic sets *sao//tu* and *bonggi//rae*:

(29)

	Ina esa naran na	The woman with the name
	Isi Tefe Reo anan na	Isi Tefe Reo's child
	Te'o esa naden na	The aunt with the appellation
	Modo Do Hano anan na.	Modo Do Hano's child.
5	Ana tu Pele-Pele Madulus	She marries Pele-Pele Madulus
	Bonggi nala anan na Pua Pele	Gives birth to the child, Pua Pele
	Ana sao Loma-Loma Malanggan	She weds Loma-Loma Malanggan
	Rae nala anan na Ka Loma.	Brings forth the child, Ka Loma.

Genealogical introductions are similar among the dialects of Rotenese. As a compositional device, they can be lengthened or shortened to suit the purpose of the poet. They can also be interwoven with other recognized formulae that describe the pregnancy and birth of chant characters in the composition. One such extended formulaic sequence describes the darkening of the breasts and the enlargement of the belly of the pregnant spouse; another uses various plant-metaphors to describe the rapid growth of the child after the birth. It is worth considering some of these interwoven formulae.

5. Formulae of Birth and Growth: Metaphors in a Botanic Idiom

In Rotenese ritual language, most of the formulae for life and death are expressed in a botanic idiom: humans are compared to specific plants and their growth (or their withering) is an expression of their life course.

In a notably erotic funeral chant, *Pau Balo ma Bola Lungi* reserved for high nobles who die young, Stefanus Amalo begins with the genealogy of the main character Pau Balo//Bola Lungi's father, Balo-Kama Sina//Ma-Lungi Lai, linking him by marriage to a heavenly origin—the rainbow and moon—through his wife, Henu Elu//Bula Sao. He then describes how Balo-Kama Sina//Ma-Lungi Lai grows up as a boy comparing him with maturing rice and millet:

(30)

Soku-la inak-a Henu Elu	They lift the woman Henu Elu
Ma ifa-la fetok-a Bula Sao.	And carry the girl Bula Sao.
De ana tu touk-a Lai Lota	She marries the man Lai Lota

	Ma sao ta'ek-a Sina Kilo.	And weds the boy Sina Kilo.
5	Boe te bongi Ma-Lungi Lai	She gives birth to Ma-Lungi Lai
	Ma lae Balo-Kama Sina.	And brings forth Balo-Kama Sina.
	De tona kale hade mai	He sprouts forth like rice
	Ma le'a bu'u bete mai	And grows up like millet
	Nama-nalu no aman	Growing long like his father
10	Ma nama-tua no toon.	And growing tall like his mother's brother.

The metaphor for growth in these lines consists of three dyadic sets *tona// le'a* ('to push, stretch'), *kale//bu'u* ('kernel, head, joint'), and *hade//bete* ('rice, millet'), which, if translated literally, might be translated as 'pushes forth a head of rice//stretches forth a joint of millet'.

In this long recitation, Balo-Kama Sina//Ma-Lungi Lai goes on to marry the woman Si Solu Hate Besi//Kona Boi Kado Lofa:

(31)

47	De ana tao neu sao sosan	He makes her his first wife
48	Ma tao neu tu ulun.	And makes her his principal spouse.

She becomes pregnant and develops food cravings. As in other recitations, these cravings both reflect and determine the character of her child. Si Solu Hate Besi//Kona Boi Kado Lofa's cravings are for lascivious foods, turtle, and sea cow meat, which foretell that her child will grow up to become the "Don Juan" of Rotenese literature. At this point, the recitation uses one of the standard formulae for describing the changes in a woman during pregnancy:

(32)

	Boe ma Si Solu Hate Besi	Si Solu Hate Besi
	Ma-siu dodoki	Her tongue craves for odd bits
	Ma Kona Boi Kado Lofa	And Kona Boi Kado Lofa
	Ana metu-ape u'una	Her mouth waters for assorted things
55	Hu tei bei ule oen-na	Because (her) belly is still like a water vat
	Ana da'a-fai Pau Balo	It enlarges with Pau Balo
	Ma su'u bei tole taun-na	And (her) breasts are still like indigo jars
	Nggeo-lena Bola Lungi.	They darken with Bola Lungi.
	Boe te nafada neu saon,	She speaks to her husband,
60	Touk Ma-Lungi Lai	The man Ma-Lungi Lai
	Ma nanosi neu tun,	And she addresses her spouse,
	Ta'ek Balo-Kama Sina, nae:	The boy Balo-Kama Sina, saying:
	"Au ma-siu bia keak	"My tongue craves chunks of turtle
	Ma au metu-ape loloa luik."	And my mouth waters for strips of sea cow."

When her husband Ma-Lungi Lai//Balo-Kama Sina manages to bring her turtle and sea cow meat, Si Solu Hate Besi//Kona Boi Kado Lofa continues to have cravings, this time for sea foods that are symbolically even more lascivious: sting ray and shark.[9] When she is finally given these foods, a ceremony is held to prepare for the birth of her child. Here Stefanus Amalo once again uses a variant of the pregnancy formula that he used earlier (compare: lines 55–58 with lines 97–100).

(33)

	Boe ma Si Solu Hate Besi	Si Solu Hate Besi
	Ma Kona Boi Kado Lofa	And Kona Boi Kado Lofa
95	Kekela neu tein	Has performed the kekela-teik ceremony
	Ma sau-masi neu su'un.	And undergoes the salt-rubbing ceremony.
	Besak-ka tei bei ule oen na	Now (her) belly is still like a water vat
	Da'a-fai bobongin	It enlarges to give birth
	Ma su'u bei tole taun na	And (her) breasts are still like indigo vats
100	Nggeo-lena lalaen.	They darken to bring forth.

Stefanus Amalo then describes the birth and growth of this child using the formulae he initially utilized to describe the birth of his father, but he expands it to a four-set syntactic formula by adding the dyadic set *kase//lai*, which designates a specific fast-growing rice and millet (compare lines 7–8 with lines 104–105):

(34)

	Boe te ana bongi-na Pau Balo	She gives birth to Pau Balo
	Ma lae-na Bola Lungi;	And she brings forth Bola Lungi;
	De loi-loi ma felo-felo.	Twisting and lashing.
	De ana tona kale hade kase	He sprouts forth like kase-rice
105	Ma ana le'a bu'u bete lai.	And he grows up like lai-millet.

The addition of the reduplicated dyadic set, *loi//felo* ('twisting//lashing'), inserted to describe Pau Balo//Bola Lungi's birth, hints at what is to come in this recitation. This dyadic set evokes the twisting of the sting ray and shark and, metaphorically, Pau Balo//Bola Lungi's later lovemaking prowess.

The initial dozen lines of Meno's funeral recitation, *Meda Manu//Lilo Losi* is a superb example of the use of a genealogical introduction that uses this same four-set formula for the growth of the child, Meda Manu//Lilo Losi:

---

[9]   In Rotenese mythological conceptions, the turtle and sea cow are adulterous female creatures; whereas the shark and sting ray are slippery ithyphallic male predators.

(35)

	Soku-la Ona Ba'a	They carry Ona Ba'a
	De Ba'a Masafali anan	The child of Ba'a Masafali
	Ifa-la Lusi Lele	They lift Lusi Lele
	De Lele Maleo anan	The child of Lele Maleo
5	De leu sao Manuama Lolok	They go to marry Manuama Lolok
	Ma tu Lasiama Baluk.	And to wed Lasiama Baluk.
	De bongi-la Meda Manu	She gives birth to Meda Manu
	De ke-fetok Meda Manu	The girl Meda Manu
	Ma lae-la Lilo Losi	And she brings forth Lilo Losi
10	De tai-inak Lilo Losi	The woman Lilo Losi
	De ana tona kale hade kase	She sprouts like kase-rice
	Ma le'a bu'u bete lai.	And she grows up like lai-millet.

6. The Localization of Language: Ritual Names for Significant Places

Where personal names occur, as in a genealogical introduction, their dual constituent elements whereby the first name of a father becomes the second name of his children, provide a knowledge of succession across generations of key characters in individual recitations, but they are especially important in origin narratives which relate characters to one another.[10] Personal names also allude to aspects of the status and origin of their bearer but are often too elusive to be easily translated.

Place names, many of which can be associated with personal names, are even more elusive. Place names permeate most recitations and thereby give a specific context—either local or imaginary—to particular recitations. The island of Rote has a variety of dyadic ritual names as do all of its historical domains. So, too, do the nearby islands—Savu, Ndao, and Timor—and the town of Kupang on Timor as well as the imagined island from which the Rotenese claim to have originated. The domain of Termanu, for example, has a succession of such ritual names that relate to different periods of its past. Within domains, prominent places of all kinds—important rice fields, ritual sites of significance, rivers, and hilltops all have their dual ritual names. The heavens, the earth and sea all have their ritual names. Place names, like personal names, are an inextricable feature of recitations. Place names can be evoked in succession to create topogenies—an

---

[10] For a Rotenese genealogy of the Sun and Moon, see Fox 1997a [reprinted in Fox 2014a:219-228].

ordered and meaningful succession of places that resemble the genealogies of persons.[11]

Narratives in many recitations involve the journeying of a chief character back and forth across the island or to other islands. The directions of this journeying are invariably indicated in the names of the places that are visited. Eastward, where the sun rises, is a favorable direction; westward, where the sun sets is less favorable. Rote itself is conceived as a creature with its head in the east and its tail in the west. In this equation, south is "right" and north is "left." This is expressed by the dyadic sets *dulu//langa* ('east//head'), *muli//iko* ('west//tail') and *ki//kona* ('north, left//south, right').

These dyadic sets are the building-blocks for more complex formulaic names, often merging person and place names:

(36)

    Dulu Oen//Langa Daen
    'East Water//Head Land'
        Common designation for eastern Rote

    Timu Dulu//Sepe Langa
    'Dawn [at the] East//Reddening [at the] Head'
        Designation for eastern Rote or the east in general

    Dulu Balaha Osin//Langa Malua Mamen
    'East Day's Garden//Head Morrow's Orchard'
        Merger of Person/Place Names: Interpretable as either

    Tada Muli ma Lene Kona
    'Tada [in the] West// Lene [in the] South'
        Designation for the Domain of Thie

    Dela Muri//Ana Iko
    'Dela [in the] West//Child [at the] Tail'
        Name for the domain of Delha

    Dae Mea Iko //Oe Ange Muli
    'Red Earth [at the] Tail//Water Flows [in the] West'
        Name for the domain of Dengka

[11] For a topogeny of some thirty-two successive ritual place names that define a circuit around the island of Rote, see Fox 1997b [reprinted in 2014a:265–276].

Thie dialect:

(37)

      Muri Loloe Olin//Iko Beku-te Tasin
      'West descending to the Estuary//Tail bending to the Sea'
         Designation for western Rote

      Inak Ku Eo Iko// Fetok Tai Le Muri
      'The woman, Ku Eo Iko//The girl, Tai Le Muri'
         Woman's Name: Merger of Person/Place Names

In effect, names, both place names and personal names, can form extended formulaic sequences much like other syntactic formulae. For example, the mother of Pau Balo//Bola Lungi who is overcome with cravings has a double dyadic name: Si Solu Hate Besi//Kona Boi Kado Lofa. The Si Solu//Kona Boi in her name may possibly be a place name affixed to her personal name but this is by no means clear.

7. Names, Formulae, Translation, and Cultural Interpretations

Names in all their variety present interpretive complexities. The poets themselves do not agree on names and continually argue about them. This becomes even more problematic as one traces the variety of names across dialects and the problem is multiplied when the names of plants, fish, birds, and spirit creatures are added to this assembly. Occasionally one element of a dyadic set will help illuminate its unknown pair. More often, however, it has been in exegesis discussions with the poets that I have been able to come to understand subtle aspects of Rotenese culture that are embodied in their poetry and through these understandings, I have struggled to arrive at appropriate translations.

Although this chapter can only touch on the array of formulae structured by the syntactic concatenation of dyadic sets, it should be evident that this is a pervasive feature of Rotenese oral composition. Parallelism in Rotenese ritual language is not simply the existence of pairs but the marshaling of these pairs in a great variety of sequential arrangements that are crucial for poetic expression.

It remains to explore the significance of this poetic language within a recognizable semiotic framework.

8. The Jakobson Legacy

The poetic use of ritual language creates a world of metaphor and imagination. Rotenese ritual language requires the use of complementary pairs and insists on their pervasive expression. Each pair, in any composition, creates a metaphoric link—a cultural correspondence—between two elements. These metaphoric links are then expressed in an ordered poetic sequence.

In *Fundamentals of Language* (Jakobson and Halle 1956:76–82), Roman Jakobson drew a contrast between the two poles of language: the metaphoric and metonymic. The metaphoric pole, linked to ideas of similarity, is associated with processes of selection while the metonymic pole, linked to ideas of contiguity, is associated with processes of combination. In linguistic terms, the metaphoric pole focuses on semantic relations of equivalence; the metonymic pole on syntactic relations of contiguity or apposition.[12]

Canonical parallelism, as in Rotenese ritual language, makes explicit the relationship between such metaphoric correspondences and their metonymic expression. As Jakobson expressly noted: "Rich material for the study of this relationship is to be found in verse patterns which require a compulsory parallelism between adjacent lines, for example in Biblical poetry or in the West Finnic and, to some extent, the Russian oral traditions" (1956:77).

In his most important single publication on parallelism, "Grammatical Parallelism and its Russian Facet" (1966), Jakobson quotes the poet Gerard Manley Hopkins:

> The artifice part of poetry, perhaps we shall be right to say, all artifice, reduces itself to the principle of parallelism. The structure of poetry is that of continuous parallelism ...
>
> Hopkins 1959:84

In this and other papers Jakobson has argued for the centrality of parallelism—particularly "compulsory" canonical forms of parallelism—in the study of poetic language. Thus, in his often quoted, "Poetry of Grammar and Grammar of Poetry," he claims: "Parallel systems of verbal art give us a direct insight in the speakers' own conception of the grammatical equivalences" (1968 [1985]:40). However, other statements of his are more elusive and subject to multiple interpretations. Among these statements is Jakobson's critically important assertion

---

[12] Roman Jakobson's publications on poetic language and on parallelism are so various and have been published and republished in so many volumes that it can be difficult to trace the development of his ideas. From the very first paper he published in 1916, he was concerned with the semantics of parallelism (see Fox 1977:59/2014a:19). A crucial paper is his "Closing Statement: Linguistic and Poetics" in *Style in Language* (1960) because it foreshadows many of his arguments in later papers. Based on personal acquaintance with Roman Jakobson and on a careful reading of his work, Linda Waugh has written a useful sketch of these ideas. Her publication (1980) includes a bibliography that gives the initial dates of Jakobson's key publications on poetics and some of the volumes in which they have been reprinted.

in "Closing Statement: Linguistics and Poetics" that "The poetic function projects the principle of equivalence from the axis of selection into the axis of combination" (1960:358).

Based on the presentation in this chapter, one might translate this statement, in notational form, as follows:

(38)

Axis of Selection   Axis of Combination
(a1//a2), (b1//b2), (c1//c2) >>>   a1, b1, c1
                                                            a2, b2, c2

Rotenese formulaic language makes this poetic function—the superimposition of similarity on contiguity—explicit in its compositions.

References

Fox, J. J. 1974. "'Our Ancestors Spoke in Pairs': Rotinese Views of Language, Dialect and Code." *Explorations in the Ethnography of Speaking* (eds. R. Bauman and J. Sherzer) 65–85. Cambridge. [Reprinted in Fox 2014a:129–148.]

———. 1977. "Roman Jakobson and the Comparative Study of Parallelism." *Roman Jakobson: Echoes of his Scholarship* (eds. C. H. van Schooneveld and D. Armstrong) 59–90. Lisse. [Reprinted in Fox 2014a:19–40.]

———. 1997a. "Genealogies of the Sun and Moon: Interpreting the Canon of Rotinese Ritual Chants." *Koentjaraningrat dan Antropologi di Indonesia* (ed. E. K. M. Masinambow) 321–330. Jakarta. [Reprinted in Fox 2014a:119–228.]

———. 1997b. "Genealogy and Topogeny: Toward an Ethnography of Rotinese Ritual Place Names." *The Poetic Power of Place: Comparative Perspectives on Austronesian Ideas of Locality* (ed. J. J. Fox) 91–102. Canberra. [Reprinted in Fox 2014a:265–276.]

———. 2010. "Exploring Oral Formulaic Language: A Five Poet Analysis." *A Journey through Austronesian and Papuan Linguistics and Cultural Space* (eds. J. Bowden and N. P. Himmelman) 573–587. Canberra.

———. 2014a. *Explorations in Semantic Parallelism.* Canberra.

———. 2014b. "Present and Future Research." In Fox 2014a:365–386.

———. 2016. *Master Poets, Ritual Masters: The Art of Oral Composition among the Rotenese of Eastern Indonesia.* Canberra.

———. 2017. "Remembering and Recreating Origins: The Transformation of a Tradition of Strict Canonical Parallelism among the Rotenese of Eastern Indonesia." *Oral Tradition* 31(2):233–258.

Frog and Tarkka, L., eds. 2017. *Parallelism in Verbal Art and Performance. Oral Tradition* 31(2), special issue.

Hopkins, G. M. 1959. *The Journals and Papers of Gerard Manley Hopkins*. Ed. H. House and G. Storey. London.

Jakobson, R. 1960. "Linguistics and Poetry." *Style in Language* (ed. T. Seboek) 350–377. New York.

———. 1966. "Grammatical Parallelism and Its Russian Facet." *Language* 42:399–429.

———. 1968 [1985]. "Poetry of Grammar and Grammar of Poetry." *Lingua* 21:597–609. [Reprinted and quoted in Jakobson 1985:37–46.]

———. 1985. *Verbal Art, Verbal Sign, Verbal Time*. Minneapolis.

Jakobson, R., and Halle, M. 1956. *Fundamentals of Language*. 'S-Gravenhage.

Silverstein, M. 2004. "'Cultural' Concepts and the Language-Culture Nexus." *Current Anthropology* 4(5):621–644.

Waugh, L. 1980. "The Poetic Function in the Theory of Roman Jakobson." *Poetics Today* 2(1a):57–82.

11

Formula and Structure

Ways of Expressing Names in
the Northern Runosong Tradition

JUKKA SAARINEN, FINNISH LITERATURE SOCIETY (SKS)

K ALEVALAIC POETRY, or *runosong*, is a form of traditional poetry that was once practiced widely in Finland, Karelia, Ingria, and in Estonia (on terms used for this poetry in different languages, see Kallio et al. 2017). In many ways, the genre resembles the Serbo-Croatian epic traditions studied by Milman Parry and Albert B. Lord. For instance, it contains narrative songs of non-stanzaic lines and has strict rules for enjambment.[1] Many lines also recur in the corpus. Because of this, they can be characterized as "formulas" or "formulaic expressions" (Lord 1960 [2001]:4; in kalevalaic poetry, see Tarkka 2013:53–75; Saarinen 2017:407–408).

In this chapter, I discuss Oral-Formulaic Theory (OFT) and the kalevalaic poetic tradition. I attend closely to the concept of formula, and also its relevance for understanding composing, performing, and acquiring tradition. I base my arguments on my studies of one of the most prominent epic singers within this tradition, Arhippa Perttunen (1769–1841), from the village of Latvajärvi, Viena Karelia.[2] A key objective of this chapter is to examine the formulas that Arhippa uses for naming persons and beings and to explicate how they function as a system.

---

[1] This has connections with the "adding style" of Parry and Lord (cf. Lord 1960 [2001]:54).

[2] These studies are published as a doctoral dissertation at Helsinki University (Saarinen 2018, with an abstract in English, pp. 3–4). Arhippa's poems were collected by three collectors (Elias Lönnrot in 1834, J. Fr. Cajan in 1836, and M. A. Castrén in 1839) and subsequently published in *SKVR*. The examples of poetic lines presented in this article derive from my reconstructed corpus of Arhippa's poems, published as part of my dissertation (in English, see also Saarinen 2013).

1. Oral-Formulaic Theory and Kalevala-Meter Poetry

OFT was introduced to Finland during the 1960s and 1970s.[3] Before this time, research on kalevalaic poetry was dominated by the comparative approach known as the Historic-Geographic Method.[4] Adherents of this method thought that any changes occurring to texts during transmission were degenerative and caused by imperfect memorization or adaptation, or both. In contrast, the oral-formulaic perspective considered variation to be a natural consequence of situated performance; it was an additive and creative processes. The performed text was not evaluated according to how well it conformed to a postulated "*ur*-text" but, instead, according to its position in the performative context.

OFT gained traction in the mid-twentieth century and promised new insights for research on runosong. The individual singer was given more credit for the performed text, and the text was now connected to the contemporary cultural context; previously, the composition of a text and its cultural context were projected into a more distant past. Not all scholars, however, were convinced of OFT's suitability. Leea Virtanen, once professor of folklore in Helsinki University, wrote that OFT is not valid for kalevalaic poetry. She pointed out that, in general, lines in kalevalaic epic poetry connect to specific songs or themes, which can be established by the fact that "a researcher can usually say without difficulty to which poem certain lines belong" (Virtanen 1968:54–55). In kalevalaic songs, lines quite often are narrowly indexical (Frog 2010:97–102; 2011:52, 58–59); they connect to particular poems and narrative contexts (cf. Harvilahti 1992a:141–142; 1992b:87–101). Paul Kiparsky pointed out in 1976 that kalevalaic singers tend to use roughly the same language from version to version:

> The important thing is that singers dispose of [...] very little floating material which can be freely inserted at appropriate points in the narration[.] Each event is unique, and most epic verses are with a particular song.

Kiparsky 1976:95–96

[3] To my knowledge, Albert B. Lord was first mentioned in Finnish studies by Matti Kuusi in 1957. Referring to Lord's presentation in *Four Symposia in Folklore* (Thompson 1953:305–311), Kuusi points out Lord's recommendation to observe metrical and syntactical formulas and different types of enjambment. Kuusi then proceeded to study enjambment as a stylistic device, but did not pay any attention to the concept of oral composition (Kuusi 1957:111). OFT starts to appear in various written studies in the 1960's, but probably was much more known and discussed by folklorists in seminars and other occasions (see Virtanen 1968:54–55; Kuusi 1970:301–302).

[4] The Historic-Geographic School, or the "Finnish School," is best known internationally for research on the folktale, but its origins are in scholarship on kalevalaic poetry.

These remarks show that runosong does not comply with two assumptions of Oral-Formulaic Theory: that formulas are versatile and that texts are rarely fixed.

In my study of Arhippa Perttunen and his son Miihkali—two famous Viena Karelian singers of the nineteenth century—I focused on inter-rendition variation. My findings agreed with Kiparsky's perspective. The text of a narrative song presented by one singer is relatively fixed. This does not mean, however, that each rendition is identical apart from "omissions" or "mistakes." On the contrary, variation is ever-present (Saarinen 1994:180–181, 194–195). It affects different aspects of the text in different ways and to different extents. Below are the four types of inter-rendition variation that I found in my research:

1. Variation is linked to the hierarchical character of the text. Elements that are subordinated in the narrative or syntactic structure (e.g. lines, motifs, episodes) can be omitted or added during performance. Central, plot-related elements (e.g. actions) tend to be stable, while descriptive elements, like a short description of a weapon or a tool utilized by the hero in a poem, tend to be more mutable.[5] One of the more marked features of poetry in Kalevala-meter is verse parallelism—repeating the central idea of a line with another line (or lines) using similar wording and syntax. As a rule, parallel lines repeat, expand, contrast, or introduce alternative equivalents to the first parallel unit, which has the full referential power of a proposition. Parallel lines augment this power (Saarinen 2017:421). This is reflected in the instability of parallel groups;[6] lines within these groups are frequently omitted (Saarinen 1994:192–193).

2. Use of the same lines and groups of lines in recurrent situations in a text, i.e. formulaic expression. Formulaic expressions range from short phrases introducing direct speech to longer passages describing a hero's preparations for a journey (e.g. by horse or boat). The latter resemble the concept of "theme" in OFT (Lord 1960 [2001]:68; see also Frog, this volume). Drawing on their formulaic repertoire, kalevalaic singers narrate recurrent situations in myriad, interchangeable ways[7] (Saarinen 1994:190–192).

---

[5] By this, I do not mean that a "description" is in any way less essential to poetic expression than action.

[6] A parallel group consists of the main line (or the first line) and one or more parallel lines that repeat the contents of the first line using the same syntax and synonymic or analogic terms (cf. Saarinen 2017:407–424).

[7] Parry used the term "thrift" to refer to singers' propensity to always use only one formula to express a certain essential idea in particular metrical positions (see Parry 1930 [1980]:266–267; cf. Lord 1960 [2001]:52–53); Parry's concept was not developed to account for poetries

3. When repeating passages in narrative discourse, singers often vary the repetition. For example, they may elide lines or sequences, or re-arrange a passage. Many traditional patterns exist for handling repetition in kalevalaic poetry (Saarinen 1994:186–190; Kuusi 1952:59–132).

4. Single words can be substituted by other words with similar metrical characteristics. Such substitutions often initiate lines, as metrical requirements are not so strict at line-initial positions. There, we often find short, stereotyped adverbs or pronouns that, despite supplying meagre semantic content, remain metrically important: <u>Oli</u> *lieto Lemminkäini* ~ <u>Tuo on</u> *lieto Lemminkäini* ('*There was* the wanton Lemminkäinen ~ *That is* the wanton Lemminkäinen'). These short segments can be easily replaced by each other and by other words.

Singers of kalevalaic poetry modify texts while learning and compiling their own versions. During this process, they exploit existing structures and borrow and mold lines and passages from other contexts and genres—even from incantation and lyric poetry (Saarinen 1994:181–191; Tarkka 2013:93–100).

Certain aspects of kalevalaic poetry lend themselves towards using pre-existing lines and formulas: lines are unrhymed; alliteration is frequent but not obligatory; and no stanzas exist, just metrically similar lines that easily alternate with each other. As a result, most lines probably do occur in more than one narrative context, if we consider the entire tradition. On the other hand, particular lines and poems strongly index one another.

Indexicality varies across the tradition. Some lines and sequences have a very narrow index—occurring in specific poems only—while others occur in many different contexts (cf. Frog 2010:97–102; 2011:52, 58–59). Challenging a common assumption of OFT, formulas and formulaic expressions in kalevalaic narrative poetry do not facilitate composition-in-performance. Rather, they facilitate *pre*-performance composition. What I mean is that they facilitate the process of learning and adopting a song. The process of selecting, compiling, and editing a song is a creative one. To understand better how singers produce kalevalaic song, we should focus on their learning and adaptation of songs, their competence as singers, and how they create meaning for their audiences (Saarinen 1994:194–195).

Genres other than narrative poetry permit more variation and creative composition, and even composition-in-performance. For examples of this tendency, we can consider Matti Kuusi's work on one gifted singer and lamenter

---

characterized by verse parallelism and it is not a good fit for verse formulas of kalevalaic poetry (Frog 2016:74–75).

from Viena Karelia, Anni Lehtonen (Kuusi 1970:293–302). Lehtonen was interviewed over the years 1911–1916 by Samuli Paulaharju (1875–1944), a renowned collector of Finnish and Karelian folklore. Kuusi described (1970:301–302) how Paulaharju occasionally would ask Lehtonen if she remembered old songs by presenting her with lines that he knew from other contexts. Lehtonen was, on the basis of those clues given to her, able to compose short, new poems based on her competence of traditional formulas, themes, and structures. Although some consider the resulting texts "fakelore,"[8] Kuusi believes that they challenge a view that was prevalent in Finland at the time; that good kalevalaic singers are passive, loyal preservers of tradition. He reminds us that Finnish researchers were originally skeptical about OFT and questions whether scholars have tried to solidify the process of oral transmission, a phenomenon that is naturally fluid (Kuusi 1970:301–302).

Other kalevalaic singers have shown similar levels of compositional competence. For example, consider Larin Paraske (1833–1904), from Northern Ingria. Paraske had the largest repertoire ever collected in Finland and Karelia. Her repertoire and compositional techniques have been studied on several occasions by Senni Timonen (1980:162, 172; 2004:238–303). Interestingly, Paraske differentiated between songs that should be sung "as they were" (i.e. without changes), and songs that could be composed by 'shoveling' (*mättää*) lines together. By 'shoveling', the singer was always able to make new compositions. Thus, it is well attested that composition by formulas—in performance—was possible in kalevalaic tradition. We should remember, however, that oral-formulaic composition as practiced in the Serbo-Croatian tradition (Parry 1932 [1980]; Lord 1960 [2001]) differs from that in the kalevalaic tradition (Kuusi 1970:293–302; Timonen 1980; 2004:238–303); they are distinct phenomena. Although, in both cases, singers use pre-existing elements and structures, the first practice involves recreating "old" songs, while the second involves creating "new" songs.

Many definitions exist for "formula," but most used for oral poetry reflect Parry and Lord's original conceptualization: "a group of words which is regularly employed under the same metrical conditions to express a given essential idea" (Lord 1960 [2001]:4). My own view is that a formula is, fundamentally, a unit of language. It is a syntactic-semantic structure that is realized within the limits of a particular poetic structure. In kalevalaic poetry, the limiting structure is the Kalevala-meter, a trochaic tetrameter showing frequent alliteration and parallelism, but having no stanzaic structure. According to Pentti Leino:

---

[8]   Paulaharju used a printed publication of proverbs for help, and presumably read proverbs for the informant enquiring if she knew them.

> [its] most striking feature is the placing of the syllables. The only metri-
> cally relevant syllable is the first one. If this is long, it is placed on a
> rise, but if it is short it must occur on a fall; however, these restrictions
> do not affect the first rise and fall of a line.
>
> Leino 1986:2

In Kalevala-meter, a basic line has eight syllables, divided into four two-syllable feet. An extra syllable or two may occur in the first foot. Syntactically, there are some restrictions on enjambment. Most lines contain a verb (predicate) with its arguments: subject, object, and adverbials. A subject, consisting of a noun phrase (NP), can form a line on its own. Likewise, an adverbial phrase can be separated from the line containing its predicate. Take the following example:

(1)

Vaka vanha Väinämöini	Sturdy old Väinämöinen
Käypi teitä asteloopi	walks striding the roads
Ympäri meren sinisen	round the blue sea

The first line is formed by the subject NP—the name of the hero *Väinämöinen* and its epithet. The second line expresses the action and contains the predi-cate ("walks"). The third line is a prepositional phrase (PP) describing where the action is situated; syntactically, it is peripheral and not obligatory. Objects appear in separate lines only under exceptional conditions, and two arguments cannot normally form a line together without their predicate.[9] The eight-syllable structure of the line sets certain limits for its syntax. Due to this, lines tend to be highly patterned and "formulaic."

2. Assessing Formulaicity

When attempting to assess formulaicity, certain questions arise. How do we detect "formulas" in the corpus of kalevalaic song, collected from thousands across a vast area, from Viena Karelia in the north to Estonia in the south? And on what bases can we judge a line to be "formulaic" or not? I view formulas as prefabricated building blocks, available both for creating "new" and recreating "old" verses. They are templates for producing parts of lines, full lines, and line groups, which are designed from older line groups and their subdivisions. We cannot say on what occasion or by whom new lines or line groups were produced in each case, but we can see the results: i.e. lines resembling each other in syntax,

---

9   This can happen in parallel lines because of an elliptical verb; see Saarinen (2018:149) for more information.

metrics, and semantics. For example, taking one of Arhippa Perttunen's poems, we see two lines in separate poems that are obviously connected:

(2)

Tako rautaisen haravan	Forged (i.e. created by forging) an iron rake
Tako rautaisen korennon	Forged (i.e. created by forging) an iron stick

The syntactic structure consists of a predicate *tako* ('forged') and an object-NP, consisting of a noun and an adjective. Only the noun changes, as required by the narrative; the other words remain constant. We cannot know which one is the original as both are quite widely distributed, but their interdependence is clear. Similarly, there are two lines in Arhippa's repertoire that depict "creation by singing":

(3)

Laulo leppäisen urohon	Sang (i.e. created by singing) an alder man
Laulo lautan lampahia	Sang (i.e. created by singing) a herd of sheep

These have the same syntactic-metrical structure: the predicate in the beginning and the object-NP at the end. They belong together. They occur in the same narrative text and show the same repetitive structure. On his way to a feast in *Päivölä*, the hero *Kaukamieli* meets a fiery eagle threatening to kill him. Subsequently, wolves and bears at the gates of *Päivölä* try to prevent the progress of his journey. *Kaukamieli* "sings" objects to be devoured by the beasts instead of him. The syntactic structure in (3) is the same as in the samples in (2), i.e. a predicate and object-NP. The metrical structure is also similar: a disyllabic verb at the beginning of the verse and a two-word NP (3+3 or 2+4 syllables) at the end. There is also a semantic similarity, since both verbs express a momentous act of producing or creating something. In the set in (2), this happens through concrete forging. In the set in (3), it happens through magical singing. Considering the possible connections between these two sets, we notice, first, that many lines share same the syntactic structure. In thinking about the covariance of syntactic and metrical structures, two things should be considered: (1) an NP (or PP) is, as a rule, undivided (i.e. a verb rarely intersects a noun and its attribute); (2) in Kalevala-meter, longer words tend to be in a line's final position (i.e. the "winnowing principle": see Sadeniemi 1951:27–39). Momentous verbs in the past tense tend to be short, so they are usually positioned at the beginning. In that position, the length of the first syllable does not matter: it can be short (*ta-ko*) or long (*lau-lo*). Thus, the "formulaic quality" of these constructions can be characterized by regular syntactic variation, which is subject to metrical constraints directing how words are positioned in the line.

Still, regular syntactic variation is not always enough to explain connections between lines. Occasionally, we must consider line function, and covariation between semantics and syntax. Some lines share no words, but still belong to the same *formula system*, to use a term introduced by Lord (1960 [2001]:35, 47–48) for a concept outlined by Parry (1930 [1980]:275–279).[10] In Arhippa Perttunen's poems, there are lines that mark the end of a journey (or being on a journey) by using a noun in the illative case (equivalent to the English preposition *to*) in a so-called temporal construction:

(4)

Pohjolahan mäntyöhö	After going to Pohjola
Kotihinsa tultuoho	After coming to his home

Only certain verbs use this non-finite construction—those with one-syllable stems—because the form adds three syllables to the stem, most commonly *tul-la* ('come') and *män-nä* ('go'). The lines in (4) have a similar function: they both express a temporal relation of one action to another. Considering their similar function, semantics (i.e. verbs of motion, nouns referring to a place) and metrical structure (4+4 syllables, participle in the end), it is clear that they are not individual formulas, but constitute a formula system. Bolstering this conclusion, it can be observed that the participles exploited—i.e. *mäntyöho* ('after going') and *tultuoho* ('after coming')—would be unusual in everyday speech. They come across as formal or archaic, and are associated with the poetic register.

To provide an example of a formula system, I present below a classification of lines expressing names in Arhippa Perttunen's repertoire. Humans, supernatural beings, and animals identified by these names are mostly subjects in sentences. Similar formulas are employed to address these beings. The Finnish and Karelian languages do not have a vocative case, per se; the vocative function of a verse can be marked by a short word like *oi* ('oh') or *sie* ('you') in the beginning of the line, as in (5), although this is not required if the name fills all eight positions:

(5)

Oi sie Anni tsikkoiseni	Oh you, Anni, my sister

---

[10] This resembles the metrical-grammatical approach to the formulaic quality of Homeric language, "based on subtle repetitions of word patterns rather than on verbatim repetition of words," suggested by Joseph A. Russo in his article, "A Closer Look at Homeric Formula" (Russo 1963:236–247).

Subjects can form lines of their own, separate of the predicate of the clause. This is not possible for all subjects, however; only active agents behave this way, i.e. a human, an animal, or a supernatural being. Name lengths vary from full lines of eight syllables to half-lines of four syllables. If a name does not fill the entire line, additional words complete it. These include the one-syllable vocative words mentioned above; adverbs like *silloin* ('then'), *niin* ('so'), and *siitä* ('thence'); pronouns like *tuo* ('that') or *se* ('it'); and occasionally the copula, *on*. Names of six syllables and shorter may occur with a short verb. As the verb and its obligatory arguments normally must be expressed within the same line, possibilities for combining subjects and predicates are very limited. Almost always, naming formulas use a "saying" verb, the most common being *sano* ('said') or *niin sanoopi* ('so he says'). Because naming formulas vary only slightly, along the above parameters, we can characterize them as a formula system.

3. Naming-Formula Types

As described, naming formulas vary along syntactic, semantic, and metrical parameters. We can group individual formulas into different categories, or *formula types*, according to the values of these parameters. Below is one attempt to do this, with each type indicated by a number and letter. Some formulas fill an entire line, while others are completed by one or two additional line-initial words, usually adverbs. Simple names of two or three syllables, without epithets, are not included. In the examples, a single dash (–) indicates a slot for one syllable, two dashes (- -) indicate slots for two syllables, and so on. Normally, every foot consists of two syllables; therefore, two dashes is equivalent to one foot. A vertical bar (|) distinguishes one syntactic-semantic unit form another, e.g. a proper name and an apposition.

Type 1. Names consisting of one noun phrase

Type 1a. A proper name + an adjective

– – vanha Väinämöini	– – old Väinämöinen
– – nuori Joukahaini	– – young Joukahainen
– – kaunis Kaukamieli	– – beautiful Kaukamieli
– – Veitikkä verövä	– – ruddy Veitikkä
– – seppo Ilmorini	– – the smith Ilmorini
– – – – Pohjan akka	– – – – mistress of Pohja
– – – – suuri Luoja	– – – – the great Creator

Type 1b. Names expressed by a relation to a proper name + an adjective

Poika tuhman Tuiretuisen	son of naughty Tuiretuini
Ruma Ruotuksen emäntä	ugly mistress of Herod
– kuulu Jumalan poika	– famous son of God
– pätövä Päivän poika	– good son of the Day (the Day = the Sun)
– – lieto Lemmin poika	– – wanton son of Lempi
– – kaunis Kalevan poika	– – beautiful son of Kaleva

Type 1c. Names expressed by referring to a place + an adjective

Ulappalan ukko vanha	old man of Ulappala
Metsän piika pikkaraini	little maid of forest

Type 1d. A proper name consisting of a first name and a surname:

Kaunis Kauppi Köyrötyini	beautiful Kauppi Köyrötyinen
– – Antervo Vipuini	– – Andrew Vipuinen

Type 2. Names consisting of two noun phrases, a proper name and an apposition

Type 2a. A proper name + apposition of a noun and an adjective

Piltti | pieni piikaiseni	Piltti | my little maid
– – Muttsi | musta koira	– – Muttsi | the black dog

Type 2b. A proper name + an apposition expressing a relation to a proper name

Iku Turso | Äijön poika	Iku Turso | son of Äijö
Vesi viitta | Vaitan poika	Vesi viitta ("water cloak") | son of Vaitta
Tillervo | Tapivon neiti	Tillervo | maiden of Tapivo
Tuurikki | tytär Tapivon	Tuurikki | daughter of Tapivo
– Luoja | Jumalan poika	– Creator | son of God

Type 2c. A common noun in the function of a proper name + an apposition expressing origin

– päivyt | Jumalan luoma	– Day | God's creation
Tiehyöt | Jumalan luoma	Road | God's creation
Tuloini | Jumalan luoma	Fire | God's creation

Type 2d. A proper name or a common noun in the function of a proper name + an apposition referring to a place

Annikki | Soaren neitoini	Annikki | maiden of the Island
Mielikki | metsän emäntä	Mielikki | mistress of the forest
Mehiläini | ilman lintu	Bee | bird of the air
Ohtoini | metsän omena	Ohtoinen [Bear] | apple of the Forest

Type 2e. A proper name or a common noun in the function of a proper name + an apposition referring to a group.

Herheläini | Hiitten lintu	Hornet | bird of Hiisis [devils]
Tahvanus | hepoisten herra	Tahvanus | lord of horses

Type 2f. A proper name + an apposition referring to an activity

Osmoini | oluven seppä	Osmoinen | smith of beer

Type 2g. A two-word noun phrase + an apposition consisting of a diminutive

Neitsyt Moarie | emoini	Virgin Mary | little mother
Ruma Ruotus | paitulaini	Ugly Herod | [wearing a] little shirt
Päivyt armas | aurinkoini	beloved Day | little sun

Type 2h. A noun + an apposition with possessive endings (only in address)

Oi emoni | kantajani	Oh my mother | my bearer
Lapseni | vakavuteni	My child | my stability(?)
Repoiseni | lintuiseni	My little fox | my little bird

Type 2i. A noun phrase + an apposition consisting of a *bahuvrihi* compound

Pohjon akka | harva hammas	mistress of Pohjola | sparse tooth
Tuonen tytti | rauta sormi	daughter of Tuoni [Death] | iron finger
Lappalaini | kyyttö silmä	The Lapp | kyyttö(?) eye

Type 3. Parallel half-lines

Mato musta | kyy vihaini	black worm | angry adder
Yön tytti | hämärän neiti	girl of night | maiden of twilight
Pihan tyttö | pellon neiti	girl of yard | maiden of field

4. Discussion

Names have a narrow distribution in Arhippa's repertoire; most of them appear in only one or two texts. On the other hand, a certain name may occur many times in a single text. Thus, names are formulas used "regularly to express a given essential idea" (Lord 1960 [2001]:4). The most common name formula, found in numerous poems, is *vanha Väinämöini* ('old Väinämöinen'). Other widely distributed names may have Christian overtones: *Neitsyt Moarie* ('Virgin Mary'), *Ruotus* ('Herod'), and his wife ('ugly mistress of Herod'), and names referring to Christ, e.g. *Luoja* ('The Creator') ~ *Jumalan poika* ('son of the God'). Most of the name formulas are single lines with no parallel lines (Steinitz 1934:41; Saarinen 2017:415–417).

Names which can be expressed with a single noun phrase often leave space at the beginning of the line. To fill the space, singers insert short adverbs, pronouns, or verbs, adapting them to the discourse. Single phrase formulas take the form of "heavy" proper names like *Väinämöini* or *Kaukamieli* (Type 1a), or express a family relation, using the word *poika* ('son') and a proper name in the genitive case (marked by -n): e.g. *Lemmin poika, Kalevan poika* (Type 1b; see also Type 1c). Rarely, these heavy names are formed through a fore-name-surname construction (Type 1d). Often, names are expressed with two noun phrases. The first phrase typically is a proper name, or a common noun functioning as a proper name in the context, e.g. *mehiläini* ('bee'). Usually, the second one is an apposition, which describes or clarifies the first (Type 2). The appositions take several forms, but a pattern can be observed. On one hand, they use the genitive case to express different types of relations: family (Type 2b), origin (Type 2c), environment (Type 2d), connection to a group (Type 2e), or function (Type 2f). Alternatively, they deploy diminutives like *emoini* ('little mother') (Type 2g), possessives (Type 2h), or so-called *bahuvrihi* compounds[11] (Type 2i). The order is regular and consistent: more exact designations (e.g. proper names) come first, and descriptive or explanatory appositions follow. The order actually mirrors the construction of parallel lines in kalevalaic poetry; the first line, or main line, expresses the referent, while parallel lines add descriptive, metaphoric, and analogic elements. In this way, the two-line formula used for "bear" follows the regular rules, although the second line opens with a *bahuvrihi* compound:

---

[11] A *bahuvrihi* compound points to a referent by specifying some characteristic or quality of the referent. *Pohjolan emäntä* ('The mistress of Pohjola') is *rautasormi* ('an iron finger'). This is not a finger, per se, but a woman with an iron finger.

(6)

| Ohtoini | metsän omena | Ohtoinen | apple of the forest |
| Mesi kämmen | källeröini | Honey paw | källeröinen (diminutive, not translatable) |

A construction with an apposition differs from verse parallelism in relation to symmetry; each parallel line is symmetrical in meaning and metrical structure, whereas the relationship between a name and apposition is asymmetrical.

How and why do oral poets employ formulas, formulaic structures, and formulaic patterns? Scholars have theorized that formulas are either a solution to the time constraints under which poets compose strict metrical lines ("mechanism"), or stem from poets' verbal artistry, attuned as they are to the special meaning that formulas derive from poetic context ("aesthetics") (Foley 1991:3–4). Foley admits that there is a compositional aspect to formulas, but states that their essence lies in how they convey meaning:

> [S]tructural elements are not simply compositionally useful, nor are they doomed to a "limited" area of designation; rather they command fields of reference much larger than the single line, passage, or even text in which they occur.
>
> Foley 1991:7

This is what Foley (1991:7) has called *traditional referentiality*. The process of generating such meaning is metonymy, "a mode of signification wherein the part stands for the whole." When looking at Arhippa's lines that contain names, we can safely speak of formulas. Furthermore, frequent names clearly connect to traditional referentiality, invoking contexts much larger than the text itself. Names like *vanha Väinämöini* ('old Väinämöinen') refer to all poems where this "eternal sage" appears. On a more general level, the name refers to the whole complex of folk beliefs about magic knowledge and persons exercising this power (i.e. as a ritual specialist called a *tietäjä*). In addition, these formulas have a compositional aspect. They can be understood as technical devices, aiding the singers in the producing the text for performance (not necessarily "in performance"). Yet the technical aspect must be seen in conjunction with their poetic significance; formulas are desirable and widely vetted expressions for singers committed to this traditional idiom. The compositional aspect of formulas is not limited to repeating identical words, but should be viewed as providing modeling structures. As models, they can create new fields of reference. Diminutives, *bahuvrihi* compounds, and using the genitive case to express relations are ways to build new name formulas or to adapt old names to other models.[12] The main point here is that singers can exploit existing structures to compose new lines and sequences at will. Arhippa uses the name *Lemmin poika* ('son of Lempi') for the hero that everyone else knows as *Lemminkäinen*. This is an idiosyncratic choice, and we do not know why he made it. The result is a name that is new on the surface, but traditional in its structure and meaning. That is the essence of formulas.

References

Sources

Cajan, J. Fr. 1–4. Archives of the Finnish Literature Society.

Castrén, M. A. Manuscripta Castreniania I. National Library of Finland.

Lönnrot, E. Lönnrotiana 5. Archives of the Finnish Literature Society.

SKVR. Suomen Kansan Vanhat Runot, I. Helsinki. http://skvr.fi.

Literature

Foley, J. M. 1991. *Immanent Art: From Structure to Meaning in Traditional Oral Epic.* Bloomington.

Frog. 2010. "Multiformit kalevalamittaisessa epiikassa." *Kalevalamittaisen runon tulkintoja* (eds. S. Knuuttila, U. Piela and L. Tarkka) 91–113. Kalevalaseuran vuosikirja 89. Helsinki.

———. 2011. "Multiforms and Meaning: Playing with Variation and Referentiality in Kalevalaic Epic." *Laulu kulttuurisena kommunikaationa—Song as Cultural Communication—Pesnâ kak sredstvo kul'turnoj kommunikacii: Proceedings from the Runosong Academy Jubilee Seminar, 8-10 October 2010* (eds. P. Huttu-Hiltunen et al.) 49–64. Runolaulu-Akatemian julkaisuja 16. Juminkeon julkaisuja 87. Kuhmo.

———. 2016. "Linguistic Multiforms in Kalevalaic Epic: Toward a Typology." *RMN Newsletter* 11:61–98.

Haavio, M. 1952. *Väinämöinen: Eternal sage.* Porvoo.

Harvilahti, L. 1992a. *Kertovan runon keinot: Inkeriläisen runoepiikan tuottamisesta.* Helsinki.

———. 1992b. "The Production of Finnish Epic Poetry: Fixed Wholes or Creative Compositions?" *Oral Tradition* 7(1):87–101.

---

[12] Cf. Russo (1963:247): "there is yet a certain freedom allowed the poet in his use of the traditional language. He is free to create by analogy, sometimes to invert traditional usages, or to build a verse counter to the expectations of his audience if it serves an artistic end."

Kallio, K., and Frog in collaboration with Mari Sarv. 2017. "What to Call the Poetic Form: Kalevalaic, *regivärs*, Runosong, Finnic Tetrameter, or Something Else?" *RMN Newsletter* 12–13:139–161.

Kiparsky, P. 1976. "Oral Poetry: Some Linguistic and Typological Considerations." *Oral Literature and the Formula* (eds. B. Stolz and R. Shannon) 73–106. Ann Arbor.

Kuusi, M. 1952. "Über Wiederholungstypen in der Volksepik unter besonderer Berücksichtigung der Edda, der Bylinen und der finnisch-estnischen Volksdichtung." *Studia Fennica* 6:59–138.

———. 1957. "Kalevalaisen muinaisepiikan viisi tyylikautta." *Kalevalaseuran vuosikirja* 37:109–128.

———. 1970. "Anni Lehtosen runousoppi." *Virittäjä* 74:293–302.

Lord, A. B. 1960. *The Singer of Tales* ed. 2. with CD. Ed by S. Mitchell and G. Nagy 2001. 2nd ed. Cambridge, MA.

Parry, M. 1930. "Studies in the Epic Technique of Oral Verse-Making, I: Homer and Homeric Style." In Parry 1980:266–324.

———. 1932. "Studies in the Epic Technique of Oral Verse-Making, II: The Homeric Language as the Language of an Oral Poetry." In Parry 1980:325–364.

———. 1980. *The Making of Homeric Verse: The Collected Papers of Milman Parry*. Ed. by A. Parry. New York.

Russo, J. A. 1963. "A Closer look at Homeric Formula." *Transactions and Proceedings of the American Philological Association* 94:235–247.

Saarinen, J. 1994. "The Päivölä Song of Miihkali Perttunen." *Songs beyond the Kalevala* (eds. A.-L. Siikala and S. Vakimo) 180–196. Studia Fennica Folkloristica 2. Helsinki.

———. 2013. "Behind the Text: Reconstructing the Voice of a Singer." *Limited Sources, Boundless Possibilities: Textual Scholarship and the Challenges of Oral and Written Texts* (eds. K. Lukin, Frog and S. Katajamäki) 34–43. RMN Newsletter 7. Helsinki.

———. 2017. "'Said a Word, Uttered Thus': Structures and Functions of Parallelism in Arhippa Perttunen's Poems." *Oral Tradition* 31(2):407–424.

———. 2018. *Runolaulun poetiikka: Säe, syntaksi ja parallelismi Arhippa Perttusen runoissa*. Helsinki.

Sadeniemi, M. 1951. *Die Metrik des Kalevala-verses*. FF Communications 139. Helsinki.

Steinitz, W. 1934. *Der Parallelismus in der finnisch-karelischen Volksdichtung*. FF Communications 115. Helsinki.

Tarkka, L. 2013. *Songs of the Border People: Genre, Reflexivity, and Performance in Karelian Oral Poetry*. FF Communications 305. Helsinki.

Thompson, S., ed. 1953. *Four Symposia on Folklore: Held at the Midcentury International Folklore Conference, Indiana University, July 21–August 4, 1950.* Bloomington.

Timonen, S., ed. 1980. *Näin lauloi Larin Paraske.* Helsinki.

———. 2004. *Minä, tila, tunne: Näkökulmia kalevalamittaiseen lyriikkaan.* Helsinki.

Virtanen, L. 1968. *Kalevalainen laulutapa Karjalassa.* Helsinki.

12

Poetic Formulae in Icelandic Post-Medieval *þulur*

Transatlantic Migration

Yelena Sesselja Helgadóttir, University of Iceland

L OAN FORMULAE are of extreme importance in Icelandic post-medieval *þulur*, a folklore genre from ca. the fourteenth to the twentieth century (hereafter 'PMÞ'). PMÞ are versified (but non-stanzaic) lists of names—or sequences of short motifs and/or longer narrative episodes—which are fragmentary, intersecting, and in free poetic form.[1] They are able to absorb both text fragments and structural and compositional devices from other genres; loan formulae are therefore a considerable part of the formulae in PMÞ. Moreover, loan formulae are of crucial importance for genre genesis of PMÞ. Quite a few such formulae came from post-medieval continental Scandinavian ('CSc' hereafter) poetry, particularly ballads and "rigmaroles," and proved to be very influential in PMÞ. CSc rigmaroles are a special kind of folk rhymes, kindred to PMÞ and known as *rim*,[2] *remser*, *ramsor*, or by similar terms in continental Scandinavian languages.

Other loan formulae come from Icelandic folk poetry, primarily from *sagnadansar* ('story-dances', i.e. Icelandic ballads). They may also come from various narrative and humorous songs, game songs, and cumulative tales, etc. These "domestic" loan formulae are discussed at length in "Migration of Poetic Formulae: Icelandic Post-Medieval *þulur*" (YSH 2021), which analyzes how formulae change between their source genres and PMÞ, adapting to a new context and metrical environment. Most loan formulae change metrically when moving into PMÞ, and changes involve all of the most relevant elements

---

[1]   I have discussed the Scandinavian roots of PMÞ in a previous article (YSH 2014), and their poetic form and loan formulae in three previous articles (YSH 2016; 2017; 2021); cf. YSH 2020:90–249 for detailed discussion of the poetic form and compositional means of PMÞ, including formulae.

[2]   *Rim* should not be confused with Icelandic *rímur*: long narrative poems with a highly elaborate system of rigorous stanzaic meters based on metrical feet, alliteration, and rhyme.

of Icelandic metrics: alliteration, beat, and rhyme. A metrical parameter that was lost in migration can be compensated by another metrical parameter. Loan formulae often become metrically richer in PMÞ (compared to their source genre), but seldom metrically poorer, despite PMÞ having fewer and less strict metrical requirements. PMÞ strive for metrically and semantically well-formed texts and formulae, avoiding both an absolute shortage of metricality and an over-abundance of metrical features. Metrical and semantic forces usually collaborate to produce balanced formulae—but where they do not, variation is contra-metrical rather than contra-semantic; increasing the metricality of a loan formula should not impair its semantics. At the same time, changes in semantics should not impair the strongest metrical element of loan formulae: the rhyme. The same is true for non-variation in PMÞ: it can be both metrically favorable and contra-metrical, but it should not impair the semantics.

In the present chapter, I carry out a similar analysis on "transatlantic" (CSc) loan formulae and consider them in terms of the complicated system of metrical and semantic checks and balances described above. I then compare the results with those from the analysis of domestic loan formulae, using the definitions and premises that I have applied in my previous research. These include understanding *formulae* as fixed or flexible verbal units in poetic composition, which have identifiable and useful metrical features (cf. Ford 2002:225) and carry distinguishable traditional meanings or associations (cf. Foley and Ramey 2012:80). Here, I also adopt Wray's (2002; 2009) approach to the formula as a prefabricated morpheme-equivalent unit. *Metrical regularity* is understood as a systematic, yet not rigorously uniform, application of a complex of phonological devices and strategies in poetic composition, rather than their uniform application to every unit, i.e. line or stanza (YSH 2016; 2020). The terms *meter* and *metrical* as referring to PMÞ in this chapter should be viewed in this light.

My research has established the special status of Icelandic ballads as a source genre for loan formulae in PMÞ. Most loan formulae come to PMÞ from *sagnadansar*, and in these formulae we observe the most metrical changes on the way from the source genre to PMÞ—such as loss of rhyme, expansion of alliteration, and line shortening. At the same time, similar changes are virtually absent in loan formulae from other Icelandic folk-poetic genres. The present chapter will touch upon CSc ballad formulae (section 1), but then primarily concentrate on loan formulae from rigmaroles (sections 2–3) and those of mixed ballad and CSc rigmarole origin (section 4). It will also discuss *passim* the peculiarities of ballads as a source of transatlantic loan formulae. Migration of CSc formulae to the Faroe Islands and their development in Faroese *skjaldur*, a folk poetry genre kindred to PMÞ and CSc rigmaroles, has not received much attention in previous work and is given more consideration here.

1. Transatlantic Loan Formulae: Migration Time and Paths

Scholars believe that ballads and other contemporary genres of folk poetry migrated to Iceland from other West-Nordic countries before 1500 or closely thereafter (cf. Gunnell 2001:38). The *terminus post quem* could be defined as 1400 ± ca. 50 years. This is based on the timing of the Black Death, which struck continental Scandinavia during the middle of the fourteenth century, and Iceland in the beginning of the fifteenth century, temporarily cutting down communications between Scandinavian countries (cf. discussion in YSH 2014:106–111). Some migration of folk poetry might have occurred before the Black Death, but it is unlikely that it was extensive, since we would expect a larger migration to have left more prominent traces in the rich medieval Icelandic sources. After the Black Death, Icelandic manuscripts significantly decreased in number (Guðvarður Már Gunnlaugsson 2016:9). Fewer materials were committed to writing for a long time, and folk songs were not prominent among them. The assessment of the *terminus ante quem* varies by ± ca. 50 years; Vésteinn Ólason (1982:105–109) assumes that Iceland became isolated from the West-Nordic linguistic community around 1530, while Jón Samsonarson (1975:427–428) believes that this happened before the sixteenth century.

Faroese folklore, including *skjaldur*, remained under prolonged influence from CSc countries, particularly from Denmark, during the early modern period. In general, Icelandic PMÞ are closer to Faroese *skjaldur* than to CSc rigmaroles (YSH 2006, 2008). This could indicate that the gate for folk song migration between the Faroe Islands and Iceland stood open somewhat longer than that for migration between continental Scandinavia and the islands of the North Atlantic. Folk song migration apparently was not linear from continental Scandinavia to Iceland through the Faroes. Some of the texts and formulae analyzed in this chapter appear, for instance, to have migrated to Iceland directly and either did not come to Faroese *skjaldur* at all or are no longer extant there (cf. (11)). Others appear to have stopped in the Faroes and never reached Icelandic PMÞ, as in (10). Yet others are common both for PMÞ and *skjaldur* (YSH 2008; 2014; cf. Figure 1).

The CSc ballads that migrated to Iceland at the time of major changes in language and literature profoundly influenced not only *sagnadansar* (Vésteinn Ólason 1982), but also, among other Icelandic genres, PMÞ. One of the major groups of loan formulae in PMÞ consists of formulae that apparently came into PMÞ directly from ballads; among these are the formulae *hest-mest* ('horse-most') and *gaman-saman* ('fun-together') (YSH 2016). These formulae are found in ballads both from continental Scandinavia and from the islands of the North

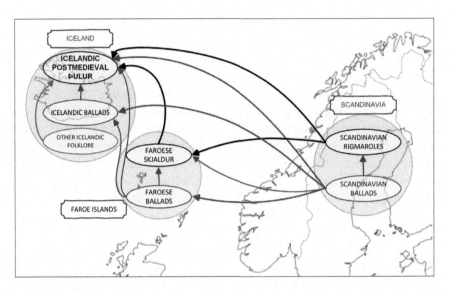

Map 1: Formula migration from Scandinavia to the isles in the North Atlantic:
Main routes and paths[1]

Atlantic, but not much in rigmarole poetry from continental Scandinavia. This indicates that the formulae at issue arrived into PMÞ immediately from ballads, without moving first into CSc rigmaroles and then into PMÞ. The question is rather whether these formulae came to PMÞ immediately from CSc ballads or intermediately through Icelandic ballads. The matter of formulae native to *sagnadansar* and formulae imported to *sagnadansar* from CSc ballads has not yet been thoroughly examined. No clear line between these two kinds of ballad formulae can be drawn with the present state of knowledge. Therefore, it can be difficult to tell whether a loan ballad formula in PMÞ comes from CSc ballads or *sagnadansar* when it is present in both. It seems nonetheless more likely that PMÞ borrowed such formulae from the Icelandic ballad tradition rather than immediately from continental ballads, in which case they would have had to overcome both the language barrier and that of the genre. Preliminary studies show a low number of formulae present in CSc ballads and PMÞ, but not in *sagnadansar*, which indicates the same direction.

The second group of transatlantic loan formulae are those that apparently were borrowed into PMÞ more or less immediately from CSc rigmaroles, though

---

[1]   The blank map of Europe that was edited by YSH for this chapter is courtesy of Daniel Feher at https://www.freeworldmaps.net/europe/europe-blank-map-hd.jpg (retrieved October 3, 2019).

sometimes under influence from ballad formulae. Some rigmarole texts were probably among the folk poetry that migrated to Iceland, possibly on a par with CSc ballads. Icelandic PMÞ, with their formulae-attracting power reaching out to both domestic ballads and other domestic genres, also proved able to borrow some formulae from rigmaroles in closely related languages. The present chapter will consider cases where adapting to new linguistic (and genre) conditions went smoothly (section 2) and some where it was challenging (section 3).

The third group of transatlantic loan formulae in PMÞ are those that are found both in CSc rigmaroles and in ballads. In many of these cases, it is difficult to say whether the formulae found in both came into PMÞ from the former or latter. In both cases, the formulae must only pass one barrier when entering PMÞ, whether that of genre but not of language, such as formulae first borrowed into Icelandic ballads as discussed above, or that of language but not of genre, like formulae borrowed from CSc rigmaroles, which will be discussed in more detail below (section 4).

In the following sections, Roman numerals and letters are reserved for formulae (e.g. Ia), while examples are numbered with Arabic numerals and letters. Language and genre, for examples of poetry other than PMÞ, are specified in block letters: N, D, S, I, F = Norwegian, Danish, Swedish, Icelandic, and Faroese, respectively; B = ballad, R = rigmarole, S = *skjaldur*. Inflected forms are indicated as relevant with Leipzig glosses in small capitals.

2. Rigmarole Formulae, Case I: Virtually No Changes

Some formulae migrate from CSc rigmaroles into PMÞ with few changes. An example is formula Ia: *There sit(s) S {and} A gold-O*, where S = subject (animate noun, NOM); A = verb of action (largely transitive, 3SG or 3PL) describing handwork; O = object (inanimate noun, largely ACC.PL), preferably rhyming with S; elements in curly brackets may be omitted while parentheses enclose a variation, whether only a word ending, as here, or alternative words or phrasing. The formula is chiefly found in Norwegian rigmaroles, where it often serves as a basis for lists organized as multiforms (cf. Frog, this volume):

(1a)

Der sit sveinanne	There sit the boys
smidar paa gullteinanne,	work on the gold-rods,
der sit møyanne	there sit the girls
saumar paa gulltrøyunne,	stitch the gold-jackets,
der sit fruenne	there sit the ladies
saumar paa gullhuvunne,	stitch the gold-caps,

der sit drengjenne	there sit the boys
spelar paa gullstrengjenne,	play the gold-strings,
lengst inn i steinanne	far in among the rocks

(NR) Støylen 1899 [1977]:38–39, #264

(1b)

Der sit frua	There sits [a] lady
saumar gull i huva,	sews gold on [a] cap,
der sit katten	there sits the cat
saumar gull i hatten	sews gold on the hat

(NR) Støylen 1899 [1977]:40, #270

In PMÞ, a very similar formula is found, except the subject and the verb are usually plural:

(1c)

þar sitja systur	there sit sisters
og skafa gullkystur	and scrape gold-chests
þar Sitja Nunnur	there sit nuns
og skafa gulltunnur	and scrape gold-tuns
þar sitja Sveinar	there sit boys
og Skafa gullteina	and scrape gold-rods

(PMÞ) Lbs 414 8vo, 92r

Besides the category of number, the differences are very few; the formula's syntax, semantics, function, and context remain the same. Most of the formula's metrical characteristics are also preserved in PMÞ. Even the formula's wording is similar between the two quite closely related languages, Norwegian and Icelandic. A similar situation can be found in the Faroes, where some formulae are also more or less calqued from CSc languages (cf. Kári Sverrisson 2000:12, #2).

PMÞ texts with the Ia formula commonly open with a version of formula Ib: *S sat in [a] well, had [a] leaf in [its] mouth* where S = subject (animate noun, NOM), usually *bokki* ('billy-goat'). These lines are most often followed by, *[it] shook its rings, asked {the} bird(s) [to] sing*, as in (2a):

(2a)

Bokki sat í brunni,	[A] billy-goat sat in [a] well,
hafði blað í munni,	had [a] leaf in [its] mouth,
hristi sína hringa,	[it] shook its rings,

bað fugla syngja	asked birds [to] sing

(PMÞ) Lbs 418 8vo, 31r

The formulae in (2a)—which are almost compounded in PMÞ—are also found in
CSc rigmaroles, mostly Norwegian. They are certainly different from formula Ia,
which is by nature quite open for variation. In Ib, variation is limited to slight
changes in the opening word in line 1 (S), sometimes in the verb in line 3,[3] and
closing words in line 4. Notwithstanding this difference, Ib also presents a case
of almost verbatim translation between languages, similar to Ia. A Norwegian
example of this formula is presented in (2b):

(2b)

Bukken stod i brunne	The billy-goat stood in [a] well
med gullblad i munne,	with [a] gold-leaf in [its] mouth,
riste paasine ringar,	shook its rings,
bad smaafuglanne syngja	asked the little birds [to] sing

(NR) Støylen 1899 [1977]:40, #271

The Norwegian formula is more open to variation, especially in the epithet
accompanying the word *blad* ('leaf') in line 2: *bleike blad* ('pale leaf'), *gullblad*
('gold-leaf, golden leaf'), etc.[4] Some variation also occurs in the verb in line 1
(and in lines 3–4). During the passage of this formula from Norway to Iceland
variation decreases, leading to some unification in the formula.[5] It is particu-
larly pronounced because the Icelandic formula hardly ever has an epithet that
goes with *leaf*. Possibly only some (few) variations of the Norwegian formula
migrated to Iceland, among them probably the one with the verb phrase *helde
blad* ('holds [a] leaf') (Støylen 1899 [1977]:40, #272), which eventually became
predominant. Some unification also takes place in the formula's function in
rigmarole/PMÞ texts. The Norwegian formula is most often an opening one, but
from time to time it is used in the middle of a text or even as a closing formula.
The Icelandic formula, in contrast, is almost exclusively an opening one. Apart
from this unification in text and function, formula Ib illustrated in (2) under-
goes virtually no substantial changes on its way from Norwegian rigmarole to
Icelandic PMÞ. Like formula Ia, illustrated in (1), it mostly preserves the syntax
of the continental formula, its meaning, metrical characteristics, and even

---

[3]   In line 1: *Blokki* (a name?) (JS 289 8vo, 29r) or *Brokkur* ('hard trotting [horse]; boor') (JS 507 8vo, p.
     31). In line 3: *taldi* ('counted') (SÁM 85/371 EF, #21604).

[4]   Støylen 1899 [1977]:40, #270, #271.

[5]   *Unification* refers here to the amalgamation of two or more modifications of a formula—or, alter-
     natively, to one or more modifications becoming predominant while others decrease or disap-
     pear (YSH 2017; 2021).

wording. Not all formulae are so well maintained. In some of them, numerous changes occurred as the formula adapted to its new climate. The next section deals with cases of substantial or even extreme changes.

3. Rigmarole Formulae, Case II: Everything Upside Down, or Is It the Same Formula at All?

In both CSc rigmaroles and those from the islands of the North Atlantic, one finds a formulaic narrative involving an unfriendly and often aggressive (old) woman, possibly an ogress (YSH 2010a; 2010b). In CSc rigmaroles, it starts with the following opening formula, identified here as IIa, which is quite open to variation: *{A/C} I came to {L} {T} {A/C} {an} old woman {(sat/stood) and} (cooked/ stirred) porridge*, where A/C = adverb or conjunction (usually of time); L = location: to the old woman, to the kitchen, home, etc.; and T = time:

(3a)

So kom eg til ei kjering	Then I came to an old woman
som stod og reidde velling	who stood and cooked porridge

(NR) Støylen 1899 [1977]:41, #275

(3b)

jeg kom ud í Kjøkkenet, der stod en Kjælling og rørte i sin Vælling

(DR) Tang Kristensen 1896:50, #483

I came to the kitchen, there stood an old woman and stirred her porridge

(3c)

När jag kom hem om qvällen,	When I came home in the evening,
hade mor kokat en välling	[my] mother had cooked porridge

(SR) Nordlander 1886 [1975]:65, #89B

Another modification of this formula has *grød* for 'porridge' instead of *velling*, which might be more exactly translated as 'gruel'. *Grød* fits well in the formula, occasionally rhyming with *sød* ('sweet') or *blød* ('thin') in neighboring lines (Tang Kristensen 1896:47, #461). This modification is observed in Sweden and Norway and is widespread in Denmark, albeit not necessarily in the same kind of rigmarole texts, cf. (3d):

(3d)
> køm i Kjøkkenet, der sat en gammel Kjælling og rørte Mælkegrød
>> (DR) Tang Kristensen 1896:50, #481

> came to the kitchen, there sat an old woman and stirred milk porridge

However, the North Atlantic island texts are dramatically different:

(4a)
| Kom ég þar að kvöldi, | I came there in [the] evening |
| sem kerling sat að eldi | where [an] old woman sat at [the] fire |

>> (PMÞ) Lbs 587 4to IX, 40r–v

(4b)
| Kom ég þar ad qvöldi, | I came there in [the] evening, |
| kerlíng sat vid eld | [an] old woman sat by [the] fire |

>> (PMÞ) Lbs 587 4to IV, 12r

(4c)
| Hann kom inn á kvøldi, | He came in in [the] evening |
| sum konan sat og rørdi | where the woman/wife sat and stirred |

>> (FS) FMD BS 340. Transcription: Birgitta Hylin

(4d)
Eg kom har eitt kvøldið	I came there one evening
har konan sat og rördi	where the woman/wife sat and stirred,
mjólk at ysta	[she was] coagulating milk

>> (FS) FMD BS 997. Transcription: Birgitta Hylin

These Icelandic and Faroese formulae have a similar context to that found in CSc rigmaroles. They begin similarly as well: the narrator comes and meets the old woman. However, the word for 'porridge' is missing both from the Icelandic and Faroese versions of this formula. It is possible that the word *vellingur* ('porridge, gruel'), which seems to be widely known in Iceland from the eighteenth century onward, was not well-known there when most of the rigmaroles migrated to Iceland and the Faroese Islands.[6] The words *grautur* (Icelandic) and *greytur* (Faroese) for 'porridge' (cf. Danish *grød*) are problematic for rhyming and therefore not used in the islands' formulae—even though they are key words in the CSc formulae. The rhyme *kælling/kjerring : vælling/velling* ('old woman : porridge'), which is crucial for the *velling*-modification of this formula, thus virtually disappears.[7] Instead, the Faroese formula keeps *rørdi* ('stirred'), frequently found in the Danish version; Faroese rhyme rules for *skjaldur* apparently allow *rørdi* to rhyme with *kvøldi(ð)* ('(the) evening'), which is also present in some cases of the rigmarole formula. For example, see (3c) above, where the key rhyme is not *kælling/kjerring : vælling/velling* but *qvällen : välling* ('evening : porridge'). The Icelandic word for 'stirred' (*hrærði*) is also problematic for rhyming; in the Icelandic formula, the key rhyme is thus changed to *kveldi : eldi* ('evening.DAT : fire.DAT'). This change likely happened under influence from Icelandic ballads, where the rhyme *kveldi : veldi* ('evening.DAT : kingdom. NOM/DAT/ACC')[8] is popular in a similar context (e.g. hero coming to a king or an earl, cf. *ÍFkv* I:43). The resulting formulae are: *(I/he) came (in/there) {in} {X} evening where {the} (woman/wife) sat and stirred {coagulating milk}* (Faroese), and *... where [an] old woman sat by [the] fire* (Icelandic), where X = a pronoun, article etc., modifying *evening*.

All these changes result in the islands' formulae being quite different from the CSc ones in form and content. The missing rhyme is compensated for, but the new rhyme does not involve the old woman, originally a key person in the formula and its surrounding narrative; she moves to line 2 instead. Another key element of the CSc formulae, the porridge, is altogether absent—or sometimes replaced by milk in the Faroes. The location, only sometimes included in the beginning of the CSc formula, becomes stable in the Icelandic formula; it moves to the end of line 2 and becomes part of the rhyme: *að eldi* ('by [the] fire'). A stable time modifier also appears in the islands' formula and becomes a part of the rhyme: *að kvöldi, á kvøldi(ð)* ('in {the} evening'), etc.

Nonetheless, the islands' formulae still involve the same protagonists (the narrator and the old woman) and core events, i.e. the narrator's coming in where the woman is sitting by the fire or even doing some cooking (in the Faroese formula). Further, the islands' formulae are metrically similar to the CSc

---

[6] I am grateful to Guðvarður M. Gunnlaugsson for pointing this out (private conversation, March 28, 2017). *Ordbog over det norrøne prosasprog* and Ritmálssafn confirm his suggestion.

[7] The rhyme *kelling : velling* ('old woman : porridge.ACC') is found, albeit rarely, in similar contexts in *skjaldur* (cf. Hylin 1971:53). It is plausible that *vellingur* was (re)introduced into active use and/ or into *skjaldur* later, when the *kvøldi(ð)* – *rørdi* modification of IIa had become established (cf. discussion on *white horse* in YSH 2016:55).

[8] Icelandic *veldi* spans a broad spectrum from 'power, authority, government' to 'state' and 'kingdom'.

ones; actually, they are metrically richer, because they have two stable alliterations in the first line and one in the second: <u>k</u>om, <u>k</u>völdi, <u>k</u>erling. Finally, they have the same function as the CSc rigmarole formulae in question—that is, they open a narrative of an encounter with an unfriendly woman. In other words, both the CSc formulae and the islands' formulae are indexed at the same place in the same (or very similar) narrative (cf. Kuiper 2009:13–21). Despite variation, this is the same formula: it has retained the same core meaning, the same function in the narrative, and even the same or similar metrical characteristics. Thus, the formula has retained its prefabricatedness and morpheme equivalence, its position as "a dedicated entry in the mental lexicon" (Wray 2009:31), and its position in the narrative's index of formulae (cf. Kuiper 2009:13–21).

The formula analyzed above covers the first element of the formulaic narrative in question: the narrator comes to a place and meets an (old) woman, or ogress. Two formulae serve the second element, which involves one of the protagonists attempting some form of intrusion or aggression, and the other one hitting the intruder in response. In CSc rigmaroles, the narrator tries to taste the porridge and the old woman usually responds by hitting the opponent with a firebrand. This is described by formulae IIb: *I took (a/her) stick and (wanted/asked) to (lick/prick) at {the porridge}* and IIc: *She took a firebrand and hit my (white/sore) hand*; see (5):

(5a)

tok eg meg ei stikka	I took a stick for me
og bad eg maatte slikka	and asked [if] I might lick
so tok hon seg ein eldebrand	then she took a firebrand
og la til meg paa kvite hand	and tried to hit my white hand

(NR) Støylen 1899 [1977]:42, #275

(5b)

a taw hend prekstek a vild i hend Grød å prek, hun taw en Illdbråend, slåw mæ øwe mi æææm Håend

(DR) Tang Kristensen 1896:47, #464

I took her stick and wanted to prick at her porridge, she took a firebrand, hit me over my sore hand

At times—although quite rarely—it is the old woman who wants to try the porridge (e.g. Tang Kristensen 1896:47, #462), and then the narration is resolved in some different way; in this case, the woman wants to try the porridge but may not do so, so she goes out and buys a cake.

In the islands' version of this narrative, no porridge is involved (formula IIa, (4a–b)). In the Faroese modification of formula IIa, milk is sometimes mentioned (4c). The narrator may ask for milk to drink, but is refused; this corresponds respectively to formulae IIb and IIc in CSc rigmaroles, as illustrated in (5). In the Faroese formula, the narrative basically ends at this point—relatively peacefully, in contrast with the versions above, as (6a) shows:

(6a)

bað hana geva mær	[I] asked her to give me
mjólk at drekka	milk to drink
Ei vildi eg givið tær	I won't give you
fyrr enn tú hevði grátið mær	before you have cried for me
við báðum tínum eygum	with your both eyes

(FS) FMD BS 997. Transcription: Birgitta Hylin

In the Icelandic opening formula, no food is mentioned, and the next part of the narrative thus must be treated differently:

(6b)

tók hún sinn bínginn	she took her heap
og hugði mig að stínga;	and intended to stab me;
eg tók þá lurkinn minn lánga	I took then my long cudgel
og lagði undir kellingar vánga	and struck under [the] old woman's cheek

(PMÞ) AM 960 4to 13, 1r

The formulae are reversed: it is not the narrator who takes a stick and wants to try the porridge, but the old woman tries to stab the narrator, and the narrator subsequently hits her with the long cudgel. The end of line 1 is clearly problematic for PMÞ collectors and their informants. Sometimes words occur that have more or less conventional meanings, like *bínginn* ('the heap.ACC'; or, possibly, Old Icelandic 'bed'?) (6b) or *pinkil* ('packet.ACC') (DFS 67 E, 421v). Alongside such words, however, are often words that are seldom (or never) attested outside of the verses. Most often these are nouns, like *pynginn* ('the purse.ACC[?]') (DFS 67 E, 424r). Sometimes these are verbs like *pyngja* ('put [s-thing] into a purse') (Lbs 418 8vo, 30v), *bíngja* (meaning uncertain) (Lbs 587 4to IV, 29r), etc., in the verb phrase *hún tók að* + V ('she took/started to' + verb.INF); no object is involved even where the verb appears to be transitive. This ungrammaticality may be interpreted as a feature of the formula (in line with Wray 2009) and is at the same time an example of the rhyme outweighing semantics in the formula's oral circulation. The Icelandic modification of formula IIb would thus be: *She (took her O / took to V) and intended to stab me*, where O = noun.M.ACC.SG, with or without an article, rhyming with *stinga* ('stab'; cf. *prek* ('stick') in (5b)) and generally starting with *b* or *p*; V = verb.INF with similar phonetic characteristics.

In formula IIb, the main issue in Icelandic and Faroese examples apparently is accommodating content and language material that is different from that of the CSc rigmaroles. In formula IIc, on the other hand, it is again the rhyme that is problematic: Icelandic *hönd* ('hand') does not rhyme with *eldibrand* ('firebrand. ACC'), and an alternative rhyme pair is inserted, resulting in the Icelandic modification of formula IIc: *I took my long cudgel and hit under [the] old woman's cheek.*

Just like formula IIa, formulae IIb and IIc have rhyme that is completely different from that in continental Scandinavia, they also involve different material and use different wording compared to the CSc formula. Moreover, they are reversed. However, the core structures of the Scandinavian and Icelandic formulae are quite similar, as observed in IIb: *(I/she) took (my/her/a) O {and} intended to prick at (the porridge / me)* and IIc: *{but} {then} (she/I) took (a/my) (hot firebrand / long cudgel) and hit (my hand / her cheek).* The formulae have similar functions in the narration: IIb is, both in continental Scandinavia and in Iceland, a prelude to the main action where one protagonist hits the other, and IIc describes the main action. Finally, the Icelandic formulae are metrically similar to the CSc ones; the idea of the rhyme in the formula is so strong in the Icelandic formulae that even the formula's meaning gives way (IIb). This leads us again to the conclusion that, despite the changes that the CSc formulae undergo on their way to Icelandic PMÞ, each formula can be considered one and the same—right across the North Atlantic.

4. Formulae Common to Continental Scandinavian Ballads and Rigmaroles

Virtually all of the formulae common to ballads, rigmaroles, and PMÞ are general in their content and wording. This quality permits additional rhymes and different contexts. Such is the case of the formulaic complex around the rhyme *land : sand* ('land : sand') which is often complemented by other rhyming pairs with CSc stems such as *strand* ('shore'), *hand (hånd)* ('hand'), and *brand* ('fire, sword, burning log'). Most of the rhyming words involved differ slightly in Icelandic and Faroese from their CSc counterparts: *strönd/strond* vs. *strand*; *hönd/ hond* vs. *hand*; *sandur, brandur*[9] vs. *sand, brand*; and CSc *land* has the plural *lönd/*

---

[9]   In NOM.SG in Icelandic and Faroese, *sand* and *brand* being ACC.SG.

lond in Icelandic and Faroese. This poses problems with rhyming for migrating formulae. We can nonetheless observe formulae belonging to the *land-sand* complex in CSc ballads, as in (7a–b), Faroese ballads, as in (7c–d), Icelandic ballads, as in (7e–f) and (11b), CSc rigmarole tradition, as in (9b), (10c), and (12b–e), Faroese *skjaldur*, as in (8c), (10a–b), and (12h–i), and PMÞ (8a–b), (8d), (9a), (11a), (12a), and (12f–g). In ballads, the formulae in this complex have several modifications connected to traveling. These include formula IIIa: *X sails away, Y stands behind on [the] (sand/shore)*, illustrated in (7a–b):

(7a)

> Kongjen han styrde sitt skip ifrå *land*,
> hass drònning stend att'e påa kvitan *sand*

> > (NB) Norsk folkediktning VII:43

> The king steered his ship from [the] *land*,
> his queen stands behind on [the] white *sand*

(7b)

> Og det var liti Kjersti, And it was little Kjersti,
> ho kom seg ned til *strand*, she came down to [the] *shore*,
> det var den skipar Håken, it was the captain Håken,
> han styrde si snekkje i *land* he steered his ship toward [the] *land*

> > (NB) Norsk folkediktning VII:38

A second modification is formula IIIb: *X (sails to [the] (sand/shore) / steps ashore), Y meets X there*, illustrated in (7c–d):

(7c)

> Fyrstur stígur Álvur kongur King Álvur first set
> sínum fótum á *land*,   his feet on [the] *land*,
> tá var tann óndi Ásmundur then the evil king Ásmundur
> kongur
> riðin niður til *strand* had galloped down to [the] *shore*

> > (FB) CCF I:377

(7d)

> Rögvaldur stóð a *sandi*, Rögvaldur stood on [the] *sand*
> þar Þiðrik sigldi að *landi* as Þiðrik sailed toward [the] *land*

> > (IB) ÍFkv I:81

Example (7e) can be considered a variation of formula IIIb:

(7e)

Biðillinn reið með *ströndum*,	The suitor rode along [the] *shores*
meyjuna rak að *löndum*	The girl washed up on [the] *lands*

(IB) ÍFkv I:90

A third modification is formula IIIc: *X approaches [the] land and (casts the anchor on [the] (sand/shore) / steps ashore)*, illustrated in (7f):

(7f)

Higar ið teirra snekkja	Where their ship
kendi fagurt *land*,	touched [the] beautiful *land*
kastaðu síni akkerini	[they] cast their anchors
á so hvítan *sand*	on such white *sand*

(FB) CCF I:377

Formulae from the *land-sand* complex occur in various contexts in Icelandic PMÞ. The closest examples to the ballad use of the formula are also tightly connected to traveling in PMÞ and belong to modification IIIb: *X arrives and Y meets X on [the] (shore/sand)*, as in (8a), which can be compared to (7d–e) above. The formula in (8a) opens the text and thus has an introductory function, noting that (7a) and (7c) above also open their respective travel episodes:

(8a)

Kom eg þar að *landi*,	I came there to *land*
sem kerlíng stóð á *sandi*	where [an] old woman stood on [the] *sand*

(PMÞ) Lbs 1057 4to q3, 182r–v

Similar use of formula IIIb is found in a different context—but also in the opening part of the texts in question—in Icelandic PMÞ, cf. (8b) and its Faroese counterpart in (8c):

(8b)

æður sat á *sandi*	[an] eider duck sat on [the] *sand*
þá blikinn kom að *landi*	when the eider drake came to *land*

(PMÞ) Lbs 587 4to III, 10r

273

(8c)

Kráka situr á *sandi* [A] crow sits on [the] *sand*
snjófuglur á *landi* [a] snowbird on *land*

(FS) FMD BS 42b. Transcription: YSH, Rannveig Winther

As is often the case for formulae that come to PMÞ from ballads, the *land-sand* formula does not change much on its way to PMÞ in this modification. However, these formulae do sometimes show text shortening and/or line shortening (YSH 2016:51–55). Another change, in content, is the formula's slightly weakened connections with traveling: the Faroese example in (8c) is actually quite static and only has an indirect connection to traveling (the lines in (8c) open a traveling episode).

A similar formula is used in a group of PMÞ texts often referred to as *Þornaldar þula*,[10] in a slightly different context: both X and Y are positioned at the same place (on the sand), but the context of the formula makes it evident that a connection with traveling is also present. This formula is nearly a rhyme-based collocation; nonetheless, the contrast of land and sand as two different locations, important for the formula under consideration, also exists in this case:

(8d)

vid saustum a landi og *eckj* a *landi*,
þad var a midium Þiörsär *sandi*

(PMÞ) AM 148 8vo, 253r

we saw each other on land, and not on *land*,
it was in the middle of the Þjórsá *sand[s]*

Examples (8c) and (8d) bring us closer to yet another context of the *land-sand* formula in PMÞ, the so-called *Tátu þula* ('Táta's þula') which lists the activities—or simply location, as in the case of this formula—of Táta's daughters (cf. 9a below). The *land-sand* formula in this modification, identified as IIId, is thus a listing formula (i.e. one built on enumerating objects); however, it still preserves the important distinction of the two locations. This use of the formula has a clear parallel in some CSc—particularly Norwegian—rigmaroles about Taate's sisters, as in (9b) (or Tora's daughters, as in Støylen 1899 [1977]:15, #78, or other similar persons):

(9a)

Segs eru á *sandi*, Six are on [the] *sand*
Sjö eru á *Landi* Seven are on [the] *land*

(PMÞ) AM 969 4to 244r–v

[10] This translates 'Þornaldur's þula'; Þornaldur is a fabled name and þula, the singular of þulur.

(9b)

og seks i *Sanda*,	and six on [the] *sands*
og sju i *Landa*	and seven on [the] *lands*

(NR) Støylen 1899 [1977]:16, #79

These rigmaroles, although relatively less common in continental Scandinavia than *Tátu þula* in Iceland, apparently provided the basis of the Icelandic formula IIId. Thus, formula IIId is a rigmarole formula that undergoes virtually no changes on its way to PMÞ, as formulae Ia and Ib above. This is, however, not the case on all the islands of the North Atlantic. Notably, the *land-sand* formula IIId in its entirety is virtually absent in this same context in Faroese *skjaldur*. Instead, its elements are used with a different rhyming word, more distantly related to the formulaic complex around the rhyme *land : sand*, described in the beginning of this section, as in (10a–b):

(10a)

tvær brendar á *brondum*	two [were] burnt by *brands*
tvær skotnar av *londum*	two [were] shot from *lands*[?]

(FS) Kári Sverrisson 2000:28, #60

(10b)

tvær liggja brendar á *brondum*	two lie burnt by *brands* [or: on *embers*?]
tvær liggja deyðar á *sondum*	two lie dead on [the] *sands*

(FS) Kári Sverrisson 2000:20, #27

These can be compared to (10c), from a Norwegian rigmarole:

(10c)

båni ligg i *brondo*,	the children lie on *embers*
brenner seg å *hondo*	get their *hands* burnt

(NR) Skar 1903–1916 [1960–1963] III:235

It is not obvious, indeed, why formula IIId is only used in such fragmentary ways in this context in Faroese *skjaldur*. This change may be due to the apparent absence of the *land-sand* formula in this context in Danish rigmaroles which were evidently somewhat influential in the Faroes. Moreover, the formula is almost absent in Danish rigmaroles in general and only incidentally used in other CSc rigmaroles. The Norwegian example (10c), strongly backed up by formula IIc, illustrated in (5) above, is likely to have been a model for this development in the Faroe Islands. However, the formula in (10c) apparently does not occur in the context of CSc rigmaroles about Taata's sisters, Tora's daughters etc., which suggests that it did not come directly from CSc rigmaroles. A possible link is the Faroese *og Sigga rakar í brondunum // við hondunum* ('and Sigga rakes up the *embers* // with [her] *hands*' [literally, 'with the hands']) in a short *skjaldur* about different household tasks (FMD BS 59a, transcription: Rannveig Winther). This *skjaldur* stands closer to the Norwegian example (10c), although the latter lists things that create emergencies in a household rather than usual household task. We should also observe that neither the Norwegian formula in (10c), nor its modifications in the Faroese *skjaldur*, seem to have reached Iceland. Neither has its context (i.e. listing the reasons why a certain farmer should hurry home). Furthermore, the rhyming stem *brand* is apparently little used in PMÞ[11]—and hardly ever in the *land-sand* formula, despite the fact that *brand* was used in Icelandic ballads, also as a part of the *land-sand* formulaic complex (albeit rarely).[12]

The second rhyming stem of the Norwegian formula, *hand*, is rather common in every genre considered here. It is widespread in continental Scandinavian, Faroese, and Icelandic ballads where these formulae apparently have connotations of (extra)marital relations,[13] as well as in rigmaroles from CSc countries (see (5) and (10c)). The stem *hand* has also made its way into Icelandic PMÞ as part of the *land-sand* formulaic complex (IIIe), despite the rhyming difficulties mentioned above. This is demonstrated by (11a), which comes from a yet different context of a PMÞ text about girls walking along the seashore. (11b) is a corresponding example from an Icelandic ballad and a conceivable source of (11a):

(11a)

taka sína brúði í *hönd*,	take his bride by [her] *hand*,
og leíða hana á önnur *lönd*	and lead her to other *lands*

(PMÞ) AM 969 4to 48v

---

[11] With the exception of the line *Brandur er a Syrlandi* ('Brandur is in Syria') (AM 148 8vo, 254v) in *Þornaldar þula* (different countries—such as Ireland, Iceland etc.—are named in some other manuscripts).

[12] Cf. *Stafrós kvæði*: *Þegar þau komu á hvítan sand, // þar felldi hann niður sinn búinn brand* ('When they came to [the] white sand, // he dropped there his decorated sword') (*ÍFkv* I: 64).

[13] Cf. these lines in a Danish ballad: *Taffvelbord reyste i fremmede Land, // Stolt Ingerlild tager en Kiøbmand om Haand* ('Taffvelbord traveled to [a] faraway land, // Proud Ingerlild takes a merchant by [the] hand') (*Danmarks gamle folkeviser* VI:266).

(11b)

> Hann tók í hennar hægri hönd: He took [her] by her right *hand,*
>
> festi frú og gaf henni *lönd* betrothed himself to [the] lady and gave her *lands*

> (IB) *ÍFkv* II:104

As in formulae IIIa–c, these examples are connected to traveling: the bride in (11a) is led to a fairytale-like land where she sits only on a silver chair, drinks only wine, etc. This correlates with the ballad use of the word *hand* in connection with (extra)marital relations and faraway lands. This *lönd-hönd* formula, however, has apparently not made its way to Faroese *skjaldur* or taken root there. This is peculiar, as the conditions for such a migration seem favorable: there are examples of *hond* ('hand') rhyming with words such as *sandur* ('sand') and stems such as *brond-* (see above) in *skjaldur*. Furthermore, there are *skjaldur* that are similar to (11a) (Kári Sverrisson 2000:16, #15).

Turning back to the *land-sand* formula without additional rhyming words or stems, it is most often found in PMÞ in the modification of *run(ning) up to land(s)*, *up to sand(s)* (IIIf), in a short runaway narrative passage in a large group of PMÞ texts typically referred to as *Sat ég undir fiskihlaða* ('I sat under a fish stack'). In this case, the formula is also related to traveling and describes its onset:

(12a)

> enn jeg að renna,
> allt uppá *land* allt uppá Biskups *sand*

> (PMÞ) Lbs 421 8vo, 36v

> and I [started] running,
> all the way onto [the] *land,* all the way onto [the] Bishop's *sand*

Similar narrative passages can be found in several CSc rigmaroles; however, the *land-sand* formula is not used there.[14] Nonetheless, the formula in question is not far away; compare this rigmarole from Norway:

(12b)

> So strauk eg aat eit anna *land,* Then I ran away to another *land,*
>
> der møtte meg ein preste*mann* there I met a clergy*man*

> (NR) Støylen, 1899 [1977]:41 #275

---

[14] E.g. Støylen 1899 [1977]:38–39, #264, and #266; Tang Kristensen 1896:38–39, #388, 47, #464, etc.

The second component of the rhyme in this fragment is different both from (12a)—because *land : mann* ('land : man') does not rhyme in Icelandic—and from CSc ballads quoted above. It is worth noting, however, that this rhyme is quite common in CSc ballads and often occurs there in the context of the *land-sand* formulae.[15] Apart from the first rhyme component, examples (12b) and (12a) have similar content: running away to another country (*land*) and meeting a cleric who will later, in both texts, provide the narrator with a cow and other things to live off.

Another formula that is used in this context in CSc rigmaroles also leads back to the *land-sand* formula, although from a different perspective: no *land* is mentioned there, the narrator runs *up and down* a bank, a road etc., for instance:

(12c)

> Upp etter bakkanne, ned etter bakkanne eg rende
>
> > (NR) Støylen 1899 [1977]:39, #264

> Up the slopes, down the slopes I ran

(12d)

> op a æ Höjgae å ned a æ Lavgae
>
> > (DR) Tang Kristensen 1896:38–39, #388

> up on a High street[?] and down to a Low street[?]

From this *up and down* formula, which is often complemented with repetitions such as *etter bakkanne* in (12c) and *Höjgae, Lavgae* in (12d), it is only a short way to the following example, where the *up and down* formula is combined with a *strand*-version of IIIf:

(12e)

Uppe i *land*	High up on *land*
og ned i *strand*	and low on [the] *shore*
sto ei liti kanna	stood a little pot

> > (NR) Støylen 1899 [1977]:18, #97

This example takes us back to PMÞ. The rhyme *land : strand* did not make its way from the CSc ballads and rigmaroles to Iceland in exactly this form, because the Icelandic word for shore is *strönd* (while *strand* means 'stranding' and 'stranded'; cf. the problem of *hönd* above). However, in PMÞ we find many cases of the rhyme

---

[15] Examples include *Dronningi genge seg neð pá sand, // der möter ho sá gamal ein mann* ('The queen walks down to/on [the] sand, // there she meets such an old man') (Landstad 1853 [1968]:586).

lönd : strönd ('lands : shore') alongside *land : sand.* The form in (12f), although the most common, is hardly grammatically correct,[16] and there have been attempts to rectify it, as in (12g):

(12f)

ieg tok ad renna	I started running
uppum *löndin*	up and throughout the *lands*[,]
Biskups *ströndin*	the Bishop's *shore*

(PMÞ) Lbs 414 8vo, 92v

(12g)

jeg tók að renna	I started running
út um *löndin* að biskups *ströndu*	off and throughout the *lands* to [the] bishop's *shore*

(PMÞ) Lbs 424 8vo, 16r

The *land-sand* formulaic complex is thus underlying, or latent, in the CSc versions of the narrative in (12b–e) and arrives to Iceland in conjunction with the *up and down* formula. In some PMÞ texts both these formulae are present, in which case the *up and down* formula is responsible for organizing the beginning of the formulaic lines while the *land-sand* formula (IIIf) takes responsibility for the ends of the lines, as in (12a). In other texts, only IIIf is present, as in (12f) and particularly (12g).

Seemingly, the *land-sand* formula (IIIf) made its way into Faroese *skjaldur* in this particular context in quite a different way; the word *land* is followed, unexpectedly, by the word *Tanga/tanga* ('tongue, spit of land, peninsula.DAT/ACC'), which has similar connotations to *sand*, but does not rhyme properly with *land(a)*, cf. (12h) and (12i):

(12h)

So fór hann rínandi og hvínandi eystur og vestur um landa at biðja sær biskop í Tanga

Then he went wailing and screeching eastward and westward throughout [the] land[?] to ask [for] himself [a] bishop in Tangi

(FS) FMD BS 996. Transcription: Birgitta Hylin

---

[16] Here *ströndin* ('the shore.NOM') should be *ströndina* ('the shore.ACC'), unless the line is understood as '[and the lands are] the Bishop's shore' or *ströndin* interpreted as irregular declination (e.g. ACC.PL.N.DEF[?]). Alternatively, the last letter of the regular ACC.SG.F.DEF *ströndina* could be missing in the manuscript.

(12i)

> So fór hann haðani, rínandi og hvínandi eystur um land at biðja sær
> biskop í tanga
> Then he went from there, wailing and screeching eastward across
> [the] land to ask [for] himself [a] bishop in [the] tongue

(FS) Kári Sverrisson 2000:42, #27

This is one of very few cases where both meaning and rhyme are affected; the latter is particularly notable because, in PMÞ, changes affecting semantics should not impair the rhyme in loan formulae.[17] This lack of rhyme is apparently also unexpected for some performers of *skjaldur*; we find a number of attempts to repair the rhyme and/or meaning, e.g. in the following examples of the second line of the formulaic couplets (corresponding to line three in 12h and line four in 12i). These range in their level of success:

- To rhyme with *land*: *bað biskoppur geva sær tand (?)* ('asked [the] bishop. NOM [*sic*] to give him [a] tooth[?] (?)') and *at biðja sær biskuppi tang* ('to ask [for] kelp for [the] bishop[?]').[18]

- To rhyme with the ungrammatical *landa* and/or to repair the meaning: *at vitja biskup í Tanga* ('to visit [the] bishop in Tangi'), and *at biðja sær Bisku á Tanga* ('to woo Biska [female name?] in Tangi').[19]

- To replace the problematic *tanga*: *til at taka biskupp úr fanga* ('to free [the] bishop from [being] prisoner[?]').[20]

It is questionable whether this is the same formula. However, the combination of the *eystur og vestur* ('to [the] East and to [the] West') formula—similar to the *up and down* formula—and the formula having *land* as one of the base words, in the context of this narrative, indicates that *land(a)-Tanga/tanga* could be classified as a modification of formula IIIf or at least as a part of the *land-sand* formulaic complex.

As for the stem *strand* ('shore'), it apparently does not occur in Faroese *skjaldur*. This is striking because, like Icelandic *lönd : strönd* (12f-g), *lond : strond* ('lands : shores') is a proper rhyme in Faroese, and it is widely used in the

---

[17] Faroese is more tolerant than Icelandic towards inexact rhymes; such rhymes are not unnatural or unusual in Faroese ballads—which are, in turn, more influential on Faroese poetry in general than Icelandic ballads on Icelandic poetry. However, this tolerance hardly extends to examples as in (12i) and (12h).

[18] FMD BS 985, transcription: Birgitta Hylin, and FMD BS 126, transcription: Jeanne Reinert Poulsen.

[19] FMD BS 42b, transcription: YSH, Rannveig Winther, and FMD BS 1222, transcription: Jeanne Reinert Poulsen.

[20] FMD BS 1018, transcription: Birgitta Hylin.

land-sand formulae in Faroese ballads[21] as well as with some other formulae of this same complex, such as *hand/hond–land/lond*. The Faroese material analyzed, however, is not exhaustive. In Iceland, on the contrary, *strönd* is a full-fledged part of the *land-sand* formulaic complex. It occurs not only in the context of (12f–g) but also in a different group of PMÞ texts as an enumeration formula. This formula is similar to the one in *Tátu þula* (9a) and is a part of a short multi-form. This is the last context of the *land-sand* formula in Icelandic PMÞ analyzed here—and sometimes it returns us to the *land-sand* formula without additional rhyming words:

(13a)

> Koma skyldu gestarnir [*sic*], prestarnir
> utanaf *löndunum, ströndunum*

> (PMÞ) AM 247 8vo 5r

> [There] should come the guests, the priests
> from the outer *lands, shores*

(13b)

> Hvenær munu pestarnir-pestarnir [*sic*]
> koma af *löndunum-söndunum*
> færa okkur mágunum tágarnar

> (PMÞ) Lbs 587 4to I, bls. 125, #138

> When will the priests, priests [or: illnesses, illnesses [?]]
> come from the *lands*, the *sands*
> give to us, [to] the brothers-in-law, the wickers

The *land-sand* formulaic complex of mixed ballad and rigmarole origin, analyzed in this section, is quite widespread. It includes both formulae that were more likely borrowed into PMÞ from ballads—as IIIb in (8) or IIIe in (11)—and formulae from CSc rigmaroles, as IIId in (9).[22] It also includes some formulae whose origin and migration path into PMÞ are obscure—even where we have clear parallels in CSc rigmaroles and/or ballads, as in IIIf in (12). Ballad-located formulae of the *land-sand* complex move easily into PMÞ and usually adapt to their new context without many formal changes, as in (8) and (11a). This is in line with previous studies on ballad formulae (YSH 2016; 2017; 2021). The main

---

[21] Cf. *land* : *strand* ('land : shore') in (7d), *strandar* : *landi* ('shore.GEN : land.DAT') in *Hørpu ríma* (*CCF* VI:104); furthermore, *strond* : *sondum* ('shore : sands.DAT') in *Høgna táttur* (*CCF* I:206); also *land* : *sand* in *Høgna táttur* (*CCF* I:207), *Arngríms synir* (*CCF* I:403, 405), *Álvur kongur* (7c), etc.

[22] Whether the latter had also originated in CSc balladry is a separate research question.

formal change in such formulae on their way to PMÞ is line shortening, as in IIIb, (8b, c). Otherwise, and especially in the formulae of mixed ballad/rigmarole origin, it is precisely the parameters of form—first and foremost rhyme—that are often the ballads' contribution into shaping the formulae in PMÞ. The content of the formulae, their function and indexing within particular texts, episodes etc. mainly comes from the rigmaroles' part, as shown in (5–6, 12). The rigmarole-located formulae of the complex that migrate as parts of larger migrating text blocks (such as IIId) also suffer few formal changes, as in (9), and sometimes small changes in content as well, as in (10a–b). Thus, their situation is similar to that of the rigmarole formulae Ia–b. It is mainly the formulae that migrate out of their text blocks, or separately from their context, that become unstable and more prone to the ballads' influence, which runs counter to the influence from other CSc rigmaroles at times. Such formulae undergo dramatic changes and sometimes only end in PMÞ or Faroese *skjaldur* in conjunction with another formula, as in (12), which can even supersede the former, as in (13). Nevertheless, the formulae that persevere—or the resulting PMÞ formulae—often become metrically stronger in PMÞ than in their source genres.

5. Transatlantic vs. Domestic Loan Formulae: Metrical vs. Semantic Variation and Non-Variation

Most of the continental Scandinavian rigmarole formulae that migrated to the islands of the North Atlantic changed upon adoption. In formulae Ia–b, which likely came into PMÞ directly from CSc rigmaroles and do not have ballad connections, changes are minimal, while the ballad/rigmarole formula IIId, conceivably also borrowed from rigmaroles, undergoes greater changes. Yet, rigmarole formulae rarely suffered changes as dramatic as those seen in formulae IIa–c, which likely migrated from CSc rigmaroles, but were under strong influence from ballads, or in some formulae of mixed ballad/rigmarole origin, such as IIIf. Many of the transatlantic loan formulae, which are somewhere between these two extremes, experience similar changes in form (and sometimes content) as the formulae borrowed into PMÞ from Icelandic ballads. As in domestic loan formulae—i.e. those borrowed into PMÞ from Icelandic folk poetry—these changes most often involve alliteration, which usually increases in transatlantic loan formulae migrating into PMÞ (cf. formula IIa above). This apparently occurs even more often than in domestic loan formulae from ballads, in contrast to formulae from other Icelandic genres where alliteration decreases. Metrical changes in transatlantic loan formulae also involve beat, especially line shortening (8b–c), although not quite as often as in domestic loan formulae. Dramatic changes in rhyme are relatively rare; examples of lost and uncompensated rhyme are found chiefly in those cases where not all rhyming sounds are located within the formula, exactly as in domestic loan formulae. Additionally, rhyme is sometimes uncompensated in formulae that also have non-rhyming modifications in CSc rigmaroles, as in (14), where the slight difference between the rhyming and non-rhyming modification lies precisely in the rhyming word, *svinger* ('[I] swing') in (14a) vs. *fly'ver* ('[I] fly') in (14b):

(14a)

må jeg låne dine *Vinger*, mens jeg *svinger* til Kjöbenhavn?

(DR) Tang Kristensen 1896:62, #544

may I borrow your *wings*, while I *fly* [lit. *swing*] to Copenhagen?

(14b)

Grågås, lån mig dine Vinger, mens jeg fly'ver til Kjöbenhavn

(DR) Tang Kristensen 1896:60, #534

Grey goose, lend me your wings, while I fly to Copenhagen

(14c)

gragiæsa módir	mother of [the] grey geese
liádu mer vængi	lend me [your] wings
svo eg geti flogid	so that I can fly
upptil födr túngla	up to [my] father's moons [*sic*]

(PMÞ) JS 289 8vo, 29r

Uncompensated rhyme is most often found in those rigmarole formulae that are not related to ballads and do not bear signs of ballad influence; in those that do, the rhyme is compensated, usually by another (ballad) rhyme. This is where transatlantic loan formulae differ from their domestic counterparts. First, formulae entering PMÞ from Icelandic ballads are likely to lose rhyme in the process. This is not the case, on the other hand, with formulae originating in CSc rigmaroles—rhyme is less important for that genre. Second, the compensating device in the case of formulae from Icelandic ballads is often alliteration (cf. YSH 2017:ex. 2a–b). On the other hand, in transatlantic loans of rigmarole formulae, another rhyme is used instead, for instance a ballad rhyme in (3–4), and see also (5–6) and (9–10) above. In general, nonetheless, the formulae from CSc rigmaroles maintain the same level of metricality or even become metrically richer in PMÞ—even more than domestic loan formulae in PMÞ.

In most cases, both metrical and semantic forces appear to be behind the changes. This is true for both transatlantic and domestic loan formulae. When either meter or meaning gives way, contra-semantic variation is readily accepted in favor of better metricality, as illustrated in (12) above. It is likely that contra-semantic variation is more readily acceptable in transatlantic than in domestic loans. The language barrier could be involved as well, but further research is needed here. Contra-metrical variation in favor of semantics seems nonetheless also accepted in transatlantic loan formulae, at least where line length is involved, e.g. *Liáðu mér vængina þína* ('Lend me your wings') (Lbs 414 8vo, 92r). This longer line disrupts the relatively regular beat of the PMÞ texts in question (14c), but is apparently accepted in order to accommodate *þína* ('your'), which most likely comes from *dine* ('your') in the Danish formula (14a). However, this contra-metrical variation does not prove stable: while the longer second line was popular in the nineteenth century, it is barely noticeable a century later. The impaired metricality of the formula may have played its part in the decline of the formula modification with the longer second line. Another reason may be the widespread tendency towards unification and non-variation in loan formulae. Additionally, there might have been less motivation to keep the wording of the formula close to its source genre, once the formula was established. A popular poem by Hulda (Unnur Benediktsdóttir), published in the beginning of the twentieth century and containing the lines: *Grágæsa móðir! // ljáðu mér vængi* ('Mother of [the] grey geese! // lend me [your] wings') (*Hulda*:101), could have served as an additional impulse towards unification in this particular case.

The tendency towards unification, non-variation, and eventually simplification, already mentioned several times, is common for domestic and transatlantic loan formulae. In transatlantic loan formulae, this tendency becomes clear when we consider that only some of a formula's modifications migrate from continental Scandinavia to the islands of the North Atlantic (e.g. IIIb, but not IIIa or IIIc), resulting in more uniform island formulae. On the other hand, the numerous borrowings of the ballad formulae, as well as chiefly ballad-located formulae of mixed origin, into different contexts in PMÞ, contribute considerably to variation in this and other formulae in PMÞ. The different development of the same formulae in Icelandic PMÞ and Faroese *skjaldur* also contributes to variation; this matter often cannot be explained by linguistic factors only. Further research is required here as well.

6. Concluding remarks

6.1. Formula migration

A considerable number of ballad formulae migrated from the CSc countries to the islands of the North Atlantic, primarily into Icelandic and Faroese ballads, but also into Icelandic PMÞ and Faroese *skjaldur*. Comparable formulae that migrated from CSc rigmaroles into Faroese *skjaldur* and Icelandic PMÞ are less abundant. It is unlikely that this lesser migration of CSc rigmarole formulae into PMÞ can be explained by less extensive migration of rigmaroles to Iceland than that of ballads, since quite a few CSc rigmaroles with very close parallels in Icelandic PMÞ are observed, as in (1–2) and (9). These rigmaroles are likely to have migrated to Iceland around the same time as the ballad texts, because the periods before and after were less conducive for such migration. This suggests that it was easier for PMÞ to borrow formulae per se, independently of their context, between genres—especially from ballads, where formulae were most actively used and had much variation and migration potential (e.g. YSH 2016). More problematic was apparently borrowing formulae between countries and languages, albeit from similar genres. One of the potential reasons is that rigmarole formulae appear to be more context-dependent than ballad formulae. They tend to travel across the sea with their context, or inside larger migrating text blocks. Thus, they are reliant on the migration of such blocks. Even where a text block migrates, and migrating conditions are generally favorable, a formula within it does not necessarily follow, as the *brand* and *strand* formulae show. Rhyming problems conceivably affected migration possibilities of the *brand* formula to Iceland—but not those of the *strand* formula to the Faroe Islands, where rhyming constraints are more relaxed than in Icelandic poetry. The formula must be missing there for different reason(s). This seems to demonstrate that rigmarole-based formulae do not adapt as well to new contexts as ballad formulae.

These findings contribute to our understanding of how well and to what extent formulaic diction can move between Icelandic poetic systems. Haukur Þorgeirsson has observed restrictions on free movement between the genres *sagnakvæði* and *rímur* (2012:193–194). Frog theorized that oral poets cannot access the formulaic diction of one type of poetry while composing or performing in another, at least not without conscious effort (2012a and esp. 2012b:52–60). Comparison of ballads and rigmaroles suggests that PMÞ performers had relatively free access to ballad formulaic diction, independent of its context, although some restrictions clearly applied (YSH 2016:54–55). This does not imply, however, that ballad performers also had free access to formulaic diction of PMÞ. Formulaic diction of CSc rigmaroles was apparently less accessible for them; it was more content-restricted and not as easily adapted to new contexts. The only exception was formulae inside larger loan text blocks, which are groups of traditionally connected lines containing sequences of names, short motifs, or both.

Another aspect of this same discussion is the low number of formulae of mixed ballad and rigmarole origin that PMÞ appear to have borrowed from the CSc countries. The *land-sand* formulaic complex (9–10) shows, for instance, that only the formulae based on the main rhyme of the complex, *land : sand*, are found in more or less considerable numbers in CSc rigmaroles, Faroese *skjaldur*, and Icelandic PMÞ.[23] The formulae of this complex thus undergo considerable simplification and unification on their way from CSc poetry into PMÞ. Primary studies show, moreover, that only a relatively small number of formulae are common for CSc ballads and CSc rigmaroles, conceivably fewer than formulae common for Icelandic ballads and PMÞ. This could indicate that the so-called formative or "creative" period (Solberg 2008:131) of rigmaroles was nearly over by the end of the thirteenth century, when ballads first spread to Scandinavia from more southern parts of Europe. This hypothesis would move the formation period of rigmaroles farther back in time.[24] Alternatively, and more likely, the low number of formulae common for CSc ballads and rigmaroles indicates that the creative period of rigmaroles was short. Subsequently, the assimilation of additional material was precluded. This latter hypothesis would not involve moving the CSc rigmaroles' formation period back in time. Yet, it does not fit in smoothly with our experience of PMÞ as texts that are quite open to new material—provided that PMÞ are closely related to CSc rigmaroles and, therefore, likely to demonstrate similar characteristics and behavior. Another possible reason for the low number of common formulae in CSc ballads and rigmaroles is that the genres were less closely connected than Icelandic ballads and PMÞ. It is possible that a greater difference existed between the registers and/or social contexts of Scandinavian ballads and rigmaroles than between those of Icelandic ballads and PMÞ. If this is true, then they might have been segregated in social practice, or not practiced by the same people. Thus, the people performing each of the genres would not necessarily have internalized the formulaic idiom of the other genre to a comparable degree (cf. Frog 2012a–b). Further research is needed to estimate which of these factors is most influential, or whether there are others yet to be discovered.

---

[23] Rhymes such as *land : strand* and *land : hand* are not used in this formulaic complex in Faroese *skjaldur*, the *brand* rhyming stem is not used in Iceland, and quite a number of rhymes, very popular in this complex in ballads, are apparently not used in any rigmaroles of the North Atlantic.

[24] In this case, rigmaroles could have migrated to Iceland even before the fifteenth century—without leaving many traces, however, in written sources (cf. the above discussion on manuscripts before and after the Black Death).

6.2. Metrics, semantics and variation

From what has been observed in the previous sections, no major differences exist between domestic and transatlantic loan formulae in terms of metrical vs. semantic variation. Most of my previous findings on PMÞ formulae are true for both transatlantic and domestic loan formulae. Metrical changes in formulae migrating between languages and genres appear to be quite similar. On the other hand, some differences can be detected between formulae apparently originating in ballads and rigmaroles. In the ballad formulae, rhyme is fundamental. Ballad formulae migrating into PMÞ maintain, first of all, their rhyme; if it goes missing, it is likely to be compensated by another rhyme or other metrical means. In rigmarole formulae, semantic and contextual parameters are paramount; formulae migrating from CSc rigmaroles into PMÞ preserve first and foremost their general meaning and their function in a formulaic narrative, if they migrate in that connection.[25] Rigmarole formulae that migrate independently of their context often become unstable and require some complementing from ballad formulae, as in formula IIa, or rigmarole formulae like IIIf. Such formulae also suffer more changes in form than both rigmarole formulae that migrate within larger text blocks and ballad formulae.

Acknowledgements

I am grateful to the volume editors, and to Susanne Arthur and Margaret Cormack who commented on previous versions of this chapter.

References

Sources

AM 148 8vo; AM 247 8vo; AM 960 4to; AM 969 4to. Manuscripts at the Árni Magnússon Institute for Icelandic Studies.
DFS 67 E. Manuscript at the Royal Library, National Library of Denmark and Copenhagen University Library.
FMD BS 42b; FMD BS 59a; FMD BS 126; FMD BS 340; FMD BS 985; FMD BS 996; FMD BS 997; FMD BS 1018; FMD BS 1222. Audio tapes in the collection of the

[25] Such formulae can, however, also travel between narratives—that is, they do not necessarily always index the same narrative. The formula *stein-bein* ('stone-bone'), for instance, indexes the narrative of the encounter with an unfriendly old woman in CSc rigmaroles, similar to the narrative in (5–6) above, but turns up in a different narrative in PMÞ, starting with lines similar to those in (8a) above.

Department of Faroese Language and Literature, University of the Faroe Islands.

JS 289 8vo; JS 507 8vo. Manuscripts at the National and University Library of Iceland.

Lbs 587 4to; Lbs 1057 4to; Lbs 414 8vo; Lbs 418 8vo; Lbs 421 8vo; Lbs 424 8vo. Manuscripts at the National and University Library of Iceland.

Ordbog over det norrøne prosasprog. http://onp.ku.dk/.

Ritmálssafn. http://www.arnastofnun.is/page/ritmalssafn.

SÁM 85/371 EF. Audio tape in the Folklore Collection of the Árni Magnússon Institute for Icelandic Studies. http://www.ismus.is/.

Editions

CCF I = Matras, Chr., ed. 1944. *Føroya kvæði: Corpus carminum Færoensium a Sv[end] Grundtvig et J. Bloch comparatum I.* Universitets-Jubilæets Danske Samfund: Skriftserie 324. København.

CCF VI = Djurhuus, N., ed. *Føroya kvæði: Corpus carminum Færoensium a Sv[end] Grundtvig et J. Bloch comparatum VI.* Universitets-Jubilæets Danske Samfund: Skriftserie 438. Kopenhagen.

Danmarks gamle folkeviser VI = Olrik, A., ed. 1967 [1895–1898]. *Danmarks gamle folkeviser VI: Nr. 316-386: Ridderviser med mandlig hovedperson, især om fejde, hævn og ulykke.* Facsimile ed. København.

Hulda = Guðrún Bjartmarsdóttir, ed. 1990. *Hulda: Ljóð og laust mál: Úrval.* Íslensk rit 9. Reykjavík.

ÍFkv = Grundtvig, S., and Sigurðsson, J., eds. 1854–1888. *Íslenzk fornkvæði*, 2 vols. Nordiske Oldskrifter 19. Kjøbenhavn.

Kári Sverrisson, ed. 2000. *Nina, nina nái: Skjaldur, ramsur og rímur*, 2 CDs and booklet. Tórshavn. (References in this chapter are made to the texts in the booklet.)

Landstad, M. B., ed. 1853. *Norske folkeviser* ed. 1968. Oslo.

Nordlander, J., ed. 1886. *Svenska barnvisor och barnrim.* Facsimile ed., supplemented and with introduction by Lars Furuland 1975. Stockholm.

Norsk folkediktning VII = Liestøl, K., Moe, M., Bø, O., and Solheim, S., eds. 1959. *Norsk folkediktning VII: Folkeviser II.* 2nd ed. (Originally published as a part of: Liestøl, K., and Moe, M., eds. 1920–1924. *Norske folkevisor.* 3 vols.) Oslo.

Skar, J. O., ed. 1903–1916. *Gamalt or Sætesdal*, 3 vols, ed. 1960–1963. Oslo.

Støylen, B., ed. 1899. *Norske barnerim og leikar: Med tonar* ed. 2 facsimile 1977. Oslo.

Tang Kristensen, E., ed. 1896. *Danske børnerim, remser og lege: Udelukkende efter folkemunde.* Århus.

Literature

Foley, J. M., and Ramey, P. 2012. "Oral Theory and Medieval Studies." *Medieval Oral Literature*. (ed. K. Reichl) 71–102. Berlin.

Ford, J. C. 2002. "A New Conception of Poetic Formulae Based on Prototype Theory and the Mental Template." *Neuphilologische Mitteilungen* 103:205–226.

Frog. 2012a. "On the Case of *Vambarljóð*, I: Comments on Formulaicity in the *sagnakvæði*." *RMN Newsletter* 5:22–38.

———. 2012b. "On the Case of *Vambarljóð*, II: Register and Mode from Skaldic Verse to *sagnakvæði*." *RMN Newsletter* 5:49–61.

Guðvarður Már Gunnlaugsson 2016. "Árni Magnússon's Initial Collection." *Care and Conservation of Manuscripts 15: Proceedings of the Fifteenth International Seminar Held at the University of Copenhagen 2nd–4th April 2014* (ed. M. J. Driscoll) 1–20. Copenhagen.

Gunnell, T. 2001. "Grýla, Grýlur, 'Grøleks' and Skeklers: Medieval Disguise Traditions in the North Atlantic." *Arv: Nordic Yearbook of Folklore* 51:33–54.

Haukur Þorgeirsson 2012. "Poetic Formulas in Late Medieval Icelandic Folk Poetry: The Case of *Vambarljóð*." *RMN Newsletter* 4:181–196.

Hylin, B. 1971. "Skjaldur: en studie över barnvisan och barnramsan på Färöarna." *Fra Færøerne—Úr Føroyum VI* (ed. O. Jacobsen) 49–65. København.

Jón Samsonarson 1975. "Vaggvisor: Island." *Kulturhistorisk leksikon for nordisk middelalder*. 19:427–428. Reykjavík.

Kuiper, K. 2009. *Formulaic Genres*. Basingstoke.

Solberg, O. 2008. "The Scandinavian Medieval Ballad: From Oral Tradition to Written Texts and Back Again." *Oral Art Forms and Their Passage into Writing* (eds. E. Mundal and J. Wellendorf) 121–133. Copenhagen.

Vésteinn Ólason 1982. *The Traditional Ballads of Iceland: Historical Studies*. Stofnun Árna Magnússonar: Rit 22. Reykjavík.

Wray, A. 2002. *Formulaic Language and the Lexicon*. Cambridge.

———. 2009. "Identifying Formulaic Language: Persistent Challenges and New Opportunities." *Formulaic Language* (eds. R. Corrigan, E. A. Moravcsik, Hamid Ouali, and K. M. Wheatley) 27–51. Typological Studies in Language 82. Amsterdam.

YSH 2006 = Yelena Sesselja Helgadóttir Yershova 2006. "Nokkur dæmi um blandað mál í færeyskum skjaldrum." *Hugvísindaþing 2005: Erindi af ráðstefnu Hugvísindadeildar og Guðfræðideildar Háskóla Íslands 18. nóvember 2005* (eds. Haraldur Bernharðsson et al.) 323–335. Reykjavík.

YSH 2008 = Yelena Sesselja Helgadóttir 2008. "Íslenskar þulur og færeysk skjaldur: Er allt sama tóbakið?" *Frændafundur 6: Fyrilestrar frá føroyskari-íslends-kari ráðstevnu í Tórshavn 26.–28. juni 2007 = Fyrirlestrar frá færeysk-íslenskri ráðstefnu í Þórshöfn 26.-28. juni 2007* (ed. Turið Sigurðardóttir and Magnús Snædal) 175–199. Tórshavn.

YSH 2010a = Yelena Sesselja Helgadóttir 2010a. "Shetland Rhymes from the Collection of Dr Jakob Jakobsen." *Jakob Jakobsen in Shetland and the Faroes* (eds. Turið Sigurðardóttir and B. Smith) 191–230. Lerwick.

YSH 2010b = Yelena Sesselja Helgadóttir 2010b. "Meira veit ég ekki um ættina… hans Grýlu?" *Guðrúnarstikki kveðinn Guðrúnu Nordal fimmtugri 27. september 2010.* (eds. Gísli Sigurðsson, Halldóra Jónsdóttir, and Torfi Tulinius) 80–83. Reykjavík.

YSH 2014 = Yelena Sesselja Helgadóttir 2014. "Retrospective Methods in Dating Post-Medieval Rigmarole-Verses from the North Atlantic." *New Focus on Retrospective Methods. Resuming Methodological Discussions: Case Studies from Northern Europe* (eds. E. Heide and K. Bek-Pedersen) 98–119. Folklore Fellows Communications 307. Helsinki.

YSH 2016 = Yelena Sesselja Helgadóttir 2016. "Formulaic Language in Minimal Metrical Requirements: The Case of Post-Medieval Icelandic þulur." *The Ecology of Metre* (ed. I. Sverdlov and Frog) 49–61. *RMN Newsletter* 11, special issue. Helsinki.

YSH 2017 = Yelena Sesselja Helgadóttir 2017. "Formulae across the North Atlantic (from Continental Scandinavia to Iceland)." *Formula: Units of Speech, 'Words' of Verbal Art: Working Papers of the Seminar-Workshop 17th-19th May 2017, Helsinki, Finland* (ed. Frog) 135–154. Folkloristiikan Toimite 23. Helsinki.

YSH 2020 = Yelena Sesselja Helgadóttir 2020. "Íslenskar þulur síðari alda". Ph.D. diss., University of Iceland. Reykjavík.

YSH 2021 = Yelena Sesselja Helgadóttir 2021. "Migration of Poetic Formulae: Icelandic Post-Medieval Þulur." *Versification: Metrics in Practice* (ed. Frog, S. Grünthal, K. Kallio, and J. Niemi). Studia Fennica Litteraria. Helsinki.

13

I Am a Fan of Hilarity

Possible Directions for Oral-Formulaic Theory and the Study of Stand-Up Comedy

Ian Brodie, Cape Breton University

Stand-up comedy straddles two forms of talk. It is a form of verbal art in so far as it is a deliberate construction of text where choices are based, in part, on the aesthetics of the words as sounds and the affectivity of the words as signifiers. Simultaneously, one of the aesthetic principles particular to the form is the seeming absence of artifice and its alignment with "ordinary" talk. It requires memorization yet needs to sound spontaneous and unaffected.

While a Hymesian breakthrough into performance might occasion a rhythmic patterning of a text, this patterning is not an inherent and expected feature of stand-up performance: absent is the tyranny of "metrical conditions" so encoded into Milman Parry's definition for formula (1930 [1971]:272). Speech may be cadenced, but would not venture into the commonly recognized categories of verse or poetry: this fuzzy boundary, Frog reminds us, results from culturally provided hierarchies of whether syntax or poetic principles are given precedence (2017b:255).[1] Without wishing to introduce a too-clever-for-its-own-benefit semantic distinction, we can suggest how metrical contexts (as opposed to conditions) emerge in performance and, indeed, are recognized and cultivated by the performer working towards honing the text for its most-perfected version as committed to a recording. Nevertheless, this is different from an audience's anticipation of the precedence of poetic principles pre-conditioning a genre performance, such as dactylic hexameter for Homeric epic or generally

---

[1] As ever, there are rare exceptions that test this general pattern. Rudy Ray Moore frequently performed his own African-American toasts like "Petey Wheatstraw, the Devil's Son-In-Law" (1971; see Labov et al. 1973) as part of his on-stage routines; throughout his career George Carlin would create pieces where the poetic principles were clearly given at least equal footing with syntax, such as "The Hair Piece" (1972) and "A Modern Man" (2006).

accentual verse forms, such as in cowboy poetry, where a specific meter is not dictated but, once established, must be used consistently.

Further, as a solo performer, the stand-up comedian does not have a practical responsibility to repeat his or her words in a predictable way and in a predictable order, so as to cue others.[2] As the owner and originator of the material, there is no moral obligation to maintain the integrity of another's intentions. Moreover, as a genre that prizes original and ever-fresh material, the stand-up doesn't need to perform material the way an audience has heard it before, or even material heard before: broadcasts and recordings are the tradition bearers of stand-up comedy's performance texts; stand-up comedians are the tradition bearers of form.

All of this suggests that the standard through-line to so-called "Classic" Oral-Formulaic Theory—of the Parry and Lord variety—is not immediately applicable to stand-up comedy (see also Frog and Lamb, this volume). That said, there seems to be *something* happening in stand-up that nestles somewhere between memorization and pure spontaneity, and *something* between a standard set of formulas and a wholly idiosyncratic verbal repertoire. Asking the question of how a comedian is able to memorize the material that goes into a five- or a hundred-minute performance is asking a parallel question to Classic Oral-Formulaic Theory.[3] What follows is, perhaps, not a first foray into this topic, but at least an indication of what directions a true oral-formulaic analysis might take.

1. "I'm Deciding When It's 'Done.'": Methodological Considerations

According to Classic Oral-Formulaic Theory studies, the performer learns the traditional materials first by listening:

> He has decided that he wants to sing himself, or he may still be unaware of this decision and simply be very eager to hear the stories of his elders. Before he actually begins to sing, he is, consciously or unconsciously, laying the foundation. He is learning the stories and becoming acquainted with the heroes and their names, the faraway places and the habits of long ago. The themes of the poetry are becoming familiar

---

[2]   For video and film recordings, especially when multiple performances are to be recorded and spliced into one, there will emerge a consensus with a director and the crew for how the set will unfold.

[3]   For a more psycho-phenomenological oriented approach to the question of memorization, see Molineux 2016.

to him, and his feeling for them is sharpened as he hears more and as he listens to the men discussing the songs among themselves. At the same time he is imbibing the rhythm of the singing and to an extent also the rhythm of the thoughts as they are expressed in song. Even at this early stage the oft-repeated phrases which we call formulas are being absorbed.

Lord 2000 [1960]:21

Similarly, the apprenticeship phase of stand-up comedy happens by listening to comedians, through recordings (Brodie 2014:210–212) and then in person, anecdotally spending hours upon hours at clubs observing more seasoned performers hone their material. Unlike when the singer of tales begins the second stage of learning by tentatively and then more confidently singing the songs absorbed in the first stage, the stand-up comedian creates new routines aesthetically shaped to conform to stylistic expectations of the genre. To determine if they are successful—if they invoke the laughter they are intended to invoke—they are performed in live contexts, checking their creative expectations against actual reception, re-evaluating the response, and returning to a live context for a further check, until such time as it sits comfortably in a repertoire knowing that it will, more often than not, "work."

I once made an oversimplification by speaking of recordings as the teleological endpoint of stand-up comedy (2014:19). My point at the time was to highlight a distinction between the recordings of stand-up comedians from those of popular music recording artists. The latter, in broad strokes, create in-studio versions of songs that will comprise their recorded output: they will introduce these songs into their repertoire for audiences who wish to hear the them, adapting performance strategies, if necessary, for the live context. Stand-up comedians, on the other hand, only have live performances as the recorded project; the aesthetics of novelty imply that once it is available in recording it will be less suitable for staying in the repertoire. The material is worked out and honed, in open mikes and in featured sets, until it has reached the desired level of readiness for recording, and it soon thereafter typically moves to a more passive repertoire, known but not in active circulation. Stand-up comedy is not a literary form, but it emerges in a post-literary age, and part of its aesthetics is based on novelty and uniqueness (Pagán Cánovas 2017:242): the broad dissemination of mediation benefits their reputation by providing an example of competency (and biography), but repeating that material in a live context could somehow abrogate the audience's expectations for the comedian. My error was implying that recording comprised the *sole* endpoint for stand-up comedy performances. As Giacinto Palmieri rightly points out, this not only privileges recording comedians and suggests that those who are not recording are engaged in something "less," it also suggests that comedians earning enviably lucrative performance fees, far more than they might by recording sales, are similarly engaged in something less (2017:28).

Nevertheless, in interview and in writing, comedians frequently refer to open mikes and tours as opportunities to prepare material for recording, and emphasize how the material performed is still a work in progress. As an illustrative example: American stand-up comedian Patton Oswalt wrote a post on his personal blog in response to his purported overreaction at being recorded during a club appearance. The precipitating incident involved a woman starting a recording halfway through a very early iteration of a personal story, "a very embarrassing recollection from my younger years that I'm very nervous about performing and still *very* unsure of how to unspool" (2012). He continues:

> I can't stress this enough: she clumsily brought the camera out and started taping after I'd done *half of the story*.
>
> So now I was facing someone walking around—a clumsily, socially blunt someone who clearly has no boundaries or sense of esthetics or shame—with *half* of a half-formed, *very* personal and embarrassing story I'm trying to hone into something good, just sitting on a device in her pocket. A device which, anytime she's had one drink too many or is in whatever weird mood she may or may not get into, can whip out and play this to—well, whoever.
>
> So in that single act I've lost control of which version of my story has been turned from signal to noise, as well as who decides when, where, and to whom it's shown.
>
> It's the equivalent, to me, of sitting at a table in a coffee shop or library, writing the first draft of a short story, or screenplay or, were I a musician, song lyrics, and having someone walk by, snap the sheet away from my fingers, snap a pic with their camera, and then say, "Hey, I'm a fan of your stuff. I want the new thing you're working on permanently on my phone now. I'm deciding when it's 'done.'"
>
> Oswalt 2012

In-person live performances comprise the vast majority of the stand-up comedian's on-stage time, but access to those performances is limited by circumstance. Barring the situational unlikelihood of working with a particular comedian and being invited to analyze their archive of personal recordings, one has few options that are feasible and respect the performer's wishes for control over their artistic production. One could follow a comedian to as many possible venues as one is able and take copious notes, but it would be a cost-prohibitive and imperfect data source (Brady 1999; Jensen 1980:13; Radick 2003). My own fieldwork with Ron James included following him on tour: I certainly experienced enough "the-same-but-not-the-same" performances to notice both patterns and creative divergences, but by agreement could not record for this type of analysis (and, were it not for his generosity in providing me some complementary tickets, I could not have done the work in the first place). Alternatively, one could avail oneself of bootlegged recordings, but that is merely rationalizing the moral proscription by laying responsibility at someone else's feet.

The stand-up performances that are most accessible for analysis *are* professional recordings and broadcasts. The recordings are, of course, of in-person performances, but ones under controlled circumstances. They are subject to editing and, in the case of video recordings, the framing of cameras, which cut between different angles on the performer and often to the audience as well. They are recorded with the intention of being verbal art directed at both an audience immediately co-present to the comedian and to a larger, less contiguous and spatio-temporally distant audience at the other end of the broadcast or recording (Brodie 2018; 2014). Techniques for building rapport will need to be applied for both of these audiences. Knowing that it will be forever accessible, the comedian works to hone the performance to his or her preferred representational version. Recordings and broadcasts are used, perhaps, as a direct source of income, but more importantly as a way of building and cultivating a reputation for comedic competency and fluency for an uninitiated audience: a list of broadcast appearances, alongside a list of appearances in curated festivals, is part of the matrix of professional comedy techniques that orients an audience's expectations prior to the comedian stepping on stage.

Therefore, one is most often limited to the sanctioned output: we do not get to see how the "unspooling" of the story is developed over time or, moving from structure to surface, how language choice is selected. Nevertheless, commercial recordings have proven themselves indispensable for the contemporary study of formula in popular cultural genres: Margaret McGeachy has demonstrated the history of their use for formula studies of African-American blues (2006:28–33), and, although we have much to learn from the David Evans / Michael Taft debate on how much the in-studio recording can serve to represent the live tradition of blues (Evans 2007; 2010; Taft 2009), we can at least take comfort in our basic observation that stand-up recordings are always recorded live.

2. "You Sort of Say Something to Take Them Down": The Initial Idea

In *A Vulgar Art*, I tentatively suggested that an approach akin to Oral-Formulaic Theory could be invoked to explain what Canadian comedian Ron James dismissed first as "laziness" and subsequently as a "technical thing": short, self-contained verbal units that can be employed in performance to complement an ongoing establishment of rapport, which require little to no adaptation. James's performances take him to small communities across Canada. He has developed his knowledge of the country into a dominant comedic theme. Consequently, in live performance, he will invoke a locally specific exoteric worldview in the form of *blasons populaire*, and simultaneously a more pan-Canadian esoteric understanding of the inherent goodness of its people living within a land so wide and savage. As an example of the former, as it appeared on *The Road Between My Ears*:

(1)

> That midway *flaunted* safety standards
> the Ferris wheel had bit of flesh and *clothing* hanging off it [L]
> *still* the scariest ride of *all*
> the *Ferris wheel*
> when you're a kid they'd keep you in that *bucket*
> that's what the ride is essentially a *bucket*
> at the very star top
> forever
> jeez I' watching *weather patterns* change over the *Gulf Stream* [L]
> family of cretins in the bucket in *front* of me
> rocking it *back* and *forth* [mimes rocking with a gormless expression] [L]

James 2003[4]

---

[4] For transcriptions, letters in [brackets] indicate audience reaction and lower- and uppercase indicates small or large, whether 'l, L' laughter, 'a, A' applause; or '→' that one reaction turns into another. Line breaks occur at prolonged pauses, audience interruptions, or to indicate the cadence of the line. Words in *italics* are specifically emphasized: *underlined* words indicate that the previous audience reaction is sustained but the performer is talking over or during it. Ellipses ('...') indicate false starts. The performer's gestures, "stage directions," and other nonverbal cues are {in curly brackets} and, when indicating tone or accent, qualify the words following, which are in double quotation marks [" "]. Text enclosed in | straight lines | denotes characterization. A more comprehensive representation of the transcription is given in Brodie 2014: xi.

In this description of the carnival rides of his youth, his specific referents vary according to the performance context: in Nova Scotia (where James spent his childhood) he evoked "the Bill Lynch Show," a local (and since disbanded) traveling amusement company, and this nostalgic reminder was greeted with applause. When I saw him in Newfoundland a few years previous, he did not use the Lynch name, and as it appears for national distribution, the more generic term *Midway* is used. Absent from *Road Between My Ears* is a dependable tag to the bit: *Easy to spot the folks from __*. For a show in Glace Bay the folks were from New Waterford, and in Pictou they were from River John: in both instances he is referring to communities "up the road," demonstrating familiarity with local sensibilities by invoking long-standing rivalries.

In a similar fashion to "Ferris Wheel," "Paid in Game" floats throughout his performances.

(2)

> there was a couple in the front row
> came backstage after the gig
> handed me a brown paper bag dripping blood
> put my hand in
> pulled out a seven-and-a-half-pound sirloin tip moose roast
> you know you've made it in Canadian show business when the locals
> > are paying you in butchered game
> don't get those perks playing Las Vegas
> people give you a brown paper bag dripping blood there
> probably has the head of a teamster in it

In performance, James locates the incident in different communities and at different times, including the week previous, when recounting his show in Grand Falls-Windsor, Newfoundland for his Halifax, Nova Scotia audience. James employs the story in interview as well as on stage (Posner 2001; MacPherson 2006): in so far as stand-up comedy is a performed biography with purposes of continually demonstrating points of communion with and relevance for an audience, how the public persona is crafted in public other than through on-stage solo performance (namely in the press, in sketch, or in acting roles) is a specific contributor to establishing a reputation and framing the interpretation of future performances.

Formula, whether as Parry's "group of words which is regularly employed under the same metrical conditions to express a given essential idea" (1930 [1971]:272) or Kuiper's "phrasal lexical item having associated conditions of use which determine its non-linguistic usage" (2009:17) implies concision: οἶνοψ πόντος ('wine-dark sea'), *kind-hearted woman, going, going, gone*. Anything longer and we start to cross the hazy border into paremiology, but proverbs also have the expectation of a certain brevity, which conditions them being thought of as pithy. The "paragraphs" of these routines are simply too long—and variable—for a strict application of standard Oral-Formulaic Theory.

But we can nevertheless consider them as units, or blocks, that collectively build a longer text, and thus consider the relationship between the whole and its parts. Identifying these routines as units having a semantic integrity that can be assembled into larger runs but, just as importantly, spontaneously recombined or resituated in different ways, should an opportunity present itself, suggests some etic path into their analysis. We can recognize that the words have been honed to a set of aesthetic criteria that occasions laughter, even if we are not quite ready to fully articulate those criteria (but see below). The process of honing takes place both on the page and on stage until such time as it is routinized: it may continue to be refined, and the interaction of performer and audience both demands and occasions fluidity, but it has nevertheless entered an active repertoire.

Sets can, thereby, be constructed, more or less spontaneously, by assembling these units dynamically. A setlist—often merely a scrap of paper with a list of metonyms—can be prepared minutes before going on stage and be the only *aide de memoire* for an entire performance: indeed, the act of writing out that setlist might be all that is needed to organize the comedian's thoughts. Furthermore, except for the courtesy of not running over their allotted time, the comedian is not beholden to that list and, should the flow of performance warrant it, a different unit can be inserted. And—as the stage is the site of practice and performance equally—new material in the process of development can be attempted between two stronger and more established blocks, knowing that, should it not be quite honed sufficiently, the audience can be "won back" with more time-tested material.

Stand-up comedy arises from the same kind of shit-talk (Bell 1983; Klein 2006) that occurs between people who are in regular ludic verbal contact with each other, save for that, as it is a professional activity, it occurs in groups other than the established reference group and is among strangers. The exercise of stand-up is about presenting oneself as akin to that reference group, while the expectation of this new audience is for the comedian to elicit laughter. Whether or not it is funny will largely be a consequence of the comedian's ability to (*a*) establish relevancy by demonstrating active participation in the worldview of the group through adverting to points of commonality; (*b*) establish interest by demonstrating active nonparticipation in the worldview of the group through the provision of a different perspective on topics of the group's concern; (c) conform to the audience's aesthetic expectations of what constitutes a "good" story; and (d) reaffirm that what is said is simply talking shit, talk among intimates (Brodie 2014:88). A known comedian has the benefit of extant goodwill, one that might actually distract from being able to assess the strength of one's material.

> When you first go on the crowd's excited to see you. But the thing with stand-up is that you can't, you can't abuse that. Like, you know, the first joke you do that's not funny, you're just like anybody else, right there. So actually I've—Chris [Rock] and I have both said that we've done this—is you try to ground their expectations. You actually do something that you know isn't gonna please them to get there quick, so you get to work, you know what I mean? Like you get on stage, they're all like [mimes excitement] because they've seen you on TV: there's nothing useful's going to come out of that. So you say something, I don't know, not insult the crowd but you sort of say something to take them down, or bore them for a minute. And then you can get an honest read on the material.
>
> Louis C. K. on Rose 2014

I raise this here (and acknowledge the concerns of whether to cite both Louis C. K. and Charlie Rose) because, while the larger project of stand-up comedy requires the establishment and ongoing cultivation of rapport, it is not a constant appeal: rather, there is value in disassociation in order to re-establish later. Similarly, there is value to be had from dividing an audience—say, on the basis of gender—and allying oneself with one over the other at various points throughout the performance, until reconciling at the end. And rapport is also built upon the liminal state of being "insider" enough to be relevant and "outsider" enough to have something to say. A future Oral-Formulaic Theory for stand-up comedy could start to categorize and more closely define various strategies of rapport-building—allegiance and disassociation, division and reunification, insider and outsider—and sections of the comedian's act as implementing these strategies. To that extent we might start to consider Parry's "given essential idea" and Kuiper's "associated conditions of use" and evaluate particular routines as fulfilling one of these strategies on this macro-level. As such, we can return to Ron James's floating routines, and how there is a recognition that they serve to re-establish rapport through, in the case of tags to "Ferris Wheel," demonstrating allegiance via invoking local *blasons populaires* and, in the case of "Paid in Game," demonstrating and re-affirming a Canadian worldview of rural hospitality.[5] Let us turn now to a more micro-level, where "given essential ideas" and "associated conditions of use" are not for grand notions of (Canadian) identity and the construction of rapport, but for the particularly effective and affective manner of expressing a simple concept.

3. "I Am a Fan of Hilarity": Non-Linguistic Conditions of Use and Crystallizing *le mot juste*

> Like most comics there's an unwritten rule that you retire your material once it's out there. And once I don't do that bit anymore that's it: that bit's finished. But if I'm still doing it, and I know—I know the beginning, middle, and end; I know all the beats; I know all the things I have to say—you can riff within that. Sometimes you get a little nugget of gold, and sometimes it's just extraneous crap, but it's never really *finished* finished.
>
> David Cross on Fox 2018

Despite the propensity for retiring material once it's "out there" on a recording, on occasion the same routine can make it to multiple mediations. On his first album, *Impersonal* (2007), comedian Paul F. Tompkins gathered together material he had been performing for years, in part as a valediction for it.

> That was the best of my stand-up from those days, and that was the stuff I would eventually do on Conan [O'Brien's *Late Night* program] and things like that, and on my Comedy Central specials. So I decided, from a vantage point of having a lot more material now than I did then, "Oh, I don't do this stuff anymore," and so I might as well finally take the plunge and put out a record and start with this stuff.
>
> Thorn 2007

Included on this album was "Peanut Brittle." Of the available versions, the earliest is from his 2003 appearance on *Comedy Central Presents*, a half-hour stand-up anthology program. Certain editions of his follow-up album, *Freak Wharf* (2009), came with a bonus CD, *Sir, You Have Fooled Me Twice* (2010): comprising looser moments from the same performance, an audience member asks Tompkins to do what she calls "Snakes in a Can" and, although he initially hesitates as it had

---

[5] Although coming from a different perspective, Rachel C. Lee (2004) takes a similar approach in her analysis of Margaret Cho's *I'm the One That I Want* special.

already been committed to recording, he relents and performs it again (and the album track is thus called "Snakes in a Can"). Lastly, he brought it out for his gala appearance at the Montreal *Just for Laughs* festival in 2012.

We have four distinct performance and recording occasions. With the exception of *Sir, You Have Fooled Me Twice*, Tompkins had deliberately selected this material beforehand knowing it was to be committed to some medium. Conversely, that spontaneous performance also exhibits a looseness, in part because the performative conceit of it being an account of a recent moment in time is so explicitly shattered. He had greater personal control over his two albums than he had over the television appearances, including liberties of time and of language, i.e. the option to use vulgarity. The albums were also Tompkins' own audience: people who had come specifically to see him. *Comedy Central Presents* would invite studio audiences to attend a taping, irrespective of whether they knew the comedian's work; similarly, the *Just for Laughs* galas are for the general festival audience with the sense of it being an "event," and who are often drawn to the evening's emcee, which for this show was *Saturday Night Live*'s Bill Hader (Brownstein 2012).

Nevertheless, we see remarkable consistency from performance to performance, as evidenced in example (3). His Labovian abstract is implicit: one could make an argument that, by virtue of already being on the stage, the abstract as a frame for what is to follow is unnecessary (Labov 1997).[6] In the orientation he locates himself in a novelty store as part of his personal and professional interests, and he reminds the audience of a particularly trite commonplace therein. He complicates that commonplace by noting the updated design, which could be new information to the audience, and he imagines the scenario through which the initiative was taken to effect that change, which brings an initial stasis of the can in its present form. This section ends in a resolution but functions as an orientation for the next, non-transcribed part of the routine, how this now-refreshed joke contrivance conditions someone falling for it in the twenty-first century.[7] Moira Marsh would classify this as a "booby trap," which "tamper[s] with everyday objects so that they are unusable or have unusual effects, and the jokes are effective only if the targets fail to notice these changes and attempt to use them in the normal fashion" (2015:27). Speaking in character as the target

[6] The abstract may indeed be implied as a conscious device for intertextually invoking a particular genre. For example, in Tompkins's "Stromboli," which is a parody of the "Vanishing Hitchhiker" contemporary legend (see Bennett 1984), he begins: "*Oh folks!* Here comes a chilling tale! I hope you're bored with the color your hair is now because by the end of this story it will be *bone white!*" (Tompkins 2009).

[7] We have vertiginously now combined Labov's use of "orientation" with Richard Bauman's particular use of it in practical joke narratives, as "the factors that bring the participants into place" (Bauman 1986:45).

(3)

The Peanut Brittle Routine by Paul F. Tompkins

Comedy Central Presents (2003)	Impersonal (2007)	Sir, You Have Fooled Me Twice (2009)	Just for Laughs (2012)	"Formulas" [and semantically consistent clauses]
		The other day I went to... I don't know why this has to take place the other day [laughs] [l]		
		I like to go [laughs]	I'll tell you what I do like	
		This was I'm gonna say this was a *week* and *a half* ago [L]		
I was in a *novelty store* the other day	Not long ago I was in a novelty store	[laughs] I went into a *novelty* store	It's I like going to *novelty* stores	[Recent visit to] "Novelty store"
			Professional curiosity I just like to see what's up	
because I am a *fan* of *hilarity* [l]	because I am a fan of *hilarity* [L]	*Because* I am a fan of *hilarity* [L]	I'm a big fan of *hilarity* in all its many forms	[Rationale] "I am a fan of hilarity"
And uh I saw that they they are still *making* the *gag* peanut brittle	*And I noticed they're still making the gag peanut brittle* [l]	*And I noticed* that they're still making the old *gag* peanut brittle can	I notice they are *still* making the *gag* peanut brittle A *can* that says peanut brittle on it	[Observation] "they are still making the gag peanut brittle"
You know what I'm talking about? You open the can of peanut brittle up and [excitedly] "snakes fly out"	You know it looks like a can of peanut brittle And then you open it up and [horrified] *"and snakes fly out"* [obnoxiously] [L] *"hahahahah What a great prank"*	[elided] "You know it's like you think it's think it's peanut brittle and you open up and" *snakes fly out* and everybody has a *great time* [l]	Then you open it up and then [excitedly] "snakes fly out of it"	"you open [it/the can] up" "and snakes fly out"

The Peanut Brittle Routine by Paul F. Tompkins (continued)

Comedy Central Presents (2003)	Impersonal (2007)	Sir, You Have Fooled Me Twice (2009)	Just for Laughs (2012)	"Formulas" [and semantically consistent clauses]
And the *time* to really get someone with this I think Was the *mid* eighteen *hundreds* [L]	I think the *best* time to get someone with *this* gag was uh... The *eighteen hundreds* [L] *you know like*	And I think this probably the best time to get somebody with *this* gag *Was the eighteen hundreds* [L]	I think the *best* time to get someone with this gag was The *eighteen* hundreds [L] *right?*	[Optimal] "time to get someone with this gag was" "the eighteen hundreds"
You know before *entertainment* was invented [l]	Before *entertainment* was invented [L]	You know before *entertainment* was invented [L]		"before entertainment was invented"
And that was the *best* they had [l]	When people just, sat around and *stared* at open *fire* [l]	Where you'd *sit around* stare at *fire* [l]		[Alternatives]
But *here's* what they've done they've updated the *packaging* on the gag peanut brittle To make it more *contemporary* [sarcastically excited] "Now it will work for sure"	What I *noticed* was they have updated the *packaging* on the *can* to make it look more *modern*	And I *noticed* that they had updated the *packaging* on the can	And I noticed something about the gag peanut brittle can They had *updated* the *font* on the *can* [l] To make it look more *modern* [l]	[Observation] "they have updated the [packaging/font] on the can"
	Because *that* was the problem [L]	As if *that* was the problem with it [l]	Because *that* was the problem [L]	"*That* was the problem"
But I love that somebody *thought* about it There was like a *guy* that said	This...	But some enterprising head of a novelty company Called his top men in	As if there was a *meeting* at the *novelty* company where the Head of the company was like	This means at some point the *head* of the *novelty* company saw this And called a *meeting*	[Segue to hypothetical scenario with] "head of the novelty company"

The Peanut Brittle Routine by Paul F. Tompkins (continued)

Comedy Central Presents (2003)	Impersonal (2007)	Sir, You Have Fooled Me Twice (2009)	Just for Laughs (2012)	"Formulas" [and semantically consistent clauses]
Gentlemen this is unacceptable	| Gentlemen this is unacceptable	| Gentlemen get in here Anyone care to explain this? [l]	| Gentlemen this is unacceptable	"Gentlemen this is unacceptable"
No one would be fooled by this outdated-looking can of peanut brittle	No one would be fooled by this outdated-looking can of peanut brittle [l]	This absurdly outdated-looking can of peanut brittle? [l] Who would be fooled by this and even open the can so as to be startled by the fake snakes? [l] Look I'm mad enough that we had to stop putting real snakes in these cans [L] But this is beyond the pale gentlemen [l] What am I paying you for? [l]	No one would be fooled by this outdated-looking can of peanut brittle We're better than this gentlemen	"No one would be fooled by" "this outdated-looking can of peanut brittle"
I want five modern fonts on my desk by five o'clock Five by five I say |	I want five modern fonts on my desk by five o'clock [L] Five by five Yes I know it's a Saturday |	I want five modern fonts on my desk by five o'clock Five by five | [l]	Now I want five modern fonts on my desk by five o'clock Five by five [L] you heard me | They must have put on a pot of coffee or something [l]	"I want five modern fonts on my desk by five o'clock" "Five by five"
And they did it	But they did it They got that shit done	And they did it		"they did it" "they got it done"
		They give it a nice new current look	They got it done And that peanut brittle can looks thoroughly up to date	

of the prank, Tompkins coincidentally gives voice to all the possible conditions for assuming the good intentions of the prankster, most notably the "quotidianness" of canned peanut brittle, followed by the terror from the snakes, and finally coming to terms with being the target of the prank.

Perhaps without ethnographic research we cannot ascertain whether it is the premise that is amusing or the way that premise is expressed (and indeed it may easily be both), but the consistencies in the performances over that decade suggest the mutually mediating conclusions that (*a*) Tompkins found the most effective ways to express the given essential ideas that lead him point by point through his story, and (*b*) the consistent reactions he gets—predictable laughs—confirm and crystallize those expressions. Anna-Leena Siikala noted the remarkable consistencies across performances of the same legend, a genre that tends towards less stylization either by meter (such as epic) or by anticipated motifs (such as *Märchen*). Of particular interest were recurring phrases, "for they seem to be hooks on which to hang a narrative in the teller's memory. Of greatest permanence are the lines the narrator usually consciously tries to repeat verbatim" (1990:84).

We may still ask a whole slew of why-questions: Why *novelty store* and *hilarity* and not *joke shop* and *amusement*? Why *the eighteen-hundreds* in both form and date? Why does the seemingly neutral *Because that was the problem* provoke such a response? What are the connotations of *Gentlemen*? Not bound by metrical necessity, of all the possible words that could be employed, Tompkins eventually chose these ones. In part, this is because they meet the expectations of meaning while simultaneously surprising us. On the very level of word choice, the familiar and strange balance is struck. How do we begin to conceptualize word choice within Oral-Formulaic Theory when we are approaching performances conditioned neither by meter nor by the routinized performances of social scripts?

Konrad Kuiper notes the difficulty in doing any sort of formula analysis on creativity:

> [Potential] phrasal coinages occur almost every time someone constructs a new phrase or clause since any phrase which is uttered is potentially a new phrasal lexical item. Creativity in terms of the coinage of new phrasal lexical items is, therefore, hard to study. As Noam Chomsky has tirelessly pointed out, speakers are being creative every time they put a new phrase or sentence together. However, that creativity is not in itself intentional.

> Kuiper 2009:191

Nevertheless, he continues, we can discern intentional creativity in spheres of action that, tautologically, are culturally framed and understood as creative, such as advertising copy or pop music lyrics, where "the coined word or phrase(s) [is] repeated so many times by its creator(s) that it becomes lexicalized" (Kuiper 2009:192). In his discussion of the cartoons of Cathy Wilcox, Kuiper suggests a methodology for the "creative artistic deformation" of phrasal lexical items. With far greater complexity than I present here, he avers that whether that deformation is structural (changing or rearranging words within a phrase) or semantic (the literalization of idioms or homophonic punning), it has "as its intent that a perceiver perceive the difference(s) between the base form and its variant" (2009:193). Because we are immersed in and fluent with the formulas of our language (the "accessibility condition"), we can hear a deformation and, provided that deformation retains sufficient perceptual clues (the "recoverability condition"), recognize the base form. There is a *frisson* between the audience's expectations of what could be said and what is actually said.

Such an approach works well for formulas, but does it work for single word choice? Elsewhere, Kuiper refers to the conditions of use associated with words, noting particularly the non-linguistic conditions, and how "native speakers share intuitions about" them. These intuitions may not be explicit or, rather, able to be specifically expressed by native speakers, but when one word is chosen over another, more anticipated word, a listener can note the momentary dissonance, recognize that it is a consequence of a deliberate choice of the speaker (particularly in frames defined by being verbal play and thus partially exercises in verbal creativity), that the seeming synonyms have slightly different non-linguistic conditions of use while maintaining semantic equivalence. On the level of word, then, we have an example of Elliott Oring's "appropriate incongruity" approach to the study of humor, i.e. "that all humor depends upon the perception of an incongruity that can be nevertheless seen as somehow appropriate" (2016:25).

Consider Tompkins's use of *Gentlemen*: as a term of address for a group of familiars it connotes a certain stodginess and anachronism. So, rather than the synonymous *fellows* (or *fellas*), *guys, folks*, or no term of address at all (and not to mention its gender exclusivity, further suggesting a holdover from some earlier era), it underscores the disconnect of the head of the novelty company with the contemporary sphere and thus the contemporary sphere of hilarity. It is incongruous insofar as it is a word with non-linguistic conditions of use that mark it as somewhat of an outlier for an anticipated "normal" word selection, yet it is appropriate once we reorient ourselves along the intended trajectory of the speaker's meaning, namely that the *head of the novelty company* is in no position either to be objective on the ongoing relevancy of the peanut brittle gag or to suggest strategies for its revitalization.

But that might be a concession to explicit characterization. When we turn to his use of *hilarity*—which he speaks in his own on-stage persona, not as an imagined other—it too has non-linguistic conditions of use: it is not a commonplace but neither is it archaic or obscure. It hovers at the edge of a vocabulary, something one would employ perhaps only in advertising copy that is trying to establish an unwarranted reputation for humor. Adding to this is the odd construction of being a "fan" of so broad a category of human experience. We could suggest any number of reasons for so deliberate a phrase and what it connotes, but that there is *some* ambiguous connotation, and so early in the routine, prepares us *in some way* to navigate the shifting trajectory of what is to follow. The efficacy, not only of *Gentlemen* as a character choice for the head of the novelty company, but also of *fan of hilarity* for Tompkins' own projection of self, is demonstrated by their continued use over the decade, and they comprise necessary moments in the text.

4. Conclusions

It is far too early to suggest any great methodological insights, as this contribution is hoping merely to point towards further avenues of exploration. Nevertheless, using the Tompkins discussion as a launching point, it might be fruitful to highlight this consideration of crystallized expressions when we examine stand-up comedy texts. They are not "formulas" in any strict sense, because they do not express the same thing in different semantic occasions. Yet, they retain remarkable consistency from use to use in the same narrative over multiple iterations, and can occasion a freedom of improvisation between the more or less verbatim phrases. To ask "Why *that* word?" is in part a consideration of why, of all possible synonyms that could have been employed, the comedian settled on this one.

These are only precursory remarks: a full oral-formulaic approach would entail access to a larger set of routine performances with both a diachronic analysis of movement from early attempts at expression to firm establishment in the active repertoire and a synchronic analysis of active performances. But it also suggests a trajectory for further analysis, namely, how humor theory can possibly circumscribe appropriate incongruity not only on the level of a piece of humor's logic but on its vocabulary: how does a stand-up routine differ from a "joke," which implies a more rigid structure, and how there is a release from not only what is meant but what is said. Moreover, routines come together to form a set that is also understood and presented as a unified discrete performance, and new material is generated within an ongoing framework of establishing rapport and reputation, pushing analysis to an entire oeuvre. Also absent is a discussion of the aesthetics of metricality in stand-up: an entire paper could discuss George Carlin's alternate use of *fucking* and *goddamn* as modifiers with respect to both their non-linguistic conditions of use and their rhythms. Lexical commonplaces that appear not only in multiple routines but in the work of multiple comedians would be of remarkable interest, although, given the imperative of innovation in a post-literate artform, the list might be somewhat thin and uninspiring.

This contribution began and thus ends in hesitancy; there seems to be *something* happening in stand-up that nestles somewhere between memorization and pure spontaneity, and *something* between a standard set of formulas and a wholly idiosyncratic verbal repertoire. Stand-up comedy texts move from essential idea to essential idea, and those ideas are expressed in a particular way because employing that particular way has been proven effective in performance, whether Ron James's *bucket* and *brown paper bag dripping blood* or Paul F. Tompkins's *novelty store* and *five by five* or countless others. To suggest that texts are not memorized but spontaneously composed by verbally navigating between these necessary expressions—whether or not we as yet choose to call them formulas—is a fruitful path of future inquiry.

References

Sources

Carlin, G. 1972. *FM & AM*. LP. Little David.

———. 2005. *Life Is Worth Losing*. Cable television live broadcast. November 5. HBO.

James, R. 2003. *The Road Between My Ears*. Television special. CBC.

Moore, R. R. 1971. *The Cockpit*. LP. Kent Records.

Tompkins, P. F. 2003. Episode of *Comedy Central Presents*. Television program. March 14. Comedy Central.

———. 2007. *Impersonal*. CD. A Special Thing Records.

———. 2009. *Freak Wharf*. CD. A Special Thing Records.

———. 2010. *Sir, You Have Fooled Me Twice*. CD. A Special Thing Records.

———. 2012. Appearance at *Just for Laughs*. YouTube. Uploaded June 24, 2016.

Literature

Bauman, R. 1986. *Story, Performance, and Event: Contextual Studies of Oral Narrative*. Cambridge.

Bell, M. J. 1983. *The World from Brown's Lounge: An Ethnography of Black Middle-Class Play*. Urbana.

Bennett, G. 1984. "The Phantom Hitchhiker: Neither Modern, Urban nor Legend?" *Perspectives on Contemporary Legend: Proceedings of the Conference on Contemporary Legend, Sheffield, July 1982* (ed. P. Smith) 45–63. Sheffield.

Brodie, I. 2014. *A Vulgar Art: A New Approach to Stand-Up Comedy*. Jackson.

———. 2018. "'I Don't Like My Work': A Response to Antti Lindfors." *Cultural Analysis* 16(2):72–79.

Brownstein, B. 2012. "Just for Laughs 2012: Review of Gala 2 with Bill Hader." *Montreal Gazette*, July 25.

Evans, D. 2007. "Formulaic Composition in the Blues: A View from the Field." *Journal of American Folklore* 120:482–499.

———. 2010. "The Blues Formula: A Response to Taft." *Journal of American Folklore* 123:218–221.

Frog, ed. 2017a. *Formula: Units of Speech—'Words' of Verbal Art: Working Papers of the Seminar-Workshop: 17th-19th May 2017, Helsinki, Finland*. Helsinki.

———. 2017b. "Formulaic Language and Linguistic Multiforms: Questions of Complexity and Variation." In Frog 2017a:252–270.

Fox, J. D. 2018. "David Cross' Squagels." *Good One: A Podcast About Jokes*. Podcast. June 4.

Jensen, M. S. 1980. *The Homeric Question and the Oral-Formulaic Theory*. Copenhagen.

Klein, B. 2006. "An Afternoon's Conversation at Elsa's." *Narrating, Doing, Experiencing: Nordic Folkloristic Perspectives* (ed. A. K. Bregenhøj, B. Klein, and U. Palmenfelt) 79–100. Helsinki.

Kuiper, K. 2009. *Formulaic Genres*. London.

Labov, W. 1997. "Some Further Steps in Narrative Analysis." *Journal of Narrative and Life History* 7:395–415.

Labov, W., Cohen, P., Robins, C., and Lewis, J. 1973. "Toasts." *Mother Wit from the Laughing Barrel: Readings in the Interpretation of Afro-American Folklore* (ed. A. Dundes) 329–352. Englewood Cliffs.

Lee, R. C. 2004. "'Where's My Parade?': Margaret Cho and the Asian American Body in Space." *TDR: The Drama Review* 48(2):108–132.

Lord, A. B. 2000. *The Singer of Tales* ed 2. Cambridge, MA.

MacPherson, G. 2006. "Ron James" (interview). Blog post. April 1. guymacpherson.ca.

Marsh, M. 2015. *Practically Joking*. Logan.

McGeachy, M. G. 2006. *Lonesome Words: The Vocal Poetics of the Old English Lament and the African-American Blues Song*. New York.

Molineux, C. "Life Memory Archive Translation Performance Memory Archive Life: Textual Self-Documentation in Stand-Up Comedy." *Comedy Studies* 7(1):2–12.

Oring, E. 2016. *Joking Asides: The Theory, Analysis, and Aesthetics of Humor*. Logan.

Oswalt, P. 2012. "It Was that Goddamned Eyeroll." Blog post, January 6. pattonoswalt.com.

Pagán Cánovas, C. 2017. "Formulaic Creativity: Connecting the Main Tenets of Cognitive Linguistics and Oral Poetics." In Frog 2017a:241–251.

Palmieri, G. 2017. *Oral Self-Translation of Stand-Up Comedy: From the Mental Text to Performance and Interaction*. Unpublished PhD dissertation, University of Surrey.

Parry, M. 1930. "Studies in the Epic Technique of Oral Verse-Making I: Homer and Homeric Style." *Making of Homeric Verse: The Collected Papers of Milman Parry* (ed. A. Parry 1971) 266–324. Oxford.

Posner, M. 2001. "Blackfly Set to Buzz." *Globe and Mail* (Toronto, ON). January 1.

Radick, G. 2003. "R. L. Garner and the Rise of the Edison Phonograph in Evolutionary Philology." *New Media, 1740-1915* (ed. L. Gitelman and G. B. Pingree) 175–206. Cambridge.

Rose, C. 2014. "Interview with Louis C. K." *The Charlie Rose Show.* Television program. May 6. PBS.

Siikala, A.-L. 1990. *Interpreting Oral Narrative.* Trans. S. Sinisalo. Helsinki.

Taft, M. 2009. "The Essential Idea of the Blues Formula: A Response to David Evans." *Journal of American Folklore* 122(483):75–80.

Thorn, J. 2007. "Interview with Paul F. Tompkins." *The Sound of Young America.* Podcast. Aug 28.

14

Formulas in Neo-Latin Poetry as a Means to Language Enrichment and Self-Representation

Language Tips and Sociolinguistics in Justus Lipsius' Poems

Hans Nollet

UNEXPECTED ENCOUNTERS lead to unforeseen associations and ideas, and, as it happens, may eventually yield unusual yet valid conclusions. Serendipity proves to be a strong ally to the interdisciplinary scholar. Hence, a casual discussion about formulaic language uncovered similarities between oral poetry and the use of rare words in Neo-Latin poems. This engendered a vivid debate and paved the way for further research, which I briefly present here.

The similarities concern poets' use of expressions learned from others that are pre-fitted to a relevant meter. A clear distinction needs to be made between the purely oral tradition of the Homeric epics, and its Latin descendants. The *Iliad* and the *Odyssey* are obviously exponents of an oral culture, comparable to the South Slavic epic tradition as documented by Milman Parry and Albert Lord, and they were, across much of the twentieth century, considered to constitute the quintessence of primary orality.[1] Within an oral culture, formulaic language can function as a mnemonic device and facilitates in-time matching of phraseology to meter in the (improvised) recitation of epics, since the singer "had readily available, in his memory, a stock of standardized phraseologies" (Havelock 1986:11; see also Reichl, this volume). In contrast, Neo-Latin poems are literary compositions, and thus verses can be formulated with careful reflection while the written form allows the texts to be available even if they are not

---

[1] Cf. Ong (1982:11): "I style the orality of a culture totally untouched by any knowledge of writing or print, 'primary orality'"; see also Parry 1971; Lord 1960; Burke 2004:93–99; Lindahl 2011.

remembered. These fundamental differences do not, however, mean that a poet did not make use of tried and tested phraseologies "readily available in his memory" in his compositions, but rather that the motivations for doing so were quite unrelated.

The approaches to formulaic language initially developed by Parry and Lord became criticized for looking at the phenomenon with blinders on, trying to isolate orality from literacy as absolute and ideal categories and interpreting metrically structured, reusable phraseology as belonging to one rather than to the other. Lord (1960:129) developed the idea of "transitional text" to describe poetry produced in writing that uses an oral-formulaic system, but the whole approach was shown to be problematic in the light of genres that could also be formulaic in spite of being based in written rather than oral composition (e.g. Blackburn 1988:24–25). Formulaic language is thus clearly not something exclusive to oral verbal art, and more recent research has shown that even written prose genres can be formulaic in the extreme (e.g. Kuiper 2009). Although many scholars today continue to think of formulaic language in verbal art as something distinctive of oral poetry, it is actually far more widespread. Phenomena like those addressed here provide valuable points of reference when considering the diversity of forms and functions that formulaic language may assume in particular forms of verbal art and their cultural and historical contexts.

The use of formulaic language in Neo-Latin poetry will be illustrated here through Justus Lipsius' (1547–1606) poems. I will first summarize the most common features associated with formulaic language in Greek and Latin, in order to distinguish these from Lipsius' *ars formulandi*.[2] I will then explore several cases of formulaic language in Lipsius' works, and finally put forward an argument that accounts for these.

1. The Process of *imitatio* and *aemulatio veterum*

Rather than relying on a common formulaic idiom related to composition in performance, Virgil, Lucan, and other epic Latin poets have imitated and emulated the Homeric diction, and built on an already existing literary (and thus written) tradition. The repeated use of certain units of speech emanates from the principle of *imitatio* and *aemulatio veterum*: the endeavor to equal or

---

[2]   For biographical and introductory information about Justus Lipsius in English, cf. Waszink 2004:3–221. The quotation of Lipsius' poems follows the numeration as used in Nollet 2015; all numbers are preceded by the abbreviation ILC = *Iusti Lipsi Carmina*.

excel the classical models (cf. IJsseling 1997; IJsewijn and Sacré 1998:1–9). In order to explain these techniques of borrowing, which constituted the basis of Western literature until the Romantic era, one is usually inclined to stress the element of tradition: the poet puts himself in a long line of predecessors and proclaims to be a worthy heir of a longstanding literary dynasty: Ennius follows Homer's or Hesiod's example, Virgil endeavors to surpass Homer, Hesiod, and Ennius; Lucan and Statius choose Virgil as their epic model.

(1)

    i.   Ἄνδρα μοι ἔννεπε, Μοῦσα, πολύτροπον,
        Tell me, Muse, of the man of many devices

                                          Homer *Odyssey* 1, 1

    ii.   Μοῦσαι Πιερίηθεν, ἀοιδῇσι κλείουσαι,
        δεῦτε, Δί’ ἐννέπετε σφέτερον πατέρ’ ὑμνείουσαι
        Muses, from Pieria, glorifying in songs,
        come here, tell in hymns of your father Zeus

                                  Hesiod *Works and Days* 1–2

    iii. Musae, quae pedibus magnum pulsatis Olympum
        Muses, who dance on the great Olympus[3]

                                  Ennius *Annales* 1, 1

    iv. Arma virumque cano   Arms and the man I sing

                                    Virgil *Aeneid* 1, 1

       Musa, mihi causas memora   Tell me, O Muse, the cause

                                    Virgil *Aeneid* 1, 8

    v.   Bella per Emathios plus quam civilia campos,
        iusque datum sceleri canimus

                                  Lucan *De bello civili* 1, 1–2

---

[3] Cf. Skutsch 1985:70, 142–147.

Of war I sing, war worse than civil, waged over the plains of
Emathia, and of legality conferred to crime

vi. Magnanimum Aeaciden formidatamque Tonanti
progeniem et patrio vetitam succedere caelo,
diva, refer.

Statius *Achilleid* 1, 1–3

Goddess, tell of great-hearted Aeacides and offspring feared of
the Thunderer and forbidden to succeed to his father's heaven

The invocation of the Muses is a topos in epic literature: by appealing to his Muse,
the performer or narrator emphasizes his close connection with the inspira-
tional divinities (cf. Havelock 1986:19–23; Minchin 1995). Homer underlines this
relationship by the use of a direct clause in the imperative mode (μοι ἔννεπε),
which is imitated by Hesiod (ἐννέπετε), and by the Latin descendants (*memora,
refer*). The Greek Μοῦσα is in Latin either transcribed (*Musa*), or paraphrased
(*diva*). Virgil's *arma virumque (cano)* is known to become extremely influential at
the outset of epics (e.g. Lucan and Statius), but we find multiple references of
this proverbial phrase also in Roman authors of other literary genres, such as
Ovid, Persius, Martial, etc. (cf. Comparetti 1908:1–33).

As for the Latin epic poets: regardless of the absence of any primary orality in
their diction, it is crystal clear that they all take extreme care over the euphonic
and rhythmical qualities of their verse. Especially Virgil is rightfully called the
master of the dactylic hexameter. In the *Aeneis* we notice (or should we say: *hear*)
undeniably a "deliberate accommodation of sound to sense" (Goold 1992:113)
and a considerable metrical "variety in repeated patterns" (Duckworth 1969:7).[4]

In the lyric genre, Catullus' poem no. 4 gained fame as soon as it was
created: we already find a witty parody in the *Appendix Vergiliana*, a collection of
lyric miscellanea written in the first century AD. Later on, humanist poets were
inspired time and time again by Catullus' iambic trifle (cf. Gaisser 1993; 2007).

(2)

i. Phaselus ille, quem videtis, hospites,
ait fuisse navium celerrimus

Catullus *carmen* 4, 1–2

---

[4] Cf. Dimsdale: "Virgil's mastery over the hexameter is unapproached" (quoted in Duckworth
1969:6; see also Schanz and Hosius 1966:90–93; Raven 1965:§§60–64, 75–77; Nougaret
1948:§§55–62).

The pinnace you see, my friends,
says that she was once the fleetest of ships

ii.   Sabinus ille, quem videtis, hospites,
        ait fuisse mulio celerrimus

Appendix Vergiliana Catalepton 10, 1–2

Sabinus yonder, whom you see, my friends,
says that he was the fastest of muleteers

iii.   In aede Penna, quam videtis, hospites,
        ait fuisse ceteris disertior

François de Montmorency *Dedicatio Pennae*
Iusti Lipsii Viri Clarissimi numeris Phaseli Catul-
liani adumbrata

The Pen you see in this church, my friends,
says that she was once swifter than any other[5]

iv.   Annaeus iste Seneca, quem vides, lector,
        ait fuisse magnus inter auctores

Justus Lipsius *Invitatio ad Senecam*

Annaeus Seneca yonder, whom you see, reader,
says that he was once important among men of letters[6]

Obviously, imitators were captivated by the fluency and the melody of Catullus'
iambic rhythm, and they carefully copied the syntactic and metrical framework:
the opening words announce the subject of the sentence in connection with a
disyllabic pronoun (*ille, iste*), and they are followed by a relative clause (initi-
ated by *quem, quam*) in which the reader is directly addressed (*videtis, vides* and
the vocative case *hospites, lector*). The second line opens with the construction
of *ait* followed by the perfect infinitive *fuisse*, and only at the very end of the
line—strategically separated from its subject—we find (preferably in its superla-
tive form) the predicative adjective which the author bestows upon the subject
(*celerrimus, disertior, magnus*). The authenticity and the charm of the imitation
resides in the choice of the subject (the first word) and its correlation with the

---

5   Cf. Papy 1992; this poem is listed as GVi 01 00 00 M¹; cf. ILE XIV, [c. 01 04 01].
6   Cf. ILC147; Lipsius 1605:f. 4v.

predicate (the last word of the second line), thus creating a tension that spans two full iambic lines.

2. Plagiarism

A third explanation, of a more practical and economic nature, concerns the repeated use of complete verses or poems with only slight changes. Obviously, this type of borrowing is to be considered as plagiarism, and it can hardly be called an artistic accomplishment.[7] The Italian papal nuncio Angelo Durini (1725-1796), for instance, copied two of Lipsius' epigrams (in which the qualities of good translations are lauded) and forged them into a new one, which served as a eulogy for his fellow countryman Pietro Metastasio, poet, librettist, and playwright at the imperial court in Vienna. Durini, who is qualified in modern biographical reference works as *abile compositore di versi latini* ('a skilled composer of Latin verse') (cf. DBI 42, 195), merely replaced the proper names and the appositions by Metastasio's name, or by the appropriate geographical and dramatic characteristics (*Petre, Romae, Etrusca, Italici, cothurnis, Theatri*).

As one can observe, Durini's poem[8] in (3.i) is in fact a patchwork, entirely composed of hendecasyllables borrowed from Lipsius' epigrams seen in (3.ii) and (3.iii). Durini's opening lines 1-2 are almost identical to the initial verses of Lipsius' epigram in (3.ii). Lines 3-4 are copied *verbatim* from lines 10-11 of Lipsius' epigram in (3.iii). Lines 5 and 7 are separate parts from Lipsius' section of lines 4-5 in (3.ii). The end of Durini's poem (lines 8-10) contains the pun and the entire content from lines 12-14 of Lipsius' epigram in (3.ii). Although extensive borrowings from classical models are not uncommon in Neo-Latin literature, Durini's procedure does exceed by far the normal practice of *imitatio* (and can therefore be labelled as plagiarism), because (*a*) Durini does not acknowledge his dependence on Lipsius' epigrams (in contrast to, for instance, example (2.iii)), which we expect him to do since Lipsius' poems could hardly be considered classical commonplace in the eighteenth century, and (*b*) he repeatedly carries out this poetic poaching of Lipsius' verses without any mention of his models (cf. Nollet 2015: *passim*).

---

[7] I will not dwell upon various kinds of humanist intellectual *Spielerei* and verbal innuendo, such as *centones*, although this type of borrowing was probably considered as a serious poetical genre (cf. IJsewijn and Sacré 1998:4, 132-133; Ford et al. 2014:II, 1137-1140).

[8] Cf. Durini 1770:69; ILC46; ILC105.

(3)

i. Angelo Durini, *Ad divinum Metastasium*

O! *Romae* decus, atque *Etrusca* siren,
nostrarum Pater elegantiarum,
quem suum veteres velint Athenae,
quem suum vetus ipsa Roma dici;
o quam nos gravibus Tuis *cothurnis*
quos haec atque alia invidebit aetas
oblectas, reficisque, rapis, docesque!
Vis verum Tibi, DIE PETRE, dicam,
te vivo *Italici* decus *Theatri*,
vivet, sed pereunte Te peribit.

O, you Jewel of *Rome*, *Etruscan* Siren,
Godfather of our refined culture,
you are a person, whom ancient Athens,
or even ancient Rome would wish to
count among their inhabitants,
o, how much delight you provide us with
your dramatic compositions,
how can you comfort, capture and
educate us, with your plays whom these
and later generations will envy you for.
Do you really want me to tell you the
truth, DIVINE PETER: as long as you live,
the jewel of *Italian Theatre* will be alive,
as soon as you are gone, also the Italian
Theatre will be gone.

ii. Justus Lipsius *Ad Ianum Hautenum: De versione eius Plauti*

Belgarum decus et *Batava* Siren,
nostrarum pater elegantiarum,
HAUTENE, unice et une mi Sodalis,
o quam nos lepida tua *Camena*
oblectas reficisque, dum Latinas
transfers ad patrium solum Camenas
et Plauti numeros solutiores
verbis et numeris ligas Batavis,
quod haec atque alia invidebit aetas.
O ioci Veneresque, o Atticorum
conditae sale collocutiones!
Vis verum tibi dici, *amice*? Dicam:
te vivo pariter sales *Batavi*
vivent, et pereunte te peribunt.

iii. Justus Lipsius, *Super S[anctorum] Patrum syntagmate noviter a Petro Pantino V[iro] R[everendissimo] et Cl[arissi]mo vulgato et erudite verso, Phaleuci*

Quis novus liber hic? Liber sacratus,
sacra nomina, res habet sacratas.
Quis auctor? Varii, vetusto ab aevo,
cum mos et pietas vetus vigebant.
Quis produxit? Et ipse moris atque
virtutis veteris: vestustiorum
gnarus artium et utriusque linguae,
PANTINUS meus. Ille, comparatae
cui nives videantur esse nigrae,
quem suum veteres velint Athenae,
quem suum vetus ipsa Roma dici,
quem meum cupio, et meum esse iacto:
cui, dum corpore mens mea illigatur,
fido et firmo adamante colligabor.
Quod SANCUS pater audiat, FIDESque.

3. Linguistic Apprenticeship

In humanist poetry, however, we come across repetitive phrasing and formulas that escape these three common patterns of formulaic language (orality, *imitatio*, copy–paste). Quite often Neo-Latin poets seem to borrow technical wording and idiomatic expressions from prose authors, ancient Latin grammar books, or obscure and unknown poets. This technique is widespread and undeniable, as evidence will show, and it can in no way be explained through any of the aforementioned arguments: Lipsius does not place himself in a literary tradition (neither epic nor lyric), since the model is a grammar book or a lexicographic compilation.[9] This *modus versificandi* does not facilitate memory, and neither does it save the author time.

In my opinion, we are dealing with a novel, purely linguistic, and didactic motive: in order to ensure a flawlessly written Neo-Latin verse, humanists considered it wise to copy a phrase, proverb or combination of words from a native speaker (read: classical author), rather than to be exposed to the risk of prosodic, metrical, or lexical errors;[10] copying from an existing ancient source, keeps you safe, and at the same time, it offers the opportunity to show off your extensive acquaintance with classical literature (*poeta doctus*).Three examples will clarify my point of view.

3.1. *Tesca loca*

When Lipsius writes the epitaph for a friend who died young, he chooses as a literary model the well-known Eucharis inscription, composed in iambic trimeter, honoring a young freedwoman who died at the age of 14.[11] Lipsius imitates

---

[9] Sometimes, we admit, ancient grammar books contain phrases of (lost) poems, from which humanists borrow. But those poetic quotes are too fragmentary to be considered as genuine models for imitation.

[10] In classical Latin verse, the metrical rhythm is quantitative, being the result of a division into long and short syllables, which is "based on the intrinsic *quantity* of different vowel-and-consonant combinations" (Raven 1965:22). Therefore, this quantitative pitch often conflicts with the natural word accent, creating a clash or tension that lends great charm to Latin verse. In the medieval era, word accent "gradually superseded quantity as a basis for rhythm, the language thus producing the models for accentual verse in English and other 'modern' languages" (Raven 1965:38). When, from the Renaissance onwards, the humanists returned to classical Latin verse as a model to be emulated, they were strongly dependent on an analytical knowledge of the language, since only native speakers would have been able to distinguish vowel quantities and audibly perceive the difference between certain long and short syllables. However, the metrical chunks or units obtained from classical poets could be easily learned and memorized, and these assured a safe passage through the metrical labyrinth by providing formulae "ready for use."

[11] Cf. ILS 5213, 1–3 = CIL, VI 10096 (pp. 3492, 3906) = CIL, I² 1214 (p. 970). The inscription dates from the Late Republican era (cf. Frascati 1997:68–71, fig. 18 [Tavole, p. VI]). See also http://db.edcs.eu/epigr/bilder.php?bild=$CIL_06_10096.jpg (accessed March 29, 2021).

the meter and the phrasing of the opening lines, but he replaces the tomb-stone's poetic phraseology of *leti domus* ('house of death') with the rare *tesca loca* ('desert, inhospitable places'), not inappropriate for someone who died far from home:

(4)

> i. *Epitaphium Francisci Martini mortui Neapoli*
> Heus oculo errante qui *loca tesca* haec aspicis,
> consistere hic te paululum Musae iubent.

> Justus Lipsius[12]

> *Epitaph for Franciscus Martinius, deceased in Naples*
> Alas! You who observe these *waste places*: as your eye dwells upon it,
> the Muses order you to stay here for a little while.

> ii. *Eucharis Liciniae l[iberta] docta erodita omnes artes virgo vixit an[nos] XIIII.*
> Heus! oculo errante qui aspicis leti domus
> morare gressum et titulum nostrum perlege.

> *Eucharis, freedwoman of Licinia's household, well educated and learned in all arts, lived as an unmarried maiden for fourteen years*
> Alas! You who observe this tombstone: as your eye dwells upon it,
> restrain your step and read through my inscription.

Lipsius borrows the formula *tesca loca* from Varro's *De lingua Latina*, a grammat-ical treatise composed in 47–45 BCE, thus bearing witness of his knowledge of the Roman antiquarian and encyclopedic author:

(5)

> Nam apud Accium in *Philocteta Lemnio*:
> Quis tu es mortalis, qui in deserta et *tesca* te apportes loca?
> [...] Quare haec quod *tesca* dixit, non erravit,
> neque ideo quod sancta, sed quod ubi mysteria fiunt attuentur, *tuesca* dicta.

> Varro *De lingua Latina* 7, 11[13]

---

[12] Cf. ILC16.
[13] Varro's suggested etymological relation between *t(u)esca* and *attueri* ("gaze at, look at") is prob-ably incorrect. Ernout and Meillet (2001:*s.v.* "tesca") state that the etymology is unknown, and mention the possible descent from either Sabine language or Indo-European.

For there is the following in Accius, in the *Philoctetes of Lemnos*:
What man are thou, who dost advance
To places desert, *places waste*?
[...] Therefore he made no mistake in calling these lands <u>tesca</u>, and yet he did not do so because they were consecrated; but because men 'gaze at' (*attuentur*) places where mysteries take place, they were called <u>tuesca</u>.

The same word combination is also commented upon by the grammarian Sextus Pompeius Festus (second century CE) in his treatise:

(6)

TESCA *loca* augurio designata. Cicero aspera ait esse et difficilia.

> Festus *De verborum significatione quae super-sunt cum Pauli epitome* 19[14]

WASTE *places* are designated by augury. Cicero [in his poetry] says this means desert and barren places.

3.2. Apollo Aperta

In an elegiac distich composed as a liminary poem or as a caption accompanying a portrait, Lipsius praises the botanist Carolus Clusius (Charles de l'Escluse), whose name invites to the antonymous pun *claudere-recludere* ('closing-disclosing knowledge').[15]

(7)

Omnia Naturae dum, CLUSI, arcana recludis,
CLUSIUS haud ultra sis, sed *APERTA mihi.
* Quo nomine Apollo priscis dictus, ab aperiendo.

> Justus Lipsius *Ad Clusii nomen lusus*[16]

---

[14] Cf. Lindsay 1913:489.
[15] The disclosure of (sacred) knowledge reserved to an initiated circle of specialists, is a classic topos (cf. Virgil, *Georgics*, 2, 173–176; for Clusius, see also Ogilvie 2006; NBW 1, 312–319; BBr 3, 759–778). According to Ovid (*Fasti*, 1, 129–130), the god Janus is called Patulcius or Clusius, depending on whether the doors of his temple were opened (*pateo*) or closed (*claudo*), as happened in respective times of war or peace.
[16] Cf. ILC44.

Since you disclose all of Nature's secrets, CLUSIUS, can you be for me
no longer CLUSIUS-THE-CLOSER, but *APERTA-THE-OPENER.
* That is how Apollo was called by the ancients, it comes from *aperire*
('to open').

Lipsius prefers the rare epiclesis *Aperta*, to indicate Apollo in his quality as the
god of prophecy and divination, as the "one who discloses and reveals oracles."
The word *Aperta* is very rare and explained by Festus:

(8)

APERTA idem Apollo vocabatur, quia patente cortina responsa ab eo
dentur.

Festus *De verborum significatione quae super-
sunt cum Pauli epitome* 1[17]

They also called Apollo APERTA, because he gave his oracles while
the cauldron [sc. the tripod] was opened.

In order to ensure the correct understanding and to display his erudition,
Lipsius decides to put a small explanatory note in the margin of his poem: *Quo
nomine Apollo priscis dictus, ab aperiendo.* Lipsius' friend Janus Dousa operates in
the same manner, when he uses this expression in a liminary poem for Petrus
Forestus' medical treatise: the name *Aperta* is annotated in the margin and even
the source of Festus is added:

(9)

IO TRIUMPHE, IO. Haud secus
et ipse, Phoebe noster, hoste de tuo
TROPAEA victor eriges,
libros, Foreste, DELPHICOS habens domi,
*APERTAE operta sors quibus
TRIPUSQUE cedat, ancipesque DICTIO.
* *Aperta*, Apollinis cognomentum, quia patente cortina
responsa dare solitus. Festus

Janus Dousa *In Dialogos Cl[arissimi] Medicinae Doctoris Petri
Foresti contra uroscopos et empiricos, iambi puri ac meri* 96–101[18]

---

[17] Cf. Lindsay 1913:21. Festus' etymological explanation is considered incorrect. The etymology of
the epiclesis *Aperta* remains unknown: it might be either a phonetic variant of the name Apollo,
or cognate with the Greek verb ἀπείργω ('keep away from, ward off') (cf. RE 3, 43, *s.v.* "Apollon").

[18] Cf. Forestus 1589: f. 9r; Dousa 1584:I.1 (pp. 4–5). Petrus Forestus was the appointed physician of
the Dutch town of Delft, situated between The Hague and Rotterdam. The name of the town is

> Io TRIUMPH, Io. And similarly you,
> our Phoebus Apollo, victorious over your enemy,
>> you will personally build a MEMORIAL TROPHY
> since you, Forestus, have your DELPHIC books at home,
>> to whom *APERTA'S concealed fate,
> TRIPOD and ambiguous DICTION must cede.
>> * *Aperta*, Apollo's cognomen, because he usually gave his
> oracles while the cauldron [sc. the tripod] was opened. Festus

3.3. *Sonticus (morbus)*

When Lipsius hurries back home from Antwerp to Leuven after feeling ill, he decides—contrary to his routine—*not* to make a stop half way in the town of Mechlin, where he usually spends a few days in transit. Therefore, he now sends his friends in Mechlin a poetical apology in choliambs with the explanation, that the real cause of this unusual behavior was his illness. In order to translate the "real cause," Lipsius uses the formula *causa sontica*, a rare expression annotated by several Roman and humanist authors. In the first place, it means "a really compelling reason," "a valid reason," or "a cause considered as real"; but it can also be used to indicate a serious or mysterious disease one could refer to in legal trials: *sonticus morbus*.

(10)

> O triste fatum! Te videre gestivi,
> et licuit ipsum te videre, nec feci.
> Quae causa? Causa *sontica* est, meus *morbus*,
> qui vexat, et tenace vinculo stringit.
> Quid dicam, amice? Ducet ad meum finem.

> Justus Lipsius *Ad Nicolaum Oudartum super*
> *propero transitu meo per Mechliniam. Scazon*[19]

> Oh, how sad is my Fate! I was eagerly looking forward to meeting
>> you,
> and there was an opportunity to do so, but I didn't.
> For what reason? The *culprit* is my *disease*,
> which causes pain and holds me in a tight grip.

---

usually translated as *Delphi (Batavorum)*. This explains the pun *libros Delphicos*: Forestus possesses books 'from Delphi' (Apollo's sanctuary) but also 'from Delft' (his hometown).

[19] Cf. ILC121.

> What can I say, my friend? This disease will ultimately lead to my
> death.
>
> Justus Lipsius, *To Nicolaas Oudaert, about my*
> *hurried passage through Mechlin. Scazon.*

Festus and Gellius explain the expression, quoting from the Law of the Twelve
Tables and from the preclassical authors Aelius Stilo and Gn. Naevius, all impor-
tant and rare sources of archaic Latin:

(11)

> i. *Sonticum morbum* in XII. significare ait Aelius Stilo certum cum iusta
> causa; quem nonnulli putant esse, qui noceat, quod sontes significat
> nocentes. Naevius ait: "Sonticam esse oportet causam, quam ob rem
> perdas mulierem."
>
> Festus, *De verborum significatione quae super-*
> *sunt cum Pauli epitome*, 18

> In the Law of the XII. Tables <u>*sonticus morbus*</u> means—says Aelius Stilo—a
> real disease with a legitimate cause; a disease that according to some
> people, does harm, since *sontes* means 'inflicting injury'. Naevius says:
> "There must be some compelling reason why you should destroy the
> woman."

> ii. Sontica causa dicitur a *morbo sontico*.
>
> Festus *De verborum significatione quae super-*
> *sunt cum Pauli epitome* 19[20]

> The expression *sontica causa* comes from <u>*sonticus morbus*</u>.

> iii. Ceteroqui morbum vehementiorem, vim graviter nocendi
> habentem, legum istarum scriptores alio in loco, non per se "morbum,"
> sed "*morbum sonticum*" appellant.
>
> Aulus Gellius *Noctes Atticae* 20,1, 27

---

[20] Cf. Lindsay 1913:372, 464.

On the contrary, a more severe disorder, having the power of material injury, the writers of those laws call in another place, not *morbus* alone, but *morbus sonticus* ('a serious disease').

Also, Erasmus comments upon this expression in his *Adagia*: he quotes Naevius' line (from Festus), and then refers to the Twelve Tables:

(12)

Translatum a Duodecim tabulis, quae *sonticum morbum* appellant non vulgarem, sed tam molestum ut reus non cogatur apud iudices comparere.

Erasmus *Adagia* 4, 10, 37[21]

The word originates in the Twelve Tables, where an illness is called '*compelling*' (*morbus sonticus*) if it is not an everyday complaint but one so serious that a defendant cannot be forced to appear in court.

3.4. Browsing books for formulas

The three aforementioned examples show how carefully Lipsius has been crafting a didactic environment that facilitates linguistic learning: the humanist embeds the unknown words in a semantically sound and meaningful context, so that the sentences appear to be self-explanatory. The meaning of 'waste places' (*tesca loca*) is announced by the context of the literary genre of the epitaph and by the reminiscence of the well-known Eucharis inscription. In the example discussed in section 3.2, any Latinist will easily associate *Aperta* with *aperire* ('to open, to uncover, to reveal'), and all the more certainly when it is opposed to *arcana recludere* ('to disclose secrets') and *Clusius* ('the Closer'). The meaning of *sonticus* (section 3.3) becomes evident by the repetition of the word *causa* and by the close semantic connection between *sonticus* and *morbus*, as annotated by Erasmus and explained by ancient grammarians. In order to find the appropriate linguistic "formulas," Lipsius is browsing through the copious number of words harvested in ancient grammar books, where the specific meaning of these words is illustrated and explained by native speakers like Aulus Gellius, Varro, or Festus. Each time, as it seems, Lipsius picks this type of locutions from the rich stock of phraseologies contained in ancient treatises that bear the label of "proof of linguistic quality" due to the authorship and the authority of their native speakers.

---

[21] Cf. ASD II-8, pp. 242–243 (ed. and annot. by A. Wesseling); CWE 36, p. 506.

4. Conclusion

Lipsius, Dousa, and other humanists are driven by an unquenchable desire to educate young people and to prepare them for citizenship and governmental functions. The adequate and indispensable tool to study and to acquire knowledge is the Latin language (besides Greek), "purified from its secular sordidness and squalor," to say it with a metaphor popular among humanists.[22] Therefore, a massive educational program is deployed, which is mainly linguistic: the ultimate goal is to write, speak, think, and reason in the language of the Ciceronian age of the Roman Republic. With a relentless energy and inspired by the true spirit of the Renaissance, humanists recreate Latin in a wide literary spectrum: drama, prose writings, and poetry.[23]

Lipsius' use of formulaic language in his poems is, I think, not so much the result of the literary procedure of *imitatio* and *aemulatio veterum*, or an easy shortcut to producing Latin poems. It is even less the symptom of an alleged propensity for obsolete words; we would not do justice to Lipsius' linguistic and educational genius, if we reduced his *ars versificandi* to a mere passion for archaism or pedantry, as has often been maintained (cf. Nollet 2015:99–102). Lipsius' motive is only partially inspired by any intent to display his erudition (*poeta doctus*). He first and foremost wishes to revitalize the Latin language, by reintroducing obsolete words, by using them in a sound grammatical and

---

[22] In a liminary poem, preceding Dousa's *Notes* to Petronius' *Satyricon* (1583:15), Lipsius exhorts his students to reap the benefits of this clean and sound piece of scientific work; the poem is entitled *Ad Iuventutem* ('To our Youth') (ILC45):

> Paedore obsitus impolitiaque
> dudum, nunc melior politiorque
> in novam properat venire lucem.
> [...]
> At tu, nostra, fave et cave, Iuventus.

> In earlier days during a long time Petronius used to be contaminated by sordidness and lack of good taste, but now he hurries and emerges in a new light,
> in better condition and more tasteful than ever.
> [...]
> But you, our young people of today, cherish him and beware of him.

[23] Cf. Kristeller's famous definition: "the word 'humanism' [...] developed from the term 'humanist,' which had been used ever since the late fifteenth century in a specific sense and which originated probably in the slang of the Italian university students of that time: a humanist was a professor or student of the *studia humanitatis*, of the humanities—as distinct from a jurist, for example" (1960:3). Burke (1987:73) questions the validity of this definition. Enenkel gives a witty paraphrase: "In fact, if one were to ask the question what a humanist is, a seemingly challenging, yet appropriate answer would be: 'a person that composes Neo-Latin epigrams and private letters'" (2009:1–2; cf. Ford et al. 2014:I, 379).

semantic context, in a formidable attempt to enrich Latin, which had become a dead language, in the sense that there had been no remaining native speakers since the dusk of Roman Empire. By providing new words and semantic values through his poems Lipsius actually offers a kind of linguistic apprenticeship, comparable with practices of oral culture: the master gives and re-gives the example, and the apprentice copies and repeats. We indeed observe identical characteristics in Lipsius' *ars formulandi* as in orally based formulas: Lipsius' poetic language features *additive*, *aggregative*, and *redundant* speech, rather than being subordinative, analytic, or linear (Ong 1982:36–41).

Whoever wishes to master a foreign language—*a fortiori* a dead language—will need to learn a substantial amount of vocabulary and precise word combinations, unless one would be satisfied with the basal level of using verbs of a general and vague meaning such as, for instance, *making* and *doing*: but you don't *do* a murder or a crime, you *commit* or *perpetrate* it. One does not *make* a poem; instead, you might *write, edit, compose, produce*, or *deliver* it. In order to practice the dynamic act of speaking Latin, the poems and prose writings of Lipsius will prove particularly helpful. Lipsius' command of the Latin language is paramount, and was universally acclaimed and acknowledged by his contemporaries. The philosopher Montaigne, himself an accomplished Latinist, exchanged letters with the Dutch humanist, and described him as *le plus sçavant homme qui nous reste, d'un esprit tres-poly et judicieux, vrayement germain à mon Turnebus* ('the most learned man now living, of a most polite and judicious understanding, truly resembling my friend Turnèbe').[24]

References

Abbreviatons

ASD = 1969–. *Opera omnia Desiderii Erasmi Roterodami, recognita et adnotatione critica instructa notisque illustrata*. Leiden.

BBr = Vander Haeghen, F. 1964–1975. *Bibliotheca Belgica: Bibliographie générale des Pays-Bas*, 7 vols. Ed. M.-T. Lenger. Bruxelles.

CWE = Grant, J. N. and Knott, B. I., eds. 2006. *Erasmus, Adages IV iii 1 to V ii 51*. Trans. and ann. Collected Works of Erasmus 36. Toronto.

GVi = Gerlo, A., and Vervliet, H. D. L. 1968. *Inventaire de la correspondance de Juste Lipse 1564-1606*. Anvers.

ILC = *Iusti Lipsi Carmina*; see note 2.

ILE XIV = De Landtsheer, J., ed. 2006. *Iusti Lipsi Epistolae, pars XIV: 1601*. Brussel.

---

[24] Cf. Montaigne, *Essais*, 2.12; ed. F. Villey, p. 578. Adrien Turnèbe (1512–1565) was a French classical scholar, famous for his knowledge of ancient Greek. What Turnèbe signified for Greek philology, Lipsius meant for the Latin counterpart.

Sources

As a rule, classical authors are quoted from the Loeb Classical Library (Cambridge, MA): *Homer* ed. and trans. by A. T. Murray (rev. by G. E. Dimock), *Hesiod* ed. and transl. by G. W. Most, *Virgil* by H. R. Fairclough (rev. by G. P. Goold), *Lucan* by J. D. Duff, *Statius* by D. R. Shackleton Bailey, *Catullus* ed. and transl. by F. W. Cornish (rev. by G. P. Goold), the *Appendix Vergiliana* by H. R. Fairclough (rev. by G. P. Goold), *Varro* ed. and transl. by R. G. Kent, *Aulus Gellius* ed. and transl. by J. C. Rolfe.

Dousa, I. 1583. *Pro Satyrico Petronii Arbitri, viri consularis, Praecidaneorum libri tres.* Lugduni Batavorum.

———. 1584. *Epodon ex puris iambis libri II.* Lugduni Batavorum.

Durini, A. M. 1770. *Selectorum epigrammatum liber ad divinum Metastasium poetam caesareum.* Varsaviae.

Forestus, P. 1589. *De incerto, fallaci, urinarum iudicio, quo uromantes, ad perniciem multorum aegrotantium, utuntur: Et qualia illi sint observanda, tum praestanda, qui recte de urinis sit iudicaturus, libri tres, per dialogismum contra uroscopos empiricos concinnati.* Lugduni Batavorum.

Lindsay, W. M., ed. 1913. *Sexti Pompei Festi De verborum significatu quae supersunt cum Pauli Epitome.* Thewrewkianis copiis usus edidit. Bibliotheca scriptorum Graecorum et Romanorum Teubneriana. Leipzig.

Lipsius, I., ed. 1605. *L. Annaei Senecae philosophi Opera, quae exstant omnia: A Iusto Lipsio emendata et scholiis illustrata.* Antverpiae.

Skutsch, O., ed. 1985. *The Annals of Q. Ennius.* Oxford.

Literature

Blackburn, S. H. 1988. *Singing of Birth and Death: Texts in Performance.* Philadelphia.

Burke, P. 1987. *The Italian Renaissance: Culture and Society in Italy* rev. ed. Cambridge.

———. 2004. *What is Cultural History?* ed. 2. 2008. Cambridge.

Comparetti, D. 1908. *Vergil in the Middle Ages* repr. 1966. London.

De Beer, S., Enenkel, K. A. E., and Rijser, D., eds. 2009. *The Neo-Latin Epigram: A Learned and Witty Genre.* Leuven.

Duckworth, G. E. 1969. *Vergil and Classical Hexameter Poetry: A Study in Metrical Variety.* Ann Arbor.

Enenkel, K. A. E. 2009. "Introduction: The Neo-Latin Epigram: Humanist Self-Definition in a Learned and Witty Discourse." In De Beer et al. 2009:1–23.

Ernout, A., and Meillet, A. 2001. *Dictionnaire étymologique de la langue latine: Histoire des mots* ed. 4 repr. with add. and corr. by Jacques André. Paris.

Ford, P. (†), Bloemendal, J., and Fantazzi, C., eds. 2014. *Brill's Encyclopaedia of the Neo-Latin World*, 2 vols. Leiden.

Frascati, S. 1997. *La collezione epigrafica di Giovanni Battista de Rossi presso il Pontificio istituto di archeologia cristiana.* Roma.

Gaisser, J. H. 1993. *Catullus and His Renaissance Readers.* Oxford.

———. 2007. "Catullus in the Renaissance." *A Companion to Catullus* (ed. M. B. Skinner) 439–460. Oxford.

Goold, G. P. 1992. "The Voice of Virgil: The Pageant of Rome in *Aeneid* 6". *Author and Audience in Latin Literature* (eds. T. Woodman and J. Powell) 110–123. Cambridge.

Havelock, E. A. 1986. *The Muse Learns to Write: Reflections on Orality and Literacy from Antiquity to the Present.* New Haven.

IJsewijn, J., and Sacré, D. 1998. *Companion to Neo-Latin Studies, II: Literary, Linguistic, Philological and Editorial Questions.* Second Entirely Rewritten Edition. Leuven.

IJsseling, S. 1997. *Mimesis: On Appearing and Being.* Kampen.

Kristeller, P. O. 1960. "Humanist Learning in the Italian Renaissance". *Renaissance Thought and the Arts: Collected Essays* (ed. P. O. Kristeller) exp. ed. 1990 with a new afterword 1–19. Princeton.

Kuiper, K. 2009. *Formulaic Genres.* Basingstoke.

Lindahl, C. 2011. "Singers and Tales in the 21st Century: The Legacies of Milman Parry and Albert Lord." *Fabula* 52(3–4):302–307.

Lord, A. B. 1960. *The Singer of Tales.* 2nd ed. Ed. by S. Mitchell and G. Nagy 2003. Cambridge.

Minchin, E. 1995. "The Poet Appeals to His Muse: Homeric Invocations in the Context of Epic Performance." *The Classical Journal* 91(1):25–33.

Nollet, H. 2015. *De gedichten van Justus Lipsius: Kritische editie met vertaling, annotatie en literaire commentaar,* 3 vols. Unpublished PhD. Leuven.

Nougaret, L. 1948. *Traité de métrique latine classique.* Paris.

Ong, W. J. 1982. *Orality and Literacy: The Technologizing of the Word.* London.

Ogilvie, B. W. 2006. *The Science of Describing: Natural History in Renaissance Europe.* Chicago.

Papy, J. 1992. "Une imitation de Catulle 4: La Dedicatio pennae Iusti Lipsi de François de Montmorency." *Les Études Classiques* 60:253–261.

Parry, A., ed. 1971. *The Making of Homeric Verse: The Collected Papers of Milman Parry.* Oxford.

Raven, D. S. 1965. *Latin Metre: An Introduction.* London.

Schanz, M., and Hosius, C. 1966. *Geschichte der römischen Literatur bis zum Gesetzgebungswerk des Kaisers Justinian, I: Die römische Literatur in der Zeit der Republik.* München.

Waszink, J., ed. and trans. 2004. *Justus Lipsius' Politica: Six Books of Politics or Political Instruction.* Assen.

15

Rhythmic Fillers in Ifugao *Hudhud*s

SERGEI B. KLIMENKO, INSTITUTE FOR LINGUISTIC STUDIES,
RUSSIAN ACADEMY OF SCIENCES

S OME ORAL TRADITIONS abound with elements that do not bear any semantic relation to the content of the text. Such elements can fulfill a variety of functions. For instance, meaningless filler words and expletives are used to create alliteration and complete the rhythm in the lament register of White Sea Karelia (Frog and Stepanova 2011:206); semantically irrelevant monosyllabic sets are used to complete rhythmic structures in the Finnish song tradition (Arjava 2017:75); expletives are used as epic discourse markers to indicate beginnings and emphases in South Slavic oral epic (Foley 2005:241, 257); the refrain *red and green grapes*, unrelated to the semantic content of the text, turns a non-ritual text into a ritual *vinogradye* song among the Pomors in Russia (Bernshtam and Lapin 2009:241); and short emotional exclamations and meaningful extended refrains in East Slavic wedding songs, with no connection to the song text, mark the end of each stanza, or the beginning or end of the song itself (Tyapkova 1995).

Such empty linguistic elements also occur in large numbers as part of formulas[1] in *hudhud*, an epic chant of Ifugao province in the Philippines. *Hudhud* was proclaimed as one of the world's most remarkable examples of oral and intangible heritage by UNESCO in 2001 (UNESCO 2014). Despite some investigation, the formulaic properties of the genre are still poorly understood, even for better-known *hudhud* texts. Furthermore, there have been no studies focused on the aforementioned semantically empty elements in *hudhud*s. This chapter aims to fill this gap by providing a description and initial analysis of such units, labeled here as rhythmic fillers.

---

[1]   Defined here as repeated sequences of linguistic elements.

In Ifugao *hudhud*, rhythmic fillers come in two kinds: (*a*) interjections and enclitic particles that are also used in everyday speech, which do not add anything to the meaning when employed in chanting, and (*b*) meaningless syllables used strictly for the sake of rhythm or epic discourse organization.

The following research questions are posed in this study: (*1*) What types of rhythmic fillers exist in *hudhud* epics? (*2*) What are the exhaustive inventories of the fillers and their typical positions in the line? (*3*) How frequent are such fillers in a *hudhud*? Additionally, an attempt is made to approach an understanding of how different *hudhud* texts vary across the languages in which they are sung (Tuwali, Ifugao, and Yattuka), across different ritualistic varieties (harvest, funeral/secondary burial, haircutting ceremony), and across individual singers, with their idiosyncratic preferences for stylistic vehicles.

1. *Hudhud*'s Background

Hudhud is an epic chant performed in a number of central and southern municipalities of Ifugao province in Northern Luzon. It is sung by a lead chanter, who narrates the events of the story, and a chorus of two or more people. The chorus finishes the line with formulas, which mostly present characters' names (Stanyukovich 2017), place names (Stanyukovich 2015; Stanyukovich and Kozintsev 2016), and time.[2]

The tradition has very strong ritual connections (Stanyukovich 1981; 1982; 2003:249; 2013:172). Performances occur only in a variety of important rituals. The protagonists of the stories belong to a group of benevolent deities (Stanyukovich 2007:64). The popular view of the tradition, however, as presented in many scholarly publications, holds that *hudhud* has no ritual significance and is a form of entertainment (Lambrecht 1960:1; 1965; 1967:267–268; Dulawan 2005; Acabado 2010; Blench and Campos 2010).

There are four situational variation categories: *hudhud di/ni*[3] *ani* or *hudhud di/ni pagi* for rice harvest, *hudhud di/ni kolot* performed for boys of the rich as part of life-cycle rituals (Stanyukovich 2013:168), and *hudhud di/ni nate/nosi* and *hudhud di/ni bogwa* for funeral or secondary burial (Stanyukovich 2007:64). A further category is *hudhud di/ni uyauy*. This is performed at weddings of the rich but is already extinct (Stanyukovich 2013:179–180), probably, due to

[2] The last of these are typical for the Tuwali *hudhud* texts published by Fr. Lambrecht and A. Daguio.
[3] The *hudhud* names are given with some variations pertaining to the discrepancy between the Tuwali Ifugao and Yattuka variants.

the fact that weddings in Ifugao are nowadays mostly patterned after the Western Christian tradition.

Hudhud is severely endangered. Only a few lead singers remain. Younger generations are no longer interested in learning the tradition, due to the disintegration of the traditional society and the fading of the native belief system, which is being replaced by Christianity and associated rituals. In addition to the total disappearance of *hudhud di/ni uyauy* ("wedding *hudhud*"), *hudhud di/ni pagi* ("rice harvest *hudhud*") has practically ceased to be performed, due to the switch to lowland varieties of rice that do not bear any ritual significance, while *hudhud ni kolot* ("haircutting ceremony *hudhud*") is performed on very rare occasions (Stanyukovich 2013). At present, there remain no more than four living Yattuka *hudhud* soloists. The most knowledgeable one died in August 2016, and was over eighty years old. All the rest are significantly younger—between fifty and sixty years old. They are considerably less competent in terms of the number of *hudhud* stories and types of *hudhuds* they can perform as lead singers, as well as the extensiveness of their knowledge of *hudhud* lexical items not used in everyday language. Apart from this, some of the living soloists do not perform *hudhud* in actual ritual settings anymore, due to their having converted to Christianity. The attitude of Ifugao Christian organizations towards *hudhud* ranges from hostile—viewing *hudhud* as a pagan practice—to supporting it to a degree, by allowing short excerpts to be performed in competitions during municipal and provincial celebrations as a symbol of their ethnic identity and cultural heritage.

Hudhud is mostly known in two closely related languages: Tuwali Ifugao (Lambrecht 1978; Klimenko 2012; Hohulin and Hohulin 2014) and Amganad Ifugao (Madrid 1980; Sawyer 1975; West 1973). They belong to the same branch of Central Cordilleran languages of the Philippine group. However, *hudhud* is also sung by two small, lesser-known ethnic groups residing in the Asipulo municipality of the same province (Stanyukovich 1997): Yattuka (Klimenko 2017) and Keley-i (Hohulin and Kenstowicz 1979; L. Hohulin and Hale 1977; R. Hohulin and Hale 1977). The latter sing *hudhud* in the Yattuka language (Southern Cordilleran). Yattuka is spoken only in two *barangays*,[4] Amduntog and Nungawa, which are in the Asipulo municipality, Ifugao province. The total population of these two *barangays* is 2,689 people (PSA 2019). Keley-i is spoken in another two

---

[4] A *barangay* is the smallest administrative unit in the Philippines. In the rural setting, it corresponds to a village together with its surrounding hamlets.

*barangay*s in the same municipality, Antipulo and Pula. Keley-i speakers sing *hudhud* only in Yattuka. *Hudhud* in Keley-i is virtually unheard of in the area.

All of the published translated texts of *hudhud* epics were recorded in the Tuwali-speaking areas of the Ifugao province, in the municipalities of Kiangan and Lagawe (see Lambrecht 1957; 1960; 1961; 1967; Daguio 1983; Dulawan and Revel 1993a; 1993b; 1997a; 1997b). As for Yattuka *hudhud*s, there are six transcribed and translated records that were made by Maria Stanyukovich (2012a; 2012b; 2012c; 2012d) and—more recently—by myself (Klimenko 2016a; Klimenko 2016b). There are also three *hudhud* texts in Yattuka that appeared in pre-print of a work by Maribelle Dulnuan-Bimohya and Ian T. Lunag (n.d.) without line breaks or translation.

2. The Language of *hudhud*

*Hudhud*s are sung in a linguistic variety differing from everyday language, as it is not meant to be accessible to the uninitiated, similar to other sacred oral traditions (cf. Grintser 1998, on properties of the sacred language of the Indian *Rig Veda*). Soloists themselves might not understand all of the unusual lexical units they sing in a *hudhud*. There have been very few studies on the formulaic properties of the genre, even for the Tuwali texts. We do know that numerous features distinguish the language of *hudhud* from the common register. The most prominent is, of course, vocabulary: many *hudhud* words are archaic, and understood only by the oldest speakers, or have never been in everyday use. Francis Lambrecht (1960:21) claims that some words in Tuwali *hudhud*s are "corrupted." However, most cases of apparent corruption are actually borrowings from Yattuka or, to a lesser degree, from Keley-i. There are also some borrowings from Tuwali in Yattuka *hudhud*s (Klimenko and Stanyukovich 2018). Most of the actual place names in the funerary *hudhud* are augmented with cryptic affixes—whose function is to render them incomprehensible—or they are substituted with different ones (Stanyukovich and Sychenko 2016; Stanyukovich and Kozintsev 2016:267–268).

Morphosyntactic differences obtain as well. Tuwali *hudhud* is said to make occasional use of uncommon case markers, demonstrative enclitics, infixes, and prefixes (Lambrecht 1960:22–29). In Yattuka *hudhud*, the archaic form of imperfective aspect constructions is predominant. Here, the aspect marker *ka* is prepended to the verb when used with third-person enclitic pronouns. In everyday language, only older speakers use such a form. Otherwise, *ka* is normally a prefix of the verb. There are, most probably, numerous other differences that remain undiscovered.

Another remarkable feature of the genre is the use of pleonastic phrases without introduction of any additional meaning (Lambrecht 1960:20–21). Many lexical units show a form of full reduplication (e.g. *olladan'da olladan* ['their yard the yard']). There are also many instances of paired synonyms (e.g. *umhep an umlah-un* ['exited exited']). This device is also applied to protagonists' names and place names (Stanyukovich 2008).

As noted by Lambrecht (1960:2–13), all *hudhud* texts also employ very similar sets of terms referring to the components of the story: locations (villages, houses, rivers, rice terraces, granaries, etc.) and events (battles, feasts, etc.). Lambrecht's list should be augmented with groups of characters (elders, the rich, commoners, girls and youngsters, etc.) and typical actions (motion within households, across the landscape, dancing, making sacrifices of pigs and chickens, serving food and rice wine, chewing betelnut, etc.).

Another prominent poetic device is the use of interjections and enclitic particles at the beginning of many lines, and meaningless rhythmic fillers that do not add anything to the content of the story, but are nevertheless an indispensable part of the genre. There have been no studies on rhythmic fillers in *hudhud*. In fact, in most *hudhud* texts, such units are not represented faithfully, even in the texts transcribed from actual recordings. Questions arise whether they can be classified and used to differentiate individual singers' styles and regional *hudhud* traditions. These queries are addressed in the following sections.

3. Scope of the Study

Primary data for the study comes from the first of fully transcribed and translated recordings of Yattuka funeral chants (*hudhud ni nosi*, in Stanyukovich 2012a). The performance was five hours long, including both *hudhud* singing proper and the *holdak* (intermission) songs. The latter are short jocular songs unrelated to the content of *hudhud*, and sung for entertainment during intermissions between *hudhud* performances. The body of the full performance runs 337 lines. The chant was performed in four parts of different length: (I) 41' 43", (II) 23' 25", (III) 7' 14", and (IV) 38' 09". Parts I, II, and IV are closed with brief *holdak* songs (0:47, 1:04, 0:39). Lines vary in duration and in the number of syllables. Table 1 presents the counts of the number of syllables for each line and the number of lines in the epic texts for each line length. The number of syllables per line varies between 21 and 79.

The text was transcribed and translated in ELAN Linguistic Annotator (Brugman and Russel 2004), glossed in Fieldworks Language Explorer, and analyzed in the corpus analysis toolkit AntConc 3.4.4w (Anthony 2018).

In (1–4), we can see the opening four lines from the *hudhud* being analyzed here. Rhythmic fillers are underlined and the parts performed by the chorus are placed in italic font.

# Syllables	# Lines	# Syllables	# Lines
36	29	28	6
33	26	23	6
37	24	26	5
35	21	27	4
32	20	49	3
40	19	48	3
31	19	47	3
34	18	25	3
39	15	53	2
29	15	52	2
38	13	51	2
45	12	79	1
41	12	61	1
42	11	58	1
30	11	54	1
43	10	50	1
44	9	24	1
46	7	21	1

Table 1. Frequencies of lines with different number of syllables.

(1)

Ay	*inay'a*	*ungngaungnga*	*apu'yu'yu*		*hi*
REAL[5]	SURP=RF	young~young	grandparent=your=RF		PRS.SG.NOM

[5] Abbreviations used in this chapter: =, clitic boundary; 12, first and second person; 2, second person; 3, third person; ACT, actor pronoun or case marker; ADJ, adjectival derivation affix; AV, actor voice; COL, collective form of nouns; CON, concessive; DEP, dependent aspect form; DIST, distal; DUR, durative; EXCL, exclusive; FUT, future; GEN, genitive; IND, independent pronoun or marker of independent position; IPFV, imperfective; LK, linker; LOC, locative demonstrative pronoun; M, minimal membership pronoun; NACT, non-actor pronoun or case marker; NEG, negative; neut, neutral aspect; NM, non-minimal membership pronoun; NNOM, non-nominative pronoun; NOM, nominative; NS, non-subject personal

Lukbut	ud'du	nandalinan'do'd'<u>do</u>	kamalig'<u>i</u>'da
PN.Lukbut	PLTM=RF	village[6]=their=OBL=RF	bench=RF=their

nidiyaan'da'<u>yi</u>	<u>a</u>'hi'd	Nobayung.[7]
home[8]=their=RF	RF=OBL=OBL	PLN.Nobayung

Your grandmother Lukbut is very young in their village on their *hagobi*[9] bench at their home in Nobayung.

(2)

Ay	olog	u	kuwan'yu'nguma	polibwat'toyu'lli'ddi
REAL	no	because	said=you=again	will_start=we=FUT=OBL

nandalinan'do'd'<u>do</u>	kamalig'<u>i</u>'da	nidiyaan'da'<u>yi</u>	<u>a</u>'hidi
village=their=OBL=RF	bench=RF=their	home=their=RF	RF=DIST.LOC

Polwitan.
PLN.Polwitan

No, because you said again that we will start at their village on their *hagobi* bench at their home in Polwitan.

---

pronoun; OBL, oblique; **PAV**, path voice; **PFV**, perfective; **PLN**, place name; **PLTM**, place and time marker; **PLV**, place voice; **PN**, personal noun; **PRS**, personal; **REAL**, sudden realization; **RF**, rhythmic filler; **RV**, recipient voice; **SG**, singular; **STEM**, stem-deriving prefix; **SURP**, surprise; **TOPCHA**, topic change marker.

[6] *Nandalinan* is a verbal form in the place voice meaning 'to reside'. The actual morphological composition of this form is irrelevant here. Some other simplifications due to the same considerations are made in the glosses hereafter.

[7] The Yattuka examples in this chapter are given in orthographic, rather than IPA transcription. An apostrophe indicates the attachment of clitics. A triple occurrence of a vowel indicates a protracted sound that is counted as one syllable. A glottal stop between vowels or in word-final position is not indicated, otherwise it is indicated with a hyphen.

[8] *Nidiyaan* is a verbal form in the place voice meaning 'to sleep over'. In *hudhud*, it is used to refer to 'home'.

[9] *Hagobi* (*hagabi* in Tuwali) is a monolithic wooden bench that is made during the most prestigious ritual of the Ifugaos (Hohulin and Hohulin 2014:145).

(3)

A	happihappit	ino'tu	hi	Inggulun	di
REAL	said~said	mother=her	PRS.NOM	inggulun	OBL

pamadingan	ni	bale'yu	gawa'na'ynoyi	a'hi'd
doorjamb	GEN	house=your	middle=its=RF	RF=OBL=OBL

Polwitan.
PLN.Polwitan

Her mother Inggulun said at the doorjamb of your house in the middle of Polwitan.

(4)

A	ungngaungnga'y	nunuingadan	nom
REAL	young~young=NOM	<RF>the_one_named	PRS.SG.NACT

Bugan'adeeeheoooy	aahay	nakaPangoiwan	ehmmm.
PN.Bugan=RF	RF	child_of<RF>-Pangoiwan	RF

The one named Bugan, daughter of Pangoiwan, is very young.

Stanyukovich 2012a

Table 2 shows the number of syllables and duration of the solo and choral parts of these four lines. The data from this *hudhud* is compared with other Yattuka *hudhud* texts (Stanyukovich 2012b; Klimenko 2016a; 2016b) and Tuwali *hudhud* texts (Lambrecht 1960; 1961; 1967; Dulawan and Revel 1993a; 1993b; 1997a; 1997b) to address the question of whether there is variation within the *hudhud* genre across the languages, ritualistic varieties of *hudhud*, and individual singers.

4. Interjections, Enclitic Particles, and Meaningless Rhythmic Fillers in Literature on *hudhud*

Lambrecht mentions "meaningless insertions of monosyllabic, disyllabic, or trisyllabic sounds (such as *eee, aaa, adna, tuwana*)" (1967:292). They are used to make lines with an insufficient number of feet longer. Such sounds, however, are not normally reflected in the texts published by Lambrecht, because they were simply written down by *hudhud* soloists and not transcribed from actual performances. As Lambrecht puts it, it is "practically impossible to write down

Line	Total # of Syllables	Total Duration	Syllables in Solo	Solo Duration	Syllables in Choir	Choir Duration
1	39	22s	17	7s	22	15s
2	39	20s	16	6s	23	14s
3	31	19s	13	5s	18	14s
4	27	24s	5	3s	22	21s

Table 2. Number of syllables and duration per line in the 4 opening lines.

a *hudhud* while it is actually being chanted" (Lambrecht 1967:292). Dulawan and Revel's texts, however, also lack many such sounds, in spite of the fact that their texts were transcribed from audio recordings.

On the other hand, transcriptions of actual recordings of Yattuka *hudhud* show that such rhythmic fillers are much more abundant than in Lambrecht's or Dulawan and Revel's texts. All rhythmic fillers in examples (1–4) are underlined: *ay, inay'a, 'yu, 'du, 'do, 'i, 'yi, a'* in (1); *ay, 'do, 'i, 'yi, a'* in (2); *a, 'ynoyi, a'* in (3); *a, <u>, 'adeeeheoooy, aahay, <a>, ehmmm* in (4).

Units without a semantic relation to the line content in *hudhuds*—or rhythmic fillers—can be divided into the following groups: non-lexical units—comprised of epenthetic and non-epenthetic units—and interjections and enclitic particles.[10] Non-lexical units are defined here as units that do not exist as independent lexemes in the language. Epenthetic rhythmic fillers are separate meaningless syllables or sequences of meaningless syllables inserted into a morpheme or between morphemes within a lexical unit. They may also be separate meaningless syllables at the beginning or the end of a lexical unit. As shown in Table 3, in the 337 lines of the *hudhud* under study here, epenthetic fillers occur in 97% of the lines. Non-epenthetic rhythmic fillers, in turn, are defined here as sequences of meaningless syllables following some lexemes in a *hudhud* line. Such units occur in about 68% of the lines. As for interjections and enclitic particles, they occur in 64% percent of the lines.

---

[10] It is typical for Philippine languages to have a set of Wackernagel enclitics, used to mark a wide range of aspect, mood, evidentiality, optativity, conditionals, emphasis, politeness, modality, iamitive, and other meanings (Himmelmann 2005:133).

non-lexical units		interjections and enclitic particles (217 lines, 64%)
epenthetic (328 lines, 97%)	non-epenthetic (230 lines, 68%)	

Table 3. Classification of rhythmic fillers.

5. Non-Lexical Rhythmic Fillers

Non-lexical rhythmic fillers occur mostly in the portions chanted by the choir. This indicates their highly formulaic nature, because a whole group of people has to share the knowledge of where in the line such units are to be used.

5.1 Epenthetic rhythmic fillers

Epenthetic rhythmic fillers are the most numerous, both in terms of their total frequency in the text (Table 3) and in the number of such units in their inventory. Such fillers normally function as infixes or enclitics, but there are also five proclitic fillers of this type. Epenthetic fillers can be word internal or external. The latter are represented here in the same way as clitics (demarcated with an apostrophe in transcription and the equal sign in glosses), although there seems to be not enough basis to classify them as such. It is impossible to assess whether such fillers bear an independent stress, as the text is chanted. On the other hand, a rhythmic break never occurs between them and the words they are shown to be attached to. Moreover, many of them either do not meet the syllable structure requirements in the language (CV(C)), or depend on another word in their sound, in cases where alliteration occurs.

Many lexemes in Table 4 are not used outside *hudhud*, while some are used in everyday language. Non-lexical rhythmic fillers never occur in everyday speech. In *hudhud*, on the other hand, most of the lexemes in Table 4 contain the corresponding fillers in all their occurrences in the text. It remains to be seen if any of the fillers are used in other genres of the Ifugao ritual literature, for instance, *alim* (Del Rosario 2013).

Filler	Literal translation	Frequency	Frequency of forms without the filler
ag<a>pawan	'to cross'	59	none
lug<u>tu	'midrib of the hagobi bench'	43	none
nun<nu>hal<a>hal<a>o	'neighboring	31	none
hinal<a>on	'neighbor'	31	none
bob<o>le	'village'	16	none
kodak<ka>lan	'river'	11	31 (kodaklan)
hi<mmanglili>mbatangan	'late afternoon'	5	none
kinnob<o>al	'side of the house'	4	none
ka-<un>dawwi	'far'	4	2 (kaddawi)
mong<u>dda-den	'to cook rice'	3	none
nowa<a>wa	'early'	1	6 (nowa-wa)
um<u>lahun	'descend from the house'[11]	1	1 (umlahun)
ko<mo>umtaggam	'dancing'	1	none
in<-ay>-om	'said "yes"'	1	none
nangngola<ha>n	'heard'	1	3 (nangngolan)
nun<u>ingadan	'named'	1	none
nak<a>Pangoiwan	'child of Pangoiwan'	1	none

Table 4. Word-internal epenthetic rhythmic fillers.

[11] Traditional Ifugao houses have posts, so one has to climb up and down the ladder to enter or leave the house.

Filler	Occurrence with Forms	Analysis of Forms	Freq.	Total freq.	Freq. of Forms Without a Filler
=yi	appawan'da'yi	RF=3NM.ACT.NNOM=RF	59	166	none
	umaldattan'da'yi	yard=3NM.ACT.NNOM=RF	43		none
	humanil-o'yi	radiate_light=RF	31		none
	nidiyaan'da'yi	<PFV>sleep_over-PLV=3NM.ACT.NNOM=RF	30		none
	algo algo'yi	sun sun=RF	3		none
=a	'law'a	=already=RF	52	118	10
	Kunelyuh'a	PN.Cornelio=RF	26		12
	Lukbut'a	PN.Lukbut=RF	19		51
	anhan'a	please=RF	5		31
	'kaw'a	=maybe=RF	4		5
	inay'a	SURP=RF	3		54
	ammulih'a	pig=RF	1		6
	awil'a	gift_animal=RF	1		9
	babuy'a	pig=RF	1		2
	bolangbang'a	gong=RF	1		none
	bokon'kattog'a	NEG=pitiful=RF	1		none
	himmardot'a	<PFV><AV>clear_sound=RF	1		3
	hinay'a	SURP=RF	1		1
	Hinlalangit'a	PLN.Hinlalangit=RF	1		54
	'ukaw'a	=CON=RF	1		none
a=	a'hi'd	RF=OBL=OBL	65	87	3
	a'hidi	RF=DIST.LOC	11		30
	a'hi	RF=OBL	7		147
	a'Hinlalangit	RF=PLN.Hinlalangit	2		53
	a'di	RF=OBL	1		239
	a'hdi	RF=DIST.LOC	1		none
=i	kamalig'i	hagobi_bench=RF	73	74	none
	gilig'i'na	edge=RF=3M.ACT.NNOM	1		none

Filler	Occurrence with Forms	Analysis of Forms	Freq.	Total freq.	Freq. of Forms Without a Filler
=du	ud'du	PLTM=RF	50	73	none
	'tu'd'du	=3M.ACT.NNOM=ONL=RF	12		9
	aggu'd'du	sun=OBL=RF	3		none
	'yu'd'du	=2NM.ACT.NNOM=OBL=RF	3		none
	batu'd'du	stone=OBL=RF	1		1
	han-aggu'd'du	one_day=OBL=RF	1		none
	koman-i-immatu'd'du	IPFV-<AV>STEM-DUR~identify=OBL=RF	1		none
	'ngu'd'du	=EXCL=OBL=RF	1		none
	'toyu'd'du	=12NM.ACT.NNOM=OBL=RF	1		none
=no	nihikyu'n'no oammod	2NM.NACT.NNOM=LK=RF elders	20	62	none
	'yu'n'no oammod	=2NM.ACT.NNOM=LK=RF elders	28		none
	'nhikyu'n'no oammod	2NM.NACT.NNOM=LK=RF elders	8		none
	hikyu'n'no oammod	2NM.IND=LK=RF elders	4		none
	'kdi'n'no oammod	=TOPCHA=LK=RF elders	1		none
	'ko'n'no umulahun	=2M.ACT.NOM=LK=RF NEUT[AV-<RF>descend_from_house	1		none
=na	kodakka)lan'na hi agapawan	(<RF>)river=RF OBL NEUT[<RF>cross-PLV]	41	54	none
	'ida'n'na oammod	=3NM.ACT. NOM=LK=RF elders	13		none
=da	'da'd'da	=3NM.ACT.NNOM=OBL=RF	36	52	6
	'na'd'da	=3M.ACT.NNOM=OBL=RF	9		none
	'ida'd'da	=3NM.ACT. NOM=OBL=RF	6		none
	'ka'd'da	=2M.ACT. NOM=OBL=RF	1		none
=do	'do'd'do	=3NM.ACT.NNOM=OBL=RF	38	49	none
	nunnuhalahalao'd'do	AV[<PFVV>STEM-RF-<RF>DUR~<RF>neighbor]=OBL=RF	4		none
	'tu'd'do	=3M.ACT.NNOM=OBL=RF	2		9
	'yu'd'do	=2NM.ACT.NNOM=OBL=RF	2		none
	kaungngaungnga'd'do	COL~child=OBL=RF	1		none
	'mu'd'do	=2M.ACT.NNOM=OBL=RF	1		6
	'tsu'd'do	=12NM.ACT.NNOM=OBL=RF	1		none

Filler	Occurrence with Forms	Analysis of Forms	Freq.	Total freq.	Freq. of Forms Without a Filler
=ya	'da'y'ya	=3NM.ACT.NNOM=NOM=RF	20	42	2
	'na'y'ya	=3M.ACT.NNOM=NOM=RF	10		none
	'ida'y'ya	=3NM.ACT.NOM=NOM=RF	7		none
	gullukay'ya	chicken=RF	4		6
	nowaawa'y'ya	ADJ-<RF>early=NOM=RF	1		none
=yo	nunnuhalahalao'y'yo	AV[<PFV>STEM-RF-<RF>DUR~<RF>neighbor]=NOM=RF	27	30	none
	mahilong'bo'y'yo	ADJ-night=also=NOM=RF	3		none
=ha	ilakhig'da'h'ha	DEP[PAV-step_over]=3NM.ACT.NNOM=OBL=RF	4	6	none
	ilakhig'na'h'ha	DEP[PAV-step_over]=3M.ACT.NNOM=OBL=RF	2		none
=ay	di'ay Kituman	OBL=RF PLN.Kituman	4	5	239
	hi'ay Kituman	OBL=RF PLN.Kituman	1		147
=yu	tsimmalan-u'y'yu	<PFV><AV>crow=NOM=RF	4	5	none
	apu'yu'yu	grandparent=2NM.ACT.NNOM=RF	1		6
=o	ingkonhob'o'da	<PFV><PAV>descend=RF=3NM.ACT.NNOM	3	4	5
	bolbalibliya'o	DUR~gaze-RV.IPFV=RF	1		none
=u	dingkug'u	RV[<PFV>turn_back_on]=RF	2	3	13
	dulung'u	floor=RF	1		none
=wa	anhan'ka'law... 'wa	please=maybe=already=RF	1	2	1
	inna-nu'wa	how=RF	1		2
=ah	Dumya'ah	PN.Dumya=RF	1	1	10
=hi	ittapi'hi	PV-NEUT~chew_betelnut=RF	1	1	3
in=	in'inhidol	RF=PAV<PFV>-go_to_edge	1	1	12
mo=	mo'mambongngad	RF=NEUTAAV-STEM-return]	1	1	none
no=	no'nokiboykat	RF=AV[<PFV>COM-go_to_feast]	1	1	3
o=	o'ida'omin	RF=3NM.ACT. NOM=all	1	1	1
=ut	Lukbut'ut	PN.Lukbut=RF	1	1	51

Table 5. External epenthetic rhythmic fillers.

A few words should be said about the fillers *=da*, *=do*, and *=du*, which are extensions of the enclitic form of the oblique case marker *=d* ('OBL') (*di* in the full form). *=du* is also used after the place marker *ud* ('PLTM')[12] (e.g. *Kunelyuh ud'du nandalinan*). All instances of *=d* ('OBL') in the chorus, except for those used with place names at the end of lines (e.g. *a'hi'd Nobayung* ['at Nobayung']), are followed by one of these three fillers. None of the instances of *=d* ('OBL') in the solo is followed by a filler (e.g. *in-ohnong'da'd pulintag*).

All three fillers occur in front of a relatively limited set of items sung in the chorus: for *=da* it is *oladan, pumbanangan, lugutu, kogawaan, kodaklan*; for *=do* it is *oladan, pamadingan, kamalig, humanil-o, kodaklan, nandalinan*; for *=du* it is *oladan, pamadingan, lugutu, hinalaon, kodaklan, nandalinan*. Since there are some common items in the three sets, the choice of the vowel in these three variants (*=da, =do, =du*) does not seem to depend on the sounds that follow them. Rather it depends to a degree on the preceding vowel, since all instances of *=du* are preceded by /u/ (e.g. *aggu'd'du, happit'tu'd'du*), all instances of *=da* are preceded by /a/, and forty-two instances of *=do* are preceded by /o/, although in six instances it is preceded by /u/ and in one instance by /a/.

Although no detailed counts have been made for other Yattuka *hudhud* texts, a cursory examination of three other texts shows that most of the units in Table 4 are also used with the same epenthetic rhythmic fillers in them. In a *hudhud ni kolot* (Stanyukovich 2012b), performed by the same soloist, the only units used without such fillers are *nowa-wa* ('early'), *koumtaggam* ('dancing'), and *nangngolan* ('heard'). In a *hudhud ni pagi* (Klimenko 2016b), performed by another proficient soloist, the only units used without such fillers are *kaddawwi* ('far'), *nowa-wa* ('early'), and *nangngolan* ('heard'), while *mongudda-den* ('to cook rice') and *komoumtaggam* ('dancing') (with the filler *mo-*) are not present in the text. In another *hudhud ni kolot* (Klimenko 2016a), performed intermittently by two significantly less proficient soloists, the only unit used without such fillers is *nowa-wa* ('early'), while *komoumtaggam* ('dancing'), *in-ay-om* ('said "yes"') and *nangngolahan* ('heard') are not present in the text.

As mentioned earlier, Lambrecht's texts of Tuwali *hudhud*s do not reflect epenthetic fillers, because, apparently, they do not bear any meaning for the lead singers who wrote down those texts. Unfortunately, it is impossible to reconstruct such fillers in Lambrecht's texts, because there are no audio records.

However, if we look at the Tuwali texts published by Dulawan and Revel in "the Philippine epics and ballads archive of the Ateneo de Manila University," we can see that they do not reflect such units either. Examples (5) and (6) show two lines from one of the *hudhud* texts published in the archive. The three

---

[12] In everyday Tuwali, this marker has the shape of *ad*. It does not exist in Yattuka.

syllables highlighted in italics are not included in the transcription published on the website and have been added on the basis of the audio recordings. One of the three fillers here is the same as in the Yattuka *hudhud*: <a> in *nak<a>-Pangaiwan* ('the child of Pangaiwan'). It should be noted, however, that in these Tuwali texts, epenthetic fillers seem to be much less frequent than in the Yattuka texts, as illustrated in the examples given earlier. The question whether this fact represents a systematic difference between the Tuwali and Yattuka traditions requires further analysis of the Tuwali texts.

(5)

Ne ugge nunmatak nunmaddikit hi Bugan aki Bugan *nanan*, ngadana, o̱ an nak*a̱* Pangaiwan.
But Bugan is not yet grown up, Bugan, dear Bugan is her name, daughter of Pangaiwan.

Dulawan and Revel 1997b[13]

(6)

Iap-ap-aptuwan yun aamod an'*na̱* bulalakkin *na*, o..*ya*, an i-Gon*no̱*-hadan *nema* o..*e*.
You are in such a hurry, ye handsome braves, o..ya, of Gonhadan nema, o..e.

Dulawan and Revel 1997b

5.2 Non-epenthetic rhythmic fillers

Non-epenthetic rhythmic fillers seem more commonly perceived as meaningful for *hudhud* performers than epenthetic ones, since the non-epenthetic fillers were not omitted in the Tuwali texts. As seen from Table 6, most non-epenthetic fillers follow only 4 items: *bulalakki* ('handsome males'), *gawa'na* ('its middle'), and *gawa* ('middle'), followed by *gawa'na* and *agapawan* ('to cross'). All of these items are always followed by some non-epenthetic fillers. In three other Yattuka *hudhud* texts (Stanyukovich 2012b; Klimenko 2016a; 2016b), the most common non-epenthetic fillers are the same, occurring with the same formula. The only exception is *neman*, not found in *hudhud ni kolot* (Klimenko 2016a).

---

[13] The original orthography and translations of the examples from texts published by Lambrecht and by Dulawan and Revel are intact here. The double full stop in Dulawan and Revel's texts represent protracted vowel sounds.

Filler	Occurrence with Forms	Analysis of Forms	Freq.	Total freq.	Freq. of Forms Without a Filler
=nnieyi	bulalakki'nnieyi	handsome_males=RF		93	none
=ynoyi	gawa'na'ynoyi	middle=3M.ACT.NNOM=RF		60	none
appawan	agapawan (d/y)appa appawan'da'yi	NEUT[<RF>cross-PLV] RF RF=3NM.ACT.NNOM=RF		59	none
dappa	agapawan dappa appawan'da'yi	NEUT[<RF>cross-PLV] RF RF=3NM.AACT.NNOM=RF		42	none
=n-ayya	gawa'n-ayya gawa'na'(da) ynoyi	middle=RF middle=3M.ACT. NNOM=RF		24	none
appa	agapawan appa appawan'da'yi	NEUT[<RF>cross-PLV] RF RF=3NM.ACT.NNOM=RF		13	none
ehmmm	see below			10	
neman	see below			9	
daynoyi	gawa'na daynoyi	middle=3M.ACT.NNOMM RF	7	8	none
	gilig'i'na daynoyi	edge=RF=3M.ACT.NNOM RF	1		none
ayya	gawa ayya gawa'na'ynoyi	middle RF middle=3M.ACT. NNOM=RF		7	none
yappa	agapawan yappa appawan'da'yi	NEUT[<RF>cross-PLV] RF RF=3NM.ACT.NNOM=RF		4	none
=nnieeeheeey	bulalakki'nnieeeheeey	handsome_males=RF		2	none
=ynooohoooy	gawa'na'ynooohoooy	middle=3M.ACT.NNOM=RF		2	none
au	au'h Urdidittan	RF=OBL PLN.Urdidittan		1	none
dahnooo	gawa'na dahnooo ohoooy	middle=3M.ACT.NNOM RF RF		1	none
ee	ee'h Urdidittan	RF=OBL PLN.Urdidittan		1	none
=nnieeehoooy	bulalakki'nnieeehoooy	handsome_males=RF		1	none
ay-ii	gawa'na'ynooohoooy ay-ii di Nobayung	middle=3M.ACT.NNOM=RF RF OBL PLN.Nobayung		1	none
aehegi	gawa'na dahnooo ohoooy aehegi'd Amduntug	middle=3M.ACT.NNOM RF RF RF=OBL PLN.Amduntug		1	none
noaynoy	gawa'na'ynoyi noaynoy nokappaynoyi	middle=3M.ACT.NNOM=RF RF RF		1	none
danooo	gawa'na danooo ooohoooy ahih hi'd Amduntug	middle=3M.ACT.NNOM RF RF RF OBL=OBL PLN.Amduntug		1	none
ayhih	bulalakki'nnieeehoooy ayhih hidi Nobayung	handsome_males=RF RF DIST. LOC PLN.Nobayung		1	none
=nnieeehe-heaaay	bulalakki'nnieeeheheaaay	handsome_males=RF		1	none

Filler	Occurrence with Forms	Analysis of Forms	Freq.	Total freq.	Freq. of Forms Without a Filler
nokappaynoyi	gawa'na'ynoyi noaynoy nokappaynoyi	middle=3M.ACT.NNOM=RF RF RF		1	none
aahay	nom Bugan adeeeheoooy aahay nakaPangoiwan	PRS.SG.ACT PN.Bugan RF RF CHILD_OF<RF>PN.Pangoiwan		1	none
daynoooohoooy	gawa'na daynoooohoooy	middle=3M.ACT.NNOM RF		1	none
inna=	inna'inna-nu	RF=how		1	2
ahih	gawa'na danooo ooohoooy ahih hi'd Amduntug	middle=3M.ACT.NNOM RF RF RF OBL=OBL PLN.Amduntug		1	none
ohoooy	gawa'na dahnooo ohoooy	middle=3M.ACT.NNOM RF RF		1	none
ooohoooy	gawa'na danooo ooohoooy ahih hi'd Amduntug	middle=3M.ACT.NNOM RF RF RF OBL=OBL PLN.Amduntug		1	none
=nnie	bulalakki'nnie	handsome_males=RF		1	none
=adeeeheoooy	nom Bugan adeeeheoooy aahay nakaPangoiwan	PRS.SG.ACT PN.Bugan RF RF CHILD_OF<RF>PN.Pangoiwan		1	none

Table 6. Non-Epenthetic Rhythmic Fillers.

Interestingly, some of the same formulas are also always used with some non-epenthetic rhythmic fillers in both Lambrecht's (1960; 1961; 1967) and Dulawan and Revel's (1993a; 1993b; 1997a; 1997b) Tuwali *hudhud* texts. However, such fillers are consistently different from those in the Yattuka texts. In some instances, the formulas in Table 8 in Tuwali *hudhud* texts are not followed by any filler. When these formulas are used in lines ending with *nema o..e* (in Dulawan and Revel's texts) or *nema eeehem* (in Lambrecht's texts), they are followed by the same filler instead of those indicated in Table 8: *o..ya* in Dulawan and Revel's texts (with the exception of *bulalakki*, which is used as *bulalakkin na o..ya*) and *eeeeeya* in Lambrecht's texts.

6. Interjections and Enclitic Particles

Now we proceed to the last type of rhythmic fillers in *hudhuds*: interjections and enclitic particles. In *hudhud ni nosi*, under study here, interjections and enclitic

Form	Non-epenthetic filler	Frequency	Total Frequency
bulalakki	=nnieyi	93	98
	=nnieeeheeey	2	
	=nnieeehoooy ayhih	1	
	=nnieeeheheaaay	1	
	=nnie	1	
gawa	=ynoyi	59	73
	daynoyi	8	
	=ynooohoooy	1	
	=ynooohoooy ay-ii	1	
	dahnooo ohoooy aehegi	1	
	=ynoyi noaynoy nokappaynoyi	1	
	danooo ooohoooy ahih	1	
	daynooohoooy	1	
agapawan	dappa appawan'da'yi	42	59
	appa appawan'da'yi	13	
	yappa appawan'da'yi	4	
gawa... gawa'na	=n-ayya gawa'na'(da)ynoyi	24	31
	ayya gawa'na'ynoyi	7	

Table 7. Most common forms preceding non-epenthetic fillers.

particle normally occur at the very beginning of the line[14] and are sung only by the soloist. The inventory of such units includes the following: *a(y)* ('REAL'), *((h)i)inay* ('SURP'), *'la(w)* ('already'), *anha(n)* ('please'), *'ka(w)* ('maybe'), *'tu-wa* ('indeed'), *woda'n* ('maybe'). These are sometimes connected with the rest of the line with the linker *'n*, which can optionally be assimilated into *'m* if followed by a labial consonant. The omission of sounds in these forms (the parts of these units that can be omitted are enclosed in parentheses) does not occur in everyday language, with the exception of *hinay*, which normally does not have the initial

---

[14] Although there are thirty-three instances of line-internal use.

Stanyukovich (2012a)	Dulawan and Revel	Lambrecht
bulalakki'nnieyi	none	bulalakkinih (adna)
gawa'na'ynoyi	gawanadna gawanay-a	gawana adna
agapawan dappa appawan'da'yi	agpawanda payawanda agpawanda (ya) numpay- awanda (oya awawanda) agpawanda nunwaawanda agpawanda (nun-/nungg-/n- nang-/oya w-/ya)awaanda agpawanda (pe) umaawanda agpawanda (nun-/oya) wa-waanda agpawanda nun-awanda agpawanda ya wawaad agpawanda nunaanda agpawanday-a	(umagpawanda/ immagpawanda) agpawanda adna
gawa'n-ayya gawa'na'ynoyi	gawana ya gawanadna gawana ya gawanay-a	-

Table 8. Counterparts of some Yattuka non-epenthetic rhythmic fillers in Tuwali *hudhud*.

/h/. A(y), ((h)i)nay, anha(n), woda'n, and 'kaw can occur alone or in combination with other units. *Inay*, '*law*, *anhan*, and '*kaw* can also be followed by an epenthetic rhythmic filler '*a*. Table 9 shows the combinations that were attested in *hudhud ni nosi* under study here. In most cases, they follow the pattern in (7):

(7)

a(y)	((h)i)nay('a)	'la(w)('a)	anha(n)('a)	'ka(w)
('a)	'la(w)('a)	('n/m)		

Violation of this order has been attested only in the following cases: *inay ay* and *inay'law ay*. In one instance *anhan* is used twice: *anhan'law anhan'la'n*. *Tu-wa* as a rhythmic filler occurs in three lines either before *anhan* (*tu-wa'anhan*) or after (*inay'law anhan'a'tu-wa'n* and *inay'law'a anhan'tu-wa'law'a*). *Woda'n* in three occasions is used alone and once in the combination *nay'law'a woda'ng*.

Filler	Frequency	Filler	Frequency
a	69	anhan'la'n	1
ay	64	anhan'law anhan'la'n	1
inay'law'a	22	anhan'law'a	1
inay	12	anhang'ka'law'a	1
anha	8	ay inay'a	1
nay'law'a	4	ay inay'law'a	1
inay'law	3	hinay'a	1
anhan	3	hinay'law'a anhan'ka'law'a	1
inay'law'a anhan	3	inay ay	1
woda'n	3	inay'la	1
a anhan'ka'law'a	2	inay'la'n	1
anhan'kaw'a	2	inay'law anhan'a'tu-wa'n	1
'kaw	2	inay'law ay	1
a anhan	2	inay'law'a anhan'ka'la'n	1
inay'a	2	inay'law'a anhan'ka'law	1
nay	2	inay'law'a anhan'ka'law'a	1
ay'law'a anhan'ka'la'n	1	inay'law'a anhan'kaw	1
'kaw'a	1	inay'law'a anhan'la'm	1
a anhan'a	1	inay'law'a anhan'la'n	1
a anhan'ka'la'n	1	inay'law'a anhan'tu-wa'law'a	1
a anhan'ka'law	1	nay'law'a anhan'a	1
a il inay'law'a	1	nay'law'a anhan'kaw	1
anhan'a	1	nay'law'a anhan'kaw'a	1
anhan'a'kaw	1	nay'law'a woda'ng	1
anhan'ka'law	1	tu-wa'anha	1
anhan'ka'law'a	1		

Table 9. Attested combinations of interjections and enclitic particles.

It seems that all *hudhud* soloists have their own slightly different set of such elements and strategy of arranging them within a line. In *hudhud ni kolot* (Stanyukovich 2012b), performed by the same soloist as the one who performed the *hudhud ni nosi* analyzed in this chapter, the use of such units seems to be the same. In *hudhud ni pagi* (Klimenko 2016b), performed by a different soloist, *tu-wa* ('indeed') is never used as a filler. Also, the text contains only a few instances of *((h)i)nay* ('SURP'), *'kaw* ('maybe'), and *'law* ('already'). On the other hand, some lines contain double or triple occurrences of *anhan*, and many lines start with the conjunction *i* ('then'):

(8)

I	*anhan'kaw'law'a*		*anhan*	numan	a
then	please=maybe=already=LK		please	then	LK

mandudug'oli'da'ngu		mabloh	a	kuwan	*ino'da'n'na*
turn_in=FUT=they=EXCL		white	LK	said	mother=their=RF

hi	*Indangunay'anayi*		*ahay*	*inPangoiwan.*
PRS.NOM	PN.Indangunay=RF		RF	wife_of-PN.Pangoiwan

> Then, please maybe already please, then they will be the ones to come, because she is beautiful, said their mother Indangunay, wife of Pangoiwan.

Klimenko 2016b

Interestingly, in another *hudhud ni kolot* (Klimenko 2016a), performed by two less proficient soloists, such interjections and enclitic particles are practically absent.

As for Tuwali *hudhud* texts, they also employ a similar set of units in some lines. For instance, some lines in Dulawan and Revel's texts start with *ay* ('REAL'), *(i)nay* ('SURP'). Also, in both Dulawan and Revel's and Lambrecht's texts, many lines contain *anhan* ('please'), which is frequently used in a number of combinations: *(k)attog anhan, (anhan) anhan kattog, kay anhan, anhaanhan*. *Kattog* expresses uncertainty, disappointment, compassion, or is used "to stress or reinforce the meaning implied" (Lambrecht 1978:286). *Kay anhan* expresses "relief about the end of something that has taken a long time" (Hohulin and Hohulin 2014:383). It is unclear, though, whether these expressions in Tuwali texts are rhythmic fillers or are part of the intended situational meaning of the *hudhud* line. The fact that they are more frequently used in the middle of the line, rather than at the beginning like in Yattuka texts, might point to the latter. For instance, in Dulawan and Revel's texts, *(k)attog anhan* is consistently used as part of the chorus, not the solo:

(9)

Inay	an	nalubyag	ka	Bugan	*an*	*hi*
SURP	LK	consoled	you	PN.Bugan	LK	PRS.SG.NOM

Bugan,	<u>*attog*</u>	<u>*anhan,*</u>	<u>*o*</u>	*an*	*in-Aliguyon.*
PN.Bugan	poor	please	RF	LK	wife_of-Aliguyon

And then Bugan was pacified and consoled, Bugan, poor one, wife of Aliguyon.

Dulawan and Revel 1997a

7. Functions of Rhythmic Fillers

The fillers in the *hudhud* under study here can perform a variety of functions, including completing the rhythm, adding to the cryptic features of the text, and poetic discourse organization. Most of these fillers seem to be used to complete the rhythmic structure of the line. The exact way in which they interact with the rhythmic formula, however, remains to be researched. It can be hypothesized that the epenthetic fillers might function to obscure the sound of familiar words, as cryptolalia is a common feature of many sacred texts, while interjections and enclitic particles might be used to mark the beginning of the line, similar to some other traditions mentioned in the introduction to this chapter.

The non-epenthetic fillers *neman* and *ehmmm* seem to have a special function in *hudhud*. They occur at the end of some lines, accompanied by some other protracted non-epenthetic fillers earlier in the line (e.g. *adeeehoooy aahay, danooo ohoooy ahih,* etc.). An example of a line containing *ehmmm* and some accompanying fillers is given below. The non-epenthetic rhythmic fillers are underlined:

(10)

Ta	gammalan'mu	inda-den	di	pammadingan
then	will_eat_with_hand=you	rice	OBL	doorjamb

ni	*bale'yu*	*gawa'na*	<u>*dahnooo*</u>	<u>*ohoooy*</u>	<u>*aehegi'd*</u>
GEN	house=your	middle=its	RF	RF	RF=OBL

Amduntug	*neman*	*ehmmm*.
Amduntog[15]	RF	RF

Then you will eat rice by the doorpost of your house in the middle of Amduntog.

Stanyukovich 2012a

In the *hudhud* analyzed here, *ehmmm* occurs only once without *neman* immediately preceding it.

Lines with *(neman) ehmmm* are not evenly distributed across the whole *hudhud*. In *hudhud ni nosi* under study here (a total of 337 lines), *ehmmm* is used in lines 4, 15, 31, 65, 70, 117, 145, 160, 185, and 221.

Part I

1. Lines 1–4: Lukbut (the main character – the dead woman for whom the *hudhud* was performed) is very young. (*ehmmm*)

2. Lines 5–15: Her family moves from Polwitan to Nobayung. Lukbut plays with other children. Many years pass. (*ehmmm*)

3. Lines 16–31: Lukbut's grandchildren are now big. She and her fellow villagers get ready for a trip to a feast in another village. (*ehmmm*)

4. Lines 32–65: They travel to Amduntog, drink rice wine and dance at the feast. Lukbut's companions leave, but she decides to stay for the night. (*ehmmm*)

5. Lines 66–70: Lukbut refuses to eat rice and only drinks rice wine. Then it is the next morning. (*ehmmm*)

6. Lines 71–117: Lukbut only drinks rice wine instead of eating breakfast. They chew betel nut. They travel to Hinlalangit for another feast, drink rice wine, and dance. Lukbut says: "I have no place to return to." It is the next morning. (*ehmmm*)

7. Lines 118–127: They get ready to travel to Monitsigging.

Part II

8. Lines 128–145: They travel to Uldidittan[16] for another feast. (*ehmmm*)

---

[15] The spelling of this place name adopted in official documentation is with "o," while it is pronounced with /u/; hence the discrepancy in the transcription and translation.

[16] Part I ends with a line where Lukbut reaches a river at the edge of Monitsigging; however, Part II starts with lines where she is walking along rice field dikes in Uldidittan.

9. Lines 146–160: Lukbut only drinks rice wine. It is the next morning. They get ready for another trip. (*ehmmm*)

10. Lines 161–185: They travel to Hinyuma-dan for another feast. It is the next morning. (*ehmmm*)

11. Lines 186–199: They travel to Hinalyapen.

Part III

12. Lines 200–221: Another feast. They meet Dumya and Baggayon (mythological figures, the conductors of souls of the deceased to the underworld), who tell Lukbut to stand on a rock in the river to wait for her children, because it is not a feast trip, but the end of her life. (*ehmmm*)

Part IV

13. Lines 222–337: One of Lukbut's children, Kunelyuh (Cornelio), goes to find his mother, passing by all the places she visited. He finds her on the rock and leads her home together with the souls of all the slaughtered pigs and chickens she had been given at the feasts. He must not lose any of them along the way. They get back to Nobayung.

This uneven distribution in Yattuka *hudhud* is in stark contrast with the distribution of similar lines in Tuwali *hudhud* epics, where such units are normally used in every second line.[17] The following example shows a line from a *hudhud* published by Lambrecht, where the counterpart of the Yattuka *ehmmm* is presented as *eeehem*, accompanied by *eeeeeeya eee*:

(11)

Motmotwaona	pakaang-angonah	Bugan	an	hi
looks=he	stares=he=PRS.NOM	bugan	LK	PRS.SG.NOM

Bugan*ana*	*eeeeeeya*	*eee*	an	panguluwana	*eeehem.*
PN.Bugan=RF	RF	RF	LK	elder_sibling=his	RF

He looks he stares at Bugan, Bugan, his elder sister.

Lambrecht 1967:366

---

[17] As Lambrecht (1967:286) notes, the *hudhud* structure consists of three-line stanzas. The second line of each stanza is said to be finished with a "long protracted *eeeee* followed by a short and low-toned *ya*," while the third line is shorter than the first two and is said to start with a meaningless *eee* and end with *eeehem* after a personal name or *nema eeehem* after a place name.

In Dulawan and Revel's *hudhud* records, the corresponding sequence is *o ... ya ... nema o ... e.*

This difference in the distribution raises the question of the function of such lines in the Yattuka *hudhud* epics. One guess here might be that they are boundary markers of "chapters," indicating transitions between different scenes, or sets of scenes considered to be separate episodes of the narrative (cf. Lamb 2015:236–237). For instance, the *hudhud ni nosi* under scrutiny here is segmented with such lines into thirteen episodes. There are only eleven occurrences of *ehmmm* in the text. In Parts I and II, *ehmmm* is used in the last line of each episode of the epic, except for the final one. Therefore, it seems to operate as a boundary marker for the episodes of these parts, and then deviation from this pattern, not using *ehmmm* in the final episode, marks the end of the part by its absence. In Part III, *ehmmm* is used to conclude the part, while it is absent from Part IV. These parts do not subdivide into episodes, making it appear that the same pattern of use observed in Parts I and II begins functioning at the higher level of structure, marking the end of the penultimate part of the epic, but not its final part.

At present, it is not entirely clear whether *(neman) ehmmm* indeed marks boundaries of different scenes in *hudhud* or it is used only to break the monotony of singing. The latter might be suggested by the fact that in some instances *ehmmm* occurs in two consecutive lines. This occurs twice in another Yattuka *hudhud* record, *hudhud ni bogwa* (Stanyukovich 2012c), which is the same in its form and content to the *hudhud ni nosi*, sung by the same soloist.

8. Conclusions

This is the first study of elements without a semantic relation to the content of lines in *hudhud*. Moreover, such units are frequently lacking from the published Tuwali texts. Rhythmic fillers in *hudhud* can be divided into non-lexical units—epenthetic and non-epenthetic—and interjections and enclitic particles. Rhythmic fillers turn out to be an important tool for drawing comparisons and exploring differences between *hudhud* texts performed both in different ethnolinguistic traditions and by different individual soloists, as numerous differences have been revealed on both levels.

Units of all these classes are significantly more frequent in Yattuka *hudhuds*. This is particularly true for epenthetic fillers, which are normally omitted in the transcription of the Tuwali texts. The reason for this omission seems to be that Lambrecht's texts were written down by soloists, rather than transcribed from recordings of actual performances. Dulawan and Revel's texts lack many of the epenthetic fillers that can be heard in their recordings, probably, because the transcribers did not deem them a necessary part of the performance. This omission supports the division of non-lexical fillers as epenthetic or non-epenthetic, as the latter are normally present in the said publications.

There are limited sets of non-lexical units and they tend to occur with the same lexemes, which are only rarely used without rhythmic fillers in *hudhuds*. The same lexemes are normally used with non-epenthetic rhythmic fillers in both Tuwali and Yattuka *hudhuds*. However, the rhythmic fillers themselves are different. The distribution and function of the protracted *ehmmm* in Yattuka *hudhuds* significantly differs from that in Tuwali *hudhuds*. In the latter, this unit is used in almost every second line, while in the former it is used very irregularly, probably bearing the function of a boundary marker, indicating transitions between different episodes.

Interjections and enclitic particles at the beginning of lines follow a strict pattern. The actual pattern in a *hudhud* depends on the soloist's idiosyncratic style. Less proficient soloists tend to omit interjections and enclitic particles altogether. Somewhat similar sets of interjections and enclitic particles are used in both Tuwali and Yattuka *hudhud* texts. In some Tuwali texts, such interjections and enclitic particles are also consistently used as part of the chorus.

The general function of rhythmic fillers in *hudhud* is to complete the rhythmic structure of the line, although the exact way in which this happens remains to be researched. It can also be hypothesized on the basis of analogy with other oral traditions that epenthetic rhythmic fillers are used as part of the means making a sacred text cryptic, while interjections and enclitic particles in Yattuka *hudhuds* are employed as markers of the beginning of a new line.

Acknowledgements

This chapter would not be possible without the help of the following people, to all of whom I am deeply grateful: Abigail Tayaban, Adeline Dillag, Aldrick Hagada, Alejandro Mondiging, Alfredo Bumaynin, Anita Pe Benito, Aya Manangan, Carmie Bilibli Guimbatan, Conchita Guyguyon, Conchita Paya-gi, Daniel Dulnuan, Davilyn Bilibli Guimbatan, Dennis Pagal, Dinnaun (Reymonda) Sipal Tayaban, Escolastica Dulnuan, Felicitas Haguy Belingon, Feliza Gumangan Paya-gi, Gayyon Timmicpao Dulnuan, Helen Tuguinay, Jan Gopeng, Hsiu-chuan Liao, Jane Cuyahon Fortich, Janet Bannot, Janni Bulayungan Albano, Jeminor Maddul Gumangan, Jenifer Gumangan, Jocelyn Uhilan Tognaon, Josephine Pataueg, Josie Duppingay Dingayan, Jovelyn Dahya, Julee Guyguyon, Julie Dulnuan, Kathleen Maulino, Kerry Faith Guyguyon Bangadon, Lusia Matabye Martin, Lynette Buhong, Maria Pullupul, Dr. Maria V. Stanyukovich, Maribelle Bimohya, Marilyn Guimbatan, Marlon Martin, Melody Tayaban, Merry Gulingay Guyudon,

Mildred Pila, Nikki Bilibli, Niza Bilibli, Paolina Ginit Pinkihan, Patrick Henry Polpog, Pio Dupingay, Renchi Piggangay, Rey Balajo, Richard Hagada Buhung, Rita Panganiban Palbusa, Roger Maddul Gumangan, Ruben Maddul Gumangan, Rudy Pallay, Sharon Guyguyon, Suzette Bilibli Aliguyon, Victor Vincent (Toto) Martin Bulahao, Virginia Bahay Maddawat, Vishna Guyguyon Nga-ngac, Zhenny Aliguyon Baniya, and others. This research was partially funded by the Fellowship for the Documentation of Oral Literature and Traditional Ecological Knowledge of the Firebird Foundation for Anthropological Research.

References

Sources

Daguio, A. T. 1983. "*Hudhud hi Aliguyun.*" *Epics of the Philippines: Anthology of the ASEAN Literatures*, vol.1, 17–66. Quezon City.

Dulawan, L., and Revel, N. 1993a. *Aliguyon nak Binenwahen*. Quezon City: The Philippine Epics and Ballads Archive of the Ateneo de Manila University.

———. 1993b. *Aliguyon nak Amtalao*. Quezon City: The Philippine Epics and Ballads Archive of the Ateneo de Manila University.

———. 1997a. *Bugan an Imbayagda*. Quezon City: The Philippine Epics and Ballads Archive of the Ateneo de Manila University.

———. 1997b. *Bugan nak Pangaiwan*. Quezon City: The Philippine Epics and Ballads Archive of the Ateneo de Manila University.

Dulnuan-Bimohya, M., and Lunag I. T. (No date). *Ifugao Oral Masterpieces, Volume 1: A Compilation of Hudhud Chants and Other Oral Literature*. Pre-print. (No place.)

Klimenko, S. B. 2016a. *Hudhud ni kolot*, field records. Poblacion, Kiangan, Ifugao, Philippines.

———. 2016b. *Hudhud ni pagi*, field records. Guisigit, Amduntog, Asipulo, Ifugao, Philippines.

Lambrecht, F. 1957. "Ifugao Epic Story: *Hudhud* of Aliguyun at Hananga." *University of Manila Journal of East Asiatic Studies* 6(34):1–203.

———. 1960. "Ifugaw Hu'dhud: *Hudhud* of Aliguyun Who Was Bored by the Rustle of the Palm Tree at Aladugen." *Folklore Studies* 19:1–175.

———. 1961. "Ifugaw Hu'dhud (Continued). Hu'dhud of Bugan with Whom the Ravens Flew Away, at Gonhadan." *Folklore Studies* 20:136–273.

———. 1967. "The *Hudhud* of Dinulawan and Bugan at Gonhadon." *St. Louis Quarterly* 5(3–4):267–365.

Stanyukovich, M. V. 2012a. *Hudhud ni nosi*, field records. Boco, Nungawa, Asipulo, Ifugao, Philippines.

———. 2012b. *Hudhud ni kolot*, field records. Lidi, Amduntog, Asipulo, Ifugao, Philippines.

———. 2012c. *Hudhud ni bogwa*, field records. Pal-iyon, Duit, Kiangan, Ifugao, Philippines.

———. 2012d. *Hudhud ni kolot*, field records. Nayon, Lamut, Ifugao, Philippines.

Literature

Acabado, S. 2010. *The Archaeology of the Ifugao Agricultural Terraces: Antiquity and Social Organization*. Unpublished PhD dissertation. University of Hawai'i.

Anthony, L. 2018 (March 24). AntConc 3.5.5w (computer software). Retrieved 10 Aug 2018, from Center for English Language Education in Science and Engineering, School of Science and Engineering, Waseda University. http://www.laurenceanthony.net/software/antconc/.

Arjava, H. 2017. "Prosodies of Music and Formulaic Language on Collision Course." *Formula: Units of Speech—'Words' of Verbal Art: Working Papers of the Seminar-Workshop: 17th-19th May 2017, Helsinki, Finland* (ed. Frog) 66-76. Helsinki.

Bernshtam, T. A., and Lapin, V. A. 2009. "Vinograd'ye pesnya i obryad." *Narodnaya kul'tura Pomor'ya* (ed. T. A. Bernshtam) 239-364. Moscow.

Blench, R., and Campos, F. 2010. "Recording Oral Literature in a Literate Society: A Case Study from the Northern Philippines." *Oral Literature and Language Endangerment* (eds. M. Turin and I. Gunn) 49-65. *Language Documentation and Description* 8, special issue. London.

Brugman, H., and Russel, A. 2004. "Annotating Multimedia/ Multi-Modal Resources with ELAN." *Proceedings of LREC 2004, Fourth International Conference on Language Resources and Evaluation* (eds. M. T. Lino, M. F. Xavier, F. Ferreira, R. Costa, R. Silva, with the collaboration of C. Pereira, F. Carvalho, M. Lopes, M. Catarino, and S. Barros) 2065-2068. Lisbon.

Dulawan, L. S. 2005. "Singing *Hudhud* in Ifugao." *Literature of Voice: Epics in the Philippines* (ed. N. Revel) 115-124. Quezon City.

ELAN (Version 5.0.0-beta) (Computer software). Retrieved 10 Aug 2018, from Max Planck Institute for Psycholinguistics. https://tla.mpi.nl/tools/tla-tools/elan/.

Fieldworks Language Explorer (Computer software). Retrieved 10 Aug 2018, from Summer Institute of Linguistics. https://software.sil.org/fieldworks/.

Foley, J. M. 2005. "From Oral Performance to Paper-Text to Cyber-Edition." *Oral Tradition* 20(2):233-263.

Frog and Stepanova, E. 2011. "Alliteration in (Balto-) Finnic Languages." *Alliteration in Culture*. (ed. J. Roper) 195-218. Basingstoke.

Himmelmann, N. P. 2005. "The Austronesian Languages of Asia and Madagascar: Typological Characteristics." *The Austronesian Languages of Asia and Madagascar* (eds. A. Adelaar and N. P. Himmelmann) 110-181. London.

Hohulin, L., and Kenstowicz, M. 1979. "Keley-i Phonology and Morphophonemic." *Southeast Asian Linguistic Studies* 4 (ed. N. D. Liem) 241–254. Canberra.

Hohulin, L., and Hale, A. 1977. "Notes on Keley-i Relational Grammar: I." *Studies in Philippine Linguistics* 1-2:231–263.

Hohulin, R. M., and Hale, A. 1977. "Physical, Temporal, and Cognitive Location in Keley-i Demonstratives." *Studies in Philippine Linguistics* 1(2):209–230.

Hohulin, R. M., and Hohulin, E. L. 2014. *Tuwali Ifugao Dictionary and Grammar Sketch*. Manila.

Klimenko, S. B. 2012. *Motion Verbs in Tagalog, Ilokano and Tuwali Ifugao*. Unpublished MA thesis. University of the Philippines, Diliman.

———. 2017. *Kategoriya zaloga v filippinskikh yazykakh (na materiale yazyka yattuka)*. PhD dissertation. St. Petersburg: Institute for Linguistic Studies, Russian Academy of Sciences.

Klimenko, S. B., and Stanyukovich, M. V. 2018. "Yattuka and Tuwali Ifugao Hudhud: Yattuka, Keley-i, and Tuwali Ifugao Interference." *Acta Linguistica Petropolitana* 9(2):585–636.

Lamb, W. 2015. "Verbal Formulas in Gaelic Traditional Narrative." *Registers of Communication* (eds. A. Agha and Frog) 225-246. Helsinki.

Lambrecht, F. 1965. "Ifugao Hu'dhud Literature." *St. Louis Quarterly* 3(2):191-214.

———. 1978. *Ifugaw-English Dictionary*. Baguio City.

Madrid, A. F. 1980. "Four Discourse Genre in Amganad Ifugao." *Studies in Philippine Linguistics* 4(1):101–143.

Philippine Statistics Authority (PSA). 2019. Philippine Standard Geographic Code. https://psa.gov.ph/classification/psgc/downloads/PSGC%20Publication%20June2019.xlxs (August 5, 2019).

Del Rosario, R. B. de S. 2013. "The Chanted Ifugao *Alim* and *Hudhud*: Ritual-Drama and Heroic Stories." *Songs of Memory in Islands of Southeast Asia* (ed. N. Revel) 129-160. Newcastle-upon-Tyne.

Stanyukovich, M. V. 1981. "Epos i obryad u gornykh narodov Filippin." *Sovetskaya etnografiya* 5:72–83.

———. 1982. *Istoricheskaya tipologiya i etnokul'turnyye svyazi geroicheskogo eposa Ifugao, Filippiny*. PhD dissertation. Leningrad.

———. 1997. "Abstract of the Final Report on the Fieldwork in the Philippines in 1994–1995 Funded by the Small Grant of the Wenner-Gren Anthropological Foundation." *Biannual Newsletter of the Wenner-Gren Anthropological Foundation*. New York.

———. 2003. "A Living Shamanistic Oral Tradition: Ifugao *Hudhud*, the Philippines." *Oral Tradition Journal* 18(2):249–251.

———. 2007. "Poetics, Stylistics and Ritual Functions of *Hudhud* and Noh." *Hudhud and Noh: A Dialogue of Cutlures* (eds. A. A. C. Umali, N. Umewaka, and R. del Rosario) 62-67. Manila.

———. 2008. "Epicheskoye skazaniye ifugao 'Aliguyon, syn Binenuakhena': syuzhet, personazhi i toponimy." *Indoneziytsy i ikh sosedi: Festschrift Ye. V. Revunenkovoy i A. K. Ogloblinu - The Indonesians and Their Neighbors: Festschrift for E.V. Revunenkova and A.K. Ogloblin* (ed. Maria V. Stanyukovich) 223-243. Maklay Publications 1. St. Petersburg.

———. 2013. "Epic as a Means to Control Memory and Emotions of Gods and Humans: Ritual Implications of *Hudhud* among the Yattuka and Tuwali Ifugao." *Songs of Memory in Islands of Southeast Asia* (ed. N. Revel) 167-197. Newcastle-upon-Tyne.

———. 2015. "Place-Names in Yattuka and Tuwali Ifugao *Hudhud Ni Nosi/ Hudhud Di Nate* Funeral Chant." *The Thirteenth International Conference on Austronesian Linguistics, July 18-23, 2015 (13-ICAL): Abstracts* (ed. anonymous) 216-217. Taipei.

———. 2017. "Anthroponymic Formulas in the Ifugao *Hudhud* and Other Epics of the Philippines." *Units of Speech—'Words' of Verbal Art: Working Papers of the Seminar-Workshop 17th-19th May 2017 Helsinki, Finland* (ed. Frog) 199-207. Folkloristiikan toimite 23. Helsinki.

Stanyukovich, M. V., and Kozintsev, A. G. 2016. "Krestiki i noliki = kroliki: O nekotorykh elementakh taynogo yazyka pokhoronnykh skazaniy yattka, Filippiny." *Radlovskiy sbornik: Nauchnyye issledovaniya i muzeynyye proyekty MAE RAN v 2015 g.* (ed. Ju. K. Chistov) 267-275. St. Petersburg.

Stanyukovich, M. V., and Sychenko, G. B. 2016. "Poetic Language and Music of the Hudhud Ni Nosi, a Yattuka Funeral Chant, the Philippines." Unpublished paper presented at Versification: Metrics in Practice, NordMetrik Conference, May 25-27, 2016. Helsinki.

Tyapkova, T. 1995. "East Slavonic Wedding Songs: Functional and Structural Characteristics and the Composition of Refrains." *Folk Belief Today* (eds. M. Kõiva and K. Vassiljeva) 490-501. Tartu.

UNESCO. 2014. "UNESCO Issues First Ever Proclamation of Masterpieces of the Oral and Intangible Heritage." Retrieved 10 Aug 2018, from UNESCO. http://www.unesco.org/culture/ich/en/RL/hudhud-chants-ofthe-ifugao-00015.

West, A. 1973. "The Semantics of Focus in Amganad Ifugao." *Linguistics* 11(110):98–121.

16

Formulaic Expression in
Olonets Karelian Laments

Textual and Musical Structures in the
Composition of Non-Metrical Oral Poetry

VILIINA SILVONEN, UNIVERSITY OF HELSINKI

T HE INTERACTION OF TEXTUAL AND MUSICAL STRUCTURES of oral poetry is multimodal and complex. While recent research has focused on metrically organized forms of sung oral poetry (Niemi 2015; Kallio 2017), this study adds perspectives of sung oral poetry lacking regular, periodic meter. I have analyzed a corpus of Olonets Karelian laments in order to treat the topic with examples. The performance of Finnic laments can be described as "tonal-textual improvisation" (Niemi 2002:708). A lamenter improvises her lament in each concrete situation by following traditional conventions and using formulaic expressions. The interrelation of variable textual and musical elements in this kind of non-metrical sung poetry creates the structural framework for composition in performance. The basic principles of composition remain consistent even though styles vary on dialectal, regional, and individual levels (see e.g. Tarkiainen 1943; Honko 1974; Niemi 2002; E. Stepanova 2014; 2015), and the performance styles vary form speech-like to song-like performances in Olonets Karelian laments.

Of the 430 laments forming a corpus in the background of this article, I selected forty-two recordings for detailed analysis.[1] In my analyses of

---

[1] The majority of the 430 laments are very fragmentary and excerpt-like. The provided transcriptions here based on textual transliteration by Helmi and Pertti Virtaranta and notations by Ilpo Saastamoinen published in Koponen and Torikka (1999). The author has checked and re-transcribed the texts and notations against the original recordings; the fluctuation of the tonal base has been removed. English translations are by the author. All transcriptions © Viliina Silvonen.

audio-recorded laments, I have noticed that the text and music of each follow their own courses but also influence one another in ways not recognized before. The overall diction of laments is complex and ambiguous, with highly metaphorical poetic language and constantly varying musical lines. However, analysis reveals that both text and music have recurring structural elements and that the interrelation of music and text is at multiple levels. To describe the phenomena I discovered in lament performance, I apply terminology from studies of lament language (E. Stepanova 2014; 2015; 2017) and Oral-Formulaic Theory (OFT) (Parry 1930; Lord 1960; Foley 1995). The organization of lament text can be analyzed through *themes, subthemes,* and *poetic lines* as well as *formulaic units.* To discuss the structural elements of the laments' melody, I use the terms *musical line, musical phrase,* and *musical motif.* Musical lines and phrases are musically coherent, rather clearly prominent units that have "a self-contained idea" (Drabkin 2001).

OFT has been discussed in many studies and the definitions of formulas are varied (e.g. Parry 1930; Lord 1960; 1991; Foley 1991; 1995; Harvilahti 1992; Kuiper 2009; Wray 2002; Kallio 2013; E. Stepanova 2014; Frog 2017). Most studies share the conception of a formula as a recurring complex form expressing "a given essential idea" (Parry 1930:80) even though the exact term used may vary from formula to formulaic sequence (e.g. Lord 1991; Foley 1991; 1995; Foley and Ramey 2012; Wray 2002; Kuiper 2009; E. Stepanova 2014; Frog 2016; 2017). Formulas act like single words; they exist in a performer's mental lexicon as "an integer of traditional meaning" (Foley and Ramey 2012:80) and can be retrieved from memory and used fluently in performance (Lord 1960:65–67; Foley 1991:6–7; Wray 2002:9). Moreover, formulas are connected to the connotative non-lexical meaning associated with their patterns of use, which accords to them what John Miles Foley describes as *traditional referentiality* (Foley 1991:6–7; 1995:27–28). In performance, they can convey profound culturally shared meanings as well as mythic knowledge (Tarkka 2005:62), and they also embody a certain kind of communication: for example, within Karelian laments, a polite, "honorific register" (Wilce and Fenigsen 2015).

Formulaicity appears on various levels in Olonets Karelian laments. As Lauri Harvilahti (1992:141–144) notes, formulas cannot be defined comprehensively and univocally because in performance the oral-poetic system is based on several simultaneous multilevel processes and the determinant parameters and features vary between genres and different forms of oral poetry. In this chapter, I understand formulaic units as complex, recurrent units characterized by an integer of meaning. In the context of Karelian lament poetry, formulaic units can be formally fixed or flexible: the number of words used to express a formula's essential idea varies, although the core remains the same

(E. Stepanova 2014:37–42, 70–74). In oral poetry that lacks a regular, periodic meter, the primary principles of organizing formulaic units are syntax and poetic and prosodic features, including music; formulaic units are based on meaning or discourse function (Niemi 2015:18; Frog 2017:255). I discuss formulaicity appearing on several levels of Olonets Karelian lament texts with the terms *minimal formula, cluster formula* (cf. Lord 1991:149–150), and *macro-formula*, which I present below (Frog 2016:63; 2017:256; this volume, section 6). Even though I do not adapt OFT directly for the analysis of musical units, the formulaicity of music is can be understood as a recurring framework of form that directs the composition of structural musical elements.

The textual and musical systems of laments are independent but their operation is interconnected. Usually, poetic lines and musical lines correspond to each other in such a way that a musical-textual basic unit is discernible. Because the mechanisms of structure of text and music are different, the correspondence is not regular. Within the smaller-scale units, there is no clear systematic correspondence between music and text, but the borders of each are interrelated: for instance, a border of a musical phrase never occurs in the middle of a minimal formula, but may appear in the middle of a cluster formula. Even though music and text each follow their own paths, in some cases a melodic pattern and textual unit, such as a cluster formula or even a complete poetic line, form a crystallized unit; however, this kind of crystallized correspondence is extremely rare.

In the present chapter, I approach the topic in three stages. First, I elucidate the formulaicity of lament texts. Second, I analyze the structural organization of lament music and its formulaic elements. Third, I compare the structures of text and music to examine their correspondence and interaction. The style of performance influences the relation and interaction of text and music. I review the interaction also in relation to emotions, which hold a central position in lament performance. Before proceeding to the first stage, I briefly introduce the Karelian lament tradition.

1. Karelian Laments

Laments (*itkuvirret*, sg. *itkuvirzi*) are considered a common Finnic tradition of verbal art and ritual practice that was in use among Karelian, Vepsian, Ingrian, Votic, and Seto populations still in twentieth century.[2] Laments were essential in rites of passage such as funerals, provided a medium and voice for collective grief,

---

[2]   Similar ritual wailing traditions are known worldwide (see e.g. Honko 1974:11–14; Feld and Fox 1994:39–43).

and equipped women with an acceptable medium for also expressing personal sorrow in non-ritual contexts. Laments were widely known and, as they were improvisatory solo performances, the ways of expression were diverse (see e.g. Honko 1974; Nenola-Kallio 1982; Konkka 1985). The traditional mythic thinking essential to the background of the lament tradition was already waning when the recordings were made during the twentieth century (e.g. Tenhunen 2006).

Karelian laments can be divided into three regional traditions, each having its own distinctive linguistic and musical characteristics, but they also share many common features and are often studied as a whole (e.g. Honko 1974; Salmenhaara 1967 [1976]; Gomon 1976; Konkka 1985; Tolbert 1988; 1990; Niemi 2002:708–712; A. Stepanova 2012:13–15; E. Stepanova 2015; 2017). The pan-regional features of Karelian laments are[3]:

- a lack of regular, periodic meter

- a metaphorical avoidance lexicon with use of diminutive, possessive and plural forms (also in cases when referring to a singular, i.e. a poetic plural) (e.g. E. Stepanova 2015)

- multilevel parallelism in both text (e.g. E. Stepanova 2017) and music

- a descending melodic outline with relatively narrow *ambitus* (tonal range of a musical line) and mostly syllabic correlation with the text, although *melismata* (several tones on a single syllable) are not rare (e.g. Salmenhaara 1967 [1976]; Niemi 2002), and

- emotion emblems, such as sobbing, voiced inhalation, a creaky voice, and actual crying (see Urban 1988:389–381; Silvonen and Stepanova 2020:214–217).

The clearest regional features of language are observed in circumlocutions (A. Stepanova 2012:13–15) and the extent of patterns of alliteration (Frog and Stepanova 2011:204–209). Regarding music, the traditions vary by the general outline of melody and differing *ambitus* (Salmenhaara 1967 [1976]; Gomon 1976).

In the present chapter, I concentrate on the Olonets Karelian tradition, which is the southernmost Karelian lament region. The special features of Olonets Karelian laments have been described only on a general level alongside those of other lament regions (see e.g. Salmenhaara 1967 [1976]; Gomon 1976; Konkka 1985; Saastamoinen 1999a; A. Stepanova 2012; E. Stepanova 2017). Besides their regional vocabulary, the distinguishing characteristics of Olonets laments are, for instance, use of alliteration over shorter stretches of text (Frog and

---

[3]   Most of these pan-regional features are shared across all Finnic lament traditions (E. Stepanova 2017:487).

Stepanova 2011:204) and peculiar variation in musical structures, even though there are several regional melodic styles (Gomon 1976:452). The most common tonal range of a musical line in Olonets Karelian laments is a sixth (e.g. from e^1 to $c\#^2$), and the melody is usually step-wise within a musical line, although larger intervals and upward elements may exist (see also e.g. Salmenhaara 1967 [1976]). In the recordings, the tempo of laments tends to be moderate; the beat is usually fast rather than slow, although it varies between lamenters and performances. The rhythm gives the impression of being rather constant; occasionally, however, a single note is approximately twice the average duration (see also e.g. Saastamoinen 1999b). A musical line that is metrically "unfixed" generally follows a descending melody, concluding with a prolonged final note, sobbing or crying, and inhalation (Rüütel and Remmel 1980:179; Tolbert 1990:88–90, 99–102; Niemi 2002:711–712). The overall tonality is unstable and it often rises steadily during a performance.[4]

2. Organization and the Formulaic System of Lament Texts

A poetic line can be considered as a basic unit of lament text. It corresponds to a clause or sentence and varies in length. A sequence of semantically parallel poetic lines expresses what is here described as a subtheme, while main themes are broader, more abstract units of semantic content (Stepanova 2014:47). For example, a theme of death can contain subthemes of changes in the environment, a description of the changes for the deceased, the eternality of death, and advice for the burial (SKNA7592:3 JFS2).[5] Themes of lament texts ordinarily follow a pattern: opening vocative theme followed by ritual, context-bound themes (funeral, wedding, conscription) and autobiographical themes. Not all laments include all of these. Ritual, context-bound laments do not necessarily include sections with autobiographical themes, and obviously laments outside of rituals consist mostly of autobiographical themes.

---

[4] The ground note and the entire musical base of a lament fluctuate. The melodic base and the ground note often vary between the two lowest notes of the scale. Analysis of the tonal or musical base and precise determination of the tonality are not possible, but, on the other hand, it would not make sense to force such a determination in the context of improvisatory oral performance that is variable by nature. (See also e.g. Tolbert 1990; Niemi 2015:24–27.) In general, the theoretical and methodological bases of musicology (Western classical music) and ethnomusicology are somewhat contradictory (e.g. Herndon 1974; Niemi 1998:29–31; see also Niemi 2015).

[5] SKNA = Tape Archive of the Finnish Language Institute for the Languages of Finland. JFS is an abbreviation of the name of a particular lamenter, Jeudokia Fedorovna Sofronova, while the number refers to the lament.

In Olonets Karelian laments, poetic lines are identified mostly as syntactic units and are distinguishable by semantic parallelism of sequential lines.[6] Poetic lines are also marked melodically, and lamenters use discourse markers—such as the interjections *oi* and *ga*, the conjunctions *i* ('and, too, or'), *a* ('but'), and *vie/viä* ('still, more, yet'), and emphatic words *kai* ('only')—to demarcate poetic lines. In the Olonets Karelian lament tradition, a single pattern of alliteration tends not to continue for a complete poetic line as it usually does in regions to the north, where alliteration has been analyzed to be one of the defining features of poetic lines (e.g. Frog and Stepanova 2011:204–209).

Texts of laments consist mostly of metaphorical circumlocutions. The language can be described as an avoidance register, a pattern believed to be rooted in naming taboos; especially people and relationships, but also objects, places, and phenomena central to laments are not named directly (Honko 1974:56–57; E. Stepanova 2015:263). Lamenters use formulaic units to express these avoided things. In funeral laments, for instance, the lamenter describes death and the different stages of the ritual with formulaic expressions. In addition to names and kinship terms, personal pronouns are among the vocabulary items avoided in laments.[7]

Alliteration occurs on the level of these formulaic units but its density is not constant. For instance, in the highly recurrent minimal formula for mother, *kallis naine kandajaženi* ('dear woman carrier.DIM.POS'),[8] only the first epithet alliterates with the core word. In general, the patterns of alliteration occur on the level of crystallized circumlocutions, as in *kiältylöil i kiälyžil* ('with voiceless. DIM.PL tongue.DIM.PL'[9]), *kylmänyžil kuvažil* ('with cold.DIM.PL image.DIM.PL') or *vilužinnu virumas* ('lying feeling chilly').[10] However, a single pattern of alliteration may extend across a whole poetic line or even a subtheme, although it is not consistent across the complete stretch of text and is interspersed with other patterns of alliteration connected with specific formulas.

The formulaic system of lament language consists of minimal formulas, cluster formulas, and macro-formulas. Each of these recurring textual units conventionally expresses an integer of meaning, but they all operate as formulaic units at different levels of scope in composition and performance. The use of cluster formulas and especially macro-formulas occurs mainly on the level

---

[6] Frog and Eila Stepanova call these units poetic strings (Frog and Stepanova 2011:204–209; E. Stepanova 2017:489–490).

[7] Some laments include direct naming and person pronouns, which I interpret to be a consequence of waning expertise in registers.

[8] DIM indicates a diminutive affix and POS a possessive suffix.

[9] PL indicates poetic plural.

[10] A similar narrow pattern of alliteration is the main mode of alliteration in laments in Vepsian, in the regions adjacent to Olonets (Frog and Stepanova 2011:208).

of idiolects, although some of the most common cluster formulas connected to ritually central subjects appear rather crystallized at a regional level. By contrast, minimal formulas tend to belong to the regional lexicon. I interpret the difference of what appears to be idiolectal or regional as related to the lack of a periodic meter, which allows greater freedom in verbal expression than poetic forms in which the number of syllables or stresses per line is regulated.

2.1. Minimal formulas

Minimal formulas are at the simplest level of verbal expression regularly used to communicate a unit of meaning (see also Foley 1995:8; Frog 2017:255). Typically, they consist of two to five words, and are reducible to a single word. For the most part, minimal formulas are circumlocutions for nouns and pronouns (see also E. Stepanova 2014:74–80). The basic form of minimal formulas for persons comprises a core word and one or several epithets. For example, the semantic unit MOTHER is often *kallis naine kandajaseni* ('dear woman carrier.DIM.POS') and FATHER *kallis armozeni* ('dear beloved.DIM.POS'). Formulas for persons are flexible in the sense that a core word may occur alone or with one to four simple epithets, or the circumlocution may form a syntactically more complex noun phrase, such as the formula *armas kuldaine yksiz i vatšoiz i vualittu kuldainen kudri* ('beloved sweet.DIM cherished in the same.PL stomach.PL sweet.DIM goldilocks'), meaning BROTHER. Although this type of formula can be expanded into a complex phrase, it can also be expressed through the core word alone.

Epithets for a lamenter's family members and beloved ones are tender, conveying a positive stance (Nenola-Kallio 1982:33; Stepanova E. 2014:74; see also Silvonen and Stepanova 2020:210–212). Diminutive and especially possessive affixes are central, marking differences between family members or close people and strangers. However, the diminutive, and in some cases even the possessive, may also be omitted from circumlocutions for close people. Formally, such omissions can create ambiguity, in which case the context guides interpretation. As with other persons, the lamenter refers to herself and expresses the ego of a lament[11] with formulaic circumlocution (A. Stepanova 2012:55). The epithets in these formulas are mostly negative, describing sorrow and misery with varying nuances, and sometimes they are semantically vague. Since the epithets are distinguished from the ones used for persons, an epithet by itself can appear as a circumlocution for the ego of the lament (see also A. Stepanova 2012:55; E. Stepanova 2014:75).

---

[11] The lamenter herself is not always the "I" (grammatical subject) of the lament; in weddings, for example, some other woman may lament on behalf the bride.

Both core words and epithets have several alternatives and their combinations may vary. Even though the patterns of alliteration are not continuous, these alternative circumlocutions enable the lamenter to compose longer patterns of alliteration. For example, minimal formulas referring to the ego of the lament alliterate with the words around it: <u>*aigamain akku*</u> *jo ahavien tuuluzien armozis* ('[epithet] woman at the mercy.DIM of biting winds.DIM') and *tuoa <u>leinä-zele</u> leibäzed i lämmäzed* ('bring warm.DIM.PL bread.DIM.PL to the <u>sorrowful-one</u>'). In the latter, a single word forms the minimal formula. In Olonets Karelia, alliteration is not predictably linked to certain classes of words (e.g. verbs) in the same way it is in lament regions to the north.[12]

2.2. Cluster formulas

Cluster formulas are units whose structure is more complex than minimal formulas. They are formulaic expressions that include several distinguishable elements, of which at least some are minimal formulas. Cluster formulas are at most the length of a poetic line. These formulaic units are very flexible in their composition. The order and number of elements of a cluster formula may vary. Usually there are more than two elements. I derive the term cluster formula from Albert Lord's term "formula cluster" (1991:149–150). With "formula cluster," Lord addresses a formulaic expression that is comprised of more than one formulaic element and used to express "'a cluster of essential ideas under given metrical conditions'" (1991:149). Lord's description is not directly transferable to the context of laments, which lack regular metrical conditions, but the idea of several elements forming a meaningful unity is applicable. On the other hand, the "group of formulas" expressing "a cluster of ideas" comes close to my conception of a macro-formula.

For example, a cluster formula for muteness, which is a circumlocution for death, is comprised of components of action, object, and manner: *huuluat kai valgeiloil vahapetšättižil petšätoittu* ('lips are sealed with white.DIM.PL wax seal. DIM.PL') (SKNA7592:3; SKNA7593:1; Fon.2781b JFS1, 2, 3, 6, 11). In addition to the formation being more complex than in minimal formulas, the actions and phenomena that cluster formulas express are more complex than minimal formulas, and yet the meaning of a cluster formula might be reduced to a single concept (in this case, TO BE MUTE meaning TO BE DEAD). In addition, emotions like sorrow and longing are also described with such cluster formulas as metaphors representing nature and the passing of time. The ego of a lament may, for example, shed tears to fill Lake Ladoga, or cry a river, or describe how the sun

---

[12] On alliteration in northern regions, see Frog and Stepanova 2011:204–209; E. Stepanova 2014:64.

has not shone on her garden since she lost the one who was dear to her (see also A. Stepanova 2012).

In Olonets laments, these cluster formulas recur in a highly crystallized manner at the level of idiolect, although variations occur. At the regional level, they mostly occur within ritual, context-bound themes. For instance, the order of components of a cluster formula may vary, as in the cluster formula *kiältylöil i kiälyžil kylmänyžil kuvažil vilužinnu virumas* (SKNA7592:3, SKNA7593:1 JFS1, 2, and 6) ('with voiceless.DIM.PL tongue.DIM.PL cold.DIM.PL image.DIM.PL lying feeling chilly'), which is also found as *kylmänyžil kuvažil kiältylöil kielyžil vilužinnu virumaz* (SKNA7592:3 JFS3) ('cold.DIM.PL image.DIM.PL with voiceless.DIM.PL tongue. DIM.PL lying feeling chilly'). In addition, along with the lack of regular metrical patterning, the lamenter may add euphonic expletive syllables, emphatic particles, or even larger textual elements. In the lament JFS6 (SKNA7593:1), the above formula includes an adjunct of time (*nämmil päivözil* ['these days.DIM']) placed before the recurrent sequence. The possibilities for variation within cluster formulas are numerous. The number of words in a component may vary, as can the order and the number of components.

Furthermore, cluster formulas may include open slots for minimal formulas for a person, for instance. These open-slot formulaic expression are stable formulaic units in which some element or elements (the filler for the open slot) vary (Frog 2016:73). The examples above can be extended to a length of an entire poetic line, including an open slot for a person. The cluster formula for muteness is comprised of an opening with a discourse marker, a minimal formula for the specific person who is deceased, and a formulaic expression for muteness: *g_on [DECEASED.GEN] kai kuldažed i kiälyäd luuhužian i lukkužien tuakse lukkoiltu* (SKNA7592:3, SKNA7593:1, Fon.2781a JFS1, 2, 3, 6, 11)[13] ('when [DECEASED.GEN] golden.DIM.PL tongue.DIM.PL is locked.FRE behind bony.DIM.PL lock.DIM.PL').[14] In my data, the crystallization of cluster formulas constituting an entire poetic line is primarily idiolectal, while narrower cluster formulas appear also regionally.

2.3. Macro-formulas

The semantic parallelism of poetic lines is a characteristic feature of laments (E. Stepanova 2017:267, 490–491). In cases when parallel poetic lines are formulaic, they can together constitute formulaicity on a greater structural level.

---

[13] Jeudokia Fedorovna Sofronova's repertoire is the largest by a single lamenter in my material (seven laments recorded in 1968, six in 1983), and thus it is best suited for analyses of formulaic expressions in terms of the greater scope, their crystallization and the complete formulaic system.

[14] FRE indicates a frequentative affix.

When these kinds of series of poetic lines are recurrent, they can be seen as a macro-formula that expresses an entire subtheme, which is itself an integer of meaning (see also Frog 2016; 2017; this volume, section 6; cf. Lord 1991:149–150). To illustrate this more complex form, I present a macro-formula that expresses the subtheme of the metamorphoses of a body through death, constituted of four poetic lines that appear in five laments (JFS1, 2, 3, 6, 11: SKNA7592:3, SKNA7593:1, Fon.2781b; here (1) the translation is simplified):

(1)

1. g_on [DECEASED.GEN] kiältylöil i kiälyžil kylmänyžil kuvažil vilužinnu virumaz
2. g_on [DECEASED.GEN] rungažiz lämmäžet kai lähtiätty sumbažed i surruttu
3. g_on [DECEASED.GEN] kai kuldažet i kiälyäd luuhužian i lukužien tuakse lukkoiltu
4. g_on [DECEASED.GEN] i huuluat kai valgeiloil vahapetšättižil petšätoittu

1. when [DECEASED.GEN] with voiceless tongue cold image laying feeling chilly
2. when [DECEASED.GEN] the warmth has left the body stiffed body
3. when [DECEASED.GEN] golden tongue is locked behind bony locks
4. when [DECEASED.GEN] lips are sealed with white wax seals

Within a recurrent macro-formula in an individual's repertoire, such as this one, the order of parallel lines may be regular, but not all lines occur in every use. JFS2 (SKNA7592:3) lacks the second line in (1), JFS3 (SKNA7592:1) lacks the third, and JFS11 (Fon.2781b) lacks the first. In addition, the lamenter may add poetic lines between those constitutive of a macro-formula. In JFS6 (SKNA7593:2), for instance, a line expressing that the lament is performed on behalf of a woman who is unable to lament herself is placed between the first two lines in (1). This variation belongs to the more general potential for a lamenter to move between subthemes during the course of a lament (E. Stepanova 2017:500–502), and lines expressing a particular subtheme are not necessarily presented in parallel (see also E. Stepanova 2014:68). Even though a poetic line may be lacking or lines of another subtheme may intercede in the series, this group of poetic lines can be seen as forming a macro-formula unit expressing the particular subtheme. The most crystallized cluster formulas and macro-formulas appear within ritual, context-bound themes.

3. Organization of Laments' Music

Laments' melody is single-lined and a musical line is comprised of one or more musical phrases, which vary in both length and shape due to the improvisatory nature of the genre. The melody of laments has three structurally significant elements: musical line, musical phrase, and musical motifs.[15] The musical line forms the basic unit of the lament's music, as it is the largest distinguishable *expressive integer of music*. By expressive integer of music, I mean a musically coherent, prominent unit that is perceived as separate from the larger whole and in that way relates to "a self-contained idea" (see Drabkin 2001, on musical theme). These types of elements of musical structure are interrelated: a smaller unit has a distinct identity with important consequences for a larger unit (see Drabkin 2001), and the segmentation of larger units is based on the distinction of smaller units.

3.1. Musical motifs

A musical motif is a small recurring musical pattern that has rather stable melodic and rhythmic features (Drabkin 2001). Because the exact form of a motif is not fixed in laments, the borders of motifs are vague and fluid. Nevertheless, motifs are discernible and important when analyzing the melodic structure of a lament.

The initial and final motifs of a musical line are prominent in the flow of a lament, being the main structuring elements of the overall musical appearance.[16] In Olonets Karelian sound recordings, the final motif is the dominant distinguishing structural characteristic of musical lines. Both the initial and final motifs have certain core notes and somewhat recognizable melodic shapes. The core notes of the initial motif are primarily the two highest in cases of ambitus of a sixth or only the highest in ambitus of a fifth. The initial motif most often begins with a repetitive use of the second highest or highest note, turning at the highest note if begun from the second highest, and then it begins to descend. Often one of the repetitive notes or the highest note is long (i.e. double the duration of others). The final motif is more stable than the initial motif: most often,

---

[15] The structures are vague and constantly varying; thus, the identification of musical elements often depends on the researcher's interpretation. Partially due to that, the terminology used in the analyses of laments is not consistent; see e.g. Väisänen 1940–1941 [1990]; Gomon 1976; Salmenhaara 1967 [1976]; Tolbert 1988:163, 172–181; Saastamoinen 1999a, 1999b; Niemi 2002:713–722.

[16] Most scholars of lament music define the initial and final motifs as fixed to some degree and the middle section of a musical line as freer (e.g. Väisänen 1940–1941 [1990]; Salmenhaara 1967 [1976]; Gomon 1976; Tolbert 1988:163, 172–181; Saastamoinen 1999a; Niemi 2002:713–722).

Figure 1. Initial and final motifs: 1. initial motif from JFS2, eighth line (SKNA7592:3); 2. initial motif from PIK1, second line (SKNA6595:2); 3. final motif from JFS2, third line (SKNA7592:1); the finalis in this motif is the second lowest note of the scale (see n. 4 above).

a final motif consists of a step-wise descending movement from a third towards the *finalis* (the ground tone), which is repeated.[17] The amount of repetition in the initial and final motifs varies by individual lamenter and by performance. The final motif is also marked with a decelerating tempo, and the repetition gives the impression of being in approximately half tempo.

In addition to these motifs at the beginnings and endings of musical lines, initial-like and final-like motifs occur in the freer middle section of a line to mark musical phrases. Initial motifs at the beginning of a line and the final motif are functionally more important than those occurring within a line, as they mark the basic units of the melody. Their form is also clearer.

3.2. Expressive integers of music

The melody of Olonets Karelian laments is comprised of musical lines that are in turn comprised of musical phrases. A principal phrase opens a musical line with the initial motif. This kind of phrase can also appear later in a musical line in a subordinated position, although this is rare. A subordinate phrase is either descending or arcing (Figure 2). A descending phrase normally begins from the highest note of the phrase, which is not necessarily the highest note of the whole line. In contrast, the melody of an arcing phrase first ascends and then descends back towards the ground note. Almost every musical phrase ends with the ground note, yet the ground note fluctuates within two or even three of the lowest notes of the used scale (see footnote 4 above). Furthermore, a lament may occasionally even go below the ground note. In some cases, the very end of a musical phrase moves upward after descending to the ground note, making an *ascending anacrusis* (a pick-up) towards a new phrase. The ascending anacrusis

---

[17] In my research material, there also appear idiolectal styles with final motifs that lack the *finalis* repetition (e.g. SKNA6593:1). In addition, among the material, one lamenter, Anastasia Fedorovna Nikiforova, uses a distinctive, individual final motif, which in a way goes around the *finalis* with *melisma* (e.g. Fon.108-I/6 and Fon.3127b).

Figure 2. A musical line of a principal phrase (M), descending phrase (m2), and arcing phrase (m3); dots and the asterisk below the stave mark emotion emblems (SKNA7592:3 JFS2, eighth line).

creates the feeling of an arcing phrase, but, in performance, the border of a phrase is clearly just after the ascent.

The overall musical outline of Olonets Karelian laments is comprised of parallel musical lines that resemble each other but differ in length and in their particular shapes; therefore, the musical lines are never identical. A composition of different types of musical phrases within a musical line can vary, while the number of phrases fluctuates from one to four per line. Two main styles of composing a musical line can be distinguished in the tradition; both are regional with idiolectal variation. In the simpler structure (e.g. KIM SKNA6593:1; PIK SKNA6595:2), a line is primarily comprised of descending phrases; in some cases, a line is only comprised of a principal phrase and several final-like motifs following it in series. In the simple line structure, a line mainly includes one or two phrases, occasionally three. The latter of the descending phrases within a line may clearly differ from those preceding it, as it does not begin from one of the few topmost notes of the scale and thus alludes to the approaching end of the musical line.

The line structure of the more complex style (e.g. JFS: SKNA7592:3, SKNA7593:1; Fon.2781a&b) ranges from single-phrased to four-phrased lines. In these laments, there are also arcing subordinate phrases (see Figure 2). The order of these different subordinated phrases is not consistent. Both descending and arcing phrases can follow the principal phrase and end a line. Yet, the arcing phrase is always in the ending position; a descending phrase never follows the arcing phrase within a line. In my material, the simpler, all-descending-phrased structure of a line is more common than the complex line.

The rhythmic appearance is rather smooth and the tempo constant. However, the flow of a lament tends to decelerate towards the end of a musical line and the final motif breaks the regular rhythm. At other junctures, namely the borders of musical phrases within a musical line, the sense of the beat continues. The change of the regular beat at the end of a line guides the separation of lines, together with the initial and final motifs.

4. Intertwined Textual and Musical Units

Laments as a genre of sung oral poetry without any regular, periodic pattern exhibit multilevel and intertwined relations of textual and musical structure that are united in performance. A consensus on the interaction of Karelian laments' textual and musical elements is that textual expression is primary and musical structures are mainly selected and organized in relation to the text, although there is some independence in musical forms (see e.g. Salmenhaara 1967 [1976]; Tolbert 1988:214–221; 1990:93–97; Saastamoinen 1999a; 1999b; Niemi 2002:712–722). Laments' textual and musical structures have different mechanisms for organizing units. These mechanisms act within structures of different scope, and the textual and musical structural units do not directly correspond to each other, which makes the interaction between them complex.

4.1. The musical-textual basic unit and the correspondence of different units

For the most part, a poetic line and a musical line correspond to each other. This unity can be understood as a basic musical-textual unit of Olonets Karelian laments. However, the patterning is not constant. In a single lament, there are usually more musical lines than poetic lines, which means that some poetic lines are divided into several musical ones. The borders of poetic lines and musical lines may co-occur, although borders of poetic lines meeting within a musical line is extremely rare. In cases when there are two musical lines vis-à-vis one poetic line, or vice versa, their borders always align with the borders of smaller-scale units. A new poetic line within a musical line aligns with the beginning of a musical phrase, and a border of musical lines within a poetic line aligns with a point in syntax that can be interpreted as a clause or some other syntactically or poetically distinguishable unit. The borders of inequivalent units predominantly appear in a later part of a lament. However, if the first poetic line of a lament is remarkably short, the first musical line may correspond to the first two poetic lines.

On a smaller scope, the borders of musical phrases do not divide minimal formulas or other collocations, but they may divide cluster formulas. For example, in *naižen kandajažen kai* /m2/ *kuldažed i kiälyäd* /m3/ *luuhužian lukkužien tuakse lukkoiltu* ('woman bearer.DIM's (*kai*) /m2/ golden.DIM.PL (*i*) tongue.DIM. PL /m3/ locked.FRE behind a bony.DIM.PL lock.DIM.PL'), or between parallel pairs *ennenkäymättömile dorogažile* /m3/ *toittšitulemattomile troppažile* ('to way. DIM.PL never-walked-before.PL /m3/ to path.DIM.PL with-no-return.PL').[18]

---

[18] Here 'm#' indicates the borders of musical phrases.

a vai näm- mik-se tu- len- tu- ker- da-žin on nai-žen kan- da- ja-žen pi- ha-žil kai ki- vi-žet kria-pos- ti-žet kir- vot-tu rau- da-žet pis- to-žed i lan- get-tu

Figure 3. An *anacrusis* (a) and a discourse marker on the border of musical phrases (SKNA7592:3 JFS2, in the third line).

The combination of musical phrases within a musical line and the composition of units of a poetic line do not have a discernible, regular correspondence. Similarly, the larger textual units (for example, macro-formulas) do not have equivalents in musical structure, since the largest distinguishable musical unit is a musical line.[19]

The interpretation of some musical and textual elements is ambiguous. For example, the ascending anacruses at the end of a musical phrase blur interpretation by fading the juncture of musical phrases (Figure 3). Similarly, the abstraction of linguistic discourse markers is occasionally vague, as they can be at the beginning or at the end of textual units. In some cases, these two appear together acting as mediators between consecutive units, and the exact abstraction is not possible, especially when appearing on the border of a musical-textual basic unit. This creates continuity and an impression of endlessness for the performance (Figure 3).

Some melodic sequences such as a musical phrase, a pair of phrases, or even an entire musical line recur with certain cluster formulas within idiolects. For instance, the cluster formula extending a poetic line in (2) recurs every time with a similar melodic contour comprised of a principal phrase followed by descending and arcing subordinate phrases (Figure 4). The variation within the musical composition is subtle; differences in the exact melodic figures, rhythm and melisma occur (SKNA7592:3 JFS2, 3 and 5).

(2)

> [opening particle] pidäy [PERSON] kaimailla /m2/ ennenkäymät-
> tömile dorogažile /m3/ toittšitulemattomile troppažile
> [opening particle], [PERSON] has to escort /m2/ onto way.DIM.PL
> never-walked-before.PL /m3/ to path.DIM.PL with-no-return.
> PL [i.e. bury]

---

[19] See Kallio's analysis (2017:esp. 344–347) of alignments and disalignments of melodic and semantic structures of parallelism in kalevalaic poetry, including the aligning of semantic units with two- or four-lined melodic structures.

Figure 4. Crystallized musical-textual unit (SKNA7592:3 JFS2, tenth line).

An interesting and similar instance of the crystallization of text and melody appears within a ritual lament for apologies (SKNA7592:3 JFS5), which thematically has an extremely repetitive pattern. In this lament, a cluster formula constituting an entire poetic line recurs almost identically in parallelism, although both open slots—the filler for to whom or what is apologized and the formula for the lamenter—vary, the former in both referent and length. Despite the fact that refrains do not appear in the Karelian lament tradition, the recurring stable elements at the conclusion of the cluster formula creates a refrain-like element (underlined):

(3)
>prostiatto [to whom/what] <u>prostiatto posl'iadnoit kerdazet k ei kelle</u>
>[lamenter] <u>vigasanažii virkelly(h) ei kelle kipakkoloi kiälyžii</u>
><u>d'iävitellyh / kielyžil i kirgailluh</u>
>apologies [for whom/what] <u>apologies last.pl time.dim.pl if to</u>
><u>someone [lamenter] said badly or said / yelled nastily</u>

The melodic pattern attached to the "refrain" is not stable but very similar across the entire section of the cluster formula's use in parallelism. Furthermore, the very beginning of the musical-textual unit is rather crystallized, as the opening word remains the same and the initial motif is stable. However, because the fillers of both open slots significantly vary in length, the composition of a musical-textual basic unit is variable.

4.2. Interaction of textual and musical structures

Text is a greater determinant than music in the composition of laments. However, the determining role of text is in interaction with music rather than unidirectionally driving it. For instance, poetic lines as compositional units are made more salient through accompanying musical features. The primary nature of the text is apparent on the level of the musical-textual basic unit: the textual content of a poetic line determines the length of a musical line (see also Tolbert 1990:93; Niemi 2002:711). The number of words within a poetic line can fluctuate greatly: the length of a line varies from approximately fifteen syllables up to more than sixty. The length of a musical line fluctuates from fewer than ten notes up to approximately fifty notes. The discontinuity of lengths is related to the inconsistency in the equivalence of musical lines and poetic lines, both of which vary across a performance.

Within the scope of more subtly distinguished units, the interaction is both text- and music-motivated. For example, the amount of repetition of the final note in final motifs depends on the text. In contrast, repetition at the beginning of initial motifs does not follow textual content. The rhythmic pattern of the overall expression is smooth and constant, and the length of the note is not tied to the length of the corresponding syllable: both short and long syllables can appear in a long note or be *melismatic* (with several short notes tied together by one syllable) (see also Tolbert 1990:93–97).[20]

The interaction of text and music may create an occasional feeling of poetic meter when a constant beat and the overall expression recur in a regular manner. For example, the expression within the theme of apologies in (3) (SKNA7592:3 JFS5) is generally regular and constant, and the lament engenders an impression of meter, but it is transient, fading away in the later part of the lament when the theme changes.

The performance style of lament is generally more song-like than speech-like, and mixed modes are also found. The style of performance affects the transmission of the text. In speech-like articulation, each word is articulated separately, while a sense of song-like performance is produced by *legato* articulation, in which notes are tied together rather smoothly. To increase flow and fluency, lamenters may add meaningless euphonic sounds—mainly /g/, /k/, /n/, and /i/—between words to bind sequential words together. In addition, melisma increases the song-like quality. Both legato articulation and melisma obscure verbal expression (see also Tolbert 1988:220; 1990:96–97).

Moreover, breathing naturally affects performance and the segmentation of both musical and textual units. In the material examined in this study, most lamenters composed textual and musical units to fit within a single breath,

---

[20] Unfortunately, I am not able to elaborate here on the more subtle interactions of linguistic and musical elements, such as rhythm (length of syllables and notes), stress (verbal and musical accentuation), etc. Yet, I want to observe that, even though laments are not organized by periodic meter, it is possible to find a phenomenon similar to the so-called *broken lines* of Finno-Karelian kalevalaic poetry (on which, see e.g. Frog and Stepanova 2011:201 and the works cited there), where metrical (musical) stress contrasts with lexical stress.

although exceptions exist. An additional indicator that breathing is not a primary determinant on unit length is that inhalations also occur in the middle of musical and poetic lines. Furthermore, inhalations within musical lines make the structure of both musical and poetic lines less clear by interrupting their beat and flow.

The structures and interaction of textual and musical forms seem to be different in ritual, context-bound and autobiographical sections of laments.[21] The length of musical phrases and poetic lines fluctuates throughout an entire lament, and the number of phrases within a line does not differ remarkably between a lament's different sections. However, in late autobiographical sections, phrases become shorter because of the increased intensity of emotion and the shortness of breath it causes. In addition, arcing phrases appear mostly in ritual, context-bound sections; in the autobiographical section of the example lament JFS2 (SKNA7592:3), there are only a few arcing phrases, and the last third of lines includes only descending phrases.

In a ritual, context-bound section, where contextually necessary themes constitute the text, the structures are generally rather consistent, and the musical lines and poetic lines form unified units. In an autobiographical section, where semantic content is more intimate and the focus is more on the lamenter's personal experiences and emotions, the structures and correspondence of textual and musical units become less regular. In this latter type of section, the display of affect becomes clearer, more audible, and more intense. Emotionality may appear during any phase of the musical-textual periods. However, the primary locus for displays of affect is at the end of a musical-textual basic unit, where the musical expression calms down and the flow of performance decelerates (see also Rüütel and Remmel 1980:179; Tolbert 1990; Niemi 2002:711–712). In general, the overall emotionality affects the expression, for example, by accenting syllables with strong exhalations and "swallowing" syllables pronounced while inhaling. Similarly, the complex interaction of text and music influence the emotionality of the performance.[22]

5. Conclusion

The present chapter has analyzed formulaic expression in relation to the structural organization and interrelation of textual and musical units in oral poetry of the Olonets Karelian lament tradition, which lacks a regular, periodic meter.

---

[21] The accessible material contains only one lament with both types of sections (SKNA7592:3 JFS2); thus, the data is not sufficient for generalizations on structural changes between these types of sections.

[22] On the emotionality of laments, see Silvonen and Stepanova 2020; Silvonen 2020.

The overall character of Karelian laments is flowing and continuous, which creates a feeling of endlessness. Only occasional, sudden bursts of affect interrupt the flow of performance.

The interaction of textual and musical units is multimodal. A musical line and a poetic line usually correspond to each other, and the length of this musical-textual unit is directed by the semantic and syntactic content of the text. However, the juxtaposition of musical lines and poetic lines is not constant and the borders of each may occur within the other, although in this case their borders will align with the borders of units of a smaller scope. Smaller units of text and music do not constitute similar continuous systems, yet the borders of these smaller musical and textual units are aligned with other borders. In general, the interrelation of musical and textual units varies constantly. However, occasionally, within an idiolect, a certain formulaic textual unit will recur with a corresponding musical unit. The formulaic expressions and the interaction of text and music are more stable within ritual, context-bound themes, and, especially, within laments attached to certain phases of a ritual, than within autobiographic themes.

The structure of text and music lacking a regular, periodic meter and the feeling of irregularity in the interaction between these make the overall structure ambiguous and unpredictable by nature. This, in turn, creates the continuity characteristic of an ongoing lament and an impression of endlessness in performance. Furthermore, the performative style influences textual content. The musical expression adds features that may hinder the interpretation of verbal expression. For example, use of euphonies and legato-like articulation complicate the separation of sequential words. In addition, audible emblems of emotion affect the structures and composition of a lament, also blurring the expression. On the levels of both text and music, varying degrees and modes of formulaicity mold the performative and affective power, ritual efficacy, and aesthetic finalization of the lament's tonal-textual improvisation.

References

Sources

Fon. — Archives of Institute of Language, Literature and History at Scientific Archives of Karelian Research Centre, ИЯЛИ КарНЦ РАН. Petrozavodsk, Karelia, Russia.

Fon.3127b/12, 18, 22, 29, 30. Five laments, Anastasia Fedorovna Nikiforova (b. unknown); recorded by V. J. Eliseev (В. Я.Елисеев) Vuohtjärvi, Karelia, Russia in 1940.

Fon.108-I/6. A lament, A. F. Nikiforova; recorded by V. J. Eliseev (В.Я.Елисеев) and T. I. Väisinen (Т. И.Вяйзинен) in Vuohtjärvi, Karelia, Russia in 1960.

Fon.2781a/1–3. Three funeral/commemorate laments, JFS8–10, Jeudokia Fedorovna Sofronova (b. 15.8.1908 Riipuškala); recorded by P. Laaksonen, E. Kiuru and T. V. Lukina in Olonets, Karelia, Russia in 1983.

Fon.2781b/16–17, 19. Three funeral/commemorate laments, JFS11–13, Jeudokia Fedorovna Sofronova (b. 15.8.1908 Riipuškala); recorded by P. Laaksonen, E. Kiuru and T. V. Lukina in Olonets, Karelia, Russia in 1983.

SKNA — The Tape Archive of the Finnish Language Institute for the Languages of Finland. Helsinki, Finland.

SKNA6593:1. Two laments, Klaudia Ivanovna Mihailova (b. 7.3.1910 Mägriä, Nekkula); recorded by P. Virtaranta in Mägriä, Karelia, Russia in 1966.

SKNA6595:2. Four wedding laments, PIK1–4, Polja Ivanovna Koroleva, (b. 1904 Kuittinen, Nekkula); recorded by P. Virtaranta in Mägriä, Karelia, Russia in 1966.

SKNA7592:3. Five funeral/commemorate laments, JFS1–5; recorded by P. Virtaranta in Riipuškala, Karelia, Russia in 1968. JFS2 available at https://journal.fi/elore/article/view/97359/58222 (in Silvonen 2020).

SKNA7593:1. Two funeral/commemorate laments, JFS6–7; recorded by P. Virtaranta in Riipuškala, Karelia, Russia in 1968.

Literature

Drabkin, W. 2001. "Motif." *Grove Music Online*. Available at: https://doi.org/10.1093/gmo/9781561592630.article.19221 (accessed April 2, 2018).

Feld, S., and Fox, A. A. 1994. "Music and Language." *Annual Review of Anthropology* 23:25–53.

Foley, J. M. 1991. *Immanent Art: From Structure to Meaning in Traditional Oral Epic*. Bloomington.

———. 1995. *The Singer of Tales in Performance*. Bloomington.

Foley, J. M., and Ramey, P. 2012. "Oral Theory and Medieval Studies." *Medieval Oral Literature* (ed. K. Reichl) 71–102. de Gruyter.

Frog. 2016. "Linguistic Multiforms in Kalevalaic Epic: Toward a Typology." *RMN Newsletter* 11:61–98.

———. 2017. "Formulaic Language and Linguistic Multiforms: Questions of Complexity and Variation." *Formula: Units of Speech—'Words' of Verbal Art: Working Papers of the Seminar-Workshop 17th–19th May 2017, Helsinki, Finland* (ed. Frog) 252–270. Helsinki.

Frog and Stepanova, E. 2011. "Alliteration in (Balto-)Finnic Languages." *Alliteration in Culture* (ed. J. Roper) 195–218. Basingstoke.

Gomon, A. 1976. "O muzïkal'nïkh osobennostyakh karel'skik prichitaniy." *Karel'skiye prichitaniya* (eds. A. Stepanova and T. Koski) 441–487. Petrozavodsk.

Harvilahti, L. 1992. *Kertovan runon keinot: Inkeriläisen runoepiikan tuottamisesta.* Helsinki.

Herndon, M. 1974. "Analysis: The Herding of Sacred Cows?" *Ethnomusicology* 18(2):219–262.

Honko, L. 1974. "Balto-Finnic Lament Poetry." *Finnish Folkloristics I* (eds. P. Leino with A. Kaivola-Bregenhøj and U. Vento) 9–61. Helsinki.

Kallio, K. 2013. *Laulamisen tapoja: Laulamisen tapoja: Esitysareena, rekisteri ja paikallinen laji länsi-inkeriläisessä kalevalamittaisessa runossa.* Tampere.

———. 2017. "Parallelism and Musical Structures in Ingrian and Karelian Oral Poetry." *Oral Tradition* 31(2):331–354.

Konkka, U. 1985. *Ikuinen ikävä: Karjalaiset riitti-itkut.* Helsinki.

Koponen, R., and Torikka, M., eds. 1999. *Ahavatuulien armoilla: Itkuvirsiä Aunuksesta.* Helsinki.

Kuiper, K. 2009. *Formulaic Genres.* Basingstoke.

Lord, A. 1960. *The Singer of Tales.* Cambridge, MA.

———. 1991. *Epic Singers and Oral Tradition.* Ithaca.

Nenola-Kallio, A. 1982. *Studies in Ingrian Laments.* Helsinki.

Niemi, J. 1998. *The Nenets Song: A Structural Analysis of Text and Melody.* Tampere.

———. 2002. "Musical Structures of Ingrian Laments." *Inkerin itkuvirret—Ingrian Laments* (ed. A. Nenola) 708–728. Helsinki.

———. 2015. "Description of Poetic Form as a Tool for Stylistic Analysis of a Traditional Song Performance: A Case of a Western Nenets Narrative Song." *RMN Newsletter* 11:17–32.

Parry, M. 1930. "Studies in the Epic Technique of Oral Verse-Making, I: Homer and Homeric Style." *Harvard Studies in Classical Philology* 41:73–147.

Rüütel, I., and Remmel, M. 1980. "Opït notatsii i issledovaniya vepskikh prichitaniy." *Finno-ugorskiy muzïkal'n'iy fol'klore i vzaimosvyazi s sosednimi kul'turami* (ed. I. Rüütel) 169–193. Tallinn.

Saastamoinen, I. 1999a. "Aunuksen itkut musiikkina." *Ahavatuulien armoilla: Itkuvirsiä Aunuksesta* (eds. R. Koponen and M. Torikka) 128–134. Helsinki.

———. 1999b. "Aunuksen itkut musiikkina: Katsaus Pertti Virtarannan kokoelmiin." *Musiikin suunta* 21(1999/3):35–44.

Salmenhaara, A. 1967. "Itkuvirsien musiikillisesta hahmotuksesta." *Paimensoittimista kisällilauluun: Tutkielmia kansanmusiikista 1* (eds. H. Laitinen and S. Westerholm 1976) 124–156. Alajärvi.

Silvonen, V. 2020. "Apeus välittyvänä, kuunneltuna ja koettuna. Affektiiviset kehät ja itkuvirsien tunteiden ilmeneminen arkistoäänitteillä." Elore 27(2), 62–90.

Silvonen, V., and Stepanova E. 2020. "Language, Music and Emotion in Lament Poetry: The Embodiment and Performativity of Emotions in Karelian Laments." In *The Routledge Handbook of Language and Emotion* (eds. S. Pritzker, J. Fenigsen, and J. Wilce) 203–222. London and New York.

Stepanova, A. 2012. *Karjalaisen itkuvirsikielen sanakirja.* Helsinki.

Stepanova, E. 2014. *Seesjäveläisten itkijöiden rekisterit: Tutkimus äänellä itkemisen käytänteistä, teemoista ja käsitteistä.* Helsinki.

———. 2015. "The Register of Karelian Laments." *Registers of Communication* (eds. A. Agha and Frog) 258–274. Helsinki.

———. 2017. "Parallelism in Karelian Laments." *Oral Tradition* 31(2):485–508.

Tarkiainen, V. 1943. "Itkuvirret." *Kansalliskirjallisuus III* (eds. H. Harmas and V. Tarkiainen) 521–532. Helsinki.

Tarkka, L. 2005. *Rajarahvaan laulu: Tutkimus Vuokkiniemen kalevalamittaisesta runokulttuurista 1821-1921.* Helsinki.

Tenhunen, A.-L. 2006. Itkuvirren kolme elämää. Helsinki.

Tolbert, E. 1988. *The Musical Means of Sorrow: The Karelian Lament Tradition.* Los Angeles.

———. 1990. "Women Cry with Words: Symbolization of Affect in the Karelian Lament." *Yearbook for Traditional Music* 22:80–105.

Urban, G. 1988. "Ritual Wailing in Amerindian Brazil." *American Anthropologist* 90(2):385–400.

Väisänen, A. O. 1940-1941. "Itkuvirsi karjalaisten kohtalosta." *Hiljainen haltioituminen: A. O. Väisäsen tutkielmia kansanmusiikista* (ed. E. Pekkilä 1990) 132-137. Helsinki. [First published in *Kalevalaseuran vuosikirja* 20–21.]

Wilce, J. M., and Fenigsen, J. 2015. "Mourning and Honor: Register in Karelian Lament." *Registers of Communication* (eds. A. Agha and Frog) 187–209. Helsinki.

Wray, A. 2002. *Formulaic Language and the Lexicon.* Cambridge.

17

Morozko

Russian Folktale Formulas in British Translations

TATIANA BOGRDANOVA, UNIVERSITY OF EASTERN FINLAND

THE FORMULAIC CHARACTER OF FOLKLORE has long been recognized as its typological universal feature (Pop 1968; Mal'tsev 1989:4). The research in the field, however, was chiefly devoted to the study of mnemotechnical mechanisms of oral traditions or to cataloguing formulas (Mal'tsev 1989:14–18, 28; cf. Nagler 1967:269–273)[1] so that the aesthetic aspect of the issue has rather been neglected (Mal'tsev 1989:2–5).[2] In his study of traditional formulas of Russian non-ritual songs, Georgii I. Mal'tsev argues that differentiation should be made between the formula as a distinct morphological type (ranging from a single word to a stereotypical situation)[3] and as a category that may be singled out on the basis of the aesthetics associated with various formulaic forms. It is in fact the aesthetic meanings that determine the recurrent and stereotypical char-

---

[1] In fact, the field of formulaic language is far more diverse, as has been indicated in the introductory chapter to this volume (Frog and Lamb, this volume).

[2] Earlier, Michael Nagler noted the absence of any coherent aesthetic theory that would help understand or appreciate the special nature of oral poetry as poetry (Nagler 1967:273). Commending his idea of "the real mental template" as underlying the production of formulas, Mal'tsev (1989:14), nevertheless, was left dissatisfied with Nagler's attempt at creating "a sound theory of the formula" to understand the beauty and meaning of the Homeric poems (Nagler 1967:274, 281).

[3] Here Mal'tsev's references are to German folklorists including A. Daur, G. Heilfurth, H. Peukert, and O. Holzapfel (Mal'tsev 1989:16–17); also, he singles out A. Wirth's morphological typology that includes stereotypical initial and final ballad formulas; binomial word-combinations; typical descriptive formulas associated with the themes of nature, feelings, and time; repetitions of numbers; as well as ballad characters, and their typical speeches (Wirth 1897; as cited in Mal'tsev 1989:28). Also, Lauri Honko emphasizes the paramount role of repeatable expressions (multiforms) in oral epic art, including descriptions of standard events (receiving guests, having a grand meal, sending a letter, etc.) that contain formulas, elaborated phrases, standard images, and minor episodic elements varying in length, degree of embellishment, and emphasis (Honko 2000:19).

acter of formulas, as well as give clues to understanding their position within a traditional canon. Thus, by way of disclosing particular aesthetic ideas associated with formulaic forms, one gets insights into the aesthetics of a given oral poetry (Mal'tsev 1989:33). For example, an experimental study of the style of Italian and Russian folktales shows a difference in their inherent aesthetic meanings: while beauty is of primary importance for Italian texts, in Russian folktales this is strength (power) (Uvarov 1973:5, cited in Mal'tsev 1989:44).

The aesthetics of formulas are the aesthetics of the general, of the typical, but they are also culture-specific, to be investigated for particular cases and poetic traditions. This is by no means an easy task, granted the "extreme complexity of codes that fund oral formulae and complexity of meanings generated or transferred by them," for example, in Serbian oral epics (Delić 2013:73). Even if identified, like ritual and ethical models or elements of social stratification, these are only the "tip of the iceberg," whose underwater massif ("hidden knowledge") is the traditional system as a whole (Mal'tsev 1989:44, 68–69; Delić 2013:73–75).[4]

But how much of this "hidden knowledge," or "the inexplicit but always implicit tradition" (Foley 1991:65), is actually rendered by translators who might or might not be folklorists themselves and who mostly deal with published texts?[5] To what extent may one expect an awareness of traditional contexts on their part, as well as an interest in conveying at least some of the aesthetics of oral-poetic traditions to their intended audiences?[6] What are the models that

---

[4]   Also, John M. Foley argues for a more faithful understanding of verbal art by attending to its "untextuality," i.e. "richly contexted array of meanings that can be communicated only through the special, 'dedicated' set of channels that constitute the multivalent experience of performance, or that can be accessed in diminished form through the augmented rhetoric of the dictated text." This means an appeal to "what lies beyond any collection of linguistic integers by insisting on the value-added signification of these integers as perceived by an audience suitably equipped to accord them their special valences" (1992:294).

[5]   Foley observes in relation to Vuk Karadžić's songs of the nineteenth century that, to the modern folklorist, these are precious but, still, only texts, "long severed from the performance tradition that gave them birth and meaning" (Foley 1991:61). Honko sees the "problematic" situation of folkloristics and printed oral poetry in terms of textualization in the fact that the discipline and its material are based on oral culture but bound to written texts, which are nevertheless "a necessary precondition for scholarly analysis on orality" (Honko 2000:3).
Here I am deeply indebted to William Lamb for drawing my attention to Foley's work, as well as for other helpful suggestions.

[6]   Of note are recent discussions of the issues related to the internationalization of oral material, i.e. examination of the range of means and devices by which an item of folklore is contextualized and recontextualized as relevant to or part of a national-level or international arena of discourse (Bauman 1993:248–250). Also, scholars in the field are more and more interested in "a full history of textualization for texts claiming orality or traditionality" (Honko 2000:3; cf. Foley 1991, 1992); translations are seen as a necessary part of these processes (Foley 2005:237). The developments are of relevance for scholars of translation studies involved in translating folklore

they follow and the strategies to which they adhere in elaborating on these texts, to add to their "literary value"?[7] These are just a few of the questions to bear in mind while focusing on the translators and translations of the Russian folktale in late nineteenth and early twentieth century.

The studies of the Russian *skazka* ('folktale'), with *skazkovedenie*('skazka studies'),[8] a special research area devoted to the genre and its formulas, may be quite advanced. Despite this, little attention has been given so far to the issue of translating folklore and folklore formulas along the lines outlined above.[9] To fill in the gap, this paper will focus on the strategies and techniques that the translators of the Russian folktale employed to render the largely strange culture and its folklore formulas within a historical scope. Due attention will be given to translated texts but also to the translators and their translation agendas (Bogrdanova 2013; 2016).

I begin with a brief introduction into the aesthetic world of Russian folktales and the approaches to the material found in the turn-of-the-twentieth-century British translations. These will be discussed in some detail, with three translated texts based on the story of *Morozko* ('Frost' or 'King Frost')[10] serving as the sources for illustrations. I will show how the translators' agendas as folklorists, editors of popular folklore collections, or authors, as well as the audiences for whom they intended their translations, were crucial in shaping their works. A contrastive analysis of the English texts in relation to one another against the background of the original folktale will be used as a helpful method in examining their distinct styles, but also for disclosing possible textual parallelisms of translations as refracted texts or rewritings.[11] This will offer a valuable insight

---

texts or theorizing about them, including an important publication of Maria Tymoczko (1995) and a more recent study of Jennifer Schacker (2003).

7   "If the oral text has any literary value, it will, after all, bloom, rather than wither, in writing. The medium itself is helpful in creating such value, even if the basic merit goes to the representative of oral verbal art, the singer" (Honko 2000:37).

8   See e.g. Propp 1946 [1998]; 1984b [2000]. Translations, if not otherwise attributed, are mine.

9   Those few publications that do contain attempts to discuss translation issues alongside lists of formulas or criticism of folklore translations largely seem to focus on the linguistic aspect of the issue (Kazakova 2003; Polubichenko and Egorova 2003).

10   A diminutive form of *moroz* ('frost').

11   According to André Lefevere, texts do not exist simply in their primary form; rather texts are surrounded by a great number of "refracted texts," i.e. texts that have been processed for certain audiences, e.g. children, or adapted to a certain poetics or a certain ideology (Lefevere 1982:13). He argues that for the general Anglo-American reader, for example, *Crime and Punishment* "is, and always will be, an amalgam" of translations, histories of Russian literature, articles in popular magazines, and theater productions (Lefevere 1982:13–14). Translation is thus understood as one form of refraction, a form of writing that is a rewriting.
Maria Tymoczko uses the discourse of retelling and rewriting as "a potent" framework for the discussion of the translation of a noncanonical or marginalized literature, such as early Irish works and traditionary tales. Translators, working with such material, face significant obstacles:

into the history of textualization and internationalization of the Russian folk-lore genre as well.

1. Formulas of the Russian Folktale

Of the great collections of Russian folktales published in the latter half of the nineteenth century and the first two decades of the twentieth, first and fore-most is that of Aleksandr N. Afanas'ev. It was first published in eight issues over the years 1855–1863 and subsequently in three volumes. With as many as 640 specimens of tales, it is still unsurpassed—at least in quantity (Sokolov 1950:386)—and serves as the main source for many translations as well.[12]

Vladimir Y. Propp, well known for his contribution to the study of folk-tale morphology, notes that it is the poetics—the style and composition of *skazka*—that makes it such a distinct genre of folklore (1984a:39). The Russian wonder tale is particularly characterized by the wealth of elaborate literary formulas: it has its own *locus communis* for every typical situation, action, and figure; being orally transmitted, they may be transformed to a degree but remain essentially the same and recognizable (Sokolov 1950:432, 489).[13] One of the first special studies devoted to the subject was that of Nikolae Roshiianu (based mostly on Rumanian folklore) whose classification of initial, medial, and closing formulas resulted from their functional analysis. While initial and closing formulas are readily distinguished by their definite positions and func-tions in the texts, medial formulas—associated with a variety of phenomena and functions—present a less clear case. Some medial formulas are used by story-tellers to attract and sustain the interest of their audience or to allow them to control their stories; others are helpful in describing folktale characters, their actions or the properties of magic objects; still others are dialogue-formulas (Roshiianu 1974:16, 91–110). A special group of medial formulas are singled out as magic because of their association with *zagovory* ('spells, incantations').[14]

---

they have to deal with issues related to material and social culture, including law, economics, history, as well as values, worldview, etc.; then, there are serious problems with the transfer-ence of literary features (genre, form, etc.), and issues of linguistic interface. For the receiving audience, the stories told by the translator are new: the more radically new they are, the more remote the source culture and literature are (1995:12–14; cf. Foley 1991; 1992; Honko 2000).

12 It was the main source for the translators under discussion in this paper.

13 Notably, Propp elaborated his theory and methodology on the basis of *volshebnye* ('wonder, magic, miraculous') tales (Propp 1928a [2001]:20; cf. Propp 1928b [1968]:19); these fairytales, best-known and most-loved in Russia, are basically oral stories about "a young man's, or less often a girl's, initial venture into the frightening adult world" (Haney 1999:8, 92–93).

14 Ryan (1999:168) notes that "some of the more elaborate Russian spells are indeed outstanding for their poetic imagery"; Propp (1946 [1998]:102–103) in his study of the historical roots of wonder tales shows that many of the motifs of such tales go back to a variety of social institutions; the

Their imagery is created by the use of imperative verbs, constant repetitions of words and expressions, diminutive forms, comparisons, rhyme, and rhythm. They associate with the sacral (magic) function of the word in folklore traditions (Roshiianu 1974:118–119). Irina A. Razumova has pointed out that, in fact, the associations between Russian folktales and spells are numerous: they go back to shared traditional ideas and especially to beliefs in the magic (material) property of the word (1991:91). Characteristic of formulas are also *skazovye stikhi* ('rhymes'), with their logical accentuation of rhyming words; these are mostly verbs, but nouns are also featured. Rhymes or rhythmic prose, alongside other euphonic devices such as assonance and alliteration, enhance the integrity, as well as the artistic effect, of formulas (Vedernikova 1975:65–66; Razumova 1991:22). But the poetics of wonder tales are not limited to traditional formulas; repetition and parallelism are equally important. Repetition serves to emphasize the meaning of this or that word in formulas, contributing to their rhythmic character and accentuating the symmetry in their sound pattern and structure: e.g. *skoro skazka skazyvaetsia, da ne skoro delo delaetsia* ('the tale is soon told but it does take time for something to be done'). There are many kinds of such formulas, including double—but usually triple—repetitions of episodes that may extend from separate words to substantial sections of texts, contributing to their fluent, sing-song character (Razumova 1991:36–53, 98).

As can be seen from this brief discussion of research in the field, formulas are understood to cover a wide variety of structural and linguistic phenomena. They are recycled from text to text, often in modified forms, and are associated with traditional aesthetic meanings to signal the implicit world of oral traditions.[15] Due to their repeated use in folklore texts, they may be relatively easy to identify. Their aesthetics, however, must be specially investigated for each particular case. For instance, in the Russian wonder tale and its translations suggested for discussion here, one may discover both initial and closing formulas, as well as medial ones, including those used for describing its eponymous character—Morozko. The types of repetitions typical of such tales include, for example, parallel episodes relating first to the stepdaughter and then to the stepmother's daughters as they encounter Morozko, who decides their destiny. These are based on dialogue-formulas, recalling the proximity of Russian wonder tales to archaic folklore forms or social institutions (Propp 1946 [1998]:21, 102).

---

most important of these is the initiation ritual; also, views of the afterlife and travels in the world of the dead play a prominent role in defining tale motifs. Thus, wonder tales are often made up of components that go back to the phenomena and ideas of early societies.

[15] Cf. Foley's view (1991:63, 65) of a formula as both a compositional and an aesthetic, meaning-bearing imperative: "as truly signifying features" formulas are to be carried over into a translation.

The tale may be of a familiar type of popular narrative, dealing with "the same expulsion of the stepdaughter and her return with gifts, the same sending of the real daughter and her punishment," representing, like the German tale "Frau Holle," the personification of winter (although in a male form). Importantly, however, in the Russian tradition it developed into a special type with its own variants thanks to its artistic vividness (Propp 1968:9). In fact, while the conflict between the stepmother and stepdaughter, in this and other stories of this type, is a more recent modification; the ideals of the Russian peasant of which the tale is illustrative are far more ancient. Yet, they remain as beautiful and compelling as ever (Propp 1984b [2000]:211).

Thus, a translator dealing with the material is to render both the letter of the poetic style and the spirit (aesthetics) associated with it. By doing so, Morozko, a Russian supernatural being who figures so dramatically in the tale, may become part of their reader's world. This objective can only be reached through the continuous effort of many translators of distinct styles and agendas who contribute to a corpus of refracted texts.

2. Translators of Russian Folktales

At the turn of the twentieth century, Russia was still a largely remote and strange country for general British audiences, when translators began retelling and rewriting Russian folktales for them. The country's rich folklore attracted both folklorists and authors in search of new, exotic material to package as consumer-oriented fairytales. William Ralston's *Russian Folk-Tales* (1873) was the most extensive collection of Russian tales in English before the mid-twentieth century (Ryan 2009:127–128).

In the nineteenth century, the British translators, editors, and tale collectors developed a number of strategies for rendering imported narrative traditions "readable, interpretable, entertaining and, most of all, relevant to the interests of their audience" (Schacker 2003:1–2). One of the key figures in this respect was Andrew Lang. While Ralston[16] made his name as an expert of Russian folklore and literature, and also as a translator of Russian folktales (Alekseev and Levin 1994), Lang is mostly remembered today as the editor of enormously popular *Colour Fairy Books*, which were published between 1889 and 1910 (Black 1988;

---

[16] Both Ralston (1828–1889) and Lang (1844–1912) belonged to the "great team of British folklorists" (Dorson 1968).The former was a founding member of The Folklore Society (London, 1878), its vice-president for some time, then a member of its Council for the rest of his life (Ryan 2009:123); Lang joined The Society on its formation and in 1889–1891 served as its President (Simpson and Roud 2003:60).

Sundmark 2004). International in character, the anthologies included Russian material as well.[17]

The translation agendas and activities of both folklorists are better understood against the contemporary folklore movement, especially in the light of the heated discussions within The Folklore Society. Notably, Ralston sided with those who were against polishing and adapting the material in popular folklore collections to please and entertain general readers. He translated the fifty-one stories of his book "as literally as possible" to produce an accurate, rather than idealized, portrait of the Russian storyteller (Ralston 1873:x–xi). Hence, his work was largely for the scholar interested in accurate recordings of folklore texts. Appreciated as "a serious scholarly exercise," it continues to be quoted as an authoritative source (Ryan 2009:127–128; Bogrdanova 2013).

Lang, on the other hand, was one of Ralston's leading opponents. Explaining his editing practice in the preface to *Orange Fairy Book*, he notes that the stories have been altered in many ways to make them suitable for children (Lang 1906:vi); Mrs. Lang "modified, where it seemed desirable, all the narratives" (Lang 1906:viii). Thus, Lang and his wife, who did most of the translations, saw to it that the tales were "steeped in the same linguistic and cultural mold"; they were to please and entertain rather than instruct their target audience (Sundmark 2004:2). With the British publishing industry expanding, and translation flourishing in children's fiction (Hale 2006:34; cf. Hines 2013:225), it seemed only appropriate that Lang's fairy books should appeal to the younger reader.

Ralston's informative and authoritative introduction into the Russian fairyland paved the way for subsequent publications, including Arthur Ransome's *Old Peter's Russian Tales* (1916). Ransome (1884–1967) was influenced by Ralston's work and left for Russia in 1913 to learn the language and write his own book of Russian tales. Fascinated by the new magic world, but dissatisfied with the way it was presented, Ransome decided that his book would not have anything to do with scholars; it would be for children, or anyone else, interested in fairytales (Ransome 1916 [1957]:vii–viii). Importantly, even if he largely subscribed to Lang's ideologies and method of fairytale adaptation, Ransome was well aware of his duty as a cultural mediator between the two worlds. Hence, he was as discriminating as possible in rendering the poetics of the Russian folktale (Bogrdanova 2016).

---

[17] Two of Ralston's translations ("Koshchei the Deathless" and "The Norka") were borrowed almost verbatim in the *Red Fairy Book* (1890) with due references to the source, but a number of other Russian tales in the anthologies are either not attributed at all or left with a short comment: "from Russian"; in fact, there is "considerable inconsistency in Lang's citation style and the spelling of source titles" (Hines 2013:268).

Having introduced the translators in question and their agendas, let us now turn to their texts. We shall examine how their ideologies and sense of aesthetics informed their translation practices; how they reshaped the original folktales to become English fairytales.[18] Additionally, we shall present textual parallels of their rewritings to show some continuities in the history of Russian folktale textualization.

3. Morozko in Ralston's Folklore Collection and Lang's *Fairy Book*

Ralston focused upon Russian wonder tales. Of the numerous stories of this class, he chose examples that highlighted, first and foremost, "mythical beings."[19] These are supernatural figures, "peculiar to Slavonic fairy-land," such as the Snake, Koshchei the Deathless, and the Morskoi Tsar or King of the Waters, on the one hand, and Baba Yaga (or Hag), her close connection the Witch, and the Female Snake, on the other (Ralston 1973:62–65).[20] Morozko belongs to this group of key folklore characters as well.[21]

Ralston singles out the Russian tale for its "striking personification of Frost." In his words, "the jealous hatred of a stepmother, who exposes her stepdaughter to some great peril," has a special importance, as well as poetical charm in these tales. This is thanks to "the introduction of Frost as the power to which the stepmother has recourse for the furtherance of her murderous plans, and by which she, in the persons of her own daughters, is ultimately punished" (Ralston 1873:214, 223; cf. Propp above). In the way he handles mythical beings, both in his straightforward, literal translations and his detailed notes, Ralston demonstrates perceptive insights into Russian folklore.

To illustrate his approach and translation practice in some detail, let us examine his version of "Morozko" against the original story and other rewritings. First, we will contrast it with the version contained in Lang's *Yellow Fairy Book* (1894:209–212) and, then, with Ransome's text. Of the two original variants, Ralston chose to give a complete translation of tale no. 95 (Afanas'ev 1855–1863

---

[18] For more detail see France (1995) and Bogrdanova (2016).

[19] Notably, three (out of six) chapters of his book deal with "mythological" stories (Ralston's term for wonder tales).

[20] They are discussed in detail in Ralston's scholarly commentaries and notes and illustrated in translations of the tales made in full, as well as in short retellings of tale variants; importantly, this indicates the British folklorist's insight into "some fundamental ethnopoetic continuities among narratives of the same tradition" (Foley 1991:64).

[21] Propp points out that "When one speaks of a tale, he first recalls, of course, Baba Yaga and her hut, many-headed dragons, Prince Ivan and the beautiful princess, magical flying horses, and many other things" (Propp 1968:87).

[1984]:113–115) and a short retelling of no. 96 (Afanas'ev 1855–1863 [1984]:116–117), which features a clairvoyant dog (Ralston 1873:214–220, 221). The latter appears as "The Story of King Frost" in Lang's anthology.[22]

It may be somewhat surprising that Frost, as a mighty supernatural being, is first introduced in the Russian story as a "wooer of maidens" (Ralston 1873:xiii):[23]

(1)

> А старуха меж тем подала в блюде старых щей и сказала: "Ну, голубка, ешь да убирайся, я вдоволь на тебя нагляделась! Старик, увези Марфутку к жениху; да мотри, старый хрыч, поезжай прямой дорогой, а там сверни с дороги-то направо, на бор, — знаешь, прямо к той большой сосне, что на пригорке стоит, и тут отдай Марфутку за Морозка." Старик вытаращил глаза, разинул рот и перестал хлебать, а девка завыла. "Ну, что тут нюни-то распустила! Ведь жених-то красавец и богач! Мотри-ка, сколько у него добра: все елки, мянды и березы в пуху; житье-то завидное, да и сам он богатырь!"

> Afanas'ev 1855–1863 [1984]:113–114, no. 95

> Meantime his wife served up a dish of old cabbage soup, and said: "There, my pigeon eat and be off; I've looked at you quite enough! Drive Marfa to her bridegroom, old man. And look here, old greybeard! drive straight along the road at first, and then turn off from the road to the right, you know, into the forest—right up to the big pine that stands on the hill, and there hand Marfa over to Morozko (Frost)." The old man opened his eyes wide, also his mouth, and stopped eating, and the girl began lamenting. "Now then, what are you hanging your chaps and squealing about?" said her stepmother. "Surely your bridegroom is a beauty, and he's that rich! Why, just see what a lot of things belong to him, the firs, the pine-tops, and the birches, all in their robes of down—ways and means that any one might envy; and he himself a *bogatir!*"

> Ralston 1873:216

[22] Its comparison with Afanas'ev's folktale (no. 96) leaves no doubt about its provenance, while the information about the source and the translator is absent.

[23] This is in fact one of the "attributes" of this tale character; attributes are the external qualities of the characters: their age, sex, status, external appearance, peculiarities of this appearance, and so forth that provide the tale with its "brilliance, charm, and beauty" (Propp 1968:87).

As one may notice, the English text is almost a literal translation of the Russian original, but the translation is rather more literary than the original's colloquial style: cf. e.g. diminutive and derogative *Marfutka* and stylistically neutral "Marfa" or jocular, but also derogative *staryy khrych* ('old git') translated as "old greybeard." The great pains that the translator takes to render every nuance of the original may produce somewhat verbose translations: cf. e.g. *skol'ko u nego dobra* ('how much good (stuff) he has') vs. "what a lot of things belong to him"; *v puchu* ('in down') vs. "all in their robes of down" or *zhit'e-to zavidnoe* ('enviable living') vs. "ways and means that anyone might envy." The connotations inherent in the Russian verbs nevertheless remain stubbornly elusive: e.g. *vytarashchil, razinul* ('stared, wide-eyed') vs. "opened his eyes wide, also his mouth, and stopped eating." Transliterations that appear in Ralston's text, like in this passage, remind the reader of its original: Frost is introduced as Morozko, though the English equivalent is used in the title and throughout the text; also, *bogatir* ('strongman, warrior') is explained in a note by Ralston as the regular term for a Russian "hero of romance" (1873:216).[24]

While nothing is said of the other, deathly aspect of the bridegroom (the wicked stepmother singing only praises to Morozko), the reaction of the poor stepdaughter and her father to the news is nevertheless quite telling: both immediately realize the evil intentions of the stepmother. Of note in this respect is the lexical item *treskuchiy moroz* ('crackling frost') in a short sentence of the original story, depicting the winter weather outside: *A delo-to bylo zimoyu, i na dvore stoyal treskuchiy moroz* (Afanas'ev 1855–1863 [1984]:113, no. 95), "Now it was winter time, and out of doors was a rattling frost" (Ralston 1873:216). Its slightly modified form *treskun-moroz* ('crackle-frost') is used in the other, shorter, variant of the Russian story, where the theme of cutting frost and death associated with it is introduced immediately:

(2)

И придумала мачеха падчерицу со двора согнать: "Вези, вези, старик, ее куда хочешь, чтобы мои глаза ее не видали, чтобы мои уши об ней не слыхали; да не вози к родным в теплую хату, а во чистó поле на трескун-мороз!" Старик затужил, заплакал; однако посадил дочку на сани, хотел прикрыть попонкой —и то побоялся; повез бездомную во чистó поле, свалил на сугроб, перекрестил, а сам поскорее домой, чтоб глаза не видали дочерниной смерти.

Afanas'ev 1855–1863 [1984]:116, no. 96

---

[24] Ralston found it important for the reader to know the key word of Russian "epic poems," the folklore genre he was so interested in as to plan a separate volume on them (Ralston 1873:x).

The wicked shrew was determined to get rid of the girl by fair means or foul, and kept saying to her father: "Send her away, old man; send her away anywhere so that my eyes shan't be plagued any longer by the sight of her, or my ears tormented by the sound of her voice. Send her out into the fields, and let the cutting frost do for her." In vain did the poor old father weep and implore her pity; she was firm, and he dared not gainsay her. So he placed his daughter in a sledge, not even daring to give her a horse-cloth to keep herself warm with, and drove her out on to the bare, open fields, where he kissed her and left her, driving home as fast as he could, that he might not witness her miserable death.

Lang 1894:209

Translated variants of the Russian idiom *treskuchiy moroz* or *treskun-moroz* as "a rattling frost" (a winter day so cold that frozen trees rattle) and "cutting frost"(one is benumbed, frozen to the marrow, with frost cutting and piecing through) may be slightly foreignizing but quite effective in emphasizing the implications of the original items. These are crucial in understanding the deathly might of Russian Frost, so perceptively understood and rendered by both translators. The example illustrates that the translation in Lang's anthology is also as accurate as possible, striving to render the original meaning and also the inherent connotation, e.g. "to get rid of the girl by *fair means or foul*," "send her away anywhere so that my eyes shan't be *plagued* any longer by the sight of her, or my ears *tormented* by the sound of her voice," etc. (emphasis added).

Of importance for understanding the character of Morozko in all his might and glory (hence the aesthetics of the formula) is the central episode of the tale. In his encounter with the poor stepdaughter, Morozko demonstrates his power and nearly chills her to death, but in the end, the "wise" words of the girl help to reveal the benevolent side of his nature. A happy ending follows:

(3)

Девушка сидит да дрожит; озноб ее пробрал. Хотела она выть, да сил не было: одни зубы только постукивают. Вдруг слышит: невдалеке Морозко на елке потрескивает, с елки на елку поскакивает да пощелкивает. Очутился он и на той сосне, под коёй дéвица сидит, и сверху ей говорит: "Тепло ли те, дéвица?"—"Тепло, тепло, батюшко-Морозушко!" Морозко стал ниже спускаться, больше потрескивать и пощелкивать. Мороз спросил дéвицу: "Тепло ли те, дéвица? Тепло ли те, красная?"Дéвица чуть дух переводит, но еще говорит: "Тепло, Морозушко! Тепло, батюшко!" Мороз пуще затрещал и сильнее защёлкал и дéвице сказал: "Тепло ли те, дéвица? Тепло ли те, красная? Тепло ли те, лапушка?"Дéвица окостеневала и чуть слышно сказала: "Ой, тепло, голубчик Морозушко!" Тут Морозко сжалился, окутал дéвицу шубами и отогрел одеялами.

Afanas'ev 1855–1863 [1984]:114, no. 95

The girl sat and shivered. The cold had pierced her through. She would fain have cried aloud, but she had not strength enough; only her teeth chattered. Suddenly she heard a sound. Not far off, Frost was cracking away on a fir. From fir to fir was he leaping, and snapping his fingers. Presently he appeared on that very pine under which the maiden was sitting, and from above her head he cried: "Art thou warm, maiden?" "Warm, warm am I, dear Father Frost," she replied. Frost began to descend lower, all the more cracking and snapping his fingers. To the maiden said Frost: "Art thou warm, maiden? Art thou warm, fair one?" The girl could scarcely draw her breath, but still she replied: "Warm am I, Frost dear; warm am I, father dear!" Frost began cracking more than ever, and more loudly did he snap his fingers, and to the maiden he said: "Art thou warm, maiden? Art thou warm, pretty one? Art thou warm, my darling?" The girl was by this time numb with cold, and she could scarcely make herself heard as she replied: "Oh! quite warm, Frost dearest!" Then Frost took pity on the girl, wrapped her up in furs, and warmed her with blankets.

Ralston 1873:217

The formulaic character of the dialogue is apparent: three times Morozko addresses the girl with the same question and three times gets the same answer, which he finds so satisfying that not only does he spare her life but showers her with riches too. Thus, her "wisdom"—her knowledge of the right word (prayer, address, formula)—allows her to pacify even such a mighty force of nature as Frost himself (Eleonskaya 1994:69–78; Lutovinova 2009:115).[25] Appropriately, the lexical archaisms and syntactic inversions of the translated dialogue-formulas emphasize the magic, spell-like character of the original. The diminutive forms

---

[25] Notably, Ralston elucidates the sacred character of this important mythological personage in his commentary to the Russian tale: "To the Russian peasants [...] Moroz, our own Jack Frost, is a living personage. On Christmas Eve it is customary for the oldest man in each family to take a spoonful of kissel, a sort of pudding, and then, having put his head through the window, to cry: 'Frost, Frost, come and eat kissel! Frost, Frost, do not kill our oats! drive our flax and hemp deep into the ground'" (Ralston 1873:221–222).

of address, so conspicuous in Russian folklore,[26] are conveyed with the help of English etiquette formulas slightly adapted for the purpose: *dear Father Frost, father dear,* and *Frost dearest.*[27]

In our examination of how the Russian character Morozko is reflected in the two portrayals of his English counterpart, Frost, of obvious relevance is the rendering of the parallel episode in Lang's fairy book (no. 96):[28]

(4)

> Deserted by her father, the poor girl sat down under a fir-tree at the edge of the forest and began to weep silently. Suddenly she heard a faint sound: it was King Frost springing from tree to tree, and cracking his fingers as he went. At length he reached the fir-tree beneath which she was sitting, and with a crisp crackling sound he alighted beside her, and looked at her lovely face.
>
> "Well, maiden," he snapped out, "do you know who I am." "I am King Frost, king of the red-noses."
>
> "All hail to you, great King!" answered the girl, in a gentle, trembling voice. "Have you come to take me?" "Are you warm, maiden?" he replied. "Quite warm, King Frost," she answered, though she shivered as she spoke. Then King Frost stooped down, and bent over the girl, and the crackling sound grew louder, and the air seemed to be full of knives and darts; and again he asked: "Maiden, are you warm? Are you warm, you beautiful girl?" And though her breath was almost frozen on her lips, she whispered gently, "Quite warm, King Frost." Then King Frost gnashed his teeth, and cracked his fingers, and his eyes sparkled, and the crackling, crisp sound was louder than ever, and for the last time he asked her: "Maiden, are you still warm? Are you still warm, little love?" And the poor girl was so stiff and numb that she could just gasp, "Still warm, King!" Now her gentle, courteous words and her uncomplaining ways touched King Frost, and he had pity on her, and he wrapped her up in furs, and covered her with blankets, and he fetched a great box,

---

[26] Diminutives are a characteristic feature of the Russian *plach* ('lament'), contributing to their highly emotional-expressive-evaluative character; while the quality of diminutiveness may be seen as a psycholinguistic phenomenon characteristic of the Russian lamentation tradition (Reznitchenko and Reznitchenko 2009:204).

[27] Clearly, Russian diminutives are an issue in English translations of Russian literature (see e.g. Menkova 2010).

[28] The original episode is left out because it is similar in many ways to the one described above (example 3).

in which were beautiful jewels and a rich robe embroidered in gold and silver. And she put it on, and looked more lovely than ever, and King Frost stepped with her into his sledge, with six white horses.

Lang 1894:209–210

This dialogue looks very familiar, because the episodes in the two original tales largely coincide, but also because Lang's translator tends to disregard the differences between the Russian tales and follows Ralston's rendering of the passage (see example (3) above). Yet, if one takes the formulas of the folklore tradition into full consideration, the distinctions, however slight, are of significance. The translator opts for something more neutral in the opening sentence of the original, leaving out the important information that indicates, again, the magic nature of the dialogue-formula: *Ostalas' bednen'kaya, tryasetsya i tikhon'ko molitvu tvorit* (Afanas'ev 1855–1863 [1984]:116,no. 96), "trembling and silently offering up a prayer" (Ralston 1873:221). Similarly, when Frost introduces himself, the girl's answer is omitted: *"Devushka, devushka, ya Moroz krasnyy nos!"—"Dobro pozhalovat', Moroz; znat', bog tebya prines po moyu dushu greshnuyu"*(Afanas'ev 1855–1863 [1984]:116,no. 96), "'Maiden, maiden, I am Frost the Red-Nosed' [...]—'Welcome, Frost; doubtless God has sent you for my sinful soul'" (Ralston 1873:221). Conversely, in his short retelling, Ralston renders the lines accurately; his literal "Frost the Red-Nosed" is more appropriate for the original cliché *Moroz krasnyy nos* ('Moroz, red nose'). This is an important attribute of Morozko and requires accurate translation.

The description of the courteous stepdaughter showered with presents is amplified by Lang's anonymous translator—compared to Ralston's short retelling—with direct quotations from the original:

(5)

> Pleased by her "wise words," Frost throws a warm cloak over her, and afterwards presents her with "robes embroidered with silver and gold, and a chest containing rich dowry." The girl puts on the robes, and appears "such a beauty!" Then she sits on the chest and sings songs.

Ralston 1873:221

Absent from example (4) are Ralston's archaisms (cf. example (3)), while the wintry aspect of Morozko is emphasized, especially through the sound effects of *rattling frost*. Also, the translator strives to render the rhythm of the original by rhyming verbal forms and sounds. This is especially effective in the repeated items concerning the lively and merry Russian magic deity.[29] Due attention is given to appellatives too: *King Frost* or *King*; *maiden, you beautiful girl*, and *little love*.

Parallelism between the two translations is especially obvious in the next important episode, as Morozko encounters the wicked stepmother's daughters. Depicted in much detail in variant no. 95, it is accurately rendered by Ralston. The dialogue with Morozko—who will decide their dreadful fate—is preceded with a protracted episode, where the girls are sent to wait for the bridegroom's presents under the same pine tree, and they spend the time quarreling (see also Ransome below). For their disrespect and rudeness to Morozko, they must suffer a severe punishment. Variant no. 96, in contrast, is much shorter and presents no such details.[30] However, the story as it appears in Lang's fairy book borrows from the parallel episode (examples (3) and (4) above), thus following the other Russian variant and Ralston's translation. For example, one can see in the following lines how the original text (6a) is amplified in Lang's variant of the story (6b):

(6a)

Пришел и Мороз красный нос, поглядел на свою гостью, попрыгал-поскакал, а хороших речей не дождал; рассердился, хватил ее и убил.

Afanas'ev 1855–1863 [1984]:116

Moroz red-nose arrived, looked at his guest, jumped and leaped around her, but no good speeches followed to please him; [he] lost his temper and struck her dead.

(6b)

In a few minutes King Frost came past, and, looking at the girl, he said: "Are you warm, maiden?" "What a blind old fool you must be to ask such a question!" she answered angrily. "Can't you see that my hands and feet are nearly frozen?" Then King Frost sprang to and fro in front

---

[29] *Prikhodit Moroz, poprygivaet-poskakivaet, na krasnuyu devushku poglyadyvaet* ('Moroz arrives, leaping and jumping and throwing glances at the lovely maiden') (Afanas'ev 1855–1863 [1984]:116, no. 96, emphasis added).

[30] Also, in tale no. 96, the stepmother has only one daughter of her own.

of her, questioning her, and getting only rude, rough words in reply, till at last he got very angry, and cracked his fingers, and gnashed his teeth, and froze her to death.

Lang 1894:212

Finally, of interest, in terms of juxtaposition of the two distinct translation styles, is the rendering of an episode with a dog foretelling a happy ending for the old man's daughter, but death for the old woman's (variant no. 96):

(7)

Just as the old man was leaving the house the little dog under the table began to bark, saying: "Your daughter shall live to be your delight; Her daughter shall die this very night." "Hold your tongue, you foolish beast!" scolded the woman. "There's a pancake for you, but you must say: 'Her daughter shall have much silver and gold; His daughter is frozen quite stiff and cold.'" But the doggie ate up the pancake and barked, saying: "His daughter shall wear a crown on her head: Her daughter shall die unwooed, unwed." Then the old woman tried to coax the doggie with more pancakes and to terrify it with blows, but he barked on, always repeating the same words.

Lang 1894:210

The translations of the dog's words illustrate the translators' different approaches to the material, in general. In contrast to Lang's translation, stressing the artistic effect of the original with the resources of the translating language, Ralston sticks to his literal strategy. Unfortunately, he dispenses with the elaborate original formulas, with verbs accentuated and rhymed to enhance the meaning and to produce the artistic effect: *Tyav, tyav! Starikovu doch' v zlate, v sérebre vezut, a starukhinu zhenikhi ne berut!* (Afanas'ev 1855–1863 [1984]:116, no. 96), "Taff! Taff! The master's daughter in silver and gold by the wedding party is borne along, but the mistress's daughter is wooed by none!" (Ralston 1873:221).

So far, we have discussed the divergent depictions of Morozko in the original tales, as a singular supernatural being, and his English counterpart {King} Frost. Informed by the scholar's agenda, Ralston introduced this character and associated key formulas in an accurate and detailed translation of a variant of the tale. He accompanied it with thorough commentary on its relationship to similar personages (and formulas) in Russian wonder tales and peasant beliefs associated with the stories. Like other tales in his collection, Ralston's rewriting of the original tale gave an accurate account of the corresponding tradition; it serves not only as a reliable source for specialists, but also as a model for subsequent translations. "King Frost" in Lang's fairy book owes much to Ralston's "Frost" in terms of inspiration, but also for the necessary background to understand and interpret key formulas of the Russian magical world. In fact, Lang's anonymous translator goes as far as to mix the two variants of the Russian tale, when borrowing from Ralston. But what makes the style of this translation distinct is the translator's conscious effort to render the repetitions and sound effects of the original, sometimes with additional detail and a level of improvisation.

As will be shown in the following section, Ransome succeeded in realizing his ambitions to bring the Russian folktale to English-speaking readers; his *Old Peter's Russian Tales*, including "Frost," have attained classic status today (Brogan 1984:110–111).

4. Morozko in Ransome's Retelling for Children

Conveniently enough for the present discussion, and probably not accidentally, Ransome (1916 [1957]:43–57) was also attracted by the singular personage of Morozko. Like Ralston, of the two variants of Afanas'ev's texts, he chooses variant no. 95, which appears under the same title as Ralston's.[31]

Interestingly, Ransome was well aware of the importance of mediating the strange culture and its folklore characters to his reader, and he added four chapters of his own. These are frame stories that introduce the reader into the world of the Russian peasant, along with explanations and elucidations that often appear in the texts of tales. For example, "Frost" begins with a short description of a Russian winter day, the storyteller and his audience (i.e. old Peter and his grandchildren). This is an appropriate and helpful introduction. It focuses upon the brutal cold of the Russian winter, the clothes required to withstand it, and the sensoria of a frozen landscape:

(8)

> The children, in their *little sheepskin coats* and *high felt boots* and *fur hats*, trudged along the forest path in the snow. Vanya went first, then Maroosia, and then old Peter. The ground was *white* and *the snow was hard and crisp*, and all over the forest could be heard the *crackling of*

[31] In other cases, though, he preferred, as well as Lang, to give his own titles to the stories in his collection (e.g. "The Fool of the World and the Flying Ship" for "Letuchii korabl'"; "Little Master Misery" for "Gore"; "Prince Ivan, the Witch Baby and the Little Daughter of the Sun" for "Ved'ma i solntseva sestra"; etc.).

the frost. And as they walked, old Peter told them the story of the old woman who wanted Frost to marry her daughters.

Ransome 1916 [1957]:43, emphasis added

In his retelling, Ransome follows the plotline closely, but adds detail and color. This imbues his story with additional nuance, in contrast to Ralston's straightforward version, as is apparent when comparing their translations. For example, consider the episode of the old man and his daughter leaving for the forest: "Early in the morning, between daybreak and sunrise, the old man harnessed the mare to the sledge, and led it up to the steps" (Ralston 1873:216). Ransome's translation of the same lines at first did not differ much: "The old man harnessed the mare to the sledge and brought it to the door," but then he adds detail absent from the original and from Ralston's text: "The snow was very deep and frozen hard, and the wind peeled the skin from his ears before he covered them with the flaps of his fur hat" (Ransome 1916 [1957]:46–47).

In preparing the reader for the events that follow, the theme of frost and cold is repeated and further elaborated by Ransome (9b), which becomes evident when compared with Ralston's text (9a):

(9a)

> After a time, he reached the forest, turned off from the road; and drove across the frozen snow. When he got into the depths of the forest, he stopped, made his daughter get out, laid her basket under the tall pine, and said: "Sit here, and await the bridegroom. And mind you receive him as pleasantly as you can." Then he turned his horse round and drove off homewards.
>
> Ralston 1873:216–217

(9b)

> The road was long and the country open, and *the wind grew colder and colder, while the frozen snow blew up from under the hoofs of the mare and spattered the sledge with white patches. The tale is soon told, but it takes time to happen, and the sledge was white all over* long before they turned off into the forest. They came in the end deep into the forest, and left the road, and over *the deep snow* through the trees to the great fir. There the old man stopped, told his daughter to get out of the sledge, set her little box under the fir, and said, "Wait here for your bridegroom, and when he comes be sure to receive him with kind words." Then he turned the

mare round and drove home, with *the tears running from his eyes and freezing on his cheeks before they had had time to reach his beard.*

Ransome 1916 [1957]:48, emphasis added

Ransome, as one can see, is very detailed in his description of the Russian winter weather, which he knew first hand and which obviously impressed him. His readers might not have had direct knowledge of the Russian frost, so he conveys it to them in rich description. The portrayal of the old man in the English text—absent in the laconic original—stresses the emotionality of the story, and helps young readers relate to the character. Duly rendered by Ransome is the formula absent in Ralston's otherwise literal translation: *Dolgo li ekhal, skoro li priekhal—ne vedayu: skoro skazka skazyvaetsya, neskoro delo delaetsya* (Afanas'ev 1855–1863 [1984]:114, no. 95) ('Whether the road was long or short is not known: the tale is soon told but it takes time for something to be done').

The description of Morozko's deathly aspect, for which Ransome's reader is now sufficiently prepared, is effectively rendered in the episode dealing with the daughters of the wicked old woman (cf. examples (3) and (4) above):

(10)

> The girls heard that some one was coming through the forest. "Listen! there's some one coming. Yes, and with bells on his sledge!" "Shut up, you slut! I can't hear, and *the frost is taking the skin off me.*" They began *blowing on their fingers.*
>
> And *Frost came nearer and nearer, crackling, laughing, talking to himself, just as he is doing to-day.* Nearer and nearer he came, leaping from tree-top to tree-top, till at last he leapt into the great fir under which the two girls were sitting and quarrelling. He leant down, looking through the branches, and asked, —"Are you warm, maidens? Are you warm, little red cheeks? Are you warm, little pigeons?" "Ugh, Frost, *the cold is hurting us. We are frozen.* We are waiting for our bridegrooms, but the cursed fellows have not turned up."
>
> Frost came a little lower in the tree, and crackled louder and swifter. "Are you warm, maidens? Are you warm, my little red cheeks?" "Go to the devil!" they cried out. "Are you blind? Our *hands and feet are frozen!*"
>
> Frost came still lower in the branches, and *cracked and crackled louder than ever.* "Are you warm, maidens?" he asked. "Into the pit with you, with all the fiends," the girls screamed at him, "you ugly, wretched

fellow!" [...] And as they were cursing at him their bad words *died* on their lips, for the two girls, the cross children of the cruel stepmother, were *frozen stiff* where they sat.

Ransome 1916 [1957]:53–54, emphasis added

One may notice in this translation that, except for one instance, Ransome follows the original that emphasizes Frost's sinister aspect, rendered literally by Ralston too: cf. "my skin is peeling with cold" (*menya moroz obdirayet*); "it's awfully cold!"(*bol'no studono*); "we're utterly perished" (*My zamerzli*); "cracked away more, snapped his fingers oftener than before"(*pushche potreskivat' i chashche poshchelkivat'*); "our hands and feet are quite dead" (*u nas ruki i nogi otmerzli*); "became lifeless forms"(*i devushki okosteneli*) (Ralston 1873:219–220; Afanas'ev 1855–1863 [1984]:115,no. 95).

Obviously, there are commonalities between the translations, in particular in their portrayals of Frost. Ralston introduces his Morozko "cracking, snapping his fingers, and leaping from fir to fir" (1873:217). Lang's translator adds detail and color: "King Frost sprang to and fro [...] cracked his fingers, and gnashed his teeth, and froze her to death" (Lang 1894:212). Ransome, perhaps inspired by the latter, is even more effective in creating an impressive image of the formidable character:

(11)

Frost hung from the lowest branches of the tree, swaying and crackling while he looked at the anger frozen on their faces. Then he climbed swiftly up again, and crackling and cracking, chuckling to himself, he went off, leaping from fir tree to fir tree, this way and that through the white, frozen forest.

Ransome 1916 [1957]:54

In striving for this artistic effect, Ransome seems to have picked up the few leads that were left by Lang's anonymous translator, such as the impressive ending of "The Story of King Frost": "At that moment the door flew open, and she rushed out to meet her daughter, and as she took her frozen body in her arms she too was chilled to death" (Lang 1894:212). But he can also be quite literal and straightforward (with a foreignizing effect), for example, in the way he renders Russian formulas of address, as in the passage above: "Are you warm, little red cheeks? Are you warm, little pigeons?" (Ransome 1916 [1957]:53); cf. *Teplo li vam, krasnyye? Teplo li, moi golubushki?* ('Are ye warm, pretty ones? Are ye warm, my darlings?') (Afanas'ev 1855–1863 [1984]:115,no. 95; Ralston 1873:219).

In fact, his diligent translations of Russian appellatives—e.g. "little Father Frost" for *batyushko Morozushko* or "little paws" for *lapushka*—invited some criticism (Kazakova 2003:288). What is important is that the translator evokes the role of such formulas in Russian tales, even if he is not quite convincing. These instances of literalness in his otherwise fluent and imaginative style may indicate a particular predilection for such forms.

Importantly, Ransome's stories are intended to entertain and also instruct. He therefore emphasizes the pedagogical aspect of the original aesthetics as much as possible. "Morozko" is quite remarkable in this aspect. According to Elena N. Eleonskaya (1994:53), it belongs to a series of Russian tales about *dobrodetel'naia devushka* ('the virtuous maiden'), who shows her positive qualities such as modesty, industriousness, obedience, patience, and courteousness in dealing with anyone, including supernatural beings, and thus succeeds in winning them over. Those who are deficient in such qualities fail, which is vividly shown in Ransome's retelling (12a), but not Ralston's literal variant (12b):

(12a)

> The old man had not time to eat even a mouthful of black bread before she had driven him out into the snow. [...] He came to the great fir, and found the two girls sitting under it *dead*, with their *anger still to be seen on their frozen, ugly faces.*
>
> Ransome 1916 [1957]:55, emphasis added

(12b)

> Before the old man could manage to get a bite he was out of doors and on his way. When he came to where his daughters were, he found them *dead.*
>
> Ralston 1873:220, emphasis added

As is evident in this version of the tale, and others considered above, Ransome manages to stress its pedagogical aesthetics via repetition, amplification, and elaboration. For example, the theme of cross daughters appears in the text again and again: e.g. when the old woman "found the bodies of her two cross daughters" and "flew at the old man in a storm of rage" he said, "My little daughter got riches for soft words, but yours were always rough of the tongue" (Ransome 1916 [1957]:55–56); cf. "You flattered yourself you were going to get riches, but your daughters were too stiff-necked" (Ralston 1873:220).

The motif of "soft words" will be further elaborated in the amplified ending of Ransome's text (13a); this is clearly seen against Ralston's variant (13b), which closely follows the original:

(13a)

> As for Martha, Fedor Ivanovitch sought her in marriage, as he had meant to do all along —yes, and married her; and pretty she looked in the furs that Frost had given her. I was at the feast, and drank beer and mead with the rest. And she had the prettiest children that ever were seen – yes, and the best behaved. For if ever they thought of being naughty, the old grandfather told them the story of crackling Frost, and how *kind words won kindness, and cross words cold treatment*. And now, listen to Frost. Hear how he crackles away! And mind, if ever he asks you if you are warm, be as polite to him as you can. And to do that, the best way is to be good always, like little Martha. Then it comes easy.
>
> Ransome 1916 [1957]:56–57, emphasis added

(13b)

> The old woman was in a rage at first, and used bad language; but afterwards she made it up with her stepdaughter, and they all lived together peaceably, and thrived, and bore no malice. A neighbor made an offer of marriage, the wedding was celebrated, and Marfa is now living happily. The old man frightens his grandchildren with (stories about) Frost, and doesn't let them have their own way.
>
> Ralston 1873:220

Thus, in Ransome's story an anonymous neighbor gets the name Fedor Ivanovitch and Marfa becomes Martha; furs are mentioned again, but also 'crackling Frost'; and grandchildren are "the prettiest children that ever were seen"—which is in fact a formula often used to describe characters in *skazka*s. Another formula, of the type that marks the ends of tales, is not forgotten either: "I was at the feast, and drank beer and mead with the rest" (left out by ever so accurate Ralston). The didactic aspect of the story is appropriately emphasized: "the best behaved," "kind words won kindness, and cross words cold treatment," "be as polite to him as you can," or "the best way is to be good always." Importantly too, repetitions are conspicuous (like in the original tales): "yes, and married her," "yes, and the best behaved," "And she had," "And now," etc. These, as well as rhyme, alliteration and other types of repetitions (*feast-rest, cross-cold, kind-kindness*) add to the rhythm of the narrative, hence rendering the overall artistic effect and aesthetics of the formulaic original.

5. Conclusion

The aim of the present paper was to examine how the beauty and poetics of the Russian folktale were understood and interpreted for British audiences at the turn of the twentieth century. At the time, folklore was striving to become a scientific discipline, while the general enthusiasm for popular folklore collections was as high as ever.

The paper focused on three major contributors to the corpus of refracted texts and on their translations (rewritings), to explore how agendas and personal stance informed their awareness of Russian "hidden knowledge" and shaped their translation practices. By examining the English texts against the original story of Morozko, and between themselves, it was possible to reveal distinctions and commonalities in their portrayals, as well as gain a useful insight into their respective textualization histories.

Ralston approached the Russian tales as a folklorist, interested in the material being recorded as accurately as possible; this contrasted with more popular adaptations. Impressed by the Russian folklorists' achievements (especially by Afanas'ev's famous collection), he took up his translation project with enthusiasm and respect for the original tradition. This shows in how he accurately rendered major mythological personages of the Russian fairyland, and how he explained and elucidated their underlying aesthetics. "Frost" was just one in his collection of Russian folktales, which served as a reliable source, not only for specialists, but also for translators that followed. As we have discussed, "King Frost" of Lang's fairy book owes a significant debt to Ralston in terms of its inspiration and its understanding of the key formulas of the Russian magic world. What makes the style of this translation distinct, however, is the translator's conscious effort to render the repetitions and sound patterns of the formulaic original, sometimes adding detail and improvisation. Lang's story, one of about fifty other tales from different traditions, was rewritten for British children in the anthologies' characteristically uniform style. Thus, Frost becomes King Frost as befits the fairytale (where characters are often kings, princes, princesses, etc.), but also perhaps to emphasize the difference between *Frost* and *frost* for the sake of the reader. The clever dog speaking in rhymes plays its own part in appealing to the target audience as well. Both Ralston and Lang were major predecessors that paved the way for Ransome's success with his *Old Peter's Russian Tales*. Informed by Ralston's introduction into the Russian magic world, but also by his own first hand experiences of the pre-revolutionary idyll of Russian countryside, Ransome rewrote his Russian folktales in the style of popular folklore collections for children. Like Lang's text, his retellings indicate a striving for artistic effect to appeal to his audience. The translator is at his best in rendering the aesthetics of the original folklore tradition with its particular folktale formulas and pedagogical implications and, also, in reproducing the rhythmic formulaic prose of the original. Thus, it is due to the translators' collective effort and the cumulative effect of their translations that much of the original aesthetics of "Morozko" has become part of the international readers' world.

Theirs, of course, was an earlier epoch, when folkloristics was still in its formative period; the translators' awareness of the folklore tradition and aesthetics they were translating was based on the insights gained through research and readings in the field, as well as travels to the country and intercultural experiences. Their contributions are of particular interest for translation studies and folklore translation, but also for the modern folklorist's discussions of "contexted" translation of formulas and textualization of published folklore materials in general.

References

Sources

Lang, A.1894 [1906]. *The Yellow Fairy Book.* London. https://archive.org/details/yellowfairybook00langiala/page/208.

Ralston, W. S. R.1873. *Russian Folk-Tales.* London. https://archive.org/details/russianfolktales00ralsrich.

Ransome, A.1916 [1957].*Old Peter's Russian Tales.* Edinburgh. https://archive.org/details/oldpetersrussian00rans.

Afanas'ev, A. N.1855–1863.*Narodnyerusskieskazki A. N. Afanas'eva*, I, ed. 1984. Moskva. http://feb-web.ru/feb/skazki/default.asp.

Literature

Alekseev, M. P., and Levin Y. D. 1994. *Vil'iamRol'ston—propagandist russkoi literatury i fol'klora: S prilozheniem pisem Rol'stona k russkim korrespondentam.* Moscow.

Bauman, R. 1993. "The Nationalization and Internationalization of Folklore: The Case of Schoolcraft's 'Gitshee Gauzinee'." *Western Folklore* 52(2/4):247–269.

Black, J. D.1988. "Andrew Lang: Master of Fairyland." *Nexus: The Canadian Student Journal of Anthropology* 6(1):24–35.

Bogrdanova, T. 2013. "Russian Folklore for the English Reader: William Ralston as an Intercultural Agent." *New Horizons in Translation Research and*

Education I. (eds. N. Pokorn and K. Koskinen) 28–44. Joensuu. http://urn. fi/URN:ISBN:978-952-61-1288-6.

———. 2016. "Arthur Ransome's Rewriting of the Russian Folktale Historicised." *Slavonica* 21(1–2):79–94.

Brogan, H.1984.*The Life of Arthur Ransome*. London.

Delić, L. 2013. "Poetic Grounds of Epic Formulae." *Balcanica* 46:51–78.

Dorson, R. 1968. *The British Folklorists*. Chicago.

Eleonskaya, E. N. 1994. *Skazka, zagovor i koldovstvo v Rossii*. Moscow.

France, P. 1995. "From Russian Tale to English Children's Story: The Case of Arthur Ransome." *New Comparison* 20:30–45.

Foley, J. M. 1991. "Strategies for Translating Serbo-Croatian Traditional Oral Narrative." *Journal of Folklore Research* 28(1):61–81.

———. 1992. "Word-Power, Performance, and Tradition." *The Journal of American Folklore* 105(417):275–301.

———. 2005. "From Oral Performance to Paper-Text to Cyber-Edition." *Oral Tradition* 20:233–263.

Hale, T. 2006. "Readers and Publishers of Translations in Britain." *The Oxford History of Literary Translation in English, IV: 1790-1900* (eds. P. France and K. Haynes) 34–47. Oxford.

Haney, J. V. 1999. *An Introduction to the Russian Folktale*. Armonk.

Hines, S. M.2013. *"The Taste of the World": A Re-Evaluation of the Public History and Reception Context of Andrew Lang's Fairy Book Series, 1899-1910*. Unpublished PhD dissertation. The University of Edinburgh. https://www.era.lib. ed.ac.uk/handle/1842/7792.

Honko, L. 2000. "Text as Process and Practice: Textualization of Oral Epics." *Textualization of Oral Epics* (eds. L. Honko) 3–56. Trends in Linguistics: Studies and Monographs 128. Berlin, NY.

Kazakova, T. A. 2003. *Imagery in Translation*. St. Petersburg.

Lang, A. 1906. "Preface." *The Orange Fairy Book*. London. https://archive.org/ details/orangefairybook00lang/page/n9.

Lefevere, A. 1982. "Literary Theory and Translated Literature." *Dispositio: The Art and Science of Translation* 7 (19–20):3–22.

Lutovinova E. I. 2009. "Obraz slova v russkikh volshebnykh skazkakh." *Vestnik Viatskogo gosudarstvennogo universiteta* 2(1):114–117.

Mal'tsev, G. I. 1989. *Traditsional'nye formuly russkoi narodnoi neobriadovoi liriki*. Leningrad.

Menkova N. V. 2010. "Russkie diminutivy v angliiskom perevode M. A. Bulgakova'Master i Margarita'."*Yaroslavskii pedagogicheskii vetsnik* 3:174–179.

Nagler, M. N. 1967. "Towards a Generative View of the Oral Formula." *Transactions and Proceedings of the American Philological Association* 98:269–311.

Polubichenko, L. V., and Egorova, O. A. 2003. "Traditsionnye formuly narodnoi skazki kak otrazhenie natsional'nogo mentaliteta." *Vestnik Moskovskogo universiteta, Seriia 19: Lingvistika i mezhkul'turnaia kommunikatsiia* 1:7–22.

Propp, V. Y. 1928a. *Morfologiia volshebnoi skazki* ed. 2001. Moscow.

———. 1928b. *Morphology of the Folktale.*Trans. L. Scott. 1968. Austin.

———. 1946. *Istoricheskie korni volshebnoi skazki* ed. 1998. Moscow. https://www.litmir.me/bd/?b=36365.

———. 1984a. *Russkaia skazka.* Leningrad.

———. 1984b. *Russkaia skazka* ed. 2000. Moscow.

Ransome, A. 1976. *The Autobiography of Arthur Ransome* (ed. R. Hart-Davis). London.

Razumova, I. A. 1991. *Stilisticheskaia obriadnost' russkoi volshebnoi skazki.* Petrozavodsk.

Reznitchenko, L. Y., and Reznitchenko, L. I. 2009. "Diminutivnost' kak etnopsihologicheskii fenomen v russkom plache." *Vestnik TGU* 11(79):203–208.

Roshiianu, N. 1974. *Traditsionnye formuly skazki.* Moscow.

Ryan, W. F. 1999. *The Bathhouse at Midnight: An Historical Survey of Magic and Divination in Russia.* Magic in History. University Park.

———. 2009. "W. R. S. Ralston and the Russian Folktale." Presidential address given to The Folklore Society, 4 April 2008. *Folklore* 120(?):123–132.

Schacker, J. 2003. *National Dreams: The Remaking of Fairy Tales.* Philadelphia.

Simpson, J., and Roud, S. 2003. *A Dictionary of English Folklore*(e-book). Oxford. http://www.oxfordreference.com.ezproxy.uef.fi:2048/view/10.1093/acref/9780198607663.001.0001/acref-9780198607663.

Sundmark, B. 2004. *Andrew Lang and the Colour Fairy Books.* dspace.mah.se/dspace/bitstream/2043/8228/1/Lang%20present.pdf.

Tymoczko, M. 1995. "The Metonymics of Translating Marginalized Texts." *Comparative Literature* 47:11–24.

Vedernikova, N. M. 1975. *Russkaia narodnaia skazka.* Moscow.

18

Opening and Closing Formulas in Tales Told in England

Jonathan Roper, University of Tartu

FORMULAS, (THAT IS SEQUENCES OF WORDS that reoccur with the same meaning and function, and *more or less* the same verbal units), have not often been a point of focus in English folklore studies. While formulas in folksong have been investigated to some extent,[1] what is the situation if we move from folk-verse to folk-prose, and search for formulas in English folktales? In contrast to fixed-phrase genres such as proverbs, folktales are a fundamentally free-phrase genre, but with the key exception that formulas appear as fixed-phrase elements within this wider free-phrase norm. Stith Thompson (1930) lists the following categories of formulaic language that can be found in folktales: opening formulas, transition formulas (*meanwhile* ...), formulaic epithets (the *green* woods, the *red* rose), formulaic numerals (over *seven* hills), formulaic synonyms for *never* (when two Sundays fall in a single week), stereotypic snatches of dialogue (usually tied to a certain character), and closing formulas.

Our first and most fundamental difficulty in identifying such elements of formulaic language comes with the thinness of our tale corpus—less than one hundred reliable records of tales recorded before World War I, documented by figures such as James Orchard Halliwell (1849), Sabine Baring Gould (1865), William Henderson (1866), Stanley Addy (1895), and Ella Mary Leather (1912), without the aid of audio-recording; and even in some instances, such as the tales presented by George Stephens (1880) and Anna Walter Thomas (Fison 1899), reconstituted years after the story was told. Elsewhere, in an outline of English folktale collection, I concluded that "the weaknesses of folktale textualization in Victorian England make it difficult for us to make any sound observations about oral folktale style" (Roper 2019:408). But it is the very clichédness of formulas

---

[1] E.g. Andersen (1985) on "formulaic narrative technique in the traditional ballads of England and Scotland."

that provides firmer ground for an investigation, especially when considering the formulas that open and close tales: to put it in a nutshell, opening and closing formulas are more likely than any other element to have survived the process of textualization more or less intact. And given the international and trans-generic fame of formulas like *Once upon a time* and *Happily ever after*, such an exercise may be of interest even given the limitations of the material. Labov has remarked that to do their job, historical linguists have to make the most of "bad data" (1994:10–11); historical folklorists too must make the most of their own bad data.

Unhappily, we know more about the folktale collectors in England than we do about the English narrators themselves. This curious inversion of priorities relative to our interests today is also evident in the record of English verbal charms (Roper 2005:78). Nevertheless, there are, at present, a couple of instances where we know the name of the narrator. The similar weakness of scholarly folk-narratological practice in England means that the only existing discussion of opening and closing formulas is the brief one by Neil Philip (1992:xxxiv–xxxv, 15–16). As might be expected, some of the best discussions of formula in prose narratives are in German. In addition to Stith Thompson's encyclopedia entry on "Formeln" (1930), which is the most comprehensive overview known to me, there are also significant mini-essays by Kurt Ranke, Gabriela Kilianova, and Bengt Holbek in the *Enzyklopädie des Märchens* on opening and closing formulas and on formulaicity (s.vv. "Eingangsformel(n)," "Schlussformel," "Formelhaftigkeit, Formeltheorie"). Johannes Bolte and Georg Polivka (1930:10–36) discuss rhyme (including formulas) in folktales near the start of the fourth volume of their *Anmerkungen*. Max Lüthi made valuable observations in his work *Das Volksmärchen als Dichtung* (1975:57–67), and the early study by Robert Petsch (1900) is still useful.

1. Opening Formulas

1.1. *Once upon a time*

What might be called "the Standard Average European (SAE) wonder tale opening" runs *There once was*, as typical examples from languages geographically close to English exemplify: German *Es war einmal* ('It was once'), Frisian *Dêr wie ris* ('There was once'), French *Il c'était une fois* ('There was a time'), Scottish Gaelic *Uair a bha siud* ('Once there was'), Danish *Der var en gang* ('There was one time'), Icelandic *Einu sinni var* ('One time was') and Italian *C'era una volta* ('There was a time'). And this is what typically happens in English too. As Joseph Jacobs observed, "some stories start off … with a simple 'Well, there was once a —'."

(1894:217). In fact, "some stories" is rather understating it, as more than twice as many tales in the collection of Addy (1895) begin with something like the SAE opening (in its various manifestations—*There was once, There once lived, It happened once,* or simply *Once*) than begin with *Once upon a time.* And given that he explicitly states that he has added nothing to the texts "except the occasional formula, 'Once upon a time'" (1895:ix), the occurrence of that formula must have been rarer still in the tales as he heard them in the north midlands of England.

And yet *once upon a time* is a formula with a long pedigree—the earliest surviving occurrence is from the fourteenth century in the *The Knight's Tale,* underlined below, where Chaucer is using it not to begin a narrative, but rather to locate a significant event in the past:

(1)

> Although thee <u>ones on a tyme</u> mysfille,
> Whan Vulcanus had caught thee in his las,
> And foond thee liggynge by his wyf, allas!

The Knight's Tale 2388–2390

Part of the subsequent fame of this formula must reside in its oddness. What the oddness consists in becomes apparent when we compare the fuller form of this formula *Once upon a time there was* (also found as *There was once upon a time*) with the "SAE opening" *Once there was.* We find the remainder to be the odd phrase *upon a time. Upon a time* is part of a formulaic complex to which *upon a day* and *on a time* (MED s.v. "once, adv A.I.2.b.") also belonged. A reference in a seventeenth-century sermon, "that *upon a time* (as *Tales* usually begin)" (Tillotson 1671:41), links the formula with the opening of narratives.

But what might this phrase *upon a time* mean? Prepositions that commonly occur with *time* include *after, around, at, before, by,* etc., but there are no other contexts where we speak of events happening *on* or *upon* a time (no other contexts besides folktale or fantastical ones that is). An answer to our question lies in the observation that the action proper does not begin with this phrase. *Once upon a time* leads not into action, but into a delineation of the protagonist. This may be a general description (*a young man, a silly man, a father who had two daughters*) or we may also be given a name. We also often receive information about the place the protagonist is to be found in (*Derbyshire, by the roadside, in the ruins of a castle that stood in the midst of a great forest*), and we may learn something of the protagonist's important relationships (if the protagonist is young, or begins the story as young, the first characters we meet are often his or her parents). While we may also get a sign of the fundamental conundrum the story will address, or of the lack that will require liquidation, we do not tend to get any more information at this stage (i.e. immediately following *Once upon a time*) about the temporal situation.

1.2. *One day*

Stories proper do not begin with *Once upon a time*. They typically begin with a specifying phrase such as *One day*. Here follows an example, with the relevant phrases marking the general situation underlined and that marking the beginning of a specific course of action in italics:

(2)

> Once upon a time there was a poor shoemaker who could not earn enough to keep himself and his family. This grieved him very much, but *one morning* when he came downstairs he found a piece of leather which he had cut out already made into a pair of shoes [...]
>
> Addy 1895:39

It is the very unusualness of *upon a time* that makes it memorable for the teller and a signal for the listeners, though the set-up can, as we have seen, be established with another, less distinctive formula, for example in the following case the simple *There was*:

(3)

> There was a farmer, and he had three cows; fine fat beauties they were. One was called Facey, the other Diamond, and the third Beauty. *One morning* he went into his cowshed, and there he found Facey so thin [...]
>
> Henderson 1866:321

Equally, the phrase that marks the shift of aspect need not always be *One day*, but can also be *One fine day*, *One night*, *One evening*, *One morning* (as here), or any other means of specifying a point in time. Note the contrast between the function of the two formulas: *Once upon a time* introduces the general situation (the protagonist, their habitual place and time—in Labovian terms, the orientation), *One day* introduces action (in Labovian terms, the complicating action). There is something similar to verbal aspect (*Aktzionsart*) being signaled by these formulas—the first formula signaling something like habitual imperfect aspect, the second something like punctual or perfective aspect. The habituality is especially obvious at the opening of "The Good Magpie" (Addy 1895:46): "There was once a gentleman who used to ride on horseback every day." Here, the time frame of our formula is supported by "used to" and "every day." In the subsequent sentence, the phrase *one day* has its specificity reinforced by the very next words "he had occasion to." *One day* introduces events which are "occasional" in the true sense of the word.

1.3. Extended variations of *Once there was*

While *Once upon a time* has but few variants, *Once there was* has more, including the same words in a different order (*There was once*, etc.), with the verb pluralized (*Once there were*), or with the verb replaced by a close synonym (*Once there lived*). But more interesting are the appearances of *Once upon a time* in an extended form. The earliest record of this seems to be in Henry Mayhew's record of London tramp storytelling. Mayhew, ventriloquizing the words of a young tramp, remarks:

(4)

> We generally begin — "Once upon a time, and a very good time it was, though it was neither in your time, nor my time, nor nobody else's time."

Mayhew 1861:391

The repetition of *time* forms a rhyme-like *terra firma* at the start of the sea-voyage into prose. Semantically, the placing of the story in a "very good time" that never was ("nor nobody else's time") signals the fictiveness of what follows. Such openings were found also in the anglophone storytelling tradition of mid-twentieth-century Newfoundland (e.g. Halpert and Widdowson 1996:78, 278, 316, etc.).

This is not, however, the only extended form we can find. At the end of the nineteenth century, according to a folklorist in Wiltshire in south-central England, "an old man" would begin his tales like this:

(5)

> There were a time, 'tweren't in my time, neither in your time, nit [=not yet] in anybody else's time; 'twere when magpies builded in old man's beards and turkey-cocks chewed bacca[2]

Powell 1901:76

[2] At this point the folklorist comments "apparently something is lost here," and indeed from other examples we might well expect something to follow that rhymes with "bacca." He also gives us the rest of the words following the break, which also seem formulaic, albeit from a

Not very long before World War I, a lifelong inmate of a workhouse in the west-central England told a visitor a version of "Jack the Giant Killer." The storyteller, William Thomas Colcombe, launched into his tale with the following virtuoso opening:

(6)

> Once upon a time—a very good time it was—when pigs were swine and dogs ate lime and monkeys chewed tobacco, when houses were thatched with pancakes, streets paved with plum puddings, and roasted pigs ran up and down the streets with knives and forks on their backs crying "Come and eat me!" That was a good time for travellers.
>
> Leather 1912:174

The wealth of food in the formula may be a negative reflection of the limited diet William Colcombe, and his fellow inmates, who were presumably his usual listeners, would receive in Weobley Union Workhouse. While some images here correspond to local ecology and to local diet: the plum puddings, the roasted pigs, the "houses thatched with pancakes," there are other things, such as monkeys, lime and tobacco, that come from another ecology. In this regard, it is interesting to note that variants of this extended opening formula have been found the other side of the Atlantic (in the following cases in the Bahamas, Belize, and coastal South Carolina, respectively):

(7)

> Once was a time
> A very good time
> Monkey chew tobacco
> An' spit white lime.
> Cockeroach jump from pint to pint
> He turn quarter never touch water.
>
> Parsons 1928:490

(8)

> This da wahn time when time was time—
> When Monkey use to chew tobacco and spit out white lime.
>
> Beck 1980:420

---

different formula: "all over hills, dales, mountains, and valleys, so far as I shall tell you to-night, or to-morrow night, or ever shall tell you before I've done, if I can" (Powell 1901:76).

(9)

> Once upon a time de goose run blin',
> Monkey chaw tobacco an' de cat drink wine.

Johnson 1930:137

This formula enters the written record much later than *Once upon a time* does. The earliest example of the formula that I have found to date is from anglophone Ireland and reported by Thomas Crofton Croker in the 1830s. It is mentioned as the way "a skilful narrator" will introduce a "fairy story":

(10)

> Once upon a time, when pigs were swine, and turkeys chewed tobacco, when swallows built their nests in old men's beards, &c.

Thoms 1834:62

This report is of interest as it associates the formula not with the entirety of folk narration, but specifically with "fairy stories," yet it is also frustrating in that one wonders what came after the "etc." Perhaps it was another clause ending in a word rhyming with "tobacco," as in this English example noted by Joseph Jacobs:

(11)

> Once upon a time when pigs spoke rhyme,
> And monkeys chewed tobacco,
> And hens took snuff to make them tough,
> And ducks went quack, quack, quack Oh!

Jacobs 1894:217

Other examples of the formula can be found from Scotland in the mid-nineteenth century (Chambers 1841:57, 81), and from mid-twentieth century Newfoundland (Halpert and Widdowson 1996:316, 461). In the F. J. Norton collection at Cambridge, we find:

(12)

> Once upon a time
> When pigs drank wine
> And bricklayers had no mortar
> I caught a little bird
> And made him drop a turd
> And mixed it up with water.

Philip 1992:xxxiv

Such ruder versions must have been more common than the surviving record suggests; after all, Joseph Jacobs explicitly said he knew "variants not so refined" as the one he quotes in *More English Folk-Tales* (1894:215), but he did not print them.

1.4. *When pigs were swine*

The earliest record of the phrase *pigs were swine* appears to come as early as 1806 in the writings of John Croker Wilson, a relative of the aforementioned Thomas Crofton Croker, and also his superior in his work at the Admiralty in London. In a satirical poem, he writes: "There was in former ages, when Pigs were Swine, / A certain Sir Henry who had a finger in the Treasury Pie" (1806:37). Here there is no direct reference to folk narration, but there still is a reference to times long past (here, a deliberately misleading one). This suggests the formula existed with its established reference (times lost past) earlier still. But what does *when pigs were swine* mean? A little light is shone upon this by another literary work from half a century later where the following dialogue imitating oral narration occurs:

(13)

> [Sir Wolfgang:] "The names of my hero and heroine were John and Jill. They lived in England, near an elevated range of hills, in the days when pigs were swine." "Stop!" cried my Lord Clodolphus. "Pigs are swine even unto this day."
>
> de Lazie 1864:333

For, after all, *pigs* and *swine* are synonyms, and there is something utterly unremarkable in that when compared with houses thatched with pancakes, birds nesting in beards, and pigs with knives in their backs. It seems rather that this is a meta-linguistic remark—the story happened at a time back in the past when what is now the slightly old-fashioned word *swine* was the unmarked way to refer to the animals we nowadays refer to as *pigs*.

In his *Mrs. Lirriper* writings from the 1860s, Dickens makes use of the formula. The use signals the start of a character's narrating: "Once upon a time, When pigs drank wine, And monkeys chewed tobaccer, 'Twas neither in your time nor mine, But that's no macker" (Dickens 2005 [1863]:124; presumably the spelling "macker" is intended to represent the word *matter* pronounced with a Cockney-style glottalized "t"). This is not the only reference to the formula—elsewhere in a later Lirriper story, Dickens includes the following allusive exchange, where the formula appears in the speech of the same character, the boy Jemmy Jackman:

(14)

"What is the date sir?" says I. "Once upon a time when pigs drank wine?"

"No Gran," says Jemmy, still serious; "once upon a time when the French drank wine."

Dickens 2005 [1864]:251

Here the formula does not begin a character's narration, but is used to indicate a "never-never" time: presumably the French have drunken wine from time immemorial. It is also a good example of the capacity of this formula to be varied playfully.

What is interesting from the folk-narratological point of view is not so much Dickens's use of the formula—we might expect him to know how folktales worked, given his interest in vernacular culture, and the fact that he preserved for us some of the tales his own nurse told him. What is of interest folk-narratologically is the expectation that his readers would pick up upon such a formula, suggesting that such a formula (and its function) was a part of common knowledge.

1.5. The *time–swine* formula

So, what can we generalize about the history of the *time–swine* formula? Firstly, as for its distribution, although we do not have a very large number of examples, there are enough to show that the formula, which was much more recent than *Once upon a time*, was to be found all over the northern half of the anglosphere: Britain and Ireland, eastern Canada, and the Caribbean. It is possible that some of these elements—monkeys, tobacco, lime—were introduced to the formula in the Caribbean and were brought east to Europe. It is also perfectly possible that the exotic ecology originated on the lips of an anglophone in Europe with the goal of evoking a never-never land. The dates of the data suggest the latter, but as the data is so thin, this is hardly sufficient to resolve a question which is perhaps ultimately unanswerable. As Daniel Crowley has noted (1966:32), some variants of this formula are echoed in the American children's rhyme that runs:

(15)

Three-six-nine,
The goose drank wine
The monkey chew tobacco
On the streetcar line.

...

If there is a genetic relation between the texts, then "three-six-nine" appears to have replaced *Once upon a time* as a result of the transfer across genres, from tale to action rhyme. This did not always happen. In a "chant" from 1950s Yorkshire (in the Hull area), we have:

(16)

    Once upon a time
    when dogs shit lime
    and monkeys chewed tobacco,
    The little piggies run
    with their fingers up their bum
    to see what was the matter.[3]

Other northern English children's rhymes like this collected in the second half of the twentieth century include the following texts (slightly re-lineated) from Liverpool and Birtley respectively:

(17)

    Once upon a time, when the birds made lime
    And monkeys chewed tobacco,
    The old women come with their fingers on their bum
    To see what was the matter.
    The matter was the bricklayers had no mortar.
    Up come a little bird and he made a little turd
    And the bricklayers had some mortar.

Shaw 1970:8

(18)

    Once upon a time when the dogs shit lime
    And monkeys chewed tobacco,
    The little dogs put on their clogs
    And went to get a cacka.
    The wind blew, the skitters flew,
    Two little doggies split in two.

Rutherford 1971:123

---

[3] Steve Gardham, electronic communication to the author, July 26, 2018.

But this kind of rhyme is not found in pre-World War I records (something likely related to its scatological nature), so the exact relation, if any, of this rhyme and its congeners to the opening formulas of tales is obscure.

There are analogous texts in other genres too. In Mummers' Plays we occasionally find echoes of the "land of plenty" motifs. For example, in a play recorded in Weston-sub-Edge, Gloucestershire in 1864, we find the following piece of dialogue, reminiscent of William Colcombe's opening motifs:

(19)

> Now my lads we've come to the land of plenty,
> rost stones [sic], plum puddings,
> houses thatched with pancakes,
> and little pigs running about
> with knives and forks stuck in their backs
> crying "Who'll eat me, who'll eat me?"

Tiddy 1923:168

Oddly, although the majority of the play is in rhyme, these lines are not, suggesting that they are a later addition to the original text of the play. Similarly, the apparently inserted nature of these lines comes out in dialogue from a Mummers' Play recorded in Cheshire just before World War I:

(20)

> I've travelled high, I've travelled low,
> Through hail, rain, frost and snow.
> Hickity, Pickity, Yorkshire and Spain,
> Three times to the West Indies,
> And back to Old England again
> Where little pigs used to run round the streets
> With knives and forks stuck in their arse,
> Crying out, "Who'll eat me?"
> Here Jack, take three drops out of this bottle into thy throttle
> And arise and fight the battle.

Broomhead 1978

While not every line in the play rhymes, the tendency is for lines to form rhyming couplets, which is precisely what we do not find with the "land of plenty" lines.

Another kind of analogy comes in the form a text printed during the Napoleonic Wars and purporting to be the rallying cry of an English officer to his troops in Flanders:

(21)

> *My Lads*, I am now going to lead you into a country where the rivers consist of fine *nut brown Ale!* — where the houses are built of hot *roast Beef* — and the wainscots paperd with *Pan-cakes*. There, my boys, it rains *Plumb pudding* every Sunday morning! — the Streets are paved with *Quartern Loaves!* — and nice *roasted Pigs* run about with knives and forks stuck in their rumps, crying out — *"Who will eat me!"* — *"Who will eat me!"*
>
> Anon 1796:4

Once again, we find no rhyme, but when we think back to Colcombe's opening, we notice that not all of that rhymes either. The first part of Colcombe's opening might be termed the "irreal formula" (*Once upon a time ...*) and that rhymes. The second part, the "absurd formula" (*When pigs were swine and dogs ate lime*), also rhymes. But the third part, the "land of plenty formula," does not rhyme. The connection between the first two formulas is by means of rhyme: *time-time-swine-lime*. The connections between the second and third formula is semantic, through the notion of pigs: *when pigs were swine* and *roasted pigs ran up and down*. There follows a final clause that is both the coda to the opening and the prelude to the story, "that was a good time for travellers," which links back to the first formula by a rhyme on *time*.

2. Closing Formulas

2.1. The *bend-end* formula

To return to our teller William Colcombe—how did the story he had begun with such a virtuoso opening formula end? The answer is, with another formula:

(22)

> Be bow bend it,
> My tale's ended,
> If you don't like it,
> You may mend it.
>
> Leather 1912:176

Colcombe had learnt the story "from an old chapbook, when a small boy" (Leather 1912:176). Detective work by Tom Pettitt (2013) has identified what must have been the chapbook edition in question. Fascinatingly, neither Colcombe's opening nor his closing formula are to be found in the chapbook version. As often proves to be the case, when we know the print contribution to a teller's narratives, the oral dimension stands out more clearly: Colcombe must have known these formulas as units independent of any story, as things suited to begin and end wonder tales.

The earliest version I have found of this *bend-end* formula dates from the 1840s:

(23)

> There was a king, and he had three daughters,
> And they all lived in a basin of water;
> The basin bended,
> My story's ended.
> If the basin had been stronger,
> My story would have been longer.

Halliwell 1846:40

A version from the 1850s runs:

(24)

> My story's ended
> My spoon is bended:
> If you don't like it,
> Go to the next door,
> And get it mended.

Halliwell 1853:79

Both of these formulas appear in a collection of "nursery rhymes," with no informant data, no geographical data, and no attached tale, but they are clearly of a piece with the formulas we find better documented later on. The first is a mock story of the sort that a weary adult might produce in response to the continued demands of a child. After "there was", the protagonists are introduced, their familial relations and social position are outlined, and they are located in a dwelling place, all in two lines. But then, instead of a story developing (there is no *one day* formula here!), there is a switch to the ending in the very next couplet. A mock apology concludes the mock story.[4]

---

4   Halliwell (1846:137) later printed another such mock story where the protagonist, Little Tee Wee, goes to sea in an open boat. Inevitably, straightway the "boat bended" and the story ended.

The second variant is more like what might be found at the end of a full tale. Indeed, a story collected in the 1960s in Port Blandford, Newfoundland, ends in just such a fashion:

(25)

>The bull's tail broke,
>An' if his tail had hung on stronger,
>My story would have been longer.

Halpert and Widdowson 1996:924

The ending here to Halliwell's example is tantalizing in its meaning. Perhaps the rhyme should be interpreted as a message from teller to audience to the effect of *I've done my share, now be off with you!!* Or, is it, with its mention of the teller's spoon, a nudge to the audience for some food (and even drink) in return for storytelling, something which is found often enough in European tales, such as those referenced by Petsch (1900)? Or should it rather be seen as the formal passing on of the duty to tell a story to the next person, i.e. should "go to the next door" be taken as a suggestion to ask the person next to the teller to now tell a story, a story that the listeners might (or might not) like better?

It is this third function that seems to the one in focus in Addy's north midland version (which he titles as "explicit fabula"), as its final two lines make clear:

(26)

>My tale's ended,
>T'door sneck's bended;
>I went into t'garden
>To get a bit of thyme;
>I've telled my tale,
>Thee tell thine.

Addy 1895:54

Although again, thyme gathered from the garden also hints towards preparing food. Food as reward is foregrounded in this version from Gloucestershire:

(27)

>A piece of pudden',
>For telling a good un;
>A piece of pie,
>For telling a lie.

Northall 1892:339

In other words, regardless of the truth-status of what they have just heard, the hearers should arrange for the teller to be fed.

Once again, various analogues of the core of this formula were to be found in, and around, the Caribbean (in the Bahamas, Antigua, Belize, plus Louisiana and Alabama, respectively):

(28)

> E bo ban, my story's en'.
> If you doan' believe my story's true,
> Hax my captain an' my crew

Edwards 1895:64

(29)

> And I went through Miss Havercomb alley,
> And I see a lead was bending;
> So the lead ben',
> So the story en'.

Johnson 1921:63

(30)

> If di pin neva ben, di stowri neva en

Escure 1982:49

(31)

> And I stepped on the wire, and the wire bent, and I left. And that's the end of the story.

Lindahl, Owens and Harvison 1997:129

(32)

> And at that time I stepped on a pin; the pin bent an' that's the way the thing went.

Faucet 1927:265

In the first example, the apostrophe present after "en" (signaling it is a form of "end") and the absence of an apostrophe after "ban" (making the word a mystery rather than a similarly contracted version of "bend"). This reflects Edwards's first hypothesis that these three syllables were probably "some forgotten African phrase" before he encountered the phrase "Be bow bended" as a closing formula for stories in England from an account deriving from *The London Globe* (1895:111). The *Dictionary of Caribbean English Usage* (*s.v.* "bend") has "and the bow/pin/nail/ wire ben[d], and the story en[d]." This formulation economically shows both invariance in the *bend-end* rhyme, and variance in the item said to bend, though it does not represent the reality of any particular rendition in the way the forms above do (nor are any sources revealed).

These *bend-end* formulas are all examples of what Petsch (1900) describes as an ending that calls attention to the teller. But there are other kinds of endings to European folktales. One of these others is a simple *c'est tout*. We find this also in the English material, e.g. Anna Walter Thomas's tale "The Gypsy Woman" (the continuation of "Tom Tit Tom") ends "An' tha's all" (Fison 1899:22). Other low-key endings involve the protagonist, or the narrator who has been observing the story (and even participating in a final feast), leaving. Thomas Keightley records a woman from Somerset who ended her tale (a version of ATU 440) with the words, "and I came away" (1834:13). A tale that Marie Clothilde Balfour claims to have collected in Lincolnshire ends "and he went off home" (1890:310).[5]

2.2. *Happily ever after?*

Petsch also noticed that some endings address the fate of the hero. While, as we know, in wonder tales the good end happily, and the bad end unhappily— quite what the happy end consists in may not be stated however. In a northern English version of ATU 563, the happy ending is only implied:

(33)
> Now lass, thou art the richest and I shall marry thee

> Henderson 1866:329

To judge by our data, such a sudden ending seems to be more common than we might imagine. But, of course, we do find the *happily ever after* formula in the ethnographic record too. One English version of ATU 510 ends with the father attending the wedding feast of a couple unknown to him, and commenting on the unsalted meat on offer there:

---

[5] Questions have been raised (e.g. Philip 1992:156-7) about Balfour's reliability as a documenter of folk narrative. Perhaps this particular example is reliable, as it comes from a story that is a Schwank rather than a true supernatural story (Balfour's favorite area for elaboration) and also because it is a formula.

(34)

> "Truly, salt is the sweetest thing in the world," he said, "though, for saying so, I sent my own daughter away from my house, and shall never see her face again."
>
> Then the bride made herself known to her father, and fell on his neck and kissed him.

Addy 1895:49

Anna Fison's nurse's version of the same tale-type also ends with the father and the youngest daughter reconciled and embracing, but ends with this additional remark:

(35)

> And so they was happy ever after

Fison 1899:29

Like *upon a time* in the opening formula, *ever after* plays a special role in the closing formula; while just about making sense, the fact that it never occurs outside the context blazons the phrase as formulaic. While *Happy ever after* is the core of the formula, it is not a sentence in itself, any more than *Once upon a time* is. To form a complete sentence, we must also have a subject (here, "they"—elsewhere it might well be "he" or "she") and a verb (here, "was"—elsewhere it could be "lived"). Note also that we have "happy" not "happily": throughout my data on this formula there is a roughly one-to-one ratio of "happy" to "happily." Given the vernacular tendency to use adjectival forms adverbially, and the propensity of collectors to correct vernacular grammar to the Standard, we are probably safe in saying that *happy ever after* is the more traditional form of the formula. And, more than that, as most rural and urban working-class speakers in England in the nineteenth century will have dropped initial "h" from words, it would have been sounded: "Appy ever after."

The changes that can be rung on the formula include making connections to the most prominent trait of the tale's protagonist. An Oxfordshire story, which combines ATU 1450 and 1384, ends with the hero convinced he has found three people as foolish as his sweetheart:

(36)

> And so he turned back, and married Moll, with whom he lived long and happily, if not wisely.

Sternberg 1852:364

In some cases, such in another variant of ATU 563, we end with the comeuppance of the bad characters, which segues into the *bend-end* formula:

(37)

> so out of the house it drove them
> through the streets
> and over the bridge
> till the bridge bended
> and my tale's ended

Henderson 1866:364

There is an interesting shift of tenses in the last clause, from "bended" to "[i]s ended," providing a return to the present for the listeners.

Another example of segueing into the closing formula was recorded from an English-born woman living in Concord, Massachusetts. The protagonists of her tale, Jack and Lady Featherflight, are married after various trials, but the story doesn't end there. A potential formulaic ending is short-circuited. The storyteller, in this case Elizabeth Hoar, narrates "the newly married pair lived happily," but, instead of an *ever after* appearing now, she follows up with "for many months, until Jack began to wish for more of the giant's treasure" (Newell 1893:59). Once again, a bridge crops up as a natural-seeming part of the narrative before being transformed into part of the closing formula:

(38)

> they could not cross the water. Lady Featherflight said, "Why not build a bridge?" And the bridge was built. They went over wagons and horses, and brought back so heavy a load that, as the last wagonful passed over the bridge, it broke, and the gold was lost. Jack lamented and said, "Now we can have nothing more from the giant's treasure house." But Lady Featherflight said, "Why not mend the bridge?"
> > So the bridge was mended,
> > And my story's ended.

Newell 1893:59

Such an early occurrence of part of the closing formula ("Why not build a bridge?" And the bridge was built") relies on the listeners' awareness of the formula to briefly tease them with the possibility that the story is going to end not long after it has begun. It also plays on the expectation that the ending formula will involve the *bend-end* rhyme, rather than the *mend-end* surprise here.

3. Conclusion

The topic of formulas in English tales would repay further investigation given that formulas found in prose have been less investigated than those found in verse, that formulas in wonder tales have been far less investigated than those found in, e.g., epics, and that formulas in English have been far less investigated than those found in, for example, German. Future research could address another of the types of formula Thompson enumerates, the typical speech of certain characters, for example, the *Fee fie fo fum* when the Giant scents Jack, or the revelatory *Nimmy nimmy not / My name's Tom Tit Tot* of the Rumpelstiltskin-character in "The Name of the Helper" tales. If the data permits, it would also be of interest to examine the tellers' own delivery by examining what formulas they use to manage the information they supply to the listeners, i.e. what their favored discourse markers are, and where they occur. Another area of interest is that of put-off formulas, which offer the promise of the tale, but do not deliver, such as:

(39)

> I'll tell you a tale.
> Shall I begin it?
> There's not much in it.

Northall 1892:339

This short rhyme comprises the tale in its entirety.

It is worth mentioning that when we look at texts for which we have very good data, such as the exemplary transcripts of Halpert and Widdowson (1996) of folktales from mid-twentieth-century Newfoundland, which are based on audio-recordings that are retained in a publicly accessible archive, we find some echoes of phenomena from our own "bad data." While it might be thought that the *Well,* in the "Well, once upon a time" that begins both of Fison's folktale presentations is mere literary affectation, an examination of *Once upon a time* as it occurs in Halpert and Widdowson's transcripts, shows that in fifteen of the twenty examples the tellers precede the *once upon a time* with *well.*[6] So Fison's *well* would seem to reflect oral storytelling practice.

Despite our "bad data," there is much we can tell about the opening and closing formulas in English wonder tales. The *time-swine* formula and the *bend-end* formula call attention to themselves and to their utterers, signaling that an extended turn of speech is now going to come, and that the narration will

---

[6]   The figure goes up to seventeen, if allowances are made for the tellers' self-corrections.

be set in an imaginary world. They stand out like islands of rhyme in seas of prose. They contain sound-patterning in the form of rhyme (or alliteration) and they can be in verse (couplets and quatrains) or, if not in verse, still more rhythmical than the prose around them. The format of the original publications has generally been followed above, meaning that sometimes the formulas have been shown lineated (like verse) and at other times continuous (like prose), but these editorial decisions were somewhat arbitrary and all the *time-swine* and *bend-end* formulas could have been displayed in a lineated form. Such an ethnopoetic layout would bring out one aspect of their poetics. There is another poetic aspect worth pondering: the core of the opening formula is thus three iambic syllables, *well once upon a time*, while at the other end of the story we have three trochaic syllables, *appy ever after*. In other words, the core formulas bookending a story have mirror-image rhythms. This is not perhaps something that has come by chance. Also, there is an intriguing mirroring and non-mirroring between the two most common formulas *was/lived once* and *lived/were happy every after*, appearing before and after the storm of the story; they both feature existential verbs, which in the first case usually applies to an individual, the second usually to a pair. The development reflects the fact that so many fairy-tales involve the individual finding their partner. It is worth remembering too that these formulas are tightly connected to the genre of wonder tale, which is the domain in which we chiefly find *upon a time* or *ever after*. When we find them in domains elsewhere, they typically reference the world of the wonder tale.

On the other hand, there is an asymmetry about the resources available at the start and ending of the stories. While *Once upon a time* is often supported by rhyme (*swine, wine, lime, blin'*, etc., etc.), *Appy ever after* is not supported by rhyme. While only words rhyming with *time* and feminine rhymes involving words such as *matter, tobacco, mortar, water, quack-o*, are found at the start of stories, there is a wider variety of rhyming pairs, both masculine and feminine, at the ends of stories: *bend-end, stronger-longer, pie-lie*, and at least one rhyming pair not mentioned yet *crew-flew* ("The cock crew / Away they flew": Henderson 1866:322). Nevertheless, it worth noting that all the pairs appear to be ordered pairs, i.e. *bend* should always come before *end*, *time* should always come before *swine* (and it sometimes comes afterwards as well).

We do not have any performance details about how the formulas were spoken in England. However, if we can apply Carl Lindahl's observations (personal communication 2017) from other anglophone traditions, there were no doubt some storytellers who bumbled through the opening formulas, as though it were something that simply had to be got through, and others who took the formulas much more seriously and relished speaking them. In one of our oldest testimonies, we find a clue to a teller's sense that formulas are necessary, but quite why remains a mystery to them: Keightley's friend from Somerset on being asked why she ended her tale with "and then I came away" could not explain: "she could not tell why" (Keightley 1834:13).

And finally, how were such formulas received by their hearers? Sabine Baring Gould, as well as having been a significant folktale collector in the 1860s, was also an author of novels and short stories. A clue as to how at least some listeners might react to these repeated formulas is suggested in one of his works of fiction A short story he published in 1888, "The Story of Jael," gives the reaction of a child (possibly autobiographical: "when the author was a child") to his nurse's use of the *bend-end* formula:

(40)

> They [her stories] began well, they proceeded well, but presently ... he perceived that all the *dramatis personæ* of the tale were converging, by various paths, to one point, and that point was a bridge, and he knew that inevitably the end of the stories would be
> > "The bridge bended
> > And so my story ended."
>
> ... How he would writhe on his nurse's knee ... and try to stay the words on her lips, or divert her thoughts into another channel, that there might be some variety in the conclusions that Jack and Jill, and Tom and Poll, and Launcelot and Guinever, might not all put their feet on that unstable bridge, and so their story go down in a tragic, yet impotent conclusion. "It is of no use, my dear boy," said nurse, "it can't be otherwise."
>
> Baring Gould 1890:82–83

Acknowledgements

This work has been supported by the Estonian Research Council (grant project PGR 670).

References

Sources

Addy, S. O. 1895. *Household Tales with Other Traditional Remains: Collected in the Counties of York, Lincoln, Derby, and Nottingham.* London.

Allsop, R., ed. 1996. *Dictionary of Caribbean Usage.* New York.

Anon. 1796. "London." *Kentish Gazette,* June 17, 1796:4.

Baring Gould, S. 1865. "Devonshire Household Tales." *Notes and Queries* 8(3):82–84.

———. 1890. *Jacquetta, and Other Stories.* London.

Broomhead, D. 1978. "Souling Play from Stapleford, Cheshire, 1908 to 1914." Folk Play Research, the website of the Traditional Drama Research Group. https://folkplay.info/resources/texts-and-contexts/souling-play-stapleford-cheshire-1908-1914 (accessed July 26, 2018).

Chambers, R. 1841. *Popular Rhymes of Scotland.* Edinburgh.

Dickens, C. 2005. *Mrs Lirriper.* London.

Edwards, C. 1895. *Bahama Songs and Stories: A Contribution to Folk-Lore.* Boston / New York.

Escure, G. 1982. "Belizan Creole." In Holm 1982:29–70.

Fauset, A. H. "Negro Folk Tales from the South (Alabama, Mississippi, Louisiana)." *Journal of American Folklore* 4(157):213–303.

Fison, L. A. 1899. *Merry Suffolk: Master Archie and Other Tales: A Book of Folk-Lore.* London.

Halliwell, J. O. 1846. *The Nursery Rhymes of England, Collected Principally from Oral Tradition* ed. 4. London.

———. 1849. *Popular Rhymes and Nursery Tales: A Sequel to the Nursery Rhymes of England.* London.

———. 1853. *The Nursery Rhymes of England, Collected Principally from Oral Tradition* ed. 5. London.

Halpert, H., and Widdowson, J. D. A. 1996. *The Folktales of Newfoundland: The Resilience of the Oral Tradition.* New York.

Henderson, W. 1866. *Notes on the Folk-lore of the Northern Counties of England and the Borders.* London.

Holm, J., ed. 1982. *Central American English.* Heidelberg.

Jacobs, J. 1894. *More English Fairy Tales.* London.

Johnson, G. 1930. *Folk Culture on St. Helena Island, South Carolina.* Chapel Hill.

Johnson, J. 1921. "Folk-Lore from Antigua, British West Indies." *Journal of American Folklore* 34:40–88.

Keightley, T. 1834. *Tales and Popular Fictions; Their Resemblance, and Transmission from Country to Country.* London.

Kuhn, S., Kurath, H., and Lewis, R. 1952–2001. *Middle English Dictionary*. Ann Arbor.

de Lazie, U. 1864. *Dreams within Dreams: A Plagiarism of the Seventeenth Century; Being like Most Visions of the Night, a Medley of Old Things and New*. New York.

Leather, E. M. 1912. *The Folk-Lore of Herefordshire: Collected from Oral and Printed Sources*. Hereford.

Lindahl, C., Owens, M., and Harvison, C. R. 1997. *Swapping Stories: Folktales from Louisiana*. Jackson.

Mayhew, H. 1861. *London Labour and the London Poor*, vol. III. London.

Newell, W. W. 1893. "Lady Featherflight: An English Folk-Tale." *Journal of American Folklore* 6:54–62.

Northall, G. F. 1892. *English Folk-Rhymes*. London.

Parsons, E. C. 1928. "Spirituals and Other Folklore from the Bahamas." *Journal of American Folklore* 41(162):453–524.

Philip, N. 1992. *Penguin Book of English Folktales*. London.

Powell, J. U. 1901. "Folklore Notes from South-West Wilts." *Folklore* 12(1):71–83

Rutherford, F. 1971. *All the Way to Pennywell: Children's Rhymes of the North East*. Durham.

Shaw, F. 1970. *You Know Me Anty Nelly? Liverpool Children's Rhymes*. London: Wolfe.

Stephens, G. 1880. "Stupid's Mistaken Cries, as Told in Essex about the Year 1800." *The Folk-Lore Record* 3(2):153–155.

Sternberg, V. T. 1852. "Popular Stories of the English Peasantry." *Notes and Queries* 1(5):601–603.

Thoms, W. J. 1834. *Lays and Legends of Ireland*. London.

Tiddy, R. J. E. 1923. *The Mummers' Play*. Oxford.

Tillotson, J. 1671. *Sermons Preach'd Upon Several Occassions*. London.

Wilson, J. C. 1806. *The Amazoniad*. Dublin.

Literature

Andersen, F. 1985. *Commonplace and Creativity: The Role of Formulaic Diction in Anglo-Scottish Traditional Balladry*. Odense.

B[alfour], M. C., and T., A. W. 1890. "English and Scotch Fairy Tales." *Folklore* 1(3):289–312.

Beck, E. 1980. "Telling the Tale in Belize." *Journal of American Folklore* 93:417–434.

Bolte, J., and Polivka, G. 1930. *Anmerkungen zu den Kinder- und Hausmärchen der Gebrüder Grimm*, vol. IV. Leipzig.

Crowley, D. 1962. *I Could Talk Old Story Good: Creativity in Bahamian Folklore*. Berkeley, Los Angeles.

Holbek, B. "Formelhaftigkeit, Formeltheorie." In Ranke et al. 1977–2015:IV, 1415–1440.

Kilianova, G. "Schlussformel." In Ranke et al. 1977–2015:XII, 88-93.

Labov, W. 1994. *Principles of Linguistic Change I: Internal Factors*. Oxford.

Lüthi, M. 1975. *Das Volksmärchen als Dichtung: Äesthetik und Anthropologie*. Düsseldorf, Köln.

Mackensen, L., ed. 1930–1933. *Handwörterbuch des deutschen Märchens*. Berlin, Leipzig.

Petsch, R. 1900. *Formelhafte Schlüsse im Volksmärchen*. Berlin.

Pettitt, T. 2013. "The Wondertale in the Workhouse: 'Jack the Giant Killer' and the Aesthetics of Parataxis." *Rask: International Journal of Language and Communication* 30:369–389.

Ranke, K. 1977–2015. "Eingangsformel(n)." In Ranke et al. 1977–2015:III, 1227–1244.

Ranke, K., Bausinger, H., and Brednich, R., eds. 1977–2015. *Enzyklopädie des Märchens: Handwörterbuch zur historischen und vergleichenden Erzählforschung*. Berlin.

Roper, J. 2005. *English Verbal Charms*. Folklore Fellows' Communications 288. Helsinki.

———. 2019. "'No Fairy Tales of Their Own?': The English and the Fairy Tale from Thoms to Jacobs." In Teverson 2019:402–414.

Teverson, A., ed. 2019. *The Fairy Tale World*. London.

Thompson, S. 1930. "Formeln." In Mackensen 1930–1933:160–164.

Index of Persons

General Index

Achilles, 14, 40, 115, 181–182
aemulatio veterum, 314, 327
African epic, 28
Alpamysh, 28, 47
Alvíssmál, 131, 143–144
Anglo-Latin, 64, 67, 70–71, 76
Anglo-Saxon, 19–20, 27–28, 45–46, 50–51, 73–79, 145–146, 148, 171
anthropology, 6, 81, 145, 242, 382, 408
Asia, 25, 28, 30, 45, 360–361
Athens, 61, 108, 319
bahuvrihi (compound), 253–255
barangay, 333–334
Beowulf, 19, 25, 27, 43, 47, 49–60, 63–64, 68–70, 72–78, 105, 143, 146, 171, 181, 192, 195, 218
Bible, the, 42, 149–155, 171–172
block of lines, 120
Bosnia, 36, 86–87, 92, 98
bylinas, 43
category-triggering, 10–11, 147–148, 151, 153–154, 170
cene under cumblum, 23
Christian, 53, 61, 64, 74, 77, 85, 87, 89, 91, 94, 98, 112, 155, 189, 254, 333
classic OFT, 1, 3–5, 10–11, 13, 16–18, 116, 119–122, 124–125, 128, 133
collocations 23, 26, 29, 96, 98, 108–109, 117–119, 127–128, 130–131, 134, 146, 274, 376

continental Scandinavia, 12, 259, 260–272, 274–279, 281–287, 290
crystallization, 17, 116, 122, 124, 133, 136–137, 371, 378
Danelaw, the, 55, 70
Dead Sea Scrolls, the, 151, 155, 172
Denmark, 261, 266, 287
deseterac, 26
dróttkvætt, 54, 74, 124–125, 127, 134, 144
Eddic poetry, 57, 77, 146
Edige, 36, 44
Egypt, 167–169
epenthetic fillers, 339–340, 345–346, 349, 353, 356
epitheta ornantia, 25
England, 14, 56, 61–62, 65, 70–73, 75, 77–79, 146, 411–413, 415–416, 418, 421, 426–427, 430, 432
Estonia, 243, 248, 431
equivalence class, 128; set, 124, 128–130
Exodus, 49–50, 54–55, 75, 155, 158, 167, 172
Faroe Islands, the, 260–261, 275, 285
Finland, 43, 243–244, 247, 256, 367, 382
formulaic blocks, 110; language, 1–4, 6–9, 11–14, 16, 18–19, 21, 60, 79, 82, 109, 111, 115–116, 120–121, 144, 146, 174, 192–195, 197–198,